THE JULY MONARCHY

The July Monarchy

A Political History of France 1830–1848

H. A. C. COLLINGHAM

With

R. S. ALEXANDER

LONGMAN

London and New York

Longman Group UK Limited,
Longman House, Burnt Mill, Harlow,
Essex CM20 2JE, England
and Associated Companies throughout the world.

Published in the United States of America
by Longman Inc., New York

First published 1988

British Library Cataloguing in Publication Data

Collingham, H. A. C.
The July monarchy: a political history
of France, 1830–1848.
1. France – Politics and government –
1830–1848
I. Title II. Alexander, R.
944.06'3 DC266.5
ISBN 0-582-02186-3 CSD
ISBN 0-582-01334-8 PPR

Library of Congress Cataloging-in-Publication Data

Collingham, H. A. C., 1947–1986
The July monarchy: a political history of France, 1830–1848
H. A. C. Collingham; edited by R. Alexander.
p. cm.
Bibliography: p.
Includes index.
ISBN 0-582-02186-3. ISBN 0-582-01334-8 (pbk.)
1. France – Politics and government – 1830–1848. I. Alexander, R., 1954– II. Title.
DC266.5.C68 1988
944.06 – dc 19

Set in Linotron 202 11/12pt Garamond

Produced by Longman Singapore Publishers (Pte) Ltd.
Printed in Singapore

Contents

List of Maps

Glossary of French Terms

actionnaire: shareholder.
Aide-toi, le Ciel t'aidera: an electoral pressure group organised by liberals to combat governmental election manipulation.
agiotage: speculation (on the Stock Exchange).
Amis du Peuple: a republican association organised during the July Revolution by Godefroy Cavaignac and Raspail.
arrondissement: an administrative and electoral subdivision of a *département*.
Association de la Liberté de la Presse: an association that provided legal and financial aid to newspapers brought to trial by the government.
atelier: workshop.
atelier de secours: public workshop for the unemployed.
branche aînée: (literally) the elder branch, the Bourbons.
caisse d'épargne: government-sponsored savings-bank.
canut: silk-worker of Lyons.
capacités: those entitled to vote by their functions, not their tax contributions.
cens (électoral): wealth qualification (determined by tax contribution) required to vote or stand for election.
centre gauche: a collection of deputies to the left of centre, but moderate in their liberalism.
charivari: a traditional form of popular protest which became increasingly political in nature during the July Monarchy.
chef d'atelier: workshop master.
compagnonnage: trade guild.
conseil d'arrondissement: an elective administrative body that worked, at least in theory, with the sub-prefect.
conseil général: same as the above, but responsible for the administration of the *département* and, hence, working with the prefect.
conseils des prud'hommes: labour relations tribunals composed of workers and employers, but usually favouring the interests of the latter.
contribution foncière: tax on landed (not commercial) property.
conventionnel: member of the Convention, the legislative assembly that

governed France from September 1792 to October 1795 and ordered the execution of Louis XVI in January 1793.
cour d'appel: appeal court.
Cour de Cassation: Supreme Court of Appeal.
département: subdivision of France, administered by the prefect.
doctrinaires: a small but influential group of constitutional monarchists known chiefly for their conservative tendencies.
entente: a policy of (diplomatic) alliance, usually cited in connection with Great Britain.
estaminet: public house, tavern.
faubourg: suburb, outlying part of a town or city.
feuilleton: serial story in a newspaper.
fonctionnaire: civil servant.
fonds secrets: funds for police purposes, occasionally used by the government to buy the support or ownership of journals.
gamin: street-urchin.
Garde des Sceaux: Keeper of the Seals.
garde nationale: citizens' militia for the provision of civil order and national defence; membership was determined by tax contributions.
gauche dynastique: opposition deputies on the left, but constitutional monarchists and not republicans.
gérant: managing editor.
gérant fictif: a man who took the title of managing editor but did not perform the function; his task was to serve prison sentences should the government successfully bring court action against a newspaper.
(les) glorieuses: the three days of the Revolution of July.
hôtel de ville: town hall.
jacquerie: peasant uprising.
juge de pays: justice of the peace.
juste milieu: the golden mean, the happy medium; in political terms, the rule of the middle classes, supposedly more moderate than the extremes of popular or aristocratic rule.
légion étrangère: foreign legion.
levée en masse: mass conscription.
loi de disjonction: a law which allowed different jurisdictions for civilians and soldiers.
mal du siècle: a term suggesting the cultural or spiritual sickness of the age, its overwhelming boredom.
mutuellisme: an association of Lyonnais silk-workers and *chefs d'ateliers* to redress economic grievances and prevent merchants from reducing pay rates.
parti de résistance: those who saw the July Revolution essentially as a change of the head of state and opposed greater constitutional reform.
parti du mouvement: those who believed the July Revolution a complete repudiation of the Restoration and pressed for significant constitutional reform.
patente: licence tax on commercial property.

pays légal: those entitled to vote by their tax contributions.
petits séminaires: Catholic secondary schools ostensibly to instruct boys for the priesthood, but teaching many who did not enter.
phalange: Utopian agrarian communities first conceived by Fourier, then developed by Considérant.
Ponts et Chaussées: government ministry responsible for transport and communications.
président du conseil: leader of the Cabinet, the minister who selects other ministers.
procureur du roi: Crown prosecutor.
procureur général: Attorney-general.
propriétaire: property-owner.
rapporteur: reporter, recorder, chairman (of a committee).
rédacteur: member of the staff of a newspaper.
rentes: government bonds.
Société des Droits de l'Homme: a secret republican society organised into cells throughout France.
Société des Familles: republican, revolutionary society led by Auguste Blanqui.
Société des Saisons: same as the above, organised after police had arrested many of the members of the Société des Familles.
tiers parti: middle party, distinct from the parties of *résistance* and *mouvement*.
tribunal de commerce: court for commercial disputes.
tribunal de première instance: magistrates court, judging minor civil and criminal cases.

Editorial Note

Historians often assert that their particular fields of investigation have been sadly neglected prior to the publication of their definitive works. They have an obvious interest in doing so and the reader, when confronted by too many such claims, naturally grows wary. But I do think that such a claim can validly be made regarding the politics of the July Monarchy. Although there is an assortment of various specialised monographs, particularly concerning republicanism and the development of socialism, available to us, Hugh Collingham's is the first book written in English to analyse Orleanist politics in anything like a comprehensive fashion.

The reader will note from the sources employed by Collingham that this study is not simply a general survey which attempts to collate the findings of recent scholarship and organise them into a coherent whole. Although the author does frequently utilise secondary source materials, the bulk of his information is derived from primary sources – archival documents, contemporary journals and memoirs. The explanation for this lies in the simple fact that a creditable account of July Monarchy politics could not have been based upon secondary sources; too little has been written on the subject. There is, then, much factual detail in this book which will be new to the reader. Yet this is a very broad study, necessitating an interpretation much more complex than that of the standard monograph. How well Collingham has told the story of the July Monarchy is, of course, for each reader to judge.

From a certain perspective, it is a sad story. Louis-Philippe came to the throne enjoying much good will, but the Revolution of 1830 gave rise to expectations which his government could not fulfil. Despite Périer's apparent initial success in stamping out the fires of revolution, successive French governments lurched from crisis to crisis. Even during the Guizot ministry, a superficial stability was maintained only by the sacrifice of reform. Confronted by massive social, economic and demographic change, the leading Orleanist politicians, including the king, resorted to political immobilism. The result was yet another violent revolution and the fall of another monarchy. Viewed thus, the July Monarchy seems an ultimate failure.

Men learn from failure. Certainly, Napoleon III drew lessons from the experience of this period. Unlike Louis-Philippe, he sought to heal the divisions of the Revolution by recourse to the jingoistic patriotism of foreign war. Like his uncle, he found himself dangerously dependent upon repeated victory. But even had Napoleon III not met defeat at Sedan, those of us who do not find anything regenerative or purifying in the spectacle and carnage of modern war cannot but view with a certain sympathy the attempts of Orleanist government to build national unity by means of the political 'middle way'. As Collingham shows, there was nothing inevitable about the failure to build consensus and a broad measure of support for parliamentary monarchy; disaster resulted from the errors and inability of the leading politicians. The failure of so many talented men is worthy of careful consideration.

Politicians, of course, do not live in a vacuum. They act in response to, and seek to direct, the social, economic and cultural forces that determine our lives. To explain the actions of politicians, Collingham therefore gives us a thorough account of life under the July Monarchy. I will not seek to judge how well the author performs this task, again leaving this for the reader to decide, but I will express my hope that others will find chapters such as 'History and Philosophy' as interesting and instructive as I have.

The additions which I have made to Collingham's text have been relatively minor ones. It was thought, by the publishers and myself, that a 'cast of leading characters' might be of some assistance to the reader otherwise unfamiliar with the period. One must always be somewhat arbitrary in such selection; I have sought to focus upon individuals who had some sort of political impact or influence. I have not included members of the royal family, believing that little confusion could arise as to their identities. Certain choices have also had to be made in the selection of sources for further reading. Although I cannot maintain that the lists provided are exhaustive, I have attempted to make them thorough, occasionally going beyond the subjects discussed by Collingham, and hope that they will give the reader useful 'starting points'. Finally, in translating the many French passages in the text, I have sought only to capture the meaning of the original in as simple and clear a form as possible. Certain terms cannot, however, be directly translated and are best left in their original form. A glossary of such terms has, therefore, been appended to the text. Any glaring omissions in the 'cast of leading characters' and 'further reading' sections or errors in translation are, of course, entirely my own fault.

R. S. Alexander

Introduction

France in 1830 was a highly fragmented society. A succession of political, social and economic changes had destroyed the old order, but no new system had won the loyalties of the majority. The Revolution had unleashed new creeds and raised classes, which might unite against opponents, but would as often quarrel amongst themselves. Broadly, political opinion divided, on the left, into those who paid homage to the liberal Revolution and those who found inadequacy in its moderation, and, on the right, into the ultra-royalists who desired to reverse the effects of the Revolution and the moderates who might deplore it but realised that the Revolution was a fact which could not be ignored.

Louis XVIII, restored to the French throne in July 1815 after Napoleon's Hundred Days, falls into the latter category. He was sufficiently astute to comprehend the strength of the middle classes and the danger of alienating them. His younger brother Charles who succeeded him in 1824, refused to understand the changes that had taken place. He and the ultra-royalists disliked the Charter by which Louis XVIII had made France a constitutional monarchy. Charles X's idea of his royal prerogative was incompatible with parliamentary government. Not only the opposition but moderate conservatives, former ministers such as Duc Decazes, Baron Pasquier and Comte Molé, found it impossible to accept the attempted retrogression to the principles of the *ancien régime*.

In opposition, the moderates combined with the centre. Around two peers, the Duc de Broglie and Baron de Barante, had formed a group of younger men known as the "doctrinaires". They followed the political philosopher Royer-Collard in attempting to combine bourgeois supremacy and parliamentary government with hereditary monarchy. The doctrinaire group included François Guizot and Victor Cousin, both prohibited from lecturing at the Sorbonne because of their liberalism, and the young men who wrote for the newspaper *Le Globe*, Rémusat, Duchatel, Vitet and Duvergier de Hauranne. All these were to play a notable role under Charles's successor.

Beside the moderate, liberal opposition in Parliament and press, existed a radical and conspiratorial opposition. There were young men like Adolphe

Thiers and Armand Carrel who could never forgive the Restoration its origins in French military defeat. This patriotic hostility had found its extreme in the vow of the assassin of the Duc de Berry, son of Charles X, to exterminate all Bourbons. Other determined, but less brutal, opponents joined the Charbonnerie, a conspiratorial organisation of republicans which infiltrated barracks where loyalty to the Emperor remained strong, and held its members in readiness for revolt. It united for a while men who, under King Louis-Philippe, would be prosecutors and prosecuted. Bazard, Guinard, Buchez and Trélat remained loyal to their hatred of monarchy, but Barthe and Plougoulm, later to become pillars of order and *procureurs généraux*, were also members. Dupont de l'Eure, Joseph Merilhou and François Mauguin played leading roles: they would all join the opposition to Louis-Philippe after 1830.

Relics of the Empire played their part in this motley opposition. Imperial soldiers and functionaries such as Généraux Lamarque, Gérard and Sébastiani posed as liberal parliamentarians. Amongst the populace, a sentimental cult of Napoleon was spread by cheap lithographs and Béranger's versification. As the Restoration accepted a conservative and pacific European order, dissatisfaction engendered nostalgia: writings on Revolution and Empire sapped loyalty and encouraged opposition, particularly amongst those too young to remember the carnage of battlefield and guillotine. Even amongst those who did not indulge these hopes nor wished the overthrow of the regime, there was social and ideological antagonism towards the aristocratic and Catholic society that the Bourbon monarchy seemed to represent. Whilst growing in economic power, the middle class frequently discovered its social and political ambitions blocked. The year 1830 was to install in power the lawyers and bankers who had attained a position of frustrated influence in preceding years. The opposition of men as fundamentally conservative as Périer and Dupin, was little more than the product of suspicion of priests and jealousy of noblemen, but, if not daring to desire its downfall, they were none the less emotionally disloyal to the regime.

The opposition to the Bourbon Restoration was drawn from a highly diverse collection of attitudes and groups, from the staid bourgeois banker to the ardent young republican, from the liberal academic to the unemployed general. On the one hand, it encouraged or condoned insurrection, whilst on the other, it posed as defender of law and constitution against the incursions of royal authority. Charles X, as king of the ultra-royalists, gave them motive to unite. In 1827 they combined to fight the elections in a cumbrously named association, Aide-toi, le Ciel t'aidera (Heaven helps those who help themselves). Guizot presided, but republicans such as Cavaignac and Bastide joined it: when it had achieved success, its right wing resigned.

The success of the opposition brought into being, in January 1828, a cabinet of moderates under the Vicomte de Martignac. This attempt to govern from the centre failed, because, in spite of his good intentions, Martignac was unable to soothe the irritations caused by his predecessors. The opposition would not give him loyal support, trying to drag him leftward: the ultra-royalists, with a cynical readiness to ally with their further antagonists which they were to show under the July Monarchy, combined with the opposition to outvote him. Upon his defeat, Charles in August 1829 asked his ultra-royalist friend the Prince de Polignac to form a ministry. To public opinion it appeared a Cabinet of courtiers, *émigrés* and traitors (the Général de Bourmont who had deserted Napoleon on the eve of Waterloo was Minister of War). Moderates, as well as inveterate enemies of the Bourbons, regarded it as an attack on their patriotism, religious liberty and political and social ambition. The opposition renewed its activity and prepared for conflict. Increasingly the existence of the regime was questioned. Comparisons were made between nineteenth-century France and seventeenth-century England: Louis XVI was Charles I, Napoleon was Cromwell, Louis XVIII was Charles II and now Charles X was acting like James II. Those who desired a parallel to 1688 looked for a French William of Orange.

Some believed they had found a candidate in Louis-Philippe, Duc d'Orléans. The Orléans branch of the Bourbon family, descending from Louis XIV's younger brother, had frequently been an affliction to the ruling senior branch. Louis-Philippe's father, called "Philippe-Egalité", had taken his allegiance to the Revolution to the length of voting for the execution of his cousin Louis XVI. Although his own political role during the Restoration had been restricted to arguments with Louis XVIII over the privileges which should be accorded to a prince of the blood, although he had opposed Napoleon and respectably married a Neapolitan Bourbon princess, he was distrusted by many royalists who could not forget his father's crime. Besides, he was suspected of holding liberal ideas, had given early support to the Revolution and had fought bravely for it at Jemappes and Valmy. It was this which recommended him to many. In January 1830, the banker Laffitte financed a new newspaper, *Le National*, in which three young journalists, Carrel, Thiers and his friend Mignet, supported by the ancient and discontented intriguer, the Prince de Talleyrand, propounded the theory of Orleanism. The comparison of Bourbons with Stuarts was taken up by the doctrinaire *Globe* and by the *Journal des Débats*, as warning and veiled threat.

The King and Polignac took no heed. The speech which Charles delivered in March 1830 was somewhat provocative in tone, and called upon the deputies to support the royal programme. An attempt by the centre right to avoid confrontation was thwarted by the ultra-royalists and the liberal opposition, Berryer speaking for the former, Guizot for the latter. A warning to the King not to overstep the limits of his prerogative was voted by 221 deputies, although surrounding their protest with assurances of loyalty. Charles felt his honour involved: the lesson he had learned from the Revolution was that conciliation brought disaster; his eldest brother's weakness had led to the guillotine. He responded to the challenge by dissolving the Chamber of Deputies. All shades of opposition united to fight the elections, which, ending on 19 July, added to their numbers. Charles would not admit defeat: he was no tyrant but a strongly principled mediocrity, who, believing the 1815 Charter to be the source of his difficulties, came to see a trial of strength as the only means of overcoming the weakness of his position. He found in Article XIV of the Charter the right to issue ordinances in times of emergency. The King and his ministers, convincing themselves that the monarchy was in danger, dissolved the freshly elected Chamber and called for new elections on a more restricted franchise, and forbade the appearance of any journal or brochure wthout preliminary authorisation. The four ordinances which Charles signed on the 25 July attacked the Constitution in spirit if not in letter.

Thus left and right walked unconsciously into revolution. The King had provoked the opposition, most members of which desired only a modification in policy, not a change of regime. The liberals for their part, frequently controlled by petty jealousies and ambitions, had weakened the centre by their attacks upon it. Yet the centre as a force was never strong: there was no moderate conservative party with popular roots, symptomatic of a monarchy which could neither repose on past traditions nor dared to ally itself with the hostile forces of progress. The forces of dissatisfaction and nostalgia held sway on left and right, especially amongst the romantic younger generation, republican, Bonapartist or royalist, which felt a temperamental dislike for compromise.

The unity of the opposition was to prove temporary. After 1830 when the insurrection provoked by his rash incompetence had forced Charles X from his throne, the opposition split between those who welcomed and propelled the July Revolution and those who merely accepted it in order to halt its progress. Many Restoration moderates rallied to the July Monarchy, but some of them never forgave the liberals their destructive opposition to Martignac. However, on 10 July, it was a group representing all shades of opinion amongst politicians, journalists and lawyers, who met at the home of the Duc de Broglie to discuss what action to take if the King acted unconstitutionally. They decided to refuse to pay taxes and to oppose the budget to force him to retreat. Most of the participants in this act of opposition hoped by the threat of resistance, to obviate the need for such measures. A few, Laffitte and Thiers for example, hoped for Charles's removal, but most feared such a result. To lose a king, however unsatisfactory, might well lead to a republic. The Duc d'Orléans was of this opinion: although he cultivated the liberals, he feared to conspire for the throne as ultra-royalists were later to assert.

Both the government preparing for a demonstration of force, and the opposition considering fiscal resistance, deluded themselves that victory would be gained within the confines of the small political world. However, economic crisis had widened the circles of the dissatisfied. France in 1830 was about to emerge from an economic crisis which had hurt the middle classes but which was disastrous for those who already lived on the borderline of destitution. Throughout the country there were bread riots, mendicancy increased, and to the hungry and unemployed in Paris was added a new wave of indigents seeking the official and private charity that was to be found in the capital. The existence of this dangerous class, crowded into the hideous slums which stretched around the centres of government, provided a high proportion of the insurrectionary army which defeated the royal troops. Ironically, they contributed as much to the speedy end of the revolution as to its success, for it was the fear they inspired which led to the determination of the politicians to impose a settlement before insurrection destroyed the social order.

In July, however, government and opposition were intent upon their political quarrel. On the 26th, the *Moniteur* published the four ordinances. The compromise upon which the Restoration had been built was destroyed: Charles, in attempting to secure the monarchy by imposing it on all factions from a base of ultra-royalism which limited the power of the bourgeoisie, brought about his own downfall and the end of the Bourbon dynasty.

1

The Revolution of July, 1830

". . . chaque enfant de Paris
De sa cartouche citoyenne
Fait une offrande a son pays."

("Each child of Paris
With his citizen's cartridge
Makes an offering to his country.")[1]

On 26 July, the Duc d'Orléans read with dismay the four ordinances published in the official *Moniteur*. "They are mad!" he exclaimed: "They are going to get themselves exiled again! As for me, I have already been, twice! I want no more of it; I remain in France!"[2] Similar consternation was expressed by other wealthy Parisian liberals. At the offices of the *Constitutionnel*, the journalists were anxiously consulting the newspaper's lawyer, Dupin. He declared that the measures were illegal, but neither he nor the majority present seemed willing to resist them. Angered by their pusillanimity, Charles de Rémusat left for the office of the *National*. It had defied the prohibition, appearing with an editorial advocating resistance by refusing to pay taxes. Its leading journalists, Thiers, Mignet and Carrel, were surrounded by an excited company, amongst whom were two opposition deputies, Auguste Berard and Alexandre de Laborde. They had come from Périer's hotel, where they, like Rémusat, had been disappointed by the caution of their colleagues.

Thiers drew up a collective protest. It called for resistance by journalists and deputies to governmental illegality, but there was no attempt to rouse the populace. "There must be leading names below this manifesto"[3] called Thiers. Many sat nervously silent, but Rémusat quietly went forward and signed his name. Gradually others followed:* eleven newspapers were

* Among the forty-four signatures were many notables of the July Monarchy: Thiers, Mignet, Carrel, Chambolle (*National*), Guizard, Dejean, Rémusat (*Globe*), Coste (*Temps*), Alexis de Jussieu, Chatelain (*Courrier Français*), Cauchois-Lemaire (*Constitutionnel*), Leon Pillet (*Journal de Paris*), Bohain, Roqueplan (*Figaro*).

represented, those who signed hoping that the journals they represented would publish the manifesto on the morrow. They separated, wondering how long it would be before the government ordered their arrest, and if the populace would support them: as yet, there seemed little sign of it.

Only slowly did Paris become aware of the King's action. The financial world had become quickly agitated, but the news had been more slow to spread amongst the population. As evening fell, crowds congregated; there were a few seditious cries, a few stones were thrown at two of the ministers, but such disorder was endemic to the city: Charles retired after his customary game of whist, confident of his triumph. A political revolution scarcely seemed imminent, especially as the deputies present in Paris (many remained in the departments where they had been fighting the election) had as yet adopted a cautious attitude. Bérard and Laborde, having left the offices of the *National*, had convened a meeting of deputies whom they hoped would emulate the journalists in a protest. Although some of the most vociferous members of the opposition were among the fourteen present, the ardour of Auguste de Schonen and Bérard was smothered by vigorous opposition from Périer and Villemain. They could agree only to meet again on the following afternoon.

On Tuesday the 27th, only four newspapers were published in defiance of the ordinance: the *National*, the *Globe* (where Rémusat called for legal resistance in rather violent terms), the *Temps* and the *Journal du Commerce* which omitted the signatures. The *Journal des Débats*, which although in opposition had failed to be represented when the protest was drawn up, and the *Constitutionnel* had applied for authorisation and, being refused, decided to act with prudence and did not appear. The timidity of the printers of other opposition journals prevented their being published. Royalist newspapers had obtained authorisation and appeared in praise of the ordinances. However, their distribution was hampered by mobs, whilst the opposition sheets which appeared were profusely distributed in wine shops, cafés and reading rooms.

The prefect of police issued warrants against the four rebellious newspapers and sent gendarmes to seize their presses. The doors of the *National* had to be broken in, whilst at the offices of the *Temps* its editor threatened the invaders with the law against breaking and entering. For a while, the crowd which applauded his harangue was able to prevent the presses being rendered inoperable: eventually force was victorious, but its evidence had aroused the population. Many employers had given their workers a free day, some from economic reasons fearing a slump, but mostly from opposition to the government, and bands were forming in the streets.

As deputies entered Casimir Périer's house, they were cheered. If the Parisians had known the caution which dominated within, their enthusiasm would have been less. Only about thirty deputies were present: many were still absent from the capital, and the two who had most influence on the result of the insurrection, Laffitte and La Fayette, had not yet arrived. Guizot had appeared, however, and added his voice to those of Périer and Sébastiani in opposing Bérard's reiterated demand for immediate formal protest and the revolutionary fervour of Mauguin and Audry de Puyraveau, who seemed to wish the deputies to rush into the streets to lead the population in insurrection. The majority of deputies remained obstinate in their indecision. Once again, action was postponed but three of the most circumspect, Guizot, Dupin and Villemain, were delegated to draft a protest. Influential Parisian liberal electors who arrived, failed to persuade them to take more positive action.

Events in the streets of Paris made talk of moral resistance increasingly irrelevant: the population had begun to seize the initiative. Mobs tore down shop signs embellished with royal arms and threw stones at gendarmes who attempted to disperse them. The first death occurred in the early afternoon when a gendarme guarding Polignac's office was killed. More followed when soldiers fired on a stone-throwing throng around the Place du Palais-Royal: the populace, crying for revenge, now had their martyrs whom they carried through the streets. Their anger was soon further increased when Charles put Maréchal de Marmont in command of military forces in the capital. To the Parisians, this name was synonymous with traitor: on his desertion from Napoleon, was blamed the capture of Paris in 1814. By this action, Charles roused patriotic emotions and gave the masses a chance to revenge themselves on a hated scapegoat.

When Marmont installed himself in the Tuileries, he found the position graver than the King, cocooned in optimism at Saint-Cloud outside Paris, had imagined. Insurrection had begun and the populace could fight on the urban terrain it understood. Marmont was successful in occupying certain strategic positions, not without difficulty. But he could not prevent the looting of arms shops and night fell with an armed populace surrounding an ill-supplied army.

Next morning, 28 July, the King received a hurried note from the commander which should have jolted him from his complacency. Crowds were forming in greater numbers, increasingly menacing; "it is no longer a riot, it is a revolution"[4]: unless His Majesty took immediate pacificatory steps, all might be lost. Whilst Marmont agitatedly awaited a reply, the situation worsened. Trees were hewn down, paving stones torn up to construct barricades. Old soldiers emerged in their imperial uniforms and some bourgeois appeared in their National Guard costume which had lain unused since Charles had unwisely dissolved that citizens' militia: they were loudly cheered.

Laffitte had arrived in Paris and his opulent salons bacame a centre for opposition forces. The banker and his friend, the poet Béranger, who possessed a popular reputation for his anti-Bourbon versifying, encouraged visitors to resistance. At last the political world provided stimulation rather than restraint. At the offices of the *National*, Thiers, Mignet and Carrel, true to the brief tradition of their newspaper, felt the time was ripe to propagate the candidature of Orléans. The young men consulted Général Sébastiani, a confidant of the Duc, and were annoyed at his counsels of patience and inaction.

Parliamentarians and important electors were congregating at Guizot's home that morning. Opinion was beginning to turn: action as moderate as legal resistance was becoming irrelevant, seeming to be treachery to the cause of the insurrection. The Duc de Broglie, like the younger and rasher Comte de Rémusat, felt that they had to be seen to act. Even Périer talked of solidarity with the Parisian population, but he also sent a personal message to Saint-Cloud urging Charles to repeal the ordinances. It was easier to debate than to agree on action, however, and further delay resulted from these deliberations. Thiers had used the opportunity to suggest to a few deputies present, that the Duc d'Orléans might be the solution to their problems.

In the streets, the position of government and army grew weaker whilst Marmont awaited orders from Saint-Cloud. The *National* and *Temps* had succeeded in printing sheets, and these and other publications encouraged insurrection. Cries of "Down with royalty" were added to the merely anti-ministerial shouts. Guard posts were attacked and the soldiers sometimes forced to withdraw. The crowds pushed into the Hôtel de Ville and Notre Dame. The tricolour flag, symbol of revolution, was raised on the cathedral's towers and the bells rang to the frantic acclamation of the crowd. "Listen to the tocsin! We are triumphing" remarked the Prince de Talleyrand gleefully: "Who are we?" he was asked: "Quiet! Not a word. I will tell you tomorrow"[5] was the reply.

Marmont heard that some of his troops were beginning to defect. He decided that only immediate action could prevent collapse, and with the Carrousel as his centre, he made plans to send his troops, in three columns, through the insurrectionary city. Progress was slow and painful in the sweltering heat, worsened by the constant need to surmount obstacles. The troops came under attack from upper windows and roofs and had the frustration of opposing an elusive and seemingly invulnerable enemy. Their ammunition began to run out. The only success was the cry of "Long live the King!" which the distribution of money by Général de Saint-Chamans elicited from some slum-dwellers; but his gold, like his troops' gunpowder, was in short supply. The first column was initially successful: the tricolour was hauled down, but the troops found themselves immured on every side by the insurrection they had with difficulty broken into and which was now closing in on them. And in the narrow streets around the Marché des Innocents, the second column was surrounded, open to the fire of men wearing National Guard uniform and the youth of the area which had been able to gain weapons. To remain meant extinction, so their commander relinquished the position gained with so much difficulty and fought his way back to the banks of the Seine. In the evening, the third column likewise returned to the centre by the left bank which was comparatively free. The columns had attained their goals but, once there, had been isolated by the forces of insurrection. Louis-Philippe's government would learn strategically from Marmont's failure.

Meanwhile the deputies' agitated discussions were beginning to reflect the reality of probable insurrectionary success. They had met at noon at the house of a wealthy deputy, the merchant Audry de Puyraveau, who had proved his revolutionary ardour by donating his carriages to form barricades and by distributing weapons. The windows were open and the listening crowd outside shouted approval or disapproval of the speeches. Laffitte was chosen president of the reunion: he had already sent an envoy to Neuilly to sound out the Duc d'Orléans but had received no reply. Mauguin invoked the solidarity of deputies and the people in a revolutionary cause and demanded a provisional government. Dupin and Sébastiani protested against any action which went beyond legality, finding even Guizot's draft protest to be rash. Guizot argued that the deputies must not act for or against the people, rather they should mediate between the King and his rebellious subjects: thus the basis of Orleanist sovereignty was expressed; it was a transaction between traditional monarchy and democracy. Guizot's draft protested against the ordinances and declared the signatories legally elected: compared with the journalists' protest two days earlier, it was mild. It was also rendered obsolete by events on the streets. As yet however, they were uncertain how the fighting progressed. The sound of gunfire on all sides seemed to presage a victory for the army and some of the foremost conspirators, Thiers, Rémusat, Mignet and Carrel, were considering flight in this eventuality.

Meeting late in the afternoon, this time at the home of Bérard, the deputies heard of the failure of their attempt to persuade Marmont to cease fire, strengthening the position of those who desired a change in regime. An editor of the *Temps* hurried in with the proofs of the protest, from which he had removed the forms of royalist respect: he declared he would publish it only with signatures. This agitated the deputies. Four of the most cautious, Villemain, Bertin de Vaux (a proprietor of the *Journal des Débats*) and two Napoleonic veterans, Gérard and Sébastiani, retired, to the jeers of the crowds outside. The discussions continued. La Fayette proclaimed that on the morrow he would establish the direction of the insurrection at the Hôtel de Ville, whilst Laffitte spoke to Périer of the suitability of the Duc d'Orléans for the Crown, in spite of his candidate's distinctly negative reply to his first soundings.

The inevitability that the protest should be signed may explain the presence of only eight deputies that evening, again at the home of Audry de Puyraveau. These were the most determinedly hostile to the Restoration, although split between republicans, Bonapartists and Orleanists like Laffitte and Bérard. These few took it upon themselves to sign for fellow deputies, including those they believed would have signed had they been present in Paris: the list that appeared on posters and in newspapers the next day comprised sixty-three names, and although Dupin was omitted, Villemain, Sébastiani and Bertin were compromised in the protest.

As for the King, he had refused continued attempts to squeeze concessions from him. Although a telescope at Saint-Cloud had enabled worried courtiers to perceive the hated tricolour floating from the towers of Notre Dame, Charles retained his confidence in Polignac. That evening he as usual played whist, while those around him discussed whether the mob would next day march on the château. In Paris, Marmont's troops, hungry and exhausted, slept uncomfortably around the Tuileries, their vulnerable citadel in a hostile city.

On 29 July, insurgents mounted the barricades early. Scarcely a street on the right bank of central Paris was free of obstacles. Mobs sacked barracks in search of rifles and ammunition. In the Rue de Babylone, students of the Polytechnique led an attack on the barracks of the Swiss Guard, unpopular because of their nationality and identification with the *ancien régime*. Périer used his authority to halt the massacre of some soldiers trapped in the Rue de Rohan. Mobs broke into a monastery, chased out the priests and burnt books and furniture. The National Guard, beginning to act as the force of order they were intended to be, turned from insurrection to prevent crowds freeing prisoners from Sainte-Pélagie, but were too late to prevent the release of those in the Conciergerie. The mobs turned their attention to the palace of the Archbishop of Paris: its valuable contents, books, manuscripts and relics were hurled into the Seine, from which eager bibliophiles were forcibly prevented from retrieving these treasures. The middle classes for the most part felt little sympathy for the Church, but impeccably secular private property might soon be threatened if the mob were allowed to develop a taste for pillage.

The politicians began the attempt to reimpose authority. At Laffitte's hotel, Thiers, Béranger and the Duc de Broglie were trying to promote the Duc d'Orléans as a means of saving monarchy without betraying the insurrection. Sébastiani rallied to this but Guizot was still uncertain, his historian's mentality less ready to overthrow a tradition. But the Duc continued to be unwilling and the republicans were attempting to gain control.

The town hall, relinquished by the army, was under the self-important protection of "Général" Dubourg, a leader who had emerged at the head of a portion of the mob and who had donned a second-hand uniform to reinforce his self-awarded rank. The arrival of a genuine general forced him to cease his pretensions when La Fayette, carried over the barricades by enthusiastic crowds, entered the building. Young republicans, amongst them Godefroy Cavaignac, Etienne Arago, Blanqui and Bastide, clustered around him, urging him to form a truly popular government, the republic "one and indivisible", whose Committee of Public Safety he would lead.

Whilst a new authority was slowly emerging, the old had disappeared. Marmont, realising the weakness of his position, the lack of provisions, the increasing desertion, sent to the King a last plea for conciliation and ordered his troops to cease fire. The rebels did not reciprocate, however, and pressed forward against the Louvre. The troops' withdrawal beneath the insurgents' bullets became a flight which carried with it the soldiers in the Place du Carrousel; they fled through the Tuileries gardens, across the Place Louis XVI and into the Champs-Élysées. Talleyrand, calmly observing the disorder, remarked: "29 July, five minutes past midday, the elder branch of the House of Bourbon has ceased to reign".[6] Meanwhile, the rebels ransacked the Louvre, destroying the contents or drinking themselves into a stupor in the cellars.

The collapse of Charles's army showed the deputies that they must rapidly organise a new authority. The radicals, Mauguin and Audry de Puyraveau, demanded a provisional government, but Guizot and the moderates, fearing the revolutionary implications of this, decided that five commissioners be sent to advise and restrain La Fayette whom many of them distrusted. Eventually Casimir Périer, Général Gérard, Baron de Schonen, Mauguin and Audry, with the young lawyer Odilon Barrot as their secretary, proceeded to the Hôtel de Ville. A lack of unity was immediately apparent. The conservative Périer issued a dry announcement demanding respect for order and property which differed entirely from La Fayette's ecstatic proclamation hailing the triumphant insurrectionaries. Mauguin nominated political friends to command the police and postal services, whilst Alexandre de Laborde, an opposition deputy for Paris whose only capacity seemed to be the speedy dissipation of the fortune amassed by his financier father, was appointed prefect of the Seine. To Gérard, theoretically in charge of troops, came increasing numbers of former National Guardsmen and deserting army officers: now that Marmont had withdrawn towards Saint-Cloud, desertion was not cowardice but politic.

The men were congregating who were willing to rally to a new regime, yet events dictated no solution. Amidst the debris of two days' fighting, in a city thick with the stench of corpses of men and horses, the triumphant populace appeared as a political force. "Down with the Bourbons!" was the cry of social dissatisfaction and of fifteen years' wounded patriotism rather than the expression of constitutional liberalism. A few republican cries were heard from the crowds, but "long live Napoleon!" was more common, expressing less a political programme than the desire to avenge a hero. There were genuine Bonapartists such as the journalist Evariste Dumoulin and "Général" Dubourg. The former on the night of 29 July composed a proclamation declaring the son of Napoleon I as emperor and attempted to rally support. The next morning, La Fayette, who, however muddled his ideas, was no Bonapartist, had the unfortunate enthusiast led into a small room in the Hôtel de Ville and kept there for a few hours while his cause waned. The Empire was an ideal, insufficiently tangible, the Bonapartist candidate being the charming and sickly Duc de Reichstadt, several days' journey away under Austrian surveillance.

The presence of a Napoleonic claimant might have rendered Orléans's candidature impossible but admirers of the first Napoleon, such as the Duc de Bassano, Maréchal Exelmans or Comte de Lobau, did not wish to risk their reintegration into the ruling circle for a mere possibility. Sentimental Bonapartists like Béranger, at Laffitte's side throughout these days, chose a constitutional monarchy under a candidate who was less than an hour's ride distant, rather than risk delay and Bourbon restoration or Jacobin republic. On the municipal commission, the Bonapartist orator Mauguin alienated possible allies by an unattractive mixture of arrogant fatuity and personal ambition. Schonen's enthusiasm at times triumphed over his natural caution but he was open to persuasion from the dominating Périer, a constitutional monarchist.

Charles X had been thrown from complacence into indecisive despair. It took repeated urging, particularly by the Marquis de Sémonville, to persuade the King to replace Polignac by the liberal Duc de Mortemart. Bearing news of this and withdrawal of the ordinances, Sémonville and Comte d'Argout arrived breathlessly at the Hôtel de Ville on the evening of the 29th. Both Schonen and Barrot later claimed to have replied to the concession bearers, "It is too late."[7]* Périer, informed that he and Gérard had been appointed ministers (a promotion he had coveted in calmer days), did not lower his guard, but seemed well disposed. Mauguin and Audry were completely hostile, the latter claiming that if Périer and Lobau talked of coming to an arrangement with Charles, he would advance to the window and summon the people. The commission in deadlock, Périer advised Sémonville and d'Argout to consult the deputies at Laffitte's home.[8] The first executive born of the Revolution resigned its powers to a meeting dominated by a small circle. Comte d'Argout struggled through crowds to the Rue d'Artois and into Laffitte's salon. The deputies listened while he again announced the King's tardy concessions. The absence of the ill and reluctant Mortemart was fatal: Laffitte was non-committal, others led by Bertin de Vaux and Sébastiani were warmer, but the hostility of the crowds outside had been roused. Amidst cries of "No more Bourbons! Long live the Republic! Long live Napoleon!", d'Argout left and rode back to Saint-Cloud.[9]

On the morning of 30 July, Mortemart and d'Argout, bearing the signed concessions, made their way into Paris avoiding the crowds. Charles X's last *président du conseil* reached Laffitte's home at about 10 a.m. but the deputies were meeting in the Palais Bourbon, a sign that they again felt themselves to be an official political body. Mortemart did not make his way there, but to the Chamber of Peers: reaching Sémonville's apartment, the sick man collapsed in exhaustion. It was impossible even to have the concessions printed because the offices of the *Moniteur* were occupied by men with orders from the municipal commission to prevent any such governmental proclamation.

Those who wished to replace Charles X with the Duc d'Orléans were in increasing control of events. The previous evening, Thiers and Mignet had drawn up a manifesto which was printed overnight, and on the morning of the 30th, copies were scattered throughout the streets. "Charles X can no longer enter Paris; he has shed the blood of the people. A republic would expose us to frightful conditions. The Duc d'Orléans is a prince devoted to the cause of the revolution"; he had fought under the tricolour at the battles of Jemappes, and he would wholeheartedly accept the charter desired by them; "It is from the French people that he would take his crown."[10] The *National* of that morning carried an article presenting Orléans as a revolutionary prince possessing qualities which should endear him to the population; he was patriotic, courageous, liberal and anticlerical. Bérard, reading out the proclamation to crowds, many of whom were illiterate, repeatedly intoned the

* Sémonville's account[8] claims that nobody uttered these words.

keywords of Orleanist propaganda: the battles of Jemappes and Valmy, the sacred tricolour, the principles of 1789. If none of this was strictly untrue, the image of the Duc being presented by his propagandists reflected neither the middle-aged man nervously hesitating in secret outside Paris nor the astute politician who would rule France for nearly eighteen years. It reflected the hopes and needs of a few members of the Restoration opposition. Prince, he would present a barrier against the egalitarian tendencies of a republic; he would legitimise a social order which they wished only slightly to modify by removing its aristocratic exclusivity; he would not offend their allegiance to 1789 whilst protecting them from 1793.

Whilst his proclamation was being distributed, Thiers accompanied by Ary Scheffer, drawing-master to the Orléans children, rode off to Neuilly, with difficulty negotiating the obstacles which littered the streets. The statement that the Duc had declared himself for the Revolution was merely anticipation. To urgent messages from Laffitte, the reply had been worse than non-committal. Orléans, fearing that some extreme royalists might attempt to take him hostage, had retreated to another of his properties outside the city. Thiers therefore faced, not the man he had come to persuade, but his wife and Madame Adelaïde, his sister. The Duchesse was aghast when she read the letters from Laffitte and Sébastiani and heard the eloquent and impassioned Thiers argue the need for her husband to mount the throne: "They will call him usurper, he the most honest of men",[11] she cried. The strong-minded and ambitious Madame Adelaïde ignored the tears of her politically incapable sister-in-law: she wasted no sympathy on Charles but listened while Thiers spoke of the necessity of preventing a republic by creating a dynasty "which owes the Crown to us and, owing it to us, resigns itself to the role that the representative system assigns to it".[12]* She replied that her family would gladly aid this just revolution and that she would obtain the return of her brother from his concealment. "Madame", responded Thiers with a phrase suited to a historic moment, "today you secure the Crown for your House."[13]

Returning to the city, Thiers found Laffitte presiding over a disorderly meeting of deputies at the Palais Bourbon, and told him that Madame Adelaide had accepted on behalf of her brother. The Orleanist solution was hawked round the Chamber: the boldest wanted the Duc to be made king immediately, but the majority preferred that he should take the title of *lieutenant-général* of the realm, as many still hoped that the legitimate line could be continued in the person of Charles's infant grandson, with Orléans as regent. A tiny number of the ninety-five deputies present would have preferred a republic: Barrot argued with them, using words later attributed to La Fayette that the Duc would be "the best of republics".[14]

A similar, but more violent, argument was taking place at a restaurant where Béranger tried to convince the young republicans Bastide, Trélat, Teste and others that France was not ready for a republic, and that a constitutional

* Thiers's account of his words was written later when it may have suited him to stress the revolutionary and contractual origins of the Orléans throne.

monarchy was temporarily necessary. Some of them became so angry that they almost assaulted the poet: they went to the Hôtel de Ville to urge La Fayette to make himself a dictator, but he merely wasted their time in pointless arguments. Signs of republican machinations, the posters, the cries of "Death to the Bourbons! Long live the Republic" had the effect of persuading deputies who still hoped for a *rapprochement* with the Bourbons, into looking for salvation to the cadet branch. Thus Dupin rode out to Neuilly, and Général Gérard sent his nephew to urge the Duc to accept the lieutenancy-general.

When an envoy from Mortemart brought the concessions to the deputies, the republicans made it difficult for him to make himself heard and Laffitte refused officially to acknowledge their reception. The liberal *idéologue*, Benjamin Constant, won considerable support when he spoke against any arrangement with the Bourbons: the Chamber had become Orleanist and Constant and Sébastiani drew up an official appeal to the Duc d'Orléans to act as *lieutenant-général*. This short and scarcely radical document did not abolish the legitimate monarchy: theoretically a regency was still possible: it merely asked Orléans to restore the tricolour and added that the deputies were concerned to execute the Charter. Forty deputies signed it, seven abstained, and three (including Villemain, a future minister of Louis-Philippe) voted against it. A deputation took it to the Palais Royal, the central Paris residence of the Orléans family, and thence a messenger took to Neuilly their request that he come to Paris. After hesitating, the Duc left quietly and at 11 p.m. that evening slipped unnoticed into the Palais Royal. At the same time, Charles and his family, fearing the proximity of the Paris mob, made preparations to move to Versailles. Increasingly the hopes of the friends of the Bourbon senior branch came to lie in a nine-year-old child, Henri, Duc de Bordeaux, son of the assassinated Duc de Berry. Most of those present in Sémonville's apartment at the Chamber of Peers were trying to further this cause. Only a few, the Ducs de Choiseul, de Broglie and de Montebello, the Comte de Montalivet and Général Dejean were truly Orleanist: most, led by Duc Decazes, Baron Pasquier and Comte Molé, all former ministers, hoped that Orléans would act as regent for Henri.

That evening it seems that the Duc himself considered this. He passionately told Mortemart that he had no desire for the throne, insisting that he would only accept a regency. He is supposed to have sent Charles a letter asserting this,* claiming that he had been brought to Paris by force. Louis-Philippe was an emotional man and at moments of crisis he could also be indecisive. On reaching Paris he was probably averse from grasping the throne, and the following morning when Laffitte led eleven other deputies to him, his first words were to desire delay.

* There is an unsolved mystery concerning this letter, over whose existence or genuineness historians have been divided. Thureau-Dangin, in the late nineteenth century, dismissed it as apocryphal, but more recently Bory in his study of 1830, implies that it is genuine. Sémonville claimed that it existed and that an urgent note the next morning reclaimed it from Mortemart. It probably did exist, but should be seen not as dishonest cunning to trap Charles (as legitimists would claim) but as an expression of indecision and confusion.

Yet it became increasingly obvious that he had to act. He had that morning already seen Laffitte and his friend Dupont (de l'Eure) (who, like Béranger, saw constitutional monarchy as the bridge to an orderly republic), Comte Molé, desirous of a regency, the Duc de Broglie, Guizot, Casimir Périer and the Comte de Rambuteau, all of whom stressed that only he could save France from anarchical republic or ultra-royalist reaction. Above all, there was Thiers who told him, "Your popularity is our only safeguard. Your refusal of royalty would serve to pave the way for a republic which would commence by devouring you, you and yours, and all of us afterwards".[15] When the deputation arrived, Bérard spoke of the republic's imminence, and Benjamin Delessert invoked the spectre of civil war; Orléans withdrew to consult Sébastiani and Dupin. A messenger hurried for Talleyrand's advice and returned with the recommendation to accept the lieutenancy. Orléans then emerged to present his affirmative to the relieved deputies. He carried with him a drafted proclamation which explained that he had agreed to become *lieutenant-général* of the kingdom, would strive to prevent civil war and anarchy, and would wear the tricolour with pride; thus the emblem of revolution decorated the Orleanist compromise. The declaration began with a lie (the Duc claimed not to have hesitated to come to share the dangers of the heroic population). It ended with a controversy, "A charter will be a testament for the future"[16]: to say "a" implied the substantial modification of the 1815 Charter, and the conservative *Journal des Débats* emphasised its belief in the essential continuity of the monarchy by printing "The Charter". The *Moniteur* claimed that this was the true version and that its first account had been an error.[17] Guizot asserts that "the" was in the original draft and that a radical deputy had altered it before printing. This controversy over the definite or indefinite article was symbolic of Orleanism, and presaged the controversy of whether Louis-Philippe became king because he was a Bourbon, or in spite of it. "The" and "because" represented the conservative claim that the Orleanist regime followed the Restoration logically, a necessary change in personnel assuring the continuation of its constitutional tradition: "a" and "although" implied that the King was chosen by the people and that 1830 represented a break from the royalist past.

This proclamation, soon to be controversial, was accepted by the 91 deputies present, and 10,000 copies of it were printed. July 1830 was indeed in many ways a revolution by the printing press, its earliest protagonists being journalists, and its victors men who knew well its powers. The deputies decided to print their own proclamation, and Constant, Bérard, Guizot and Villemain (who had accepted the *fait accompli*) were delegated to draft it. The presence of the first two ensured that the demands of the more radical elements would be advocated. Thus after the obligatory panegyric on Parisian heroism and the liberal and patriotic qualities of the Duc d'Orléans, it contained, against Guizot's will, the words "He will respect our rights, because he will take his from us"[18]: the deputies' proclamation thus claimed to be making a king. All the deputies present having signed, they set out for the Palais Royal where Laffitte read it and the Duc accepted it.

All realised that if republican forces were not quickly stifled, this agreement was worthless. A strange procession therefore left the Palais Royal: the Duc d'Orléans rode at the head, then came Laffitte in a sedan chair (he had injured his leg), followed by ninety deputies. Negotiating obstacles, hemmed in by a curious and friendly crowd, the Duc bestowed smiles and handshakes to right and left; "In my opinion, the Prince fraternises a little too much with a crowd of individuals of the lowest class of people"[19] wrote Bérard, who if progressive was no democrat. As the procession, followed by a disrespectful band of small boys, neared the Hôtel de Ville, glowering republican faces were observed and some cries of "Long live the Republic" and "Down with the Duc d'Orléans" were heard. Yet the predominant feeling of the crowds seems to have been goodwill mingling with confusion. "Who is that gentleman on horseback? Is he a general? Is he a prince?" the deputy Viennet heard someone ask, and another say "I hope it's not another Bourbon."[20]*

La Fayette emerged to greet the Duc; then, to a diverse audience, amongst which extremes of pleasure and disapproval were manifest, Viennet read the proclamation and the Duc again accepted. It was then that Dubourg exploded unexpectedly into history and shouted that they would know what to do if these promises were not kept: as many versions of the Duc's reply, delivered with restrained indignation, exist as do memoirs by those present on the occasion. La Fayette saved the situation by taking Orléans's arm and guiding him towards the balcony: here, the two men, holding a large tricolour flag which had been handed them, embraced amidst crowd's acclamations. This was the new monarch's popular sanction: "The republican kiss of La Fayette made a king",[21] remarked Chateaubriand. The Parisians had made Louis-Philippe king, Barrot would later claim,[22] but rather this was an ignorant population in a fit of enthusiasm ratifying the adhesion of their naive hero to the manœuvres of a few politicians.

On the next day, the *lieutenant-général* tried to charm some leading republicans who had protested against the *fait accompli*. He urged the necessity for compromise and in answer to their demand for war against the 1815 settlement, for peace in Europe. Cavaignac's only concession was to admit that Louis-Philippe's father, like his own, had voted for the death of Louis XVI, which separated him from "the others". The embarrassed reply was that some events should only be remembered that they might not be imitated.[23] Declaring that they would never support him, the republican group went to complain to La Fayette who under their influence drew up a programme: national sovereignty would be recognised in the Constitution, hereditary peerage and suffrage restrictions would be abolished and the magistrature completely renewed. This became known as the programme of the Hôtel de Ville and it was claimed by republicans to have been accepted by the future King only to break it. Yet Louis-Philippe would claim there was no engagement, although he admitted promising La Fayette "a monarchy surrounded

* Some Orleanist propaganda posters argued speciously that their candidate was not a Bourbon but a Valois: this dubious compliment avoided an unpopular name, but as a descendant of Louis XIII, the Duc d'Orléans was as much Bourbon and as little Valois, as Charles X.

by republican institutions",[24] a guarantee he probably thought sufficiently ensured by the abolition of hereditary peerage. The existence of an agreed programme is probably a republican myth, although La Fayette was charmed into exclaiming that Orléans was a republican like himself. And Bérard was told by the *lieutenant-général* that he entered his new functions without pleasure; "I have always kept an old republican sentiment at the bottom of my heart."[25]

Whilst expressing his republican regrets to the left, Orléans spoke to the friends of the senior branch of his grief at their fall. To Chateaubriand who came to him on 1 August to plead the cause of a regency for Henri V, he regretted that facts were against this desirable outcome. "I read in his face the desire to be king",[26] comments the writer bitterly. But it would have been difficult for Orléans to thwart the desires of men to whom he owed his position by imposing a child king upon them. And if the boy died, he would stand accused; "I would be stigmatised for ever. . . . I have suffered enough for my father."[27] For fear of exacerbating the hatred that ultra-royalists bore his regicide father, through Louis-Philippe, the Orléans family committed a last fatal wrong against the senior branch.

Having withdrawn to Rambouillet but refusing to attempt to continue fighting amidst the more royalist population of the Loire, Charles decided to appeal to the honour of his relative. On 2 August he formally proclaimed his grandson's accession, then signed his abdication, his younger son, the Duc d'Angoulême, also renouncing his rights in favour of his nephew, Henri V. On receipt of this, the *lieutenant-général* returned only a polite acknowledgement noting the abdications and replying that he would consult Parliament in whose archives he placed these.

The following day he wrote that it was necessary that Charles and his family leave France, but the old King was obstinate, and on Barrot's advice it was decided that a manifestation of the National Guard might speed their exile. The origins of the march of a Parisian mob to Rambouillet are unknown: the legitimists accused Louis-Philippe of fomenting it, but more probably it was a spontaneous expression of mob hatred for Charles. The *lieutenant-général* ordered the National Guards to accompany and control this crowd and sent three commissioners, Barrot, Schonen and Maréchal Maison, to persuade Charles to leave. As Barrot left Orléans in tears, bitterly lamenting that he should be the instrument of his relatives' exile, the Duchesse declared with pride, "Look at him, he is the most honest man in the realm."[28]

At Rambouillet, the commissioners urged Charles and his family to leave before the procession arrived. The King asked how many there were: possibly as many as 80,000 replied Maison, exaggerating the number at least fourfold. Some urged the King to use the 10,000 armed men he still had: "blood, always blood!"[29] lamented Charles and decided to leave. Resistance by royal troops could well have destroyed the rabble as Général Jacqueminot, one of those theoretically in command of them, later admitted. On this occasion, they were prevented from looting: many of them, reaching the château after the royal family had left, slept in the park and then rode back to Paris in carriages commandeered from the royal stables, singing the "Marseillaise". Without conflict, the crowd had scored its last victory in the 1830 Revolution.

Slowly, escorted by the commissioners and a few troops, the royal convoy made its way towards the coast. Sometimes the Duc de Bordeaux and his sister, not understanding events, graciously saluted, as they had been taught, the silent and inquisitive crowds who thronged the villages. Eventually, on 16 August, at Cherbourg, the royal party bade a tearful farewell to those who had remained loyal, and left for England and exile.

Throughout France the old authorities had collapsed and new ones taken their place. Generally, this change was peaceful, reflecting events in Paris, but without violence. As the first news of the protests arrived in large provincial towns, crowds appeared on the streets, shouted their approval of the Charter, their opposition to the King, and raised the tricolour. At Bordeaux, a crowd seized the prefecture and town hall in imitation of Paris. At Lyons, workers went into the streets, the authorities evacuated the town hall, and an aged Napoleonic general arrived to head the National Guard which had formed as soon as news of the victory in Paris was received. At Metz, the commander of the garrison decided not to resist when he learnt that Charles's army had evacuated Paris and handed over authority to the National Guard. Only Nantes saw bloodshed, for royalism and liberalism were extreme here, the authorities did not cede, and barricades and attacks on the army were needed before news from outside led to the collapse of the Restoration authority. The commander at Clermont shot himself rather than cause bloodshed or dishonour himself by surrender to a civilian militia. Elsewhere, however, the pattern was the same: old uniforms were proudly donned by bourgeois who formed committees to sit in the vacant chairs. Rarely was the Revolution strikingly popular in the provinces: at Lille, for example, a few manufacturers, hearing of the fall of Charles in Paris, told their employees to protest, and having frightened the municipal government, took its place. The departmental revolution was more obviously a bourgeois take-over of power than in Paris. From Bayonne, the liberal economist Bastiat wrote proudly that wealthy and prudent men had sacrificed their interests and their lives to acquire order and liberty.[30] But although no lives were lost in this small town and, as elsewhere, the sacrifice of interests amounted only to the loss of a few hours passed parading, it was a group of bourgeois in National Guard uniform who raised the tricolour on the citadel. Doubtless they felt they had played a historic role, sharing in the heroism of the Parisian population: even bourgeois revolutions need their mythology.

The Orléans Monarchy has been accused, since the date of its inception, of being a betrayal of the Revolution. The July insurrection was not, however, a single revolutionary republican movement of the majority of Frenchmen. The destruction of royal authority was accomplished by a section of the Parisian population, hostile to Charles, but otherwise without a political focus. Thus a determined few were able to impose a change in regime, acceptable to a majority for fear of the alternatives. Louis-Philippe was a necessary barrier to a Jacobin republic, but he also prevented a royalist reaction which remained a possibility until Charles reached Cherbourg. Without the lieutenancy-general, men like Périer or Sébastiani would have sought an arrangement with the senior branch. Orleanism betrayed not so much the republicans as the royalists whom it disarmed by appearing to protect their interest. They had little chance of recapturing Paris, but might have held much of the rest of France. Whomever he betrayed, Orléans almost certainly saved France from civil war.

Men such as Laffitte, Béranger, Bérard and Marrast thought that in Orléans they had found a king content with small powers, a rich man needing only a small civil list, a liberal to provide the decorative pinnacle to a bourgeois society. His strength lay in the youth of Henri V, the absence of Napoleon II, the fears roused by the republic: he represented a way that was none of these and yet seemed to participate in all of them. He was prince, patriot and liberal. He represented the dualism in the majority of middle-class Frenchmen, from the small shopkeeper to the banker; adherence to the principles of the 1789 Revolution and fear of its consequences.

Of course it was not the bankers and journalists who had died in *les trois glorieuses* as the days of insurrection came to be known. Most of those who fought were artisans or skilled workers. The lowest sections of society played a much smaller part, and as Général de Saint-Chamans had found, would cheer anyone who distributed bread or money, whatever their politics. The proportions had been estimated* (from the list of recompense distributed to relatives of the 211 dead and 1,327 wounded) as containing almost 1,000 of the artisan class (especially carpenters and stonemasons), less than 300 labourers and servants, 54 shopkeepers and 85 professional men. Evidently the role of the middle classes in the fighting was not large, but significant, given their proportion of the population. In a revolution without leaders (and where leaders were scarcely necessary as instinct led the insurgents into tactics perfectly suited to the urban battlefield), a few bourgeois in National Guard uniform, former soldiers and polytechnicians acted as officers. The part that the student played, however, like that of the *gamin* (street urchin), is one of the myths of 1830. Only three students were among the dead, and in spite of the bravery of Arcole who died on the bridge which bears his name, the revolutionary contribution of small boys was not as great as Delacroix's famous picture would have one believe. None the less *Liberty leading the People* brilliantly portrays the myth of a population united in heroism, a city in arms, vanquishing tyranny. It was the spirit which Casimir Delavigne, working hurriedly to provide an Orleanist alternative to the revolutionary and provincial "Marseillaise", embodied in "La Marche parisienne"; a song so popular it caused Nourrit, leading tenor of the Opera, to destroy his voice singing endlessly of Paris rising against slavery, marching against enemy cannon.

* By D. H. Pinkney, *The French Revolution of 1830*, Ch. VIII.

If the Parisian working man risked his life, journalists like Thiers and Rémusat, politicians like Laffitte and Bérard, believed that they risked at least their liberty if the insurrection failed, an eventuality which at times seemed probable until 29 July. The Revolution was also inaugurated because men as conservative as Périer and Molé were willing to resist the ordinances by measures of non-co-operation. Orleanists therefore claimed that the Revolution was consistent from its inception in the salons to its conclusion in Louis-Philippe's coronation. Gratitude to the insurrectionaries rarely suggested any duty to defer to their wishes. Indeed, some found the popular involvement a dangerous embarrassment: Périer refused to sign the municipal commission's proclamation congratulating the Parisians on having chosen a king. Others, whilst relieved at the victory of constitutionalism, regretted the event itself; Royer-Collard, for example, "sad amongst the victorious"[31] or Guizot who lamented that in France resistance became revolution and that every storm became a deluge.[32] But there were also conservatives who welcomed the Revolution; Broglie for example, or Rémusat who saw it as a middle-class constitutional movement from beginning to end.[33] Yet essentially, as the socialist Louis Blanc claimed, the Revolution was brought about by the *haute bourgeoisie* who feared it, and accomplished almost unwittingly by the populace,[34] which ambiguity meant that these events remained controversial throughout the lifetime of the July Monarchy.

Laffitte's justification, although intended as an argument against republicans, implied also that Louis-Philippe's kingship derived from the people: at the Hôtel de Ville, he had presented the Duc to the National Guard and the populace and their acclamation legitimised the choice.[35] And La Fayette who like Laffitte was later to oppose the King, claimed that popular assent was shown not only by the population of Paris, but by the stream of deputations from towns and villages all over France.[36] To the conservatives, this was scarcely relevant: they believed that only the person of the head of state had changed. Between the extremes of Orleanism, one side believing that no political revolution had occurred, the other that the people had chosen its king, there stretched a variety of nuances, and outside there lurked the hostile extremes, legitimist or republican, which would not accept the event as final. The optimism of July was soon to evaporate as men realised that the birth of a new regime had not put an end to divisions between Frenchmen.

REFERENCES

1. C. Delavigne, *Œuvres Complètes* (1885), 521.
2. Prince de Joinville, *Mémoires* (1894), 41.
3. J. Simon, *Thiers, Guizot, Rémusat* (1885), 35.
4. Maréchal de Marmont, *Mémoires* (1840), III, 242–3.
5. J. L. Bory, *La Révolution de Juillet* (1972), 363.

6. P. Mantoux, "Talleyrand en 1830", *Revue Historique*, LXXVIII (1902), 272.
7. Odilon Barrot, *Mémoires posthumes* (1875), I, 118.
8. Marquis de Sémonville, "Souvenirs", *La Revue de Paris* (September 1894).
9. J. Laffitte, *Mémoires* (1932), 172.
10. S. Bérard, *Souvenirs Historiques sur la Révolution de 1830* (1834), 112.
11. A. Trognon, *Vie de Marie-Amélie* (1872), 183.
12. Papiers Thiers, Bibliothèque Nationale, nouvelles acquisitions françaises 20602.
13. Ibid.
14. Louis Blanc, *Histoire de Dix Ans* (1840), I, 35.
15. S. Berteaut, *M. Thiers* (Marseilles, 1873), 26–7.
16. Bérard, op. cit., 136, 1779–80, and Laffitte, op. cit., 189.
17. *Le Moniteur*, 3 August 1830.
18. F. Guizot, *Mémoires pour servir à l'histoire de mon temps* (1858), II, 37, and *Le Moniteur*, 1 August 1830.
19. Bérard, op. cit., 144–5.
20. L. Viennet, *Journal* (1955), 103.
21. Vicomte F.-R. de Chateaubriand, *Mémoires d'Outre Tombe* (1948), III, 631.
22. Barrot, op. cit., I, 125.
23. Chateaubriand, op. cit., III, 632.
24. E. Lemoine, *Une visite au Roi Louis-Philippe* (1849), 21.
25. Bérard, op. cit., 144.
26. Chateaubriand, op. cit., III, 653.
27. Sémonville, op. cit., 96–7.
28. Barrot, op. cit., I, 133.
29. Marquis A. de Bonneval, *Mémoires Anecdotiques* (1900), 204.
30. F. Bastiat, *Œuvres Complètes* (1881), I, 20.
31. Baron P. de Barante, *Vie Politique de M. Royer-Collard* (1861), II, 53.
32. Guizot, op. cit., II, 4.
33. Comte C. de Rémusat, *Mémoires de ma vie* (1958), IV, 355.
34. Blanc, op. cit., I, 30.
35. Laffitte, op. cit., 144, and A. Pépin, *La Royauté de Juillet et la Révolution* (1837), 63.
36. Marquis M.-J. de La Fayette, *Mémoires* (1838), VI, 471.

2

The Foundation of a Regime

"Oh! l'avenir est magnifique!
Jeunes Français, jeunes amis,
Un siècle pur et pacifique
S'ouvre à vos pas mieux affermis. . . ."

("Oh! the future is magnificent!
Young Frenchmen, young friends,
A century pure and pacific
Opens to your firmer steps. . . .")[1]

"Et puis vient la cohue, et les abois feroces
Roulent de vallons en vallons;
Chiens courants et limiers, et dogues et molosses,
Tout s'élance, et tout crie: Allons!
Quand le sanglier tombe et roule sur l'arène,
Allons, allons! les chiens sont rois!"
("And then comes the mob, and the ferocious barking
Rolls from dell to dale;
Running dogs and bloodhounds, watchdogs and mastiffs,
All bound forward, and all cry: Let us go!
When the wild boar falls and rolls on the sand,
Forward, forward! the dogs are kings!")[2]

Paris in early August enjoyed a political fête. Crowds stood around the Palais Royal awaiting the emergence of the Duc d'Orléans: he would frequently appear to beam at them and to beat time while they roared the "Marseillaise". "La Parisienne" was its close rival in popularity: it extolled the Parisian population and the *lieutenant-général:*

"Soldat du drapeau tricolore
D'Orléans, toi qui l'as porté. . . ."

("Soldier of the tricolour flag
D'Orléans, you who have carried it. . . .")

Everywhere the three colours replaced the Bourbon white, the symbols of the old monarchy were defaced and the municipal authorities rechristened those streets which had laboured under names associated with the deposed family: the Rue du Duc de Bordeaux became the Rue du 29 Juillet, the Place Louis XVI became the Place de la Concorde; the Rue Charles X was now known as Rue La Fayette and Laffitte, who lived in the Rue d'Artois, henceforth honoured it also with his surname. The festering corpses of men and horses had been cleared, with more haste than efficiency in their burial: the remains of the citizens who died in *les glorieuses* were later buried beneath the July Column which was erected where the Bastille had stood.

A commission was created to grant compensation to those who had suffered losses during the Revolution: the shopkeepers in particular claimed recompense for the pillage inflicted by the heroic populace. Liberal bourgeois donated generously in a fit of enthusiasm for proletarian bravery, but the distribution of pensions and medals proved difficult as vast numbers deemed themselves worthy. Meanwhile the Queen and her daughters visited the wounded in the hospitals, the politically tactless Marie-Amelie showing an unfortunate tendency to encourage the recovery of the soldiers who had fought on the wrong side.

"I love this people that has shown that its education is complete"[3] wrote Saint-Marc Girardin in the *Journal des Débats*. Yet it was soon to be proved that the people had not fought to profit liberal politicians, and heady enthusiasm quickly dissipated as the divisions always inherent in the Revolution began to emerge. As yet unnamed, but evident in the first week of August, were the broad groupings which would become known as the *parti du mouvement* and the *parti de résistance*; the first believing that July had been more than a dynastic alteration and was a complete repudiation of the Restoration, the other determined that the Parisian insurrection should not become more than the accompaniment of a change in the head of state which would produce an improved practice of constitutional principles. The conservative liberals were apprehensive lest popular energies turned to make greater political and social demands, and that many of the politicians so suddenly hurled into prominence would prove weak barriers to them. With Parliament in demoralised disorder, they looked to the *lieutenant -général*. However, Orléans was not yet ready to free himself from the radicals. He dissatisfied them by dissolving the municipal commission which had issued directly from the insurrection (called a *pétaudière* (bear garden) by Schonen, one of its members, who believed that no order could be re-established whilst demagogues chattered on at the Hôtel de Ville) but accepted most nominations which that commission had made. Yet the weakness of the *parti du mouvement* was a lack of talent, and the appointment of conservatives was unavoidable. If Baron Bignon and Dupont (de l'Eure) were of the *mouvement*, Général Gérard weakly in the centre, there could be no doubt that Baron Louis, Amiral de Rigny, Périer and Guizot were of the *résistance*. Gérard, Rigny, Louis and Dupont remained where the municipal commission had placed them, at War, Navy, Finance and Justice respectively. The Duc de Broglie moved to the Ministry of Public Instruction, the Guizot replaced him at the Interior, entering as Périer, nervous of office, left. The incompetent Laborde was maintained as prefect of Paris, but the radical appointee at the police prefecture was changed for a moderate. A further dilution of the revolutionary content occurred when Bignon, briefly given responsibility for Foreign Affairs, was replaced by Maréchal Jourdan, one of those ageing dignitaries of the Empire who were soon to occupy many of the pinnacles of the regime: in this case the occupation was fleeting, but was an early sign of Louis-Philippe's determination to control foreign relations. The provisional ministry thus haphazardly achieved was, with modifications, to remain uneasily in office until November, when its incompatibilities forced its collapse. It was a coalition of the wide range of opinions which was Orleanism. The differences between them were soon revealed during the debates to decide on constitutional changes.

The *lieutenant-général* opened the parliamentary session on 3 August. Peers and deputies met together for this inauguration, but only 69 of the 331 peers were present, and scarcely half the deputies, 240 instead of 430. The absences reflected the disapproval of a large number of politicians for the Orleanist capture of the Crown. Those present did not wear the rich parliamentary uniform, but sported tricolour cockades on their frock-coats. The emotional colours, symbol of revolution, had been draped over the fleur-de-lis on the central dais. There, the Duc d'Orléans delivered his speech. He congratulated Paris on its "heroic courage" in defending freedom against the "deplorable violation" of the constitutional Charter and he asked for Parliament's guidance in re-establishing liberty and the rule of law. He gave a list of reforms on whose necessity there was general agreement – the organisation of the National Guard, the application of the jury to press infractions, administrative changes and the abolition of Article XIV of the 1814 Charter, "so odiously interpreted". But Orléans took care to stress the need for peace and stability, for the respect of law and established interests. Charles's note of abdication was mentioned and placed in the archives of the Chamber of Peers, but no allusion was made to the Duc de Bordeaux. The murmurs of the group of twenty who supported Henri V, were drowned by the enthusiastic applause of the majority. The *lieutenant-général* had begun tread to the middle way. He was still an unknown quantity: those who hoped he would prove the malleable figurehead to a radical government and others who expected him to reflect and lend authority to their conservative opinions, still did not know whether the man they would soon make king was of the *mouvement* or the *résistance*.

Yet some radical Orleanists were already dissatisfied at the direction of events. For example, the nomination of Baron Pasquier, minister of Napoleon and Louis XVIII, to the presidency of the peers and his invitation to the two eldest sons of the Duc d'Orléans to sit amongst them, seemed to prove that the spirit of the former regime still lingered on. A number of deputies, meeting at the home of Laffitte on the evening of 3 August, declared that there ought to be considerable changes in the Charter. This initiative was a sign of the weakness of the heterogeneous Cabinet and of the fears of the radicals that the revolutionary spirit would be diluted. It was decided that the deputy Bérard should draw up a project for reforming the Charter, showing clearly that the new dynasty based its rights on the will of the people.

Bérard's draft strongly attacked the Bourbons and stressed that the new throne was founded upon the principle of popular will, not dynastic right. Orléans would win the throne by accepting the equality of all religions, the expulsion of foreign troops (this was a reflection of patriotic hatred for the Swiss Guard), a democratic civilian militia (the National Guard), electoral reforms and the total reconstruction of the peerage. This radical bourgeois had originally desired the abolition of aristocracy, but had been persuaded that this would create too many enemies.

When Dupont, most radical of the ministers, supported the project before the others, he met determined resistance. Bérard, who had been told that he would be consulted, was persuaded not to present his project to the deputies and to wait inactively, while Broglie and Guizot remodelled it. The two conservative theorists omitted the woolly phraseology with its hints of popular sovereignty and introduced their own conceptions, modelled on the situation of England in 1688. They stressed the vacancy of the throne, created by abdication rather than by revolution. Guizot placed Charles's abdication in the parliamentary archives (an act which was to anger the left who claimed this gave validity to an act which had none). An attempt to save hereditary peerage was made by replacing Bérard's threats with the promise to cast out the creations of Charles X. The provision for the election of National Guard officers was omitted. They agreed with Bérard to increase certain parliamentary rights and to reduce the age at which a man might vote or stand for Parliament, but they wished to retain the 300 francs annual tax voting qualification, and the 1,000 francs required to be eligible to stand for deputy. Guizot and Broglie thus believed that fifteen years had proved the worth of the Charter, but they were in an illogical position for they had concurred in a revolution and the proclamation of 31 July which Guizot had drawn up had admitted the principle (to which he now objected) that the King held his rights from the people. Bérard was no more logical, for his project proclaimed not only the Duc d'Orléans to be king, but his male heirs to succeed him by law, a negation of that popular choice in which Bérard claimed to believe.

On receiving his project, so substantially revised, Bérard altered it further. "You have wished to establish legitimacy", he told Guizot, "as for me, I have returned to the truth by making it usurpation."[4] It was not a complete return, however: if he restored the promise of franchise reform, the anti-Bourbon violence and democratic phraseology had largely vanished. The first Orleanist compromise had been achieved.

It was speedily accepted by Parliament. Nervous of the Hôtel de Ville where La Fayette held court amidst dissatisfied republicans, the deputies were anxious to establish the new regime as quickly as possible. On 4 and 5 August, they examined the conduct of the elections, the "verification of powers", and chose Casimir Périer as their president. When Bérard presented his project for revising the Charter, with the exception of those faithful to the fallen King and some members of the left who believed the people should be able to vote for their king, there was a general disposition to accept the compromise. A committee hurriedly made some slight modifications and Dupin, its president, presented the new draft at 8 p.m.

During the day, the Palais Bourbon, seat of the deputies, had been almost under siege. A crowd, mostly of students, had gathered outside with various demands, notably for the suppression of the hereditary peerage, a controversial question absent from the varying projects. La Fayette and Constant, two deputies sympathetic to the protesters, had eventually persuaded them to cease their harassment by virtually promising the acceptance of their demands. Noisy meetings occurred on the 7th, and the *lieutenant-général* decided that the hereditary peerage had to be sacrificed. Guizot and Bérard were strongly opposed to abolition but he convinced them that he could not use force to maintain unpopular heredity. The issue was therefore postponed, a delay which made abolition unavoidable. This was the price paid La Fayette for exerting his pacifying influence over his republican friends.

On 7 August, Dupin read out the project as altered. With one exception there was no debate amongst the hurried deputies. The magistrature had not been mentioned and Mauguin and Salverte led the left in demanding a complete reorganisation and wholesale purge, with the tacit support of the Garde des Sceaux, Dupont; they were, however, opposed on this issue not only by the conservatives but also by the centre who saw the magistrature as a symbol of the stability of the social order. Led by the lawyer Dupin, they defeated the amendment by a large majority.

The preamble to the Charter as it was adopted on 7 August reveals the uncertain compromise of the July Monarchy. Popular will and divine right were equally absent. The Charter had been violated, it declared, and so the deputies "considering . . . that as a result of that violation and the heroic resistance of the citizens of Paris, His Majesty Charles X, His Royal Highness Louis-Antoine, the Dauphin, and all the members of the elder branch of the Royal House, depart French territory at this moment, – Declare that the throne is vacant in fact and by law, and that it is indispensable to provide for it."[5] Thus the departure of Charles was presented as being almost voluntary, and the Duc d'Orléans made to appear the legal candidate to the vacant throne. He and his heirs were summoned by "the pressing universal interest". His kingship was dependent, not upon the people's will, but on his acceptancs of the Charter and its revisions.

The changes reflected the conservative liberalism of the deputies. The articles guaranteeing individual liberty and freedom of conscience were retained. The clause in the 1814 Charter which declared Roman Catholicism the religion of state was abolished but it was, against the desires of some anticlerical radicals, described as "professed by the majority of Frenchmen", giving it a pre-eminent status. Louis XVIII's Charter had granted freedom of the press, whilst qualifying it with reference to possible abuses. In the aftermath of a revolution in large part the work of journalists, the press seemed wholly admirable. The qualification was therefore removed and the bold declaration made, "Censorship can never be re-established."[6]

The excuse used by Charles, "state security", was removed as a motive for royal action. The King could make ordinances for the execution of laws, "without power either to suspend the laws themselves or to dispense with their execution". Formerly the King proposed legislation on his own initiative or on the advice of the Chambers: now he shared initiation with the deputies and peers. Similarly an amendment no longer had to have royal approval before it was made. Each of the three constitutional powers could inflict a veto as before. The deputies made public the sessions of the peers (as their own already were), nullified Charles's nominations to that Chamber and promised to examine the question of hereditary peerage. Also to be the subject of separate legislation was the extent of parliamentary franchise, but they lowered the qualifying age of a deputy from forty to thirty and the voting age from thirty to twenty-five. Electors, not the King, were to choose the presidents of electoral colleges. Similarly, as they had in fact just done, the deputies won the entire right to choose their president.

The constitutional changes wrought by the July Revolution were symbolised by Article 65. Instead of making an oath to the deity, the King and his successors would swear fidelity to the constitutional Charter before Parliament, depriving them of any aura of divine right. As in the 1791 Constitution, he was "King of the French", supposedly a more democratic title than "King of France". Yet his actual power had been only slightly decreased. The King was head of state: commander of the armed forces, he declared war and made peace; he made public appointments and ordinances, proposed laws and might veto them. The constitutional significance of July 1830 lies less in the textual changes in the Charter than in the conviction of the deputies that they were, in fact and by right, the most powerful element. The peers had remained in the background during the Revolution and constitutional revision: mutilated by the removal of some of their number, their hereditary nature was doomed. It was the deputies who made the 1830 Charter and who in their own estimation had become the constituent power for the future. This conception of the constitutional superiority of the Chamber of Deputies was not held by the King and there was nothing in the 1830 Charter which legally bound him to act as if it were. The hasty compromise was to provide many opportunities for later discord and was too vague in its terminology ever to serve as sole arbiter. In politics, as in society, the 1830 Revolution was not so much an obvious displacement of power as a change of mood. To Bérard and Guizot, the Charter in which they both played such significant roles, represented very different constitutional conceptions.

The report was debated for six hours and then accepted by the huge majority of 219 to 33. Only one legitimist, loyal to the fallen Charles, spoke against the new King, and from the left, François de Corcelles's[4] demand for the changes in constitution and monarch to be submitted to popular vote, were speedily rejected. Vicomte de Cormenin abstained from voting and shortly resigned, asserting that deputies had no power to make a king; after a revolution power returned to its popular source. Yet when Orléans had accepted with fervent approval the Chamber's declaration and appeared on the balcony of the Palais Royal between Laffitte and La Fayette, the applause of the enthusiastic crowds appeared to represent a popular sanction. After this, the approval of the Chamber of Peers, by 89 to 10, with 14 abstentions and about 200 absentees, seemed of small relevance. Legitimists, for the moment, feared social revolution more than they hated Orleanist usurpation. The perfunctory debate was enlivened only by an eloquent protest of loyalty to the fallen Bourbons from Vicomte de Chateaubriand.

The speed of this constitution-making seemed offensive to some[7] but to the Orleanist Rémusat it had "something stirring and romantic which is entirely characteristic of the nation's genius".[8] It was the result of fear, however, as well as of enthusiasm. All Orleanists hastened to establish their king before they lost control of the situation, whilst moderate republicans and legitimists failed to use their potential strength for fear of alternatives they feared more. Grievances were removed rather than the Constitution truly reformed, but so confident were conservatives such as Broglie and Guizot that a perfect constitutional system now existed that no provision was made for revision, and the majority who desired stability readily agreed.

The hastily arranged ceremony which officially inaugurated the Orleans Monarchy on 9 August showed how dissimilar was its tone from that of its predecessor. None of the feudal trappings or religious symbolism which had adorned the coronation of Charles X in Rheims cathedral was present in the tiered hemicycle of the Chamber of Deputies. The Duc d'Orléans sat on a folding stool below the throne, listening to the declaration of the deputies read by their president, Casimir Périer, followed by the adherence of the peers. The Duc swore to observe it as *roi des Français*. Four marshals presented him with the symbols of his office, and the new King from his throne promised to obey the laws and observe the Charter. This was a king making a contract with his people, not ascending his throne to receive their submissive loyalty. He left to cheers of "Long live the King" and of "Long live Louis-Philippe I" from those who knew that Broglie's desire to mark the essential continuity of the Orléans Monarchy with the title Philippe VII had been ignored.

Being now king, Louis-Philippe was able to establish and regularise the administration. Judges took the oath to the new monarch and courts began to administer justice in his name. The deputies and peers likewise swore loyalty, often with speeches to explain their conduct or soothe their consciences. On 11 August he officially constituted his first ministry, refusing as before to put his authority on the side either of *résistance* or *mouvement*.

This unhomogeneous Cabinet differed from its stop-gap predecessor in the introduction of Comte Molé as Foreign Minister. He was a cultivated aristocrat, highly conservative and politically experienced, having been a minister of both Napoleon and Louis XVIII. His reception of the new monarchy had been unenthusiastic and his promotion came as proof that, if the King vacillated within France, he was resolved to present a conservative face to Europe. Broglie as Minister of Public Instruction and Guizot at the Interior continued to provide the backbone of *résistance*. Baron Louis retaining charge of Finance was too immersed in solving the commercial problems resulting from revolution to provide much support outside his own department at which he was aided by Thiers as secretary-general. Comte Sébastiani who entered the Cabinet as Minister of the Marine was drawn right by prudence, leftwards by weakness, and Général Gérard as War Minister was still more inclined to follow popularity. None the less, of the departmental ministers, only Dupont, remaining at Justice, was truly of the *parti du mouvement*. To satisfy other notables who had contributed to the Orleanist settlement, there were four Ministers without Portfolio, two mutually inimical conservatives, Dupin and Casimir Périer, and the more radical Bignon and Laffitte. Such a Cabinet could have no chief, or *président du conseil*, a role which the King fulfilled, allowing him to maintain his independence by manœuvering between the conflicting groups.

The ministry of 11 August symbolises, and perhaps rather exaggerates, the changes brought to French politics by the 1830 Revolution. Instead of a minister being almost invariably a nobleman, as had been the case under Louis XVIII and Charles X, the aristocratic minister became rather an exception (a change evident in altering the form of address from *Monseigneur* to the more bureaucratic *Monsieur le Ministre*). However, the presence of Comte Molé and the Duc de Broglie, two *grands seigneurs*, shows that there was no wholesale exclusion. The triumph of the middle classes is seen in the rise of the lawyers, Dupin and Dupont, the bankers Périer and Laffitte, and in Guizot, an academic with brief official experience in 1815. Louis had a long ministerial career behind him and an imperial title. Gérard was a general of the Empire but, unlike many of Napoleon's generals who served the Restoration, he had risen from the ranks. Similarly Sébastiani, like Napoleon a member of the Corsican gentry, had served under the Emperor and gained a title. On the whole, it was a Cabinet of technical capacity rather than social position.

The first task of the ministry was to establish an Orleanist bureaucracy. In a country where regimes founded on differing principles had succeeded each other in violence, an apolitical administration had not been able to grow: moreover, the increase in numbers of an educated bourgeoisie, the vast expansion of the state under Napoleon and its ensuing contraction, meant more applicants than jobs. Thus began the *curée*, the rush for positions. "Everyone wants a piece of the cake",[9] wrote Auguste Barbier in a poem which became famous for its excoriating disgust. Two weeks before, Frenchmen had fought for liberty behind the barricades; now occurred "the uprising of petitioners",[10] as the *Journal des Débats* dubbed it. Officers removed in 1815 came with exaggerated demands to the War Ministry, believing that fifteen years spent on half-pay, grumbling about the Bourbons, should be counted as active service. Petty lawyers crowded into Dupont's bedroom early in the morning, and late at night sleepy spectators feigned admiration for Laffitte's playing of piquet in hopes of a post or a pension. No one who was believed to have influence, whether in palace or ministry, was safe from a siege of voracious and persistent office-hunters.

Though many were shocked that greed had so speedily replaced idealism and others aggrieved that they had not gained what they considered their due, the replacement of personnel imparted to the administration an Orleanist character necessary to the regime's survival. Within three months Dupont had removed over 400 magistrates, notably the *procureurs généraux*, whose highest posts were taken by important deputies, such as his friend Merilhou, Barthe, Schonen, Dupin and other liberal advocates of the Restoration. Judges were unmovable but about 100 refused to take the oath and were replaced. At the Interior, Guizot eventually created 79 new prefects (out of a total 86) although only 24 were quite new to the post, many having been prefects of the Empire or of the Restoration's liberal phase. He also replaced 196 of the 266 sub-prefects and a large number of their assistants. Some of these sudden promotions were successful, if incongruous; the journalist Dunoyer, the Comte de Gasparin who had contributed to Guizot's *Revue Française*, and the minister's friend Amédée Thierry, the historian, were rewarded with prefectures. But in the haste, some errors were made, for example the two sub-prefects who, having celebrated their promotion, danced to the Palais Royal, were speedily dismissed. Almost all mayors of large towns were replaced, and the extirpation descended through the administration as the new men replaced the protégés of the fallen with their own friends, relations and clients.

The changes, as in politics, assisted the ambitions of the middle class. The predominantly aristocratic nature of the prefecture gave way to a body of men who were officials by profession or bourgeois by birth. In only a few cases was this new class commercial, the main examples being a few mayoralties where a nobleman gave way to a wealthy man of commerce. It was the lawyer who seemed predominant in these promotions. Général de Castellane expressed ironic surprise that no lawyers captained vessels or commanded regiments, so frequently did the profession seem to qualify as sufficient experience. In the army and diplomatic corps the changes, although considerable, do not possess much social significance; sixty-five out of seventy-five generals, and a similar number of colonels, were replaced, usually by men who had been retired by the Restoration for having been loyal to the Emperor for a little longer than the others. In the diplomatic corps, where there were many resignations, the new appointees were equally as aristocratic as the former holders.

None the less the upper echelons of the *parti du mouvement* received large rewards, and not only in posts. Audry de Puyraveau received 200,000 francs to assist his business: Louis-Philippe paid Benjamin Constant's gambling debts, the decrepit liberal *idéologue* carefully informing the King that he would feel no political obligation for having accepted the bribe; since he died in December, his inevitable opposition had little time to develop. In another act of politically motivated generosity, Louis-Philippe bought the forest of Breteuil from Laffitte at double its value, in order to support the banker's tottering finances. Ironically, it was the *parti du mouvement*, later to suffer from the conservative dominance of government and administration, who were most determined to purge the state of those of whom they politically disapproved: it was Dupont's circular of 29 October 1830 to all *premiers présidents* and *procureurs généraux* of the courts telling them to employ only sincere Orleanists, which was later used by the *parti de résistance* to support its own purge of the radicals it distrusted.

The administrative changes widened the gap between Orleanists of left and right. Laffitte, La Fayette and Dupont accused the conservatives of preventing the destruction of the Restoration which the Revolution had fought for, inveighing against the manner in which servants of earlier regimes, Pasquier, Molé and especially the inevitable Talleyrand (now ambassador to Britain) had insinuated themselves into high office.[11] When the *parti du mouvement* indignantly asked Broglie if he knew what a Carlist was, his mocking definition was that it was someone holding a position coveted by another man.[12] And for their part, the conservatives complained at the promotion of some of Dupont's republican friends and feared that the weakness of men like Barrot and Laborde encouraged continued disorder. Indeed the July Monarchy seemed so precarious, that a number of conservative peers less dogmatically Orleanist than the doctrinaires, notably Pasquier, Molé, Mortemart, Sémonville and Decazes, discussed the possibility of installing Henri V if the experiment proved unsuccessful.

None the less, if tempers were heated in the post-revolutionary situation and fears exacerbated, the party lines were not yet as sharply divided as they would later become: the conservatism of Orleanism had not yet smothered its revolutionary origins. Some members of the *résistance* could still see themselves as progressives and idealists. "We supported the *résistance* in administration and the *mouvement* in legislation", claimed Guizot.[13] The compromise of Orleanism was not purely external but was, as Guizot's words suggest, an attempt by a group of men to reconcile within themselves the conflicts of various national traditions, to combine loyalty and ambition, reason and emotion, order and freedom. Their task, wrote the Comte d'Argout, was to create a government "and to base it in good measure upon the consent and by the hand of the revolutionaries".[14] The problem was greater still than this, because the conservatives, by their encouragement of revolution, or acceptance of it, destroyed the logic of their position.

REFERENCES

1. *Journal des Débats*, 19 August 1830.
2. Auguste Barbier, *Iambes* (1898), 11.
3. *Journal des Débats*, 16 August 1830.
4. S. Bérard, *Souvenirs Historiques sur la Révolution de 1830* (1834), 221.
5. Archives Parlementaires, 6 August 1830.
6. Ibid., 7 August 1830.
7. Louis Blanc, *Histoire de Dix Ans* (1840), I, 82.
8. Comte C. de Rémusat, *Mémoires de ma vie* (1958), IV, 361.

9. Barbier, op. cit., 11.
10. *Journal des Débats*, 16 August 1830.
11. Bérard, op. cit., 151, 175, and Marquis M.-J. de La Fayette *Mémoires* (1838), VI, 515.
12. Duc V. de Broglie, *Souvenirs* (1886), IV, 67.
13. Rémusat, op. cit., IV, 363.
14. Archives Nationales, Fichiers de ventes d'autographes, Argout à Paulze d'Ivoy.

3

Post-revolutionary Disorders, 1830–1831

"Et l'Émeute parait, l'Émeute au pied rebelle,
Poussant avec la main le peuple devant elle;
L'Émeute aux mille fronts, aux cris tumultueux,
A chaque bond grossit ses rangs impetueux,
Et le long des grands quais où son flot se déroule,
Hurle en battant les murs comme une femme soule."

("And Riot appears, Riot in rebel feet,
Pushing by main-force the people before her;
Riot in a thousand faces, with tumultuous cries,
At each bound grows her impetuous ranks,
And along the grand quays where her wave lashes,
Howls and strikes the walls like a drunken woman.")[1]

On 29 August 1830, King Louis-Phillipe attended a huge review of the Parisian National Guard. This citizen militia, disbanded by Charles X, had been reconstituted under the command of La Fayette. To him, it was a symbol of patriotism, the populace in arms: for conservatives, the National Guard represented the order-loving bourgeoisie, ready to protect property and society against republicans and socialists. The *égalité* which La Fayette had inscribed on its banners had been removed at the request of the prefect of police: now there stood only the words *liberté, ordre public*. In 1848 many Parisian National Guards were to decide that they preferred their conception of liberty to the requirements of public order, for some guardsmen enjoyed the political privileges of the prosperous, whilst the service of others was repaid only by the right to wear a gaudy uniform. But the reception they gave Louis-Philippe in August 1830 led him to regard them as an adamantine pillar of his regime. He distributed flags to the legions amidst enormous enthusiasm, wrote Cuvillier-Fleury, tutor to the King's third son: the King chosen by the deputies, recognised by the people on 31 July, "was consecrated that day, that is the word, by the acclamations of fifty thousand bourgeois, who devoted their swords to him".[2]

National Guardsmen were even welcome at the King's table. The Court in autumn 1830 was still a place of great informality, the palace of a true citizen king, where if the guilt-ridden Queen was pale and depressed, her lady-in-waiting wafted a huge tricolour fan; and where Louis-Philippe would tolerate the gross familiarity of Général Gérard who, complained the Austrian ambassador, presented the appearance of saying constantly, "It is I who has placed you where you are."[3] And Rémusat, a relative of La Fayette, describes how the hero's family would dine with that of the King: "One would have said there were two dynasties at the table: the civilities did not come from our side."[4]

Louis-Philippe still felt the need to court his popular base, but he and his conservative ministers increasingly feared republican disorder. Semi-secret societies and clubs such as the Francs Régenérés, often predominantly student in membership, sought an opportunity to complete the unfinished work of July. More durable were Les Amis du Peuple who, by presenting themselves as a pressure group opposing the conservative direction of the government, rather than an armed conspiracy, were able to attract the patronage of deputies, La Fayette, Général Lamarque, Audry de Puyraveau and Dupont. Represented by the *Tribune*, the society gave lectures and produced propaganda. Amongst its members can be found most of the future republican leaders, Étienne Garnier-Pagès, Godefroy Cavaignac, Marrast, Guinard, Auguste Blanqui, Raspail and others.

The activities of these groups maintained Paris in ferment throughout the summer. They were behind the republican demonstration of 4 August when 4,000 protested outside the Chamber of Deputies; they were responsible for the incendiary posters – "Those whom we have put in power betray us. Let us arm ourselves!"[5] The resentment felt by the middle classes at this continuing disorder was shown in a violent manner when a large band, mostly of shopkeepers, many in the National Guard, invaded the hall in the Rue Montmartre where a section of the Amis du Peuple met nightly. They forced out the clubbists and prevented them from meeting there again. This action emboldened the authorities to prosecute and the club was dissolved by order of the police tribunal. As a result it became more of a secret organisation, which was to play an important role in fomenting unrest during the forthcoming trial of Charles X's ministers.

When on 25 September a demand was made that the clubs be closed in the interests of order, Guizot, Minister of the Interior and himself member of an opposition organisation during the Restoration, dared only promise to use the government's legal powers: even this was attacked by Constant as illiberal. In spite of the firm words of Périer, most deputies feared to compromise themselves by allowing the *parti de résistance* a free hand, as did the King who was perpetually attempting to heal rifts between his ministers. The Cabinet was under attack from all sides: the *National* spoke for the left in finding it untrue to the generous spirit of *les glorieuses* whilst the *Journal des Débats* and the *Constitutionnel* criticised its failure to control the radicals. It was, complained Saint-Marc Girardin, "a government which does not govern, but humbly begs to obey".[6] Neither King nor Parliament was yet willing to act decisively.

The deputies had to replace those who had resigned and re-elect those who had received governmental appointments, 113 in all. The *parti du mouvement* which had ceased to regard the 221 opposed to Charles as heroic liberals, now deemed them relics of the Restoration, called for total re-elections but was outvoted, and in October the Chamber adjourned for partial elections. Determined to avoid the faults of his predecessor, Guizot, who had retained the property qualifications but removed the much disliked double vote, instructed the prefects to be strictly impartial: the different factions within the ministry and the prefectoral corps did of course make a governmental line impossible. None the less, deputies of all opinions used their powers of promoting to offices of local profit within the customs or postal service, to try to win votes. The effect of the elections was to return mostly Orleanist deputies of moderate opinions: for many, notably Barrot, Hippolyte Passy, Achille de Salvandy, Rémusat, Martin (du Nord), Persil, Barthe and Thiers, these elections were their entry to parliamentary life. Legitimists were still stunned and inactive, the left disorganised outside Paris. In so far as changes in class can be measured, there was a shift from the aristocratic landowner to the professional, and to a lesser extent, to the commercial man. In terms of wealth possessed, there was little alteration.

Four of Charles's ministers had been able to escape from France, but Chantelauze, Guernon-Ranville and Peyronnet were captured near Chartres, and Polignac, dressed as a servant but attracting attention by his good breeding, had been arrested on the Normandy coast before he could cross the Channel. The government regretted the inefficiency of these fugitives, but took care that they did not fall into the hands of the populace. By the end of August all four were incarcerated in the grim fortress of Vincennes. After the bloodshed of July the demand for vengeance was strong. A leftist deputy, Eusèbe de Salverte, promptly proposed an accusation of treason and the committee elected as a result drew up a list of offences. On 27 September the deputies approved trial by a huge majority. Only Berryer, at the beginning of his brilliant career of opposition to the July Monarchy, attacked the measure, denying the right of a Chamber born of illegality to try ministers of a legitimate king.

Popular hatred of former ministers was encouraged by some on the left, such as Carrel in the *National* who saw the desire for clemency as typical of a general tendency to placate French Carlism and European conservatism. Agitators like Blanqui strove to turn mass hatred into a republican insurrection. Throughout October the crowds grew more menacing and on the evening of the 18th, a large crowd gathered at the Palais Royal. When they shouted insults at the King and republican slogans, "Death to the old ministers or the head of King Philippe",[7] and tried to enter the palace, the National Guard cleared the courtyard. Then the cry "To Vincennes!" arose and the mob turned and marched south-east through the suburbs of Paris to arrive at the fortress late at night. The general in command firmly refused the demand to surrender his charges, and in the early hours, the tired and partially drunken mob marched back to demonstrate again outside the King's residence, where many of them were arrested.

Frightened by the spectacle of the mob, unsure of the National Guard, the ministry dared not accede to the deputies' request that the death penalty be abolished for political crimes, much as the King was determined to save the lives of the former ministers. Odilon Barrot, prefect of the Seine, tried to appease the populace by a proclamation which, whilst appealing for calm, implied criticism of clemency, and promised that the prisoners would receive fitting justice. Barrot, son of a *conventionnel*, had more than any other, turned the Marquis de la Fayette towards acceptance of a constitutional monarchy, but he reproached the new government and especially the Minister of the Interior, his supposed overlord, for their conservative timidity, holding an unshakeable conviction that the people held a benevolent liberalism similar to his own.

The conservative ministers were furious at the proclamation which vented these ideas, even though Guizot prevented its official publication. He argued for Barrot's dismissal but Dupont refused even to be a party to his disavowal, whereupon Guizot and Broglie resigned. The uncompromising doctrinaires, Guizot later admitted, had become very unpopular, "more compromising than useful".[8] Louis-Philippe had considered wooing the left by giving ministries to Mauguin and Bignon, but no important conservative would remain in such a Cabinet. He was forced to accept Broglie's proposal that a politically united ministry should be achieved by nominating a *président du conseil* who would select the ministers. Broglie also advised the King to turn to the *parti du mouvement*, allowing it for a brief period to prove its incapacity, so that the conservatives united by the proximity of disaster, might return to government in greater strength. Louis-Philippe may not have accepted this argument completely, but he decided it was tactically wise to turn leftwards and asked Laffitte to become *président*. He owed his throne to him more than to any other, yet the banker had a pompous amiability which implied he would not threaten royal predominance. Although Laffitte was moderate compared with Dupont, whom he disliked, Molé, Périer, Louis and Dupin speedily resigned. The centre, however, in the persons of Gérard and Sébastiani, remained.

After some difficulties, the ministry came officially into being on 2 November. Laffitte, as well as being *président*, took over Louis's Ministry of Finance and its secretary, Thiers, who gained increased responsibility because of his minister's dual function. Dupont remained at Justice, and his protégé Merilhou succeeded Broglie at the Ministry of Public Instruction: the rigid Broglie believed that Merilhou's personal character should at least have disqualified him from the responsibilities for religious matters which the post carried with it. An imperial relic, Maréchal Maison, replaced Molé: purely a stop-gap, he was there until Sébastiani felt able to take the position; to have done so at once would have allied this ambiguous politician too firmly with the *mouvement*. The most important promotion demonstrated the King's determination to save the life of the former ministers and was made at his request. A young hereditary peer, Comte Camille de Montalivet, was a moderate conservative uncompromised by alliance with the doctrinaires, and a popular colonel in the National Guard.

Once the deputies had voted to prosecute Charles's ministers, the Chamber of Peers became a court of justice and began collecting evidence. The authorities considered measures for maintaining order during the trial. Many of the National Guard saw their role as ceremonial and were unwilling to risk their lives in this cause, and on 12 December others joined students and workers' deputations in a long, unruly funeral procession for Benjamin Constant (the first of a number of dead notabilities selected by opponents of the regime as symbols of an alternative system); the unreliability of the bourgeois militia was evident.

The trial opened on 15 December. After three days spent in examination of the evidence, Persil, former liberal lawyer, *procureur général* and deputy, opened the case for the prosecution. Although later to be a severe Minister of Justice, in his demands for a severe penalty, attacks on the Bourbons and defence of revolution, he seemed to be addressing himself to public opinion rather than to the 163 peers gathered to administer justice. Replying to Persil, Vicomte de Martignac delivered a masterly oration in defence of Polignac who had replaced him as *président du conseil*. He pleaded that Charles's ministers had acted in good faith; that it was not for a monarchy founded on a different base to judge the past and, pleading for mercy, he warned that to shed blood would open an abyss which might never be closed, an admonition aimed effectively at those who had lived through 1793. Hennequin, defending Peyronnet, used the legitimist argument that the ordinances were legal. He was followed by a brilliant young lawyer from Lyons, Sauzet, a future deputy, who won the first of his many oratorical triumphs: if the ideological basis of his defence of Chantelauze, his former protector, was extremely vague, his moving plea for mercy and French unity brought tears to the eyes of the more emotional peers and President Pasquier had to try to prevent an excessive display of approval from the judges.

Outside, the crowds seemed aware of the peers' inclination towards mercy. On 20 December, the National Guard had difficulty in holding back a mob shouting "Death to ministers!" The last lawyer for the defence, Adolphe Crémieux, fainted before ending his plea: beneath his robes he wore the National Guard uniform, doubtless in case of emergency. Shouting could be heard from outside, and the session was closed for fear it might be ended violently. The ex-ministers escorted to their prison could hear the murderous cries, whilst the mob threw stones at the coaches of the departing peers.

That night, preparations were made for the completion of the trial on the morrow. Montalivet's decision to put the more reliable army into the grounds of the Palais du Luxembourg, displeased La Fayette who saw it as an insult to the National Guard and to the people of Paris. He had met leaders of hostile groups and plied them with flattery and humanitarianism: it offended him to be told that this was insufficient. Similarly, the prefect of the Seine had appealed for acquiescence in the verdict, whilst suggesting a vague sympathy with popular demands. Montalivet had less faith than Barrot and La Fayette in their hold on popular affection and readily accepted Pasquier's proposal that the accused be spirited back to Vincennes before the verdict was given.

Thus on the 21st, after a particularly virulent speech from the third prosecutor, the crowds growing larger and more threatening, the four defendants were hustled from the Chamber. An immediate transfer to a waiting carriage being rendered impossible by La Fayette having allowed suburban guardsmen, particularly hostile to Polignac, to occupy a strategic position, Montalivet returned the ministers to their prison. Hurriedly he sought an alternative but received no assistance from La Fayette and Barrot fearful of unpopularity, and only the authorisation to do as he thought best from Laffitte who would put nothing in writing. So Montalivet found two reliable colonels of the National Guard and stationed them with a small force outside the prison: to obtain silent acquiescence, he implied that the ministers were being removed to their deaths. He sent the intended carriages to another exit as a feint and brought his own liveried coach to a nearby gateway. Then having forced the concierge to free the prisoners, he led them past the silent guards to his coach: he himself rode in the small mounted escort which took it slowly through the crowded narrow streets of the Latin quarter, and then into the deserted suburbs whose turbulent inhabitants were at the Palais du Luxembourg awaiting the sentence.

Meanwhile a verdict had been reached; 136 peers found Polignac guilty and 20 innocent. A vast majority (only four voted for the death sentence) decided that the four ministers should receive life imprisonment and *mort civil*. When at 6 p.m. the cannon at Vincennes announced the safe arrival of the ministers, the rumour ran that this signified the death penalty. But when the truth finally reached the crowds, there was anger: some National Guards threw down their rifles in disgust and La Fayette could only dismiss them. In the dark streets, disappointed mobs vented their fury by breaking windows and lamps.

On the next day, Paris seethed with rumours of conspiracy and *coup d'état*. Groups from republican clubs tried to rouse the populace to insurrection. An attempt by some demonstrators was prevented by the National Guard, most of whose members, although displeased by the verdict, appeared in response to the summons, having no wish to see the infant regime give way to a republic. The government, still distrustful, put the army in the most vulnerable spots, but although there was shouting and stone-throwing, the danger was over.

The July Monarchy had surmounted its first great crisis by cunning, but the trial also makes evident the weak foundation of the regime. It was a reluctant concession to public opinion, demonstrating how, almost against its will, Orleanism could not avoid its revolutionary basis. The prosecutors' speeches assumed the legitimacy of popular revolt. Avoiding mention of the death sentence, the demands of these three, none of them radical, show Orleanism at its most pusillanimous; placating public opinion whilst relying on the peers' preparedness to accept unpopularity. None the less the event had considerable influence on the regime's direction. The King and Montalivet gained credit amongst conservatives who were angered by Barrot's proclamations and La Fayette's ambiguous cajolements. Though still a hero for many liberal bourgeois, the Marquis had lost his credit with the republicans and he attempted to regain it with an *ordre du jour* to his troops, suggesting that the government had promised more liberal policies as a result of the National Guard's having maintained order. The King ordered the official *Moniteur* to publish a denial of any engagement.

La Fayette was no longer indispensable, but the *résistance* party wished to punish him for having been so. A majority of deputies voted for changes which made impossible the general command which he held and reduced the National Guard to a parochial peace-keeping force, destroying his conception of a citizen army ready to fight counter-revolutionary Europe. But when the Marquis announced his resignation, the King, then Laffitte and Montalivet, fearful of the effects, tried to persuade him to remain and offered him an honorary command. However, with his usual aristocratic courtesy, the Marquis had begun to make the democratic demands of the "programme of the Hôtel de Ville". Neither the King nor Laffitte would accept such dictation and the resignation was accepted. Montalivet quickly discovered a replacement in the Napoleonic veteran and former opposition deputy, Général Mouton, Comte de Lobau. Finding him conservative and efficient, the deputies then abrogated their abolition of the general command.

On parting, La Fayette issued a final *ordre du jour* urging the National Guard to continue their devotion to order and liberty. His speech in the Chamber of Deputies claimed that the republican institutions promised around the popular throne had not been granted and that public opinion should demand them. However, the deputies were relieved that there was no appeal to direct action and, there having been no more than a student demonstration, they could afford to cheer La Fayette as he left his post to enter increasingly embittered opposition. Dupont resigned from the Cabinet in sympathy, further weakening the radical element in the government. The triumph of order during the trial and removal of La Fayette represented a success which persuaded the *parti de résistance* that compromise was unnecessary, a reaction which would often be repeated.

The growth in confidence of the conservative majority placed the Cabinet in an increasingly weak position, lacking as it did a common policy or a capable leader. However, it was feeble rather than radical: the changes which had taken place since its formation, had moved it away from the *parti du mouvement*. Sébastiani had replaced Maison at Foreign Affairs and his replacement at the Ministry of the Marine had been the conservative Comte d'Argout. When Gérard resigned because of ill-health, his substitute was Maréchal Soult, Duc de Dalmatie. Soult was no more a party politician than Gérard, yet he was a strong believer in discipline and order, and this he imposed with an efficiency he had not always shown on the battlefield. Dupont's replacement was Merilhou, who held similar opinions but was of lesser integrity and influence. To the Ministry of Public Instruction went Félix Barthe, a lawyer and former *carbonaro*, an example of the young revolutionary becoming a middle-aged conservative. With the exception of Merilhou, these new ministers were to hold office under Laffitte's conservative successor, Périer. Although Laffitte's ministry has been described as the only Cabinet of the *mouvement* of the July Monarchy, its membership reveals this to be untrue. It was divided: Dupont, while a minister, had often disagreed with the president, and deputies following Mauguin and Lamarque found the Cabinet insufficiently radical. Conservatives disliked the presence of Dupont and Merilhou and feared the weakness of Laffitte: inside the Cabinet, d'Argout and Soult were his "supervisors much more than his colleagues".[9]

The Revolution had raised Laffitte to the political heights, whilst ruining the finances of his over-extended bank. His talents were those of an imaginative speculator; politically he had no real convictions. Son of a carpenter, he ostentatiously revelled in his wealth and popularity, naively believing that money and charm would solve all poblems. The puritanical single-mindedness of Dupont and woolly idealism of La Fayette were both alien to him: his own liberalism was merely a combination of instinctive good nature and bourgeois jealousy of the aristocracy. Even had he been politically able, Laffitte could not simultaneously manage his own financial concerns, a difficult ministry and preside over the Cabinet. It was Thiers, *sous-secrétaire d'état* at Finance, who with the advice of Baron Louis, the former minister, conducted tbe French economy in this time of crisis. The young man, one of the many who believed that Louis-Philippe owed his throne primarily to them, certainly did not lack confidence, believing that the writing of a history of the French Revolution had qualified him to administer finance, conduct foreign policy and wage war.[10]

The conservative ministers were frustrated by Laffitte's failure to lead. In particular, the Comte de Montalivet, following an energetic policy against conspiracy and disorder, was frequently angered to find that orders from the Ministry of the Interior were ignored or countermanded by the prefects of the police and the Seine. The majority of deputies sympathised with his frustration. The Chamber had shown its conservatism in electing Casimir Périer as its president by a large majority. It found leaders for its fear of disorder and European war in the coarse commonsensical Dupin, and in Guizot who clothed his ideas with oratorical grandeur and the appearance of philosophical profundity. Around him was forming a group of doctrinaire conservatives, "furiously moderate"[11] claimed La Fayette. From the left there were also assaults on governmental weakness. It was "government by abandon"[12] wrote Carrel in the *National*. Lacking a permanent stable majority, the ministry lived by expedient and has few achievements to its credit; a law organising the National Guard, a municipal law, various financial and military measures, the agreement that the state would pay Jewish priests as it paid Catholics and Protestants, and, most important but little to do with the government, the

Berenger commission's speedy report on electoral reform.

The conservatives were gaining confidence and cohesion in Parliament, but with governmental inaction and the *parti du mouvement* in control of important posts in the law and administration, conspiracy flourished and disorder was tolerated. As Rémusat wrote, "France fails to recognise her own peril and, completely enchanted by her victory, tolerates all disorders as signs of pardonable enthusiasm."[13] In spite of its victory over the mob in December, Orleanism was still close to its revolutionary origins.

Hostility to Catholicism as a buttress of the Restoration made many an anticlerical bourgeois a revolutionary sympathiser. Hostility to the Church was one of the motive forces of the Revolution. Throughout France, crosses had been destroyed and pamphlets published, attacking Bourbons and clergy, alleging that Charles X had become a Jesuit or retailing obscene libels concerning the Archbishop of Paris, Hyacinthe de Quélen. On 14 February was performed the annual rite commemorating the assassination of the Duc de Berry in 1821. Since he was the father of the Duc de Bordeaux, the child who for legitimists was Henri V, the requiem could scarcely avoid political implications. Montalivet had prevented its being held in one church in central Paris, but the organisers were able to transfer the ceremony to the church of Saint-Germain l'Auxerrois, opposite the Louvre. On the 14th, a holiday in Paris, the attention of the crowds was drawn by the liveried carriages outside the church. The ceremony was unprovocative, but when it finished, one of the congregation laid a portrait of Henri V on the catafalque. When news of this reached the crowds, a wave of anger and hatred swept through them and they began to sack the neighbouring vicarage and then the church itself. Altars were overturned, paintings slashed, statues and stained glass shattered and the cross on the roof torn off: some pranced through the streets in the holy vestments. The congregation escaped and the clergy were escorted to safety by the National Guard, but the latter made no attempt to prevent the destruction of the church. The mayor of Paris seemed to take pleasure in the scene, whilst Thiers and Baude, the prefect of police, watched indifferently from the balcony of the Hôtel de Ville.*

Baude had taken no precautions in spite of Montalivet's warnings, nor, after this, did Barrot, prefect of the Seine, take measures to prevent attacks on other Parisian churches. On 15 February, attention turned to the Archbishop's palace. Facing no resistance, a mob burst in and threw furniture, sacred ornaments, vestments and manuscripts into the Seine. Seeing its role as political, not criminal, it prevented a few bibliophiles from rescuing the precious manuscripts from the river. Having virtually demolished the Archbishop's town residence, a crowd pursued their hatred of him to the length of travelling out to Conflans to sack his country retreat. Other Parisian churches were damaged and ecclesiastic property threatened throughout the

Ed. Note. For a recent account of Thiers's role and ambiguous motivation, see J. P. T. Bury and R. P. Tombs, *Thiers 1797–1877, a Political Life* (London, 1986), pp. 44–5.

country, but nowhere did the authorities attempt to prevent the devastation. However, republican agitators were unable to turn this violent anticlericalism into an attack on the regime: perhaps the authorities were wise not to associate themselves with the unpopular Church. They blamed the destruction upon the Church's association with Carlism. To anticlericals like Baude and Barthe, Minister responsible for Religious Affairs, the populace had been provoked. Even Montalivet authorised the *Moniteur* to go no further than to regret that the people had been "carried away by a legitimate indignation".[14] The Church was not recompensed, instead concessions were made: at Laffitte's insistence, Louis-Philippe unwillingly decreed the erasure of the fleur-de-lis from all public places lest its Bourbon associations angered the mob. Périer was disgusted that having retained it after a revolution, this escutcheon should now be cast away because of a riot.[15]

Having temporarily lost his nerve and considered putting himself completely in the hands of the *parti du mouvement* by making Barrot, Mauguin and Salverte ministers, the King recovered and moved in the opposite direction. The sack of Saint-Germain proved a turning-point, the rout of the Orleanist left. Benjamin Delessert and Guizot expressed their anger at the event and informed the government that conservative tolerance was at an end. Barrot, facing parliamentary onslaught and his superior's demand for his dismissal, resigned. He had gained a reputation for weakness and incompetence, which was only partially justified, but which was to exclude from office for the remainder of the reign both Barrot and the Orleanist left, the *gauche dynastique*, whose leader he became.

This and the replacement of the ineffectual prefect of police brought the ministry a brief lease of life, but although the deputies hesitated to overthrow the Cabinet at a time of unrest, it was itself falling apart. Laffitte and Merilhou wished to bring more radicals into the government and fight a general election with the aid of the left. Strongly opposed by other ministers, they found excuses for resignation. Laffitte chose the favourable ground of royal usurpation of ministerial authority which was to become a favourite theme with the opposition. From Vienna, the French ambassador had written asking for authorisation to assure Austria that France would attack her if she entered the north Italian principality of Modena. The King and Sébastiani, his self-effacing Foreign Minister, kept this note from Laffitte: they feared its effects on the French war party if the request became public. Louis-Philippe had no wish to fight a revolutionary war over an insignificant principality. The *président du conseil* discovered the existence of the note, however, obtained a Cabinet discussion and demanded that troops be sent to north Italy to resist the Austrians. The King, supported by most ministers, bluntly refused and Laffitte resigned on 12 March, later claiming this as a protest against a pusillanimous foreign policy.

Increasingly isolated in Cabinet and Parliament, Laffitte had either to fight elections or resign, but it may be doubted if he truly desired to move far towards the left. If, out of office, he was to repent, as did La Fayette, his role in creating the July Monarchy, it was under the influence of resentment against the King, the result of festering disappointment, not of intellectual conviction. Laffitte had flattered the King and accepted money from him, but had been unable to find a majority to grant a civil list and by his weakness had humiliated the new regime. With his reputation for honesty and competence tarnished by the manner in which the Treasury had compensated him for his miscalculation in lending money to the defaulting government of Haiti, his personal affairs in even greater disarray than those of the state, "Jacques Laffaillitte" (Jacques the Bankrupt)[16] left office with the *parti du mouvement* in discredit. It had disapproved of riots but it had tolerated them, it had advocated a foreign policy of aggression to a bankrupt nation, threatened revolutionary war with an army in disarray, whilst its own economic caution, its inability to be truly democratic, had deprived it of real popular support. The conservatives had established themselves behind the radicals' muddled rhetoric and, finding that rhetoric dangerous, forced the radicals out: the *parti de résistance* had captured the July Monarchy.

REFERENCES

1. Auguste Barbier, *Iambes* (1898), 60.
2. A. Cuvillier-Fleury, *Journal Intime* (1900), 1, 272.
3. Comte R. Apponyi, *Journal* (1913), I, 356.
4. Comte C. de Rémusat, *Mémoires de ma vie* (1958), IV, 373.
5. Maréchal de Castellane, *Journal* (1895), I, 381–2.
6. *Journal des Débats*, 24 October 1830.
7. Apponyi, op. cit., I, 343.
8. F. Guizot, *Mémoires pour servir à l'histoire de mon temps* (1858), II, 134.
9. Ibid., 187.
10. Rémusat, op. cit., 364.
11. Archives Parlementaires, 20 February 1831.
12. *Le National*, 11 March 1831.
13. C. Périer, *Discours*, ed. C de Rémusat (1837), I, introduction.
14. *Le Moniteur*, 16 February 1831.
15. A. Laya, *Etudes de M. Thiers* (1846), I, 145.
16. A. Challamel, *Souvenirs d'un hugolâtre* (1885), 63.

4

The Attack on Liberalism: Saint-Simonism and the *Avenir*

"Il n'y a pas d'année qui fait autant de théories sur l'homme que n'a fait cette année 1832 en un seul de ses jours."

("There has never been a year which has seen as many theories on men as this year of 1832 has seen in a single day.")[1]

The constitutional changes resulting from the Revolution may have been slight; the psychological effects were enormous. The compromises, the return of routine politics bitterly disappointed those who had seen 1830, not as the completion of 1789 but as proof that the French were still a revolutionary people. Disillusioned with the conventional means of improving society, they sought a variety of spiritual panaceas. Dissident Catholics, prophets of new religions, Utopians, socialists and republicans, offered a refuge from humdrum constitutional politics. "At that time one had the choice of so many illusions",[2] wrote the Comte d'Alton-Shée. However fundamentally they differed from each other, the proponents of these remedies for the problems of a dislocated civilisation, were united in their dissatisfaction with the *juste milieu*. The followers of Saint-Simon and the Catholics of *L'Avenir*, for example, both saw the bourgeoisie as a source of spiritual disorder and repression in Orleanist liberalism. In the latter they saw what the new vocabulary described as *égoisme*, and they proposed to destroy it with their own varieties of *association*.

The Comte de Saint-Simon had died five years before the Revolution which was to assist his ideas to such prominence. A strange combination of eccentric speculation and practical acuity, this forceful personality had gathered around himself a group of disciples. To them he preached that industrialists were the new aristocrats and that intellectuals were the new priests of a religion combining science and philanthropy. Pierre Bazard, Prosper Enfantin and

Olinde Rodrigues, the leading disciples, maintained the faith after the master's death, published his writings and gave lectures. They made a few converts, especially amongst the students of the École Polytechnique, yet they might gradually have disappeared, the new recruits fading away as had previous interested men such as Auguste Comte and Armand Carrel, had not a revolution breathed fresh life into the cause. True, the population took little note of the proclamation they issued on 29 July and La Fayette spurned the request made by Bazard's deputation that he should become dictator of a society re-formed on Saint-Simonist lines. However, in the following month, Saint-Simonism began to attract a larger following, especially amongst students and dissatisfied intellectuals. The insurrection had shown the power of the working classes, but, the Saint-Simonians were among the first to point out, their economic situation had in no way improved. They claimed to be able to lead the proletariat to a society where unjust class differences would have no place. By lectures and the distribution of tracts, they gained some support among the artisans of Paris and Lyons, although their attempt at putting their doctrines immediately into practice with communal workshops was an utter failure. They took over the *Globe*, previously the organ of the doctrinaires, and Michel Chevalier, a brilliant young engineer and former polytechnician, became its editor and main contributor. Although it had only about 500 subscribers during its short period of publication, January 1831 to April 1832, free copies were distributed in large numbers to students and workers.

Desiring to make the state a co-operative concern, in which exploitation (although not inequality) was removed, the Saint-Simonians saw themselves as a microcosmic example of the future and lived as a family; leading it were two *Pères*, Bazard and Enfantin. They represented different tendencies within the sect which would soon divide it. The severe and idealistic Bazard was a former *carbonaro* and republican conspirator against the Restoration: like Leroux and the former Saint-Simonian, Buchez, he found pure republicanism an insufficient response to the ugly competitiveness of a commercial society, and advocated a strong authority capable of radically reforming society. Enfantin, a former polytechnician from an unsuccessful commercial background, developed the spiritual aspects of Saint-Simonism. A handsome young man of great charm and enormous conceit, he responded to his generation's desire for a Christ figure.

To those who had lost religious faith but felt the deprivation, the sect was able to offer an authoritarianism and mysticism of which their souls were starved. It rejected Voltairean aridity whilst avoiding the discomforts of Christianity. It advocated the rehabilitation of the body, whilst its preaching of human brotherhood possessed a religious aura. Thus it attracted men like Hippolyte Carnot, member of a notable republican family, but who wanted to go beyond politics, or like Arlès-Dufour who combined business ambitions with a mystical temperament. By its attack on unearned privilege and inherited wealth, its scorn for the aristocracy (in spite of worshipping a founder who claimed descent from Charlemagne), Saint-Simonism appealed to the young of the middle classes. Eugène Humann is an example; son of the wealthy merchant and industrialist who later became Finance Minister, he found in the sect a cause, a brotherhood, and a refuge from pessimistic doubt. Also searching for a faith, the poet Alfred de Vigny and, even more briefly, the critic Sainte-Beuve found optimism in this creed of man's ability to perfect himself.

Many members of the sect were also Jewish, notably Chevalier, d'Eichtal, Pereire and Rodrigues (a fact of which Toussenel made great play in his anti-Semitic and anti-capitalist tirade, *Les Juifs, Rois de l'Époque*). Some scientists enjoyed the idea of a priestly role and many cultists, leaders like Enfantin and Chevalier, or temporary followers like Louis de La Moricière, were members of the technical élite produced by the École Polytechnique. Of course there were those who were probably attracted only by the sudden vogue (the Comte d'Alton-Shée, for example, who attended one meeting but was repelled by the ugliness of the female followers), but Saint-Simonism was able to respond to many of the needs and desires of the time and at its peak attracted many men of great talent, poetical and financial.

It offered a reconciliation of order, accompanied by progress, and liberalism, without bourgeois egoism. It saw poetry in machinery and God's spirit at work in the engine. Industrialists would create wealth, aided by capital from the state: class conflicts would disappear as man exploited nature rather than his fellow man. Saint-Simonism claimed to be based upon scientific fact: its theory was positivist and its religious elements free of metaphysics. Historicist, it stated that the industrial era had replaced a feudal age and that man's ills resulted from the politician's usurpation of the governing role which should belong to the entrepreneur. Most Saint-Simonians retained some belief in this, their fundamental doctrine, even when their cult had fallen in ruins.

Although Enfantin's attacks on the *oisifs* (idlers) living off their land or rents and the *Globe*'s exaltation of the *travailleurs* (workers) made Saint-Simonism indistinguishable from Babeuvism to the conservative mind, the creed was in fact hierarchical and authoritarian. A new hierarchy of capacity replaced the old one of inherited wealth. Command and material rewards were given in proportion to worth and work: the élite controlled culture and economy alike, measuring everything by its social purpose. The totalitarian implications were cloaked by constant invocation to love and fraternity. But beside the Utopian visions, there were imaginative and practicable proposals. The demand for cheaper credit was soon echoed by businessmen and some bankers tried to supply it. The "Mediterranean network", product largely of Chevalier's fertile brain, contained fantasies but also far-sighted schemes for a Paris–Marseilles railway and Suez Canal to open the unexploited wealth of the East to French industry.

Saint-Simonism's scientific and religious tendencies might be combined in one person, but gradually began to produce divisions, exacerbated by the jealousy between the two *Pères*. Bazard approved the basic Saint-Simonism doctrine of rehabilitating matter, but objected to Enfantin's mystical defence of promiscuity. As Enfantin put more stress upon "the priestly couple", man and woman acting as one unit with a strange combination of sexual and spiritual qualities, he increasingly alienated the less Bohemian members. In November 1831 Bazard finally found his colleague's character and doctrines insupportable. Amidst emotional scenes and bitter accusations he left, followed by others including Carnot, Leroux and eventually Rodrigues, disillusioned when the doctrine of free love destroyed his own conjugal happiness. Although Bazard died soon after this and other important disciples remained, the movement was seriously weakened.

Already, before its temporary prominence in 1831, Saint-Simonism had lost one important disciple. Buchez, a Catholic, had been attracted by their anti-competitive ideas and stress on improving the lot of the poor, but whilst sharing a typically Saint-Simonist belief in the magical properties of credit, he was unlike them hostile to the entrepreneur and advocated workers' co-operatives. He held meetings in rivalry to the Saint-Simonians and his journal, *L'Européen*, propounded Christian socialism. Some co-operatives were formed, although only the Association of Gilded Jewellery Workers founded in 1834, survived long, and this body of skilled artisans in a luxury trade could hardly provide the motive force for the peaceable social revolution which Buchez desired. Some Saint-Simonians, leaving in the wake of Bazard, turned to this form of socialism: others like Leroux followed their own individual paths. The bizarre Utopianism of Fourier attracted others, and within a few years would command a popular following which Saint-Simonism never possessed.

Thus weakened, the remnant now found itself under governmental attack. The cult never extended further than a few hundred intellectuals and artisans in Paris and Lyons and discussion groups in a few smaller provincial towns, but was none the less suspected of being a force for disorder. In advocating the end, albeit peaceful, of the parasitical bourgeoisie, in seeking to gain converts amongst the working classes, Saint-Simonians seemed more of a social threat than pure republicans. The government, armed with the legal code which prohibited associations of more than twenty people, prosecuted them for troubling public order and closed their hall in January 1832. Enfantin and his forty disciples retreated to Menilmontant where *Le Père* instituted a rigid monastic regime which combined housework, lofty thinking and ceremony. The group wore a symbolic costume: a sky-blue smock opened on a white waistcoat which buttoned at the back to remind each man of his reliance upon his fellows; a leather belt, white pantaloons, red beret and revolutionary beard completed the ensemble.

Enfantin had boundless faith in his mission as herald of a new dawn: he proclaimed Saint-Simon the successor and equal of Moses, Christ and Muhammad. He himself claimed only to be the precursor of a female Messiah, although his behaviour showed little humility. The *couple prêtre* was an extreme development of the conceptions of synthesis which had been inherited from Saint-Simon. Now body and soul, man and women, were one, and politics, science and art combined in one indivisible fount of progress. But the former fashion had become ridiculous and its disciples dwindled to a group of argumentative eccentrics. In April 1832, the *Globe* ceased publication, bidding farewell to an unconcerned public with a panegyric to Enfantin: "the world sees its Christ and still does not recognise him; and that is why he retires with his apostles from your midst".[3]

Enfantin and Chevalier tried to turn their trial into an attack on bourgeois values. Enfantin censured society for frowning on fornication but permitting prostitution: the prosecutor replied with an attack on the Saint-Simonians for endangering morality, the family and property. The defendants argued that the judges could not give justice because they were unable to understand them: certainly the jury could not, and the two were sentenced to a year's imprisonment.

Events had exacerbated their growing differences, and when released after seven months, they went their separate ways amidst mutual recriminations. Chevalier was able to re-enter the Department of Mines and commenced a brilliant career. He, who had written to Louis-Philippe trying to persuade him to cede his throne to *Le Père*, became a writer for the *Journal des Débats* where, disavowing his former friends, he used the practical ideas of Saint-Simonism, notably in advocacy of state finance for public works. He became a respected economic commentator, in 1838 *conseiller d'état* and later advised his former co-disciple, the financier Pereire, on building railways. Enfantin's return to respectability was never so complete. He left France for Egypt with the remaining followers, now calling themselves "Les Compagnons de la Femme": in theory they sought the female Messiah, *La Mère*; in practice, they contented themselves with less exalted specimens of womanhood, joyfully abandoning the chaste rigours of Menilmontant. Succeeding neither in interesting the pasha of Egypt in their plans for a Suez canal, nor in finding *La Mère*, most of them disconsolately returned home. This final adventure was the end of Saint-Simonism. Enfantin was helped to return to conventional society by the philanthropic business man and sympathiser with his earlier less eccentric ideas, Arlès-Dufour. The former prophet accompanied a government mission to Algeria in 1839 and deluged the administration with letters suggesting vast schemes of colonisation. He then became the administrator of railway companies and secretary-general of the great Paris–Lyons line, playing a significant part in building large concerns by the fusion of small companies. Many other Saint-Simonians, their youthful fantasies forgotten, pursued careers in finance or technology. But the movement had always contained divisions between those who stressed the importance of increasing national prosperity and those who attacked the injustice of the inequalities of wealth, and others followed Buchez and Leroux who had passed through the movement, learnt its vocabulary and adopted some of its conceptions. One of the first of many nineteenth-century attempts to fuse hostile forces, revolution and authority, democracy and élitism, science and religion, Saint-Simonism had died by 1834, but in the most unlikely areas, at opposite ends of the social and political spectrum, it had left traces of its meteoric vogue.

The Saint-Simonians were not alone in their belief that the 1830 Revolution demonstrated that society was undergoing dissolution. A group of dissatisfied Catholics had begun to form before 1830, but the Revolution freed them from the restricting loyalties of their royalist backgrounds and impelled them to wage battles in a new world. The insurrection was anti-Catholic, the authority emerging from it was anticlerical, and so these loyal children of the Church found themselves in opposition to the state and to bourgeois society.

The Abbé de La Mennais had risen to sudden fame under the Restoration with the publication of his *Essai sur l'Indifférence en Matière de Religion* in which he eloquently argued that the only salvation for society was in basing itself entirely upon the Christian revelation. He saw the alliance of throne and altar as oppressive, demanded that the Church be entirely free and that full liberty of conscience, press, association and education should be allowed that Catholicism might profit. The Church Militant needed a head, and La Mennais exalted the role of the Papacy, at the expense of the bishops who repudiated his ideas. A small man with a sad, pinched face, the Abbé de La Mennais had a febrile eloquence and charisma which brought to him a group of younger men, laymen and liberal priests. Amongst the latter was Père Lacordaire, of bourgeois family, a former law student and converted sceptic, who, becoming a priest, was discouraged by royalist religion, but dissuaded by the Revolution from accepting a position in America.

Events of 1830 proved to La Mennais and Lacordaire that the Church should welcome liberty. Association with the Bourbons had led the populace to destroy its altars and crosses, but in Belgium and Poland, Catholics were the popular leaders in the struggle for freedom. Religion could use the weapons of the present, association and education: all it needed from the state was liberty, the freedoms promised by the Charter. With that faith in publicity so typical of the time, a newspaper was founded in October 1830: *L'Avenir* aimed to change men's minds to win their souls.

"God and Liberty", the epigraph of the newspaper, proved a dangerous slogan. *L'Avenir* achieved the remarkable feat, for a Catholic production, of being twice seized by the police in its first five months. Although it promised Catholicism without legitimism or Jacobinism, divorced from party politics and changing regimes, its social reformism and demands for liberty placed it with the opposition. It proposed Church–state relations modelled on those of Belgium whose rebellion against Protestant Holland it applauded. It gave support to Catholics in Ireland and Poland and even called for reforms in the Papal States. It placed itself firmly on liberal ground. "Liberty of conscience and of teaching, liberty of the press and of association, civil and political liberties, liberty of work and of industry, such are our natural and acquired rights"[4] declared La Mennais in *L'Avenir*. The new King was warned to keep his promises, or forfeit his right to obedience. Soon it would attack the government for not granting freedom of education, it bitterly mocked the states choice of bishops, it encouraged the monks of a Breton abbey in their resistance to the attempts of the authorities to close it. It accused the government of trying to destroy the faith by illegal intervention in Church affairs in a violent article which led to its prosecution: defended by Janvier, La Mennais and Lacordaire were acquitted amidst scenes of enthusiasm. Above all, the newspaper appealed to the priests to free themselves from the dead hand of the state, to become men of their time, to conquer the masses by joining the side of progress and liberty – "Priests of Jesus Christ, what does one make of you? Civil servants, paid for their services, submit to whatever their commander deign. . . ."[5]

Not all his associates accepted the full radicalism of La Mennais's ideas – universal suffrage, for instance, horrified Montalembert. As in Saint-Simonism, the school of *L'Avenir* was dominated by a powerful personality who, by innate ultraism or personal vanity, felt compelled to draw principles to an extreme conclusion. However, all united in demanding the separation of Church and state. The young Comte de Montalembert and the Abbé Lacordaire wrote most of the journal, La Mennais contributed the resounding leading articles for which it became celebrated and the Comte de Coux supplied comment on political economy, criticising the effects of liberal capitalism upon the lower classes. Other contributors included Gerbet and Baron d'Eckstein. It was a talented but frequently violent-sounding production.

The radicalism of *L'Avenir* made it enemies everywhere. Legitimists were angered by its assault on the alliance of throne and altar, its attacks on European monarchs and its unfairly blaming them for provoking a mob into sacking Saint-Germain. It displeased the bishops by its ultramontanism, its radicalism and by its attacks on their quiescence, and above all it earned the hostility of the government. This opposition limited the circulation of *L'Avenir* to a maximum of 2,000, until its disappearance in November 1831. But during that year, it had made a considerable impact, especially on Catholic students and younger members of the priesthood.

The men of *L'Avenir* were not satisfied merely to argue. They pursued their campaign for the right to teach without state interference. To open a school it was necessary to obtain the preliminary authorisation of the Université, a body hated as representative of the authoritarian secular state. In December 1830, La Mennais, Lacordaire, Gerbet, Montalembert, de Coux and others created the Agence Générale pour la Défense de la Liberté Religieuse whose prospectus was published in *L'Avenir*, its declared primary aim being to attack the secular monopoly of the Université in education. Local associations were encouraged, an early attempt to create a Catholic movement at ground level. Under its auspices, defying the law but appealing to the reformed Charter which declared education free, an unauthorised primary school was opened in Paris in May 1831.

After Lacordaire had delivered an inaugural speech to twenty children and a body of well-wishers, the teaching began: it lasted only two days before police expelled the children, and Lacordaire, Montalembert and de Coux as the teachers were prosecuted and fined. At this moment Montalembert became a peer on the death of his father, heredity not yet having been abolished, and at the instigation of La Mennais who wanted publicity for the cause, the young man appealed against the verdict to his fellow peers. The three appellants, dressed in full mourning, faced the peers in their blue judicial robes. "Charles de Montalembert, schoolmaster and peer of France" as he described himself when asked his name and profession, made a resounding speech, the first of many to agitate the fusty Chamber. Lacordaire demonstrated that Catholics, like legitimists and republicans, would not hesitate to contrast the confessed principles of the regime with its behaviour, asking why they should not use the liberties which the 1830 Charter promised them. Although the peers upheld the verdict, Montalembert became a national figure, lionised in the provinces when he travelled on a mission of propaganda for free education.

By 1832 the *Avenir* group had reached that difficult position which had faced the Saint-Simonians: in spite of the effect caused, the spiritual revolution had not occurred and the movement risked loss of impetus and indiscipline. Enfantin's followers sought a female Messiah in Egypt; the three leaders of liberal Catholicism made almost as irrationally optimistic a pilgrimage. Part of La Mennais's vision was that the Papacy would lead the oppressed people – "Soon a calm and powerful word spoken by an old man of the Holy City will give the signal that the world awaits – for the final regeneration."[6] But the conservative Gregory XVI was not one to understand such Utopianism.

The three intended to ask the Pope to dissipate the suspicions concerning their orthodoxy, but others wished to stifle these trouble-makers. Montalivet, as Minister of Public Instruction, was responsible for religious affairs, asked the Comte de Sainte-Aulaire, ambassador in Rome, to persuade the Pope to refrain from giving the slightest approval to "the revolting absurdity" of Mennaisianism.[7] Austria and Russia, who objected to the support given to Polish rebellion, also put pressure upon the Pope. The Archbishop of Toulouse, Mgr d'Astros, drew up a list of propositions from La Mennais's writings for which he desired papal condemnation and sent them to Rome with the support of other bishops in southern France. Although this arrived too late, Gregory was not unaware of the hostility of the French hierarchy.

The encyclical *Mirari vos* appeared on 15 August 1832, a vaguely worded papal repudiation of the ideas for which *L'Avenir* had stood. Montalembert received the news with an angry disappointment which gradually abated: he submitted to papal authority but felt it unnecessary to deny his ideas. La Mennais's reaction was one of despair leading to a nervous and spiritual crisis. At first submitting and closing the Agence Générale, he became disillusioned with the Catholic Church. He increasingly believed that God would care for religion, that man should concentrate on reforming the political world which he held responsible for his repudiation. None the less, the conciliatory efforts of his fellow Breton, Hyacinthe de Quélen, Archbishop of Paris, produced further submission, even to the papal brief *Litteras* which suggested that the promised obedience had been incomplete. Gregory had been pushed to this by Mgr d'Astros and by Metternich who had been angered by the contributions of Montalembert and La Mennais to the *Livre des Pélerins polonais*, a work of Catholic insurrectionary nationalism by the Polish poet Mickiewicz, published in Paris in 1833.

Late that year, La Mennais finally told a distressed Montalembert that he had lost his Catholic faith. He was at work on the expression of a new philosophy where the ideas of *l'Avenir* were taken to an extreme, with the backbone of orthodox dogma removed. In April 1834 appeared *Les Paroles d'un croyant*. Its author declared it destined for the people. It was a bitter attack upon kings, a call to the oppressed to rally to the Gospel which would lead them to the reign of equality, the peaceful role of a universal republic. Written in a simple, biblical style, the work sold swiftly. Lamartine admired its beauties of language but saw in it "the Evangelist of insurrection, Babeuf made divine",[8] whilst Saint-Marc Girardin declaimed in the *Débats*, "It is Ezekiel disguised as a Jacobin; it is Marat dressed up as a prophet."[9] The former Abbé de La Mennais had become the republican pamphleteer Lamennais, his religion the brotherhood of democratic deism.

A new encyclical, *Singulari vos*, utterly condemned any such invocation of Christianity in revolutionary causes. Montalembert after much heart-searching submitted, believing that whatever its political errors, spiritual peace could not be found outside the Church. He could not convince Lamennais of this, nor could the rebel make his former disciple realise that Catholicism was only a dying form of the eternal religion. Lacordaire used *Les Paroles* as the excuse to publish his own separation from Lamennais and for an attack on the more extreme elements in Mennaisianism. The school was now definitely at an end. Sadly, sometimes angrily, his associates left their mentor to the rather suspicious republicans.

Lamennais continued to plead his cause, and in *Les Affaires de Rome* (1836) attacked the Pope, attempting to destroy what once he had adored. An extreme vehemence of his affirmation covered a painful scepticism: there was no moderation in his ideals, whether it was a progressive Papacy or fraternal proletariat following the precepts of a democratic Christ. Opposed to the Restoration from the far right, from the far left to the July Monarchy, to both he lent the bitter splendours of his poetical prose. The initial crisis once over, his desertion affected Catholicism little. A star might be extinguished, said Gerbet, but the universe remained.[10] It had been a very bright star, however, as the Catholic journalist Louis Veuillot realised: Lamennais was first to proclaim the doctrines of militant Catholicism, "he has made the breach through which we will try to pass".[11]

Lacordaire, personally almost as tormented a being as Lamennais, but less prone to political extremism, was not repelled by bourgeois society as was the aristocratic Montalembert, and came to terms with Orleanism: in 1834 he began the public preaching that was to make religion almost fashionable. Montalembert despaired that after the defeat of the *Avenir* school, the French Church would fall into utter disgrace as "the protégé of the most infamous power that has ever soiled the face of the earth".[12] Yet he recovered to play a significant intellectual and political role, albeit a rather isolated one, between Catholic legitimists and anticlerical liberals, "Jacobin in the eyes of one party, and bigot in the eyes of the other".[13] However, the 1840s would see him the leader of a renewed movement to gain educational freedom, possessing a national role because he had never ceased to believe that the Church and liberty were not antagonists, but allies.

If *L'Avenir*, like Saint-Simonism, had collapsed in the disappointment of its excessive aspirations, it had similarly released many influential ideas. It had educated part of the élite of a generation: it had helped fit Catholicism for a new age, making it aware of social problems, allowing it to throw off the dead weight of a royalist past and encouraging it to conquer public opinion.

REFERENCES

1. Alfred de Vigny, Otello (*Œuvres Complètes*, Editions Du Seuil, 1965), 349.
2. Comte E. d'Alton-Shée, *Mes Mémoires* (1869), I, 81.
3. *Le Globe*, 20 April 1832.
4. *L'Avenir*, 30 October 1830.
5. Ibid., 13 November 1830.
6. Ibid., 22 December 1830.
7. Affaires Etrangères, Rome 969, f°. 319, 19 November 1832.
8. A. de Lamartine, *Correspondance* (1882), I, 337.
9. *Journal des Débats*, 24 May 1834.
10. Abbé Gerbet, *L'Université Catholique*, January 1837.
11. L. Veuillot, *Correspondance* (1884–92), I, 327.
12. G. Goyau and P. de Lallemand (eds), *Lettres de Montalembert à Lamennais* (1932), 35.
13. Bibliothèque Nationale, nouvelles acquisitions françaises 21536.

5

Mouvement and *Résistance*: The Triumph of Périer

"Mon volcan tant prédit a dechaîné ses laves;
Là voilà devant nous la guerre des esclaves!
De nouveau Spartacus sortent des ateliers,
Les conscrits de la faim s'enrolent par milliers."

("My volcano, as so often predicted, has unleashed her lava;
There it is before us, the war of slaves!
Once again Spartacus comes out of the work-shops,
The conscripts of hunger enrol by the thousand.")[1]

The July Monarchy faced two main threats in the early months of its existence; one in Paris which expanded, the other in the provinces which contracted. If much of France had remained indifferent or uncomprehending whilst Bourbon authority passed into other hands, the population of certain areas remained predominently loyal to the senior branch. Many priests, resigning or dismissed army officers, courtiers who lost pensions, and staunch squirearchs, were unwilling to reconcile themselves to the new order. In the deep south and west of France there was mass support for this hostility. Legitimist hotheads, such as Comte Ferdinand de Bertier, unenthusiastically put in command of French royalists by Charles X, believed that the partisans of Henri V should strike before they lost heart: he confidently expected assistance from the Tsar and King of Spain, both of whom wished to see the usurper dethroned. Although Charles put primary responsibility for a restoration in the hands of God, many legitimists hoped that European war would give them an opportunity for successful uprising. To this end they collected and concealed arms.

The relationship of legitimists and the new authority differed from area to area. Where the prefect was moderate and conservative and the legitimists regretfully resigned to the position (the Eure, for example, where Antoine Passy was prefect) relations were usually calm and conciliatory. Elsewhere, if the prefect were more radical, the legitimists more uncompromising, open and sometimes violent hostility existed. In ultra-royalist Toulouse, for example, the purge of officers, including the most insignificant clerkships in the office of weights and measures and the municipal library, had torn apart the mesh of royalist patronage, had forced the town into an Orleanist mould by creating unemployment, imparting to it the feeling of a beleaguered fortress. In towns of the Midi, the lower orders were often Carlist in feeling and were Catholic, whilst the Orleanist bourgeoisie was frequently Protestant. It was an area with many old grievances to be revenged and religion exacerbated the bitterness of political divisions. Working-class support gave legitimism a violent tendency. Nîmes, where Catholic authorities had been replaced by a liberal largely Protestant establishment, was the scene of attacks on Protestant employers, which the prefect claimed were often inspired by the priesthood. The countryside of Nimes and Alais and the towns of Uzès and Sommières saw many disturbances amongst a populace who attacked authorities doubly disliked as Orleanist and bourgeois.

Dupont, Minister of Justice, took the strictest measures against Carlists in the administration and against expression of legitimist opinion. He put the department of the Gard, scene of the worst disturbances, under a state of siege in order to grant the authorities greater powers of arrest and search. However, the immovable magistrature meant that in many places the courts were anti-Orleanist. Juries throughout the departments of Hérault and Gard would frequently fail to find guilty those whose political opinions they shared. Courts at Alais and Nîmes imposed ludicrously small fines on men convicted of attacking and, in one case, killing members of the National Guard.[†]

Troubles of legitimist origin were not limited to the south. In the Morbihan department there were continued troubles for which the royalist clergy were often blamed, and authorities noted the collection of arms. In the Maine and Loire, late in 1830, poor grain circulation was used by Carlists to encourage the population against the merchants; an ecclesiastical school at Sable was dissolved as a centre of conspiracy. By mid-1831, however, with economic recovery and establishment of authority, the disturbances grew fewer and less dangerous. The legitimists had missed their opportunity: when in spring 1832 the Duchesse de Berry led a rebellion, she faced a monarchy fortified by the energetic government of Casimir Périer.

The fact that the Church withheld its support from the regime was not as serious as it would have been in an earlier age, but did much to prevent the rallying of conservative opinion and to maintain the hostility of the peasantry in areas where Catholicism retained its hold. Although one section of the Church accepted the Revolution and embarrassed the regime by going further in demanding fuller liberty, the majority of priests regretted Charles X, usually with resignation, but sometimes with overt hostility to the usurping monarch. The anticlericalism of many of the new authorities manifest in failure to prevent mob destruction of Church property, maintained

Ed. Note. As B. Fitzpatrick has shown in his *Catholic Royalism in the Department of the Gard, 1814–1852* (Cambridge, 1983), ultra-royalism in the Gard was motivated at least as much by competition for local power between members of the two faiths as by any great attachment to the Bourbons. Nevertheless, Catholic royalists were generally hostile to the government of Louis-Philippe.

the mutual hostility, led on the Church's side by Hyacinthe de Quélen, Archbishop of Paris.

The first difficulty arose when three bishops nominated by Charles X were being installed and refused to take the oath to the new King: the Gallican Dupin demanded that their episcopal revenues be confiscated until their surrender, but the Duc de Broglie, Minister responsible for Religious Affairs, adopted more conciliatory methods and was eventually able to persuade the three to swear allegiance. The Catholic Broglie tried to restrain the frequent tendency of prefects to anticlericalism, and was rewarded by success in persuading most bishops to have prayers for the new King said at mass, but the anticlericalism of his successor Merilhou put an end to the hesitant *rapprochement*. The failure of Laffitte's government to prevent the sack of Saint-Germain l'Auxerrois, the refusal to offer apology or (until 1837) compensation, produced open enmity from Archbishop de Quélen who was refused permission to rebuild his residence on the grounds that the site was provocative. The government of Casimir Périer at least was willing to brave popular anticlericalism and to take steps such as the reopening of the seminaries of Metz and Nancy, which had been closed because their existence had provoked mobs to attack them in October 1830 and February 1831. Yet Périer remained suspicious of the priesthood, and asked prefects to have mayors report on unexplained absences of priests: as a result, several anticlerical authorities saw Carlist conspiracy in every conversation between two *curés*. Various arbitrary acts against the Church, and the first episcopal nominations made by the government, showed disregard for ecclesiastical opinion.

As well as facing hostility from the clerical and Carlist right, the government had from its inception been criticised by those who felt it was excessively favourable to legitimists. The 1830 Revolution had raised hopes among the lower classes which it could not fulfil. The realisation of their political power had brought with it a growing consciousness of their economic weakness. The Revolution had aggravated a financial depression and workers found that fighting for the political triumph of the liberal bourgeoisie had been to their own economic disadvantage. When a poor harvest in 1830 and high bread prices created riots throughout the country, the prefect of police in Paris reported the complaints of the populace that the Revolution had been stolen from them: hunger was a bad counsellor, he remarked. However, in spite of the efforts of republicans and Saint-Simonians to educate them, the working classes as yet had scarcely any conception of political action founded upon class or upon economic demands. They could be moved by the negative passions of hostility to priesthood or Bourbons but a positive programme attempted by co-ordinated action was alien to their traditions, as it was to a style of life whose predominating feature was the battle for physical survival.

In the early days of good relations between the regime and the population of Paris, working-class demands usually took the form of polite petitions to the authorities to compel employers to increase wages. When there were disorders, some isolated cases of machine breaking for example, Orleanist newspapers tended to blame them upon Carlist provocation. It was the typographers, the first workers to join the revolutionary fray in July, who showed the most organisation. Their strikes over the introduction of new machines created havoc in the Parisian press in the autumn of 1830 and inspired other workers to follow their example. Orleanists, liberal and conservative, were at first almost pained to see the working classes fight for their own interests without regard for the dogma of *laissez-faire*. Girod (de l'Ain), the prefect of police, economists such as Charles Dupin, newspapers from the *Journal des Débats* to the *National*, argued the blessings of enterprise free from state control and the requirements of progress which was eventually of benefit to all.

As the manifestations continued and unemployed or striking crowds seemed to endanger order, the authorities became sterner, although not wholly negative. Girod's ordinance of 25 August 1830 attacked reunions as a source of disorder and commanded all to return to work. Parliament voted large, if inadequate, sums in an attempt to encourage industry. The prefect of the Seine provided paid work in *ateliers de secours*. As with Louis Blanc's socialist workshops in 1848, these attracted immigration; there were too many unemployed for the money and work available and, as a potential source of disorder, they were closed down. When the republicans interested themselves in the working classes for political ends, the government became increasingly heavy-handed, going so far sometimes as to make arrests for the mere presentation of a petition. Orleanism as the force of the beleaguered centre tended to see all dissent as fundamental attack. Périer's war against anarchy was based upon the conviction that only conservative Orleanism could maintain the regime and that those not holding his beliefs were either conscious traitors or their unknowing tools: his ministry attempted to make *résistance* a national cause.

In the aftermath of the July insurrection, the Paris authorities had frequently done little more than confirm the position of those who had seized control in 1830. Local power was therefore a reflection of opposition to the Bourbon government and was often more republican than Orleanist. At Metz, for example, a town of Lorraine where patriotism had been republican or imperialist, radical thinking was strong in the new local government. The sub-prefect of the area and the mayor of Metz encouraged the anticlericalism of the National Guard, which indulged in bullying the priesthood. There were noisy protests urging the government to aid the Polish rebellion: clubs were formed, notably the Association Nationale pour Assurer l'Indépendance du Pays et l'Expulsion Perpetuelle de la Branche Ainée des Bourbons, which was joined by the mayor and members of the administration and National Guard. These groups focused their attack upon the prefect, Baron Sers, unpopular for having served the Restoration and for his opposition to the militaristic patriotism manifest in the National Guard. Périer's government removed the mayor, the army commander and many functionaries, which enabled the conservatives to gain control of the municipal council and two of Metz's three electoral colleges. The National Guard, with its strong *petit bourgeois* element, continued to be troublesome however: its delegate, a former *avocat général*, dismissed by Périer, harangued the King, demanding the republican institutions promised in 1830, and after officers had supported a petition for electoral reform, it was dissolved.

At Bordeaux, which was one of the few areas where there was a movement similar to that in Paris, the new authorities at once began to divide. The mayor, the Bonapartist Marquis de Bryas, had acted the role of a provincial La Fayette and kept the town in the control of the *parti du mouvement*, until his dismissal by Périer. The elections of 1831 saw a fight between the Bordeaux supporters of the *mouvement* led by Bryas, and conservatives with government aid. Both sides had their own newspaper, the former demanding a democratic and aggressive foreign policy, stricter repression of priests and royalists, whilst the conservatives argued for internal order and external peace. Although he won the election, Bryas lost the Hôtel de Ville, and wealthy merchants such as Guestier and Wustemberg were able to gain control of the city.

In Bordeaux, as frequently elsewhere, the battle was one of class as much as of opinion; the conservative upper against the lower bourgeoisie. The potential class divisions within Orleanism were obvious in a superficial but revealing instance when, on the morrow of the victory of 1830, wealthy Orleanists of Lyons gave a ball for the King's eldest son, carefully pricing the tickets above the means of most *petit bourgeois* National Guardsmen. Such divisions came to underlie political conflicts. If the middle classes had captured the July Revolution from the workers as the latter claimed, it was not yet completely certain which section of the middle class would obtain predominant possession.

The King sent for Casimir Périer immediately upon the resignation of Laffitte, at Montalivet's urging, although he realised that he would not rediscover the compliance he had enjoyed in Laffitte. Montalivet had already opened negotiations with the man whom he believed alone capable of saving the country from a descent into anarchy. Périer was difficult to persuade: he wished to punish Frenchmen for their insubordination by allowing chaos to grow until all cried out for order to be imposed; and he was not sure that the ultimate moment had arrived. There was also disgust with power which had become sullied by its humiliations at the hands of the mob: "now that it cannot be done without dirtying one's hands, you want me to take it up! . . ."[2] he complained, and he held a neurotic conviction that office would kill him; "I will leave the ministry feet first."[3] He felt a mission to destroy the ferment of revolution in France, but despaired of its success. He was "bold despite doubt and even sadness",[4] wrote Guizot; but boldness triumped.

Then began the task of finding ministers. Sébastiani happily remained at Foreign Affairs where both King and *président du conseil* desired a man of moderation and application but without a domineering personality. It was not so easy to persuade the aged Baron Louis to return in order to reform the Finance Ministry after the depredations of the prodigal Laffitte, but the Comte d'Argout took charge of Commerce to lessen the burden. Maréchal Soult, who felt a reciprocated antipathy for Périer, hesitated to accept the War Ministry until the threat that it would be given to a rival. Barthe retained Justice and Montalivet took over Public Instruction, for Périer himself, showing where he believed the great tasks lay, added the Interior to the responsibilities of the presidency.

Although in personnel the Cabinet of 13 March resembled its predecessor, its policies were very different. Périer imposed solidarity upon his ministers before their appointments were signed, and had wrenched from the unwilling King, as a condition of accepting office, permission to hold Cabinet meetings without the Duc d'Orléans, liberal-minded heir to the throne, and on occasion without the King himself. Nor might the King tamper with the official journal: the *Moniteur* would be under sole direction of the president. Even when all this had been gained, Périer, on the day after his official appointment, rushed to the King to resign, claiming he could not govern when the Court was hostile: the King, his sister and more reluctantly his son, all assured the premier of their support and implored him to remain.

Yet Louis-Philippe could never like Périer, nor the latter trust the King. It needed constant mediation by Périer's *chef de cabinet*, the Comte d'Haubersaert, and his colleague, the King's confidant, Montalivet, to keep the two on speaking terms. Louis-Philippe with his dilettante interests and voluble charm could not understand the other's uncompromising and logical temperament, and complained of his narrow intellect, his banker's soul, padlocked like a strong-box.[5] His view resembled the republican Louis Blanc's claim that Périer was mean-spirited beneath his haughty exterior; opposing the Restoration because jealous of the aristocracy, whose graces he lacked, but fearing and loathing the people. A great gulf divided Périer from Laffitte, his fellow banker, perhaps the result of their different origins: the latter had been born humbly and had won a precarious fortune by luck and unscrupulous energy: Périer was born into a bourgeois dynasty, of secure and massive wealth and connections with the imperial administration and liberal aristocracy (although the fact that he was the youngest of ten children perhaps accounted for the extreme susceptibility which accompanied a consciousness of his own superiority). For Laffitte, 1830 was the crowning speculation to conquer a system which had tried to exclude him at birth, but Périer accepted the results purely to maintain order. He told Barrot that France's misfortune was that so many, like him, believed there had been a revolution. "No, Monsieur, there has not been a revolution; there is simply a change at the head of state."[6]

By sharply dividing friends from enemies, Périer disciplined the wavering, but also united in opposition moderates like Barrot and extremists. "Let us go and fight these scoundrels", he declared one day, and when the more moderate Broglie remonstrated that adversaries was a fairer term, replied gruffly, "I know what I am talking about, for I have been one of them."[7] His own supporters he respected little more. Presenting a manifesto of resistance to the deputies, he told them that the promised concessions had been made law. Disorder would produce no more, rather it would lead to disaster, "it is good to speak the truth to nations as well as kings".[8] He obtained the vote of confidence he demanded.

Périer's government began to turn the administration into an arm of the *parti de résistance*. Excessively liberal mayors and *sous-préfets* were replaced and generals who had tolerated disorder in the name of patriotism, removed. Périer would not allow office-holders to belong to radical pressure groups and forced the King to suspend his aide-de-camp, the deputy Alexandre de Laborde, for being a member of L'Association Nationale. Seeking re-election, Laborde had, like forty other deputies, joined what appeared to be a patriotic movement with the stated aim of combating the elder branch of the Bourbons and foreign powers, "by means of all personal and pecuniary sacrifices".[9] But as well as being an attempt to unite supporters of the *mouvement* as a political party, it served as a cover for republican activities. Laborde left it after the 1831 elections and returned to his place at Court, but others, especially in the army, lost their posts permanently: Barrot was removed from the Conseil d'État, Général Lamarque lost his command and Bérard was dismissed as director-general of the department of roads and bridges. Henceforth both the responsibilities and the rewards would go to members of the *parti de résistance*. The gaps were filled by men who could be expected to enforce order with rigour. The most notable appointment was that of Gisquet as prefect of police in November 1831. A former employee of the Périer bank who had worked his way to the top from the most humble of backgrounds, he was the first capable figure to fill this vital post. He had, however, more energy than probity and the alleged profit he made on the order of a consignment of rifles made the "Gisquet rifles" a scandal which the opposition were quick to use against this unpopular figure.

The left were not only forced from power, they were continually opposed in Parliament. It was a weakness of the regime, and one which Périer shared, to put the parliamentary struggle before all else. Journalists he despised, and he left to his supporters the responsibility of trying to win public opinion. In the Chamber of Deputies he would not delegate authority: he would constantly spring to his feet to answer Mauguin, Barrot and Lamarque when they made apologies for riots and accusations that the government was deviating from the spirit of 1830. He tried to crush the myths of the left, especially by stressing that the programme of the Hôtel de Ville had never existed. Lacking adroitness in debate and profundity in philosophy, he commanded the assembly by his personality: gaunt, handsome, glaring fiercely, a clenched fist held high, he quelled mutiny and attacked the spirit of fear which led moderates to compromise with the destructive passions of the radicals.

Périer had the support of three considerable orators, later to become mutually inimical, but who in 1831 were able to act together. Dupin, archetypal bourgeois lawyer, had the ability to make a commonplace sound profound and by appealing to the pacifism and desire for order of the tradesman and property-owner, did much to make Périer's conservatism acceptable to the average deputy. Guizot, on the other hand, gave it a philosophical justification, concerned to combat not only the disorder of the streets but the ideological anarchy which he believed gave it birth. Thiers was less dogmatic in his conservatism, but admired Périer as a man of action, and brought his wit and verve to attack the losing cause of the left.

Yet even Périer recognised the limits to conservatism in the average Orleanist deputy. He accepted a wider extension of the franchise than he had personally desired. And in August 1831, less haughty than usual, with lowered head, he announced that the peerage would cease to be hereditary. Personally a believer in the hereditary principle, he none the less realised that to save the Upper Chamber as other than the elected body which the left wished, it had to be abandoned: consultations with members of his majority showed insufficient support, nor was the King willing to fight on the issue. Once he had made the decision, Périer applied it with characteristic vigour: to ensure acceptance of the bill, he created thirty-six peers who would vote for it. So in late December, the peers accepted their emasculation. A conservative ministry had reluctantly helped pass a measure desired primarily by the Orleanist left and centre. Similar motives prevented Périer reopening Saint-Germain or taking a strong lead concerning the King's civil list. Many deputies were willing to support the cause of order as long as their bourgeois susceptibilities were not wounded.

That cause had yet to triumph outside the Chambers. The fortnightly political chronicle of the newly founded *Revue des Deux Mondes* was entitled "the revolutions of the fortnight", a reflection of the atmosphere of riot and political instability which pervaded Paris in 1831 and 1832. Never had newspapers attacked a monarch with such virulence, and the Restoration offered no precedent for the offensive which Périer opened against the press. More than eighty press trials were inaugurated by the government, on accusations of provocation to sedition. The *procureur général*, Persil, pursued a constant feud against the extreme *Tribune*, which underwent the majority of trials at this time. Two of its editors, Marrast and Sarraut, served prison sentences of several months, and the newspaper had to pay fines of up to 3,000 francs. If penalties were severe, verdicts were far from sure. Often juries, intimidated by republican threats, their names published in the opposition press, would acquit the accused. The very violent Jacobin–Bonapartist *Révolution* was found guilty in only eight of thirty trials.

The government suffered similar failures when it prosecuted clubs. Thus Evariste Gallois who, at a republican banquet, had brandished a dagger and cried "For Louis-Philippe if he betrays us!" was acquitted of any threat to the King. Many of the accused used the tribune to attack their judges and the monarchy, making acquittal a political triumph. In December 1832, when Godefroy Cavaignac and other leaders of the Amis du Peuple were accused of forming an association in defiance of the law, the jury agreed that the transgression had occurred, but still chose to deliver a verdict of not guilty. It was left for another ministry in 1834 to win the battle in the courts with the aid of new laws.

In the streets of Paris, the government was involved in a constant battle for order. In May 1831, republicans and Bonapartists gathered in the Place Vendôme to protest against the inscription "given by the King of the French" on the medals given to those who fought in July. When the crowds became unruly and refused Général de Lobau's summons to withdraw, the commander of the National Guard used water-power from the hose-pipes installed against fire to drive the demonstrators from the square. Students were a permanent force for disorder, on one occasion hurling stones at Barthe, the Minister of Justice, and *procureur général* Persil when the two ventured to the Sorbonne. The emotional issue of Polish independence provided a rallying cry for the opposition on several occasions. The news of the Russian victory over the rebellion, announced by Sébastiani in unemotional (but frequently misunderstood) words, "the latest news is that calm reigns in Warsaw",[10] produced serious riots in Paris in late September for almost a week. On the 30th, Périer and Sébastiani were forced from their carriage and threatened with violence: Périer's impassive bearing impressed the crowd and the two walked on unmolested.

In January 1832 took place a bungled attempt to produce insurrection by ringing the bells of Notre Dame. It was followed within a few weeks by a legitimist débâcle, the Rue des Prouvaires plot, where royalists distributed arms to republicans with the intention of seizing the Tuileries and overthrowing the King. Accompanying these spectacular failures were many minor disorders, protests and plots which lacked sufficient determined support to turn into insurrection: the government was vigorous and the Parisian National Guard loyal.

The disorder was not restricted to the capital. Carlist troubles seemed less serious, but republicanism, with the aid of the alienated Orleanist left, turned many provincial towns into areas of conflict. At Metz, Polish refugees added to the unrest already fomented by Bonapartist and republican groups. The most serious troubles here were the 1832 grain riots caused by high prices: the army and National Guard, which inclined towards the opposition, only acted when increasing pillage seemed to presage a social and not merely a political revolt. Strasbourg was very similar. Bonapartist sentiment was strong here and inflamed the discontent felt for the conciliation of the regime toward the autocracies of Europe. As at Metz, the National Guard was infiltrated and on 4 October 1831, a revolt broke out involving Guardsmen and the workless. An attack upon a customs post was combined with declamations on foreign policy: for the second time that year, the troops were called out. The prefect reduced the duty on cattle to try to placate the crowds: he was promptly dismissed by the central government by telegram. With the army steadfast, the riots gradually dissipated.

At Grenoble, however, in March 1832, the prefect Duval who had proved ruthless in suppressing grain riots in the Pyrénées-Orientales department (as he was to be when confronting legitimists in the Vendée) provoked riots by attempting to arrest students who were manifesting hostility to the regime during a carnival procession. Using troops against them, the injuries caused so angered the populace that he had to take refuge in the barracks. Périer, showing that he admired strength in the prefects even when unaccompanied by wisdom, refused to remove Duval or to allow the commander to withdraw his troops in an attempt at conciliation. It was the lack of real purpose in the insurrection that ended it, but administrative heavy-handedness had helped turn Grenoble into a centre of opposition.

The worst disorders occurred at Lyons where the revolt had a power and discipline which the demonstrations lacked elsewhere. Although revolt in a provincial city, even the second largest in France, could not overthrow the government, it was an important event in working-class history, and terrified the propertied classes. Lyons had suffered enormously during the first Revolution; republicanism was associated with a particularly bloody provincial example of Jacobin terror. Class antagonism fed upon problems in the silk industry upon which almost half of the city's 180,000 population depended and which was acutely suffering from the national depression. Saint-Simonian preaching against the unprofitable middleman was especially well received here, where the merchants held considerable power, providing the raw material to small workshops and selling the finished product.

As well as its dissatisfied labour force, Lyons had a large number of Piedmontese refugees. Their sympathisers formed an association, the Volontiers du Rhône: like that at Metz, it was semi-military, pledged to defend the fatherland against the Bourbons and other forces of European reaction. Early in 1831, it undertook a march towards the Italian frontier to aid rebels against the King of Piedmont, but on the orders of Montalivet (then Minister of the Interior), it was turned back by the army.

As in Paris, Périer's policies had turned many radicals into republicans. Carrel of the *National* had lost faith in the regime and similarly Anselme Pétetin, editor of the *Précurseur*, had moved into opposition, heading a group of republicans, intellectuals and lawyers (including the young Jules Favre) in the Association Lyonnaise pour la Liberté de la Presse. Opposing them was the city's wealthy governing group, notably mayor Prunelle and the deputy Fulchiron.

When in October 1831 the chiefs of workshop petitioned the prefect, Bouvier-Dumolard, for an increase in payment, the latter assembled a committee from both sides which negotiated a new tariff. Acclaimed by the workers, the *canuts*, many merchants refused it and protested to the government. Périer disapproved of state intervention, especially on the workers' behalf, and ordered Bouvier-Dumolard to cancel it. The prefect was forced to announce that the agreement was in no way legally binding and so very few merchants observed it. The *canuts'* leaders decided upon a strike and on 21 November held a mass demonstration. The National Guardsmen present were mainly merchants and their clerks who fired at the crowd when stones were thrown at them. In the usual way, insurrection began with a call to arms and the building of barricades. National Guards in the working-class Croix-Rousse district, many of them *chefs d'atelier*, joined the insurgents bringing weapons. The capture of Bouvier-Dumolard, attempting to negotiate a truce, and the failure of the army commander to co-operate with the civilian authorities, deprived the latter of power. On the 22nd, the insurgents spread from the working-class suburbs on the hills, down through the alleyways to the centre of the town. That evening, the exhausted army retreated, and on the 23rd, the insurrection occupied the Hôtel de Ville: it was master of the city.

The Lyonnais workers had shown considerable strategic sense in capturing barracks and telegraph installations and in holding captive the prefect for a few vital hours, but the revolt had no leader and, with victory achieved, the next step was bound to be divisive. Some wished to inaugurate a new social order. Influenced by journalists of the left-wing *Glaneuse*, Lacombe, head of the Volontiers du Rhône, which had provided an informal leadership of the insurrection, became provisional chief of staff and printed a proclamation vaguely promising a corporative society: but then lost courage and sent a counter-proclamation to his fellow *chefs-d'atelier*, many of whom were worried by the radical course of events. The revolt was splitting between the majority of *chefs d'atelièr* who were not inclined towards socialism and the *Glaneuse*, the radical minority of workshop owners and the majority of workers; although the greater number of the latter were interested only in the tariff and not in the extreme republicanism of the *Glaneuse*.

On the 24th, the moderate insurgents, fearing the extreme elements, made terms with the authorities and by means of their collaboration, the prefect was able to regain control. On 3 December, an army sent from Paris under Maréchal Soult and the Duc d'Orléans entered the town to assert governmental authority. There was no resistance and Orléans took care to prevent the worst effects of military occupation. Accompanying the display of strength came the King's order for a large quantity of silk for upholstery.

Governmental action, as always under Périer, meant the removal of those who had proved inadequate. Bouvier-Dumolard was replaced by Comte Adrien de Gasparin, a proven administrator and believer in rigorous *laissez-faire*: he began a stricter surveillance of working-class activity. The National Guard, many of whom had deserted or shown unwillingness to risk themselves in the defence of order, was virtually dissolved. The army, which in the government's view had behaved discreditably, also underwent changes. The weak commander was replaced and Colonel Magnan and Lieutenant-Colonel Cavaignac, who had aroused suspicion by their contacts with insurgents, were transferred. Under Géneral Aymard, there were improvements in discipline and living conditions, and strategically placed forts were built to prevent the city again falling to an uprising.

This brief success had resulted from the authorities' weakness, an unenthusiastic army and National Guard, only 300 of the 2,000 having responded to the summons to arms. The insurrection was economic in origin, masters and men having common grievances against the merchants. It was never completely republican; many were indifferent and others Carlists. Although the provisional government set up in the Hôtel de Ville on 23 November was republican, it was betrayed by other republicans fearful of its Jacobinism. The differences between the intellectual *Précurseur*, the masters'

Écho de la Fabrique and the violent *Glaneuse*, fully revealed when the insurrection was successful, destroyed it at the moment of its victory.

In Paris, newspapers of the *mouvement* agreed that the uprising had to be crushed. Only the most left-wing republicans showed approval and legitimists argued that a revolutionary government had no right to destroy revolutions. The Comte de Montalembert in the *Avenir* sympathised with the insurgents and pointed out that the Lyonnais, unlike the Parisians, had respected the Church. Such words and Chateaubriand's praise for their heroism, brought from liberals the claim that the insurgents had been encouraged by priests and Carlists. The majority found their spokesman in Saint-Marc Girardin who wrote in the *Journal des Débats* the famous cry of the possessing class: Lyons had revealed the "grave secret" of the antagonism between those with property and those without. "The barbarians who menace society are neither in the Caucasus nor on the steppes of Tartary; they are in the faubourgs of our manufacturing cities."[11] He asked republican and legitimist middle classes to join the Orleanists to defend their property. The other part of Saint-Marc Girardin's message, that society should concern itself with the fate of its lower orders, was forgotten. A large majority of the Chamber of Deputies saw in the proletarian problem merely a threat to order, and called for repression with all the powers of the law.[12]

Périer's majority was nourished by disorder. The problem of Orleanism was that, lacking a true philosophical base, its strongest motive force would always be the defence of order. Périer's struggle, febrile, incessant and ending in his death, gave an air of grandeur to feelings which were merely negative. The battle on the streets was necessary to retain unity in Parliament, for the conservative majority always threatened to split or to weaken. This was seen during and after the elections of July 1831, the first fought under the new electoral law.

These elections were a further means for the government to form a united party of resistance. Whereas in the partial elections of November 1830, the government had declared its impartiality between Orleanists, on this occasion there was no such neutrality. Périer's circular to the prefects in May told them that the government, believing its principles to be in the national interest, would not be neutral, nor should the administration be.[13] He did, however, stress disregard for minor variations, and obedience to the law. Action usually took the form of restrictions upon government employees inclining toward the opposition, and a vigorous campaign was fought against the Aide-toi, le Ciel t'aidera society, resurrected as the electoral organisation of the Orleanist left.

From these noisy and disorderly elections emerged a conservative majority, but one of uncertain numbers. A high proportion of wholly new deputies meant an uncertain party structure: men entered Parliament with no strong convictions, waiting to make up their minds or to mould their opinions to their profit. A new recruit did not wish to bind himself immediately to Casimir Périer, as the latter was to find when the deputies came to vote for the president of the chamber. The ministerial candidate beat Laffitte only narrowly, a sign that he was still seen as a leader even by some moderate conservatives, and Dupont was elected vice-president. Périer felt that the government lacked a strong majority and resigned. This frightened the deputies who had just shown their independence, and many begged him to remain in office: there was confusion and despair amongst the conservatives. A sudden crisis in foreign policy, the Dutch invasion of Belgium, caused Périer to resume his post.

His necessity proved, Périer continued his way without deviation or flexibility. "It is time that uniform governmental action put an end to the culpable ambitions of our enemies, whoever they may be",[14] he announced, demanding a firm majority on 23 July; he received it. The debates on the deputies' *adresse* to the King were bitter, the left invoking France's generous revolutionary tradition, conservatives replying with accusations that the opposition was undermining the social structure. Again Périer demanded and received a vote of confidence, 282 to 73. Although the number of abstentions was large, many deputies preferring not to involve themselves in a conflict which would lose them popularity or independence, it was obvious that the left must abandon its hopes of a parliamentary dominance. The first assembly returned by the widened franchise, accepted by most of the Orleanist left, was fundamentally conservative: the hopes raised by the election of a radical vice-president were dashed by the vote on the *adresse*, reinforced by the physical victory of order at Lyons in November.

As 1832 opened, Périer could see a strong and effective administration, improved finance and tax collection regularised, a parliamentary majority and an increasingly disciplined army. In foreign affairs, France, if still mistrusted by the conservative powers, was no longer the weakly anarchic force she had been the previous year and European war had been avoided, to the chagrin of the left. The spirit of revolution had not been destroyed, but Périer's struggle had made riot less common and less destructive. He himself, however, was exhausted by his constant efforts. Suspicious of allies and colleagues, he often spoke of resignation, partly from the intention to establish his continued dominance by proving his necessity, partly from his obsessive fear that the burdens of office would kill him. His colleagues begged him not to retire: "You wish my death? Very well! I shall sacrifice myself",[15] he replied. Early 1832 was troubled by plots and rumours of plots, and especially by evidence that the legitimists were planning an uprising. And to add to the internal sickness of France, there came in February the cholera.

By March 1832, it had arrived in Paris, and by the time it had gone, six months later, 18,402 people had died. The disease spread outwards from the capital. By 5 April it had reached Douai, on the 10th Saint-Quentin and Rouen, within the next week cases were discovered at Amiens, Abbeville and Dunkirk; it went thence to Cambrai, Valenciennes and to Lille in late May. It claimed most victims in the grim industrial quarters with their crowded unhygienic houses. At Metz, 800 died, the same proportion of the population as in Paris, and some nearby villages lost a quarter of their population. Emigrants from the capital carried it to other departments. The disease hit

Bordeaux in early August and Arles in autumn, but it was capricious; Marseilles was spared in 1832 but in the winter of 1834–35, over 3,000 died there,and another 200 in a second smaller invasion of cholera in 1837.

Medicine was powerless to deal with the disease. The cartloads of corpses added an additional sinister quality to the contorted streets of the Parisian slums in which the cholera found the majority of its victims. Unemployment increased and there were unpleasant scenes of mob hysteria. Rumours that the authorities were trying to destroy the population by poisoning them were encouraged by some republicans: others preferred to present priests or royalists as the villains. The latter view was encouraged by no less a personage than the left-wing mayor of Paris, a physician, Cadet-Gassicourt, who put up a proclamation suggesting that if there were poisoners at work, they were Carlists. The poisoning idea was given further credence by a clumsy proclamation by Gisquet, prefect of police, intended to reassure, which told water-porters and food-sellers to cover their merchandise. Doctors were very unpopular and were occasionally attacked, and on one occasion some innocent bystanders were torn apart by a mob who suspected them of sprinkling poison on water.

Amidst the flight from Paris, the royal family and the government remained at their posts. The King visited hospitals while his womenfolk worked on clothes for the sick: the Orléans family gave 500,000 francs to help the victims. The Comte d'Argout, responsible for public health, bravely toured the worst areas: he caught the disease and almost died. On 1 April, the Prince Royal and Périer toured the wards of cholera victims at the Hôtel-Dieu, encouraging and even shaking hands with the sick. Three days later, Périer fell gravely ill. It seemed as if he might conquer this enemy as he had others, then came a relapse, followed by days of delirium when his mind was obsessed by the mob hysteria and murders; he despaired for the future of France and was bitter about his own failure. In words half-madness and half-sense, his mind ranged from his sick-bed hatred of the "scoundrel"[16] Dupin, against whom he warned the King, to his frustrated personal mission for guaranteeing European peace by international disarmament. At last, on 16 May he died.

Some jealous politicians such as Sébastiani, were happy to see the authoritarian *président* removed. The King had mixed feelings: if he disliked the way in which the tight-lipped banker had given him orders, he had at least felt confident in his government. "Is it good news? Is is bad?"[17] he apparently asked himself on hearing the news: he wished for Périer's system without Périer. Unloved but admired, Périer became for Orleanist conservatives a martyr to the cause of order. A statue was erected at Père Lachaise: it is a fitting memorial to the man; his left hand on the Charter, Périer, with a determined expression, raises his clenched right fist in a threatening oratorical gesture.

REFERENCES

1. M. Barthélémy, *Némésis, Satire Hebdomadaire* (Brussels, 1832), 270–1.
2. Comte P. de Ségur, *Mémoires* (1873), VII, 392.
3. Comte C. de Montalivet, *Fragments et Souvenirs* (1899), I, 319.
4. Archives Nationales, 42.AP.15, and F. Guizot, *Mémoires pour servir à l'histoire de mon temps* (1858), II, 211.
5. Victor Hugo, *Choses Vues* (1887), 85.
6. Odilon Barrot, *Mémoires posthumes* (1875), I, 215.
7. D. Cochin, *Louis-Philippe, d'après des documents inédits* (1918), 213.
8. Archives Parlementaires, 18 March 1831.
9. Duc V. de Broglie, *Souvenirs* (1886), IV, 228.
10. Archives Parlementaires, 20 September 1831.
11. *Journal des Débats*, 8 December 1831.
12. Archives Parlementaires, 23 December 1831.
13. Broglie, op. cit., IV, 254.
14. Archives Parlementaires, 23 July 1831.
15. L. Viennet, *Journal* (1955), 269.
16. Mme F. Dosne, *Mémoires* (1928), I, 8.
17. Barrot, op. cit., I, 267.

6

The Orleanist Constitution

"Quelle constitution donner à un peuple qui est trop éclairé pour supporter un gouvernement absolu et trop corrompu pour un gouvernement libre?"

("What constitution to give to a people which is too enlightened to support absolute government and too corrupt for free government?")[1]

The conservative Guizot expressed to the King his disapproval of the frequency with which His Majesty had joined crowds in singing the revolutionary "Marseillaise": "Do not concern yourself, Minister," the King replied, "I stopped saying the words long ago."[2] Similarly, Orleanism's revolutionary claims became an ever more hollow pretence, finally destroyed by Périer. Orleanist electoral law was completed during the latter's rule, but was the product of the months when *mouvement* and *résistance* were locked in bitter argument, undefined though the terms of it usually were. There was dissatisfaction with Restoration electoral processes and a vague desire to widen the franchise: yet the demands of the *parti du mouvement* were scarcely radical. A commission of eight was chosen by the government* and the results of their deliberations introduced to the deputies in December 1831. Two important principles had already been made law in the revised Charter: the lowering of age qualifications so that to vote, it was necessary only to be twenty-five, not thirty, and to qualify as a deputy, only thirty instead of forty, an obvious gain for the young men of July; and the necessity of standing for re-election on being promoted in the state service, including ministerial office.

The government had planned to double the number of electors (94,000 under the Restoration), adding to those qualifying by wealth, those who fulfilled a professional standard of capacity. The commission believed this *cens*

* A cross-section of Orleanist opinion, consisting of the deputies Benjamin Constant, Augustin Périer, elder brother of Casimir, Thiers, Dejean, Comtex Xavier de Sade, Destutt de Tracy and de Rambuteau, and the peer Baron de Barante.

variable too complicated and susceptible to administrative misapplication. They preferred a fixed census, and suggested an annual taxation payment of 240 francs. Many thought this too high and a figure of 200 francs was agreed upon, and 500 francs to be eligible as a deputy. Some of the more conservative, such as Périer, Royer-Collard and the King, who neither liked nor understood the *petite bourgeoisie*, feared their possible incursion into the electorate, and felt that even 200 francs was too little. As to universal suffrage, the Orleanists saw it as the first step to a Jacobin republic, whilst the left feared the conservative prejudices of the peasant majority. In the debate, it was two legitimists, the deputy Berryer and the Marquis de Dreux-Brézé in the Chamber of Peers, who demanded democratic primary assemblies, confident that the rural masses would vote for the local landowner, likely to be a royalist.

The number eligible under the 1831 law remained tiny, 166,583 men, 0.5 per cent of the French population. The number grew as incomes increased, to 240,983 (0.7 per cent) in the 1846 elections. Those eligible as deputies formed a yet more restricted group of 4,200 men earning about 3,000 francs a year; less than ten potential candidates for each seat. Unfortunately for the regime, not all of these were Orleanist. About another thousand were enfranchised by their capacities, corresponding members of the Institute, and retired military officers paying 100 francs in tax (but not magistrates, for too many of these were legitimists). If an *arrondissement* contained fewer than 150 fulfilling the qualifications,* the most highly taxed had to be included to achieve this minimum: nationwide, these *complémentaires* numbered fewer than 1,500. Lastly, a few property-owning women, usually widows, could nominate male proxy voters. Scarcely a radical reform, removing power from the very rich to share it amongst the wealthy, none the less the electoral force of France was substantially changed.

Before the law received the royal signature on 19 April 1831, a painful process of redistribution had taken place. It was considered necessary to add to the 430 deputies, taking account of recent growth in certain areas. The commission decided as best it could what proportion of deputies each of the eighty-six departments deserved. Although these had developed an administrative tradition, they were highly unequal in population and wealth. But the deputies objected to the changes in *arrondissements* which returned them, and developed a system which left these areas almost unchanged but added twenty-nine new ones. Out of the ensuing stalemate, came a combination, more unsatisfactory than either plan: department by department, the Chamber considered which scheme was the better.

This compromise was not a cunning plot, but it suited the majority and the administration too well for them to desire the removal of its anomalies. There were vast inequalities between *arrondissements*, especially between country and town. The electoral rearrangement tended to separate towns from surrounding rural areas, thereby creating Orleanist islands separate from the

* It had been only 50 under the Restoration.

countryside: this was particularly true of the royalist south. The small town was most favoured by the system; large towns, in spite of the improvement effected, were usually still under-represented. Paris, for example, with one-tenth of the electorate, had only 3 per cent of the deputies. And within Paris, surprisingly it was the wealthier areas which were under-represented: in the IIe *arrondissement*, 23 in every 1,000 could vote, less than half this in the poor VIIIe (which included the Marais and Sainte-Antoine districts) and only 5 in every 1,000 in shabby suburban Saint-Denis.

Twenty-three electoral colleges had over 1,000 electors, including 10 of Paris's total 12 *arrondissements* and 2 in Lyons; whilst in the department of the Basses-Pyrénées for 1,300 electors there were 5 *arrondissements*. Thus about as many voted for five deputies in the Basses-Pyrénées as voted in Paris for one. In the poor department of the Creuse, 4 deputies represented scarcely 900 voters: in the rich Seine, 14 represented over 18,000. The Bouches-du-Rhône had over 15 electors for every 1,000 men, whilst Corsica had less than 2. Similar contrasts existed between the Calvados and Côtes-du-Nord, the Seine and Hautes-Pyrénées; Émile de Girardin had 150 electors at Bourganeuf (in the Allier) and was returned to the Chamber of Deputies by only 85 of them in 1839, while the IIe *arrondissement* of Paris had *c.* 2,870 electors. The average *arrondissement* had 500 electors, but in 1846, 60 had more than 800 and 77 had less than 300. This maldistribution enabled Orleanist officials to win elections in small towns in the south, but itself compensated the parties in other areas. It was estimated[3] that of the 129,153 votes in 1837, 38,346 elected 216 ministerial *juste milieu* deputies; 18,909 elected 120 deputies of the centre and *tiers parti*; 4,115 elected 25 legitimists and 17,543 elected 101 of the various shades of the opposition: there is no striking dispoportion here.

The electoral system tended to heighten a local feeling already strong due to absence of a firm party structure. The so-called middle-class electorate, complained the conservative publicist, Henri Fonfrède, was a mixture of several classes and interest groups whose deputies were guided primarily by local factors and reflected "parochial" opinions.[4] (Of the two notable fictional elections of the period, the petty intrigue of Balzac's Arcis is more typical than Stendhal's Lucien Leuwen's desperate campaign against a huge opposition majority.)

Usually only about three-quarters of those eligible actually voted, further limiting the size of the electorate. On only two occasions did the proportion voting reach 82 per cent: in 1839, when the parliamentary coalition of left and right against the Molé government encouraged political interest, both roused passions against the government and made many unpolitical people vote against the immorality of the coalition, and again in 1846 when many legitimists and Catholics went to the polls because of the current issue of educational freedom. Only about 200,000 therefore voted in 1846, 41,000 having abstained. Most of the abstainers would have been legitimists, who were unwilling to register and take the oath to the *roi des Français* which the process of voting required.

The prefect had the decisive role in registration. The procedure to find those eligible was complicated. None the less, electoral lists were more impartial than under the Restoration and there were in this respect at least few valid complaints at the behaviour of the authorities. Both sides, however, would occasionally have an elector register in an *arrondissement* where his vote was of most value, rather than that whence came the bulk of his income.

Attempts were made to remove certain grievances against Restoration voting behaviour. By law, the electors chose officers from amongst them, to conduct the elections. Voting was public: the elector, on a table which was supposed to be sequestered (but the law was often not observed on this point) would write on a piece of paper the name of his chosen candidate, fold it and give it to the president who would drop it into the ballot box. When this was completed, they were counted and then burned. Since the polls were insufficiently policed, there was plenty of opportunity for the laws on secrecy to be infringed. And procedure was open to corruption or error when there was no victory or the majority was less than a third and there had to be another vote: only on the third occasion was a simple majority sufficient, and the voting took place on separate days which was an invitation to conspiracy. Since the first vote was often for a national celebrity who would be standing elsewhere, it was common for an absolute majority not to be reached at the first vote.

Most of the 200,000 who in 1839 were entitled to vote, did so because of the land they owned. The *contribution foncière* was primarily a tax on the soil, and landed property was taxed at a higher rate than industrial and commercial property. Thus, although the law of April 1831 aided the commercial bourgeoisie by putting the *impôt de patente*, the licence tax on commercial property, on the same level as the land-tax for electoral purposes, the nature of the tax made land a better investment for a man wishing to vote or become eligible for election. The *patente* allowed many of medium wealth to become electors and it was possible to qualify by adding it to land-tax, but over the country as a whole, the vast majority, about 180,000, were enfranchised through the latter. There were exceptions, Paris being the greatest: of its 18,000 voters in 1846, 6,000 were involved in commerce: 35 per cent paid by *patente* alone, 43 per cent by land-tax alone, and 22 per cent by mixed taxation. Those who voted as a result of the *patente* predominated in the commercial *petit bourgeois* areas of the III, IV, V, VI and VIIe *arrondissements*, whilst the *contribution foncière* provided a clear majority of voters in the wealthier more aristocratic and more conservative areas of the Ier and X^{e} *arrondissements* (the Faubourgs Saint-Germain and Saint-Honoré). Large *patentes*, where contributions were over 500 francs, were found in areas of great commerce, notably in the IIe *arrondissement*. Because the capital city was more highly taxed than the provinces, a Parisian voter might well be poorer than his counterpart. In Paris, one inhabitant in fifty was an elector, and in the wealthy IIe *arrondissement*, one in thirty, much higher than the national average. The small businessmen given preponderance by this were mostly *gauche dynastique*, and three-fifths of the Parisian electors voted for the opposition which in 1842 won ten of the twelve seats.

Over most of the country, however, the Orleanist voters were a body of men whose claim to vote rested preponderantly upon wealth obtained from land. This wealth had of course often been invested in land or *rentes* after an official, professional or commercial career. Because a high proportion had attained or inherited their eligibility only in middle age, the average age of electors was high, higher than that of the deputies whose average age was forty-nine.

This difference in local wealth, the contrast between industrial and agricultural areas, between fertile and poor land, the varying styles of ownership, meant that the Orleanist electorate did not present a universal class structure. One may say that the middle class predominated, but this class was wide, varied and lacked uniformity of wealth and life-style. The contrast is obvious between a wealthy *arrondissement* of middling farmers, close to their peasant origins, providing a large electorate with a tendency to opposition, and a poorer *arrondissement* where the farms would be larger and more often in aristocratic hands. A similar difference occurred in towns, between the small *arrondissement* with its predominance of professional men, and a city like Marseilles, where artisans and shopkeepers of humble origin had obtained the vote. At Wissembourg near Strasbourg, the habit of dividing farms into small portions meant that the franchise had to sink below the 200 francs *cens*, but it could in no way be compared with backward Corsica. In most of Paris, the *petit bourgeois* achieved dominance, but in a small provincial town the bourgeois elector would be a lawyer or doctor more often than he was a shopkeeper. A reversal in fortune could of course remove a man's voting rights with his financial security. In times of prosperity, many *petit bourgeois* earned more, paid more in taxation and gained a vote. The 1846 financial crisis, following a reform of the *patente* in 1844 which disenfranchised almost 2,000 Parisian electors, grocers, butchers and tailors, deprived many of the franchise, and must have wounded their civic pride in addition to causing economic difficulties.

During the July Monarchy, electoral methods, publicity and propaganda became more modern, and to some extent, more democratic. In this transitional phase between the modern party system and the world of traditional personal relationships, electoral behaviour varied enormously from place to place. There were a large number of *arrondissements* where only one candidate stood, and others where the opposition was purely nominal. On the other hand, loose party distinctions and strong personal rivalries often produced a competition between candidates of similar views. Since there were no limits on the number of seats for which a candidate might stand, some, like Thiers, Barrot or Lamartine who claimed to be national figures, might be elected four or five times. Political enmities also prevented the growth of a simple party structure which would be reflected in elections. The tendency of legitimists and republicans to vote together against the Orleanist candidate was frequent, for example the election of the republican Arago at Perpignan with legitimist aid. At Villefranche in the Aveyron in 1834, Thiers and the legitimist came equal, and the prefect asked the opposition candidate who had come third to persuade his supporters to vote for the anti-legitimist historian of the Revolution. Although the candidate agreed, his more extreme supporters did not obey and the legitimist was elected. In other areas, however, where the legitimists were not so violent or where historical factors prevented their *rapprochement* with their extreme opposites, conservatives friendly and unfriendly to the regime might unite against the Orleanist or republican left.

Where party distinctions were blurred, and individuals frequently stood as local notables and not as representatives of a national idea, there were few real preliminary engagements. *Professions de foi*, although they became more frequent, were generally vague, often no more than a promise to be independent which was quickly broken: or there might be an emotional plea of being a "native son". After 1839 *réunions préparatoires* became more common; indeed in the *arrondissements* of Paris they became the rule. A group of important electors would ask the candidates to attend a meeting, make a speech and answer questions. Some commentators such as Fonfrède and conservative doctrinaires saw this as a dangerous step, an encroachment of democracy upon the conscience of the deputy who might be forced to make engagements of his vote to his electors.

In the early days when reaction against the Restoration was still a powerful motive, the idea that the administration might in any way intervene in the electoral process, was repulsed with pious horror. Guizot's circular of September 1830 declared that the government should remain entirely apart from the partial elections which were about to take place. The situation soon changed, however, because the continuation of a politicised administration gave any government a means of exerting electoral influence. Périer told the prefects in 1831, as if it were an obvious truth, that the administration could be no more neutral than was the government, and the conservatives were surely justified in believing that Laffitte had intended to use against them all the advantages of office when he demanded elections. With its internal enemies, to a regime facing the constant threat of rebellion, electoral management seemed justified. Indeed some supporters felt the government behaved with unwise moderation. Thomas, prefect of the Bouches du Rhône, lamenting the election of legitimists in 1831, claimed that more determined government action could have prevented this. And indeed governments began not only to intervene more positively in elections, but to do most on behalf of their strongest supporters. Périer had told the prefects that: "An honest man devoted to King and Charter is always a good deputy."[5] But in 1834, Broglie was anxious that his friends remain in office to fight the election, fearing the result if the *résistance* relinquished its control: the destructive neutrality of the central *tiers parti* meant that better conservative credentials were required. The 1837 and 1839 elections saw a further narrowing in governmental electoral aid. The moderate conservative Molé loathed Guizot and his doctrinaire supporters: thus centrists and moderates were helped or tolerated whilst the doctrinaires, formerly assisted by the administration, often found it working against them. Government action thus varied considerably. Much depended on the prefects, instructions to whom were often left deliberately vague lest clumsy execution compromise the government. Other administrative agents were usually expected to do little more than not to oppose the administration, although he who hoped for promotion in magistrature or bureaucracy was well advised to provide more assistance than silence.

In the disorderly years before 1834, a typical circular sent by a prefect to the mayors of his department would refer to the government's war against anarchy, and the duty of all the state's employees to continue it electorally, using their influence to obtain a good result. However, if the prefect considered intervention counter-productive or disapproved of the government's instructions, he might well remain inactive or act independently. Thus in 1839, when the conservatives were split, the doctrinaire prefect at Grenoble refused Molé's instructions to fight Alphonse Périer whom he had previously supported, and similarly the prefect of the Cher aided Duvergier de Hauranne as before, in defiance of the ministry. Not all prefects willingly entered an electoral campaign or showed skill at it.

Where the prefect was efficient and determined, the *procureur du roi* and *juges de paix* would be called into action, and in a small *arrondissement* it was quite possible for these men or the sub-prefect to visit every elector to persuade him of the merits of the candidate or remind him where his interests lay. The prefect might choose election time to make a tour of duty, often taking the governmental candidate with him. Promises to build roads, schools, canals and bridges would be made. If there were soldiers stationed in the town, it might be rumoured that they would have to be removed to a rival town, to the detriment of local tradespeople, were the opposition candidate to win. The King could send a gift of money to repair the church; the Ministry of Public Instruction might make a gift of books to the municipal library or the Department of Roads and Bridges remove a toll: the means which were used were many and effective. The Comte de Montalembert, leading a campaign for educational freedom in 1846, wrote in his *Devoir des Catholiques dans les Élections* that to vote Catholic was to act with honour and independence against a system where the taxes they paid were redistributed as humiliating bribery: a protest against "this odious system, in which . . . all that the state undertakes (and what does it not undertake?), from a railway to the repair of a village bell-tower, is transformed into an electoral ploy, into political merchandise".[6]

The most effective method was the promise of a job or a promotion. The state had vast numbers of offices in its gift, and tradition, reinforced by the events of 1830, made even the tiniest employment in the customs or town hall an object of political consideration. Usually official employment gave security and prestige and, at a time of increasing unemployment, such posts were much in demand. Thus Tocqueville wrote bitterly to his friend Gustave de Beaumont in 1836 about his electoral opponent at Cherbourg, who, as well as pleasing to the anticlericals as the offspring of a nun and a *curé*, had also the enormous advantage of being an official in the Justice Ministry and could promise posts as tax collector or *juge de paix* in return for votes: "In

Normandy, as in all of France, there is a great hunger for government posts, even the most insignificant."[7] If the deputy were not so close to the fount of official regard, he was often reduced to promises which he had to pester the government to redeem. As Karr wrote in *Les Guêpes*, "the French candidate gives nothing, he promises – not his own money – but to one person the glory of our armies and a tobacco-shop licence, and to another the frontiers of the Rhine and a grant for his son . . . etc."[8] Corruption, varying in seriousness and flagrancy, might also be the personal work of the deputy, governmental or opposition. An independent candidate was not necessarily without influence on the ministry, and some officials who became deputies were able to retain their neutrality whilst using the government's powers on their own behalf. Obtaining favours often appeared to deputy and electors as praiseworthy local patriotism. "I do not wish to obtain a *collège royal* for Mâcon in order to become a deputy, but I would like to become a deputy of Mâcon in order to obtain a *collège royal* for my native region",[9] declared Lamartine. The superficial plausibility of such a claim enabled men who believed themselves independent to obtain and receive gifts. At the port of Lorient in 1843, the electors decided that a *conseiller* at the Cour de Cassation was less useful to them than an official at the Ministry of the Marine: they asked LaCoudrais, director of the ministry, to present himself as a candidate and he was successful.

In 1844, the *arrondissement* of Louviers showed even greater determination in the pursuit of its economic interests. The candidate, Charles Laffitte, nephew of the banker, publicly promised in the *Courrier de l'Eure* that he would use his position as railway financier to have constructed a railway to the town from Rouen. Elected by a large majority, he was attacked in the Chamber of Deputies for corruption and the election was overruled. The voters persisted, however, re-electing him four times until the Chamber finally allowed him to take his seat. The Marquis de La Valette, former chargé d'affaires in Egypt, delegated to accompany the son of Mehemet Ali from his Pyrenean spa to Paris, made a diversion to Bergerc where he was candidate: the inhabitants enjoyed the spectacle of Ibrahim Pasha's large retinue, while the caterers whose expenses were paid by the government, found his passage profitable and expressed their gratitude with their votes.

Corruption by the opposition would be somewhat different in nature. Bribery and promises might be used, but slander and force were not uncommon. Thus Tocqueville complains of the behaviour of his opponent Le Marois, who provided three days' free drinking in the *cabarets* at Valogne and whose supporters led drunken peasant voters to the poll to the cries of "No nobles!" Physical force was more frequent after the election when mobs sometimes gave a charivari to the conservative candidate or broke the windows of the prefecture. In *arrondissements* where the vote extended fairly low down the social scale, the sort of behaviour faced by Tocqueville was common. Mérimée describes with disgust an election he observed in 1846. "Bad wine is drunk, glasses clink, speeches are made, meanwhile several stagger to the dunghill to relieve themselves of all that embarrasses them. I am horribly aristocratic when I see democracy and its disgusting manners."[10] Conservatives might argue with some justice that to lower the franchise would increase such behaviour.

The opposition was not averse from trying to counter promises with threats, especially effective if the issue of the elections seemed in doubt. This was the case in 1839 when the opposition coalition produced a circular addressed to all higher officials, announcing that the coalition would be forming the next government and asking that they should not weaken their positions with it by supporting the present Cabinet. It hinted that there might need to be many changes and that those who erred would be replaced. The government found it disgraceful that an unformed ministry should make such threats, whilst justifiable for itself to demand the loyalty of its employees. The circular probably had some effect, for many officials carefully remained neutral to emerge later on the winning side. On a more minor scale, an opposition address at Béthune warned that the secrecy of the ballot would not be able to protect functionaries who had "the culpable weakness to vote for a candidate of whom their conscience disapproved".[11]

The prefect was the most important link between the government and local administrative and electoral machinery, but was little liked. Thiers disdained the Ministry of the Interior because, says Véron, the prefects he had to receive were "neither sufficiently well-bred, nor of families of sufficiently good standing".[12] There was the occasional exception like Lautour-Mézeray, "the man with the camelia" who had spent a fortune on buttonholes and, forced by his debts to become a sub-prefect, pursued against great odds the life of a Parisian dandy in the provinces: his use of his previous reputation to pursue the women of the Limousin almost brought him to grief, but he redeemed himself by a successful electoral campaign against the republican deputy Cormenin. The job of the prefect was a deadly serious one; as representative of the government in a department, he had to uphold its dignity at all times. The reward was the contempt of those who found them bourgeois or bureaucratic: the image of the prefect in the literature of the time, in Balzac's works, Stendhal, and Mérimée in *Colomba*, is always unfavourable.

Noble prefects were as exceptional as diplomatists who were commoners. Those who, like the Comte de Lezay-Marnésia, had *ancien régime* aristocratic origins, were frequently attacked for being crypto-legitimists and found themselves in conflict with bourgeois Orleanism represented by the mayor and National Guard. Towards the end of the regime, a slight reversal of this trend may be observed as young members of legitimist families began to rally, and it came to be seen as good training for a political career: when in 1846 the son of the Baron de Barante gained a prefecture, it was symptomatic of a growing belief that the politician needed administrative experience. The great exception to the generally bourgeois nature of the service was the Comte de Rambuteau, prefect of the Seine for most of the period, but the Paris Hôtel de Ville was no ordinary prefecture. Rambuteau lived there in splendour, an opulent host and peer of political importance: not surprisingly he preferred this to an unstable Cabinet post which he refused.

Of the eighty-five other prefectures, there were only about ten noblemen in 1840, and of unimportant families. The previous professions of all had been official and bourgeois, with only two who were purely landed proprietors. Lawyers were the largest contingent with sixteen, but there were a comparatively large number of businessmen, eleven, and, apart from eight who had been men of letters, the remainder were former functionaries.

If not well paid, the position was powerful when it had governmental support, but weak in the face of political pressure. Thus Lezay-Marnésia was kept waiting for three days by Montalivet, often a somewhat casual Minister of the Interior, and his complaints met with the threat of dismissal. He almost suffered this at the hands of Duchâtel also, when he proposed asking the Duc de Bordeaux as owner of Chambord, to contribute to road building in the department of Loir-et-Cher: it was politically tactless, for the government did not wish it known that the legitimist pretender possessed land in France. Weakness and mere bad luck could also lose the prefect his post. Périer was particularly strict, and the Guizot ministry behaved similarly when in June 1841 riots broke out at Toulouse: two prefects were removed, one for allowing it to happen, and his stronger replacement because he fled from a crowd threatening him with death.

The prefectoral service was frequently criticised. The conservative *La Presse* published[13] an article naming twenty-two prefects who were inadequate and attacked the nepotism involved in their selection. The Duc d'Orléans, when touring the provinces, often complained about their incapacity and blamed the local power of the deputies. It was vital for a political notability that he should have the support of the governmental power invested in the prefect. Thus the Sébastiani family in their Corsican fief maintained an inefficient and unpopular prefect, against the wishes of the government. The Delessert family had Guizot send a relative, Edouard Bocher, to the Calvados. Périer made his relative, Achille Chaper, a capable and severe man, prefect in Dijon, and his brother Alphonse maintained Pellenc at Grenoble where he was deputy. Dupin was not a ministerial supporter but his powerful position kept the prefecture of the Nièvre under his control. The historian Amédée Thierry was a friend of Guizot, and Thomas assisted Thiers in land speculation. Sometimes deputies would lend their support to the government in order to have a prefect or sub-prefect replaced. The result was that in some places prefects became well established, but in others were constantly being changed. Governmental upsets could have a severe effect on them. The war of the Molé ministry on doctrinaires (and since prefects were generally very strong conservatives many of them came into this category) cost many of them their posts. The return of Guizot to power in 1841 meant a removal of many of the centrist elements introduced by Molé between 1837 and 1839 and by Thiers in 1840. The prefect had many duties. Sometimes he had to perform a police job, such as Duval sent to the Vendée to capture the Duchesse de Berry; the prefect of the Cher had to keep surveillance on the Spanish pretender; and, on a less exalted plane, the sub-prefect of Carpentras had to maintain a permanent watch lest Thiers's troublesome father should suddenly leave for Paris to embarrass the young politician. The prefect had his important electoral duties, and had the task of overseeing the subsidised governmental newspaper of his department. In this way he was a local mouthpiece for the ministry, supposed to reflect its policy. The prefect, like the *procureur du roi*, was also expected to report to the government on the state of public opinion, his relationship with the clergy, the activities of republicans and legitimists and the price of foodstuffs.

There were 278 sub-prefects, mostly with no ambition but to earn a salary in their native area. Those like Haussmann who were promoted to prefect were the exception. Again, he was exceptional when as sub-prefect of Blaye he dined weekly with the Marquis de Lamoignon, alone except for the footmen, to confer with this mayor and great landowner on the best measures to be taken for the area. Most sub-prefects did not win this esteem, and if they had instructions to limit the local power of a grand notable their life could be difficult, as it was for the sub-prefect of Libourne struggling against the dominance of Duc Decazes.

Local elections were set on a wider base than the national system. The law of March 1831 on municipal elections gave the vote to one in every ten electors, to 14 per cent if the population of the commune was over 1,000, reaching 19 per cent if over 15,000. They were chosen in order of wealth, to which were added a group of *capacités*, certain officials, including army and National Guard officers. These were the most democratic institutions of the monarchy, but the powers of which they disposed were not large. The mayor was chosen by the King from the elected municipal councillors, or by the prefect if the commune had a population under 3,000. In a town like Lyons or Bordeaux, it was a position of great importance, and elsewhere a situation symbolic of local prestige which a deputy might covet. Almost 40 deputies in 1837 were mayors.

The municipal law usually worked well, selecting a liberal group in each area larger than the narrow national electorate. But in areas of opposition to the regime, they were often troublesome. At Metz, for example, the *conseil municipal* was reduced to stalemate by its stormy sessions where *mouvement* and *résistance* continued to face each other. At Marseilles, the electoral system had given the vote to *petit bourgeois* wine-shop owners and small craftsmen, usually legitimist, who, with republican aid, obtained a majority on the municipal council.

In 1833 *conseils* of *arrondissement* and *conseils généraux* were made elective, and their electoral body was between the national and local in size. The *conseil général* was a departmental body usually with thirty members. The law of 22 June 1833 elected them by canton, creating an electorate of the fifty wealthiest men, which in a poor canton would be of low standard. The majority of cantons had to go below the 200 franc *cens* to find the requisite numbers. The *conseils généraux* had been the local instruments of Bonapartist centralisation, but the Orléans Monarchy extended their powers and they often became spokesmen for the department against the state. The laws of 1833 and 1838 gave them the right to deliberate on tax contributions, on the distribution of the budget, to inform the government of departmental needs, discuss ways of helping the populace, improving prisons, hospitals and agriculture. They did not always respect their administrative limitations, sometimes refusing to debate a question presented to them by the prefect on the government's behalf: in 1841, nine of them denied the legality of Finance Minister Humann's tax reforms. Under the influence of Lamartine, the *conseil général* of the Saône-et-Loire constantly thwarted the prefect and opposed the government. In 1847, eighteen councils expressed with varying degrees of strength their desire for electoral reform. On the whole, however, they were governmental and acted in collaboration with the prefect.

The fact that their role was restricted to local problems, meant that those legitimists who were elected, and there were many, were generally prepared to play a constructive role. The *conseils généraux* reflected the views of the grand notables and the type of property-owner dominant in the area. Thus that of the Haut-Rhin was dominated by great industrialists, such as Schlumberger, Hartmann, Dollfuss and Koechlin. Merchants, especially of wine, were powerful in the Gironde. Land was generally the source of prestige and dominance, although in areas where the *gauche dynastique* was strong, a greater proportion of doctors and lawyers is noticeable. Inside the council, peers and deputies would generally play the leading roles, and in 1838 about 110 deputies and 120 peers were *conseillers généraux*. For Bignon at Nantes, Barrot in the Aisne, Maréchal Soult in the Tarn, Duc Decazes in the Gironde, Dupin in the Nièvre, the presidency of the *conseil général* was the symbol of their position as national notables reflected in their departments. This is why the struggle between Duvergier de Hauranne and Montalivet for influence in the Cher was of such importance. Dynasties tended to form: sons would succeed fathers, or, in the case of the death of Antoine Schneider, his brother replaced him as deputy and as *conseiller général*.

Another institution reformed by the July Monarchy and given a more liberal nature was the Conseil d'État. Although the Garde des Sceaux presided over it and the conseillers were nominated by the King, its tone was less authoritarian and *étatiste* than previously. Its primary role was to advise on legislation, on disputes arising from it and to decide on complaints against the state. Although closely connected by its membership with Parliament, it had lost its political attributes, and was dominated by conservative liberals but never became enfeoffed to any ministry. As well as this body advising the Ministries of Justice and the Interior, there were councils of lesser importance which gave legislative assistance to the other ministries, forming a close connection between the judicial system and the bureaucracy.

The judicial system was that of the Empire and the Restoration. Although here as elsewhere an obvious grievance, the creation of special courts, was removed, in other respects nothing changed. The conservatism of the legal profession was one of the bases of the July Monarchy, represented at its head by the political Court of Peers, and by the Cour de Cassation, staffed with members of the established legal bourgeoisie, amongst them eleven peers and nine deputies, notably Dupin, the *procureur général*. In spite of its proximity to the government, the Cour de Cassation was capable of acting with independence on important occasions, and this it had in common with the magistracy as a whole. It resulted from the continued presence of many legitimists and men of the left in such cities as Strasbourg and Metz, and the strong feeling held by many lawyers that they were a caste with the right to use the government but with the duty to protect certain hallowed legal principles against its incursion: the failure of the government to gain a majority for the *loi de disjonction* in 1837, for example, was due to the refusal of many lawyer deputies, on other issues loyally obedient to the ministry, to abandon the principle that civilians and military men, accused of a crime in common, should all be judged by the same civilian court.

The worst consequences of a political magistrature did not occur under the July Monarchy, but it is none the less evident that the profession was the prerogative of a few men. Usually they had to be wealthy, for the pay of a magistrate was not high, and this maintained the position within established families. In the Cour des Comptes, which controlled the accounting of public expenses, the complexity of the issues to be decided meant that the *conseillers* had to be drawn from those who understood finance, thus creating a group of rich specialists.

There was as yet little concept of an apolitical administration. The continuation of aristocratic attitudes meant that it was heretical to suggest that deputies or mayors be well paid, or that other positions in administration or magistrature be entered because they were profitable. The ideal may have been laudable but in practice some mayors illegally gave themselves a salary from communal funds, and many deputies surrendered some of their independence for the sake of a governmental salary. Ambitious men also became deputies in order to prosper in their careers. In 1834, fifty-eight deputies were magistrates, in 1846 the number was sixty-six. In particular the government prosecutor, playing a constant role against press offences and conspiracies, had to think in political terms. *Procureurs généraux* tended to be young and often militantly conservative: three of the most important became deputies and later Gardes des Sceaux, Persil, Martin (du Nord) and Hébert. The principles of political choice extended to the base of the legal system, when the government asked its prefects to avoid putting legitimists and republicans on jury lists: enemies of the social and political order could not be allowed to judge it.[14]

The July Monarchy shows the difficulty of founding a liberal regime upon autocratic and revolutionary traditions. With a constitutional system imported from England in 1815 and grafted on to a powerfully centralised country of radically conflicting passions, many of them hostile to the freedoms upon which the monarchy had attempted to base itself, it is scarcely surprising that corruption was necessary to provide a discipline otherwise lacking. Yet stability was not a rule of the period as the brevity of many Cabinets proves. Personal factors limited the uniformity which might have resulted from governmental influence. As the genuine liberalism of many Orleanists prevented the regime becoming authoritarian, so independence of mind stopped corruption becoming an oppressive force. To a friend wanting a favour, Mérimée wrote that the deputy who would help him was in "quasi opposition" which was "a favourable moment to obtain something, because in the country in which we live one gives to those one fears, rather than to those one likes".[15]

There was a variety of interest groups which had to be satisfied. The extensions of the franchise in national and local voting had not created a political public or an Orleanist class: they had made a complex situation more so. "Society . . . is in the position of an inverted cone",[16] complained Molé in 1833 to the Baron de Barante, one of the makers of the new law on *conseils généraux*. Molé, in the department of Seine-et-Oise, had just been defeated by a small property-owner: under the Restoration twenty-five of the thirty *conseillers généraux* had been aristocrats, but now the nobles had only half a dozen representatives. But in the Auvergne, the previous order had not been turned upside down. New forms of wealth were rare, the provincial agricultural bourgeoisie accepted the rule of the nobility, and at Barante the position of its baron was secure. The electorate mirrored Orleanism in its lack of uniformity. It reflected middle-class dominance in a variety of ways, at the same time allowing the continuing existence in some areas of aristocratic preponderance. The compromise was in many ways unsatisfactory, but a delicate balance had been achieved.

REFERENCES

1. Comte J. Pelet de la Lozère, *Pensées morales et politiques* (1873), 96.
2. J. Bertaut, *Le Roi Bourgeois* (1936), 100–1.
3. F. Chatelain, *Sept Ans de Règne* (1837).
4. H. Fonfrède, *Du Gouvernement du Roi* (1838), 77–8.
5. *Le Moniteur*, 5 April 1831.
6. Comte C. de Montalembert, *Devoir des catholiques dans les élections* (1842), 62.
7. Comte A. de Tocqueville, *Œuvres*, ed. J. P. Mayer (1967), VIII, 170–1.
8. A. Karr, *Les Guêpes* (1858), III, 46.
9. A. de Lamartine, *Discours politiques* (1878), II, 76.
10. P. Mérimée, *Correspondance générale* (1941), IV, 501.
11. Archives Nationales, BB^{18} 7583 (A^{8}).
12. Dr L. Véron, *Mémoires d'un bourgeois de Paris* (1854), III, 207.
13. *La Presse*, 13 May 1837.
14. Archives Nationales, F^{1a*} 2089.
15. Mérimée, op. cit., II, 25.
16. Baron P. de Barante, *Souvenirs* (1890), V, 72.

7

Parliament: Deputies and Peers

"M. Hulot fils était bien le jeune homme tel que l'a fabriqué la révolution de 1830: l'esprit infatué de politique, respectueux envers ses espérances, les contenant sous une fausse gravité, très envieux des réputations faites, lâchant des phrases au lieu de ces mots incisifs, les diamants de la conversation française, mais plein de tenue et prenant la morgue pour la dignité. Ces gens sont des cercueils ambulants qui contiennent un Français d'autrefois; le Français s'agite par moments, et donne des coups contre son enveloppe anglaise, mais l'ambition le retient et il consent à y étouffer. Ce cercueil est toujours vêtu de drap noir."

("M. Hulot Junior was very much the type of young man produced by the revolution of 1830: his spirit infatuated by politics, respectful towards his aspirations, containing them in a false gravity, very envious of reputations made, uttering phrases instead of incisive words, the diamonds of French conversation, but very tenuous and taking hautiness for dignity. These men are walking coffins which contain former Frenchmen; the Frenchman grows agitated upon occasion, and strikes against his English envelope, but ambition restrains him and he consents to suffocate himself. This coffin is always dressed in black cloth.")[1]

After 1830, the Chamber of Deputies discarded their ceremonial costume and debated in frock-coats. A change which was more than purely symbolic was that the deputies gained full power to elect a president and the King lost the role he had previously played in the selection. The Chamber had increased its powers slightly in law and, by ratifying the selection of a new king, had gained in confidence and ambition. Under the July Monarchy, parliamentary life was vivid and dramatic, but to some it appeared futile, whilst to others it was the arena of all significant events.

In social terms, the July Revolution was significant. The proportion of landed proprietors sank from 31 to 23 per cent whilst deputies from professional and business backgrounds rose slightly. After 1830, as before, however, the largest professional group was that which held public official functions. More obvious is the increased bourgeois nature of the Chamber. At the end of the Restoration, 41 per cent of the deputies were noble, and resignations and the 1831 elections reduced this proportion to 24 per cent.

It stayed around this level until the 1842 and 1846 elections when the number rose from 110 to 125.

Such a figure must be taken with some scepticism, however. The complexities of the French social situation in the eighteenth century, the search for, and inevitable discovery of, aristocratic pedigrees, the buying of *terres* (lands), invention of titles, often legalised by the Empire, make it difficult to discover the true aristocracy of the *ancien régime*. The 110 includes some 20 of doubtful origins, whilst excluding those of pretensions, such as Salvandy, and the imperial nobility if in no way previously aristocratic. In 1837, 112 deputies had titles, three-quarters of which were imperial or later in origin, and only half of this number was previously noble. If we add those married into the aristocracy, it is evident that we have a large aristocratic contingent, but one of different traditions, reflecting social confusion and change rather than stability. The aristocrats tended to be of the more obscure families who had supported the moderate revolution or served the Empire. There were a few representatives of the great nobles of the *ancien régime*; for example, the Duc de Fitz-James who sat on the legitimist benches, the Comte de Chastellux, *chevalier d'honneur* to Madame Adelaïde, deputy for the Yonne where he possessed vast properties, and two other members of great families who were courtiers, Comtes Anatole de Montesquiou and Jules de La Rochefoucauld who had entered Orléans service under the Restoration and remained in it after 1830. Other examples were present but none the less the sons of peers and the heirs of ancient names no longer littered the ministerial benches.

Similar difficulties exist in defining *propriétaires*: to speak of them as of a cohesive social or economic group is highly misleading. A landowner might be a noble, a lawyer whose father had made successful speculations or a former industrialist who had bought a château. To call Guizot an academic or Thiers an author and journalist merely describes their pre-political careers. How does one classify Comte Charles de Rémusat, hereditary landowner, journalist before 1830, then politician and writer, or Général Bugeaud whose seat in the Chamber for the Dordogne owed more to his local landownership than to his military prestige? Lamartine, with a large acreage of vineyard, described himself as a *propriétaire*, although it was his writing of history and poetry which subsidised his poorly managed estate. In finance, the multiple interests overlap: the Périers, for example had interests in banking, mining, industry and were also landowners. For this was an age without specialisation, when the merchant becomes a banker and the banker an industrialist: when a doctor or lawyer prefers to describe himself as a *propriétaire*, when the politician writes history or philosophy, and the young aristocrat makes an excursion into diplomacy or the army before retiring to the château or entering politics.

It is probable that, in the 1837 Chamber, for about 20 per cent of deputies land or property was the main source of income. Significantly, about half the legitimists fall into this category, and a third of the doctrinaires. If the latter are separated from the other 230 governmental deputies, there are no great differences between them, the central *tiers parti* and the far left. The *gauche dynastique* has a slightly higher proportion, and one might suggest that an independent source of wealth caused conservatives to join the élite doctrinaire group, and others to enrol in the moderate left.

To be a deputy meant to be wealthy: an income of over 2,500 francs was necessary to produce the qualifying 500 francs *cens*. Few doctors could be expected to earn that, and a *lycée* teacher earnt insufficient at around 1,500 francs. One hundred or more deputies paid between the minimum 500 and 800 francs, and only about 30 came in the very rich category of over 5,000 francs, a far smaller proportion than amongst the peers.[2] On the whole, the parties of the left were poorer, but even here there were many very rich men. Of the extreme left group of 20, at least 4 paid over 3,000 francs *cens*, actually a higher proportion than amongst conservatives. The centre, whilst it had a larger proportion than legitimists or conservatives paying the minimum, also had, due to its support from wealthy merchants, a higher proportion of the very rich than they did. Wealth and party are thus not easily equated.

To remain a deputy as well as to become one, demanded wealth. Lamartine estimated that being a deputy and living in expensive Paris cost him 22,000 francs a year[3]; but not all deputies were as extravagant as Lamartine, running a salon and subsidising a newspaper, nor did they find it necessary to order their kid gloves by the dozen. Being an important minister cost more than the allowance it brought: Broglie, Molé and Guizot all left office poorer, or at least without financial gain. Lack of fortune did not prevent men such as Guizot, Persil or Martin (du Nord) becoming ministers. The July Monarchy was not a plutocracy, but it nevertheless gave increased prestige and influence to wealth. Hartmann, a rich manufacturer, paying almost 8,000 francs *cens*, attained a social position and by his ownership of a Paris *hôtel* with a salon sufficiently large to accommodate large numbers, became organiser of back-bench meetings. Fulchiron and Ganneron, rich financiers, fulfilled similar roles, gaining by their money an importance which would have been denied them under the previous regime.

Men such as these made or inherited their wealth and used it on politics, but others entered the Chamber of Deputies to further their careers. Become a deputy, was the wry advice one Minister of War, Général Bernard, gave an aspirant for promotion.[4] Général de Castellane constantly rails in his diary against the prevalence of political means to military success, claiming, with some reason, that Bugeaud's success was primarily due to his position as a deputy. This was even more true of the magistrature. To become a *procureur général*, to attain a seat in the Cour de Cassation, it was important to be a deputy. The Chamber contained many whose political interest was slight and whose pursuit of promotion made them natural supporters of the government. The career of Felix Réal was a model: the Restoration *carbonaro* became a deputy of the *mouvement* and *avocat général* after 1830: as *maitre des requêtes*, he joined the *tiers parti*, emerging as a loyal ministerial deputy when in 1837 he was made a *conseiller d'état*.

In 1834 there were about fifty-eight deputies who were active magistrates, rising to sixty-six after the ministerial victory in the 1846 elections. Former magistrates totalled another twelve. About a quarter of ministerial and conservative deputies were active magistrates. Beside the 18 per cent of the Chamber who were members of the magistrature, over 13 per cent were *avocats*, independent of the government: fifty-three in 1837 to whom may be added a handful of notaries, members of the *gauche dynastique*. Some administrative officials also had legal training, and the total accounts for over a third of the deputies. If the magistrature was governmental, the *avocat* was generally a member of the opposition, a mere 5 per cent of the total ministerials, but 20 and 30 per cent of the membership of the legitimist and republican parties. Amongst them were found the most notable leaders: Sauzet, Billaut, Chaix-d'Est Ange of the centre; Odilon Barrot, Étienne Garnier-Pagès, Martin (de Strasbourg) on the left; Hennequin and Berryer on the right. The legal profession imparted its spirit to the deputies' proceedings, responsible for much oratorical ability and a legal expertise which was sometimes responsible for effective legislation, sometimes producing mere quibbling obstruction.

As well as the magistrature, two other functions depended upon the government, the administration and the armed services. Current or former officials provided about 12 per cent of the Chamber, and soldiers or sailors almost as much. If on active service they mostly voted for the government, but there were exceptions. Clauzel, the only Marshal to sit in the Chamber of Deputies, and his aide-de-camp were members of the opposition, and a few members of the *tiers parti* and *gauche dynastique* were active in administration. Possibly true to the left-wing tendencies of the Polytechnique, these more radical officials had technical functions.

To be a member of the opposition did not necessarily preclude profiting from the system: friends and relatives might be helped by the use of political connections, even if an opposition deputy took nothing for himself. Thus the legal career of Barrot's nephew was remarkably speedy. Nepotism was neither the monopoly of one party, nor of the regime.

There were a few more *fonctionnaires* amongst the small literary and academic contingent. Two or three teaching law were ministerial, as was the chemist Gay-Lussac, but Arago and his fellow astronomer and brother-in-law Mathieu sat on the far left. There were also other deputies in the arts and sciences, half a dozen doctors, and a few journalists, notably Chambolle of the *Siècle*, Girardin of the *Presse* and Pagès (de l'Ariège) of the *Temps*. There were others who wrote, although their main income came from elsewhere, such as Étienne and Viennet. Many deputies such as the Vicomte de Cormenin and Duvergier de Hauranne were also journalists or pamphleteers.

The Chamber was dominated by the liberal and governmental professions. In 1837, 19 per cent were magistrates, 13 per cent lawyers, 12 per cent in administration, 11 per cent in the armed services and 5 per cent in teaching, journalism or art. Twenty-one per cent were primarily property-owners, and the remaining 13 per cent belonged to commercial professions, 12 per cent of whom had predominately financial interests, the remainder being industrialists. The financiers tended to be the more conservative, although the forge masters, the largest group amongst industrialists, proved highly successful in uniting to protect their interests. Men who were purely capitalist were thus a minority, although many others, as investors, producers of raw material or representatives of a locality, would on occasion become spokesmen for a particular commercial interest.

Family alliances were strong in the two Chambers representing a small political world where the reflexes of traditional order were still strong. The imperial nobility and new official and industrial wealth had allied with the *ancien régime* aristocracy to produce a characteristically Orleanist class. Thus the two Paillard du Clairet, father and son, forge owners, were related by marriage to the Comte de Montalivet, and Anisson-Duperron, Napoleonic administrator, had married the daughter of the Baron de Barante. Within the Chamber of Deputies, two dynasties are outstanding. The Périer family had five brothers as deputies during the July Monarchy, two of whom became peers. The son of Augustin stepped out of line by pretending to be a republican and marrying into the La Fayette clan. But Casimir Périer's son, diplomat and then deputy, followed the family tradition, and Casimir's nieces married various notabilities such as the prefect Achille Chaper, the deputies Contre-Amiral Christian de Hell, Charles de Rémusat, Louis Vitet and Baron de Chabaud-Latour. The Comte de Rémusat forms a link with the other great family, the La Fayettes. The general had one son, the Marquis George de La Fayette who had a son Oscar, both of whom followed his example in becoming deputies. The general's daughter was mother of the deputy Jules de Lasteyrie, whose sister was Rémusat's second wife. George de La Fayette's two daughters had married deputies of the left, one of whom, Tocqueville's friend Gustave de Beaumont, was himself related to the deputies Francisque de Corcelles and Général de La Moricière. Through cousins and distant relatives by marriage, these relationships can be extended to cover all parties and social groups.

Both the Périer and La Fayette families had an influence which was more than the sum of individuals. The prestige of the leading member, salon reunions and a family tradition, gave them extra importance, even though not all the La Fayettes professed exactly the same ideas, unlike the Périers, united in their conservatism. Family politics were not always amicable: for much of the period, the ministerial Emmanuel de Las-Cases saw his Bonapartist father, the memorialist Comte Joseph, on the benches of the far left. The fact that the fanatical legitimist Duc de Valmy, non-conforming member of a liberal family, was brother-in-law of Louis-Philippe's Minister of Marine, Amiral de Mackau, shows the limitations of family relations. The deputies did not hunt in family packs. The entry of the apolitical Comte de Champlâtreux to support his father-in-law Molé was unusual, and the conservative Molé failed in his attempts to attract his independent liberal relative, Alexis de Tocqueville, into his orbit. Yet family political traditions and local influence were still important. It was not rare for a son to inherit his father's electoral seat. Thus, when Vicomte Duchâtel reached the age of thirty and became eligible, his father resigned and the young man simply succeeded him. The sons of Persil, Étienne and Comte Anatole de Montesquiou similarly took over when their fathers were promoted to the Chamber of Peers.

A singular spectacle, exclaimed Madame de Girardin, "men who, individually, are nearly all capable, and who, when united, seem paralysed".[5] The Orleanist Parliament contained a vast array of talent and the lack of progressive legislation and the proliferation of pointless intrigue in what Salvandy referred to as the "bull's-eye" of democracy[6] is thus the more striking. The lack of strong party structure or programme meant that personality became all-important and deputies regarded themselves not as legislators so much as the makers of ministries and electors of Cabinets. "Instead of occupying itself with national affairs, the Chamber occupies itself all year long with determining whether it will kill the ministry or allow it to survive",[7] wrote Fonfrède, a vehement critic of the deputies' indiscipline. The "paralysis" resulted from that mixture of stability and instability which characterised the July Monarchy. At an election 100 or, as in 1839, 150 new deputies would enter, many with unknown views: but many others had faced no serious opposition, and a quarter of the deputies sat continuously from 1830 to 1848. Passive negativism and place-seeking were frequent amongst ministerialists: a determination to oppose, often amounting to desire for destruction, was present in the opposition. "By using all sorts of regime", remarked Metternich, "France more or less dissolves itself into oppositions."[8] Every succeeding regime had its partisans and within these groups were nuances of extremism or loyalty. Added to this, the strength of local factors, interest groups, family traditions, combined with the absence of established political discipline, meant that often, as Barante remarked, "individuals believe themselves principles".[9] It was common for deputies to declare themselves independent without party engagement. A party was often seen not as an association of common opinions but as a nefarious faction. It was held that the Restoration had become a party when it had offended the wishes of the nation, as defined by Orleanists. Molé attacked "the parties" in 1839 when various oppositions gathered in a coalition against him: he wished the conservatives and ministerialists to develop a party discipline in response to attack, but saw them as a party in no other sense. The term often used was "the majority", for conservative Orleanism claimed to represent the majority of the nation. It was therefore justified in administratively opposing the parties in elections for they represented interests and hostile ambitions, not the national will as expressed in 1830.

It was only at election time that the motive for temporary unity and strong central organisation was sufficiently strong to overrule individualism. The far left was most advanced in its electoral methods. In September 1837 it created a Comité Central de l'Opposition Constitutionnelle, headed by Garnier-Pagès. It sent out circular letters to win support, formed local committees in common with the central body, found candidates, provided lawyers to help with the registration of left-wing electors and to find flaws in the registration of their opponents. In 1840 Laffitte formed a Comité Réformiste with Dupont as vice-president, François Arago, Martin (de Strasbourg) and Joly as secretaries. It was an unwieldy body of forty-five members which was intended to organise elections and fight for electoral reform which was by this time the main platform of the left. However, it was only possible to organise such committees for an election or a campaign, after which differing opinions and clashes of personality would end the life or the effectiveness of such committees.

This was equally true of the right. Montalembert's electoral campaign in 1846 knitted together a temporary alliance of Catholics, but there was no chance of making it a party. Conservatives and ministerialists occasionally met in the salon of one of their wealthiest colleagues to discuss a matter in which they wished to influence the ministry, or make a public statement, but it needed a crisis to provoke them, and the electoral role of ministerial deputies was largely passive: their campaign was organised in the offices of the *président du conseil* and Minister of the Interior. Certainly the coalition of 1839 heightened conservative unity and determination: Molé observed in them for the first time "the ardour, the energy of a party",[10] but this lasted scarcely longer than the election. However, the word "party" was beginning to lose its derogatory overtones and Guizot in the 1840s would speak with reverence of "the conservative party" as if it were an established organisation with a united creed and a formal tradition, which it was not.

"The independent deputy can pass himself off as a chef: anyone can sit at his table."[11] These were the attractions of independence. A sudden sign of opposition from a governmental supporter would increase his importance. Thus the tendency for small groups to form and be recognised, around a family, around a nuance or an idea. To give the numbers of the parties (which in 1837 we may suggest are 21 legitimists, 27 doctrinaires, 233 ministerialists, 64 *centre gauche* and *tiers parti*, 91 *gauche dynastique* and 23 republicans) does not account for the misty divisions and cross-currents. In contrast to the chaos of nuances in the lower Chambers, the peers present a stable and solid governmental majority.

In 1831, the principle of heredity had not died undefended. Royer-Collard argued that the destruction of legitimism had created a void which the quasi-legitimacy of the doctrinaires could not fill. The increasing power of democratic elements would absorb all others and, in its tendency to violence and demand for equality, would destroy order and liberty. He appealed to the deputies to take this last opportunity to prevent the bankruptcy of the philosophical liberalism, aristocratic in its nature, which he had espoused throughout his long life. The majority was influenced neither by this, nor by the more constitutional arguments of Thiers and Guizot who spoke of the need for a balance on the English model, to mediate between the democracy of the Lower House and the sovereignty invested in the monarch. Only 86 voted for heredity, 206 were opposed.

The peers' arguments were similar, but the deputies' decision made them still more futile. Molé spoke of "the American level" which would be merely a stepping-stone to the destruction of property, the natural effect of an abolition which proscribed inequality as privilege. Life peerage was a contradiction in terms, a mere political transaction: "We will be lifetime civil servants only."[12] The Duc de Fitz-James defended heredity as a fount of continuity which ensured respect for traditions by echoing a noble past, the Duc de Broglie argued the utility of a group able to think on a higher plane because removed from the vulgar demands of electoral combat, and others pointed out that as an ultimate court of appeal, the peers needed the guarantee of independence which heredity gave. All knew, however, that their rhetoric was in vain. Opposed as Périer had been to abolition, his creation of peers showed that he would accept no obstruction. He was the more determined because he feared that La Fayette and Laffitte might win approval for their proposed elected assembly.

It was decided that peers should be chosen by the King, for life, selected from certain categories. An amendment proposed by the opposition deputy, the Comte de Mosbourg, added six years' service in an elected body, *conseil général* or chamber of commerce, as eligibility to the wealth qualifications – much to the disapproval of Ducs Decazes and de Broglie, who argued that peers should at least be independent by reason of their wealth. The bill became law in December 1831, many peers abstaining, and sixteen, notably the legitimist Fitz-James, resigning in protest.

Predictions of a loss of independence were proved correct. Suffering from its loss of prestige and self-respect, the Chamber of Peers, wrongly believed to be aristocratic, remained unpopular and rarely dared use its powers. On some notable occasions during the Restoration the peers had shown their independence from the government: under Louis-Philippe their rare signs of independence were in opposition to the Chamber of Deputies. On a few occasions when a majority of deputies voted for an issue not desired by the ministry or not official government policy, the Upper House prevented its becoming law. On divorce, the peers, more conservative and more Catholic than the deputies, refused a majority to an attempt to facilitate the process. And when, against the wishes of King and ministers, the deputies repeatedly voted to lower the interest on *rentes*, government bonds, the peers as regularly outvoted the proposal. Susceptible to royal influence, the Chamber was fundamentally governmental and disliked crises. Thus it both disapproved of Guizot when he attacked the Molé ministry in 1839, and of Molé when he attacked the Guizot ministry in 1846, even though the occasion of his bitter censure was one of the few when its proceedings attracted a large audience. In spite of this occasion and the drama surrounding Montalembert's oratory in defence of Catholicism, the noisy and radical speeches by the Comte d'Alton-Shée and Marquis de Boissy, who even criticised the King, and Vicomte Dubouchage's advocacy of working-class rights, the Chamber as a whole justified Molé's charge that its motto was "death is the supreme good".[13]

Many criticisms were directed at the Orleanist Chamber of Peers, not least from its members. An unsatisfactory compromise, however, is often maintained by inertia and the fear of renewed conflict if it were destroyed. "You would like, by means of the peerage, to have a constitutional aristocracy; you have, due to the inherent vice of categories, a hierarchy of retired civil servants",[14] wrote the conservative commentator and deputy Saint-Marc Girardin in 1845, but the remedy he suggested, a partial reintroduction of heredity, was complex and controversial. It is noticeable that the most independent elements were amongst those twenty-two who entered by heredity in the first months of the July Monarchy, before it was abolished: such were the Marquis de Boissy and de Dreux-Brézé, Comtes d'Alton-Shée and de Montalembert, Vicomte Dubouchage and the Prince de La Moskowa. On the whole, the peers were an elderly body; only 12 per cent were under fifty years old, which was the average age of the deputies.

The Chamber grew less aristocratic in its membership, whilst the deputies became slighly more so. Of the total of about 550 men who were peers between 1830 and 1848, just over 300 were nominated by Louis-Philippe, and most of these were state functionaries. The majority of men who were not, and who were mostly nobles, were those who remained peers from the Restoration. The nobility of *ancien régime* origins became increasingly a minority and most titles were imperial in origin. After 1830, thirty-seven peers were created who had no title. The regime was sparing with titles; most of those given were to diplomats such as Bresson, Boislecomte and Pontois who needed to move in European society. Amongst the 550 peers were about 190 military men, of whom about 80 were on active service: 40 magistrates, 30 of them retired, and 6 active prefects, 30 diplomatists, about 50 *conseillers d'état*, 20 high officials and a few academics and scientists. There were, not necessarily exclusive of the above, over 150 former deputies justifying Alton-Shée's taunt that the Palais du Luxembourg was a "Hôtel des Invalides" for those wounded in electoral battle. There were also many *conseillers généraux* and mayors. More than half the peers had served the Empire, and some, especially the soldiers and also the Prince de Talleyrand, had previously served during the Revolution. Its *président*, Baron Pasquier, made Duc and given the title of Chancelier by Molé in 1837 in an attempt to increase the dignity of his office, had been a minister of both Napoleon and Louis XVIII as had Molé himself. "The peerage has become the triple receptacle for the corruptions of the Bourbon Monarchy, the Republic and the Empire",[15] sneered Chateaubriand, who resigned rather than take the oath to Louis-Philippe. For him, the former Jacobins, the decaying generals, the vapid courtiers, were time-serving mediocrities. A different attitude might discover in the Luxembourg praiseworthy moderation, an attempt to ensure peace and stability and in some, perhaps, an ideal of patriotic service.

The peers were not only predominantly old and experienced men, they were also rich. It is true that one peer, Cousin, did not pay enough tax to qualify for the franchise, that two others, Comtes Rossi and d'Alton-Shée, were not eligible as deputies, but on the whole the Chamber of Peers was much wealthier than the Chamber of Deputies. A dozen paid more than 10,000 francs in annual taxation, the Duc de Valençay, heir to Talleyrand, paying over 24,000 francs, Broglie almost 13,000. This vast wealth was basically in land, although the regime did make peers of a few merchants, such as Guestier and Wustembourg, and manufacturers, such as Hartmann. Eighteen peers were *actionnaires* of the Banque de France, and the Comte d'Argout, a former minister, became its governor. Wealth, unaccompanied by experience of an official position or electoral office, was insufficient qualification to be created a peer, however, and the Chamber contained a considerable amount of expertise. As well as the 44 per cent[16] of peers who in 1840 were active in official posts and those retired, there were agricultural and scientific experts, such as the chemist Gay-Lussac. There were academics and members of the academy and in 1840 Victor Hugo, Vicomte as he liked then to be known, entered the assembly. Debates were therefore often less political, but frequently more expert, than those of the deputies.

The peers were more royalist than the deputies. Those who did not resign in 1830 included a great many who accepted the Orleans Monarchy with regret, *légitimistes ralliés* such as Baron Mounier, and moderate legitimists such as the Duc de Noailles. The legitimists had also the more extreme but oratorically effective Dreux-Brézé. The strong proportion of imperial relics gave the Luxembourg a vague but powerful residue of Bonapartist sentiment, overt and active in one or two figures such as Général Exelmans. Catholicism was also a stronger force than amongst the deputies: d'Alton-Shée's confession of his atheism created horror. There was also a strong contingent of Protestant southern noblemen, such as the Comtes de Gasparin and de Preissac, and the Barons de Daunant and de Jaucourt. These factors gave the peers a different character from the deputies: the ambiguities of Orleanism were dulled by the conservatism of the Palais du Luxembourg.

As well as being a legislative element, theoretically equal to the Chamber of Deputies, the peers, who generally numbered about 360, were a political magistrature. The 1830 Charter promised to define their role as the highest court of state, but because of the complexity of the issue, none of the five attempts was successful: so this most important role was left without a ruling on the crimes to be judged, procedure followed or penalties given. When the first cases arrived, they acted by precedent – they sent the Comte de Kergorlay to prison for six months for publishing a violent legitimist diatribe against Louis-Philippe, and accepted the task of judging Charles's ministers. To be a peer still gave the right to be judged by that body as shown in the cases of Kergorlay, Montalembert and the Duc de Praslin. When Victor Hugo was caught in *flagrant délit*, he claimed the privileges of a peer to avoid arrest, and the husband was bought off to avoid the embarrassment of a trial in the Luxembourg. The peers also tried crimes of state, the insurrections of 1834 and 1839, Prince Louis-Napoleon's attempted coup in 1840 and four would-be regicides. On the whole it performed these difficult and unpleasant tasks conscientiously.

Although Orleanist liberals believed in a balance of powers, their revolution had actually destroyed this: government and deputies had increased their powers at the expense of the peers. To belong to the Upper Chamber was a political disadvantage, as was shown in the careers of Broglie and Molé. In February 1848, the latter said ruefully to his fellow peer, the Comte de Saint-Priest, that he heard that revolutionary crowds had chased out the deputies with rifle butts: he feared they would only kick out the peers. "You flatter yourself," replied Saint-Priest, "they won't even bother."[17]

REFERENCES

1. H. de Balzac, *Cousine Bette* (Garnier edition, 1967), 46.
2. A. J. Tudesq, *Les Grands Notables en France, 1840–9* (1964).
3. A. de Lamartine, *Correspondance* (1882), III, 103.
4. Vicomte P. de Pelleport, *Souvenirs militaires* (1857), 191.
5. Mme D. de Girardin, *Lettres Parisiennes* (1857), II, 61.
6. Duchesse D. de Dino, *Chroniques* (1909), III, 33.
7. H. Fonfrède, *Du gouvernement du roi* (1838), 118.
8. Prince C. W. von Metternich-Winneburg, *Mémoires* (1883), VI, 33.
9. Baron P. de Barante, *Souvenirs* (1890), VI, 158.
10. Ibid.
11. Mme de Girardin, op. cit., III, 34.
12. Archives Parlementaires, Chambre des Pairs, 22 December 1831.
13. Barante, op. cit., IV, 53.
14. M. Saint-Marc Girardin, "La Chambre des Pairs", *Revue des Deux Mondes*, XII (November 1845), 537–62.
15. Vicomte F.-R. de Chateaubriand, *Mémoires d'Outre Tombe* (1948), III, 659.
16. A. J. Tudesq, "Les Pairs de France", *Revue d'Histoire Moderne et Contemporaine*, III (1956), 268.
17. A Sommain, *La Pairie en France au 19e Siècle* (1903).

8

Louis-Philippe and his Court

"Ayant compris la lassitude des temps et la vileté des âmes, Philippe s'est mis à l'aise."

("Having understood the lassitude of the times and the poverty of souls, Philippe put himself at his ease.")[1]

"Un grand roi, bien qu'il ressemble plus à Ulysse qu'à Ajax."

("A great king, although he resembles Ulysses more than Ajax.")[2]

In appearance, the King was slightly plump, with heavy, characteristically Bourbon, features. Indeed, his resemblance to Louis XIV was frequently commented upon, but instead of hauteur his expression often seemed to say "I am more wicked than all of you, and know the dark secrets of each of you!"[3] Yet he also had "that natural nobility",[4] wrote Alfred de Vigny, which was typical of the Bourbons. The heavy jowls gave his head the pear-shaped quality which the caricaturists made famous: he was perhaps the most caricatured King in history. But a caricature, for all its brilliance, is not necessarily more than superficially true, and the myths which arose around Louis-Philippe have often obscured a truth less simple and less easily explained than verbal or pictorial caricature.

He was, said Odilon Barrot, who liked him in spite of political differences, a man whose faults and qualities reflected a stormy life: a strange mixture of bourgeois simplicity and masterfulness, of free thinking and prejudice of rank, revolutionary sentiments and fears of the Revolution.[5] Louis-Philippe himself spoke of the difficult dualism of his upbringing, instilled with semi-republican principles but also made very aware that he was a prince. There was the traumatic experience of the execution of his father Philippe-Égalité, who having betrayed Louis XVI was himself killed by the Revolution he tried to serve. Montalivet, the closest of all to this friendless man, said that Louis-Philippe referred to his father only twice in all the time he knew him.[6] His exile in youth remained an ineradicable memory. At Eu in 1843, he surprised

Queen Victoria by taking a penknife from his pocket to skin a peach for her, saying that it was always possible his experiences might be repeated.[7] His loquacity and charm were the façade of a very private person, and perhaps of an insecure one. His upbringing and maturity had paralleled France's own history: he had suffered from her revolutions, his personality was moulded by her instability and his character had ambiguities and contradictions similar to those manifested by the July Monarchy.

Almost all commentators agree on Louis-Philippe's tendency to appeal to men's self-interest. For some, he was a man of benevolence, humanity, morality and probity whose attitude to mankind had been warped by seeing so many consciences bend.[8] Certainly he was often cynical, and romantics did not like this or the eclectical tastes and realistic obedience to necessity which in him replaced the passions, antipathies and warm sympathies which they admired. Accusations of deviousness, however, were exaggerated. "He has been called false, but I never found him so",[9] said Guizot. Thiers agreed the King was "sharp and wily" but "false he was not"; he might use indirect, but not treacherous, means.[10] He was a man of expedients, preferring, said Barrot, "indirect means" to a straight route.[11] It is interesting to note that both Thiers and Guizot claimed that Louis-Philippe preferred himself to the other: the truth is probably that the King was more at ease with the former, and had more respect for the latter, and was able to convince both that this was a preference.

In his personal dealings, the King was generally kind and considerate. The republican Martin Nadaud noted his courteousness to the workmen in the Tuileries.[12] As he grew older, however, he grew irritable with politicians and critics and impatient with little things although he retained his patience in great issues. Inculcated with eighteenth-century humanitarianism, in him a mild Catholicism was combined with a mild Voltaireanism, but he retained a passionate hatred of all bloodshed from foxhunting to capital punishment. He was painstakingly conscientious in examining the death penalties given, and used his right to commute whenever possible. He much regretted his failure to spare the lives of his would-be assassins, Fieschi, Pépin, Morey and Alibaud, but was successful in applying his "right of clemency" to those others sentenced to death for trying to kill him.

Louis-Philippe, believing it a sign of democratic spirit, would spare nobody his monologues. A fluent and often entertaining speaker, he felt a political need to propagate his opinions, which, allied to natural garrulity, made him talk too much and listen too little. The same faults were revealed in his reading. The bitterness of the hostile press upset him, and the frequently inadequate defence of supposedly amicable journals angered him. This man, genuinely attached to constitutional principles, had difficulty accepting the criticism involved in constitutional practice. He avoided reading the French press, unlike Metternich who examined scurrilous sheets as well as serious journals; instead he perused only *The Times*, where he found a grave approval of the principles of his foreign policy. Because he was not surrounded by the flattering tongues of aristocratic courtiers, he felt he could ignore those he believed to be ill-informed and ambitious critics: the error cost him his throne. Comprehending the need to conciliate the bourgeoisie, he slightly resented it, claiming that the *grande bourgeoisie* owed him more than he owed them, but he made the mistake of not looking beneath them.

Louis-Philippe was political man enthroned. From the moment of rising at 8 a.m. to retiring at 2 a.m., he was almost entirely occupied with affairs of state. He read all despatches carefully, wrote frequently to the ministers and talked to deputies and diplomatists. He attained by these means a grasp of affairs, in particular of foreign relations, which could be rivalled by scarcely any of his ministers. He would doubtless have concurred in the verdict of Lord Granville, the English ambassador, that he was "by far the ablest man among them".[13] The King grew increasingly contemptuous of politicians. "In general," he told his son-in-law, Leopold of the Belgians, "our politicians have an over-abundance of courage and audacity when they are in opposition, but as soon as they become part of the ministry they are *feigherzig* [timid] and always on the verge of cowardice."[14] He excepted Guizot from this general blame, thus his increasing tendency to believe him infallible. The ministers were like truant schoolboys, the King told Hugo, unwilling to attend to their business, lacking consistency and persistence.[15] Especially he felt they did not properly defend him, whilst preventing him from defending himself.[16]

Accusations of political cowardice, not dissimilar from those he levelled at politicians, were made against the King by Thiers and Guizot. Thiers's accusations were directed at the King's "passion for peace"[17] or his "mania for peace", but one might suggest that there was more courage in resisting popular opinion on this issue than in surrendering to chauvinism. Guizot's accusation was slightly different: "Though personally brave," he told Nassau Senior, "he was politically timid; he preferred address to force; he always wished to turn an obstacle instead of attacking it in front."[18] And he said that Louis-Philippe regarded the Republic "as some Asiatic nations do the devil, as a maleficent principle, to be flattered and propitiated, but not to be resisted".[19] Certainly there is much truth here: Louis-Philippe had learnt during a dramatic life how to manœuvre and to conciliate, and he continued to do so as king. He had a partiality for those politicians such as Comte Molé, who preferred conciliation to confrontation. In 1848 also, a fatalistic attitude caused Louis-Philippe suddenly to surrender to the insurrection.

Of all the reasons for Louis-Philippe's lack of popularity, the most unfair were the accusations of avarice. The King was, whilst himself simple and abstemious in his tastes, a generous host. Although he was not confident of his own or his dynasty's future, he had scarcely any private savings, or funds invested abroad which the republicans accused him of having. Had he been ostentatiously extravagant, he would no doubt have incurred blame for this. Enemies spread calumnies about the monarch's character in order to undermine the authority of his government, claimed Montalivet, intendant of the royal finances.[20] And Rémusat, no apologist, says that the reputation for parsimony was three-quarters false and very harmful to both king and monarchy.

Louis-Philippe wanted a civil list of 18 million francs annually, a sum only slightly more than half that received by Charles X. Although Laffitte promised him this, and even Dupont had expressed a willingness to propose 15 millions, the hostility of some of their followers caused them to remain inactive. When Périer came to power he was unwilling to sacrifice popularity for the King's sake and submitted to the deputies a blank for them to fill. The King received only 12 millions which infuriated him: he accused the deputies of wishing to annihilate him, and certainly there were many who by restricting his wealth wished to limit his power.

It was the attempts to have the state provide for his children which roused the most hostility. Although the Orléans' property was vast (it included the Palais Royal, Dreux and Eu united to the former Crown domains, amongst them Versailles, Rambouillet and Fontainebleau), the revenues went to the state whilst the upkeep was paid from the civil list. The King was concerned that his sons should have suitable properties: Orléans, it was presumed, would inherit most of it, Aumale was heir to the last Prince de Condé, but the other three had nothing. Louis-Philippe made a determined attempt that Rambouillet be given to Nemours, either as hereditary possession, or, when this proved unpopular, with a grant. The proposal in 1840 to pay Nemours an annual sum led to the collapse of the ministry. Even Guizot could not succeed: his proposals in 1844 were so unpopular in committee that he withdrew the Nemours financial measure rather than risk a parliamentary defeat. The King did not much help his own cause; he objected to being obliged to ask these financial favours and so became domineering and tactless. He regarded generous finance as his right, but the deputies were not sentimentally royalist and only spent very grudgingly. Discussion on royal finance resembled deciding the price of a machine destined for a while to be the government, said Guizot.[21] Princesse Marie refused to be verbally mauled in the Chamber of Deputies and so her father paid for her dowry himself.

The King paid tax on his property. Moreover he was careful about its upkeep. His favourite relaxation was to tour the rebuilding with his architect, Fontaine. Whatever the views on some of his additions at Versailles, Louis-Philippe saved it from becoming a military hospital and, at the cost of over 23 million francs, restored the building, dedicating it "to all the glories of France" to save it from destruction in any possible future revolution (which was the fate which befell his beloved Neuilly in 1848). The creation of a museum in Louis XIV's palace may have displeased royalists, but its celebration of the achievements of the *ancien régime*, Revolution and Empire as well as "the comforts of peace and the benefits of liberty"[22] given by the constitutional monarchy was a typical piece of Orleanist eclecticism. Large sums were spent on other works, such as the building of Fontaine's chapel for Saint-Louis at Carthage, buying paintings, subsidising the Sèvres factory and improving the royal library. The King was also generous to his servants, secretly paid off the debts left by Charles X and gave financial assistance to Constant, Audry de Puyraveau and Laffitte, even after the latter had joined the opposition. He donated large sums to the poor, especially in the appalling winter of 1830–31. Montalivet suggests a figure of 43 million francs in royal charity during the reign, half of which may be seen as politically motivated munificence, such as gifts to repair churches and help hospitals, but the remainder was not made public. As well as the King, the Queen and her children were generous in donations to charity. Thus in 1848, the King, supposedly miserly, was found to have debts of 27 million francs. "The King has done more than he could," wrote Montalivet, "the state less than it should."[23] A modern historian has estimated that France under Louis-Philippe had one of the cheapest monarchies in Europe, costing two-thirds the sum which the British monarchy cost the British taxpayer.[24] And yet so successful were the pamphlets of the republican Vicomte de Cormenin attacking royal greed and the feudalistic attempts to provide for his children, that in spite of their manifest factual errors, it was believed by many Frenchmen that their monarch was both expensive and niggardly.

Because the July Monarchy was coexistent with its king, the monarch was even more closely identified with the system than in absolutist states. The first controversy over the King's legitimacy showed how Louis-Philippe had become a symbol and how he would be attacked or supported in order to oppose or approve the government. Some conservatives claimed that the Duc d'Orléans had not been chosen but had mounted the throne by the abdication of Charles X and his son. They not only ignored the rights of Henri V, but in claiming that they made a compact with "a prince whom we found next to the throne"[25] they denied the notion of popular choice in which less monarchist Orleanists claimed to believe. Thiers asserted that they possessed a monarch "who can search for his legitimacy only in that of the nation".[26] He and men who thought similarly claimed that a wholly new monarchy had been created in August 1830. Dupin attacked the conservatives' attempts to create "quasi-legitimacy": Louis-Philippe, he claimed, was king "although a Bourbon" not "because a Bourbon". His birth was a happy accident not the source of a right.[27] These polemics were the focus of an argument about what form of society France would be, and became less important once the Charter was established and firm divisions had appeared between the parties of *mouvement* and *résistance*.

The question of the extent of royal power was less theoretical. It had not been decided by the Charter which did not alter the powers of the King save by the removal of Article XIV, yet the parliamentary origins of the regime had persuaded many deputies that they were the dominant power. (Previous constitutional orthodoxy had held that King and two Chambers were equal, if dissimilar, in authority.) The commentators provided no real assistance as their views on the Charter differed according to the party they supported. Many saw the King as a simple convenience, a figure-head. For Berriat Saint-Prix, the people were sovereign, and the King's role reduced to one of mediation between the two Chambers, between ministers and deputies.[28] The doctrinaire Rossi, however, saw the King as a "supreme national magistrate", a source of impulsion, limiting and co-ordinating other powers. Others, such as Fonfrède and Roederer, put the King's role even higher.[29] They formed an extreme towards which conservatives (such as the *Journal des Débats* and some doctrinaires) sometimes swung. Influenced by their fear of *petit bourgeois* ambition, disgusted by parliamentary manœuvres, they put Bonapartism into Orleanism. For them the King was inviolable, not because, as for the left, he was powerless, but because he represented "social unity".[30] He was sovereign, not in word merely: in practice all executive power emanated from him, and this school believed the political problems of the July Monarchy resulted from the deputies' refusal to acknowledge this.

The controversy over royal powers came to life during the ministerial crises of 1834–35. The failure of the party politicians to produce strong, stable government, enhanced the King's role. The anonymous pamphlet of Comte Roederer, a functionary of the Empire turned fanatical Orleanist, *Adresse d'un constitutionnel aux constitutionnels* of 1835, created a furore. It argued the primacy of royal power, and regarded ministers as administrators who accepted responsibility for the King's acts. Parties had no right to force their wills upon the King who represented the national will. Those who wanted strong government, as many of the doctrinaires did, thus believed sovereignty, even if limited, to be held by the monarch. They pointed out that the King had the right to nominate to office, to decree ordinances, to convoke and prorogue the Chambers, to sign treaties without Parliament (save for financial clauses therein) and to refuse to make a bill law, although in practice he never did so. If the King himself had removed the formulae "because such is his pleasure" and "of his own full authority", he none the less held huge powers whilst remaining "sacred and inviolable". They claimed that even if he did not hold abstract sovereignty, the King did more than merely reign. Thus Persil could speak in fulsome terms: "The King is our cult . . . we do not separate him from France, of which he is the saviour and providence."[31] Yet other doctrinaires felt more sympathy for the Whig than for the royalist or Bonapartist traditions. Some of them resented the King's manifestation of hostility to the Duc de Broglie and were more sympathetic to Thiers's doctrine that the King reigned without ruling.

Roederer's pamphlet gave the left the opportunity to claim the King was breaking the 1830 contract by trying to make himself absolute. When his disagreement with Thiers resulted in the latter's removal from office, an important recruit was gained for this opinion. It was with the Molé–Guizot ministry of 6 September 1836, which Barrot called "the triumph of personal government by the king",[32] that royal political power became a matter for parliamentary discussion. The method by which the King had changed Cabinets, and the fact that he did so when Parliament was not in session, laid him open to accusations of unconstitutional behaviour. None the less, the King knew that most deputies supported him. The problem was that as political incompatibilities increased, Louis-Philippe had to choose between rivals, which brought him the enmity of those excluded. The Coalition of

1838–39 chose royal power as its focus for attack, because in taking Molé as his *président*, the King had a ministry which included none of the outstanding leaders of the Chamber of Deputies. Molé had a majority but he lacked strong parliamentary support, and so the position of the King again became prominent. Although, as Granier de Cassagnac wrote, when it suited him Molé had the same "parliamentary pretensions" as his rivals, he was forced by circumstances to become "the able and resolute champion"[33] of the liberty of the throne. The opposition, which included not only the left, but those conservative groups excluded from power, combined on a constitutional issue for party reasons. By attacking the King, they hoped to destroy the ministry to which he had given his support.

The pamphlet war of 1838 and 1839 ranged around the controversies earlier raised by Roederer. Fronfrède's *Du Gouvernement du Roi, et des limites constitutionelles de la Prérogative Parlementaire* (1839) attacked the Coalition for its destructive opposition, telling the deputies that not they, but the King, represented the country. The more that the Chamber was dominated by local interests, the greater the need for "a stable, certain, central direction at the heart and head of society".[34] Duvergier, however, argued that the Chamber of Deputies had primacy because by election it represented the country. The King had a representative function as a symbol of permanence. The monarchy would seek to increase its powers, but if it did so at the expense of other bodies, he argued in his *De la Chambre des Députés dans le Gouvernement Réprésentatif* (1838), they would obtain a system which possessed "the inconveniences of absolute monarchy without the advantages".[35]

The campaign against the King's political role had a destructive effect upon royal prestige but in no way decreased royal power. The effect of political divisions in 1839 necessitated the formation of a provisional government by the King, the most evident manifestation of his prerogative. And in 1840 he again forced Thiers from office over a disagreement on foreign policy. This inaugurated a period of stability and royal interference appeared less noticeable as a result. Guizot, who profited from the royal action, approved this use of the prerogative, forgetting the part he had played in the Coalition. The King "firmly using his prerogative, has changed his Cabinet . . ."[36] he announced, thanking Louis-Philippe for thereby saving France from war. He accused the opposition of substituting for "the King can do no wrong" which was the principle of royal inviolability, the unjustifiable "the King can do nothing"..[37] And he expressed a regret at the decrease in monarchical power, because, holding office himself, he could only welcome royal support and exercise of the prerogative in his favour.

The opinions of ministers changed according to circumstance. The left had not attacked the royal prerogative until it had been removed from power, nor was Thiers concerned to limit its use when he himself held office. Most believed that the instability of France, the frequent lack of a strong parliamentary majority demanded some form of central direction. Thus during the debates on the regency in 1842, Thiers, despite his talk of the King merely reigning, supported the Duc de Nemours against the claims of Princesse

Hélène. Another centrist deputy, Vivien, asked, if the throne were occupied by a figure-head, who would govern.[38]

Tocqueville accused Louis-Philippe of being true only to the letter of the Charter, but warping its spirit.[39] Yet given the debates amongst Orleanists, this spirit was not easy to define. The King prided himself on his faithfulness to the Charter. He justified his dismissal of Thiers in 1840 by his command of the army, his power to declare war and peace, but stated he would accept the Chamber's will in the matter.[40] Indeed, Louis-Philippe never claimed, as did Roederer and Fonfrède (whose arguments he, never a theoretically minded man, may have found more embarrassing than useful), the right to ignore the will of the deputies. He did, however, claim the right to try to influence them. At the Court soirée, the King would "buttonhole the deputies".[41] as he called it, trying to convince them if they disagreed with him and to charm the recalcitrant into supporting the government. The monarch had also some direct power in the *banc de cour*, about ten deputies who voted ministerially because of loyalty to him. They were men like Vatout, his librarian (who also claimed to be an illegitimate son of Philippe-Égalité and thus more closely tied than by mere employment), or the controller of the royal forests, or, as were most of them, aides-de-camp to various members of the royal family, such as the Comtes de Montesquiou and de La Rochefoucauld. Only Liadières and Vatout spoke frequently and they were certainly more than mere spokesmen. The *banc de cour* in fact was simply part of the ministerial body, but none the less it caused some resentment, and was a useful subject of attack as a symbol of royal interference in the parliamentary system.

The King has been blamed for prolonging ministerial crises but there is very little truth in this. In 1835, he tried to avoid the return of Broglie but surrendered after brief resistance. In fact, personal antipathy and favouritism played remarkably little part in his political decisions. "He only obeys the force of circumstance, necessity",[42] remarked Heine, although one striking, and perhaps fatal, exception was his hostility to the appointment of Bugeaud to command the army against insurrection in February 1848. Louis-Philippe may have preferred Molé to Guizot in 1837 for personal reasons and because his confidant, the Comte de Montalivet, would serve with the former, but once Guizot was installed in power, Molé's attempts to overthrow the ministry annoyed the King, nor did the latter make any attempt to force Montalivet into the Cabinet. Indeed, evidence would suggest that rather than cause instability, the King much regretted it. It was a wearying task trying to harness eight horses, and he could not always achieve the team he preferred, he told Viennet. "But I wind up adapting myself to them, and it is then that a parliamentary storm takes them from me."[43]

It was Casimir Périer who had forced the King and his family to move from the Orléans home, the Palais Royal, to the Louvre, more easily defended, but with its memories of murdered and exiled kings. To avoid mob attacks and to protect Louis-Philippe from ill-natured curiosity, a moat was dug in front of the building, and, reinforcing the fortress-like atmosphere, a subterranean passage was constructed so that the King might walk in the Tuileries gardens. The strolls through Paris with his wife and the famous umbrella became impossible once it grew popular to try to assassinate him and it is ironical that this monarchy of popular inauguration should within two years be forced thus to immure itself, whilst absolute rulers walked unmolested amongst their subjects. Louis-Philippe escaped frequently to the more relaxed atmosphere of his house at still-rural Neuilly.

If the palace seemed isolated, within it was liberalised. Louis-Philippe forbade the use of the word "court" with its *ancien régime* associations. At first, uniforms were abolished, even for footmen, with the result that the King would occasionally mistake them for deputies and ask them which department they represented. However, within two years the earlier elements of democracy had been considerably limited, women of fashion no longer found themselves dancing with their tailors or shoemakers who had become National Guard officers and thereby gained entry to the Tuileries. "The throne has made a devilish comeback since July",[44] cried Général de Castellane with joy after one splendid ball where formal Court dress was worn by the majority of guests. Yet in spite of attempts to conciliate the old aristocracy the majority of the Faubourg Saint-Germain continued to ostracise the Orléans Court. "There is more difficulty in getting people to my court entertainments from across the Seine than from across the Channel", Louis-Philippe complained to an Englishman.[45] None the less, the Court, if it never rivalled the extravagance of the *ancien régime* or the two Empires, frequently presented a brilliant appearance, especially at the fancy dress balls which the Orléans children arranged with great flair, and where not only society figures, but luminaries of the worlds of art and entertainment gathered. In the evenings when there was no entertainment at the Court, the Queen and the princesses would sit around a circular table and sew, each in front of her personal drawer. This close family life provided the happier side of Louis-Philippe's existence.

The Queen made little impact on France. Although Marie-Amélie was a Neapolitan Bourbon, she showed little of the Italian temperament so evident in her niece, the Duchesse de Berry: instead she owed more to the Habsburg strain in her ancestry. She disliked politics and played scarcely any part in them although she concerned herself with some ecclesiastical promotions and was said to have gained the Comte de Jarnac the post of First Secretary at the London embassy. Her role was a family one: she was an excellent and much-loved wife and mother. Pious and charitable, she prevented the immorality of her sons' personal lives from infecting Court life.

Very different was Madame Adélaïde, the King's sister. She was "the female version of the King",[46] with the same political passions as her brother whom she occasionally advised on affairs of state. She had been the boldest of the family during the July Revolution, and the King much relied upon her moral support throughout his reign. At the Pavillon de Flore she held a small court where a group of intimates such as Talleyrand, Sébastiani, Gérard, Dupin and Flahault gathered. Whereas the Queen felt most at home with members of the Catholic aristocracy, such men were more truly Orleanist, without the traditional or religious attitudes of which Marie-Amélie approved. Unconsciously, the two women represented two of the main facets of Orleanism.

The Prince Royal, the King's eldest son, who became Duc d'Orléans when his father ascended the throne, gained a popularity which Louis-Philippe was never able to attain. Twenty years old in 1830, tall, elegant and handsome, he had a lively, somewhat restless mind. Immensely popular with women, he made full use of his charm. On one occasion, an insurrection broke out surrounding his place of assignation and he had to pretend to build a barricade before slipping away to his military headquarters to return with the municipal guard to destroy it. It was such incidents which endeared him to those who found Louis-Philippe's domesticity to be dull. In the early years of the monarchy, Orléans shared many of the ideas of the *parti du mouvement* and of his generation, and occasionally expressed them to the annoyance of the King who told him that they were not sufficiently well established for the Prince Royal to play at being a Hanoverian Prince of Wales.[47]

Although the English aristocracy admired his noble, somewhat cold tenure and one observer remarked that he was essentially "more princely in that he does not wish to assume airs",[48] Orléans felt strongly the need to conquer prejudice against princes. The army, the element "the least touched by corruption and worldliness that surround us", provided him with a means of doing so, and in Algeria he escaped the squalid squabbling of the deputies, "our masters".[49] He not only demonstrated considerable skill, but, he said, because to be pardoned for his birth he needed to do more than others, sought the most dangerous areas of fighting. A friend suggested that he did this because having a presentiment of his tragic early death, he sought a more glorious end. "He had too much insight to have any grand illusions about his future."[50] True or not, his courage won him great favour in the army, which was echoed by public opinion. On his tour through France in 1839 he was well received even in strongly legitimist areas. Rémusat said that he knew nobody more suited to mount the French throne.[51] His marriage to the Princess Hélène de Mecklembourg-Strelitz in 1837 was a popular event: it also proved highly successful in spite of the fact that the husband had not seen his bride before she crossed the French frontier. The birth of a boy in 1838, "that final offspring of an ancient race, that first-born of a glorious revolution",[52] seemed to promise the dynasty a secure and brilliant future. Yet almost too much hope had been put in the prince, and the future of Orleanism seemed to collapse when in July 1842 he died in an accident, aged thirty-two. "France has lost the one man who could have brought her out of this mediocrity",[53] said Thiers. His brothers despaired of their future: ". . . where will our focus be?" asked the Duc d'Aumale, "God, in taking him from us, has decapitated our family."[54]

"These days, princes cannot be weaklings, fools or madmen",[55] wrote Princesse Louise, and the children of Louis-Philippe were not only devoid of these drawbacks but possessed remarkable qualities of their own. Unfortunately, the oldest of the four brothers who remained after the death of Orléans was the least suited to replace him. "The appearance of the Duc d'Orléans was noble, that of the Duc de Nemours is nobiliary",[56] commented Heine. The Prince Royal's younger brother had not the easy charm and extrovert qualities of Orléans, but instead an excessively stiff dignity. Nemours, said his father, "was a born archduke".[57] Etiquette was stricter at his salon, when after 1842, aged twenty-eight, he gained an official position as probable future regent, than it was at his father's Court. Although he combined this with a taste for sexual alliances with women of all classes, for all the Orléans princes shared a common physical bravery and energy, his appearance of hauteur, largely due to shyness, made him unpopular.

The next son, the Prince de Joinville, was a contrast. An independent and bold character, he decided not to follow his brothers into the army, and instead embarked upon a naval career. In 1845, however, he left the service in disgust, having written a brochure of transparent anonymity attacking the government for its neglect of the navy. In contrast to the Saxe-Coburg marriage of Nemours, his wife was the daughter of the Emperor of Brazil who brought an exotic touch to the Court by such actions as a request for soup made from parakeets. After the poor scholastic performance of Joinville, the Duc d'Aumale had brilliant success at the Collège Henri IV, the school which all the princes attended. He became a remarkable and courageous soldier and, when only twenty-seven, successfully administered Algeria. The youngest brother, the Duc de Montpensier, most resembled his father, having less openness than his brothers and a more political mentality. Those who believed his father parsimonious, claimed that Montpensier's habit of dressing in an old and dirty coat and hat to search the shops of sellers of bric-à-brac, hunting for bargains, proved that he had inherited this quality. His marriage to the sister of the Queen of Spain caused a diplomatic crisis, and his role in making his father abdicate in 1848, would be much criticised.

Of the daughters, Princesse Louise was married to King Leopold of the Belgians, and thereafter paid only short visits to her family. Princesse Clementine married yet another Saxe-Coburg. The most interesting of the three daughters, however, was Princesse Marie, neurotic and artistic. A promising pupil of the Orléans drawing-master, Ary Scheffer, who also gave Joinville lessons to good effect, she sculpted a sentimental statue of Joan of Arc which received the homage of being much copied at the time. She was the first of the eight children to die, in 1838, aged twenty-five. With her mystical ideas, she went furthest in her romanticism. All the Orléans children showed sharply the contrast in artistic ideas between their father's generation and their own. The princes were "followers of Hugo" whilst Louis-Philippe on the whole retained the prejudices of traditional classicism.

The Orléans family never lost a feeling of the instability of their situation. The Prince Royal said that he was always conscious, when in Algeria, that France might suffer serious agitation and he would be obliged to return to Paris, "sword in hand".[58] Rémusat was amazed when Princesse Marie informed him that she kept a collection of portable valuables ready, "should we fall".[59] The feeling of insecurity did not significantly lessen with the duration of the monarchy: at least, the Duc de Nemours, always prone to pessimism, became convinced, after the death of his brother, that the dynasty was doomed.

Louis-Philippe came to see himself as a barrier against war and disorder, a feeling which must have been heightened by the continued attempts to assassinate him. He told the Austrian Emperor that his mission was to save France from the scourge of anarchy and preserve European peace. Thus he tried to turn his back on his revolutionary origins, yet whilst ceasing to be the citizen King, he never gained the dignity of hereditary right. Lamartine wrote that Louis-Philippe was a man remarkable in many ways, clever, studious, prudent, a good father and model husband, kind, humane, peace-loving and brave, "one could say that nature and art have endowed him with all the qualities which make a king popular with one exception: grandeur".[60] Yet perhaps grandeur was a luxury he could not afford. It was 1830 which had truly destroyed the mystique of kingship. Louis-Philippe was probably right in saying that the French would be merely contemptuous of a figure-head king, but by being seen to wield power he attracted to himself the odium of every fault. He realised the impossibility of his situation. "Justice will be rendered to me only after I am dead",[61] Louis-Philippe used to say, but even this was perhaps an excessively optimistic anticipation.

REFERENCES

1. Vicomte F.-R. de Chateaubriand, *Mémoires d'Outre Tombe* (1948), III, 82.
2. H. Heine, *Lutèce* (1866), 144.
3. Comtesse C. de Boigne, *Récits d'une tante* (1921), III, 70.
4. A. de Vigny, *Journal* (1867), 194.
5. Odilon Barrot, *Mémoires posthumes* (1875), I.
6. Comte C. de Montalivet, *Fragments et Souvenirs* (1899), II, 7.
7. J. Bertaut, *Louis-Philippe intime* (1936).
8. Barrot, op. cit., I, 250.
9. N. W. Senior, *Conversations with M. Thiers, M. Guizot and other Distinguished Persons during the Second Empire* (1878), II, 389.
10. Ibid., I, 10.
11. Barrot, op. cit., I, 252.
12. M. Nadaud, *Mémoires de Léonard* (Bourganeuf, 1895), 202.
13. H. L. Bulwer, *The Life of Viscount Palmerston* (1870), II, 35.
14 *Revue Rétrospective* (1848), 397.
15. V. Hugo, *Choses Vues* (1887), 85.
16. Montalivet, op. cit., I, 145.
17. Senior, op. cit., I, 130–1.
18. Ibid., II, 389.
19. Ibid.
20. Montalivet, op. cit., II, 231.
21. Archives Nationales, 42.AP.36.
22. Montalivet, op. cit., II, 40.

23. Ibid., II, 24.
24. J. J. Baughman, "The financial resources of Louis-Philippe", *French Historical Studies*, IV (Spring 1965), 63–83.
25. F. Guizot, *Mémoires pour servir à l'histoire de mon temps* (1858), I, 26.
26. Papiers Thiers, Bibliothèque Nationale, nouvelles acquisitions françaises 20602, 48.
27. J.-J. Dupin, *La Révolution de Juillet 1830* (1835), 22.
28. F. Berriat Saint-Prix, *La Charte constitutionnelle* (1840).
29. H. Fonfrède, *Du Gouvernement du Roi* (1838).
30. Ibid., 2.
31. Archives Parlementaires, 5 April 1835.
32. Barrot, op. cit., 363.
33. P. Granier de Cassagnac, *Histoire de la Chute du Roi Louis-Philippe* (1857), 18.
34. Fonfrède, op. cit., 13, 19.
35. P. Duvergier de Hauranne, *De la Chambre des Députés dans le Gouvernement réprésentatif* (1838), 33.
36. Archives Nationales, 42.AP.212.
37. Ibid.
38. Archives Parlementaires, 12 July 1842.
39. Comte A. de Tocqueville, *Souvenirs* (*Œuvres*, XII, ed. J. P. Mayer, 1967), 13.
40. Montalivet, op. cit., II, 49.
41. L. Viennet, *Journal* (1955), 103.
42. Heine, op. cit., 144.
43. Viennet, op. cit., 84.
44. Maréchal de Castellane, *Journal* (1895), III, 92.
45. A. D. Vandam, *An Englishman in Paris* (1892), I, 63.
46. Barrot, op. cit., 153.
47. D. Cochin, *Louis-Philippe intime* (1918), 17.
48. Baron P. de Barante, *Vie Politique de M. Royer-Collard* (1861), V, 63.
49. Duc F.P.L.C.H. d'Orléans, *Lettres* (1890), 83.
50. Ibid., 85–6.
51. Comte C. de Rémusat, *Mémoires de ma rie* (1958), IV, 18.
52. A. de Musset, *Correspondance* (1879), 161.
53. Ibid.
54. F. H. G. Limbourg (ed.), *Correspondence du duc'd'Aumale et de Cuvillier-Fleury* (1910–14), II.
55. Louise-Marie d'Orléans, *La Cour de Belgique et la Cour de France* (1933), 59.
56. Heine, op. cit., 267.
57. Cochin, op. cit., 83.
58. Orléans, op. cit., 86.
59. Rémusat, op. cit., V, 63.
60. A. de Lamartine, *Souvenirs* (1871), 93.
61. Hugo, op. cit., 93.

9

The Doctrines of Orleanism

"Je trouve en France, deux ou trois grandes maisons de commerce qui se disputent le monopole des faveurs sociales; dois-je m'enrôler dans la maison Henri V et Cie, ou dans la maison le National et Cie? En attendant le choix que je pourrais faire plus tard, j'ai accepté un petit intérêt dans la maison Louis-Philippe, la seule qui soit à même de faire des offres réelles et positives, et moi, je vous l'avouerai, je ne crois qu'au positif."

("I find in France two or three great houses of commerce which dispute amongst themselves the monopoly of social favours; should I enrol myself in the house of Henri V and Co., or in the house of the National and Co.? In awaiting the choice that I can make later, I have accepted a small interest in the house of Louis-Philippe, the only one which can make positive and real offers, and I, I must admit to you, believe only in the positive.")[1]

"Les révolutions ne sont jamais arretés et closes que par des mains qui y ont pris part."

("Revolutions are only ever stopped and closed by the hands that have taken part in them.")[2]

"We shall seek to hold to a middle way, equally distant from the abuses of royal power and the excesses of popular power",[3] Louis-Philippe told a deputation in January 1831. This phrase, expressing a novel conception of government, basing a regime upon a party programme, became immediately adopted; by the left, as revealing a reaction against *les glorieuses*, by conservatives as an expression of constitutional liberalism. The *juste milieu* was an Orleanist illusion; the belief that there was a permanent, stable middle ground on which a regime could be founded to withstand the assaults from factions of both sides. Furthermore, conservatives came to associate themselves with this *juste milieu*, and believing the Orleanist left to be an extension of the republican party forced it, after 1831, into permanent opposition. Thus the July Monarchy, founded as a guarantee of parliamentary government, rejected the natural concomitant of multi-party or bipartisan rule.

Orleanism was a compromise, but not one which emerged from an expressed national desire. However wise the attempt to extinguish conflict by finding a middle way, the new monarchy was imposed from above. So had

Bonapartism been, but it had found real popular support. The July Monarchy lacked the evils of the Empire but also its strength. It depended upon a willingness to compromise politically which did not exist, and upon constitutional reflexes which were not established in France. It wished to replace paternalist Catholic kingship with constitutional monarchy. Unfortunately this primarily intellectual idea had no united philosophy behind it. In the absence of a coherent creed, Orleanism invoked a date, July 1830, and to replace the doctrines of legitimism stressed the necessity of Louis-Philippe, who alone was able to save the monarchy from the results of Charles X's folly and provide the benefits of republican liberty without its Jacobinical consequences. Thiers admits that in 1830 some wanted Napoleon II, others the Republic, but "there was something else which, without inspiring enthusiasm, but rather by force of necessity seized and led the public reason".[4]

Reason and need were not, however, forces as powerful as enthusiasm. Even Louis-Philippe could not regard mere necessity as sufficient. He liked to claim for himself a legitimacy from Henri IV who, with William III of England, was a patron saint of the July Monarchy, conservative but not reactionary, and healer of national rifts. Pépin, a pamphleteer close to the King, represents the regime as successor to the Consulate, Louis XVIII and Martignac,[5] and Guizot also sees Louis-Philippe continuing the constructive conservatism of Louis XVIII. But whatever its historical exemplars, there could be no doubt that the July Monarchy was of illegitimate birth. It tried to play down its revolutionary origins: by 1835, the King no longer speaks fulsomely of *les glorieuses*, the "Marseillaise" has been buried as far as possible and official art portrays the King enthroned at the deputies' request and not by the people's will. The official view, presented by Pépin, is that Louis-Philippe ascended the throne on the grounds of national sovereignty, which he vaguely describes as "the conjuncture of all reasonable and intelligent opinion", aided by popular energy. It was necessary to be vague to try to stifle dangerous controversies, to speak of "the effective intelligent majority" represented in Parliament and present the *juste milieu* and bourgeoisie as identical. "The *juste milieu* is the jury; it is the National Guard; it is the electorate",[6] said Pépin, trying to prove that the regime represented the majority. Yet the *juste milieu*, rather than increasing in strength, was the prey of the extremes. Belief in government from the centre was a distinguishing factor of Orleanists; unfortunately they differed as to where that centre lay.

It was natural that Orleanism, a political *juste milieu*, should find a base in the middle orders of society. This is not to say that it was a middle-class creed, restricted to the bourgeois from whom it emanated, but that the historical compromise was by its nature more attractive to this class than to any other. Most republican leaders were bourgeois, there were many middle-class legitimists, but the bulk of the class preferred the Orleanist *juste milieu*. The *laissez-faire* economics of its academics, its distance from Catholicism, its superficial adherence to revolution combined with its service to order, satisfied a class which lacked loyalty to the past or radical demands for a changed future. Some aristocratic Orleanists such as the Comtes de Rémusat and

Ségur, like ideologists of bourgeois origin such as Guizot or Cousin, accepted the middle classes as a powerful reality, regarding them as a force for stability without disastrous aristocratic retrogression or lower-class violence. Thus the *grand notable* class, new wealth in land and commerce, official eminence together with liberal nobles, replaced the former élite.

Not all aristocratic Orleanists fully accepted such a favourable view. Men like Molé, or Tocqueville in spite of his democratic ideas, retained a personal aversion from the bourgeoisie, but both in different ways accepted the reality of middle-class power; the former in his belief that for conservatism to be successful it had to rest upon great industrial and financial fortunes as well as upon the great landowners, the latter in his realisation that the democratisation of society automatically placed preponderance of power in middle-class hands. The class was of course very complex and its lack of unity would prove fatal to Orleanism; it is noteworthy that *classe moyenne* is rarely used with precision: Guizot and Barrot, for example, meant very different things by it, the first an intellectual élite, the second a radical *petite bourgeoisie*. It was the Orleanist who invented his middle classes, not Orleanism which was the simple product of a class.

The Orleanist bourgeoisie could tolerate, even admire, aristocrats as individuals whilst disapproving of aristocracy as a system. Similarly it needed a king, whilst distrusting royalty and abhorring the atmosphere of courts. Orleanism was a monarchy without royalism, oligarchical without aristocracy, accepting religion as a force for order but distrusting its mysticism. Its mainstream drew its philosophy from Voltaire and its politics from 1791. Many conservative deputies supported the policy of order whilst retaining the anti-clerical, anti-aristocratic prejudices more fundamental to left-wing Orleanism. For example, in 1831, a majority of deputies accepted the proposal of the left for the ending of 21 January, the day of Louis XVI's execution, as a day of mourning, as decreed by the Restoration: the peers, lacking the deputies' hostility to royalism, limited the import of the decision by finding a formula which ended the official aspect but which declared the deepest regret for the event. The deputies showed the same spirit in 1832 when they erupted in fury over Montalivet's use of the word "subjects",[7] and the sitting had to be suspended. The majorities for abolition of the hereditary peerage, for the restriction of the King's civil list and decrease in the ecclesiastical budget, sprang from similar prejudices.

Orleanism did not attempt a mass following. It held that the Restoration had fallen because it alienated the middle classes. The King firmly believed that his throne rested on the bourgeoisie and in the early years of his reign, regarded the *petite bourgeoisie* of Paris as its main bulwark. Increasingly, however, he came to allow the notables to become their spokesmen and listening only to the opinions he wanted to hear, neglected to pay attention to *petit bourgeois* dissatisfaction. With this group alienated, Orleanism became a minority party, without popular support in areas of Carlist dominance or in republican towns. Yet the strength of indifference, the desire for order and prosperity gave Orleanism a passive majority. The local notables reflected this in a more political manner, and the reality of their strength was to be demonstrated by the conservative majority elected by universal suffrage in face of the 1848 Revolution. In July of that year, in about half the municipalities, the mayors in office before the Revolution were re-elected with the greatest changes in the legitimist south and south-west and the most successful Orleanist survival in the north and north-west.

Orleanists may be divided roughly into two age-groups: those whom Tudesq[8] calls the Orleanist generation, that 50 per cent of the deputies of 1846 who had been born in the last decade of the eighteenth century, the liberal young of the Restoration reaching an age of political participation around 1830, and those of a generation sufficiently old to have served the Empire. The latter group contained men such as Molé, Pasquier and Broglie who had been brought up during the Revolution, and in a few cases, notably Talleyrand, had served it. What Odilon Barrot, son of a member of the Convention and born in 1791, dismisses as the "phantom of the Terror" remained a hideous reality for many of an older generation who suffered very directly from the Revolution. The fathers of the King himself and of three of his *présidents du conseil*, the Duc de Broglie, Comte Molé and Guizot, had been guillotined, and many others had lost parents or relatives, suffered privation or persecution. Fear of Jacobin terror, Barrot claims, brought areas of blindness to a mind as intelligent and in other respects open, as that of Louis-Philippe, and partly accounts for his disastrous weakness in the face of revolt on the morning of 24 February 1848.[9]

The ambiguity of the July Monarchy results from this. Brought about by popular action, it is scarcely surprising that it was created "more against insurrection than by it"[10] as Lamartine wrote in 1831. Some, like Molé, frankly abhorred revolution and all pertaining to it, but blamed the Restoration for producing it. Broglie with greater allegiances to liberalism saw 1830 and 1789 as heirs of the British political revolution of 1688. Guizot and other bourgeois drew a distinction between the achievements of the French Revolution and its excesses: "I am one of those who were raised by the ardour of 1789 and who will never consent to descend."[11] After 1830 confirmed what he believed to be the gains of 1789, he regarded "the spirit of revolution" as a dangerous force, which liberty must break with, as order must be separated from absolutism.[12] Yet Guizot was unpopular because he refused to use rhetoric appealing to those whose hearts were revolutionary whilst their purses were conservative.

Those Orleanists who suffered from the Revolution had rarely emigrated, but had rallied to the Empire, the cradle of the July Monarchy. Not that all who held office under Napoleon fully approved the regime, but they accepted it as necessary to heal the ravages of the Republic. From old and new élites, the Emperor created a new ruling class and its second generation sat beside those older men who had themselves held office in state or army. Such were the Comtes de Montalivet, son of a Minister of the Interior, d'Haussonville, son of an imperial chamberlain and Broglie's son-in-law, the Passy brothers, sons of a high official, Duchâtel and Rémusat, Amiral de Rigny, nephew of

Baron Louis, the Dupin brothers and many others. The Restoration had not been such a healthy period for them. Some servants of the Empire such as Molé, Pasquier and Decazes, enjoyed office briefly in ministries of the centre. Others were offended by their exile from power and, alienated from Charles X, looked for a change in regime. Most Orleanists sincerely believed in hereditary monarchy, but as a profession and not a possession. Constitutionalists such as Broglie and Guizot regarded 1830 as a necessary imitation and as a final step. The revision of the Charter according to the *Journal des Débats* was final: the July settlement was "the normal state for the future".[13] Even the less doctrinaire Thiers believed the compromise a "definitive transaction",[14] because the *juste milieu* would survive, whereas Republic, Empire and Restoration monarchy had perished by exaggeration of their principles. All liberals, he declared in 1831, rallied to the government, which itself was the liberal party.[15] But this identification of Orleanism with liberalism disguised the fact that the latter contained two scarcely compatible brands: the one moral in nature, basing constitutionally guaranteed freedoms upon religious concepts of freedom of conscience; the other anticlerical, anti-aristocratic and for constitutional liberties only in so far as autocracy was associated with the Bourbons, thereby persuading many Bonapartists that they were liberals. Combined in criticism of Charles, this alliance was bound to dissolve under the strains of power, especially when determined opposition, not abiding by constitutional conventions, forced the liberals to begin to jettison their ideals, and the conservative Orleanists triumphed over those of the *parti du mouvement*, more in tune with the Revolution. The orthodoxy established under Périer based itself on the hesitant and inactive of July, and those, like Rémusat and Thiers, who had played leading roles, gained political prestige not for that, but for their defence of order.

Attitudes towards legitimism varied considerably amongst Orleanists. One doctrinaire told Bérard that they had more confidence, in defending the July Monarchy, in those who had wished to defend the Bourbons than in those who had overthrown them.[16] And Salvandy in his verbose pamphlet, *Seize Mois, ou la Révolution et les Révolutionnaires* (1831), regards the Orleanist left as a republican Trojan horse, and asks the monarchy to try to win over the legitimists. Others believed a closer link with legitimists to be possible and necessary. Molé discussed with Berryer in 1837 the possibility of electoral reform which would aid the latter,[17] and the legitimist leader tells us that Guizot too wished to come to terms with them, desiring to strengthen conservatism by extending it to the right, and, he claims, to this end was open to the electoral changes which were, however, continually prevented by a group of his political allies. And although the King distrusted them and took great exception to signs of legitimist sympathies, he was constantly preoccupied with the need to win them away from their allegiance, and after 1848 blamed his fall upon the division in monarchist ranks.

There was a group known as "rallied legitimists" who unwillingly accepted the new regime. They stood between their fears and their regrets, a hatred of disorder and dislike of legitimist alliance with the extreme left persuading them to support the government. There were about twenty deputies, for the most part not very significant, although Lamartine (until his journey to republicanism), Royer-Collard and Salvandy may be considered to have links with them. There were many more in the Chamber of Peers. Disliking Louis-Philippe as a usurper, they often refused to visit the Tuileries but would play a constructive if minor role in Parliament.

There were also those who, whilst in the position of serving the Restoration, had not only rallied to its successor but obtained high office in the new regime. A name had to be found for them, and men such as Talleyrand, Decazes, Pasquier, d'Argout, Sémonville and Molé were lumped together in the "'politique' party" or "governmental". These men believed in order, without possessing the dogmatic philosophy of the doctrinaires. Indeed, with the exception of Talleyrand, they regretted the fall of the Restoration and ascribed to the doctrinaires some of the blame for this. There was amongst them, says Pépin critically, a "complete absence of political principles in relation to institutions".[18] Of greater weight and more ambition than the *légitimistes ralliés*, these individuals, with no party around them, none the less gained power and influence.

The group known as the doctrinaires was more often attacked than described. There was perhaps a doctrinaire tone rather than a strict set of policies. The insulting designation had been applied under the Restoration to a group of its critics, a circle around Guizot, Broglie and, at that time, Royer-Collard. Their arguments were academic and philosophical in nature. They opposed ultra-royalists who put sovereignty in the King and republicans who saw it in the people. In 1830 it was they who, anxious not to abandon the traditions of royalism but eager to found a constitutional monarchy, invented what came to be known as "quasi-legitimacy": the Duc d'Orléans, claimed Guizot, was found at the steps of the throne and public interest demanded that he mount it. The year 1830, said Broglie, was the revolution of the doctrinaires as 1793 was of the Jacobins.[19] In this claim lies their philosophy and their presumption. For them, the July Monarchy and its Charter were a consummation, and not a beginning. For Guizot, their thought was a "mixture of philosophical elevation and political moderation",[20] whilst Thiers, the pragmatist, dismissed it as theorising which neglected reality.[21] Their mixture of German philosophy and English political theory, their frequently religious cast of mind, often Protestant, made them unpopular. None the less they exerted considerable influence, because of an intellectual superiority, fully recognised by themselves, and by their desire and ability to act as a party. Only a group of thirty deputies, they included not only Guizot, but Rémusat, Duvergier, Jaubert, Duchâtel and others capable of influencing opinion by tongue or pen. The dominance of Guizot and Broglie between 1832 and 1835 at a time when moderate opinion was frightened into conservatism, enabled them to become leaders of the majority.

For the governmental majority was not a party but a large group of over 200, whose dominant characteristic was interest in firm quiet government, broad but undogmatic loyalty to the 1830 settlement and, frequently, a wish to gain or retain profitable posts. They had spokesmen, but leadership tended to come from without, from individuals like Molé who had no real party, or from groups like the doctrinaires or *tiers parti*.

The latter, or *centre gauche*, finding leaders in Thiers and Dupin, stressed the revolutionary, anticlerical and anti-aristocratic nature of Orleanism. To their left were the *gauche dynastique*, men of the *parti du mouvement* who remained loyal to the Orleans dynasty. In the case of Odilon Barrot, this loyalty was fervent, for he regarded constitutional monarchy as "the only form of government, not merely desirable, but possible in our France".[22] It too stressed the revolutionary birth of the July Monarchy, and in some respects went further, in demanding a more democratic system, an extension downwards of the political participation of the bourgeoisie by widening the franchise and an aggressive foreign policy. After other figures, such as Mauguin or Laffitte, had lost respect or moved leftward, Barrot emerged as leader of the party. Mild, vague and indecisive, his essential moderation and loyalty to the monarchy hindered fully effective opposition in the eyes of his more extreme followers: he was "minister of the department of opposition"[23] scoffed one journalist. This unintended resemblance to an English opposition leader did not impress his contemporaries. But he had great oratorical talents, and was highly popular in the country: with free elections, wrote the pamphleteer "Timon" (Vicomte de Cormenin), Barrot would be returned by 200 *arrondissements*, "So much is he the expression, the formula, the real truth of the bourgeois monopoly!"[24] Barrot, more than any other political leader, represented the Orleanism of the majority of French bourgeois. Suspicious of monarchy, Church and aristocracy, fearing republican violence, uninterested in social or economic reform, it regarded 1830 as a class triumph rather than a philosophical or ideological victory. Yet this most typical Orleanist was ousted from office in 1831 and thereafter was permanently in opposition.

The July Monarchy represented neither popular sovereignty nor legitimate monarchy. The doctrinaire attempt to present it as something above two fallacious concepts, had no real success. To its enemies it appeared a transaction. Mediocre hacks, "eunuchs of the quasi-legitimacy", Chateaubriand called the servants of the July Monarchy: traitors to every cause, men without honour or dignity, governed only by ambition, "they will die only after exhausting their oaths to all possible regimes, and only after spilling the last drop of blood on their final post".[25] Another legitimist, Alfred Nettement, saw Orleanism as hatred by the *haute bourgeoisie* for the aristocracy: to gain power they pretended to be egalitarian: cunning, they spread errors by which they were not duped, illusions they did not share and, like calculating croupiers, impassively profited from the losses of others.[26]

There was, however, more than place-seeking and class envy to Orleanism. A desire for moderation and peace was general: a true belief in liberty and constitutional government, if rarer, was not uncommon, and many Orleanists proved this by their refusal to serve the shabby autocracy of Napoleon III. The criticism made by the Duc d'Orléans that the class which had triumphed in 1830 was corrupted by success and that its dominance had destroyed the nation's *élan* has some validity.[27] But so does the defence made by his younger brother, Aumale, twenty-five years later, that the July Monarchy spoke less of the principles of 1789 than the Second Empire, but as a truly constitutional regime, more genuinely practised them.[28]

REFERENCES

1. Stendhal, *Lucien Leuwen* (Martineau edition), 89.
2. Comte J. O. d'Haussonville, *Histoire de la politique extérieure du gouvernement français* (1850), II, 48.
3. A. Pépin, *La Royanté de Juillet et la Révolution* (1837), I, 421.
4. A. Thiers, *La Monarchie de 1830* (1831), 129.
5. Pépin, op. cit., I, 136.
6. Ibid.
7. F. H. G. Limbourg, (ed.), *Correspondence du duc d'Aumale et de Cuvillier-Fleury* (1910–14), II, 5–6.
8. A. J. Tudesq, *Les Grands Notables en France, 1840–9* (1964), I, 108.
9. Odilon Barrot, *Mémoires posthumes* (1875), I, 218.
10. A. de Lamartine, *Sur la politique rationnelle* (1831), 78.
11. F. Guizot, *Mémoires pour servir à l'histoire de mon temps* (1858), II, 37.
12. Ibid., 3.
13. *Journal des Débats*, 21 January 1831.
14. Thiers, op. cit., i.
15. Ibid., 150.
16. S. Bérard, *Souvenirs Historiques sur la Révolution de 1830* (1834), 19.
17. Archives Nationales, 223.AP.26.
18. Pépin, op. cit., II, 320.
19. Duc V. de Broglie, *Souvenirs* (1886), IV, 340.
20. Guizot, op. cit., I, 57.
21. L. Vivien de St-Martin, "Souvenirs", *Le Correspondant*, 25 September 1905, 1057.
22. Archives Nationales, 271.AP.23.
23. Charles Alexandre, *Souvenirs sur Lamartine* (1884), 29.
24. "Timon" (Vicomte L. M. de Cormenin), *Livre des Orateurs* (1847), 188–9.
25. E. Biré, *Dernières Années de Chateaubriand* (1902), 106.
26. A. Nettement, *Histoire du Journal des Débats* (1842).
27. Duc F. P. L. C. H. d'Orléans, *Lettres* (1890), 149.
28. H. d'Orléans, Duc d'Aumale, *Lettres sur l'histoire de France* (1861), 30.

10

Legitimism and the Vendée, 1832

"Châtelaine
Vendéenne
Quande finira le temps de peine
Au milieu d'un cortège éclatant se verra,
Et sur un cheval blanc, le vainqueur saluera
De sa main jeune et souveraine
Châtelaine
Vendéenne."

("Castellan
Vendean
When the time of hardship finishes
Will see himself in the middle of a brilliant procession,
And on a white horse, the conqueror will salute
With his young and sovereign hand
Castellan
Vendean.")[1]

Legitimism shared in the contrasts of the times. Those loyal to the *branche ainée* extended from genteel sulkers to avid conspirators. Men who believed in stability and custom were forced to become rebels; trusting in the dignity and sanctity of hereditary power, they had to attack a monarchy. Their cause was not yet lost, but it seemed increasingly anachronistic and they hovered uneasily between anger and resignation. There was a division between those, led by Berryer, who wished to play the parliamentary game, and others who regarded participation in the Parliament of the usurper as tantamount to treason. There was a rift between old and young, between rigorous conservatives and daring romantics, and the traditional conflict between aristocratic piety and hedonism, recast in the nineteenth century forms of religiosity and dandyism.

Whereas the republicans attacked both the regime and the principles on which it was based, the legitimists had to try to attack the July Monarchy without damaging royalism itself. They faced the additional complication of differences over exactly who was their true king. For many, the abdication of Charles X was not valid. Charles would give no guidance on this, his main motive appearing to have been distrust of his daughter-in-law, the Duchesse de Berry. In his desire to retain control over his grandson, Henri, Duc de Bordeaux, he continued to act as king in exile until his death in 1836, when his younger son, the Duc d'Angoulême, who had also abdicated in favour of Henri on 29 July 1830, assumed the role of head of the family, taking no royal title, but not renewing his renunciation of the throne. Some of the older and more conservative legitimists thus remained loyal to Charles and his son, Louis XIX, although the majority recognised the abdications. Indeed, a young king appealed to the romanticism of many. Henri V was the symbol of that royalism "young, poetic, French, national"[2] which Albert de Bertier de Sauvigny asked Balzac to help create.

Legitimism was held together by an almost religious faith. It had its pilgrimages: bands of believers travelled to Prague in 1833 to celebrate the Duc de Bordeaux's thirteen years, some went six years later to Rome for Henri V's first journey abroad (from Austria) as claimant to the French throne, and large numbers visited the prince in London in 1843. It also gained martyrs, those who died in the Vendée in 1832; it had its exiles and those who were imprisoned for it. Sadder still were the wasted lives; that, for example, of Tocqueville's friend, Comte Louis de Kergorlay, whose ardent legitimism cut him off from a world in which his talents would have made him shine, powerless, frustrated and sick at heart, his life destroyed in July 1830. Because of the chivalric loyalties of Restoration royalism, the mystical elements which gave it strength, legitimism possessed a sustaining power which prevented compromise. As one republican remarked, many of his fiercest fellow-thinkers had deserted the cause after 1830 to become "philippistes enragés" (fierce supporters of Louis-Philippe),[3] but the legitimists were more faithful to their cause and 1830 produced few defections amongst them. It could involve real sacrifices – for example, the Duc des Cars who spent all his wealth in the cause. A silent but rash man of action, he despised the salons and hated any idea of parliamentary participation and passed the last years of his life in expensive and fruitless conspiracy.

Legitimism meant attachment to a family, to a person, and for this reason many legitimists, with an acumen proved correct by events, feared Bonapartism more than republicanism as resting upon similar principles to its own. Whereas the partisans of Napoleon II or III paid lip-service to the Revolution, royalists invoked the traditions of French history and a monarchy which had been created by France whilst creating the nation itself. Legitimacy was a historical contract, the source of order within a hierarchical state, symbol of morality and justice, whose essential continuity had twice been broken in modern times, in 1792 and 1830, with disastrous results. Also, unlike Bonapartists, legitimists were for the most part decentralisers. Aristocratic traditions of the *ancien régime* had been strengthened by distrust of revolutionary Paris and most royalists desired a diminution of the capital's authority. Béchard, deputy for Nimes, in his *De l'administration de la France* attacked centralisation and advocated provincial self-government. And local assemblies were part of the programme declared by the Duchesse de Berry in 1832.

The legitimist view of the state was organic. It respected corporations and traditional groupings opposed to bourgeois and liberal individualism. This was true in economic affairs as in political: in 1845, for example, Berryer defended carpenters accused of coalescing against their masters. A party which was primarily aristocratic naturally inclined towards hostility to what it saw as bourgeois egoism. In *La Quotidienne*, the aged philosopher of ultra-royalism, the Vicomte de Bonald, attacked "a bourgeois monarchy, and a sovereign bourgeoisie".[4] According to him, the bourgeoisie had moved from the rightful place in the state to dominate society, they had proletarianised the population in their search for industrial wealth, and had materialised modern civilisation. The doctrine of *laissez-faire*, the financial struggle of capitalism was opposed to the idea of property as a moral force in society in which the legitimists claimed to believe.[5] And because they were so strongly based upon the land, they were generally out of sympathy with industrialisation. They saw the faults of the system more clearly than did most Orleanists, but nostalgia and prejudice often prevented readiness to pursue practical remedies. A notable exception was Vicomte Alban de Villeneuve-Bargemont, prefect of the Restoration, who after participating in the Vendean fiasco, turned to works of charity, and was largely responsible for the first factory legislation in France. Young royalists, often inspired by the social conscience of *l'Avenir*, participated in Catholic charitable associations. And the romanticism of Chateaubriand, aesthetically hostile to the prosaic vulgarity of the *juste milieu*, inspired many with lofty if nebulous ideals of a society reformed by loyalty to its true prince. They feared that the bigoted atmosphere of the Court in exile at Goritz, would irredeemably separate their young king from his people, a distrust repaid by the Court and its representative, the conventionally ultra-conservative Marquis de Pastoret who administered Henri's French property and whose ideas were expounded by *La France*.

The parliamentary party represented a tendency between the static mourning of Goritz and the poetic extremism of younger activists. Berryer was its acknowledged leader in the Chamber of Deputies. Cormenin considered him the greatest French orator after Mirabeau (but remarked that orators should be heard not read.)[6] Berryer's ability to inspire and to influence members, not only of his own party, was due to the beauty of his voice and nobility of movement, the alternation of charm and drama: the theatrical technique so admired by this generation, dispelled the rather vulgar appearance, stout and swarthy, of one lacking the aristocratic refinement of so many of his persuasion. He looked like a clever Irish priest remarked Greville disparagingly.[7] Berryer, generous and a *bon viveur*, had sacrificed what would have been a hugely profitable career as a lawyer to the cause, although since legitimists believed that their leaders should have châteaux, one was bought for him as the result of subscriptions. Inspiring devotion in some, others distrusted his moderation, fearing that legitimism would be corrupted by participation in parliamentary intrigue. They believed his speeches were more show than substance: "He is a colourist"[8] scoffed the Vicomte de La Rochefoucauld. Nor was it always easy to lead a party of individualistic aristocrats, even when numbering only twenty-five, and with the loyal assistance, until his death in 1838, of a *grand seigneur* and former peer, the Duc de Fitz-James, himself also an outstanding parliamentary performer. The impatient or extreme failed to comprehend Berryer's aims – to manœuvre to create disorder, vote to cause damage, skilfully to exacerbate the illogicalities of Orleanism rather than charge into the fray always waving the white banner of Henri V. Many conservative legitimists outside Parliament objected to his alliance in 1838 with their enemy Thiers against the less objectionable Molé, unable to understand Berryer's motive which was to damage the monarchy by humiliating the King through the defeat of his chosen minister. Simpler legitimists saw it only as a vulgar and debasing political tactic.

Although Berryer desired a certain measure of electoral reform, and indeed in 1837 discussed with Molé, the *président du conseil*, a slight enlargement of the franchise which they both hoped would return more wealthy landowners to the Chamber of Deputies, he was not sufficiently radical to accept the democratic measures increasingly espoused by a section of the party. The legitimists were at one and the same time a party of conservatism and a party of revolt, and some regarded large-scale electoral reform as a means of re-establishing the *branche aînée*. The Abbé de Genoude, who led this opinion, was even more than Berryer an anachronistic figure in the party. Short and fat, with an enormous head and eccentric appearance, he was a fervent Catholic who had written a book on the faith which the Papacy had put on the index. When widowed, Genoude had taken orders, but had then thrown himself violently and energetically into politics. In control of the *Gazette de France* and its provincial satellites, he entered a surprised Chamber as deputy for Toulouse in 1846. He was isolated here, but his arrogant strength of character and purpose enabled him to support this. He struck a note independent of Berryer, and there was rivalry between the two, although prolonged disagreement never led to an official split. However, a polemic began in the royalist press between his *Gazette* and the *Quotidienne* and *La France* which found his ideas destructively revolutionary. Alfred Nettement, *rédacteur* of the *Gazette*, wrote an "Appel aux Royalistes contre la division des opinions" in which he tried to heal the breach by propagating Genoude's ideas whilst praising Berryer's talents: however, he found the parliamentary activities of the latter pointless because the Chambers were entirely divorced from the nation: they needed an O'Connell, he claimed. Yet the hostility of Charles, and the failure of Henri to offer more than vague adherence to the more prescient or more radical, prevented the unification of the party around a forward-looking programme.

The strength of the legitimists was primarily the strength of the landowning aristocracy. Although like others this was a divided class, a majority of its members were legitimist in sympathy, if not in action. When in the Chamber of Peers, the Marquis de Boissy asserted that five-eighths of the surface of France was owned by legitimists, his claim created uproar, but none seriously disputed the proportion. Of course this surface area could not be translated into simple political support, but it represented huge potential influence. The drawback was that many satisfied their honour by retiring to their châteaux and would do no more. This "internal emigration" might withdraw strength from the regime but would deliver none to the legitimist opposition. Many legitimists deprived of the fruits of power contented themselves with agriculture, restricting their public role to membership of a farming society or an archaeology or local history association. Frequently they would not even vote, being honourably unwilling to take the necessary oath to the usurper. This attitude received the consecration of Chateaubriand and Baron Hyde de Neuville who both refused to become deputies from these scruples, but was under continuous attack by Berryer. At every election the *Quotidienne* and *Gazette* would plead for all eligible royalists to vote but with limited success. In Aix-en-Provence in 1839, there was an abstention of 44 per cent, most of which was legitimist. In the Vendée the general abstention rate was 30 per cent, and in some *arrondissements* it sometimes rose above 50 per cent. Such scruples are in contrast with the attitude of those magistrates who had taken the oath, and harassed the Orleanists from their invulnerable seats in the *cours royales* of Toulouse, Aix, Bordeaux and Marseilles. Because the electoral system tended to favour the town bourgeoisie at rural expense, legitimists were often stronger in the *conseil général* of a department than the number of deputies they possessed would seem to indicate.

Legitimism was strongest in the aristocracy, but remained in certain areas a potent force among the lower classes and a significant minority of the middle classes. These middle-class legitimists were usually of long-established families, often of lawyers or doctors who had close links with the nobility, or old merchant families in well-established commercial centres. New industrial man was generally Orleanist and there were few exceptions such as Benoist d'Azy, legitimist deputy of the Nièvre, who having given up his administrative career concerned himself with coal-mines and railways. The de Wendel family of Thionville, wealthy forge owners, were legitimist, their royalism a long-established tradition based upon strong Catholicism.

In certain areas the legitimists had a more popular base. Particularly in the Vendée, the peasantry remained loyal to religious and monarchical traditions, although the townsfolk were inclined to be Orleanist. But in the south, especially in the Gard, Hérault and Bouches du Rhône departments, much of both town and country was legitimist in feeling. The prefect of the Vaucluse estimated it as seven-eighths of the population of the department.[9] Here Protestant nobles tended to be Orleanist, creating that isolated upper echelon which legitimism formed in such areas as Alsace. Working-class hostility to Protestant manufacturers added religious to political bitterness in towns like Nimes where Catholic aristocrats and workers were ranged against Protestant liberals who had profited from 1830. The legitimists were strong in these southern towns: two of the three deputies of Toulouse were theirs, and two of the three deputies of the Ariège. The Bouches du Rhône sometimes had four legitimist deputies out of six, including Berryer in Marseilles. They were in a majority on the municipal council of some towns like Montpellier, Agde and Pezénas, and Marseilles where most classes were legitimist, the poorest amongst the most enthusiastic. In many of these southern towns a strong Carlo-republican alliance developed: at Arles and Tarascon they used regularly to elect a deputy from either side who would oppose the regime. At Toulouse, this gave a democratic tinge to legitimism which returned Genoude in 1846 and had previously elected a pro-Catholic republican. The Hérault, Tarn, Gard, Ariège, Haute Garonne and Bouches du Rhône departments had majorities which were positively hostile to Orleanism. These were areas of successful legitimist journals like the *Gazette du Languedoc* at Toulouse or *Gazette du Midi* of Marseilles, both of which had over 1,000 subscribers, a large readership for the provincial press. With a wide popular base, legitimists tended to be more active than in the north, and Orleanism relied upon rural rotten boroughs, not on the towns.

They were strong also in the mountains of central France where two of Haute-Loire's three deputies were usually legitimist, and the Loire, Haute-Vienne, Puy and Corrèze usually returned one each. Unlike the south, the battle here was the more simple one between conservative countryside and Orleanist urban bourgeoisie. At Limoges, there were active legitimists supported by the bishop, and the talented journalist Alfred de La Guéronniere gave the *Gazette du Centre* a certain notoriety but the party was without the strong popular support it found further south. In the north, legitimism was strong in some parts of Flanders, Picardy and the Somme where the influence of the great property-owners would sometimes return legitimist deputies such as Villeneuve-Bargemont, who as a successful former prefect was popular in the area.

Legitimism, like Orleanism and republicanism, relied on the *grands notables* of an area. The Church might be important: there was, for example, a noticeable difference between legitimist activity at Arras where Bishop de la Tour-d'Auvergne was a supporter, and Cambrai where Belmas was hostile. The Catholic vote at Epinal (the Vosges) split the bourgeoisie and sometimes elected a legitimist deputy. Although the east was not royalist the presence of a powerful Carlist family, the de Bertier, and the legitimist sympathies of the *maitres de forge*, the de Wendel family, gave them a stronger position at Thionville than they possessed in similar towns. In the east and most of the north, however, they were a definite minority.

Legitimists would not always ally themselves with republicans against an Orleanist. There was a tendency for many of them to vote for a conservative candidate who would do his best not to alienate them, men such as Janvier or the Catholic Comte de Carné. Versailles and the aristocratic Faubourg Saint-Germain (Xe Paris) tended to elect legitimist-inclined or aristocratic Orleanists such as Laurent de Jussieu. Some deputies like Lahaye-Jousselin managed to be legitimist in their *arrondissement*, in his case in the Loire-

Inférieure, and to support the government in Paris. Thus the party reflected the variations in French political behaviour and exacerbated the divisions in French society.

After 1830 many legitimists left for their estates: financial reasons, the loss of their jobs or pensions, often necessitated rural retrenchment, the return to the sources of landed wealth. Others remaining in their Parisian salons maintained a constant criticism of the regime and its monarch. This source of opposition, although confined to a social élite within the small area of the Faubourg Saint-Germain, was damaging. It meant that the upper echelons of French society lost the coherence necessary for the maintenance of an undemocratic regime. The representatives of a Europe royalist and aristocratic found in the salons an argument against the July Monarchy. The salons were a barrier between Louis-Philippe's acceptance by France and Europe. Périer, waging war on this as on greater issues, once summoned the Austrian ambassador and told him that if Comtesse Apponyi expected the Duc d'Orléans to attend her soirées, the King asked that she should not invite those who did not go to the Tuileries. Apponyi replied that she could not entertain on such a condition: only fifteen women of society went to the palace.[10] Gradually Orleanism broke down some of this hostility as the regime became better established and more monarchical in tone, but there were always a few great houses of the Faubourg Saint-Germain which kept legitimism alive in the midst of Orleanist and republican Paris.

In July 1830 several of the more extreme royalist – notably the Duchesse de Berry – had wanted to fight in the Vendée to recapture the lost throne. To a romantic generation, the Vendean wars against the Republic were an inspiration. The royalism of the Vendean peasantry was combined with a strong religious faith, and the priesthood largely remained fervently loyal to the fallen Bourbons. In the heart of the area, of thirty-two *curés* only five were sufficiently loyal to the regime to sing "Domine salvum fac regem Ludovicum-Philippum" at mass. Some priests would play an active part in the 1832 revolt and churches provided a meeting place between the minor gentry of the area and the peasants. The anticlericalism of many Orleanist authorities strengthened the alliance between the Vendean altar and the Bourbon throne.

The suspicion in which the July Monarchy held the royalist west, was shown by the presence of large numbers of troops. Under Général Lamarque, a leftwards inclined general, the tone of the command was conciliatory towards Vendean feelings. When Lamarque became increasingly disillusioned with Louis-Philippe, he had to be removed: legitimists had approached him and it was feared he might lend himself to their schemes. But the government's attempt to disarm the peasantry was poor psychology: they banded together, skilled at avoiding the patrols. There were some horrifying acts by the soldiers, occasionally abetted by their commanding officers who hated the Vendée from the first Revolution, or were taking revenge on the Restoration. In return the *chouans* would occasionally trap patrols or shoot spies in their midst. The liberal press of Angers and Nantes tried to represent the royalist peasantry as brigands and smugglers, which was rarely the case: brigandage, like the strength of traditional beliefs, was the product of the environment, but was not identical with royalism. Although old loyalties still lived, the Vendée was less favourable to insurrection than it had been. The towns had grown in size, with a bourgeoisie hostile to legitimism, some former aristocratic leaders had lost prestige because they had rallied to the Empire, and anticlerical though the Orleanist authorities might be, this could not compare with the attempts of the Republic to extirpate Catholicism. None the less faith overrode reality, and in 1831 Vendean royalists, ashamed at being caught off guard in July, were begging the Duchesse de Berry to come to lead them in revolt.

For the Duchesse the boredom of the ageing court in exile was insupportable, and the resignation preached by her father-in-law was alien to her passionate Neapolitan temperament. To place her son on the throne of his ancestors was her mission. She was encouraged by the most fanatical and impractical of the younger legitimists as she travelled around Britain making plans, writing letters to Bertier, Kergorlay and other supporters in France. With a succession of false names, her correspondence incessantly changing codes to outwit the agents of Louis-Philippe, she passed through Europe in the summer of 1831. When her presence in Piedmont became known, the French government in possession of some of the Duchesse's conspiratorial letters, forced King Charles Albert, a tacit supporter of her cause, to expel her from his domains. Travelling through Italy and failing to obtain any aid from her half-brother, King Ferdinand II of Naples, who was also nephew to Queen Marie-Amélie of France, she eventually settled in the principality of Modena, whose Duke had not recognised the French change of throne. From here, the Duchesse and three legitimist leaders, the Comtes de Bourmont, de Kergorlay and the Duc des Cars, made plans for a legitimist uprising in France the following spring.

Already, a Vendean nobleman, the Baron de Charette, son of a leader of the first Vendean war, had secretly arrived in his province to organise the Vendean army which was expected to provide the focus of a national rising. The difficulty which all conspiracies faced confronted the royalists. Enthusiasm was high in many quarters. The news of imminent uprising roused unoccupied young legitimists and retired officers of the Garde Royale from their sulky lethargy and flung them into preparation, not always discreet. It was, in particular, difficult to collect and store a sufficient quantity of arms in any great secrecy. As the republicans were to discover, for a conspiracy to be secret it has to be tiny.

Some legitimists were in touch with Bonapartists in Paris. The Bonapartist Général de Montholon, later to become a conspirator for Louis Napoleon Bonaparte, considered the Duc de Reichstadt an impossibility and preferring Henri V to Louis-Philippe, was willing to lead his friends with legitimists in a coup, even though the Duchesse de Berry refused to accept the superimposition of the imperial eagle on the white Bourbon flag. Prince Louis Napoleon, whose motives as so often are hard to fathom, but perhaps hoped for a civil war, gave this co-operation his blessing. There were also *pourparlers* with the pro-republican Général Clausel who, whilst well disposed, was unwilling to compromise himself until after an attempt proved successful.

However, the whole attempt was riddled with various spies and *agents provocateurs*; in particular Vidocq, the great ex-criminal, was working for the government. It was perhaps for this reason that royalist leaders decided to act. On 2 February 1832, less than 1,000 men, fewer than hoped for, mostly royalists, gathered near the meeting place in the Rue des Prouvaires. Many were former royal soldiers, especially members of the dissolved Swiss Guard. A key to the Louvre had been obtained by bribing a concierge, and the plan was to break in and capture the King. While they were arming, the police entered. A mêlée ensued, but the conspirators were surrounded and outnumbered. There were various brave but unequal struggles as the legitimists tried to avoid being taken, but by 3 a.m. it was all over and many conspirators were simply collected from neighbouring cafés.

This fiasco persuaded the Duchesse to put all her trust in the Midi and the Vendée. She was encouraged by Berryer who felt the moment was ripe since the regime was weakened by the cholera, the death of Périer and the Belgian crisis. There were promises from the Netherlands that a Dutch army would begin an offensive against Louis-Philippe if her revolt showed any signs of success. The rulers of Spain and Portugal also promised later assistance, and the King of Piedmont allowed a ship under his flag to carry the Duchesse and a few supporters from Italy to Marseilles. The French government discovered this but failed to stop the boat on the high seas.

On the morning of 29 April, the Duchesse, with Bourmont and a few others close to her, landed on the south French coast. Marseilles had been chosen as the starting place of the uprising, from whence the revolt would be carried through the royalist areas of Provence and the Midi into the Vendée. The Duchesse had sent word to the Vendean leaders to prepare to rise on 3 May.

In comparison with their hopes, the measures of preparation taken by the conspirators were small. The leader at Marseilles, the Duc des Cars, had fixed the rising for 4 a.m. but only sixty men gathered. To summon the expected numbers, the white flag was planted on a church tower, and the bell rang wildly to no avail. Men hesitated to join openly a revolt about which they suddenly felt apprehensive. Des Cars led his men through the streets to attempt to capture various important positions, but at the Hôtel de Ville, the Orleanist troops, prepared for such an attempt and better armed, easily routed them. The royalists and the republicans, misled by the success of insurrection in 1830, were to attempt many more times to overthrow the regime from the streets, not understanding how difficult it was to rouse even a well-disposed population to attack a prepared authority.

Madame, however, was not weakened in her resolve by this ignominious collapse. Her romantic mind saw in the Vendée the forces of chivalry against which the troops of the usurper would fight vainly. In the coach of the Vicomte de Villeneuve-Bargemont, posing as his wife with her elderly adviser the Comte de Mesnard as her father and a marquis disguised as a footman, she travelled towards the Vendée. Here, she donned the traditional garb of a male Vendean peasant, blue trousers and black jacket, with black woollen cap. From various hideouts, moving continually to avoid discovery by the enemy troops, she made contact with the Vendean leaders, the Marquis de Coislin, Charette and others: a young lawyer from Nantes, Achille Guibourg, brought her news that Maréchal de Bourmont had arrived in that town. She sent out new orders for the uprising to begin on the night of 23 May.

Her supporters, however, had been losing confidence since the failures in the Rue de Prouvaires and Marseilles. Berryer, representing the council which the Duchesse had nominated as provisional government when the July Monarchy fell (it also included Chateaubriand, Fitz-James and Hyde de Neuville) sought to prevent the rising. On 22 May he arrived at Nantes, where he had little trouble convincing Bourmont that insurrection would prove disastrous, and what was virtually a counter-order was issued to the troops. Berryer then proceeded on a long, uncomfortable journey along the rough tracks, hearing the peasants calling to each other with the owl-like cries which had gained them the name of *chouans*, to ensure the route was clear of Général Dermoncourt's patrols. Eventually reaching the hideout of the Duchesse, he attempted to fulfil his mission. It took three hours and profuse tears from both parties before she surrendered. But next morning, encouraged by false reports of risings in the Midi sent by fanatics determined that the insurrection should not be stifled, she retracted her promise, declaring that honour commanded her to fight. She sent out an order stating that the insurrection would take place, but postponing it yet once more to the morning of the 4 June. The despairing Berryer wrote from Nantes restating his arguments: the royalists would be defeated, and the Orléans throne thereby strengthened. He begged Madame to wait until the regime succumbed, forced to choose between republican riots and a nationalistic policy leading to disastrous European war. A desperate note from the Parisian council, signed by Chateaubriand, informed her of the distance between her hopes and reality: civil war would not only be deplorable in itself, it would alienate much support. But all appeals to reason were useless.

Berryer meanwhile was under arrest after his Parisian home had been raided and material discovered which linked him with the Duchesse de Berry. The meaning of his visit to Nantes was misinterpreted: the government believed he was encouraging the rebellion. Also arrested for "plotting against state security" were Hyde de Neuville, Fitz-James and Chateaubriand. The elderly vicomte, doyen of French letters and former Foreign Minister, spent twelve hours in a grimy cell, listening to the cries of the prisoners, the sounds of locks, chains and closing doors – "the hideous machines that drive the world".[11] Then he was taken to the more suitable surroundings of the Prefecture of Police where the Gisquet household kept him in comfortable sequestration for a fortnight. The arrest of Chateaubriand created some outcry, not merely in the legitimist press: the *Journal des Débats* published a protest by Armand Bertin against his imprisonment. As Alfred Nettement wrote in the *Quotidienne*, it was strange to see a minister who was a former *carbonaro* (Barthe), formerly revolutionary *procureurs du roi* and policemen arresting MM. de Chateaubriand, Hyde de Neuville and de Fitz-James for undermining the monarchy.[12] Once freed, Chateaubriand took responsibility for the messages. Berryer was examined, described his intentions and was released. The arrests had actually been no more than a clumsy method of preventive detention, the government having seen these men as potential leaders of insurrection. The government could afford to release them, for by this time the rebellion had collapsed.

It had not started well. Many Vendean royalists made no secret of their pessimism. If they fought, it was from honour and not confidence. As one of them said, with a wry allusion to the Duchesse's romantic illusions – "It things do not go well for Madame one must die, and that will be the end of it, and then . . . go hang Walter Scott, for it is he who is the true culprit."[13] The failure in the Midi and the postponements had sown despondency and confusion. A group who had not heard of the cancellation of the outbreak planned for 23 May, began to assemble under their white flags. On the 24th they met a highly superior force, and many were captured. This unofficial beginning of hostilities encouraged the energetic Général Dermoncourt to take action. He was justly suspicious of his superior, the corrupt Général Solignac, open to bribery, who had shown a lack of enterprise, although Solignac would later attempt to recover his position by harsh measures against the royalists. On his own initiative he searched a château of a legitimist nobleman and discovered the plans for the insurrection. The element of surprise, vital in a guerrilla campaign where the badly armed faced a superior force, had been lost. Dermoncourt informed Soult, Minister of War, who returned the good advice to the general to concentrate his troops. The army had learnt from its past mistakes, but the Vendeans had gained no similar advantage.

Another presage of disaster was the death of Cathélineau, son of the leader of the first Vendean war, traced by the army to a farmhouse: forced from his hiding place by the torture of the farmer concealing him, his head was beaten in by a rifle butt. The brutal death, by removing a popular leader, further weakened her cause: the Duchesse had felt a kindred spirit in Cathélineau whose political stance was not far removed from brigandage. Madame herself was also in great danger as was shown when troops shot a young Vendean noblewoman escaping from a captured farm, probably believing her to be the princess. Amidst so many tragedies and disasters, the news that the Tsar promised aid once the insurrection showed signs of success, was small consolation.

On 2 June, she sent out a rallying cry, appealing to "this people of heroes" to follow her in fighting for the throne of Henri V. On the night of the 3rd the royalist forces began to assemble, the peasants congregating at the châteaux of their leaders. The gentry were not susceptible to the claims of strategic discipline, and many acted with an enthusiastic precipitation which was disastrous. By the 5th, a few small engagements had taken place. In some the insurrectionaries were dispersed and captured, but in others they were successful: Charette skilfully manœuvred to avoid the superior Philippist forces, but was unable to assemble all the rebel army. The storms of that night were the final blow: in this primitive army, cartridges were carried in pockets, and torrential rain both soaked ammunition and prevented the exhausted rebels from sleeping. The government was better prepared. It had proclaimed a state of siege in the most involved departments, the Vendée, Maine-et-Loire, Loire-Inférieure and Deux-Sèvres. In Paris, the *Quotidienne* was prevented from appearing for three days by "the terrorist *juste milieu*"[14] and preventive arrests were made.

On 6 June, battle was conclusively engaged: the Vendeans under Charette fought with great bravery, but soon found themselves encircled by greater forces, and with insufficient ammunition. Charette decided to disband his troops, who, knowing the countryside, were able to escape the net, and turned his attention to aiding the escape of Madame, who had with difficulty been restrained from joining the battle, and had been occupied in treating the wounded. Other small engagements took place, in which a similar hopeless bravery was shown. The Duchesse was escorted to Nantes, still in peasant disguise, to be concealed for five months in the home of two fervently legitimist Nantaises. In spite of urgent commands by Charles X that she leave France, she stayed on, hoping for a republican rising or a Dutch offensive.

Louis-Philippe and his wife desperately desired the Duchesse's escape, not wanting the embarrassment of another political trial. It seems that the King even sent word to his wife's niece to assure her that she would be allowed to get away, and possibly royal pressure prevented Montalivet from availing himself of the means of treachery offered him whereby the place of concealment might be discovered. In that area of tight-knit loyalties, all police attempts at bribery to discover her whereabouts and all searches had proved vain until an offer was made to the government. Thiers, Montalivet's successor at the Interior (in the ministry of 11 October) was not squeamish. The traitor was a Jew of German origin named Deutz, who had been converted to Catholicism, enrolled into the legitimist cause and used on secret missions. He offered to sell the government his knowledge of Madame's whereabouts. Thiers agreed to give him half a million francs and Deutz left for the west. The minister ignored the Court's feelings and decided to satisfy instead the anti-royalism of the deputies by seizing the fugitive. To the Comtesse de Boigne who warned him of the dangers of making a royal martyr, he replied, "Royal tears and even royal blood are not worth as much as you suppose." The advance of civilisation could be measured by the decrease in awe for royal personages.[15] The moderate Comte de Saint-Aignan was removed from the prefecture of the Loire-Inférieure, being considered too honourable for the task of capturing the Duchesse, and was replaced by the arrogant bourgeois Maurice Duval, celebrated for the force he had used at Grenoble. He was greeted at Nantes with boos and the banging of kitchenware, a charivari which lasted two days. Deutz, claiming that he had important news to impart, eventually obtained an interview with the

Duchesse, the house was surrounded and finally after a concealment of the most excruciating discomfort from which she was driven by two cold gendarmes lighting a fire in the chimney behind which she and three others had hidden, one captivity was exchanged for another. On 7 November, the Duchesse was led to the castle of Nantes, and thence by corvette to the fortress of Blaye on the Gironde: the government could not keep her amidst the legitimists of the Vendée or risk sending her, like Charles's ministers, towards the republicans of Paris. Général Bugeaud was sent to guard her and prevent all contact with her supporters.

The imprisonment of the Duchesse shocked legitimists, gave distress to the King and even more to the Queen: "Ah, if only she had wished to profit by these six months of patience to take herself away when he was master",[16] she cried. The royalist journals protested at this new enormity perpetrated by the government of the usurper. Chateaubriand published in late December a pamphlet *Mémoire sur la captivité de madame la Duchesse de Berri*, whose eloquent "Madame, your son is my King!" inspired royalist hearts, and presented a challenge the government could not ignore. A league of legitimist youth presented to the author a medallion in gratitude, the leader of the deputation, a student named Victor Thomas, made a speech of loyalty to Henri V, published by legitimist newspapers and so in February, the author, the student and a selection of journalists found themselves on trial for sedition. This gave Berryer, defending the *Quotidienne*, the opportunity for one of his most magnificent orations. The jury brought in a verdict of not guilty. The crowd outside cheered Chateaubriand loudly: their acclamations disproving the claim of Persil, the *procureur général*, that without the protection of governmental forces, the mob would tear him apart.

By this time the government, embarrassed on the question whether or not to hold a political trial, had found a way out of its difficulty. It appeared that Madame was pregnant. The republican press eagerly published the rumours. When the *Corsaire* was guilty of what he considered to be a slur on the honour of the Duchesse, an editor of the legitimist *Revenant* challenged a journalist on the republican sheet to a duel. The example was catching as chivalrous young journalists rushed to defend the reputation of impugned virtue. The *Tribune* and *National* offered a mass duel, but the *Quotidienne* rejected this as ridiculous. Instead, Laborie of the *Revenant* fought Carrel of the *National*, both were wounded, the latter seriously, and republican journalists clamoured for more duels in revenge. Amidst this atmosphere of romantic farce, the government obtained from the Duchesse a declaration of a marriage she claimed had taken place secretly in Italy before the Vendean expedition. In fact, the Duchesse, with child by Guibourg, the lawyer who had shared her long concealment at Nantes, had, by means of the priest who catered to her spiritual needs, smuggled out news of her predicament to a royalist who had searched for a suitable husband. A candidate was found in a young Neapolitan diplomat of good family: a compliant priest married them while the Duchesse pined within the fortress on the Gironde.

Sure now of its facts, the government announced the marriage in the

Moniteur of 26 February 1833. Her followers refused to believe it. Many were persuaded, like the legitimist newspaper of the Gironde, *La Guienne*, that Madame's declaration was a forgery. Others let their anger rise against Louis-Philippe for allowing a relative to be thus attacked, truly or untruly, and turned their attention to the health of the captive, suffering a long imprisonment in an unhealthy castle. Never, declared Chateaubriand, with absurd exaggeration, had there been such an example of moral torture: "If she dies captive, since her enemies have dug into her vitals we shall bestir her ashes."[17] Others, not strictly legitimist, opposed her incarceration, Tocqueville and Beaumont being amongst those who publicly protested against this imprisonment without trial.

The Duchesse did not die, but on the morning of 10 May gave birth to a girl. The process had been almost as public as the birth of her son Henri, but instead of courtiers, the mother was surrounded by the petty officials of Bordeaux and her military gaolers. The government was determined that none could credibly assert that the birth was its own invention. The legitimists were astounded, many were furious: a martyred Duchesse had been turned into an undignified and undisciplined woman. "She has cuckolded her own cause", remarked Chateaubriand bitterly,[18] although he was not to abandon her as many would.

The Orleanist government had as so often before found a political solution to its problems, a compromise wholly satisfying to none, but avoiding the worst aspects of a more honest or more brutal course of action. The left could not easily demand the trial and execution – although many did – of a pregnant woman, and the descent of her cause from heroism to comedy was deemed sufficient punishment. She was taken to Naples and released, her political importance destroyed. As for the other leaders of revolt, since they were tried in the area where captured, they frequently faced sympathetic juries or magistrates and received only slight penalties. Charette and Bourmont were exceptional in being condemned to death in their absence, but in 1837 they too received amnesty.

The adventure had ended in that mixture of the romantic and the ridiculous with which it had always been invested. The Vendean insurrection of 1832 may be seen as a symbolic battle between religion and scepticism, chivalry and compromise, aristocracy and bourgeoisie, and as such it is significant. Yet it was always more symbol than reality, the last brief flare of an ancient loyalty lit by the dying embers of the loyal Vendée. The Orleanist government fought this spirit with modern weapons: it built roads through the territory to open it to trade and industry, and, if again necessary, to an army. The prefect Duval, failing to raise his hat to Madame, was the entry of a new world into the Vendée. Old loyalties could not vanquish the new forces, although the government continued to keep a close and nervous watch on members of the Charette and Bourmont families.

The year 1840 briefly gave legitimist conspirators hope: a European conflict would give them an opportunity and there were preparations in the Morbihan for an uprising, but war was avoided and nothing came of the plots. Most legitimists hoped that the regime would collapse of its own contradictions or be overthrown by a short-lived republic. Legitimism thus became less conspiratorial, but it remained on the outskirts of legality. Few leading legitimists escaped the attentions of the police. In 1837, the arrest of Vicomte Walsh, director of *La Mode*, found carrying letters to the exiled court, led to the examination of Berryer, Genoude and Nettement, but no case could be made for a trial for conspiracy. The extraordinary consequences for the higher classes are exemplified in the imprisonment of the Vicomte de La Rochefoucauld for having written a violent pamphlet against the regime: in gaol he was visited by several members of the aristocracy, including his aunt and her stepdaughter, the Comtesse Anatole de Montesquiou, whose husband was *chevalier d'honneur* to the Queen. (The different La Rochefoucauld branches congregated annually, but it was upon the understanding that politics were not mentioned: the violence of their feelings would have destroyed the amicability of family reunion.)

Passions were tending to cool, however, especially as the Church became less hostile to Louis-Philippe. The need to find a career brought the scions of previously uncompromising families into the Orleanist fold. The defection of the Duc de Guiche in 1846, the eldest son of a great royalist family, caused a sensation in the salons of furious legitimists. Yet the occasional defection made legitimism no less uncompromising. The struggle for educational freedom and the government's clumsy attack upon its honour after the pilgrimage of many of its leaders to visit Henri V in London, did much to maintain its passion. After 1848, both Louis-Philippe and Guizot blamed the failure of the July Monarchy on legitimist opposition. Given that the monarchy fell in the streets of Paris, this is to grant too much force to psychological factors, but it is evident nevertheless that legitimism played a large part in preventing the firm establishment of the regime. Few Orleanists would have contemplated the sacrifices which were made for Henri V, and however anachronistic it may have been, some of the Vendean spirit would have been invaluable to Louis-Philippe when his monarchy crumbled in 1848.

REFERENCES

1. Jules de Rességuier, 'La Chatelaine de la Vendée', in E. Asse (ed.), *Les Petitis Romantiques* (1900), 185.
2. H. de Balzac, *Correspondance* (1964), III, 701–2.
3. A. Saint-Ferréol, *Mes Mémoires* (1887), 125.
4. *La Quotidienne*, 2 January 1838.
5. Ibid., 10 September 1836.
6. "Timon" (Vicomte L. M. de Cormenin), *Livre des Orateurs* (1847), 218.
7. C. F. Greville, *Memoirs* (1874), III, 380–1.
8. Vicomte de la Rochefoucauld, *Mémoires* (1837), x, 228.
9. Archives de Guerre, E^5 146. Archives Nationales F^{19} 5601.
10. Maréchal de Castellane, *Journal* (1895), II, 486.

11. Vicomte F.-R. de Chateaubriand, *Mémoires d'Outre Tombe* (1948), v, 281–2.
12. *La Quotidienne*, 29 October 1832.
13. Chateaubriand, op. cit., v, 278.
14. *La Quotidienne*, 25 June 1832.
15. Comtesse C. de Boigne, *Récits d'une tante* (1921), IV, 76.
16. Ibid., 87–8.
17. *La Quotidienne*, 20 April 1833.
18. L. Viennet, *Journal* (1955), 136–7.

11

The Republicans, 1831–1834

"Moi dont la main brisait un trône
Quand elle peut combattre encore
Irai-je la tendre à l'aumône?"

("I whose hand smashed a throne
When it can fight again
Am I going to tender it for alms?")[1]

Général Lamarque, one of the more illustrious victims of the cholera, had been a deputy and leading orator of the left. An impressive funeral was arranged as a political demonstration, and generals and deputies in sympathy with the *mouvement* led the procession. Thousands followed the cortège through the streets on 5 June 1832: some republicans, unknown to most of their leaders, had decided to provoke an insurrection, and legitimists, hoping for a diversion to aid the movement in the Vendée, had distributed arms. The crowds grew whilst La Fayette orated, the mood changing from funereal to riotous. Revolutionary speeches succeeded official orations, and a red flag surmounted by a Phrygian cap appeared: La Fayette and the other notables disappeared. Some republicans attacked the troops brought out to prevent riots. There were false reports that the Hôtel de Ville had been captured, shooting began and barricades were erected. At Saint-Cloud the King heard of what became the first serious insurrectionary threat to his throne: "Amélie, there is trouble in Paris: I am going there",[2] he told the Queen and rode that evening into the capital. The troops under Général de Lobau had been able to keep the insurrection within the Saint-Merri–Marché des Innocents area, although they could not prevent the looting of munitions shops and an arms factory.

On 6 June, the government declared a state of siege in order to facilitate the work of repression. Some liberals such as Broglie were worried by the constitutional aspects of this, and Louis-Philippe himself was unenthusiastic, but a majority in the Cabinet agreed with the army leadership that it was necessary to ensure the punishment of all involved in the attempt. It quickly became obvious that the insurrection could not succeed. The republican leadership was divided: most of those who met at the offices of the *National* decided to wait rather than encourage the revolt, and although Général Clauzel wavered, he refused to place himself at its head. The insurrection lacked leadership, the middle classes were hostile and the workers gave it little support. It did, however, possess the strategic superiority given by street fighting: from barricade to barricade, house to house, the rebels sniped at the invading troops hampered by their unwieldy cannon. Losses were severe on both sides, 800 men died or were seriously injured. Around the Cloître Saint-Merri a desperate group of insurgents resisted the army until late afternoon. Their eventual defeat was the end of what had briefly threatened to be a republican version of 1830. After its failure, the victors regarded it rather as a parody, and the regime was strengthened by the manifestation of determination by the army and National Guard.

Because of the state of siege, insurgents went before *conseils de guerre*, which were for the most part not excessively severe in their penalties, although more certain to convict. The opposition press, however, was outraged and compared the siege with the four ordinances, overlooking the fact that they had supported Dupont in taking such measures against Carlists. One of the convicted appealed to the Cour de Cassation, a body which contained some lawyers of legitimist as well as conscientiously liberal dispositions. The court found the appeal justified on the basis of the clause in the revised Charter which forbade exceptional tribunals, and the government, embarrassed by this verdict, bowed to the decision. As a result, defendants went before the courts, where, after long trials, the penalties were often harsher.

On the second day of the Lamarque riots, 6 June, three leaders of the left, Laffitte, Barrot and the republican Arago, went to the Tuileries bearing a document known as the *Compte rendu*. This had been drawn up in the interval of the 1832 session by a committee where republicans dominated, including as it did La Fayette, Mauguin and Cormenin as well as Barrot and Laffitte. The document which received almost 140 signatures, had obtained republican adhesion by the omission of all monarchical formulae and signs of respect for the sovereign. It claimed that insufficient rigour was being used against the legitimists, and complained that "a bad will" (by which it meant the King) had obstructed the *parti du mouvement*. It argued that the civil list was too high at 12 million francs, Laffitte seeming to have forgotten that he had initially asked the deputies for 18, and protested against the word "subject" which was not in official use. It found French foreign policy excessively weak towards Austria in Italy, and Russia in Poland, criticised the organisation of the army as Carlist, and objected to the measures taken against the National Guards of Lyons, Perpignan and Grenoble because of their opposition tendencies.

Louis-Philippe rejected the criticisms with some vivacity and blamed the recent bloodshed on rioters who used a funeral to fire on the troops. When

Laffitte said that the monarchy should be popular, he replied that he had done nothing to make it less so. He had become king to save France from anarchy and would continue his mission, in spite of daily slanders in the press. Had there ever been, he demanded, "a person against whom more calumnies have been vomited?"[3] To Barrot's and Laffitte's remonstrances that a few republicans near the centres of power were less dangerous to his throne than the reactionary measures of the Périer ministry, and to the more vehement attacks of Arago on the Orléans system, the King replied reiterating that the programme of the Hôtel de Ville was "an infamous lie"[4] propagated by the left: he had kept all his promises, it was a hostile press which was responsible for the nation's troubles.

The failure of both force and persuasion on 6 June 1832 forced the left and the republicans to reconsider their methods. Laffitte and others in opposition withdrew their allegiance from the monarchy and moved towards the republicans, whilst the latter learnt that insurrection was not as easy as they had believed, that it needed to be prepared and organised. It did nothing to lessen the appeal of violence which emerged in a new way. On 19 November 1832, the King was riding to open the parliamentary session when a pistol shot rang out. He lowered his head instinctively, then waved to show that he was unhurt. The would-be assassin was a republican, Bergeron: he was acquitted by a jury and became a hero to those who felt, as he did, that the speediest way to inaugurate a republic was to shoot the monarch. Many other assassination attempts were to follow this, and the constitutional King became a prisoner in his palace, denied the freedom enjoyed by the autocrats of Europe who could walk safely amongst their subjects.

The republican movement was predominantly bourgeois. Its leaders were frequently children of notabilities of Republic or Empire, such as Godefroy Cavaignac, Joseph Guinard or Hippolyte Carnot, son of the Jacobin minister. The older generation had frequently served these regimes and retained their allegiance, Voyer d'Argenson, for example, or Général Lamarque. Doctors and medical students were common in republicanism because, whilst suffering the general dissatisfaction of the lower middle classes as members of an overcrowded profession, they also came into contact with the ills of society. Vignerte, Raspail and Trélat were renowned for their generous service to the poor. Five members of the governing committee of the Société des Droits de l'Homme were doctors: another two were aristocrats, the Breton ex-officer the Comte de Kersausie and the Marquis Le Voyer d'Argenson, an imperial prefect of advanced views. Another two were sons of republican luminaries, and only one, the obscure public crier Delente, could be considered of humble background. Lawyers, journalists and dissatisfied intellectuals, students, refugees, especially Polish and Italian, and retired soldiers or non-commissioned officers were other significant professional groups within the movement.

Although the gap between republicans and working classes somewhat narrowed in the 1840s, it still remained. They had little impact on the true proletariat of the new industrial centres, and elsewhere, such as Marseilles and

Toulon, their influence on the lower classes was restricted by the continuance of a royalist tradition. Their support was most often found amongst the artisans of Paris and Lyons, and they had difficulty in altering this established pattern. When they were honest, the republicans admitted that they were a minority: Sarrut confessed that "the mass of the nation rejects republicanism and wishes order at any price. . . ."[5] They were, admitted another republican Sébastien Commissaire, "a weak minority in the country",[6] and this remained true until the allegiance of the *petite bourgeoisie* to the Orleanist order weakened in 1847. Republicans were also divided amongst themselves: they might unite on hostility to monarchy, but many of them were in reality Bonapartist, others Jacobins and others liberal: some were concerned with liberty, others with national aggrandisement, and others with social needs. They were an élite, basically of the petty official and intellectual classes finding a support in the dissatisfied artisan, and society's alienated or ill-rewarded. This élitism was reflected in the authoritarian or hierarchical structure of most republican organisations; its minority nature fostered a lack of realism which it had in common with legitimism.

Following the events of July 1830, republicans retained for a while the atmosphere of parliamentary opposition, the air of reason which had opposed a regime claiming the sanction of religion, a bourgeois moderation hostile to aristocracy. The society, Aide-toi, le Ciel t'aidera, merely asked that the people's will should be observed, and found this compatible with a property qualification. Carrel in the *National* with his mistrust of popular conservatism and disdain for fellow republicans, retained the parliamentary tradition and opposition to royal power. Yet as these became associated with the failures of 1830, the ex-prefect, Barrot, the dispensable minister Laffitte who hesitated to break finally with the system, and La Fayette who had kissed the new monarchy into life, liberal ideology became discredited. Voltaire, the former hero, was enthroned now as deity of a free-thinking but conservative bourgeoisie, so Rousseau, more inspiring to a romantic generation, and his concept of "general will" entered the republican vocabulary.

Although the republicans were as bourgeois as were Orleanists, the 1830 revolution had made them more conscious of the power and the problems of the lower classes. The programmes of the Amis du Peuple, published in September 1830, attacked bourgeois egoism and spoke of a need to improve the conditions of the worker: but it stressed respect for property and its formulae were more Saint-Simonian than socialist. More radical were the ideas of the aged conspirator Buonarroti, enabled by 1830 to return to Paris. Keeping alive the cult of Robespierre, through him the ideas of Babeuf were spread to Charles-Antoine Teste, Vignerte, Voyer d'Argenson and others. Voyer, a *grand seigneur*, stepfather of the Duc de Broglie, was one of the first to claim publicly that the workers should profit from the Revolution. His pamphlet of 1833, *Boutade d'un riche à sentiments populaires*, asked the poor why they did not rise against their oppressors. No palliatives would suffice: whilst there was inequality there would be poverty and oppression of the poor by the rich. Its author was prosecuted by the government but acquitted by the jury. Charles Teste, brother of Louis-Philippe's future minister, went further in showing not only reasons why the poor should revolt, but also the way to create equality. His *Projet de Constitution républicaine* put all property in the hands of the state, as a result of which, laziness was theft. To inaugurate the reign of virtue a dictatorship would be necessary to destroy opposition by means of terror. Adding the social ideas of Babeuf and Buonarroti to Robespierre's politics, he helped make Jacobinism intellectually respectable amongst republicans.

Buonarroti believed in undermining the social and political structure by means of an élite which, whilst ready to act at the right moment, would meanwhile convert the working classes to republican virtue, a quality more important than ideology. His Charbonnerie Démocratique Universelle, existing in Paris and Lyons where it brought under his influence future revolutionary leaders, professed a Robespierrian radicalism of vaguely socialist nature. Its strongly hierarchical organisational methods were highly influential and were to be seen in the Famille and the Saisons more geared to action than Buonarroti's movement. When he died in 1837, the massive funeral, packed with republican notabilities, was conducted by Teste, and orations by Trélat and others testified to his influence. Buonarroti had indeed done much to spread the cult of violence and conspiracy, teaching contempt for individual rights in the face of the greater good of "social morality".

Yet liberal republicanism continued to be an important part of the movement, although not the most active or broadly influential. Reviled by opponents as "fayettisme" because espoused by the aristocratic La Fayette, it was strong in the parliamentary party, and was represented by Armand Carrel's *National*. Carrel, with Garnier-Pagès, Barthélemy Saint-Hilaire and Cauchois-Lemaire, by 1831 dominated the Aide-toi, le Ciel t'aidera, a pressure group with corresponding associations in thirty-five departments. Generally observing the law, it assisted selected electoral candidates, published brochures, aided "patriotic journals" and gave legal aid. Believing in universal suffrage, but uninterested in social questions, it was very much a group of notables without real roots. The 1834 law on associations was fatal to it: its members had each to decide whether to join an illegal association or not to participate in republican organisational activity.

To educate, one of the intentions of Aide-toi, was the primary aim of the *Association pour l'Instruction Gratuite du Peuple* founded in 1831. Cabet became secretary-general in 1833 but most other influential figures in it were moderates, Barrot, La Fayette, Dupont, Audry, Garnier-Pagès and Cormenin. It was purely Parisian, resulting from the admiration for the workers felt by such men, and initiated by students who did the teaching. Amongst the lecturers were Auguste Comte and Berrier-Fontaine; Victor Lechevallier gave instruction on physics and Laponneraye taught history with a strong republican bias. At its peak, as many as 2,500 adults were receiving courses on a variety of matters, but enthusiasm ebbed as it became less fashionable and more difficult to recruit people who would teach without payment. Implicated by the government in the Lamarque riots, the authorities were highly suspicious of its worker–student links and it succumbed in 1834. It had been a novel endeavour, and typical of a new mentality amongst republicans. Many of those who were patrons of this venture also played a role in the Association pour la Liberté de la Presse. The Vicomte de Cormenin was the moving spirit of this body, designed to give aid to the newspapers of the left which suffered from government prosecution: it too died in 1834.

Many members of these groups also belonged to associations which were directly political in activity and more openly republican. The Société des Amis du Peuple was the first to be created, in the midst of the July insurrection itself. It formed around a nucleus of young men, notably Cavaignac, who desired a republican France and who set about creating it in an unrestrained way which won them the hostility not only of the *Journal des Débats* but also of Carrel's *National*. It tried to whip up the crowds in the summer of 1830 to achieve a more radical constitution, to produce large-scale riots during the trial of the ex-ministers. When in September 1830 National Guardsmen in the neighbourhood of the Rue Montmartre invaded one of their declamatory and inflammatory sessions, their meetings became less open, but they were none the less far from being secret. The main activity was speech-making, in a vocabulary combining Jacobinism and Saint-Simonism, vehement demands were made for vague changes in society, and opposition to the bourgeoisie was primarily political. Raspail when president of the society attempted to make members more conscious of working-class problems by suggesting, unsuccessfully, that they each adopted a number of poor families.

The dominant figure was Godefroy Cavaignac, an eloquent speaker with the appearance of an austere soldier, extreme in his idealism and contemptuous of the vulgar and petty amongst his followers as in the opposition. "He warmly loved but did not esteem his party, which, on the other hand, esteemed but did not love him."[7] As with his hero Robespierre, fraternity for him was more abstract ideal than personal practice. A strong, centralised government and universal suffrage he believed would achieve moral reformation of mankind: monarchy was an evil force which impeded the progress of the human spirit. These ideas were broadly accepted by the society, but the doctors Trélat and Raspail had greater interest in implementing social reforms. Other leading figures were the violently conspiratorial Blanqui and weak well-intentioned Guinard. With these differing personalities and no real discipline, the Amis could form nothing like a political party, and their achievement was the spread of ideas, precise only in allegiance to Robespierre and Marat.

Shortly after the Amis du Peuple, the Société des Droits de l'Homme was created. At first obscure, its organisation survived the Lamarque riots of June 1832 when the government took strong measures against the Amis. Cavaignac succeeded in merging the two and producing a tightly organised society, its structure designed to withstand governmental attack and to enable a large association to exist with the appearance of conforming to the law, which declared associations of over twenty members illegal. The Droits de l'Homme formed sections of less than twenty men each, based on districts of Paris.

With 163 sections, at its peak it had about 3,000 members and the affiliation of clubs throughout France gave it as many more, probably the most important being the *mutuellistes* of Lyons. The sections were grouped in quarters, the quarters in *arrondissements* which obeyed a central committee, whose members' names were unknown to the ranks. It included Cavaignac, Guinard, Kersausie, Lebon, Vignerte, and three deputies, Audry de Puyraveau, Voyer d'Argenson and de Ludre. The secrecy reveals a certain organisational sophistication and approval of conspiratorial action, for as well as spreading the republican gospel, it was organised for action: it attempted to arm each of its members with a rifle and twenty-five cartridges. It made, in the garrison towns where it had branches, determined efforts to infiltrate the army, bribing soldiers to desert or stay and join the Droits de l'Homme. Homage to Jacobins and regicides was represented in the names of its sections: Robespierre, Louvel, Guerre aux Châteaux, Mort aux Tyrans. It had also a communist side, represented by Lebon and Vignerte, and it published a vaguely communist brochure by Cabet. Some of this *babouvisme* may have been a conscious means to attract the working classes, for, whereas the Amis du Peuple had been largely student in its membership, the Droits de l'Homme now aimed to attract workers and was fairly successful: many an artisan was, like Martin Nadaud, flattered at being addressed as an equal by a well-educated bourgeois. Yet complete egalitarianism was not officially professed by the whole society which indeed had no definite programme save belief in strong central government and universal suffrage. Its manifesto published in the *Tribune*, 23 October 1833, added to this a demand for fairer treatment for the workers, and propounded the need for a republican education. But there was a widening gap between Raspail and those stressing good deeds to show republican virtue in action, and others, notably Lebon and Vignerte, who called for immediate action. When the latter demanded an insurrection to celebrate the anniversary of the Lamarque riots, the committee refused, but produced a violent *ordre du jour* which spoke of the people's merciless justice and of watering the tree of liberty with blood.

The moderates, always hoping for support from the Orleanist left, carefully distanced themselves from the ultra-republicans. In the Chamber, Garnier-Pagès disavowed Voyer's socialism, and similarly Carrel wrote favouring universal suffrage but put social reforms vaguely in the future. An elegant, somewhat dandified young journalist, Carrel had been an early deserter from Orleanism, finding it insufficiently radical and excessively pacific abroad. The *National* became republican with him: it appealed to those moderates who preferred the United States to the Jacobins as a model, and its offices served as their headquarters. Although the *National* criticised the immoral egoism of the very rich, it was in no way egalitarian. For the Société pour la Défense de la Liberté de la Presse, Carrel produced a disapproving report on the *Tribune*'s manifesto, criticising in particular the idea of progressive taxation. This led to angry polemics between the two. Marrast and Sarrut, the *Tribune*'s leading contributors, delivered a wider attack on society, and wrote more crudely than the stylist Carrel, but for many were still too moderate.

Within the Droits de l'Homme itself divisions were increasingly apparent. Government prosecution for its attempts to rally popular opposition to the fortification of Paris weakened the society, and during the trial in December 1833 real differences emerged between Raspail and Vignerte. The latter, with Caussidière and Lebon, formed a Société d'Action whose violence frightened less ferocious spirits such as Audry and Voyer. Similar divisions developed wherever republicans were sufficiently numerous. The Lyons branch of the Société des Droits de l'Homme, after being inspired by Cavaignac and affiliated to Paris, soon split between moderates and the extremist men of action led by Baune who gained dominance.

In spite of these divisions, 1833 saw a determined effort to politicise the working classes. Much material was distributed in the workshops, brochures were published and Cabet's *Populaire*, addressed to a lower-class readership, obtained a wide circulation. Determined efforts were made to win support in the army, which 1832 had shown to be a source of strength for the regime. A pamphlet by the left-wing Bonapartist Briqueville was widely distributed in garrison towns in 1833. It exalted the role of the French army and attacked its present small size and leadership. Republicans attended the cafés of the military, republican National Guardsmen at Metz asked officers to banquets. The government were sufficiently worried to order the immediate arrest of any soldier found to belong to the Droits de l'Homme. The non-commissioned officers were not only offended in their patriotism, but their promotion prospects were hindered by a pacific foreign policy. Troop reductions in spring 1834 led to unrest in the army, and an NCO conspiracy was revealed at Lunéville in April, but its collapse showed the limited influence these *petit bourgeois* had over the troops.

In the *cabarets* of Paris republicans gathered to drink and debate or to drink and sing. Often the *goguettes*, singing societies, were republican institutions, specialising in radical songs and where the singer frequently introduced his performance with a political discourse. At Les Infernaux, the most famous republican chansonnier Hegesippe Moreau sang songs like "Le Peuple a faim" or "Le Prolétaire", in which he prophesied the triumph of the working poor over the wealthy. Such poems as his elegy for the Lamarque rioters who had died express his idealistic view of working-class attitudes and an exaggerated view of their role in republicanism. Other songs were less noble. One of the most popular, by Altaroche, who became chief editor of the *Charivari*, was about the King, an equivalent in rhyme to Daumier's cartoon Gargantua:

"Gros, gras et bête
En quatre mots, c'est son portrait:
Toisez le des pieds à la tête,
Aux yeux de tous, il apparait,
Gros, gras et bête.

Gros, gras et bête,
En pelle s'élarge sa main,
En poire s'allonge sa tête,

En tonneau croît son abdomen,
Gros, gras et bête."[8]

("Gross, fat and stupid
In four words, that is his portrait:
Measure him from foot to head,
In the eyes of all, he appears,
Gross, fat and stupid.

Gross, fat and stupid,
Into a shovel grows his hand,
Into a pear grows his head,
Into a barrel grows his abdomen,
Gross, fat and stupid.")

There was a multitude of newspapers, which reached a readership in wine shops and reading rooms. Carrel's *National* was the leading republican journal, with an intellectual readership. Its rival, the *Tribune*, with about 1,500 subscribers, spoke a more violent language and, because undergoing almost permanent prosecution by the government, was the largest recipient of the charity of *L'Association pour la Liberté de la Presse*. Other newspapers were more personal in tone. The *Bon Sens* was created, shortly after the Lamarque riots in June 1832, with the intention of republicanising the workers. The editor, Cauchois-Lemaire, was, however, too moderate for many of his backers, and the writing which had originally been simple reverted soon to a more typical journalistic style. It was soon overtaken by *Le Populaire* of Cabet, an inexpensive weekly journal, catering better for the working classes by clear, effective writing, and was able to gain a readership of 12,000 for a short while. Raspail, however, needed substantial aid from his admirer Kersausie to be able to publish the *Réformateur* in 1834: it presented his programme for total reform of the state, less centralist than those demanded by his fellow republicans, and he also differed from them in his pacifism.

There were almost sixty provincial journals by 1834. Most depended upon benefactions: few had over 1,000 subscribers and some, like the *Sentinelle des Vosges* at Epinal, had less than 100 and extremely brief existences. Often one man would do everything, such as Trélat at Clermont, who edited and wrote alone *Le Patriote* which served central France. These newspaper offices served as public committee rooms for the local republicans. At Nancy, for example, the republican deputy, the Comte de Ludre, supported and directed the *Patriote de la Meurthe*, led the party and recruited *sous-officiers* from the Lunéville garrison. Other garrison towns, notably Metz and Strasbourg, had strong republican groups and newspapers. The influence of Lyons was felt in nearby industrial towns, such as Saint-Étienne where Caussidière was leader. The republicans were a powerful minority at Grenoble where the local Droits de l'Homme organisation had 400 members, and where Garnier-Pagès was deputy. There were enough republicans in legitimist Marseilles to produce *Le Sémaphore*, and in Toulouse to return a republican deputy, Joly. In the far south-west in the military bases at Bayonne and Perpignan, where Arago held a leading role, republicanism was influential. Brittany had a few thriving centres, notably Rennes. At Rouen there was an extremist society affiliated to the Droits de l'Homme, and Berrier-Fontaine had some success organising small groups in his native Orne department.

Throughout most of France, republicanism was a tiny urban minority. Only in the north-east could it be considered potentially equal to Orleanism and stronger than legitimism. Lyons and Paris were its great centres of strength, but it had little success in recruiting the proletariat of the towns of the industrial north. Perreux estimates that in the 60 departments of centre, south, north and west there were barely 10,000 active republicans, hardly as many as in the 20 departments of the east. Republicanism very much depended over most of France upon a rich or influential man: it varied between groups gathering in cafés and those associations of Metz or the Jura which drilled for revolution or war: it was split between liberals and terrorists, Girondins and Jacobins, exemplified in Paris by *National* against *Tribune* and in Lyons by *Précurseur* against *Glaneuse*.

Gérard de Nerval was briefly imprisoned in Sainte-Pélagie, and describes how the authorities took care to separate the republicans into dormitories with regard even to nuances of opinion: there were the centralists, the federalists, and socialists, not numerous as yet.[9] There were also a few Bonapartists, and legitimists, particularly in the aftermath of the Rue des Prouvaires and the Vendée, the Swiss troops disbanded in 1830, "the plebs of the legitimist party".[10] Some inmates crossed political boundaries: the Vicomte de La Rochefoucauld organised concerts for both parties, and formed a strong friendship with Germain Sarrut, editor of the *Tribune*. But for the most part the two sides kept apart in their distinct quarters. They would sing to maintain their spirits. The legitimists celebrated Henri V's birthday with their song,

"Non, non, Philippe, ah! garde toi jamais
D'en concevoir la coupable espérance!
Par la bassesse, achetant des succès,
Tu peux, Philippe, être roi des Français,
Mais Henri Cinq est roi de France."

("No, no, Philippe, ah! guard yourself from ever
Conceiving the culpable hope!
By baseness, purchasing success,
You can, Philippe, be king of the French,
But Henri V is king of France.")

whilst republicans chanted with more bloodthirsty flair,

"Louis-Philippe a merité
D'avoir le poing coupé et la tête tranchée.
Aux armes! Aux armes!
Vengeons-nous, vengeons-nous ou mourrons!"[11]

("Louis-Philippe has merited
To have his hands and head chopped off.
To arms! To arms!
Let us revenge ourselves, revenge ourselves or die!")[11]

REFERENCES

1. Hégesippe Moreau, "Le Prolétaire", in P. Brochon (ed.), *La Chanson Française* (1956), 129–30.
2. F. Guizot, *Mémoires pour servir à l'histoire de mon temps* (1858), II, 347.
3. Archives Nationales, 300.AP.32.
4. Ibid.
5. Vicomte de La Rochefoucauld, *Memoires* (1837), XII, 325.
6. S. Commissaire, *Mémoires et Souvenirs* (Lyons, 1888), 77.
7. L. de la Hodde, *Histoire des Sociétés Secrètes* (1850), 51.
8. Altaroche, in Brochon, op. cit., 155.
9. Gérard de Nerval, *Mes Prisons* (in *Œuvres*, Pléiade edition, 1952), I, 76.
10. Ibid.
11. T. Muret, *A Travers Champs* (1858), 75–83.

12

The Ministry of 11 October 1832 and Ministerial Instability, 1834–1835

"A mesure qu'ils ont fait une Constitution
écrite avec de l'encre, ils s'écrivent:
'En voilà pour toujours'. . . ."

("As soon as they have made a Constitution
written in ink, they cry:
'And here it is forever' . . . .")[1]

"En ce moment, vous changez des ministres comme un malade change de place dans son lit. Ces oscillations révèlent la décrépitude de votre gouvernement. Vous avez un systeme de filouterie politique qui sera retourné contre vous, car la France se lassera de ces escobarderies. . . ."

("At this moment, you change ministers like a sick man changes positions in his bed. These oscillations reveal the decrepitude of your government. You have a system of political fraud which will be turned against you, because France tires of these hypocrisies. . . .")[2]

After the death of Périer in April 1832 his Cabinet continued in office. The King relished the position of control which the absence of a *président* and the compliance of Montalivet (who had been appointed to the Ministry of the Interior), Soult and Sébastiani gave him. Yet the suspicious failure to capture the Duchesse de Berry, the clumsy arrest of leading legitimists and the Cour de Cassation's adverse decision over the state of siege cast doubts on the government's ability: Talleyrand, ambassador in London, said that a leaderless France was losing prestige abroad. The King resigned himself to replacing Périer, and hoped that Dupin, formerly his legal adviser, would fill the post, after his first candidate, Talleyrand, declined it. Throughout the summer a tiring succession of negotiations proceeded, a duet of royal caresses and coquettish refusals by Dupin, who, happiest playing to the gallery when in opposition, had little desire for office. His demands, the removal of Sébastiani and Montalivet, and a more centrist orientation of policy, increasingly angered the King who eventually accepted the advice to turn to the Duc de Broglie, whom Talleyrand and Thiers recommended because of his reputation for probity and good relations with English politicians. But Louis-Philippe found it hard to accept Broglie's terms, the replacement of Montalivet by Guizot, and made a last attempt to form a ministry with Soult, Thiers and Dupin. Failing, he resigned himself to the doctrinaires' dominance, but he had made Broglie, like Périer, suspicious that royal preference was for the centre.

However, Thiers did not accept Guizot's entry gladly, and even tried to persuade him against it. Before agreeing to become Minister of the Interior, he obtained the inclusion of Humann as Finance Minister to strengthen the non-doctrinaire element. Maréchal Soult made no difficulty about adding the presidency to his defence portfolio. Without strong views or party affiliation, he was stern, even brutal, to his subordinates, but obsequiously flexible towards the King, if his *amour propre* were flattered, which was a constant task. A firm and efficient administrator, he possessed important authority in the army, but his political incompetence could make him a liability. At least his prestige helped cover the unpopularity of the doctrinaire ministers, Broglie who became Foreign Minister, and Guizot at Public Instruction. Because Guizot was a practising Protestant, it was believed he could not be responsible for religious affairs and these went to the nominal Catholic Barthe who remained Garde des Sceaux. Comtes de Rigny and d'Argout stayed at the Marine and Commerce, and early in 1833 Sébastiani was to re-enter the Cabinet as Minister without Portfolio. The Cabinet was officially announced on 11 October 1832.

Although he was not *président du conseil*, the dominant figure amongst these able men was the Duc de Broglie. Few disputed his intelligence and nobility of character, but equally none of his friends would have disputed his own admission that he was "unskilled in the management of men".[3] Too high minded to deceive, too proud to flatter, disadvantaged by an appearance of hauteur and, unlike his fellow aristocrat Molé, unprepared to mitigate it with charm, Broglie secretly disliked politics and despised politicians. Although a laborious and effective administrator and capable of delivering magnificent statements of principle, making concessions and seeking popularity disgusted him. He abhorred absolutism and legitimism, showing this in the cold civility with which he treated the *corps diplomatique*: only with British ambassador Greville was he on friendly or confident terms. His own rigorous ideology was a development of English Whiggism. Barrot, a political opponent, speaks of "the elevation of his sentiments, his true liberalism",[4] but whilst his ideas were not essentially different from mainstream Orleanism, they were combined with religious and ethical thinking which the average deputy found antipathetic. Guizot, who admired him, upheld similar beliefs with less rigour and greater personal ambition. Lacking popularity, his intellectual and oratorical talents none the less made him leading spokesman of the *parti de résistance*. Bitter against the men of disorder who had destroyed the liberal vision of 1830, he was concerned to repress them by force, but also to destroy their ideological roots.[5] The task of the *résistance* was, he claimed, not only vast but entirely novel: in fighting revolution in spirit and action, "it undertakes to conquer entirely by laws, and by laws rendered and applied in the presence of liberty".[6]

As 1833 opened, it seemed that the government might be able to proceed undisturbed with the work of establishing the July Monarchy and in converting France to conservatism and liberalism. The Duc de Reichstadt was dead, taking Bonapartist hopes with him; the Duchesse de Berry was discredited and the Carlists despondent; the republicans had been defeated and were weakened by division. Guizot could confidently declare to the deputies, "Uprisings are dead, clubs are dead, revolutionary spirit, that spirit of blind warfare that seemed momentarily to have seized the entire nation, is dead."[7] A furious opposition compared the new ministry with that of Polignac, but conservatives were relieved, especially as the ministers were able to introduce themselves to the Chambers with two *faits accomplis*. Broglie had despatched an army to assist the Belgians against the Dutch, and Thiers, on his own initiative, had taken the unscrupulous but effective action which captured the Duchesse de Berry. Furthermore, the latter's pregnancy enabled the government to brave the fury of the left and avoid a trial.

Yet although the ministry won majority support, the election of Dupin to the position of president of the Chamber had put an opponent of the Cabinet in a position of influence. During the summer of 1832, Guizot wrote, the two Frances of the *Journal des Débats* and the *Constitutionnel*, represented by himself and Odilon Barrot, had struggled for the indefinable soul of Dupin. The latter had refused to give himself to either side. To be able to launch sarcasms right and left, to betray friends and attack enemies, presenting this in the guise of judicial fairness, delighted him, and the president's chair gave him an effective platform for eight years. Jean-Jacques Dupin appeared a caricature of the provincial bourgeois, although he was son of an important imperial functionary. Even when calling upon the King, he wore the heavy, clumsy boots which persuaded the inhabitants of Clamecy that he remained a loyal son of the Nièvre. "A trimmer of the worst kind"[8] Rémusat called him; he could change directions in mid-oration if he saw that opinions were against him. Broglie, whose philosophical conservative liberalism seemed metaphysical and abstruse to him, referred contemptuously to arguments "in the manner of Dupin, with street-corner logic".[9] But his method of expressing commonplaces with self-confident pungency gained him a popularity which the other never possessed. He was more the symbol than the leader of the *tiers parti*: indeed he would claim that this did not really exist but was rather the more independent deputies of the majority. Guizot described it in his memoirs as a mixture of "indecisive honest men and meticulous intriguers", the timid and the ambitious, the weak and the vain, which troubled the cohesion of the conservatives.[10] They were united essentially by dislike of the doctrinaires, but had no wish to compromise themselves by joining the opposition.

When the three leading personalities of the Cabinet, Broglie, Thiers and Guizot, were in accord, as usually they were, the King found himself impotent and neutralised. "It is Casimir Périer in three persons",[11] he claimed. This more widely spread strength, however, enabled the Cabinet to surmount intrigue and fight routine parliamentary battles whilst making 1833 extremely productive in legislation. There was Guizot's law on primary education of 28 June, which provided the basis of a free national education system. A law on *conseils généraux* and *d'arrondissement* made these bodies elective. Broglie reformed the consular service, making it less a form of foreign sinecure and integrating it with France's international political and commercial needs. The government of the colonies was reorganised to make it more regular, constitutional and less dictatorial. Thiers, whose imagination was fired by public works, passed laws to facilitate expropriation for acts of public utility, with indemnity decided by a jury, a law to aid state public works, and a programme of large expenditure which he pushed through the parsimonious Chamber of Deputies. Finance Minister Humann fretted but continued the work of Baron Louis in restoring French finances to health.

There soon came proof that prophecies of the end of internal disorder were premature. This was not entirely unwelcome to the doctrinaires, for their ability to lead the conservatives depended upon crisis which would remove the deputies from leaders amongst less dogmatic conservatives and men of the centre. Disorder concentrated minds and encouraged discipline: "We always need a little danger to make us reasonable",[12] Rémusat wrote to Guizot. Amongst conservatives, the acquittal of Bergeron and the Cour de Cassation's ruling on the siege had added to their dislike of juries and their suspicion of the magistrature. Increasing disturbance in spring 1833 led to demands for stronger legislation: "Present legality kills us",[13] cried the deputy Viennet.

The question of fortifications provided the opposition with a rallying cry. The King and his War Minister were both firmly convinced of the utility of fortifications round Paris for both defence and internal security reasons. Soult took his enthusiasm for the forts to the extent of spending money on preliminary work which his budget had not granted. Humann objected to this expenditure and the doctrinaires, who found Soult troublesome and were rewarded by his bluff military dislike, did nothing to support the scheme. The issue was seized upon by the opposition press as a plot to destroy liberty by the building of Bastilles, and there was a campaign which revealed itself in some cries of "Down with the forts!" from National Guardsmen during the generally successful celebrations which commemorated the July Revolution. Viennet had the *Tribune* brought to trial by the deputies for insulting them as "a prostituted Chamber". It was pointed out that Barthe, now Garde des Sceaux, had acted for the defence, when the Restoration had taken similar action. None the less, the paper was convicted. Cavaignac and Marrast defiantly repeated their accusations of corruption in the faces of the shocked deputies; and in a trial of members of the Droits de l'Homme for plots against the state, the accused hurled outrageous insults at the court, and were then found innocent by the jury. A further humiliation for authority occurred when Gisquet, prefect of police, tried to prevent public criers hawking inflammatory brochures. He had no legal justification, as Rodde, an editor of the *Bon Sens*, proved when dressed as a crier he braved the police and distributed republican brochures to crowds outside the Bourse. It was obvious too that laws on association were being thwarted not only by the Société des Droits de l'Homme but by a growing number of workers' societies of primarily economic purpose who created divisions of twenty numbers, which would delegate representatives to a central committee to treat with employees. It appeared to the middle classes that the structure of society was threatened, and the government was reminded by such events as the seizure of 600 rifles in July, part of a plot by ammunition-manufacturing polytechnicians, that conspiracy remained a threat.

That summer the King undertook journeys in the provinces, which in his words were "very happy, very fatiguing and highly gratifying",[14] and it appeared that the new dynasty had at last established itself. Security and relaxation, however, made the unpopularity of the doctrinaires more irksome as their unyielding conservatism appeared less necessary to those just as interested in repressing disorder but unwilling to adhere to a consistent philosophy. None the less, when the 1834 session opened, a large majority welcomed the first of the Ministry's restrictive measures, Barthe's bill on public criers. Municipal authorisation was made obligatory and it could be revoked for misconduct. A tax was imposed on productions of more than two sheets, infractions to be tried, not by jury, but by a correctional tribunal. Violent protests erupted, but the police, the *sergents de ville*, with some brutality, kept rioting under control. This week of disorder gave the government a favourable opportunity to introduce a more important bill stating that associations of over twenty members were illegal, whether or not they were subdivided, and even if they met irregularly. In the case of infractions, fines were increased and the possibility of imprisonment added for all members, and not only the leader, as before. All associations were subject to the law, including those which appeared wholly inoffensive, for fear that the republicans might use them as a cover for seditious activities. Distrust of the jury was again manifest in the removal from its jurisdiction of offences connected with associations. In the case of crimes against the state, the Court of Peers would be called upon to judge, and lesser offences would go before the *tribunaux correctionnels*.

The liberal advocates of these laws were following the Revolution's restrictive legislation of 1791, and the Napoleonic *Code Civil*, but apart from their own consciences, were in danger of infringing a stipulation of their own 1830 Charter which demanded that political offences be tried by jury. So the tribunals could play only a limited role concerned with infringements of regulation on public crying and association, although governments often tried to interpret this widely. As it was, the ministers and their supporters defended their law, not on principle, but as a necessity to save the state. Guizot spoke with sorrow about the hopes of liberty defeated by disorder, for which he blamed republicans and their *gauche dynastique* apologists.[15] Yet their opponents could reply, as did Berryer: "There is something more hideous than revolutionary cynicism; it is the cynicism of apostates."[16] Under the Restoration, Guizot had been a member of Aide-toi, le Ciel t'aidera, Broglie had founded an association to protect the freedom of the press and Barthe had been a *carbonaro*: now these men stamped upon liberties they had formerly demanded. To the doctrinaires, sure of their liberal credentials, their actions seemed impeccable. They thought more about the intellectual and philosophical aspects of the problem than did one like Thiers who believed in the power of the state above all else. The doctrinaires also differed from average conservatives, claims Rémusat, in that they did not lose faith in liberty itself, but because of their faith were the more severe on the faults committed in liberty's name.[17] Few save the doctrinaires found such reasoning very convincing, but the argument during the debates presenting the very existence of the regime as being in the balance, seems to have been an effective appeal, for the bill became law by 246 to 154 votes.

On the whole the July Monarchy used these considerable new powers mildly, attacking only dangerous enemies, leaving untouched religious and political associations, which, albeit hostile, were no real threat in terms of force. The law was primarily intended to frighten enemies: thus there could be no limitations in its terms or length of applicability. The ministry responsible for it fell not long after its triumph. In March 1834, an unexpected parliamentary reversal would bring about its modification and inaugurate a period of political instability. In its one and a half years, the Ministry had accomplished much at home and abroad, but had failed in its ambition to defeat philosophical and political anarchy. Its inability to create a stable majority was shown by its defeat in the Chamber of Deputies, and as Broglie left office, republicans were preparing for another effort in the streets.

It is unsurprising that men with secure positions, such as the Comte de Rambuteau, prefect of Paris, or the Comte de Sainte-Aulaire, ambassador to Vienna, should not have wished to exchange them for the brief power of a minister. In its eighteen years, the July Monarchy had seventeen ministries, fifteen of them in its first ten years, and numerous single changes of portfolio besides. However, the instability was to some extent superficial. Guizot, for example, held office for thirteen of these years, and other ministers were members of several Cabinets, Thiers and Persil, for example, or Duchâtel, holding a record with eight ministries. The prime cause of this instability was that Cabinets were coalitions of nuances, rather than representatives of united parties. Attempts to increase one's faction from within (as when Guizot destroyed the Molé Cabinet in 1837 by insisting on a doctrinaire Minister of the Interior), or pressure from outside, when deputies insisted on a post for one of their group as the price of their support, occasioned constant change. A homogeneous Cabinet such as Molé's second, based upon one section of the conservative party, risked losing its majority.

"To make a ministry", wrote Stendhal, "it is a question above all of pleasing the King, pleasing the Chamber of Deputies almost as much and, finally, not shocking the poor Chamber of Peers too much."[18] Perhaps this overstates the role of the King for there were many occasions when he had to resign himself to ministers he disliked, but the monarch undoubtedly played a large role, almost invariably constructive. For a time in 1835 he opposed the formation of the Broglie–Thiers–Guizot ministry, but such opposition to the will of leading politicians was rare. Usually he attempted to end their bickering and speedily to create a new ministry. The King was needed to provide in the Cabinet a discipline which was otherwise rarely present amongst individuals not bound by party loyalties. When in summer 1836 Thiers, in conflict with the King over Spain, advocated a Cabinet resignation, some ministers were indignant at this attempt to bind them. Humann's unilateral action over *rentes* in 1835 was an extreme form of ministerial independence, but there were many other smaller instances, embarrassing but not fatal to the Cabinets concerned. The King was often necessary to discipline recalcitrant ministers, to impose a common line on them, or to charm them from submitting resignations when they were upset at being thwarted.

The *président du conseil* had no established legal position, nor was he an official party leader. The first ministry of the July Monarchy, a collection of founding fathers who regarded themselves as equals, had no *président*, but Dupont as Garde des Sceaux was given an honorary pre-eminence. After the death of Périer, there was no *président* for some months, nor was there in the emergency Cabinet of specialists which the King formed in a period of political crisis in March 1839. These are exceptions: it became a political necessity for a Cabinet to have a head. A pattern was never imposed, but the *présidents* of the July Monarchy are of two basic varieties, the military figure-head and the politician. The Cabinet of 11 October 1832 gave the presidency to Maréchal Soult because he provided a covering prestige for an unpopular ministry, and because to have granted any of the politicians pre-eminence would have been dangerous (as was shown when Broglie took it in 1835). Soult became an embarrassment, and 1834 saw a succession of unsatisfactory "illustrious swords". With Broglie, Thiers and Molé, the system then reverted to the *président* being a genuinely political figure, but the difficulties of this were shown in 1837 when Guizot and Molé struggled for pre-eminence. The year 1840 produced at last a stable arrangement whereby Guizot dominated a fairly homogeneous ministry, whose figure-head *président* was again Soult. This combination of the two systems produced a secure ministry, but the dangers of this immobility were perhaps greater than those of the instability of 1834.

Besides the presidency, there were eight portfolios: Foreign Affairs, the Interior, Finance, War, Navy, Commerce with Public Works, Public Instruction, and Justice, either of which two last was accompanied by responsibility for religious affairs. In 1839 Dufaure was put in charge of a separate Ministry for Public Works, and this separation thereafter became the rule. There were also ministers without Portfolio, as compensation for Sébastiani and de Rigny left without posts in 1833 and 1835, and in 1830 to add the political weight of Périer, Laffitte and Dupin to the first Cabinet of the regime. There were also under-secretaries, often young men of promise helping an overworked minister, such as Thiers at Finance in 1830, and Rémusat, under-secretary for the peer Gasparin, Minister of the Interior in September 1836, or to add extra political support, which explains the presence of Malleville and Billaut as under-secretaries in Thiers's second ministry. When the *président* was a politician he was usually also Minister of Foreign Affairs. Because of its political role and electoral importance, the Interior was the other most important ministry, and was for the same reason the worst organised and most unwieldy. When an "illustrious sword" was *président du conseil*, he was also War Minister.

The personnel of the ministers reflects the Orleanist political world, but not with complete faithfulness. There were more peers, twenty-two of a total of sixty ministers, than the lesser political importance of the Upper House would suggest. Under Laffitte, and in Thiers's first and Molé's second ministries, both Cabinets without a party majority, peers were equal in number to deputies: in the latter case, the fact that the most important posts were held by peers was a serious weakness. However, the number of aristocrats was small. Comte Molé and the Duc de Broglie were the only true *grands seigneurs*: the Comtes de Montalivet, d'Argout and de Rigny were of lesser families which had become prominent since 1789, and Sébastiani and Duchâtel had less convincing claims to nobility. Most ministers had held official posts, prefectoral or political. The Ministers of War and the Marine had careers in the services, and the Gardes des Sceaux were invariably drawn from the legal profession. There was frequently professional experience to be found in the Ministry of Public Instruction, where Villemain, Cousin (both peers) and Guizot had all been lecturers at the Sorbonne. If simple landowning aristocracy was less important amongst ministers than it was in Parliament as a whole, the economic professions were perhaps rather more so. Two presidents, Périer and Laffitte, were bankers, as was Alexandre Gouin, Thiers's Minister of Commerce in 1840. Humann was a wealthy former merchant with important interests in iron, as had Comte Jaubert. Gautier, briefly Minister of Finance in the King's non-political crisis ministry of March 1839, was a merchant, and Cunin-Gridaine, responsible for commerce throughout the 1840s, was a wealthy textile manufacturer at Sedan. In all ministries, therefore, the regime tended to seek professional expertise, and the standard of legislation and administration was high, perhaps at the expense of originality and imagination. It also tended to install the interest groups at the summit of government, thereby virtually making them official. The interests of the legal profession or of forge owners might easily appear identical with the interests of the nation. The largest interest, however, cutting through party and faction, was that which disliked high taxation and distrusted governmental expenditure. Because Broglie had not stooped to amicable conspiracy in the corridors of the Palais Bourbon and his rigid hauteur ruffled the *amours propres* of the deputies, the ministry of 11 October which had just received a massive vote of confidence, proved vulnerable to this.

Reparations to America for ships seized by Napoleon proved one of those unpopular measures, removed from the simple choice between *mouvement* and *résistance*, which at various intervals would temporarily ally the government's less faithful friends with its permanent enemies. The Restoration had avoided the issue, but the July Monarchy, needing allies, had agreed in 1831 when Sébastiani was Foreign Minister, to pay the United States 25 million francs: a substantial sum, in return for which an agreement favourable to French wine exports was only slight compensation. Only in March 1834 did the matter finally come before the deputies. In the course of a long and virulent debate, far right and left united to attack what they claimed was Broglie's pusillanimous policy. Berryer, by his well-argued speech, seems to have swayed deputies outside his own party and some felt it difficult to be less patriotic than the Restoration. The feeling that the payment was humiliating, dislike of any expenditure, and a wish to snub Broglie (it was noticed that friends of Soult, who had come to loathe Broglie, abstained from voting), produced a parliamentary revolt: to the general amazement, the government proposal was defeated by eight votes. Broglie immediately resigned, congratulating himself that he was no Soult threatening continually to resign but never doing so, and was followed by Sébastiani. Rightly seeing the vote as a whim on the part of a few deputies rather than a vote of no confidence, Broglie persuaded the other ministers to remain in office, particularly as internal order appeared threatened, and elections appeared inevitable. In April 1835, the deputies, frightened of the consequences of another act of rebellion, were to give Broglie's reparations proposal an enormous majority.

Broglie hoped that he had given a salutary lesson to the political world, but in fact his resignation led to undignified squabbles and a period of uncertainty. The King, happy to lose the difficult Duc, hoped to replace him by Molé who had ideas closer to his own on foreign policy, but this was thwarted by Guizot's refusal to serve with him. Instead "the Guizot society"[19] as the King termed the doctrinaires, ousted those who did not share their views, Barthe and d'Argout who were consoled by the presidency of the Cour des Comptes and the governorship of the Banque, replacing them by the strongly conservative Persil and brilliant young Comte Duchâtel. The latter took only Commerce, however, and Thiers, displeased by the increase in doctrinaire representation, was compensated in his architectural ambitions by adding Public Works to the Interior Ministry. The main weaknesses were that Amiral de Rigny, who replaced Broglie at Foreign Affairs, was of insufficient stature for his post, and in the continued irritations provoked by that bulky figure-head, Maréchal Soult.

The ministerial crisis which ended with the announcement of the new ministry on 4 April had been short, lasting only four days. This was as well, because on 9 April insurrection broke out in Lyons, followed by serious trouble in other towns, including the capital. Thiers repressed the disorders with vigour, and the Cabinet fought elections in June 1834 with success. This achieved, the politicians could again take up the business of intrigue. Guizot and Thiers seized the first opportunity of ridding themselves of Soult, finding a pretext in the controversy over how Algeria should be governed. The Minister of War felt there was no alternative to a military governor: Thiers and Guizot, claiming, with some justice, that such government had been unsuccessful heretofore, demanded a civilian government, and promoted the candidature of the influential Duc Decazes. This led to angry arguments, and when Soult threatened to resign, the ministers cheerfully persisted. His bluff called, the Marshal went to the Tuileries and, weeping, submitted his resignation. The King warned that Gérard's incapacity would prove more embarrassing than Soult's irritations, but, pressed by the ministers, he charmed the hesitant soldier into accepting the presidency and on 18 July 1834, the *Moniteur* announced the replacement of one "illustrious sword" by another. Shamelessly, Guizot and Thiers quickly realised the inconvenience of a civilian governor in Algeria and acceded to the demand of the new Minister of War that control should remain with the military: Decazes was compensated with the position of *grand réferendaire* of the Chamber of Peers.

The conservative government had weakened itself at a critical juncture. Soult had been a buttress to the politics of resistance, Gérard was not. Averse from public speaking, he feared the unpopularity incurred by association with the doctrinaires. Like his friends in the *tiers parti*, he desired an amnesty for political prisoners, especially the insurgents of April 1834, but Thiers and Guizot and the doctrinaires refused to contemplate the idea. On 29 October, after only three months as *président du conseil*, Gérard seized the opportunity to resign, precipitating the longest ministerial crisis yet.

It was complicated by the *tiers parti*, grown in numbers, many of the newly elected wishing to avoid making engagements. Some notable recruits joined it: Léon de Maleville because he found the doctrinaires insufficiently liberal; two offshoots of the imperial aristocracy, the charming Comte Mathieu de La Redorte and dandified Comte Roger, who found the doctrinaires personally uncongenial and already possessing a superfluity of talented young politicians; the "oratorical animal"[20] Sauzet, personable, eloquent but of pliant opinions; and the more considerable figure of Dufaure, an advocate who had earned enough to enter politics, and then retired, liberal and independent.

It was Etienne, editor of the *tiers parti Constitutionnel*, former censor of the Empire, turned liberal under the Restoration, who drew up the 1834 *adresse* which was to take its place in doctrinaire demonology. Rigid conservatives were in a minority on the commission, and the *adresse*, the Chamber's reply to the King's speech, contained hints of disapproval of the ministry beneath a vague endorsement of conservative policy. The government could not oppose such an indefinite document, but once it had passed, the *Temps* and *Constitutionnel* led the opposition press in stressing and exaggerating its covert hostility. When Gérard's brusque resignation opened a new ministerial crisis late in October 1834, the *tiers parti* was no longer disposed to adopt a passive attitude.

As before, the King sent for Molé, not wishing, he said, to cede his throne to "His Majesty M. de Broglie and His Royal Highness M. Guizot".[21] Faced with Guizot's refusal to serve under anyone but Broglie and Dupin's excessive demands, Molé abandoned the attempt. The ministers themselves were indecisive and divided: amidst the journeys to the Tuileries and the salon plotting, personalities became more incompatible and the crisis deeper. The doctrinaires engaged confidently in strategic war with the King, joking about his predicament. With the exceptions of Persil and Jacob, they resigned, recommending the King to accept a *tiers parti* ministry: they expected this to fail and, on their return, to be able to overcome any monarchical opposition.

Louis-Philippe's annoyance with the doctrinaires caused him briefly to favour the ludicrous attempt. Dupin helped assemble a *tiers parti* Cabinet but would not compromise himself as a member, although he pushed his brother, the statistician Baron Charles Dupin, into the Navy Ministry as a sign of his support. The ministry was improvised with hurried and confused negligence. It included Passy at Finance, Teste at Commerce and Sauzet at Public Instruction: in addition, Bresson, ambassador in Berlin, was called to fill the post of Foreign Affairs, and Persil, equally devoted to office and to the King, the only conservative member, remained Garde des Sceaux. Most members were fairly insignificant, and none more so than the man chosen to lead it and also to be Minister of the Interior, Hugues Maret, Duc de Bassano. A high-ranking administrator under Napoleon, he had the disadvantage of considerable debts. Learning that with his allowance as *président du conseil*, Bassano would at last have an income, queues of creditors gathered expectantly outside his home. The new ministers had little confidence, and fear of ridicule led Teste and Passy to tell the King they could not serve after all. Meanwhile Bresson had speedily refused the unexpected appointment. Thus ended "the day of the Dupins": the ministry announced on 10 November collapsed three days later and the unfortunate Bassano sank back into insolvent obscurity.

The King, always disgusted by ministerial crises, when in face of "the antipathies, the predilections, the demands, the coteries", he experienced "cruel wranglings and immense embarrassments",[22] had unwisely encouraged an attempt which could not succeed. As for Dupin and the *tiers parti* who had demanded that royal power retreat before the Chamber of Deputies and a *président* with real authority, they had tried to create a ministry under an unknown, ageing nonentity, whose War Minister and interim Foreign Secretary, Général Bernard, was a royal aide-de-camp, and which included Persil, as staunch an upholder of the royal prerogative as the King himself. The attempt severely damaged *tiers parti* hopes and prestige, as the doctrinaires had expected.

The impossibility of government leaving conservative hands having been shown, the King had to look to his former ministers. Because he and Thiers did not wish for Broglie as president, they again resorted to an "illustrious sword" in the person of Maréchal Mortier, Duc de Trévise, another of those brave Napoleonic officers promoted above their talent in times of warfare.

Honest and timid, wrote Rémusat, "not one of his words announces the least intelligence".[23] On 18 November a new ministry was constituted, different from that which existed before the crisis only in Mortier and a new Navy Minister, Amiral Duperré. Thus a three-week crisis, whilst failing to produce any real change, had none the less weakened the system. In particular, Thiers, his ambitions exacerbated by the aged Talleyrand during his visits to the salon of the Prince's niece, the Duchesse de Dino, was increasingly chafing at the dominance of the doctrinaires. Whilst agreeing with them on action necessary to maintain order, he feared their unpopularity and disliked their rigid philosophy. He endeavoured to distance himself from Guizot by stressing his own revolutionary allegiance at a time when the other was accused of being an *émigré*. None the less, the ministers jointly attacked the *tiers parti*, demanding and obtaining a vote of confidence which removed some of the uncertainties caused by the ambiguous *adresse*. On the decision to hold a mammoth trial of insurgents of the previous April, they obtained a majority only of twenty-eight, less than half that received on the vote of confidence, a sign of nervousness amongst governmental deputies.

The sudden resignation of Mortier in late February precipitated a new crisis. So timid he could scarcely speak in the Chamber, unable to dominate the Cabinet, the Marshal left office on the brink of nervous collapse. The politicians were determined to avoid another such expedient. The King's choice for *président*, Comte Molé, being again rendered impossible by the refusal of Thiers and the doctrinaires to contemplate the amnesty for political offences which he demanded, the usual advisers were summoned to the Tuileries; Dupin and Gérard, Soult from his estate at Saint-Amand, and Sébastiani from London where he was now ambassador, but all these counsellors could not alter the inevitable result. Soult, turning to the left, interviewed Barrot and Mauguin, and proposed Bignon as a minister which Louis-Philippe refused to contemplate. A meeting of vociferous conservatives at the home of the rich deputy Fulchiron showed that there was a growing demand for the farce to cease and a strong ministry be chosen. The King understood and, although he had claimed in November that he would rather his hand should wither away than sign the readmission of Broglie, he now told Guizot wryly, "It is definitely necessary to submit to your yoke, messieurs *les doctrinaires*."[24] Guizot protested against the expression, but there is no doubt that the younger doctrinaires at least, angered by a pamphlet by Roederer which exalted the constitutional role of the sovereign, were determined that the ministers should rule and that these ministers should be members of their party, led by Broglie. After three weeks' haggling, the ministry was reconstructed: Broglie became president and Minister of Foreign Affairs, and Maréchal Maison was brought from St Petersburg to fill the Ministry of War, as requested by Thiers, who had unwillingly rejoined the Cabinet.

Thus a year after Broglie's resignation which had inaugurated this period of ministerial crisis, the political situation was virtually unchanged. The doctrinaire group had reinforced their dominance, but had increased the enmity felt toward them by Molé and his supporters. They who preached the necessity for a united Cabinet and for ministers to respect the will of the deputies, had in April 1834 promoted Duchâtel who had strongly defended the bill which had brought about the Cabinet's defeat, and shown themselves ruthless conspirators, willing to acquiesce in the constitutional inadequacies of a succession of figure-head *présidents*. The recurrent crises lessened the King's regard for politicians. If he did not create or prolong crises as his enemies claimed (and the politicians were happy to allow it to be believed because it concealed their own internecine feuding), he none the less attempted to safeguard his own personal prerogatives. On this occasion he failed, and with forced good grace accepted the reimposition of the uncongenial Duc de Broglie. As for the country, "it is during these sorts of interregnum that she is most tranquil",[25] remarked Viennet. France looked on with varying degrees of amusement and disgust. The harm done was not so much practical as psychological. In the "vacuum of power" of twenty-five weeks which Charles Pouthas has estimated France suffered between 1832 and 1839,[26] the longest being the ten-week crisis of 1839, the previously incumbent ministers usually continued to transact vital business. And if during 1834 too much ministerial energy was spent in intrigue, the important posts of the Interior and Justice remained, except for Bassano's three days, in the same hands. Thus the April uprisings were crushed without undue difficulty, the trial of the insurgents prepared and the restrictive September laws were passed. The policies of the *parti de résistance* were maintained amidst parliamentary anarchy.

REFERENCES

1. A. de Vigny, *Otello* (*Œuvres complètes*, Editions du Seuil, 1965), 349.
2. H. de Balzac, *Z. Marcas* (Pléiade edition), 757.
3. Cited in P. Thureau-Dangin, *Histoire de la Monarchie de Jullet* (1897), II, 168.
4. Odilon Barrot, *Mémoires posthumes* (1875), I, 285.
5. Archives Nationales, 42.AP.29, 30.
6. F. Guizot, *Mémoires pour servir à l'histoire de mon temps* (1858), III, 186.
7. Archives Parlementaires, 16 February 1833.
8. Comte C. de Rémusat, *Mémoires de ma vie* (1958), III, 116.
9. Thureau-Dangin, op. cit., II, 27.
10. Guizot, op. cit., III, 196.
11. Barrot, op. cit., I, 284–5.
12. Guizot, op. cit., III, 220.
13. Archives Parlementaires, 23 March 1833.
14. Bibliothèque Nationale, nouvelles acquisitions françaises 3021.
15. Archives Parlementaires, 23 March 1834.
16. Ibid., 21 March 1834.
17. Rémusat, op. cit., III, 71.
18. Stendhal, *Lucien Leuwen* (Martineau edition), 574.
19. Rémusat, op. cit., III, 73.
20. Ibid., III, 123.

21. L. Viennet, *Journal* (1955), 144.
22. J. J. Dupin, *Mémoires* (1860), III, 222.
23. Rémusat, op. cit., III, 113.
24. Viennet, op. cit., 145.
25. Ibid., 139.
26. Charles Pouthas, "Les Ministères de Louis-Philippe", *Revue d'Histoire Moderne et Contemporaine* I (1954), 112.

13

April Insurrection and September Laws

"L'insurrection, qui fut le plus saint des devoirs pour le duc d'Orléans, est devenue le plus horrible des crimes contre le roi des Français."

("Insurrection, which was the most holy of duties for the Duc d'Orléans, has become the most horrible of crimes against the King of the French.")[1]

The Société des Droits de l'Homme had tried to act as a party organisation, and to some extent succeeded. It had no united direction, no common finance, but its committee kept in contact with the branches and with other republican clubs throughout France. This centralisation was new, but at its source the small committee was prone to division. The Lebon faction seemed to have established its dominance, when, more extreme still, the supporters of Kersausie, who wanted the society to deal in more than mere propaganda, built up their own pseudo-military Société d'Action during 1833. Attempts by de Ludre and others to impose uniformity failed, and the Société d'Action became virtually independent, when the government's law on association made it impossible for propaganda associations to function as semi-secret societies, and dissolution or resistance were the only choices. The majority of the committee, led by Cavaignac, agreed with Carrel, La Fayette, Garnier-Pagès and most republican deputies that immediate insurrection was unwise; but many members, supported by the *Tribune*, were attracted by the militants' arguments. There was more violent talk than effective action: Louis Blanc admits: "In general, devotion did not rise to the level of agitation."[2] News of a rising at Lyons forced action upon the Parisians.

Mutuellisme in Lyons was a well-disciplined force modelled on the Droits de l'Homme, but with primarily economic purposes. Although younger and politically radical elements controlled their journal, the *Écho de la Fabrique*, by no means all *mutuellistes* were fervent republicans. About 40 per cent of *chefs d'atelier* were members and conflicts between them and the merchants were growing increasingly bitter. The prefect Gasparin made constant efforts to maintain the conseil des prud'hommes as a forum for discussion, but it became a battlefield. The authorities put pressure on the merchants but dared go no further, and in February 1834 the *mutuellistes* decided, by a rather small majority, to strike against a reduction in the pay rate for the makers of felt for hats, due to falling demand. With the support of the journeymen who threatened the reluctant into solidarity, they succeeded in halting the industry for a week: 20,000 men ceased work, a remarkable manifestation of unity. However, the merchants held firm, Gasparin, unlike his unlucky predecessor, refused to intervene, and the only attempt at mediation was made, unsuccessfully, by the moderate republican Petetin. The strikers found they could not afford to deprive themselves of income any longer, and, despite a minority of diehards especially among the journeymen, the *canuts* returned to work, not only defeated in their strike but potentially disarmed by the law on associations. The *Écho de la Fabrique* printed a protest, which it claimed had been signed by over 2,500 men, stating a belief in association as a human right and the determination not to cease organising.

The Lyons economy, damaged by the strike, was further aggravated by a financial crisis in the United States. Many of the unemployed were present outside the Palais de Justice on 5 April 1834 for the trial of six *mutuellistes*, arrested for their part in recent strikes. Noisy protests forced the postponement of the trial, and some republicans, encouraged by this first victory, prepared for insurrection. Lieutenant-Général Aymard and Gasparin believed a show of strength would be sufficient to deter intending insurgents. The socialist Louis Blanc is wrong in suggesting that the authorities provoked the 1834 uprising.[3] From the government came orders for moderation, and Gasparin was a rigid but not cruel man. It was the failure of the deputies to grant credit to aid trade with America which angered the Lyonnais and the recent Cabinet crisis which persuaded many that the right moment for revolution had occurred.

When the trial reopened on 9 April, the demonstrators found the authorities prepared. Opposite the court a republican was distributing revolutionary handbills, and the crowds prevented his arrest. Soldiers who tried to dismantle a barricade had cobbles thrown at them, and responded by firing. At the sound of shots, barricades were speedily hurled together in La Croix-Rousse, a working-class district on a hill outside the centre. This became the stronghold of the revolt, but its inhabitants were prevented from linking with allies elsewhere in the city by the fortifications which had been improved since 1831. On the 9th and 10th, the army, capably led by Lieutenant-Général Aymard, succeeded in containing the insurrection in a few areas confined to working-class districts on the right of the river. The insurgents had firearms, but in ballistic strength they had nothing to equal the army cannon. Their strength lay in their mobility, in their knowledge of the dark tortuous alleys of their own neighbourhoods and the long narrow covered walks peculiar to Lyons, constructed so that silk could be carried undamaged from the place where it was woven down into the mercantile centre. These provided traps for the soldiers, and many troops were lured to their deaths between barricades before army tactics changed to mass movement and wholesale destruction of the houses used by the enemy.

The insurgents probably numbered about 3,000: they were not as well supported as they had hoped. A large proportion were under thirty and unmarried, and were the journeymen weavers, generally with stronger political opinions than their masters, the *chefs d'atélier*, and with less to lose. The other leading occupations, although the silk workers provided the largest proportion, were also of the artisan type with strong associations – carpenters, masons and tailors. These were not men brought together by a common political faith, although republicanism was the preferred form of government of most of them, but by social injustice. Rebelling against new economic facts, they lacked a positive programme. Lyons showed the weakness of the republicans whose moderates disapproved of the rebellion.

On 11 April, outnumbered and surrounded, the rebels' position grew desperate as the army took the offensive. In one of the city churches, they manufactured ammunition, melting lead for bullets, the wounded brought into a side chapel to be tended by priests. One of these, victim of the anticlericalism of the authorities and their desire to make the revolt unpopular by finding Carlist connections, was kept in prison without trial for nine months on the unjustified charge of fomenting rebellion. As legitimist and Catholic journals noted, the Lyons revolt was not anticlerical, but desperation caused it to become increasingly extreme in its republicanism. Jacobinically, it dated its proclamations Germinal, An XLII de la République.

On 12 April, whilst republicans elsewhere were in ferment, the army in Lyons was engaged in the final efforts. Thiers believed that any transaction would leave insurrection ready to burst forth again, and demanded complete surrender. On the 13th, all lingering pockets of resistance were crushed and the uprising came to a bloody end in La Croix-Rousse where it had first taken root. The troops had lost 130 men, the rebels at least 170, and about 20 innocent civilians had perished during the five days' fighting.

The *Tribune* on 11 April reporting the outbreak of fighting at Lyons, declared the courage of the insurgents to be "a grand example."[4] The next day they announced "The people are masters of the city",[5] and on 13 April, that revolution was occurring throughout the provinces and had already conquered at Chalon, Beaune and Dijon.[6] These misleading reports, akin to the false news of rising in the Midi given by fanatical legitimists to prevent the Duchesse de Berry leaving the Vendée in June 1831, were a reflection of the determination of extremists in the Droits de l'Homme to create a national revolution. The outbreaks which occurred on 12 and 13 April were more purely republican in nature, and as such even more minority movements than the Lyons uprising. At Lunéville, a group of *sous-officiers*, led by Clément Thomas, who was in contact with republicans at Épinal and Nancy, encouraged by reports of revolt elsewhere, tried to raise the garrison to join other regiments and march on Paris to declare the Republic. Thomas's eloquence obtained no more than forty followers, however, and through betrayal by a sergeant's mistress, the conspirators were easily arrested. De

Ludre was implicated in this foolish attempt at a provincial military *coup d'état*, but was later released for lack of evidence.

Elsewhere in France there were lesser riots, usually fomented by the clubs. The attempts to rouse the masses met popular apathy and governmental force. At Saint-Etienne, the Caussidières, father and son, provoked violent demonstrations from the ribbon makers and miners on 11 and 12 April. The republicans at Artois behaved as if they were masters of the town for a day, but took fright when the extent of their illusion was revealed. At Marseilles, Clermont-Ferrand, Grenoble, Chalon-sur-Saône and Vienne rioting took place and arrests added to the large number of prisoners from Lyons, Paris and Lunéville.

In Paris, Cavaignac, leading the less extreme faction of the Droits de l'Homme, had given assurances that Paris would aid the Lyonnais if they revolted but he was in fact unenthusiastic. It was the Société d'Action, with about a third of the membership of the organisation, which grasped the initiative and set in motion the conspiratorial machinery. Thiers meanwhile had taken preventive measures. An army of 40,000 troops and National Guardsmen had been assembled under Maréchal de Lobau. The *Tribune*, "the *Moniteur* [the official government paper] of the insurrection" as Louis Blanc described it, albeit a highly misleading source, was temporarily closed on 13 April, lest its optimistic accounts of the Lyons insurrection encourage further rebellion. Although revolt broke out in Paris on the 13th as planned, many of the leaders of the Droits de l'Homme had been put under preventive detention, and it was ill led. The insurgents were limited to a fervent few, outnumbered by the army: as in Lyons, their only assets were their courage and the narrow streets where they constructed their barricades. On the morning of 14 April, the government forces attacked the quartier Saint-Méry, the slums of which were the republican citadel. Thiers was present, giving orders and riding boldly through the most dangerous areas. The fighting was brutal and brief.

One of the dark streets, the Rue Transnonain, was the scene of an event which Daumier's lithograph has made unforgettable. Troops had entered to destroy a barricade and were removing a wounded officer on a stretcher when shots were fired from an upper storey killing him. A group of angry soldiers rushed into the building and indiscriminately shot a dozen of the inhabitants, including a child and a woman. The republicans, using the atrocity as propaganda, blamed it upon the military command: Bugeaud in particular, already "the gaoler of Blaye," incurred greater odium as "the executioner of the Rue Transnonain." The generals, however, were not to blame: the massacre resulted from a spontaneous act of uncontrollable anger, and the hatred of the troops, most of them from small towns or the countryside, for a city they feared and an enemy they could not see. The Duc d'Orléans wrote to his sister, the Queen of the Belgians, of the horror at seeing corpses draped on the remains of barricades and the trickling of blood from a second storey down the whitewashed walls:[7] but however hideous, the uprising was small in comparison with that of Lyons and earlier Parisian revolts.

The various risings had been the result of unity in optimism: fanatics and conspirators had by means of tenuous connections convinced themselves of their strength, and at a certain moment had seized the initiative and overruled the moderates, but there was no centrally led revolt. Most republicans had projected future revolution, but probably in 1834 the majority had not truly desired it. To the government however, especially Thiers, this appeared an organised national conspiracy. The Société des Droits de l'Homme, inefficient and divided as it was, seemed to the government to have directed the rebellion. The needs of Orleanist propaganda, added to a genuine tendency to regard all protest purely in political terms, persuaded it that the societies alone were responsible, and Thiers instructed prefects to use all possible means against them. Gasparin waged war on the Lyons republican press, even the moderate *Précurseur* which succumbed to legal attack. Later, during the trial in Paris, the government stressed republican conspiracy and limited working-class grievances to a minor role, which in Lyons, scene of the largest rising, was an incorrect analysis. Determined to damn republicans in the eyes of France, it decided to try all the accused as part of one conspiracy; this seemed to be justified by the archives of the Société des Droits de l'Homme which gave names of members, and details of expenses which included ammunition-buying. It also allowed it to bring them before the Chamber of Peers, removed from the indulgence of local juries because participating in a great crime against the state.

Lengthy and exhaustive examinations reduced the original 2,000 accused to the 121 considered most guilty, 59 of whom were Lyonnais and 42 Parisian. The prisoners were separated according to their origin, thereby reinforcing the differences in regional temperament to be manifest during the trial. Republican newspapers made accusations of ill-treatment, but in fact the prisoners were allowed considerable freedom. Some did not hesitate to avail themselves of the favoured treatment permitted those who could pay for it: the aristocratic Kersausie was able to indulge his taste for fine wine, the fastidious Marrast was brought a nightly bath. All were allowed internal freedom of meeting and it was the most extreme who dominated the discussions on the conduct of their defence.

The republicans determined to make of the trial a gigantic political manifestation, to carry the fight from the barricades into the dock. To this end, they drew up a list of 150 republican luminaries to defend them, including representatives of all shades of opinion; not without difficulty, as the anticlerical Cavaignac strongly objected to the inclusion of the Abbé de Lamennais. However, Baron Pasquier, president of the Chamber of Peers, ruled that only established lawyers might conduct the defence, although legal resistance caused him to cancel the declaration that the court had the right to nominate counsel. The disqualified defenders formed a "committee of defence", republican newspapers hurled imprecations at Pasquier, caricatures vituperated the peers and idolised the defendants. Some tried to frighten the government by sending a letter, purporting to come from a legion of National Guardsmen refusing to serve outside the Palais du Luxembourg. An attempt to stir up riots in the Saint-Denis and Saint-Martin areas failed amidst energetic police measures and public indifference.

When on 5 May 1835 the trial finally commenced, the agitation outside the Luxembourg was as nothing compared with that inside. From the beginning, the accused loudly refused to recognise the court which denied them the right to choose freely their defenders. When, on the second day, the *procureur général* Martin (du Nord) read out a declaration that the court would not allow its justice to be impeded, his voice was drowned by the protesting accused, whilst above the uproar rose the stentorian voice of Baune, pouring contempt upon the court, claiming that its justice was founded upon bayonets. The red robes, the dignity of court ritual, had not impressed the defiant prisoners as some peers had naively hoped: the guards could scarcely keep them under control. Unwillingly, the peers declared that a defendant could face his trial alone, and by a tiny majority decided that evidence might be given against a defendant in his absence, if his behaviour made this strictly necessary. Even this had little effect on those who were determined to make a farce of the trial. However, it was becoming evident that the republicans were divided. Half the Lyonnais showed themselves prepared to co-operate in the trial, and were accused of putting city before party. To encourage resistance, imprecations against the deserters were accompanied by promises of monetary compensation for the faithful. Some members of the "committee of defence" met, and Michel (de Bourges) drew up a letter of exhortation to solidarity which attacked the peers in forcible terms: "the infamy of the judge makes the glory of the accused"[8] it ended. Those present, about thirty, signed it, not only for themselves but for their comrades, whose adhesion they did not doubt. On 11 May the letter was published by the *Tribune*, with a list of signatures, amongst which were those of two deputies, Cormenin and Audry de Puyraveau: the name of Garnier-Pagès failed to appear due to a printing error. After some agitated debate, the peers decided not to accept this new insult. They authorised the arrest of the *gérants* of the *Tribune* and of the *Réformateur*, Raspail's journal which had also published the letter, and of its signatories, genuine or not. In the latter category came the two deputies, and the Lower House had to grant permission for the peers to try them. Cormenin claimed that he had not signed and was absolved: Audry admitted as much, but was more offensive and was sent to answer to the peers, despite Dupin and Barrot's attempts to rouse prejudice against the aristocracy. The Chamber also proceeded to its own persecution of the republican press by causing the *gérant* of the *Réformateur* to be fined and imprisoned for a month for an insulting attack. By their resolution the two Chambers were proving that the weakness on which the republicans had relied did not exist.

Only four serious sentences resulted from the *Tribune–Réformateur* trial, but not before the republicans had again divided between the cautious and the rash over the question of whether those who had not actually signed their names might disavow the false signatures. Raspail was absolved because the peers were touched by his sentimental mysticism. Michel and Trélat of the *Tribune* took the responsibility and received the biggest penalties. Trélat told the peers that they could not judge him bccause of the world of political enmity between them. "Condemn me, but you will not judge me, because you cannot understand me." Their conflict was "the revolution fighting against the counter-revolution, the past in battle with the future and the present, egoism versus fraternity, tyranny versus liberty".[9] This eloquence sent Trélat to prison for two years: Michel because less offensive, received a lighter punishment.

In spite of Trélat, this trial was little more than an incident. The peers returned to the mammoth trial and the question whether to sentence the more co-operative defendants before proceeding with the recalcitrants. The decision to do so, if fairer to those examined, was legally questionable. Three peers, Villemain, Comtes Molé and de Flahaut, ceased to sit at this point, joining Maréchaux Gérard and Maison and other *tiers parti* and legitimist peers, who refused to form part of the court. The majority of peers were uneasy, but determined to proceed. Some accused refused to appear, others were insulting rather than defensive, but increasingly, the Lyonnais, less purely republican and less susceptible to Parisian discipline, were participating. They were ably defended by the young lawyer, Jules Favre, who argued that the revolt was spontaneous, and, less justifiably, that in so far as there was a conspiracy, as the prosecution claimed, it was by *agents provocateurs*.

The morale of the accused, already damaged by divisions, now received a shattering blow. Some of the prisoners had succeeded in digging a tunnel from the cells of the Sainte-Pélagie prison into the cellar of a neighbouring property. On 12 July, twenty-eight of the prisoners crawled to freedom, emerging into the street and entering carriages which had been brought there. Some of the most important thus escaped into exile; they included Cavaignac, Marrast and Guinard. A few of the élite, notably Kersausie, had chosen to remain for those reasons of solidarity which all had once proclaimed. There was rejoicing in the party that the authorities had been so neatly outwitted, but the escape of the generals left the troops leaderless and divided. The trial proceeded laboriously but on the whole calmly. The sentences on the escapees of July were the last to be given. The punishments were fairly severe. Eighteen, including Baune and Kersausie, with some who had escaped, were sentenced to deportation: others were sent to prison for periods of one to twenty years. The amnesty of 1837 would cancel these penalties. After almost a year, from fatigue or scruple, nearly fifty of the original judges had absented themselves. Yet under the guidance of President Pasquier, who after his initial shock at the insolent violence of the accused had behaved with sedate strength, concealing occasional ruthlessness beneath *ancien régime* courtesy, the peers had persevered, enabling the government to triumph over disorder on a public stage.

The insurgents of April 1834 had suffered a fate common to those remaining too long before the public eye; they had been almost forgotten, especially when the intriguing case of Lieutenant de La Roncière, accused of raping the daughter of a general, provided a new sensation. The republicans had demonstrated courage, disinterestedness, stoicism and eloquence: there had also been vanity and discord, fanaticism and violence. "Fools! Blockheads! Envious men! Weaklings! How much time must pass before this country is ready for a republic"[10] cried Carrel, who told Berryer that the republicans had no political sense, no discipline; "We commit error upon error."[11] He wrote an eloquent obituary in the *National* for La Fayette who died in May 1834, mourning in him a true friend of liberty, a republican who was alien to the insane violence which had led the party to disaster. To the extremists, however, the Marquis's decision to be buried next his wife in the Picpus cemetery, where lay many of the noble victims of the French Revolution, was a last insult to their beliefs.

Failure taught the republicans the need for better organisation and discipline, for patient education and propaganda, and the need to master "the science of social revolutions",[12] as Louis Blanc put it. It also made them more willing to enter into alliance with the legitimists. Previously the two groups fought: now, both vanquished in revolt, they often formed tactical alliance. In 1831, said Thomas, prefect of the Bouches du Rhône, republicans would have torn Berryer to pieces; now they voted for him, so three of the department's six deputies were legitimist.[13] Conspiratorial groups emerged from the wreck of the clubs in 1834, but they were smaller and better disciplined. Socialism developed after it had been shown that insurrection was insufficient and that greater support was necessary from the working classes. More sinister, the failure of rebellion inspired the assassins: as Bergeron's attempt had followed the crushing of the Lamarque riots, so the defeat of the April insurrection was succeeded by the Fieschi plot.

If the Orleanists tended to exaggerate the role of conspiracy and the influence of the press, the corresponding republican error was to see Louis-Philippe as a linchpin whose removal would cause the July Monarchy to crumble. To have allowed the Duc d'Orléans to succeed his assassinated father would probably have strengthened the regime, but to fanatical republicans the King was a potent symbolic figure. With the return to Jacobin extremism and the increased readership of the works of Saint-Just, regicide seemed an essential republican virtue. From August 1830 onwards, many began to contemplate assassinating the King. At a pro-Polish banquet in Lyons in February 1832, incendiary speeches were made, one of which included a quotation from a poem,

"The breast of kings, is it therefore so hard
That the blade of a dagger cannot penetrate it?"[14]

The first to do more than play with the idea was Bergeron, whose acquittal made him a republican hero. The increase in republican bitterness, the failures of April 1834, again put assassination into men's minds. The rumours, the hints in the republican press in spring and summer 1835, showed the intention to be more than the reflection of mental derangement. For some it was a subject for jest. "Yesterday", wrote *le Charivari* on 26 July 1835, two days before Fieschi's *machine infernale* was fired, "the citizen-king returned to Paris, with his superb family, without being in any way assassinated along the way."[15] After the Fieschi attempt, many republican papers condoned it, as they had seemed previously to offer encouragement to assassination. The *Patriote du Puy de Dôme*, for example, wrote that the Republic was something "so beneficial and so holy that it can accept its triumph by whatever means" and regretted that its arrival had failed by half a second.[16]

On 28 July 1835 the King rode through the streets for the annual review to celebrate *les glorieuses*. His three eldest sons, Orléans, Nemours and Joinville, were beside him, then Maréchaux Mortier and de Lobau, followed by the ministers and officers. News of plots had been reported and all were nervous. Thiers had inaugurated police searches of suspected houses but the protests had been such that it was abandoned without success. As the procession rode down the Boulevard du Temple, a burst of shots rang out. This assassination attempt was no ordinary one: Fieschi and his accomplices Morey and Pépin had created a *machine infernale* in which twenty-five rifle barrels were simultaneously fired. The resulting hail of bullets killed eighteen and seriously wounded another twenty-two. Mortier and several officers were amongst the dead: the object of the attempt received a bullet in the arm and a graze on the forehead which caused some fever and headaches. His horse was wounded and Joinville quickly led it forward away from the chaotic scene. The Duc de Broglie received a bullet which flattened on the star of the Légion d'honneur on his chest. The shocked crowd enthusiastically acclaimed the King who continued with the ceremony. The republicans with their red carnations disappeared. All were amazed by the King's courage and calm. Returning to the palace after the review, he finally wept at the death of Mortier.

A moving requiem was performed for all victims, from the Maréchal de France to a child of the people. Fieschi had been caught trying to escape across the roofs. The trial was a calm affair but his impenitence sickened those present. He and his accomplices were condemned to death. The complicity of a section of the republican party was obvious. Morey and Pépin, members of the Société des Droits de l'Homme, had obtained finance for Fieschi's plot and Pépin had fully informed the republican leader Recurt of its progress.

In the aftermath of the Fieschi attempt, the Broglie government was able to use the revulsion to pass unpopular laws. After the April insurrections, severe penalties had been imposed on weapon hoarders and barricade builders, and supplementary credits given to help the army suppress internal disorder. The bills which the government now put forward, the September laws as they became known, went much further. The doctrinaires were given their opportunity to try to influence men's minds. Fieschi had convinced the hesitant, including the King, that stricter laws were necessary, his act of violence had weakened dogmatic liberalism and his unashamed evil set many in search of order, physical and spiritual. The ministers quickly drew up and submitted three proposals in early August 1835. The number necessary to produce conviction by a jury was reduced from eight to seven out of twelve: there was to be secrecy in voting to try to limit the efficacy of threats: a higher court had the right to order a retrial if it believed a miscarriage of justice had occurred. Another facilitated the task of the *procureur général* in trials for rebellion, and gave the courts power to continue a trial against a violent defendant in his absence, the result of experiences during the April trials. The most important bill concerned the press: incitement to insurrection, to hatred of the King and attacks on his authority were classed as crimes against the state, which could be tried by the peers and not by a jury, and which were punishable by imprisonment and fines up to 50,000 francs. It was forbidden to demand a change of dynasty, invoke the fallen Bourbons, call for a republic or show adherence to another form of government, attack property rights, the laws or the Constitution, also to publish the names of jurymen or to give an account of the jury's proceedings. A newspaper was suspended from publication if condemned twice for these offences within a year. Caution money, like terms of imprisonment and fines, was increased. To end the *gérant fictif*, the man who lent his name to the newspaper's administration and who took responsibility for infractions although he was purely a token figure, it was declared that the *gérant* had to divulge the name of an author of an incriminating article, and to print the response of a libelled person, and official documents if so asked by authority. A newspaper could not exhibit and sell engravings, but ordinary prints and theatre plays were not covered by the law.

With the bitterness of illusions shattered, Broglie rushed into legal repression with an exhilaration in his hatred and contempt for the enemies who forced him to renege his early ideals and with the self-righteousness of a man who surrenders what he cherishes for the public good. He tacitly admitted the dangerous principle of the law when he declared that it was just and politic only whilst the constitutional monarchy was in power. The liberals of the ministry, notably Guizot and Broglie, were not without doubts, especially concerning the jury measure, where Persil and Thiers eventually convinced them of its necessity, but the atmosphere of the discussion created overstatement rather than moderation on all sides. Broglie saw disorder as a wild beast, prevented from dictating its will through the clubs, fought in the streets, eventually tracked to its dark conspiracies, "it is now in its last resort; it takes refuge in the fractious press". Its claims to the right to discussion were hypocritical, for its violence destroyed reason and orderly liberty, which alone allowed true discussion.[17] Guizot used the same argument against accusations of tyranny. He told the deputies that "the policy of the *juste milieu*, is essentially the enemy of absolute principles and extreme ends".[18] They, who had fought for liberty in 1830 and had retained it whilst fighting for order since then, had the right to say this.

In spite of Salverte, Garnier-Pagès and Barrot's accusations of censorship, of Lamartine's attack on "a law of iron . . . the reign of terror against ideas",[19] of the opposition press comparing Broglie unfavourably with Charles X and Polignac, the majority were willing to be convinced. Sauzet, although a member of the *tiers parti*, had been rapporteur of a commission which had increased the penalties proposed by the government, and, as deputy for Lyons, he eloquently invoked "my city twice bloodied by the excesses of the press".[20]

Dupin admits in his memoirs that scandalous acquittals and the behaviour of the accused during the April trials, had necessitated some action. However, he spoke against putting the peers in charge of press offences and claimed the law on the jury was against the Charter. Garnier-Pagès claimed that juries acquitted so frequently because the government's political trials were too numerous: "Finding that it is sometimes injust, the bourgeoisie withdraws her assistance from you."[21] However, the most notable contribution to this debate was made by Royer-Collard. The aged liberal who had come to dislike his former pupils, the doctrinaires, especially Guizot, broke his silence to deliver an attack on the judicial aspects of the press law. It was a sensation because Royer-Collard was a member of the *parti de résistance*: but his lack of enthusiasm for the 1830 Revolution undoubtedly provided a motive for his attack on the government. With his liberalism uncontaminated by the necessities of power, he proclaimed it an immoral subterfuge to turn press offences into state crimes to remove them from the jury. These "baleful remedies" were "legislative inventions that breathed trickery".[22] He reminded the deputies that the ills of anarchy were bred by revolution and that many present conservatives had formerly supported rebellion. This intervention caused uproar but could not prevent the bills being passed with large majorities. The law on the jury obtained 224 votes against 149, the law on the press 226 to 153. The peers quickly passed them, the only notable opposition coming from Villemain. In the country, most of the forces of order gave their enthusiastic approval.

The law certainly changed the nature of the press, but the hope expressed by Persil that only the Orleanist press could survive it was proved unfounded. Implication and innuendo replaced violent attack: perhaps in the long run it was more effective. The King could be insulted under sarcastic pseudonyms, and Broglie was correct in pointing out that no limits were imposed on attacking the ministers. About thirty of the most demagogic newspapers considered it pointless to continue publication: other opposition journals took care to censor themselves lest infringements should bring them speedily to destruction. The change in law made juries more ready to convict, the processes of judgment were no longer so favourable to the accused, and political trials grew less violent and less interesting. Guizot was to argue that all human societies needed fixed points, "unassailable bases",[23] yet the September laws could do nothing to create these. The vulnerable compromise of Orleanism was more susceptible to criticism than to violent attack. In the long term, the September laws must be considered a failure, but whatever the results, as the most extreme legal act of the *parti de résistance*, they became a political touchstone. They had split the *tiers parti*: Sauzet had voted for the government on the press but against it over the jury; a handful of idiosyncratic conservatives, notably Lamartine and Royer-Collard, had opposed them, but on the whole the September laws increased the distance between the parties of *résistance* and *mouvement*. Thiers's continued loyalty to the laws for which he had spoken so firmly divided him from the *gauche dynastique* even when in opposition in the 1840s.

REFERENCES

1. H. de Balzac, cited in J. Crépet (ed.), *Pensées, Sujets Fragments* (1910), 39.
2. Louis Blanc, *Histoire de Dix Ans* (1840), IV, 153.
3. Ibid., 184.
4. *La Tribune*, 11 April 1835.
5. Ibid., 12 April 1835.
6. Ibid., 13 April 1835.
7. Cited in F. Bonnet-Roy, *Ferdinand-Philippe, Duc d'Orléans, Prince Royal, 1810–1842* (1947), 130.
8. *La Tribune*, 11 May 1835.
9. Blanc, op. cit., IV, 284–5.
10. Comte E. D'Alton-Shée, *Mes Mémoires* (1869), I, 81.
11. Ibid., 163.
12. Blanc, op. cit., IV, 295.
13. J. Vidalenc (ed.), *Lettres de J. A. M. Thomas* (Aix-en-Provence, 1953), 73.
14. *Le Précurseur*, 18 February 1832.
15. *Le Charivari*, 26 July 1835.
16. *Patriote du Puy de Dôme*, cited in Archives Parlementaires, 28 August 1835.
17. Archives Parlementaires, 24 August 1835.
18. Ibid., 28 August 1835.
19. Ibid., 21 August 1835.
20. Ibid., 26 August 1835.
21. Ibid., 17 August 1835.
22. Ibid., 25 August 1835.
23. F. Guizot, *Mémoires pour servir à l'histoire de mon temps* (1858), III, 311.

14

The Press

"Malheureuse Monarchie! pensa le comte de Vaize. Le nom du roi est dépouillé de tout effet magique. Il est réellement impossible de gouverner avec ces petits journaux qui démolissent tout. Il nous faut payer argent comptant ou par des grades. . . . Et cela nous ruine: le Trésor comme les grades ne sont pas infinis."

("Wretched Monarchy! thought the comte de Vaize. The name of king has been stripped of all magic. It is truly impossible to govern with these little journals that demolish everything. It is necessary to pay one off with ready money or with offices. . . . And that ruins us: the Treasury, like offices, is not limitless.")[1]

The July Monarchy was a great age for the press, as was to be expected of a regime which originated in a protest by journalists. There was a hunger for information, a mass of incompatible nuances demanding to be satisfied, a plethora of ambitions, each desiring a mouthpiece. The evolution from salon politics to those of public opinion, provided a generation of individualists with a variety of readerships. The capital published about thirty dailies and ten times as many reviews and periodicals to cater for this voracity for newsprint. Technical innovations changed printing methods; the expansion of capitalism provided it with the commercial role of advertising; political and literary battles gave it a permanently changing scene to describe.

The regime both loved and loathed the press. Because so many of the new men of August 1830 had been contributors to journals which had struggled for press freedom during the Restoration, the government initially promised this. "Censorship can never be re-established", declared Article Seven of the 1830 Charter. The laws of the land were now the only restrictions, and the logical consequence of this was the law of 8 October 1830 which made juries alone competent to judge press offences. The law which followed in December allowed a man to hawk pamphlets and prints by means of a licence from municipal authorities, and caution money, stamp duty and postage rates were lowered during the governmental honeymoon with the press. Within five years almost all this liberalisation and relaxation would be reversed. In spite of a sincere desire for press freedom, government intervention in journalism as in elections was too habitual and too convenient to be easily abandoned. The government would also declare it necessary, for one matter on which *résistance* and *mouvement*, legitimists and republicans, were all agreed, was the influence of the press. The Laffitte ministry prosecuted the legitimist press which at this time was most vociferous in opposition to the regime. Under Périer, as republicans became more overt in their hostility and the government determined to create a strong combative party of resistance, attention turned against them. Garde des Sceaux Barthe's circular of 2 July 1832 blamed the press for inciting revolt in Paris and the Vendée, and he and his successor Persil ordered local *procureurs généraux* to use all legal means against incendiary journals of left and right.

The government's powers were considerable but double-edged. To send republicans and legitimists into the witness-box, gave them and their advocates the opportunity to make speeches. When the regime prosecuted Chateaubriand, the main government prosecutors Persil, Franck-Carré and Martin (du Nord), were easily made to appear as mediocrities persecuting genius. Defending the *Quotidienne* in 1834, Berryer, the legitimist lawyer, read the offending article aloud, and succeeded in bursting into tears when he came to the sentence most complained of – "The legitimate successor of our legitimate kings is Henri V. . . ."[2] This caused a sympathetic outburst of emotion in the auditorium. A trial, even if a conviction were obtained, was often a moral victory for the defendants. And an acquittal was the repudiation of the government by a section of public opinion, even when such a verdict was obtained, as it often was, by threats against members of the jury and publication of their names and addresses. In areas of strong opposition, a verdict of guilty was almost impossible to obtain: in Toulouse, for example, combinations of legitimists and republicans on the jury prevented successful prosecution of the violently legitimist *Gazette du Languedoc*. Of the 520 prosecutions which the government attempted against the press from 1831 to 1835, there were 332 acquittals.

However, a verdict of guilty could ruin a newspaper. Two or three fines of 1,000 francs or more might destroy a small one. The *Tribune*, which with 111 prosecutions to its credit, was the most persecuted of newspapers, finally succumbed to its twentieth condemnation in May 1835. Although it had avoided penalties on many occasions, it had still in 4 years paid fines totalling almost 16,000 francs and received for its various *gérants* a total of 49 years in prison. The *Quotidienne* and *Gazette* and the more moderate republican *National* followed far behind with fifteen prosecutions each. Some *gérants* went so often to prison that special, fairly pleasant, quarters in Sainte-Pélagie were allotted to them. Some newspapers ingeniously attempted to avoid such action. The *Cancans*, for example, lived a short, brilliant life, appearing at odd intervals, printed and published in different places, appearing with different titles, *Les Cancans inexorables*, *incorrigibles*, *flétrissants* and so on, pretending to be different publications, before police harassment proved finally successful. For the same reason, in January 1834, the *National*, to escape the consequences of prosecutions against its former self, changed its name to *Le National de 1834* and obtained two new *gérants*. The legitimists relied upon private subscriptions to maintain their weaker publications: the republicans had the Association de la Liberté de la Presse, which provided legal and financial aid for threatened journals.

The government increasingly felt restricted in its fight. As the old liberal reflexes disappeared under the repeated blows of insurrection, as the activities of rioters and assassins discredited freedom of expression, the ministers introduced restrictive measures, notably the 1835 September laws which, since censorship was supposedly outlawed, widened the definition of crime, making provocation to revolt an act of treason which could therefore be tried by the peers. Where trial by jury remained, the voting would be secret to avoid intimidation, and a bare majority would suffice. Caution money was increased to 100,000 francs deposit for those newspapers of the capital appearing more than once a week.

The opposition press avoided some of the restrictions: the King, whom it was forbidden to mention when discussing governmental actions, might be referred to with ironical respect as "an august personage", in the opposition rags as "thing", most frequently by using the impersonal "one". But the laws were death to certain productions. The preliminary authorisation for drawings (a form of censorship which, it was asseverated, did not infringe the Charter) at once caused Philipon to close his *Caricature*, whose success was based upon the immediacy of its often brutal political cartoons: the last copy satirically asked liberty for the ministers of Charles X who had harmed the press less than the government which had replaced them. The July Monarchy has been much censured for its press measures, yet it is worth noting that even after September 1835 the press of the extreme opposition continued to be able to attack the regime with more violence than most countries without censorship have to accept. The difficulty facing the July Monarchy was that, as so often, the liberal principles on which it was founded were incompatible with complete freedom. The press law was the weapon of a regime on the defensive, and after the comparative relaxation of the Thiers and Molé ministries between 1836 and 1840, the Guizot ministry was to use it frequently, especially in the aftermath of the diplomatic humiliation of 1840, which was also a year of industrial unrest, and in 1847 when it felt threatened by the united forces of the left demanding electoral reform.

For the journalist, the struggle for freedom of expression lent an aura of nobility to a calling which had only recently emerged from frivolous scurrility, and the financial demands of the government for caution money even from journals whose politics were impeccable, made running a newspaper an expensive occupation. "Journalism is war"; a way of fighting without killing men and a way of running a newspaper without losing money had yet to be invented, lamented Montalembert.[3] Lamartine found that his mouthpiece at Mâcon, *Le Bien Public*, cost him 15,000 francs a year.[4] Other newspapers had patrons – Raspail's *Réformateur*, for example, was financed repeatedly by the republican Comte de Kersausie, but not even his generosity could help this small-circulation journal overcome three heavy penalties within a brief period and the imprisonment of all its staff. Others found a patron might be compromising: Montalembert preferred to borrow from money-lenders who would refrain from telling him how to run the *Univers*. To make a profit, a paper needed 4,000 subscribers and, to cover its costs, at least 3,000. In 1836 fewer than half the leading fifteen national newspapers had sufficient readership to be able to make a small profit, and much of the press therefore required outside aid. For opposition newspapers, there was the patron or group of wealthy supporters: for the others, there was the government.

The *fonds secrets*, a sum voted annually for police purposes, provided a fund which could be drawn upon to subsidise friends and bribe enemies. Sometimes the government would simply try to buy a journal: thus in 1842 Guizot offered the director of a newspaper which supported Thiers, the sum of 100,000 francs from the *fonds secrets* if it became ministerial,[5] and Thiers paid 120,000 francs to Walewski for the unprofitable *Messager*. Other methods were also used: the ministry of 6 September 1836 promoted a dancer at the government-run Opéra because she was the mistress of the editor of the left-wing *Courrier Français*, and a change of political opinion was promised (but never occurred). Molé subsidised the *Revue des Deux Mondes*: he also gave its editor Buloz charge of the Comédie Française, to oblige him voted against Sainte-Beuve's election to the Académie, made its political commentator Lerminier a *conseiller d'état* and another contributor Loève-Veimars consul in Baghdad. Relationships between politicians and the press were not simply financial but political and personal. Generally, a journal would only sell itself to someone it wished to be bought by, and would rarely abandon total independence. The tiny *Charte* might be simply bought and directed by the ministry, but the *Journal des Débats*, whilst receiving subsidies, retained the right to criticise. Thus in 1838 when Molé supported Britain against French Canadian rebels, the *Débats* annoyed him by its attacks: the English ambassador believed the minister's assurances "that he cannot control the direction of the Paper".[6]

Not only conservative newspapers accepted governmental money. In 1837 on the occasion of the Duc d'Orléans's marriage, some republican journals were paid for a few days' silence, proof of the government's belief in the power of the press to rouse hostility. And the deputy Viennet describes with indignation how an opposition journalist who had printed libels about him, came to offer the cessation of this in return for assistance.[7] If professional ethics were frequently low, this may be largely ascribed to the political passions of the age and insufficiency of libel laws which meant that the wildest accusations could go unchallenged. The Feuchères case, when the last Prince de Condé was found hanged in 1830, provided legitimist sheets like the *Cancans* with material for the most outrageous attacks upon the Orléans family, to whom he had left the bulk of his fortune.

So this "modern divinity", as the legitimist Balzac called it, had destroyed a monarchy: it perpetrated lies, corrupted institutions, warped patriotism, making France "a little town where one is more concerned by what is said about it than by national interests".[8] Similarly, Théophile Gautier the aesthete claimed, only half in jest, that Charles X alone had understood the question: the dethroned King had tried to serve civilisation by suppressing newspapers. Criticism came between audience and artist, nation and monarch, making poetry and royalty impossible, journalism rendering only the dubious compensation of a daily sheet of cheap paper covered with bad writing, poorly printed.[9] The greatest press proprietor of the age, Emile de Girardin, spoke of the daily newspaper as "the most arbitrary of absolute powers, the most anarchic of revolutionary agents. . . ."[10] Even sincere liberals like Tocqueville felt limited enthusiasm for the freedom of the press, accepting its destructive violence, believing censorship to be an even greater evil.[11] This power was novel, and it was natural that there should be a common feeling that it was misused. The press was a suitable scapegoat to be blamed for political instability, low moral standards and corruption in artistic taste, but this was a controversy which appeared in the press itself. Général Bugeaud, whilst hurling anathema on all journalists, felt compelled to read several newspapers of all opinions each day, at the same time violently fulminating against their dishonest libels and inaccuracies.

The journals of the July Monarchy were the productions of a remarkably small number. Indeed, the staff of some tiny provincial newspapers consisted of an 'editor' with a pair of scissors, who would take up the pen only to describe local matters, placed among the extracts freely culled from others. Even the larger productions maintained informal links with the worlds of politics, art, society and commerce: usually the barriers between owning and directing, editing and reporting, were blurred. The driving force of the newspaper, the man responsible for its political line, with whom the ministry would discuss terms, might be a proprietor not contributing to the writing, he might be a *gérant* who played a commanding role, or he might be the *rédacteur en chef*, most considerable of the contributors, for the larger papers had several editor-contributors. The *Siècle* had a board of financial proprietors whose main concern was commercial and who accepted its moderate left stance as being most profitable, whilst its rival, the *Presse*, with Emile de Girardin as owner and contributor, was much more personal in organisation and tone. The *Journal des Débats* was run by the Bertin family who, whilst never contributing, imprinted it with their strong convictions. Thus a newspaper could be a commercial adventure, the instrument of one man's ambition or the organ of a party. This variety reflects the political complexities and the technical advances of the period.

The most important part of the paper was the *premier-Paris*, critical comment on a piece of current news; "the slice of bread and butter that every day must be placed at the head of a public paper, and without which, it would appear, the intelligence of subscribers would starve, for lack of nourishment",[12] sneered Balzac. The divisions between readership of newspapers were primarily political rather than social: a doctor, banker or lawyer might read any number of papers. That he should prefer the pro-Thiers anticlerical *Constitutionnel* to the pro-doctrinaire *Débats* or pro-Molé conservative

Presse, that he read the *gauche dynastique Siècle* rather than the less moderate *Courrier Français* or moderate republican *National* or again the pro-Berryer *Quotidienne* rather than the more radical *Gazette de France*, was decided by his preference for the *premier-Paris* and would define with some precision his political views. The writer of this vital column, Balzac described as the leading, albeit anonymous, tenor of the operatic ensemble that was a newspaper staff. Sometimes there was more than one, and often it would be contributed from outside. The *Journal des Débats* as well as its regular journalists (most notably the deputy Saint-Marc Girardin) also received occasional contributions from men like Salvandy or Rémusat. Politicians in control of a newspaper would not only decide its general policy but sometimes dictate its leading article: Thiers was particularly energetic in this respect.

Other pieces of news took very much the second place, and were often reprinted in the barest terms. Frequently, if external, they would simply be translated from foreign papers. Other important contributors were those who organised the deputies' debates according to the colour of the publication, correcting the grammar of the nation's representatives, adding "sensation" or "profound sensation" at vital points in friends' speeches, "murmurs", "denials", "uproar" in those of enemies. There would then be the judicial section – of great professional importance to a large section of the readership and of interest to many others. There would be economic and commercial specialists and a section on the Bourse. And there would be the art and literary critics: "the public loves to be served three or four authors spat upon like dogs and loaded with ridicule each morning",[13] wrote Balzac with the bitterness of experience.

It was from the press of fashion and education that the new political press found its origins: it took its gimmicks and its advertising from the one and high circulation and low prices from the latter. The public was increasingly regarded not as a political congregation, but as a market. Hippolyte de Villemessant, editor of *La Sylphide* (a fashion journal which took its title from Taglioni's popular ballet), light-heartedly unscrupulous, understood well what his readers wanted. Once he wrote of a *grisette* who, preferring death to dishonour, had left her canary with a note tied round its tiny neck begging someone to care for it: the next day, a canary had to be purchased to satisfy the sentimental public who flocked to the editorial office where the story had been invented. On another occasion all the copies were perfumed. Villemessant's contempt for his audience, that of the dandy and the modern public relations expert, made him a pioneer of advertising. An article could be paid for twice: the *arriviste* would pay for a flattering account of her soirée, her couturier would be mentioned in it, and the public would enjoy reading of it. Advertising had to be unsubtle: Guerlain felt he was not having his money's worth when he was described only as "the demigod of perfumes".[14] But when the brilliant publicist had an accident and was unable to work, his frothy mixture fell flat and *La Sylphide* went bankrupt.

Émile de Girardin began similarly to Villemessant. The illegitimate son of a courtier of Charles X, his need to prove himself and overcome parental neglect lent a febrile strength to his determination to conquer the world of journalism. Having sold his fashion journal *La Mode* after the change of dynasty (it became a legitimist publication mixing politics and *haute couture*), he founded the *Journal des Connaissances*. It was to cater for the desire for self-instruction amongst the *petite bourgeoisie*. The formula, with its strongly technical bent, its encouragement to self-help (notably *caisses d'épargne*), its schemes (such as a bank for insurance against cholera, augmented by contributions from the newspaper) and printing innovations, made it a profitable concern, reaching for a while the huge circulation for the time of 130,000. It suffered from the rivals it created and was closed in 1837. Less successful was the *Garde Nationale* created in September 1830 with the aid of another colourful, although less substantial, adventurer, Latour-Mézeray. It was intended to appeal to what Girardin considered the new élite, but was short-lived. Latour-Mézeray had also created the first children's periodical, the *Journal des Enfants*, which at its peak sold 60,000 copies and owed much of its success to its low price and the fact that it was posted to every child with his name on the wrapper.

The year 1830 thus coincided with a development of printing techniques and advertising: it heightened the desire for newsprint by increasing political controversy and awareness. Girardin and others understood that a new class needed journals, and the first, somewhat imperfect, attempt was made by Léonce de Lavergne, an associate of Guizot. In the opening issue of the *Journal Général de la France*, 15 March 1836, he wrote "Today everyone needs to read a journal",[15] and the annual subscription was 48 francs (instead of the customary 80). This attempt to save the lower-middle classes for conservatism obtained a readership of about 3,000.

It was *La Presse* and *Le Siècle*, however, which were the true inaugurators of the new era of journalism, being more innovatory in matter and technique. The *Siècle* which appeared on the same day as the *Presse*, 23 June 1836, was its rival. Dutacq, its director, had been collaborating with Girardin, but the two had quarrelled. The *Siècle* was far less personal in its production, and suffered from a succession of management difficulties. None the less, from the start, it obtained a huge market, by judging its readership well. "In all matters, the right market has become the indispensable condition of success. . . ."[16] it declared: the press must accept this law to appeal to the new class who wanted to read a paper. So it charged 40 francs a year, and had a policy to match. This was one which was basically *gauche dynastique*, and it appealed to the *petite bourgeoisie* and artisans by its opposition, flattering their dissatisfactions by being energetic in theory. "It is a fearful tribune which dreads the sound of its own voice"[17] mocked Alfred Nettement. It reflected the moderation of its *rédacteur en chef* Adolphe Chambolle, a deputy and close follower of Odilon Barrot who sometimes contributed to it, and whose brother wrote on legal affairs for it. Its criticism was not to the standard of the *Presse* or *Journal des Débats*, but this probably did no harm to the "Journal of wine merchants"[18] as it was contemptuously called by intellectuals. Its circulation, approximately 11,000 in 1836, was 30,000 in 1840 and 35,000 in 1845, making it the most read newspaper in Paris. It had thus overtaken the *Presse* whose more conservative politics may have lost it readers, although in some ways it was a more radical publication, showing an awareness of social problems which was not general in Orleanism. Articles such as those of Granier de Cassagnac on the proletariat brought working-class problems to the middle-class home for the first time in an unpolemical manner. The *Presse* tended not to take the bourgeoisie as seriously as the *Constitutionnel* or the *Débats*: it was friendly to the legitimists, its conservatism was socially progressive and anti-liberal, and it was independent on economic policy. It was critical of the English alliance, and more friendly towards Russia. Some of this was due to the character of the Girardins and of Théophile Gautier, its literary critic. Madame de Girardin who, under the pseudonym of the Victomte de Launay, contributed an amusing and irreverent chronicle to the paper, also held a salon where political and literary notabilities such as Montalembert, Molé, Pasquier, Hugo, Lamartine, Musset and Mérimée congregated. Supporting Molé's government may have lost it readers (whilst assuredly gaining it aid from the *fonds secrets*) but when it followed Molé in his bitter attacks on Guizot after 1846 its circulation rose to 30,000. Girardin continued to lead the way in innovation: he was, for example, the first to give titles to articles. But his was a turbulent career. His support of Molé made him unpopular, and his election as deputy was twice vigorously contested on the grounds of electoral malpractice and the possibility that he was Swiss and not a French citizen. The new, cheaper newspaper which he had pioneered had itself roused considerable animosity. In the left-wing *Bon Sens*, Capo de Feuillide published a virulent criticism of him, attacking not only his price-cutting as materialistic, but also his illegitimacy. When Carrel in the *National* joined the attack, Girardin, who had begun prosecuting Capo for defamation, replied in the *Presse*, using a phrase, possibly unintentionally, which suggested that Carrel was dishonest. The latter, ever prompt to arms, sent a challenge. The two men met in the Bois de Vincennes: Girardin was gravely wounded, but Carrel received a bullet in the stomach and died two days later. Thus the prosaic economics of the new press were accompanied by bloodshed. Carrel's death was a serious deprivation for journalism but his *National* could not avoid lowering its subscription.

The *Journal des Débats* remained at 80 francs a year, appealing as it did to a wealthier readership, but others reduced their prices, the *National* and *Gazette* to 60 francs, the *Quotidienne* to 40 francs in 1843. This was a very dangerous price for a paper without a large circulation, making it more dependent upon outside financial aid. Advertising took on an increased importance: Girardin's successful gamble was based on the assumption that advertising, attracted by a large circulation, would compensate for the halving of subscriptions. Because of the price revolution, the total publication of national newspapers rose from about 110,000 in 1836 (not very different from what it had been in 1831) to 180,000 in 1845, showing particularly sharp jumps at times of political excitement such as the 1839 Coalition and the

1840 Eastern crisis. The concept of news itself became a replacement for political comment, partly because of the increased speed of transport. Charles Havas founded an agency with correspondents in different countries, and carrier pigeons hastened the latest events in Vienna or Frankfurt to the Parisian breakfast table.

Girardin's example inspired imitators. Besides the *Journal Général* and the *Siècle*, there was the *Globe*, set up in 1841, directed by Granier de Cassagnac, which in 1846 became *L'Époque*. Less successful than the *Presse* whose pro-Guizot rival it was intended to be, it none the less had a readership of 10,000 to 12,000. It developed a new style with larger pages, clearer divisions between subjects and frequent supplements. The ministry gave it considerable contributions from the *fonds secrets*.

The profitability of the mass circulation newspaper inspired Docteur Véron, a publicist and adventurer in the Girardin mould, to acquire the *Constitutionnel*. He and a group of investors bought it in 1844 for 432,000 francs. The readership, small bourgeoisie and shopkeepers, had often deserted to the *Presse* or *Siècle*, and the once great journal, the terror of the Restoration, had sunk to a circulation of about 3,500. Véron maintained its favourability to Thiers, its *petit bourgeois frondeur* spirit, its anticlericalism, although he put new attack into it, but it was not politics or editorial policy which quadrupled the circulation before the end of the year, increasing to 25,000 in 1845, nor was it purely the result of the overdue price reduction to 40 francs. The success was the result of that new incursion into the world of journalism – the serial.

Ironically, it was the staid *Journal des Débats* which was one of the first to include a daily slice of fiction. Needing a way to repel the challenge of the cheap press without lowering its price, it had followed the lead of Girardin who had, in October 1836, published Balzac's *Vieille Fille*. With Sue's *Mystères de Paris*, the *Débats* had an immense success which kept its impatient readers faithful, and again in 1845 *Le Comte de Monte Cristo* increased its readership. It was Sue's *Juif Errant* which was the salvation of the *Constitutionnel* although when Véron paid the author 100,000 francs for it, it was no more than a title.

Some journals refused to print serials: the *National* and Nettement's *Gazette*, on opposing political sides, agreed that modern fiction was a source of corruption and that such frivolity besmirched a serious journal. The *Quotidienne* published only a few, which, since they had to conform to strict moral standards, were tedious and unsuccessful. Another legitimist paper, the *Union Monarchique*, began publishing Balzac's *Député d'Arcis* but the protests were such that it ceased printing it (and the author ceased to write it). The serial seemed like the newspaper itself, fascinating and dangerous. The same criticisms were made against it: it lowered the standards of fiction as the press generally debauched literature and philosophy. The *Presse* printed a story from that suspect figure, the Comte de Courchamp, gourmand and transvestite. The *National* discovered that *Le Val Funeste* was lifted from an old novel, and simultaneously with the *Presse*, printed the last instalment; the two proved almost identical. There was universal laughter whilst the *Presse* prosecuted the luckless plagiarist.[19]

It was a period of an increase in the numbers of newspaper, an overall increase in sales and a tendency for periodicals to become dailies. Receiving a newspaper every day became a habit: Émile de Girardin quickly changed his determination that the *Presse* should not appear on Monday bccause there had been no news on the Sunday. A paper reached a wider audience than that which subscribed to it. The *estaminet* provided a copy, usually republican or opposition, and there were political clubs in many towns. There was also the reading room where all opinions could be daily consulted on payment of a subscription and where the latest fiction could be read. The rise in the daily press made the pamphlet and brochure less important than had been the case under the Restoration, but the republican pamphlets published by Pagnerre at 50 centimes usually sold widely, and writers like Lamennais and Cormenin could expect to sell 10,000 copies.

In 1845, the *Siècle* was the leading paper as it had been almost as soon as it was born, with 23 per cent of the total readership, 21 per cent going to the *Presse*. The revived *Constitutionnel* followed with about 12 per cent of the total. Then came the *Débats* whose share was 7 per cent a substantial relegation from the days when it had led Orleanist opinion: with only 6,571 subscribers, it had suffered from *L'Epoque* which had almost as large a proportion. The fusion of legitimist papers, *L'Union Monarchique*, had 5 per cent, *La Quotidienne*, *Le National* and Catholic *L'Univers* about equal with slightly less of the total. Thus only the *Débats* and *L'Epoque* with one-sixth of the readership of Paris supported the Guizot ministry, the conservative *Presse* being as bitterly hostile as the organs of the left. That the *Siècle*, the most popular Parisian newspaper, and the *Constitutionnel*, together selling over one-third, were opposed to the generally conservative principles into which the monarchy had fallen, should have been a warning, as was the fact that over 180,000 Parisians read a newspaper whilst less than a tenth of these could vote. Yet the poor showing of republican newspapers is noticeable, only the distinctly moderate *National* finding a low place amongst the leading newspapers of the capital.

The *Journal des Débats* is usually seen as the newspaper better than any other representing Orleanism and encapsulating the opinions of the *haute bourgeoisie*. The famous Ingres portrait of Louis François Bertin, one of the two brothers who directed it (and who owned a four-sevenths share in it), has become an image symbolic of the Orleanist bourgeois. Thumbs on knees, obese, shrewd and self-confident, he stares out on the world. Yet the Bertins were too individualistic to be typical and the paper they produced was in some respects unconventional. It was read by the upper-middle classes, property-owners, lawyers, bankers and academics: manufacturers tended to read the *Temps* or the *Presse* which was protectionist, whilst the *Débats* was for free trade in tune with its academically liberal ideas. It was read by some deputies but disliked by others, not only of the opposition, for the scorn with which it treated the provincial deputies. The *Débats* was élitist, with no sympathy with mediocrity or the distrust for superiority felt by many conservatives in face of Broglie or Guizot. Although conservative, it had little sympathy for legitimism and was anticlerical. It tended to support the doctrinaires because it found in them the intellectual stringency it admired, but it never placed itself unreservedly at the disposal of any group or party. Although the *Débats* gave support to every ministry, it retained a certain independence. Whilst accepting a grant from *fonds secrets*, even from Thiers whom it supported in the most lukewarm way and sometimes criticised, it always spoke with a characteristic voice. It was governmental rather than dynastic, for example when in May 1844 it criticised the Prince de Joinville for writing a pamphlet on the navy which showed hostility to the Guizot ministry. Yet it had links with the Court: Auguste Bertin de Vaux, son of the younger of the two founding brothers, was *officier d'ordonnance* of the Duc d'Orléans. (This was one of the reasons that the *Débats*, rather against its will, supported thc fortifications of Paris.) Bertin de Vaux's father became a peer and Armand Bertin, the son of Bertin (*l'aîné*), was a college friend of Montalivet whose acquaintance he maintained. The newspaper was thus part of the highest Orleanist political echelons. This made it an excellent target as being a symbol of a class otherwise difficult to define. Alfred Nettement, the legitimist journalist, wrote a *Histoire du Journal des Débats* (1842), describing its *haut bourgeois* egoism, its revolutionary cynicism against the Restoration and its selfish complacency when enjoying the fruits of power. This invective could not alter the high quality of its writing. Amongst those providing the *premier-Paris* (often contributed by some notability), were Silvestre de Sacy and the deputy Saint-Marc Girardin (whose attacks on Russia over Poland embarrassed the government, and brought the conservative journal the distinction of being banned in Russia). Cuvillier-Fleury (tutor to Aumale), Xavier Doudan (protégé of the Duc de Broglie) and Philarète Chasles contributed to the *variétés*: Jules Janin wrote on the theatre and Delécluze on art. Berlioz, who taught Bertin's talented daughter, was an unenthusiastic but brilliant music critic. The former Saint-Simonian, Michel Chevalier, wrote on economics. If the politics of the *Débats* were conservative, it was none the less progressive in art and finance.

The *Débats* overshadowed all conservative rivals until the *Presse* established itself in 1836. The *Moniteur Universel* was official, reporting debates and making government announcements. Most of its 2,000 copies went free to officials. The others tended to be party organs, often very personal and usually short-lived. There was the *Charte de 1830*, an evening paper, which merged in 1838 with another of small circulation, the *Moniteur Parisien*. Created by doctrinaires to oppose Thiers, receiving from Duvergier de Hauranne a daily account of events in the Chamber of Deputies, it could not resist the financial blandishments of Molé and came to oppose those who had created it. Its continued ministerialism and need for finance returned it to the doctrinaire fold after 1839. Similarly a title put to different uses was the *Journal de Paris* which was printed between 1836 and 1840. If any readers read it throughout this period, they must have become sadly confused for, having originally been pro-Thiers, it was sold to the doctrinaires, turned highly conservative but anti-doctrinaire under Fonfrède when it reached its peak of *c.* 2,000 subscribers, and then returned to doctrinaire hands and oblivion.

Thiers founded the short-lived *Nouvelliste* to be deliberately extreme in his favour to rouse other journals. He also helped Walewski who bought for 140,000 francs in May 1838 the *Messager des Chambres*, which had a circulation of less than 1,000, and made it pro-Thiers. It never prospered, however, and his main organ was the *Constitutionnel*. In 1830 this had been the leading newspaper of Orleanism with a middle-class readership of 23,000 and, more active in July than the cautious *Débats*, it regarded the regime as its own creation. Rivalry, and its increasingly uninspired writing, had drastically reduced its readership until Docteur Véron, having been a powerless *actionnaire*, became director and *gérant* and resurrected it. Thiers helped Véron, obtaining finance from industrialists by promising them that it would follow a protectionist policy. It had a readership of the *petite bourgeoisie*, minor officials, clerks and shopkeepers: its tone was anticlerical, socially conservative but politically irreverent. It had also been conventionally classical in its artistic criticism because two conservative Academicians, Étienne and Jay, associates of Thiers in the Chamber, were *actionnaires*, and its guiding spirits in literature. Véron destroyed their predominance, and as he had rejuvenated the Opéra with Meyerbeer's *Robert-le-Diable*, so he revived the *Constitutionnel* by daily bringing his readers the drama of Sue's *Juif Errant*.

The *Temps*, the other main newspaper of the centre, had died before a Véron could save it. It had a strong commercial bias and had possessed many readers amongst moderate business men. It reflected the undogmatic conservatism common to such people, disliked the doctrinaires heartily and for most of the 1830s, found its hero in Dupin. Its leading writer, Pagès (de l'Ariège), made it a supporter of Molé, then it turned to Passy and Dufaure and lastly to Thiers. In 1842 it disappeared, its circulation down to almost 1,000, a substantial decline from its 1830 total of 8,000 when it, like the *Constitutionnel*, had gained prestige from its role as a proponent of insurrection.

The legitimists had several journals, reflecting their different nuances. The *Quotidienne* tended to support Berryer and the Duc de Noailles in Parliament. It was loyal to the exiled Court and its Catholicism was ultramontane. Laurentie, its editor for much of the period, took care not to offend the landed proprietors who formed a substantial part of its readership. The large proportion of its readers who lived outside Paris gradually turned away as the provincial royalist press increased its efforts. The decline in readership of the *Quotidienne* from about 6,000 in 1831 to half this, persuaded it to join with the smaller and more reactionary *La France* and the *Écho Francais* to produce in February 1847 the *Union Monarchique*, directed by Laurentie and Henri de Riancey, and printing about 7,000 copies.

When an attempt had previously been made in 1841 to create unity in the royalist press, the *Gazette de France* had refused to co-operate. Under the Abbé de Genoude, it followed an idiosyncratic course advocating universal suffrage and association with radicals rather than parliamentary behaviour. Genoude even went so far as to form with Laffitte and others an anti-Orleanist journal demanding electoral reform. The *Gazette* attracted the more extreme but less conservative legitimists, and had a circulation of about 5,000. Also legitimist was the fashion journal *La Mode* edited by Vicomte Edouard Walsh, then Nettement, who interspersed its elegant drawings with violent and sometimes witty royalist polemics.

The republicans and left had a wide range of newspapers. The *Siècle*, created in 1836, would be the most widely read, the spirit of opposition of the lesser bourgeoisie. The *Courrier Francais* would suffer from its competition and its readership decline from 8,000 in 1831 to a fifth of this in 1845. It was further to the left than the *Siècle*, and somewhat dull: Léon Faucher was for most of the time its political writer, and Adolphe Blanqui, leading economist and brother of the revolutionary Auguste, made it a serious and estimable production. More eccentric was the *Journal du Commerce*, a paper with a circulation of under 3,000, of which the left-wing Bonapartist Mauguin was usually a guiding force. There were two other Bonapartist organs, both short-lived: *La Révolution de 1830* which appeared in 1831–32, and *Le Càpitole* which ran from June to December 1840. The local *Progrès du Pas-de-Calais* also showed republico-Bonapartism in action by publishing articles from the pen of the pretender, Prince Louis.

Of the variety of openly republican newspapers, the *National* was the leader. It retained a fairly consistent readership of 4,000 consisting of middle-class republicans and patriots, students, soldiers and a few prosperous artisans. Its social policy was conservative, it opposed strikes and it favoured universal suffrage only in the distant future. What he regarded as a pusillanimous foreign policy had persuaded Armand Carrel, its chief contributor, to take it from its liberal Orleanism into republicanism in 1831. Whereas Carrel had refused a prefecture from his erstwhile collaborator, Thiers, and become a republican, Marrast, his successor, had become a republican after he had asked for a prefecture and been refused. A superb stylist like Carrel, like him he was also dandified, somewhat arrogant and snobbish, but without the other's genuine and idealistic devotion to liberty. When a contributor to the *Tribune*, the more extreme competitor of the *National*, between 1831 and 1835, he had written violently: when Carrel's stormy life came to an end in a duel with a fellow journalist, he replaced him and followed his more moderate line. As Paris became more radical, a greater proportion of the *National*'s subscribers were provincials.

The successor to the *Tribune*, killed by the trials against the republican press, was the *Journal du Peuple* (1839–42), edited by Dupoty with a committee of republicans behind him of varying shades of opinion, including Louis Blanc, Godefroy Cavaignac and Audry de Puyraveau. It was succeeded after it too died as a result of prosecution, by *La Réforme* of Ledru-Rollin. Edited by Flocon, it received contributions from Etienne and François Arago, Cavaignac and Blanc. It had a more socialistic complexion than its predecessor, whilst avoiding any ideological consistency. Revolutionary in its ethos, like the *Tribune*, and unlike the *National*, it openly admired the Jacobins and had about 2,000 subscribers.

A large number of other socialist and republican journals were published on a narrow base such as Blanc's *Revue de Progrès* (1839–42), propagating his ideas on the organisation of labour. The individualist Raspail had his own mouthpiece and Vinçard's *Ruche Populaire* had Saint-Simonian tendencies. There was Cabet's *Populaire* which propounded his system of communism from 1841 onwards and the Fourierist journals of Considérant, the *Phalange* and the *Démocratie*, the latter achieving over 2,000 subscribers, unusually high for such productions. There were also the working-class papers, notably Buchez's *L'Atelier*, founded in 1840, although the *Bon Sens* had been the first to include working-class contributions and to aim particularly at this audience. A conservative attempt to reach the lower classes, *Le Conservateur*, financed by Gabriel and François Delessert and other friends of the government, died in 1847 for lack of subscribers. Finally, amongst the daily papers, one may notice the *Estafette*, appearing after 1836 to cater for the 3,000 who wanted all opinions by simply giving extracts from other newspapers.

Political in nature were also the satirical and caricature magazines. The king of this world was Charles Philipon, who had a small drawing ability but an even greater one for organising the talents of others. *La Caricature*, which began like so many other news enterprises in the autumn of 1830, employed Daumier, Grandville, Mounier, Carlet and Devéria amongst others. Philipon and Louis Desnoyers, who wrote the text, imparted to this production a bitter personal hostility towards the King, whom it attacked for *lèse–nation*. In caricature, the shape of his head was made to resemble a pear, which quickly became a popular joke. On 7 June 1832, jesting concerning the King's proneness to assassination attempts and a project for *un monument expiapoire* to be erected in the event of a successful one, led to prosecution. In court Philipon claimed the resemblance of the sovereign to a fruit was a coincidence and attempted to prove it diagrammatically. This feat did not prevent his imprisonment for six months, but sales of a print showing the royal head becoming a pear in four stages paid for the fine which was imposed. The September laws on caricatures and prints made it impossible for *La Caricature* to continue, and Philipon also sold his *Charivari*, the first illustrated daily established in 1832, which had delivered a bitter daily satirical attack on the government, and turned to the profitable and safer field of "comics" less political in tone. Its work was continued by the *Corsaire*, absorbing another small sheet in 1844 and becoming the *Corsaire-Satan*. It had some brilliant contributors in Alphonse Karr (famous for his satirical *Guêpes* which retailed scandal and mocked everyone and everything), Henry Mürger, Jules Sandeau, Louis Champfleury and Léon Gozlan. It lived an insecure existence, however, and gave the impression of being written by boulevardiers for their own amusement, which was largely the case.

Other interest groups were provided for. The journalist discovered the existence of women and children. As well as the fashion journals, there were serious productions for women such as the *Tribune des Femmes*, Saint-Simonian in nature, and for children a host of edifying and instructive journals. The *Journal des Economistes*, founded by Adolphe Blanqui in 1841, was the organ of the liberal economists: it sought to propagate principles of free trade. Most of its contributors were also writers for other papers – Chevalier for the *Débats*, Dussard for the *Temps*, Faucher for the *Courrier Français* and Wolewski for the *Siècle*.

Of a much wider readership was the *Gazette des Tribunaux*, which catered exhaustively and more frankly than the daily papers to the public voracity for criminal cases and scandal. There were also the religious journals. The *Ami de la Religion* was the organ of the bishopric of Paris, the *Correspondant* was a serious, weighty and moderate monthly, but most remarkable was *L'Univers*. Begun as a Catholic daily in 1836, it struggled for a few years with under 2,000 subscribers, annexing the doctrinaire *Journal Général* in 1840. Then the entry of Veuillot brought to it a brilliant polemical talent and the struggle for freedom of education gave him a cause: by 1847 this now belligerent religious paper had obtained a circulation of 6,000.

The period saw the expansion of the literary journal. In François Buloz the literary scene had one of those entrepreneurs in which the Orleanist artistic and journalistic world was so rich. He became director of the *Revue des Deux Mondes* in 1831, attracting to it contributors from amongst the foremost names of the day, although this created difficulties, most of which Buloz overcame. It was necessary to moderate critics in order to retain the contributors: Balzac refused to write for it after Gustave Planche criticised his *Contes Drolatiques* for obscenity. Moderately romantic, it presented high-quality material to a middle-brow readership: Buloz turned down an article on Kant by Cousin because he himself could not understand it. Basically literary, it contained articles on social questions and a political commentary, of centrist opinion. Although it had a readership of 2,000 it could not make a profit on its own, and Buloz relied upon the subscription which the Ministries of the Interior and Public Instruction took out for their dependent bodies, and to accept governmental aid which forced him unenthusiastically to support Guizot. The *Revue de Paris*, founded in 1834, was of a slightly lower standard and greater actuality. It began to print excerpts from novels. A left-wing answer appeared in 1841, the *Revue Indépendante* of George Sand and Pierre Leroux who in it pronounded their mystical brand of socialism.

The provinces reflected similar opinions to those of Paris but of their approximately 500 newspapers most were very small. Only about 30 printed over 1,000 copies (6 of which were republican) and those of over 2,000 were rare. There was, for example, the dynamic *Courrier de la Gironde*, vehemently but unorthodoxly Orleanist under Fonfrède and catering to the spirit of particularism of Bordeaux, selling 4,000 copies. The republican *Courrier de Lyon* had 3,500 and Lille possessed a huge newspaper readership, shared between three, of which the two largest were in opposition: the legitimist *Gazette de Flandre* sold 4,000 copies and the *Écho du Nord* was *gauche dynastique* of the left, anticlerical and sold to the commercial and industrial bourgeoisie of the area. With 6,000 readers, it was the largest provincial newspaper and put the conservative Orleanist rival into a poor third place.

The large towns, Marseilles, Nantes, Le Havre, Lille, Strasbourg, had two or three newspapers like this, and Bordeaux, Lyons and Rouen each supported four dailies. Thus at Strasbourg there was the *Courrier du Bas Rhin*, nationalistic and moderately republican, and *L'Alsacien*, extreme left and revolutionary: opposing them was the *Journal du Haut et Bas Rhin*, formed in 1832 by the prefect with the assistance of manufacturers to support the conservatives. Many such local ministerial papers were prefectorally inspired, and suffered from the need to follow the governmental line. They did have the advantage of being able to print judicial announcements, but on the whole Orleanist notabilities seemed to be little interested in the press, perhaps because too involved in the sweets of power. The conservative Orleanist press also had the disadvantage that the more talented of its contributors would automatically be attracted by the capital and the prospects of a career. Even the ardently Girondin Fonfrède spent some years in Paris, and the humbly born Veuillot began his career in a local paper at Rouen, then became editor of Bugeaud's mouthpiece at Périgeux before moving to the capital and the *Univers*. Similarly Léonce de Lavergne of the *Journal de Toulouse* became *chef de cabinet* of the Comte de Rémusat, the local Orleanist notability, and after some ministerial journalism in the capital, fell into an official career becoming a deputy and *sous-directeur* at the Ministry of Foreign Affairs.

The legitimists on the other hand had a wealth of provincial talent which could not pursue official careers. About forty legitimist newspapers were spread through thirty-one departments. Alfred de La Guéronniere at the *Avenir National* of Limoges, Armand de Pontmartin with the *Gazette du Dauphinée* and others, gave small productions an unexpected flair. The bureau of these was often the local party headquarters and sometimes the editor was also director and proprietor. Republican newspapers were published in most great towns, especially in the east, but were rarer in the west and south-west, where opposition was legitimist. The problems and controversies were the same as in Paris. In Marseilles, the *Peuple Souverain* came to an end when Maillefer, its editor, was arrested, compromised in the plots of April 1834. Divisions between socialist and moderate political republicans were frequently bitter. So the *Censeur* of Lyons accused socialists of diverting the working classes from political action, and in its turn was accused of being egoistically bourgeois. None the less, provincial journals enabled republicanism to become a national movement after 1830, and legitimism maintained its strength through a vital local press. Orleanists should have worried more about their weakness in this arena. The manner in which the provincial press conforms to that of the capital, follows its divisions, reflects its controversies and often copies its words, shows how, in spite of occasional lingering particularism, the country was increasingly becoming an intellectual unity. Frenchmen liked their information and opinion to come through a local mouthpiece, but nothing could alter the fact that news was Parisian.

REFERENCES

1. Stendhal, *Lucien Leuwen* (Martineau edition), 422.
2. C. de Lacombe, *Vie de Berryer* (1895), II, 84.
3. Comte C. de Montalembert, *Correspondance* (1905), 183.
4. H. de Lacretelle, *Lamartine et ses amis* (1878), 75.
5. L. Vivien de St-Martin, 'Souvenirs', *Le Correspondant*, 25 September 1905, 1058–9.
6. Public Records Office, Foreign Office Papers, 27.559 (Granville to Palmerston, 12 January 1838).
7. L. Vienne, *Journal* (1955), 103.
8. H. de Balzac and Laurent-Jan, *Monographie de la Presse Parisienne* (1843), 78.
9. Théophile Gautier, *Mademoiselle Maupin* (Charpentier edition, 1922), 34–5.
10. E. de Girardin, *De l'instruction publique en France* (1842), 457.
11. A. de Tocqueville, *Démocratie en Amerique* (1835), Part II, Ch. 2.
12. H. de Balzac, *Cousine Bette* (Garnier edition, 1967), 46.
13. Ibid., 77–8.
14. H. de Villemessant, *Mémoires d'un journaliste* (1872), 96.
15. *Journal Général de la France*, 15 March 1836.
16. *Le Siècle*, 23 June 1836.
17. A. Nettement, *La Presse Parisienne* (1845), 49–50.
18. A. Challamel, *Souvenirs d'un hugolâtre* (1885), 335.
19. T. Muret, *A Travers Champs* (1858), 75–83.

15

Foreign Policy, 1830–1835

"Sombre quatre-vingt-treize, épouvantable année,
De lauriers et de sang grande ombre couronnée,
Du fond des temps ne te relève pas!
Ne te relève pas pour contempler nos guerres,
Car nous sommes des nains à coté de nos pères."

("Sombre '93, frightful year,
A great shadow crowned by laurels and blood,
From the abyss of the times do not raise yourself!
Do not raise yourself to contemplate our wars,
Because we are dwarfs alongside our fathers.")[1]

In the aftermath of revolution, the chanting of the "Marseillaise" and sudden blooming of a Napoleonic cult in Parisian street theatres reflected an exuberant and bellicose patriotism. Many believed with Carrel that the peace treaties of 1814 had been destroyed together with the monarchy that military defeat had restored to France.[2] The *parti du mouvement* was united in desire for an aggressive foreign policy, confident in the belief that absolute monarchs would be dethroned by their subjects if they dared fight democratic France. Audry de Puyraveau led demands for a *levée en masse* to begin the European revolutionary struggle. A new popular diplomacy, predicted La Fayette, would replace the conspiratorial bartering of nations' welfare behind palace doors.[3]

They were to be disappointed. Louis-Philippe from the beginning showed himself a lover of peace, and directing external relations he considered his prime duty. He was prepared to use secret means to do so. Constant vigilance was necessary lest the diplomatically inexperienced relics of the Empire who had attained positions of importance provoked a crisis by their clumsiness, or events in Belgium, Poland or Italy initiated a European conflict. He triumphed, but at the expense of his popularity. Laffitte in 1831 and Thiers in 1836 and again in 1840 left office, criticising the King and his foreign policy. He attracted to himself the odium of "peace at any price",[4] and his greatest claim to Europe's gratitude became the foremost cause of his unpopularity in France.

The appointment of Molé as Foreign Minister in August 1830 revealed the King's conservative intentions. Not even Apponyi, the Austrian ambassador in Paris who foresaw terrible consequences of the July days, believed that this *grand seigneur* would encourage Jacobinism. Special envoys were despatched to the Courts of Europe with letters justifying the new monarchy and asserting its devotion to peace and existing treaties. Général Athalin, sent to St Petersburg, had the most difficult task. It was only in late September that Tsar Nicholas I, who regarded himself as the guardian of legitimacy, sent an ungracious letter of recognition to Louis-Philippe, addressing him not in the terms usual between monarchs as "Monsieur my brother", but as "Sir". Other rulers had accepted him more speedily, although Ferdinand VII of Spain had been compelled by the threat not to prevent Spanish liberal refugees forming an army on the border. The only exception was the Duke of Modena, whose royalist principles forbade him to compromise with revolution; but his acceptance was dispensable.

When late in August revolution in Belgium against union with Holland overthrew the barrier which had been erected against French expansion in 1815, European prejudice against the new regime seemed justified as the left hailed it as the initiation of the destruction of the Vienna settlement. The July Monarchy, caught between nationalist passions and the need to placate other governments, was led to enunciate the central principle of its diplomacy, which it chose to term "non-intervention" and to seek the friendship of Britain, which unsatisfactory alliance was to be the pivot of its foreign policy. Fearing that a European power might militarily assist the King of the Netherlands crush the revolt, Molé declared that such action would force France to aid the Belgians. This improvised response to a crisis became a general principle: France promised to respect the status quo, if other powers did the same. Talleyrand called non-intervention "an abstract and politic word which virtually means intervention".[5] Certainly, in a continent where the great powers habitually interfered in the internal affairs of the smaller states, the term could scarcely mean what it said. However, it stated clearly what actions would be regarded as a *casus belli*. Sébastiani stated that his *circonscription* of areas where the principle applied were France's neighbours, Belgium, Piedmont, Spain and the Rhineland provinces. Here, France claimed the right to particular influence (unsuccessfully in Piedmont) whilst refusing it to others.

Britain like France objected to the Northern Courts claiming the right to give military assistance to any threatened conservative government. The two countries also had their constitutional ideology in common, but commercial interests and rivalries of influene constantly threatened their *entente*. For many Orleanists, notably Broglie, the alliance of the two liberal powers was a moral and philosophical necessity. As his son-in-law, the Comte d'Haussonville, wrote when the two promoted the regular development of "modern institutions, we have the advantage of fulfilling our liberal mission without appearing revolutionary".[6] This alignment was an equivalent in foreign policy to the *juste milieu* and its essentiality to Orleanism was shown by its maintenance in spite of the fact that France clashed directly with Britain more than with any other power. Guizot was essentially correct in saying of the *entente* that "England, strongly sympathetic to France, pushes her ministers in a favourable direction; France, although a little surprised, follows her King in the same direction".[7] Nowhere more than in foreign policy were the Orleanists so much separated from public opinion, for they regarded England as France's natural ally, whilst to the average Frenchman, she was the natural enemy.

Of all the early actions of the young regime, the appointment of the Prince de Talleyrand to the London embassy was that which most horrified radical opinion. If the aged statesman's reputation for astute duplicity was vast, to the idealists of 1830 he exhaled all the corruptions of the *ancien régime*. The doggerel of Barthélemy, suspicious of all French ambassadors and "their hidden policy in accord with the sovereigns", reached a peak of vitriolic disgust when he came to describe

> *the lie incarnate, the living perjury,*
> *Talleyrand-Périgord, Prince of Benevento!*"[8]

The Paris opposition was disgusted; Molé, who realised the danger the prestigious figure presented to his control of the ministry, was displeased, but most conservative opinion approved the choice. Louis-Philippe, surprised by the hostile reaction, was satisfied by Talleyrand's reception in Britain where "the plain good sense of John Bull appreciates that this nomination is the most sage and happy for the two countries".[9] If his appointment was not one to popularise the *entente* in France, the new ambassador was indeed enthusiastically received in England. "The July Revolution is sometimes a little bourgeois in Paris, but, thanks to M. de Talleyrand, it takes a very high tone in London",[10] wrote a contemporary. With his niece, the Duchesse de Dino, in command of his salon, the lame, wrinkled prince could from this vantage point deliver his mordant witticisms, dispense conservative wisdom to a European audience and rule French foreign policy with Louis-Philippe's assistance (if the minister were the compliant Sébastiani or de Rigny).

The government tried to show its good faith by action against ths plots of refugees: it dispersed an Italian army gathering at Lyons in February 1831, stopped the collection of arms by Spanish liberals, and prevented the *parti du mouvement* from involving France in the struggles of Belgians and Poles. However, those who desired war were not only on the left. There were many who, believing that the defeats of 1814 were a mere incongruity in the designs of Providence, felt that a war would best establish the new regime. The servants of Napoleon, many of whom occupied high office in the aftermath of the July Revolution, had adopted his belief in the grand design and the short victorious campaign. So such a conservative as Bertin de Vaux, briefly ambassador at The Hague, recommended a war against the Netherlands: Maréchal Maison, ambassador in Vienna, favoured an attack to drive the Austrians out of Italy, and in Constantinople, Général Guilleminot planned an Ottoman–Polish attack upon the Russian Empire. The King kept watch on these, moderated Sébastiani's despatches when they sounded bellicose and restrained those such as Soult, who, although unwilling to compromise themselves, sometimes seemed not averse from the prospect of war. Even the Prince Royal expressed his willingness to fight to destroy the 1815 treaties and create a new Europe. The Continent was dangerously close to conflagration and much of the credit for peace must go to Louis-Philippe. If Périer's obsessive desire for European disarmament was doomed to frustration, as his more realistic monarch realised, there was a grandeur in the concept as there was in the King's preparedness to risk his own popularity for peace.

After Belgium, events in Poland and Italy maintained Europe and the young regime in perilous crises. On 28 November, insurrection broke out in Warsaw. The Poles believed that France, fresh from her own revolt, would come to their aid. Almost all Parisian newspapers were favourable to the Poles and hostile to their Russian masters. The *National* called for a declaration of war, not only on the Tsar, but on Prussia and Austria also, using revolutionary means. The Catholic *Avenir* saw a Catholic revolt against oppressive heretics and believed that France should provide material assistance, whatever the cost. Delavigne followed the *Parisienne* with the *Varsovienne* and crowds identified themselves with the Poles by singing emotionally.

> *"For old brothers in arms*
> *Have you only tears?"*

an implied criticism of their own government. In March 1831, Parisian crowds attacked the Russian embassy and insulted the ambassador.

From the beginning, the French government recognised itself powerless. Even had it wished to fight, to do so was geographically and militarily impossible. Louis-Philippe assured Polish envoys of his government's good offices but promised no more than this, and his envoy to Russia, the Duc de Mortemart, similarly attempted to impress upon the leaders of the insurrection that France would not provide military assistance. The rebels, however, would not hear of compromise, putting their trust in the influence of La Fayette and the triumph of the *mouvement*. Early in 1831 Prussia was asked not to assist the Tsar's troops in repressing the insurrection but to no avail. Britain was little more helpful, since Palmerston refused pleas to offer joint mediation: what little influence France had, disappeared as Nicholas grew increasingly angry at the presence of Polish refugees in Paris, and the revolutionary bellicosity of the French press. Mortemart could have no effect in Saint Petersburg although he continually counselled moderation and concession, as instructed by his government. France would do no more than argue for the maintenance of congress Poland.

The capitulation of Warsaw on 7 September created an upsurge of anger, directed more against the government than against Russia. Sébastiani became "the Corsican who represents the executioner of Poland"[12] and a misrepresentation of his embarrassed announcement of the Polish defeat became for ever associated with his name. It produced three days' rioting in Paris and further attempts to storm the Russian embassy. In later years, the government would find itself regularly defeated when proposals sympathetic to Poland were made during debates on the King's speech: many ministerialist deputies, like the *Journal des Débats*, were Russophobic and enjoyed the opportunity for displaying their generous emotions. The left, for its part, ignored the fact that Laffitte's ministry had done as little for Poland as had Périer's. On this issue, French opinion continued to display a lack of realism which was not shared by its government.

Italy was in theory an area within the French sphere of non-intervention, but in practice the peninsula was under Austrian domination, and the entry of Austrian troops into Piedmont was the only action likely to produce war. None the less, France and Austria fought for influence throughout the period. Fear of revolution caused the Italian princes to reinforce their links with Austria, who crushed the risings of 1831, causing a crisis in the affairs of the two countries. The French ambassador in Vienna, Maréchal Maison, urged his government militarily to protect the policy of non-intervention, risking war whilst Austria was poorly prepared. The fall of Laffitte enabled Louis-Philippe to impose his peace policy with less difficulty, for even Sébastiani had wavered in this in the face of his growing unpopularity and lack of Cabinet support.

Périer believed in resistance abroad as at home. When Habsburg troops entered the Papal States, France protested and made some bellicose gestures but, as Périer knew, she was powerless. The characteristic Orleanist position, facing the hostility of both conservatives and progressives, centrist in her foreign relations as in her internal affairs, is shown in all its weakness in Italy. France was distrusted by the legitimist princes and Austria, whilst her failure to aid the revolutionaries brought upon her accusations of selfish egoism from Italian radicals. In spite of their talent and moderation, neither the Baron de Barante nor the Comte de Sainte-Aulaire, ambassadors at Turin and Rome, were able to gain the confidence of the Piedmontese or papal governments. Their instructions were to advocate reform and compromise, and to encourage the Italian rulers to establish their independence from Austria. Périer, facing elections, was anxious to obtain the withdrawal of Austrian troops from papal territory. In discussions at Rome, France and Britain demanded reforms against an obstructive Austria and a vacillating Papacy. The French government felt the Catholic Sainte-Aulaire was too indulgent to the Papacy but was less concerned with reforming the Papal States than with freeing them from Austrian presence. Périer accepted a compromise reform programme whose implementation was not enforceable; determined to obtain Austrian evacuation before the new Chamber of Deputies commenced its session late in July 1831, he sent a French squadron to the Italian coasts. The Papacy, fearing a war between France and Austria (for Sébastiani's despatches, albeit moderated by Louis-Philippe, sounded threatening), agreed to French demands, and Metternich, not desiring the fall of the conservative Périer, promised to withdraw the troops. It appeared that the middle way, strengthened by threats, had triumphed, and the King's speech announced the evacuation, "Just as I have demanded",[12] a phrase which offended Metternich.

Italy remained an embarrassment, however, for no liberalisation took place, nor did disturbances decrease in the Papal Legations. The Pope's inability to control them led him to appeal to Metternich, and on 23 January 1832 Austrian troops again crossed into papal territory. Périer was furious and took the action promised as the inevitable French reaction to an Austrian advance. Orders were given for a French force to sail to the Adriatic and and to take possession of the papal fortress of Ancona. Talleyrand thought it was "a stupidity"[13] but obtained English acquiescence: Sainte-Aulaire, facing papal protests, found the expedition "deplorable"[14] but public opinion and indeed France's reputation as a great power demanded some such assertion.

On 23 February 1832 1,500 men under Colonel Combes occupied Ancona and the tricolour was hoisted on the citadel. Whilst Sainte-Aulaire and the expedition's titular commander, Général Cubières, assured the Pope that France wished to protect him and would do nothing to exacerbate revolutionary discontent, Commandant Gallois, the naval chief, made a proclamation which announced that his force preceded a French army which would aid them in fighting for that liberty desired for them by Napoleon. Gallois was quickly withdrawn. His independent act had merely heightened the ambiguity of a manœuvre which was not revolutionary but purely anti-Austrian. As La Fayette asked, for whom and against whom was the expedition? Its effect was more conservative than otherwise for, to obtain papal recognition of its temporary occupation, the French government abandoned its zeal for reform.

In Belgium, however, military conflict, albeit on a small scale, could not be avoided. The left led by Lamarque, Bignon and Mauguin, demanded that France simply occupy Belgium, a conquest justified as being within the "natural frontiers". They were furious when France co-operated with representatives of the four other powers in the London Conference, even when Laffitte presented as a great triumph Talleyrand's success in having the fact of Belgian separation recognised. Many Belgians desired unification with France, but French commercial interests feared the competition. The deputy Cunin-Gridaine, spokesman for the textile manufacturers of the north, warned how the industry would be damaged, and the mayor of Elbeuf wrote to the mayors of other industrial towns calling upon them to join in repelling the advances of a commercial enemy. It was, however, the diplomatic factor which determined the government's attitude. It desperately desired to find something to give public opinion, but it was impossible to dispense with British support. The illegitimate son of Talleyrand, the Comte de Flahaut, was sent to urge his father to attempt a partition of Belgium between France and the Netherlands. Louis-Philippe refused a Belgian proposal that his second son, the Duc de Nemours, should sit on the Belgian throne, but the storm of protest aroused by the candidature of Leopold of Saxe-Coburg sent him looking for a Bourbon candidate who would not be so offensive to Britain as one of his own children. As later in Portugal and Spain, he produced a Neapolitan prince in rivalry to a German. Talleyrand's attempts to gain territorial concessions, varying from a couple of border fortresses to partition, angered Palmerston. This was the central weakness of Orleanist foreign policy: her only ally was jealous and suspicious. In the face of this, Sébastiani became both desperate and indecisive. He tried to assure the Chamber of Deputies that, although it meant war at that time, in the future Belgium would be bound to join France, whilst sending Talleyrand recriminating letters accusing him of insufficient energy in obtaining concessions.

The threat that the Belgians would choose as their king the Duc de Leuchtenberg (a Beauharnais, which was tantamount to being a Bonaparte), produced in Louis-Philippe a reaction of horror. As a result, Bresson, French representative at Brussels, was allowed to foster the candidature of Nemours, which he did successfully. He himself developed one of those lunatic schemes which tended to flit through the minds of Frenchmen from Polignac to Napoleon III: he suggested that the Prince of Orange, the Tsar's brother-in-law, be put on the throne of rebelling Poland, which would compensate the Netherlands for Belgium being ruled by an Orléans. Far from any such plan, the French government after some indecision, disavowed Bresson. As Palmerston remarked of them, they "cannot make up their minds to be honest with stoutness or to play the rogue with boldness".[15]

With the arrival of Périer, French policy became rather more coherent. Périer, whilst determined to prevent any German action in Belgium, was impatient with Belgian intransigent territorial demands: pressure was put on Brussels to accept the terms decided in London, and no resistance was made to the Saxe-Coburg candidature. It was, however, the Dutch King who, on 1 August, broke the armistice and attempted to reconquer his former territory. Périer, feeling his parliamentary position insecure, had been about to resign but the invasion compelled him to change his mind. In response to an appeal from the King of the Belgians, Maréchal Gérard led a France army into Belgium and quickly forced the Dutch troops to withdraw. The French attempted to use their position to gain a small but strategically important territorial concession, but failed in the face of British hostility. France gained some reward for her military withdrawal in the demolition of certain border fortresses, whilst the marriage of Louis-Philippe's daughter, Princesse Louise, to the Belgian King helped diminish the fear that the new state would be a British or German satellite.

The Netherlands still refused to accept Europe's verdict and retained Antwerp which had been granted to Belgium. When, in October 1832, the Duc de Broglie accepted the Foreign Ministry, it was with the understanding of his friend, the British ambassador, Lord Granville, that military action in Belgium was necessary to gain the conservative Cabinet parliamentary support. Broglie threatened Europe with the *parti du mouvement* if this were not allowed him. Britain agreed, a substantial achievement for Talleyrand, that other means of persuasion having failed, a French army should be used against the Dutch. On 19 November 1832, Gérard began the siege of Antwerp. At the first shots, old soldiers sang songs of the Empire, and the Ducs d'Orléans and de Nemours joyfully greeted their baptism of gunfire. After five cold muddy weeks, the Dutch surrendered and evacuated the city. Three days later the French army began the homeward march. Broglie was conscious of the importance of keeping his word, and the speedy withdrawal impressed Europe.

The Belgian question remained in suspension for five years until in 1838 the King of the Netherlands expressed his willingness to accept the European decision. The finalising of the question thus came to Comte Molé who had been Foreign Minister in 1830 when the rebellion had begun. He unsuccessfully attempted to obtain an increase in Belgian territory. The difficulty was, as it had always been, that without strong British support, a pacific France was fundamentally impotent. Some persistent negotiation gained a few points, as had Talleyrand's incessant demands, but nothing of significance. The mere fact of Belgian independence, however, was a gain in itself; a barrier created against France had been removed; and however much they had struggled to obtain some additional satisfaction for public opinion, the King and Talleyrand determined that this should never lead to war or destroy the English alliance.

When late in 1831 Mehemet-Ali, Viceroy of Egypt, attacked his sovereign, the Ottoman Sultan, he had French support. Not only did public opinion approve the revolutionary (and Napoleon's Egyptian adventure held a place in the French imagination which Mehemet-Ali took care to foster), but the government, for once in agreement, believed that it was in their interests to support him. However, although hostile to the Turks in the south, part of whose Empire she herself had seized in Algeria, France wished the Sultan strong in face of Russian ambitions. She tried to use Britain to strengthen Ottoman resistance to Russian influence, but Palmerston was suspicious of her intentions. The Orleanist government therefore had little influence in Constantinople.

It was significant that Broglie's government should send a man of action as ambassador to the Sublime Porte. Amiral Roussin, who had recently dealt energetically with the Portuguese, arrived in February 1833 with instructions to limit Russian influence, and immediately tried to remove the naval presence which the Sultan, fearful of the threat presented by his rebellious vassal, had called to assist him. Roussin, like his predecessor Général Guilleminot, who had been withdrawn because he had tried to provoke a war between Tsar and Sultan, was extremely anti-Russian. Initially attempting an unsuccessful bluff by threatening to leave if the Russian navy did not, he then exceeded his instructions in another direction, promising to persuade Mehemet-Ali to accept the Sultan's terms and sending threatening notes to the Egyptian ruler. French policy in the East already presaged the diplomatic disaster of 1840: it was Turcophile, or rather Russophobe, in Constantinople, whilst very favourable to Mehemet-Ali in Alexandria. And because of the latter factor, the Porte preferred Britain or Russia to France. Roussin's alternation of bluster and promise had no effect: the Convention of Unkiar-Skelessi signed in July 1833 between Russia and Turkey was a defeat for France, but also for Britain, and brought the two countries together. However, the fact that a British navy played the leading role in halting Mehemet-Ali's advance was an ominous sign of Britain's intention to keep command of the Mediterranean, and of her hostility to the man who was increasingly to become a French protégé.

The Convention of Münchengratz in September 1833 showed that the suspicion of the Northern Courts towards France had not yet abated. There was much in this meeting of the sovereigns of Russia and Austria and Prince Royal of Prussia and their ministers that was defensive, still more that was a ploy by Metternich to restrain Russia and exalt his own position. Nevertheless it was France who provided the common enemy. A convention was drawn up which restated the rights of the three powers to intervene in support of sovereigns against rebellious subjects. After some resistance, the King of Prussia, not so ill-disposed to Louis-Philippe, agreed to join the Tsar and Habsburg Emperor in submitting to France notes recording the decisions taken at Münchengratz. The Duc de Broglie, now Foreign Minister, behaved with even more than his customary hauteur to the three ambassadors. He strongly repudiated the insinuations that France encouraged revolutionary movements. He argued against intervention as a right, and restated that any intervention by another power in Belgium, Switzerland or Piedmont would lead to war. Metternich tried to pretend that the latter had not been included as a *casus belli*: Sainte-Aulaire immediately declared that Austrian intervention in Piedmont would bring forth a French army and Broglie was quick to back him up in despatch. This created a small war of words which, to Louis-Philippe's distress, worsened French relations with Austria. Because Münchengratz seemed to reveal unchangeable hostility to the Orléans Monarchy on the part of the Northern Courts, it turned further towards Britain, approving Talleyrand's suggestion of a formal alliance as a reply to Austria and Russia, and as a rallying point for the small states seeking to repel pressure of larger neighbours. But Palmerston was averse from such an entanglement: the weakness of Orleanist France was that usually she could have no ally other than Britain, but Britain, especially under Palmerston, did not feel so drawn to France. It was the struggle in the Iberian peninsula which was to produce a modified version of the formal alliance with which liberal France hoped to counterbalance absolutist Europe.

Spain in the 1830s was of great interest to her northern neighbour. She presented in a lurid form the conflict of tradition and modernity, of absolutism and liberalism which France also experienced. Spanish culture was of increased interest as shown in Louis-Philippe's collection of Spanish painting, advised by Baron Taylor, and by authors such as Prosper Mérimée and the Marquis de Custine. To the latter, Spain was what France had recently been, whilst the United States was what she was to become, and he loved in Spain those elements, such as an aristocratic sense of honour, which were becoming lost in his own country. Others were less sympathetic, because

Spanish Carlism seemed even more reactionary than their own Vendean royalism. If there were disagreements on the message, all agreed that Spain was an example. For Louis-Philippe the lesson learnt had led to characteristic prudence: Napoleon's "Spanish ulcer" had shown the dangers of involvement, nor was Louis XVIII's royalist expedition an encouragement. Yet to leave Spain to its own devices was impossible. It was axiomatic that it was within the French sphere of influence, and a Carlist or republican triumph could not but influence events in France. To support constitutional monarchy in the Iberian peninsula was for Orleanist France not a mere matter of preference but of vital concern to her own internal security. Spain was the most important issue in foreign affairs in these years, and Anglo-French alliance reached both its closest co-operation and its nadir of distrust.

Both Iberian countries had parallel situations. In Spain and Portugal, reactionary uncles contested the rights to the throne of young nieces whose supporters were more moderate and constitutional in ideology. Britain and France supported the latter, and the Northern Courts encouraged the former. France was willing to recognise Britain's paramount influence in Portugal, but had from the first shown hostility to Don Miguel, who as regent had deprived his young niece Maria of her royal rights. When he ill-treated some French inhabitants and refused compensation, Périer with typical energy despatched in May 1831 a squadron to the river Tagus. It captured the Portuguese fleet and eventually, after Amiral Roussin threated a war, forced Miguel's government to grant reparations. The action had been brief and was accepted by the British government which had itself previously taken similar measures. The two constitutional powers agreed in their dislike of Miguel's regime, although France had perhaps the stronger political motives: Miguel had been markedly hostile to the July Revolution and was receiving aid from Spanish and French Carlists. In the civil war which was taking place, France gave aid to Maria and tried to prevent Spain from helping her uncle. France became concerned also with the question of a husband for Queen Maria: a similar problem was to create a crisis in Spain in 1846. Louis-Philippe desired a Bourbon on the throne as sign of French prestige, and because public opinion would resent a German. He had a Neapolitan candidate, in order to avoid the hostility of Britain to an Orléans. France asked Britain to prevent the candidature of the Duc de Leuchtenberg, and the King was very angry when this member of the Bonapartist clan whom he had so feared in Belgium, was successful in obtaining the young Queen's hand. Even when Leuchtenberg died in 1835, he was unable to prevent a German marriage to an inevitable Saxe-Cöburg. Portugal was of small importance, but Louis-Philippe could not risk such a marital defeat in Spain.

King Ferdinand VII of Spain died in September 1833 at a moment when in neighbouring Portugal Don Miguel was almost vanquished. The situation was very similar: Ferdinand's heir was his daughter Isabella, three years old. Don Carlos the dead King's brother, denied the right of a woman to succeed: the legal question was confused, but it was above all a struggle of parties which formed round the Regent, Queen Maria-Christina, and her daughter, and the girl's uncle. The supporters of Carlos were in their turn supported by the Northern Courts and French Carlists, whilst the Cristinos looked to Britain and France. The Spanish Cristinos decided that Miguel and Carlos both had to be defeated and appealed to Britain early in 1834. A triple alliance was speedily negotiated between Britain, Portugal and Spain, and was signed on 15 April 1834. France was kept in ignorance and the Comte de Rigny, Foreign Minister at that time, was surprised to hear of the treaty. Palmerston suggested that France should accede to it, but Talleyrand protested that his country could not accept such a secondary role. Rigny demanded a new treaty and Palmerston, unwillingly, was forced by other Cabinet ministers into a negotiation with the French ambassador.

The Quadruple Alliance as it finally emerged on 22 April 1834 was thus born amidst mistrust. Portugal and Spain would give mutual aid, Britain grant naval assistance and France would contribute if asked. The terms were very vague: for Broglie they were an Anglo-French European commitment to constitutional government; to Talleyrand it was a diplomatic ploy to strengthen the French in Eastern Europe; to Palmerston, it meant the French promised to give in Spain what assistance he wished. Louis-Philippe, fearing to alienate the Northern Courts, tried to diminish its weight and declared he would not intervene. There were divisions within the French Cabinet: some, like Thiers, saw the alliance as basis of a military campaign in the Iberian peninsula, but others opposed any such engagement. Maréchal Soult in particular feared French troops could only be humiliated in the face of Carlist guerrilla warfare.

Whilst in Portugal the demoralised Miguelists soon surrendered, the forces of Don Carlos continued fighting with some success. Additional articles in August 1834 strengthened border control between France and Spain, and French ships prevented aid reaching the rebels. But when in 1835 Spain, supported by the French ambassador, the Comte de Rayneval, asked for direct military aid, Broglie (again Foreign Minister) returned a prompt refusal: French opinion was unfavourable, the King and Talleyrand were utterly opposed, Humann feared the effect on the budget and the Bourse fell at the thought. Broglie feared it would destroy the Anglo-French *entente* whilst being unpopular in Spain itself. Although Maréchaux Gérard and Maison supported him, Thiers's arguments that mutual hostility to Carlism bound France to give every possible military aid to the Cristinos were to no avail, reinforced as his opponents were by the assurances of financiers, notably the Rothschilds whose interests had been damaged by the Spanish government, that any such action would lead to a collapse of French credit. Louis-Philippe repeated that he did not want his soldiers fighting beside republicans[16] and his view prevailed, after much noisy argument in the Cabinet. He was, however, unable to prevent Broglie taking the initiative in allowing the French *légion étrangère*, fighting in Spain, to recruit in France.

In spite of the Quadruple Alliance, relations between Britain and France were not easy. Especially when the weak Rigny was at the Foreign Ministry, frequently submitting to the King's influence, France tended to support more conservative groups amongst Spanish and Portuguese politicians. There was a struggle for influence in Greece, and ill-feeling over Algeria. Broglie realised the difficulties in the relationship of the two countries, Britain's insularity and Palmerston's "harassments",[171] but he believed that correspondingly greater wisdom and responsibility from France would compensate for this, and that the effort was worth while. For the King, however, the alliance was not a moral necessity, and it was not so popular in the country that he would make sacrifices for it. He was encouraged in this attitude by Talleyrand, increasingly hostile to Palmerston and sceptical of the worth of the alliance he had striven to create.

As Louis-Philippe and his regime became more conservative, friendship with Eastern Europe became more attractive. During 1833, the King began to flatter and charm the ambassadors of the Northern Courts, to make sallies against Palmerston and even against Broglie. In 1834 he commenced a secret correspondence with Metternich. He told the Chancellor he wished, by alliance between France and Austria, to render war impossible. "I attach the glory of my reign to that pacific work. . . ." and explained how he lost popularity in restraining "national *élan*".[18] Broglie was happy for France to be a liberal power distrusted by conservative Europe, but Louis-Philippe had no wish to remain a parvenu king and was hoping for the marriage of the Prince Royal with an Austrian archduchess. The *rapprochement* could not go far, however, when Broglie seemed to take pleasure in coldly insulting the Austrian Chancellor and his ambassador. Thus the King rejoiced when the Duc's gaucherie led to a parliamentary rebuff and his resignation: he hoped that Thiers would prove more amenable to his policy.

Talleyrand's role in the promotion of Thiers in 1836 was his last diplomatic action. In 1835 the Prince had submitted his resignation and was replaced by the similarly aged but less competent Sébastiani; apoplexy replacing dropsy, as Daumier mocked in one of his cartoons. "Thanks to you, Sir, I have gained a place in Europe for the Revolution of July."[19] There was some truth in this claim: if there was suspicion of France, it was at least less active than three years before. To some extent this was due to the increasingly aristocratic nature of French diplomatists. The Comte de Sainte-Aulaire became ambassador in Vienna in 1833 instead of Maréchal Maison, son of a grocer, and the Baron de Barante had replaced Mortier in St Petersburg. Ambassadors who were not noble became exceptional after 1832, and were usually political notabilities. Such were Guizot, ambassador to London in 1839; Comte Mathieu de La Redorte, a second-generation Bonapartist noble sent to Madrid in 1840 by his friend Thiers; his successor Salvandy, and Rossi, ambassador at Rome in 1846. Titles were bestowed upon those such as Rossi, de Pontois and Bresson who lacked them. The entry into the profession of Casimir and Eugène Périer, son and nephew of the minister, and the sons of Duc Decazes and Humann, showed that the new ruling élite considered this a suitable field for their children's ambitions. The aristocratic nature of the career meant a strong tendency to patronage. Very often sons joined their fathers, as was the case with both Barante and Rayneval. The Comte de Sainte-Aulaire fostered both his son and son-in-law and similarly Albert de Broglie was helped by his father.

It was necessary in London as in St Petersburg to show that the July Monarchy was not bourgeois. In the case of the Comte de Flahaut, ambassador to Vienna in the 1840s, his social graces were more important than the diplomatic skill he was rarely asked to use. Also, diplomacy, if prestigious, was not remunerative; the allowance was rarely sufficient to cover the expenses of running an embassy, and ambassadors like Flahaut or Montebello, who tried to win a social position, did so from their own pocket. Those, like Sébastiani in London, who refused to do so, received the censure of the capital they thus deprived of hospitality. Occasionally bad choices like the latter were made, and some, like Salvandy, received embassies for purely political reasons. On the whole, however, although it showed the Orleanist ruling class at its most closed and hierarchical, French diplomatists were a highly skilled and accomplished group.

The weaknesses of Orleanist foreign policy derived from the vulnerability of the French position in Europe and also from political instability, the continual change of incumbents in the Foreign Ministry until Guizot's arrival late in 1840. Thus from St Petersburg, Barante wrote to Thiers in 1836, "Our ministerial evolutions are distressful for a poor ambassador who sees the effect that they produce. . . . Hold on, therefore, my dear minister",[20] a wish that was unfulfilled. There were factors of continuity, however, even in Paris. The King, although thwarted by Périer and Broglie and twice in serious conflict with Thiers, played an important role in foreign policy, reading despatches, talking to his own representatives and foreign diplomats, and sometimes corresponding with them. And there was in the Boulevard des Capucines the shadowy but powerful figure of Desages, director of political affairs at the Foreign Ministry. Industrious, with a remarkable grasp of detail, he had the confidence of the King and refused offers of embassies, preferring to work behind the scenes. None the less, these men and the successive ministers had a capricious Chamber of Deputies and the most vociferous public opinion in Europe to contend with. Orleanist France could not join the diplomatic game as an equal partner.

REFERENCES

1. Auguste Barbier, *Iambes* (1898), 17.
2. *Le National*, 3 October 1830.
3. Archives Parlementaires, 28 January, 16 November 1831.
4. N. W. Senior, *Conversations with M. Thiers, M. Guizot and other Distinguished Persons during the Second Empire* (1878), I, 130–1.
5. T. Raikes, *Journal* (1858), I, 64.
6. M. O. d'Haussonville, *Histoire de la Politique Extérieure du Gouvernement Français, 1830–1848* (1850).

7. F. Guizot, *Mémoires pour servir à l'histoire de mon temps* (1858), II, 261.
8. M. Barthélemy, *Némésis, Satire Hebdomadaire* (1832), 270–1.
9. Guizot, op. cit., II, 89.
10. Baron P. de Barante, *Souvenirs* (1890), V, 57.
11. C. Delavigne, *Œuvres completes* (1855), 521.
12. Archives Parlementaires, 20 December 1831.
13. C. M. de Talleyrand-Périgord, *Mémoires* (1892), IV, 433.
14. Barante, op. cit., V, 17.
15. H. L. Bulwer, *The Life of Viscount Palmerston* (1874), II, 44.
16. Foreign Office, F.520; Granville to Palmerston, 18 March 1836.
17. Raikes, op. cit., II, 7.
18. Marquis H. C. de Flers, *Le Roi Louis-Philippe* (1891), 308–9.
19. Talleyrand-Périgord, op. cit., V, 478.
20. Barante, op. cit., V, 336.

16

The Brief Supremacy of Thiers and Parliamentary disorder, 1836–1839

"Puis nos discours pompeux, nos fleurs de bavardage
L'esprit européen de nos coqs de village,
Ce bel art si choisi d'offenser poliment,
Et de se souffleter parlémentairement. . . ."

("Then our pompous discourses, our flowers of chatter
The European spirit of our village cocks,
That fine art carefully chosen to offend politely,
And to insult in parliamentary fashion. . . .")[1]

"Trois voleurs se réunissent pour voler un homme possesseur de ce beau diamant qu'on appelle le pouvoir; une fois l'homme à terre comment s'y prendront-ils pour se partager le diamant?"

("Three thieves meet to rob a man possessing that beautiful diamond called power; once the man is brought down, how will they manage to divide the diamond amongst themselves?")[2]

The achievements of the Broglie ministry were not purely restrictive in their nature. If 1835 had been overshadowed by the April trials and by the September laws, Broglie had achieved some foreign policy successes, and demonstrated his liberal conscience by taking preparatory steps for the abolition of slavery. Duchâtel proved a reforming Minister of Commerce, and there was legislation to improve trade and assist road-building. By the end of 1835, the country was calmer and more prosperous, so that the deputies, released from fear, ceased to look for strength in the government and felt free to indulge in political exercises. The general elections of June 1834 had shown France tiring of strenuous government by increasing the number of centrist deputies. The doctrinaire Duvergier called such men "faint-hearted":

to Guizot they were "cowards",[3] and he feared that with relaxation might come a growth of personal pretensions, for without some danger "each believes himself . . . free to think, speak and act as he pleases".[4] And indeed, when the 1836 session opened, the deputies chose as vice-presidents the ministerial Martin and three centrists (all shortly to become ministers under Thiers) and delivered a reply to the King's speech which was less than whole-hearted in its support for the government.

Within the Cabinet too, divisions and dissatisfaction were increasing. Broglie himself was undergoing a recurrent disaffection with politics, distressed by his poor relations with the King and some of his colleagues. Even his political ally, Guizot, was impatient with his rigidity and his scruples. As for Thiers, the third member of the triumvirate which dominated the Cabinet and led the ministerial party, he, although agreeing over policy, found these two personally uncongenial and their confident and dogmatic young supporters intolerable. However, it was Humann, the dogged Minister of Finance, concerned only with the administration of his department, whose tactless action created a crisis. Believing that the interest paid on government securities was too high, he advocated the conversion of *rentes*. National Guardsmen, the *petit bourgeois* of Paris, were often *rentiers*, and Louis-Philippe who believed his Crown depended upon them, was unwilling to offend them for the sake of economy, a subject which interested him little. Instead of discussing the issue in the Cabinet where he probably realised it would fail, Humann on 14 January 1836, when reading a routine document on the budget, suddenly declared the necessity for lowering interest rates. This appeal for the support of the deputies astounded them. It also infuriated his colleagues, and Humann, who had not expected such a furore, resigned. The Comte d'Argout was quickly put in his place.

The proponents of conversion would not let the matter rest. The ministry was repeatedly pressed to commit itself to introduce a bill. Broglie, irritated by the attempt to ensnare him, was at his most haughty. "We are asked whether the government intends to propose the measure in this session. I answer: No! Is that clear?"[5] The last phrase, spoken slowly whilst looking scornfully round the hemicycle, infuriated the deputies. It produced, wrote Barrot, "the effect of a *grand seigneur's* rudeness and was not forgiven".[6] So when Gouin, a *tiers parti* banker deputy, forced a discussion, many deputies approached the issue, their minds dominated by resentment against the aristocratic disdain of the Duc de Broglie. It was an issue where provincial deputies, including ministerials, saw high interest rates as yet another example of greedy Parisian dominance. The ministers dared not oppose conversion outright, and asked for an adjournment of the matter. It was refused them, by the narrowest of margins. The opposition had retained its numbers, whilst some ministerials, notably Humann, had abstained or voted against the government which lost by two votes. All ministers immediately handed their resignations to the King.

The events of 5 February opened a sixteen-day crisis which radically changed Orleanist politics. The defeat on the irrelevant issue of *rentes* destroyed the system of 11 October and split the triumvirate which, united, had dominated Parliament since 1832. The rift could not be patched up as it had been after the parliamentary defeat in 1834. Broglie left office declaring that he was no longer a party leader, and never again held office. The defeat and the roots of the new ministry came from the *hôtel* of Ganneron, rich candle manufacturer and deputy, where disaffected conservatives met members of the *tiers parti*. The meeting proved that many ministerials had lost their faithfulness to uncompromising resistance, and its doctrinaire spokesmen.

Again the King called first upon Molé to form a new Cabinet but, as before, the latter was unwilling to head a purely *tiers-parti* ministry and the doctrinaires would not serve with him. Guizot was too unpopular, and Thiers, in spite of his youth (he was not yet forty) was an obvious candidate. His refusal to continue with the doctrinaires made the latter impossible, and strengthened his own candidature. Talleyrand, who with genial condescension had been grooming this *petit bourgeois* for leadership, both encouraged the King to choose him as *président* and Thiers to grasp his destiny. Louis-Philippe, happy to rid himself of the doctrinaires, willingly turned to Thiers. To Viennet, who remarked on the inconveniences of descending from *grand seigneurs*, Louis-Philippe replied that he was indifferent to this, "to me birth is nothing".[7]

Thiers's had certainly been a remarkable rise, from journalist with a humble provincial background to head of government in six years. His appearance was against him; myopic and bespectacled, his round owl-like head on a small pudgy body, he appeared to Princesse Louise as "the odious little dwarf".[8] Thiers had the misfortune to be plagued by relatives who were a vivid reminder of his origins: an embarrassing father who was kept far from Paris, sisters who had to be prevented from opening cafés under the family name, two illegitimate brothers who were sent to very distant parts as consuls, and a mother who could not be allowed to be present at the wedding of her son. His loveless marriage, witnessed by the outstanding figures of the July Monarchy, gave Thiers a secure place in the *grande bourgeoisie* and through financial security encouraged his political success. The father of the bride, sixteen when the thirty-six-year-old politician married her, was a wealthy financier. His second wife held an undistinguished salon which had provided a home for the young journalist, where he had won his first admirers by putting their conventional anticlerical and anti-Bourbon sentiments into brilliant conversation. Madame Dosne became Thiers's mistress, and the complaisant husband rewarded him with loans and eventually with the gift of his daughter by his first marriage, the erasure of debts which Thiers had incurred in buying his large house in the Place Saint-Georges, and a dowry of 300,000 francs. Here the vivacious and loquacious Madame Dosne and the more silent but decorative Madame Thiers provided a court where the notables could appear: the journalists, the seekers of favours and makers of alliances flocked to join the *habitués* such as Fould and Ganneron, Etienne and Mathieu de la Redorte who had decided to attach their careers to Thiers's destiny. Thiers would charm and dazzle, and after dinner, with that unconventionality which he had not lost in his social ascent, would recline on a sofa and sleep for two hours while conversation continued around him.*

Thiers's career was not unblemished. The assistance he had given his father-in-law, the closeness to him of several leading financial figures, his own property speculation, inspired much gossip which, if it exaggerated the corruption, none the less was based upon the evident fact that Thiers was willing to profit financially from his political career, like his mentor Talleyrand, and in a way which Broglie, Molé and Guizot sedulously avoided. There was also the *affaire* of Grandvaux in autumn 1835. Thiers and Duchâtel joined a shooting party on the estate of the wealthy deputy Vigier. The Minister of the Interior promised his host, "one of the greatest house destructions that has ever been seen,"[9] and was true to his word, over-enthusiastically entering into the spirit of the drunken gathering. The scandal was considerable and the opposition press made the most of it. The *Quotidienne* chose to present the affair as a political parable, with Thiers as the grotesque symbol of the triumph of the middle classes: revolutions had robbed, guillotined, France had suffered forty years of catastrophe "and all of that so that M. Thiers would come, after drinking, to show France his backside by candle-light".[10]

Thiers's social circle was not distinguished: it is noteworthy that with very few exceptions the aristocracy kept him at a distance. Lamartine and Tocqueville had a strong dislike for him which was an important factor in their political behaviour. For Tocqueville, Thiers represented intrigue and insincerity.[11] His anticlericalism and questionable role at Saint-Germain l'Auxerrois in 1831, his anti-Bourbonism and use of the traitor Deutz against the Duchesse de Berry, his chauvinistic admiration for Napoleon and tolerance of many of the worst aspects of the Revolution whose historian he had been, was antipathetic to many. What particularly annoyed Tocqueville was that his strength lay in his ability to adorn the vulgar thoughts of mediocre men. Thiers represented the revolutionary prejudices of the bourgeoisie whilst conservatives such as Guizot tried to dampen them. Thiers as a member of the party of resistance was moved simply by the desire to protect property and by order to strengthen the state. Doctrinaire liberalism had no interest for him: he believed in facts and had no repugnance for resorting to force. As Rémusat wrote, "he does not base practice upon theory and has never done so".[12]

To the anti-clerical who admired the hierarchy of Roman Catholicism, it seemed no contradiction to say "I am a revolutionary, but a man of order".[13] Thiers's revolution was political and bourgeois, not social or working class, and he had absolutely no interest in the latter. His popularity, the Duchesse d'Orléans astutely remarked, lay in that the French were emotionally revolutionary, but resigned to government as a practical necessity, and Thiers

* *Ed. Note.* There can be little doubt that Thiers took his career ambitions fully into consideration when marrying, but in their recent biography of Thiers J. P. T. Bury and R. P. Tombs give a much less scathing account of this alliance and discount the charge of adultry. See J. P. T. Bury and R. P. Tombs, *Thiers 1797–1877, a Political Life* (London, 1986), pp. 45–52.

was "at base a revolutionary who truly believed himself a liberal".[14] As a statesman he had two sides, one was romantic, ambitious and chauvinistic, the other bourgeois caution. "His imagination disturbs his judgement",[15] remarked Guizot. He sought adventure but feared to find it, twice embroiling France in foreign adventure. The King forced him from office in 1836 and again in 1840, but whilst venting his annoyance and increasing his popularity at the monarch's expense, on the second occasion at least he was not unhappy to be removed from the dangers into which his impetuosity had led him. He retreated to the writing of history, producing after 1840 an account of his great hero, Napoleon, with whom one side of his character identified itself. His view of power was aesthetic and dramatic, not moral or administrative. Talleyrand remarked on the nature of Thiers's ambition and said it was a pity that he could not be made a cardinal.[16] Louis-Philippe well understood Thiers whom in many ways he resembled. Thiers was less difficult than the *grands seigneurs*, his predecessor Broglie and successor Molé, and was better company than Guizot. The King treated his "dearest president"[17] with greater affection and familiarity than the others, finding him more congenial, respecting him less.

Thiers's parting from Guizot and the doctrinaires necessitated, and his own character facilitated, a strong *tiers parti* element in the Cabinet. Sauzet became Garde des Sceaux and Passy Minister of Commerce. The two military offices were held by incumbents without strong political convictions, although both Maréchal Maison and Amiral Duperré were attached to Thiers, who in his Bonapartist sentiment and pragmatic conservatism, had an appeal for soldiers. In their eagerness for office, the *tiers parti* were willing to accept an element of royal influence, against which they had formerly protested so vociferously, in the Comte de Montalivet as Minister of the Interior. Another independent conservative, the Comte d'Argout, who had replaced Humann, was retained at Finance. The Cabinet had little political coherence and was utterly dominated by Thiers. Nor did it possess a strong majority, a fact which did not much worry the *président du conseil* who was confident of his skill in the arts of expediency. He was aided by the fears of the conservatives that if they were to attack the ministry, they would alienate the middle ground. The danger lay in the doctrinaires, a group of thirty or forty, highly displeased at being displaced from playing a leading role. The younger doctrinaires, more extreme, less politic, created a newspaper, the *Charte de 1830*, whose role was to attack the concessions made by the ministry to the left and to present an opposition which the milder *Journal des Débats* was unwilling to undertake. Jaubert, Duvergier de Hauranne and Piscatory occasionally openly spoke against the government during the session, but the men who desired stability, the diplomats, the financiers, the great officials who groaned at each ministerial crisis, were in accord with those deputies whose jobs rested upon ministerial approval, in their unwillingness to risk a new period of instability.

Thiers could not afford to alienate conservative opinion and strongly rebutted the fears that he might compromise with the *parti du mouvement*.[18] As for the *gauche dynastique*, it was happy to see the government move into the centre and, hoping it might be seduced further leftward, behaved with moderation. As for the *tiers parti* and *réunion Ganneron*, over 100 deputies with a strong representation in the Cabinet, they were happy to have their first taste of power. The *Constitutionnel* and the *Temps* ceased to be newspapers of opposition and became virtually official.

If Thiers was supported by a wide spectrum, he was also its prisoner. He had constantly to reassure each group. His inaugural speech promised the conservatives that the September laws would be the base for his ministry but informed others that conciliation would replace combat. Guizot's speech enmeshed Thiers in conservative support, praised his guarantees to the resistance, whilst Barrot thanked him for abandoning the divisive policies of the past. The ministers sat embarrassed whilst the two orators duelled for the government's soul. On the issue supposedly under debate, the *fonds secrets*, the budget annually voted for police purposes whose exact spending the government did not have to divulge, the new Cabinet won a huge majority. It signified weakness rather than strength and showed the various groups on right and left being consciously but menacingly patient. This game continued throughout the session, which as a result was barren. Thiers amply proved his skill in manoeuvre: he eloquently concealed the vagueness of his promises to left and right, and he established himself as the oratorical equal of Guizot and Berryer. Sometimes the *président* would say one thing reassuring to the conservatives, whilst his Garde des Sceaux, Sauzet, would promise radical changes to the left.

Such legerdemain precluded action. There could be no amnesty for political prisoners. Conversion of *rentes*, the issue which had defeated Broglie and brought Thiers to power, was theoretically agreed but postponed. A dowry for the King's daughter, the Queen of the Belgians, owing since her marriage, had been promised the King, but the Cabinet dared not ask its unstable majority to vote on an unpopular matter involving expenditure. A few business measures were all that the ministry had to show for its period in office, and even here any radical change was precluded by the disagreement between Passy, inclined to free trade, and Thiers, a strong protectionist.

Before the question of Spanish intervention destroyed the Cabinet, there were other causes of dissension. As the session progressed, impatience on both sides grew and became evident in the Chamber of Deputies. Sauzet was disgruntled that his liberal promises had not been fulfilled. Montalivet and Comte Pelet de La Lozère, Minister of Public Instruction, found Thiers's bumptious predominance wounding to their vanity. Jaubert, a leading doctrinaire deputy, led an attack on the expense of the programme of public works which Thiers had undertaken since 1833. The latter was also pursuing a policy of expansion in North Africa. Not only did deputies from all sides attack this, but within the Cabinet Passy agreed with Thiers's opponents.

A chance event strengthened the Cabinet's conservative critics. On 25 June, Louis-Philippe after inspecting works on the Louvre was leaving in his carriage when a bullet lodged in the panelling five inches from his head. It was another miraculous escape; this of all the attempts on the King's life came nearest success. The would-be assassin, Alibaud, a solitary republican fanatic, immediately became a hero whose exploit was celebrated in poems and prints. He became a martyr also when, against the King's will, he was executed. Louis-Philippe had driven calmly on, but the Queen and her daughters were not so tranquil. Neither was Thiers: he feared a new attempt if the King were to inaugurate the completed Arc de Triomphe as planned. The ceremony and the National Guard review were abandoned. The King strongly resisted these attempts to protect him which resulted in virtual imprisonment; "To live thus is to live not at all!"[19] but the majority of the Cabinet overruled him. The retreat depressed spirits, and Alibaud's attempt, together with renewed activity of republican conspirators, led to talk of the need for a return to resistance and rumours that the doctrinaires would re-enter the Cabinet. By the time of the parliamentary vacation in summer 1836, the Cabinet was in an obviously weak position, and few thought it capable of surviving another session.

The flexible Thiers had lent himself to a change in foreign policy, advocated by Talleyrand who had become furious with Palmerston ("a man who does not have the ability to reason")[20] and welcome to the King who wished to break the "matrimonial blockade", preferably by marrying the Prince Royal to the Austrian archduchess. So Thiers encouraged *rapprochement* with the Northern Courts by moderating those tendencies in French foreign policy which previously had alienated them. When their troops occupied the independent Polish republic of Cracow to quell disorders in February 1836, Thiers made no protest: since the opposition did not wish to cause him trouble, no great objection arose over this acquiescence. In Switzerland, he pleased Metternich by his stern attitude against radical refugees. Similarly in Spain, although not committing himself for the future, Thiers refused English pressure to increase intervention. He made assurances to Prussia and Austria and suggested, to Palmerston's annoyance, that the young Queen of Spain be married to the son of the Carlist pretender. With the Comte de Rayneval and his English counterpart struggling for influence in Madrid, and similar conflict between the allies taking place in Portugal, Greece and Turkey, Thiers believed that the alliance was often "a vain word rather than a reality",[21] and for the moment made no effort to change this state of affairs.

In spite of his efforts, the projected marriage failed. Orléans and Nemours made an excellent impression in Berlin and Vienna, but powerful cliques at the Habsburg Court were opposed to a marriage with the family of a usurper, and Alibaud had demonstrated the threats which French royalty faced. Thiers was angered: "they will have reason to repent it at Vienna", he wrote, France's true friend was England.[22] By August 1836 then, Thiers's policy had bifurcated: he would be conservative at home, whilst to please the left, he would turn abroad to what he called "our true principles".[23] Thiers felt always the desire to make a dramatic gesture and was more concerned with public opinion than other Orleanist leaders. To intervene in Spain offered him a method of revenge on the Northern Courts and suited his anti-legitimism. Even when on 12 August a military coup forced the Spanish Queen Regent to accept a new more radical constitution and change of government, Thiers did not alter his determination.

He wished to increase the *légion étrangère* from 3,000 to 10,000 men by voluntary means, and to attach to this 10,000 Spanish troops, all to be commanded by a French general, Clauzel or Bugeaud. He believed this force would suffice to crush the Carlist guerzillas. The King was opposed; each concession Thiers won was after lengthy argument and threats of resignation.[24] The King told him that the concessions he made proved his affection, but Montalivet was instructed to watch the *président* closely, and Thiers in return did not scruple to deceive the King.

The Cabinet meetings of mid-August were stormy. The *président* had believed he completely dominated the *conseil*, but Montalivet and Pelet strongly supported the King against anything resembling direct intervention. When Louis-Philippe refused to allow Bugeaud to take command of the *légion étrangère* in Spain Thiers resigned and tried to make his Cabinet follow him. An unsuccessful attempt was made to find a compromise, but Thiers was persuaded to remain in office, and for a week both sides manoeuvred to obtain their own way. The King asked Thiers to dissolve the troops forming on the Pyrenees. The *président* refused and asked Bugeaud to take command of them. Louis-Philippe would not be frightened into submission whilst his foreign policy collapsed. His confidant, Montalivet, had begun to negotiate the formation of a new ministry. The announcement by the general commanding the *légion étrangère* that direct intervention was being prepared, provided Louis-Philippe with the opportunity for his initiative. He and Montalivet had the *Moniteur* publish a denial of this and a dissociation of the general from French service. When Thiers discovered this, he resigned and on 29 August his Cabinet left office.

His ministry had no striking achievements to its credit, at home or abroad, but Thiers retired with a considerable, if spurious, liberal reputation. Having begun as the King's man and pragmatical friend of Austria, he left with a reputation for independence towards the royal will, and associated with a liberal and anti-Austrian foreign policy. The Northern Courts admired and enthused over Louis-Philippe's action, but in France suspicions grew that royal power was dangerously increasing, and Thiers and his followers enlarged their popularity at the monarch's expense. A section of basically conservative opinion now chose to criticise the King, and attacks on Orleanism's excessive pacifism and on friendship for the absolutist powers ceased to be the sole property of the left.

In forming his ministry, Thiers had irrevocably split himself from Guizot, preparing the eventual dominance of the latter and the resulting fall of the monarchy. To gain office and revenge, Guizot had formed a tactical alliance with Molé, a man with whom he was personally and ideologically incompatible. The doctrinaire believed that his small party should lead the conservatives behind a programme of unwavering resistance, although his younger followers, like Duvergier, believed that the evils of deviating from the policies of resistance had not been sufficiently felt and they should wait until the ministerial and conservative majority was begging to be saved from disorder.[25] Molé had won some popularity by declaring his desire for conciliation and compromise, but having no party support, he needed the doctrinaires. They for their part could not rule alone and hoped that this peer would prove no more than a figure-head.

The short-lived ministry which was announced on 6 September 1836 with Comte Molé as its *président* and Foreign Minister was dominated by the doctrinaires. Even though Guizot restricted himself to the minor portfolio of education because he felt guilty entering a Cabinet presided over by a man whom his ally Broglie vehemently disliked, he had no intention of abandoning the moral and intellectual leadership which he believed rightly his. The Comte de Gasparin, peer and former prefect, went to the Interior with Charles de Rémusat as his under-secretary; Persil was again Garde des Sceaux, and Duchâtel became Minister of Finances. The other ministers carried little political weight. Amiral de Rosamel was possibly the most significant of the regime's navy ministers. Genéral Bernard, at War, was a capable administrator but hardly an "illustrious sword", being as Rémusat said "a timid embarrassed man who resembles a schoolmaster".[26] Martin (du Nord) who completed the Cabinet as Minister of Commerce, had impeccable conservative credentials as former *procureur general*, but was not part of the doctrinaire clique.

The incompatibility of Molé with the latter was soon manifest. The *Débats* was considered almost an official organ and Molé found intolerable the way in which those whom he believed his subordinates used it to present their own ideas. The doctrinaires' own journal, *La Paix*, even went so far as to criticise Molé's handling of foreign policy which it found insufficiently favourable to Britain. In control of the Interior and Justice departments, they removed some *tiers parti* officials, and replaced them with men of their own party. They refused the amnesty for political prisoners which Molé desired. Persil indulged in arguments to left and right, recommencing the legal attack on opposition journals and engaging in a vituperative exchange with the Archbishop of Paris. They made obvious their disapproval of the King's speech opening the 1837 session, in which Molé and Louis-Philippe hinted at a new direction in politics: "Time has already calmed many hatreds and each day softens the duties that circumstance has imposed upon my government."[27] In fact, the doctrinaires were increasingly out of touch with the majority. The favourable reception given the King's conciliatory words and the victories of the centre in the election of parliamentary officers showed that the former *parti de résistance* was losing its cohesiveness and conservative will.

If political differences within the Cabinet were real, it was incompatibility of personality which made Molé increasingly detest Guizot and his followers. Snobbishly noting Guizot's attempts to compensate for his undistinguished ancestry, the aristocrat found the younger man's brusque self-assertion a constant irritation to his own vanity. So when Gasparin, efficient administrator but incompetent parliamentarian, resigned, Molé was determined that no other doctrinaire should replace him, whilst Guizot insisted on taking the post himself. Stalemate was turned into crisis by events resulting from the first of Prince Louis Napoleon Bonaparte's attempts to overthrow the monarchy at Strasbourg on 30 October 1836. The first signs of opposition ended the farcical *putsch* and the pretender was put on a ship for America, King and Cabinet being united in finding exile a better solution than trial and punishment, but the aftermath of the affair was to destroy the ministry. According to French law, all accused had to undergo the same process of justice, and Louis Napoleon's accomplices, although mostly soldiers, had included civilians. All the accused therefore went before a jury at Strasbourg, a town of strong Bonapartist affections, where the population was hostile or at least indifferent to the constitutional regime. The jury found them innocent and they were freed amidst scenes of wild enthusiasm. This, says Rémusat, was "one of those extremist movements that brought about the triumph of Guizot".[28]

The government decided to bring in a law which allowed different jurisdictions for civilians and soldiers (*disjonction*). Two lesser bills made it a serious crime not to divulge information on attempts on the King's life, and proposed to create a prison on a West Indian island. The *loi de disjonction* provoked a long and violent debate. It emerged that the bill was most strongly supported by the doctrinaires, and that many moderates disliked a measure which tampered with what they believed to be legal orthodoxy. Royer-Collard and Dupin lent their prestige to the argument that all defendants in a case should be tried by the same body. The doctrinaire Jaubert, supporting an amendment which toughened the proposals, attacked those *députés fonctionnaires* who were hesitating to support the government and who accepted "the sweets of power along with the favours and honours of the opposition . . .".[29] This tactlessness was counterproductive: even deputies with paid official functions liked to believe themselves independent. By a narrow margin the government was defeated.

Simply replacing Gasparin proved impossible and the two rivals began the search for colleagues. Louis-Philippe asked them both to present their proposed Cabinet lists to him, finding himself in the enjoyable position of arbiter. Guizot's weakness was that he could come to no agreement with Thiers, "engaged up to the neck with the left"[30] as he said with annoyance. Montalivet agreed to serve with Molé and the King had to choose between a pure doctrinaire ministry and a Cabinet which, if omitting the great orators of the Chamber of Deputies, none the less seemed by moving towards the centre to be more representative of the political mood. After some hesitation the King chose the latter. Thiers was pleased for he was convinced that this ministry, whose only considerable figures were peers, would soon need to replaced. Guizot, however, who had negotiated clumsily misjudging men and situations, had left office, the leader of a dissatisfied and isolated group and his bitterness was soon to be manifest.

The ministry of 15 April 1837 retained the non-doctrinaire elements of its predecessor and placed two peers, Montalivet and Barthe, at the Interior and Justice, and introduced two deputies without previous ministerial experience to the Ministries of Finance and Public Instruction, Lacave-Laplagne and Salvandy. Molé had thus attained complete predominance in the Cabinet, resembling that which Thiers had possessed. Montalivet was not one to challenge it: a capable man, he was also lazy and had a habit of disappearing to shoot partridge at the expense of routine matters. Lacave-Laplagne was more conscientious, "as good a Minister of Finance as any other".[31] Salvandy was a salon wit and *littérateur*, a snob with a fondness for legitimist noblewomen: representative of a section of conservative opinion, he frequently irritated Molé by his indiscipline.

The predicament of the Cabinet resembled that of Thiers the previous year. Forces to right and left of it offered their tolerance on certain conditions. Dupin's supporters and the *Temps* gave it support. Thiers and his followers in press and Parliament expressed some contempt for "the little ministry" as they called it, but welcomed the expulsion of the doctrinaires. These latter, for their part, were even more angry than they had been against Thiers. Although Guizot was restrained and tried to establish himself as the leading conservative by "protecting" the ministry as he had done Thiers, the younger doctrinaires, notably Jaubert and Duvergier, criticised the ministry for the "frightening weakening of authority"[32] which it represented. They objected to the withdrawal of the restrictive measures introduced under the preceding Cabinet: they were furious with the promotions to official posts of *tiers parti* figures which Molé made in an attempt to widen his basis of support. They felt they were being displaced from their natural position as leaders of the majority. The left blamed Molé for staying in power as head of a conservative ministry when the system of resistance had been defeated, whilst the doctrinaires blamed him for weakening the policy of resistance when it most needed upholding. The story of the next two years is that of the doctrinaires coming to accept the left-wing thesis albeit with occasional hesitations and a resulting loss of cohesiveness and integrity.

Molé's early actions had been concessions revealing the weakness of his position. His refusal to present a programme was admitted with frankness: "Messieurs, the programmes presented from the Hôtel de Ville to the present have never proved anything but vain"[33]; but this did not disarm the opposition. On 9 May 1837, the government took a courageous step in declaring an amnesty for all political prisoners. This produced a real, if temporary, relaxation in public life and added to the popular rejoicing and warm atmosphere in which the marriage of the Duc d'Orléans was celebrated. Yet the action, although welcomed by the centre and by moderate conservatives, was disapproved by the doctrinaires and their sympathisers: the *réunion Hartmann*, a meeting of the most conservative ministerialists, expressed apprehensions. The *Débats*, whilst accepting the amnesty because approved by the King, clearly showed its lukewarm attitude to the Molé Cabinet and its concessions, telling the deputies that their firmness and energy were necessary to strengthen the government.[34]

Molé aimed to be "the man of truce and reconciliation amongst parties":

he desired to "restore the King to France and France to the King".[35] Thus the lavish marriage for the Prince Royal and a highly successful *grade nationale* parade which the amnesty had ensured: the King was able to stroll unharmed around the Botanical Gardens cheered by the population of the neighbouring slums. Promotions for members of the *tiers-parti* were counterbalanced by gestures to the right, notably the restoration of the Church of Saint-Germain l'Auxerrois, closed since its sack by a mob in February 1831. Mgr de Quélen, Archbishop of Paris, who had been sulking since the event, visited the Tuileries to thank the King, and Molé gained the gratitude of the Queen and other Catholics. Using charm and more palpable rewards, Molé added to his majority: *fonds secrets* were distributed to newspapers, and the *Journal des Débats* and, in particular, the *Presse* gave him firm support. But the "politics of the see-saw"[36] as the *National* called it, could not be indefinitely continued: after initial successes, the various groups began to demand more than could be given them. The ministry lasted the session, however, and Molé, inspired by his hatred of the doctrinaires, was determined that it should continue to survive. However, he had already suffered his first defeat as a result of their hostility. A bold scheme for state construction of a railway network had met not only the opposition of a few local interests who considered themselves unsatisfied and the objections of the habitual opponents of expenditure, but the doctrinaires had joined them to defeat the government. A similar combination of interests would combine in the 1838 session to prevent another large-scale railway plan.

In the meantime the doctrinaires received further reasons to dislike Molé. He had decided the moment was suitable for holding elections, the economic situation being healthy and France seemingly relaxed. In the elections of November 1837, the government played a less active role than was usual, even though the *centre gauche* and doctrinaires asked for its support. In a few cases, however, it went so far as to aid moderate opponents of the doctrinaires, a fact which revealed how deep had become the rift within the conservative party. Guizot's friends could not forgive Molé and Montalivet for this. The mood of relaxation had helped the centre and *gauche dynastique* at the expense of firm upholders of resistance. A disorganised Chamber emerged from this election fought without strong principles, said Guizot: the great government party which began to form under Périer, damaged by the defection of Thiers, suffered additional weakening.[37]

Guizot believed in a cohesive and disciplined force, led by a small group; Molé believed in a more flexible, pragmatic approach where the Cabinet chosen by the King represented the breadth of forces which comprised the majority. Thus, during the 1838 session, Molé attempted to bring representatives of the *centre gauche* into his Cabinet, but he faced the inevitable obstacle of Orleanist party behaviour. Thiers wanted the Foreign Office, which Molé would not vacate, and refused lesser posts and embassies when offered them. The groups of the centre would not allow a member singly to join a conservative Cabinet, but demanded a more significant representation. This the King refused: he was growing increasingly conservative, and willing as he was to make certain concessions, he was determined they should be made by the *parti de résistance*. In spite of pleas from Molé, the King resisted any significant change in the Cabinet. The *président du conseil* hinted at resignation as, during the 1838 session, his position grew increasingly desperate and his Cabinet was immobilised by the parliamentary Coalition forming against it.

Molé, ill-fitted for parliamentary leadership, showed skill in dealing with foreign affairs. A realist without philosophical trammels, he felt that public opinion should be kept as far as possible from diplomacy, whilst his elaborate courtesy made him more acceptable to the *corps diplomatique* than Broglie or Thiers. He understood the isolation and weakness caused by excessive reliance upon the British alliance. Molé's refusal to intervene in Spain, his insistence that the French representatives support the Queen but in no way aid the radical government, seriously weakened the latter and pleased the Northern Courts. In Switzerland, he continued the conservative policy begun by Thiers. Under the latter's government, an *agent provocateur* and spy, Conseil, had been sent into Switzerland to report on the behaviour of French republican conspirators there. When the Swiss discovered his identity, they accompanied his expulsion with insults to their larger neighbour, beginning a quarrel between the two countries which Molé inherited. He ended it, obtaining a bare apology by the threat of force. This was again needed in 1838 to compel the expulsion of Prince Louis Napoleon Bonaparte who had returned to Switzerland from America and had begun conspiring against the Orleanist government. Although threats only had been used, Molé's government showed greater similarity to the ideas of the Holy Alliance than to its own professed creed of non-intervention. Above all, it was Molé's action in immediately withdrawing French troops from Ancona when the Austrians had eventually evacuated the papal territories which pleased Metternich. Molé was simply obeying the promise made by Périer but the French opposition none the less blamed him for having failed to extract any concession from Austria or from Rome. It was, however, just such an obedience to diplomatic laws combined with an absence of revolutionary rhetoric which pleased conservative Europe and strengthened France's position. The French diplomatic corps were thus extremely hostile to the parliamentary Coalition and anxious for Molé's success.

The exception to this favour lay in Britain. Molé had no wish to destroy the English alliance but the manner in which he came to power, ending Palmerston's hopes of seeing a French army aid Spanish radicals, and his intention to limit the exclusivity of the *entente*, meant that the English Foreign Secretary was ill-disposed. During the three and a half years of Molé's government, relations were generally tepid, occasionally interspersed by outbursts of anger or distrust, on other occasions becoming warm and co-operative. Differences over Portugal and Spain where Britain supported more radical factions, strong opposition to Palmerston's plans for free trade between Britain and Spain which would have damaged French commerce, made the Iberian peninsula the cause of most ill-feeling. The triumph of moderate forces in Spain meant that Molé and not Palmerston was successful here. However, Molé gave no aid or support to the French Canadian rebels and was able to prove the meaning of the alliance at no real cost. His measures of gunboat diplomacy, to obtain redress from Mexico, Buenos Aires and Haiti, for tyrannical actions against French subjects, were pursued with moderation and co-operation with Britain. Although for the sake of Spain, Palmerston would have preferred to see Thiers in the Boulevard des Capucines, the relationship never sank as low as Molé's parliamentary opponents tried to claim. The Foreign Minister had improved his country's diplomatic position, he had protected the French monarchy against conspiracy in Switzerland and given it a moderate neighbour in Spain. He had completed the founding of the Belgian state with improved financial terms, and by personal supervision had inaugurated a new and successful strategy in Algeria. Yet none of this was sufficiently sensational to impress public opinion, and its broad conservatism of approach gave the opposition the pleasing opportunity to pose as radicals.

One day, Guizot strode into Odilon Barrot's study and proposed that they united to combat "this personal government; it is time to put an end to those favourite ministers . . .".[38] Similarly, Thiers, although he waited longer in the hope that he could force some arrangement on Molé, ceased to restrain his followers in their opposition. As soon as the 1838 parliamentary session opened, the attack began, the left laying down the lines it was to take. The ministry, claimed the *gauche dynastique* Comte de Sade, was "outside of all the known conditions of representative government",[39] being of no party, having no real support save that of the Court, existing only through the mutual jealousy of the opposing parties.

Molé appealed to the newly elected deputies to help him govern without the parties and fanatical opinions.[40] He was to find this an impossibility. Other politicians were growing impatient at their exclusion from office. They had no alternative ministry with a majority, but hoped that Molé's resignation would lead to a political reshuffle which would be to their profit. Thus they harried the government. They denied it a majority on its railway proposals and forced it to agree to lower the interest rate on *rentes*, although to their extreme annoyance, the Chamber of Peers reversed this. Molé and Montalivet had been favourably disposed to a small enlargement of the franchise, but no electoral measure could be introduced with such an unstable majority. Some useful laws, however, were passed for the more humane treatment of lunatics, and on prisons; there were measures concerning bankruptcy and commercial tribunals, and, most important, a limit to centralisation in laws extending the powers of justices of the peace and of *conseils généraux*. Other bills were blocked in committee. Molé tired of "this war so hateful and so personal".[41] He swung from extremes of determination to discouragement, and wrote emotional letters to the King alternately blaming him for insufficient support and promising him untiring resistance to their common enemies.

The Coalition began with a "collusion of epigrams" between doctrinaires and *centre gauche*. The younger doctrinaires, Jaubert, Rémusat and Duvergier, increasingly took their line from Thiers, more frankly aggressive in the struggle, more spirited and more entertaining than their leader, Guizot. This alliance was to have important effects in the future. Thiers imparted to them some of his own hostility to the King. "My dear friends," he told them, "the King mocks us all." If they were united, the "ministry of lackeys" would collapse at once.[42] The doctrinaires were becoming ever more impatient and the most enthusiastic were able to carry the more hesitant, such as Guizot and Duchâtel. An attack on royal power suited both their claim to parliamentarianism and the tactical need to satisfy their allies on the left.

Duvergier de Hauranne developed the theories of the *centre gauche* in a way that would not too greatly alienate his own group, but imbued them with a violence of tone which made them acceptable to the radicals. An energetic intriguer and violent party man, Duvergier was physically unprepossessing, bald, ugly, with darting myopic eyes, and he was an ineffective orator, which explains why, in spite of his ambition and his talent, he never attained ministerial office. He was, however, a brilliant pamphleteer. "The fight pleases and warms him", wrote his associate Rémusat, who never quite shared the "battling logic" with which Duvergier invested any struggle into which he was thrown. Rémusat also made a criticism which was not only true of Duvergier and most doctrinaires, but could be levelled at Orleanism itself: his friend was "too constitutional", in that he believed constitutional legality to be a panacea. This idea of importing "all the agitation of a free country" without provoking, indeed in order to avoid, social crises, wrote Rémusat later, was typical of most of them.[43] The Coalition is an extreme manifestation of this tendency in Orleanism. Thiers's slogan, "the King reigns but does not govern", was adopted by the Coalition as a whole. Legitimists and republicans looked on with satisfied amusement. Supporters of the ministry such as Fonfrède's *Journal de Paris*, attacked the alliance of right with left, "a moral anarchy which surpasses anything one could have imagined until now . . .",[44] and Philippist pamphleteers wrote rejoinders to Duvergier and Rémusat. Never had there been such a nauseating exhibition of personal ambitions,[45] wrote Bresson, ambassador to Prussia, who noted that European diplomatists were remarking that the French revolutionary spirit had not been quenched.

A sign of the fluidity of the Orleanist party structure was that Molé did not know, before the 1839 session opened, whether or not it would give him a majority, although he warned the King that he would be defeated unless the ministry were substantially modified. His chances of survival were destroyed when Dupin, having used ministerial votes to obtain his re-election to the presidency of the Chamber which he gained by an extremely narrow margin, deserted the Cabinet. Only three of the nine members of the Commission de l'Adresse were ministerial supporters. Thus for the first time, a government of the July Monarchy faced a hostile *adresse*: indeed the latter attacked not only the ministry but also the King by referring to "the intimate union of powers contained within their constitutional limits".[46] The ministers fought to have adopted, not this hostile reply to the King's speech, but a set of amendments proposed by the minority on the commission. The burden of this could rest only upon Molé. He, who had prided himself upon not being an orator but on plain and business-like debating, was forced by anger into eloquence. Day after day he mounted the tribune to answer the attacks of Guizot, Barrot, Thiers, Berryer and other leading parliamentarians. Although seconded by his ministers, the only supporter who could equal the leaders of the Coalition was Lamartine. At this stage in his vagrant political career, he, who had not long left the ranks of royalism, claimed to be a progressive conservative. The aristocrat in him felt an affinity for Molé and the lack of oratorical skills on the benches of the ministerialists gave him the chance to shine. He eloquently seconded Molé's defence of the royal prerogative, whilst denying that it had overstepped its limits, and he contrasted the moderate conservatism of the Cabinet with the destructive ambitions of the immoral Coalition.

Majorities varied on each clause, but the final vote was a government victory, 221 to 208. "I do not believe", wrote Louis-Philippe to his minister, "that the parliamentary annals of any country contain a battle comparable to that which you have just undergone with so much honour and success"[47]; but although Molé had emerged with an increased reputation and had inspired his supporters into becoming a united and determined body, the majorities he achieved, which fluctuated from thirteen votes to four, were not sufficient for strong government. On 23 January, Molé submitted his resignation.

The governmental impotence caused by the passions exacerbated by the Coalition now became fully evident. The 221, meeting frequently at the home of the wealthy Jacqueminot, presided by Cunin-Gridaine, were not only the largest group in the Chamber but the most united. Angry with all members of the Coalition, they would not tolerate any one of them as their leader. The King was right to try to form a Cabinet based upon them and Soult was the obvious candidate to approach. Such a choice, however, would not produce the radical alterations the Coalition now desired: Soult could make no progress and the King returned to Molé, whose Cabinet again entered office. It did so in order to hold an election to end the stalemate. The Coalition was furious: Louis-Philippe was compared with Charles X and Molé with Polignac. Yet the action was fully constitutional, for the largest party had not a sufficient majority to ensure strong government.

The elections of March 1839 were probably the most bitterly fought of the July Monarchy. Both sides used every means of persuasion and influence available to them. The ministerial deputies subscribed money, established a committee to correspond with local supporters and published propaganda. All prefects were summoned by the Minister of the Interior who instructed them to spare no efforts to combat the Coalition candidates. Some office holders who supported the opposition were dismissed to encourage others. The *Journal des Débats* and *Presse* were printed in large quantities and circulated throughout France as ministerial manifestos. The parties of the Coalition also founded committees. The leaders tried to co-ordinate their separate campaigns and produced a common programme: the latter, in the interests of unity, had to continue to attack the Crown and the ministry, rather than suggest any alternative policies or the Cabinet which would emerge from its electoral victory. Pamphlets and newspapers were published and distributed. A circular letter was addressed to officials warning them not to jeopardise their futures by supporting the Cabinet.

"The conservative party" as it was increasingly calling itself, as one man, warned that the Coalition triumph could destroy the regime and social order. "It is the spirit of revolution", cried Royer-Collard in his electoral speech: "I recognise it in the hypocrisy of its words, in its mad arrogance, in its profound immorality."[48] Lamartine warned that the Coalition would unleash a European war. The *Débats* hysterically told its readers that the Coalition, which included its former heroes, Guizot and Thiers, menaced the Charter of 1830 in the name of Henri V or of Brutus: "after having legitimised anarchic passion, these yet remains for them to unleash it upon your properties, upon your industries, upon your families!"[49]

Occasionally there was violence as crowds, usually supporting candidates of the left, attacked the prefect or governmental supporters. Often fighting broke out amongst the electors themselves, so high had passions run. The ministry lost about fifteen supporters, most of whose seats were gained by the *centre gauche*. The conservatives remained the largest party but with an even smaller majority. The opposition triumph was tactical, due to the temporary uniting of its various components against the government. On 8 March Molé and his Cabinet handed their resignations to the regretful King. This time there could be no recall.

The Coalition's electoral triumph did not produce that strong parliamentary government which its members had demanded. By increasing incompatibilities, it made this more difficult, but its attacks on the King had lessened royal prestige. Guizot came to regret his role and admitted that the doctrinaires had been too extreme.[50] His reputation emerged diminished, many regarding the former defender of monarchical order as no more than "a vulgar power-seeker".[51] His party were divided: some had criticised Molé for weakening government by moving towards the centre whilst others accused him of making the executive excessively strong. Duvergier and Rémusat in particular had become used to taking orders from Thiers, and were soon to be lost to Guizot with serious results for the monarchy.

The *gauche dynastique* deputy, Faucher, editor of the *Courrier Français*, had written that Louis-Philippe, by uniting men who had believed themselves separate, had done the constitutional cause a real service. "I hope that before a year has passed the King will have turned in his sword. To tame the prince the most intoxicated with his own ability and the least constitutional imaginable, without revolution, is not a small undertaking."[52] Yet although the attacks added to the King's unpopularity, they extended his influence during the following year, and paradoxically, by strengthening the left, the Coalition removed them from power by increasing conservative resentment. The Coalition had accustomed the centre to attacking the King. The arguments of the republican Vicomte de Cormenin "are only the extension of our own position",[53] wrote the *Constitutionnel*, for example. Thiers remained conservative, but learnt to speak like a radical. The Coalition, which included men as conservative as Guizot, Thiers and, one might add, Barrot, speaking the language of revolution, was fully in the tradition of French politics: in particular, it was a return to the Orleanism of 1830. To many who considered themselves true conservatives, however, this appeal to revolutionary passions prevented French politics ever finding stability. They came to see 1839 as a dress rehearsal for 1848, the Coalition as leading to the fall of the monarchy. After the resignation of Comte Molé, due to "shameful causes" wrote Chancelier Pasquier, the decadence of power became daily more obvious and the exacerbated divisions amongst Orleanists assisted the revolutionary opposition.[54]

The Coalition created the longest ministerial crisis that the monarchy knew. It lasted over two months and was only ended by the fear created by the Blanqui conspiracy on 12 May 1839. Thiers believed that since both conservatives and *gauche dynastique* would be bound to support him against the other, he was master of the situation, and refused to allow Guizot to take the Interior, but Guizot would accept no lesser place. The *gauche dynastique* rank and file would only allow their leader Barrot to enter office with other supporters, and the conservatives were not willing to allow the left to obtain such a foothold in power. Barrot claimed that the Coalition victory was a vote for reform and that measures should be taken against deputies holding paid official functions, which he asserted to be the source of the royal power. Thiers was not yet interested in reform, however, and still less was Guizot. Although some of the doctrinaires, Duvergier, Rémusat and Jaubert, were sorry to see the alliance between their group and the *gauche dynastique* broken, the more conservative, notably Duchâtel, were relieved when the compromising connection was brought to an unfriendly end.

Obviously a coalition ministry containing the three leaders was impossible. After the failure of Soult, the King approached the Duc de Broglie, who, refusing office himself, proved unable to persuade Guizot and Thiers to serve together. When Soult again attempted to form a ministry with Thiers, the latter destroyed the Cabinet which seemed to have formed by demanding intervention in Spain, to which his potential colleagues, Soult, Humann and Passy, were as opposed as the King. By the end of March, Soult was declaring that "there was an abyss between himself and that little man"[55] and was struggling to form a ministry with a few figures of the *tiers parti*. The King was growing increasingly distressed and in the face of the politicians' impotence, on 31 March 1839 he formed a provisional ministry.

This Cabinet had no *président* and was created merely to conduct official business. The Duc de Montebello, peer and ambassador, was made Minister of Foreign Affairs; the Comte de Gasparin returned to the Interior; Girod took Justice, Général Cubières and Baron Tupinier filled the military ministries, the banker Gauthier was in charge of Finance and Parant was at Public Instruction. It was this Cabinet of officials and obscure politicians which faced the Chamber of Deputies when, amidst continuing rumour and intrigue, the new session opened, with the former allies now able to carry their quarrels into a public forum. Political problems had coincided with a financial slump: unemployment increased, there were disorders in the streets, the Bourse sank and the salons spoke of revolution. The political world was still in stalemate whilst on 10 May the Chamber of Deputies discussed, without result, the proposition of Mauguin that the King should be asked to form a Cabinet which was not provisional. The left was enjoying the self-inflicted problems of the Orleanists and trying to aggravate them.

On 12 May, a group of extreme republicans, led by Barbès and Blanqui, seized the opportunity created by the disorder in government to create an insurrection. Their attempts failed miserably, but it was enough to bring the political world to its senses. "Marshal, I believe this is the moment to go fishing", the King said; "In troubled water",[56] replied Soult. The ministry of 12 May was quickly formed as pretensions, suspicions and ambitions waned in the face of the crisis. The King and Soult knew that the deputies exhausted and frightened as they were, would hesitate to defeat a Cabinet, even though it contained none of the leaders of the Coalition. It was, however, although largely inexperienced, not an untalented ministry. Duchâtel, pleased to hold office without Guizot, took the Interior. Passy became Minister of Finance, and Dufaure, able and independent, received Public Works. A worse choice, imposed by Soult, was that of Teste as Garde des Sceaux; a clever and confident speaker, he utterly lacked the integrity of the nervous Dufaure. Cunin-Gridaine, a spokesman for the 221, was persuaded to enter as Minister of Commerce in the hope that conservative support would be given the ministry. Villemain was brought in as Minister of Public Instruction to give additional oratorical support. Général Schneider and Amiral Duperré took the Military Ministries. Because the great names would, or could, not join the Cabinet, Soult himself, in addition to being the *président* was Minister of Foreign Affairs, a post for which he was utterly unsuited.

This ministry's long survival seemed unlikely and its vast majority was a sign of the deputies' exhaustion, not of their confidence. Duchâtel and Cunin-Gridaine would provide insufficient anchor on the right for a Cabinet based on the centre but attracting only provisional support from Thiers. Guizot, too, might present a threat, but he found his parliamentary position embarrassing and both sides were therefore pleased when, in February 1840, Sébastiani was compensated with a marshal's baton and Guizot was sent as ambassador to London. The ministry lacked direction and was weakened by continuing rumours of reshuffles. The King was more powerful than ever. Soult was inexperienced in the ways of diplomacy, and Passy and Dufaure could easily be persuaded by the monarch's stronger will: "Since they have dined at the table of a gentleman of good family, they have become as supple as gloves",[57] remarked Mérimée. Such was the result of the Coalition, but it had not been of Louis-Philippe's seeking.

In these circumstances the debates on the *adresse* when the 1840 session opened were highly confused. The speech from the throne was weak and promised no action save hinting at hostility to England over the threat which the Pasha of Egypt again presented to the Ottoman Empire. Thiers attacked the tendency to weakness over foreign policy and Barrot spoke of reviving the spirit of 1830 by finding a patriotic cause. Thus out of dissatisfaction with internal politics and lost direction, arose the desire for triumph abroad. A vote of 212 to 48 on the *adresse* showed huge abstentions and the Cabinet obtaining a wide basis of unenthusiastic support. Opposition found an excellent issue on the proposal of a grant to the Duc de Nemours. The King's request was not unreasonable as his second son was recently married, but Nemours was not very popular, and Thiers wanted revenge on the King and on the ministry which, by supporting Sauzet against him as candidate for the presidency of the Chamber of Deputies, had led him to a humiliating defeat. Moreover, a section of the conservatives, which, still loyal to Molé, felt hostile to the Cabinet as the product of the Coalition, led by Desmousseaux de Givré with the encouragement of the *Presse*, wished to overthrow the ministry. On 20 February, in a secret ballot, a majority of twenty-six defeated the proposition. It was a brutal insult to the King who felt it bitterly: "Never has a sovereign been as afflicted as I",[58] he lamented. Against his will, the ministers resigned, expecting that their rivals, as before, would be shown to be powerless, so that the Cabinet would be returned to office with a strengthened position. They were wrong: Thiers was at last able to master the situation. He put an end to the damaging period of parliamentary disorder, but at the expense of leading France to diplomatic disaster.

REFERENCES

1. A. de Musset, *Sur la Paresse*, (*Poésies nouvelles*, Editions Garnier Frères, 1962), p. 144.
2. Stendhal, *Correspondance*, (1908) III, 228.
3. Archives Nationales, 42.AP.25.
4. Comte C. de Rémusat, *Mémoires de ma vie* (1858), III, 181.
5. Archives Parlementaires, 18 January 1836.
6. Odilon Barrot, *Mémoires posthumes* (1875), I, 291.
7. L. Viennet, *Journal* (1955), 188.
8. Princesse Louise-Marie d'Orléans, *La Cour de Belgique et la Cour de France* (1933), 44.
9. Archives Nationales, fichiers de ventes, Thiers à Vigier, 23 September 1835.
10. *La Quotidienne*, 19 October 1835.
11. Comte A. de Tocqueville, *Œuvres*, J. P. Mayer (ed.) (1967), VIII, 603.
12. Rémusat, op. cit., II, 364.
13. R. P. Droulers, "La Nonciature de Paris et les troubles sociaux-politiques sous la Monarchie de Juillet", *Saggi storico intorno di Papato* (Rome, 1959), 432–3.
14. D. Nisard, *Souvenirs* (1888), I, 39–40.
15. N. W. Senior, *Conversations with M. Thiers, M. Guizot and other Distinguished Persons during the Second Empire* (1878), II, 389–90.
16. Victor Hugo, *Choses Vues* (1887), 85.

17. Bibliothèque Nationale, Papiers Thiers, nouvelles acquisitions françaises, 20601, f. 31.
18. Ibid., 20602, ff. 11–12.
19. Comte J. Pelet de La Lozère, *Pensées morales et politiques* (1873), 86.
20. T. Raikes, *Journal* (1858), II, 7.
21. Papiers Thiers, nouvelles acquisitions françaises 20602, f. 9.
22. Ibid., f. 20.
23. Ibid., f. 50.
24. Ibid., f. 48.
25. F. Guizot, *Mémoires par servir à l'histoire de mon temps* (1858), IV, 173.
26. Rémusat, op. cit., III, 176.
27. Archives Parlementaires, 27 December 1836.
28. Rémusat, op. cit., 199–200.
29. Archives Parlementaires, 7 March 1837.
30. Rémusat, op. cit., III, 207.
31. Ibid., 211.
32. Archives parlementaires, 18 April 1837.
33. Ibid., 2 May 1837.
34. *Journal des Débats*, 24 April 1837.
35. Baron P. de Barante, *Souvenirs* (1890), VI, 20.
36. *Le National*, 23 May 1837.
37. Guizot, op. cit., IV, 281.
38. Barrot, op. cit., I, 321.
39. Archives Parlementaires, 8 January 1838.
40. Ibid.
41. Barante, op. cit., VI, 78.
42. Cited in P. Thureau-Dangin, *Histoire de la Monarchie de Juillet* (1897), III, 225.
43. Rémusat, op. cit., III, 243.
44. *Journal de Paris*, 18 March 1838.
45. Duc E. de Noailles, *Le Comte Molé* (1925), VI, 171–2.
46. Archives Parlementaires, 4 January 1839.
47. Noailles, op. cit., VI, 216.
48. Cited in Baron P. de Barante, *La Vie politique de M. Royer-Collard* (1861), II, 524–5.
49. *Journal des Débats*, 1 March 1839.
50. Guizot, op. cit., IV, 292.
51. Cited in Thureau-Dangin, op. cit., III, 232.
52. L. Faucher, *Biographie et Correspondance* (1875), 76.
53. *Le Constitutionnel*, 20 February 1839.
54. E. A. G. de Pasquier, *La Révolution de 1848* (1944), 12–13.
55. J. J. Dupin *Mémoires* (1860) IV, 15.
56. Rémusat, op. cit., III, 257.
57. P. Mérimée, *Correspondance générale* (1941), II, 247.
58. Maréchal de Castellane, *Journal* (1895), III, 212.

17

Diplomatic Disaster, 1840

"Ma patrie est partout où rayonne la France,
Ou son génie éclate aux regards éblouis!
Chacun est du climat de son intelligence;
Je suis concitoyen de tout homme qui pense:
La vérité, c'est mon pays!"

("My homeland is everywhere where shines the light of France,
Where her genius bursts upon dazzled regards!
Each man lives within his own intelligence;
I am a fellow citizen of every man who thinks:
The truth, that is my country!")[1]

The political crisis of 1839 was succeeded the following year by the most dangerous diplomatic crisis that the new Monarchy had to face. Indeed, the Eastern problem was more than an external affair, and the defeat France suffered was more than a mere check for her diplomatists, but an injury to the monarchy, to the soul of the country itself, which for a few months had become unusually united over its duty to uphold the pretensions of Mehemet Ali, Pasha of Egypt. The involvement of France led her to face Europe alone, to try to bluff; then, the attempt failing, to see her unity dissolve before the threat of war. From the defeat arose the ministry dominated by Guizot, determined to recover lost ground by diplomatic means, by playing the game the other powers wished to play. In this it faced a body of opinion whose disapproval of the pacific foreign policy of the July Monarchy was embittered by the humiliation of 1840, for which they demanded a revenge.

Whereas the British were hostile both to the Pasha and to French influence throughout the Ottoman Empire, France supported the Sultan against Russia, but favoured Mehemet Ali, who in 1833 had attacked his overlord and added Syria to his pashalic of Egypt. This ambiguity led Roussin, ambassador in Constantinople, to complain of the lack of direction he received from Paris, whilst Egypt's development was increasingly financed with French capital and her army modernised by French officers. Of foreign ministers, only Molé was fundamentally hostile to this new power, sharing with Sainte-Aulaire in Vienna, a distaste for rebellion, and agreeing with Barante at St Petersburg that France was threatened by a peaceful coalition which would conquer her diplomacy in the embassies of Europe and destroy her influence. Thus, when in 1838 Mehemet Ali stated his intention to declare himself the independent hereditary ruler of Egypt and Syria, Molé led a willing Palmerston in threatening naval measures to prevent any such declaration. Wisely, Mehemet Ali waited; he did not have to be patient for long. In April 1839, with the reckless hatred of a dying man, Sultan Mahmoud flung a Turkish army into Syria. Maréchal Soult's ministry of 12 May faced an Eastern question which was no longer a vague and distant threat, but a dangerous and urgent problem. Egyptian troops had swept to the frontiers of Turkey and only been stopped there by French promises of intervention.

In Paris, the King, with the advice of Desages, director of political affairs at the Foreign Ministry, decided French policy. Soult, with the mind of a soldier not a diplomat, spoke vaguely to the Chambers of glory with peace, to the diplomats of European concord. The government took care to act with Palmerston's aggreement, and accepted the suggestion of a combined Anglo-French fleet to keep the peace. Louis-Philippe believed that Franco-British alliance could curb Russian influence by replacing the treaty of Unkiar-Skelessi, and that France could rebuff Russian attempts to isolate her. This brilliant result rested upon the illusion that France could mediate between Porte and Pasha and that Britain would allow Egypt to retain its conquests and become independent. Palmerston wanted Mehemet Ali to give up Syria in return for the hereditary possession of Egypt: the Marshal did not dissent. "Soult is a jewel, nothing can be more satisfactory than his course with regard to us",[2] wrote Palmerston to Granville in July 1839. But, continued Bulwer, secretary of the embassy at Paris, reporting this euphoria, "When we came to action on that agreement all accord ceased."[3]

French public opinion favoured Mehemet Ali. He was a rebel, and most Frenchmen approved of revolution if disliking some of its consequences. They approved his admiration for Napoleon and his offensive on the stagnation and superstition represented by the Ottomans. More soberly, Saint-Marc Girardin pointed out in the *Journal des Débats* that as Britain's ambitions increased in Asia with the taking of Aden, France should at least maintain her influence in the Levant. On the left, the *National* wanted more than influence: Egypt should become a French colony, and Near Eastern difficulties used as an opportunity to seize the Rhine frontier. When in June the deputies came to discuss the credit that the government asked to augment French Mediterranean forces, the commission approving it tried to push the ministers into a more energetic policy. In the debates, moderates and conservatives showed that the influence of the Orient was potent upon minds otherwise prosaic and pacifist. Carné called upon the government to protect Egypt against Ottoman military despotism, and also the "maritime despotism"[4] of England. Tocqueville, in his first speech in the Chamber, declared that England was no natural ally and recommended an "Anconade" to support Mehemet Ali, landing troops somewhere on the Turkish coast: he did not feel that Britain or Russia would risk war. With Lamartine, the debates arrived at "a thousand and one nights", as Guizot[5] described his ideas for partition of the Ottoman Empire between the Christian powers. If less poetic, the ideas of other deputies were scarcely more realistic. It was left to a legitimist, the Duc de Valmy, to point out the perilous illogicality of the French position: enlightened by his prejudices against rebellion and favourable to Russia, he saw the contradiction of remaining in alliance with Britain whilst supporting the dangerous cause of Mehemet Ali. He was an exception: the credits were voted by an immense majority.

Whilst the deputies talked, the Sultan's army was being routed at Nezib, and on 4 July his navy deserted. Its treacherous commander, leading his fleet out of the Dardanelles, encountered French ships under ths command of Amiral Lalande, a Russophobe who had made plans for an Anglo-French attack on Sebastopol which he regarded as a likely development of the crisis. He and the Prince de Joinville, who was serving under him, were delighted to hear that the fleet was being removed from Constantinople because of Russian influence there and was sailing to strengthen Mehemet Ali, deceiving the British who believed the expedition was against Egypt. Lalande allowed the fleet to proceed and it sailed direct to Alexandria, where its kneeling commander presented it, and less valuably, his loyalty, to the Pasha.

European diplomacy lagged behind events. France was particularly damaged by this, for Soult was unable to imprint any unity upon French diplomacy, and Roussin, Lalande and Cochelet, the consul at Alexandria, frequently took initiatives according to personal rather than governmental policy, which officially was to favour neither Turkey nor Egypt but to mediate between them. Roussin compromised his government by signing, with representatives of the other powers, a collective note proclaiming that they would act in unity, an action which in supporting the Sultan went against the official policy of "from Turk to Turk" as Mehemet Ali expressed it[6] treating suzerain and rebellious vassal as equals. The battle of Nezib had proved to Palmerston that Egyptian power needed to be diminished: it convinced France that Mehemet Ali was invulnerable. So she refused to accept the British proposal of south Syria added to Egypt for Mehemet Ali, Louis-Philippe telling Granville that it would be impossible to dislodge Ibrahim's army. Mehemet Ali would resist if the Porte's concessions were insufficient, claimed the French government which proposed hereditary Egypt and Syria: but this was too much for Palmerston and too little for Mehemet Ali. Palmerston was infuriated by the desertion of the Turkish fleet and demanded that Lalande repair his earlier inaction by assisting the British to compel Egypt to surrender it, but France refused to do more than lend persuasion. Soult ignored warnings from French diplomats in London and St Petersburg that those two were becoming increasingly friendly. Nicholas I, in his desire to destroy the alliance of the two liberal powers, showed himself flexible, whilst the government of his pragmatic enemy Louis-Philippe moved towards disaster with uncompromising blindness.

Ambassadorial and ministerial changes could not greatly improve the position. Although in October, Roussin, the headstrong and unsubtle sailor, returned to the arid dignity of the Chamber of Peers (whence he was recruited into Thiers's March 1840 Cabinet) and was replaced by a career diplomat, the Comte de Pontois, the French position had been already lost at the Sublime Porte; and without it, the "from Turk to Turk" policy Pontois was intended to strengthen was doomed. In February 1840, Comte Sébastiani, considered too favourable to the Sultan and not sufficiently independent towards Palmerston, was replaced, after some resistance from Louis-Philippe, by Guizot. It was hoped that France could recover her position in London by means of Guizot's diplomacy, yet the new ambassador carried with him instructions which made this impossible: France still required all of Syria to be added to Egypt as hereditary in Mehemet Ali's family. Guizot was reduced to trying to frighten Palmerston with the Russian spectre, in which he had no success. Meanwhile, relations between Russia and France, which had improved under Molé, were at an extremely low level. Some tactless words in the Chamber of Deputies from Soult on Poland and an anti-Russian editorial from the *Journal des Débats* (the Tsar as an absolute ruler could not understand that French newspapers were not written in ministerial offices) had angered Nicholas and made him more than ever favourable to Britain.

After its parliamentary defeat, the weak ministry of Soult had to be replaced. The absence of Guizot had enormously strengthened the position of Thiers. Louis-Philippe had wanted either to retain Soult, or to return to Molé, but he could not avoid commissioning Thiers to form a Cabinet, for the little man's dominance in the Chamber of Deputies was obvious. The formation of the Cabinet of 1 March 1840 occurred with remarkable ease. Without Guizot, and with the disinterested Duc de Broglie aiding his efforts, Thiers, taking the presidency and Foreign Affairs for himself, was able to recruit doctrinaires. The Comte de Rémusat attained high office with the Ministry of the Interior. Duvergier de Hauranne, who had also played a leading role in uniting doctrinaires to *centre gauche* during the Coalition, was considered unsuitable, but his brother-in-law, Jaubert, was made Minister of Public Works. Rémusat realised this split would probably end "the association known as the doctrinaire party",[7] for the more conservative were hostile to any members of the group allying with Thiers in a Cabinet which would have to placate the left. None the less, Rémuseat, although typically regretting his action to the point of being struck down for a while with nervous depression, had now joined his fate to the *centre gauche*.

The other ministers were an assortment taken from the centre. Besides Roussin, there was Général Cubières, Minister of War, who had held this post in the provisional Cabinet of March 1839. A respected figure connected with the imperial aristocracy, he was unusual in both being a brave soldier and having good manners. This reputation he was to lose in the most humiliating circumstances. Cousin, philosopher and influential academic, Minister of Public Instruction, was friendly with Thiers and held a vague position between conservatives and the *tiers parti*. Alexandre Gouin, Minister of Commerce, was a banker, and constant campaigner for the reduction of interest on *rentes*. "A thrifty guardian of the public's coffers" with what Rémusat called "bourgeois ideas"[8] on state finance, and in this he resembled the new Finance Minister. Comte Pelet de La Lozère was a very wealthy man in a Cabinet which, by including Gouin and Jaubert, was one of the richest and most financially expert of the regime. Pelet was a somewhat rigorous Protestant, and personally antipathetic to Thiers, but his reputation for probity was a useful adjunct to the ministry.

Thiers immediately set about his previous methods of rule from the centre. Rémusat's circular to the prefects told them frankly that the Cabinet would follow "a policy of transaction"[9] and told them to protect conservative interests with conciliatory language.* Rémusat in fact hoped to create a new *juste milieu* for he realised that the doctrinaires could no longer appeal to confrontation,[10] and he replaced a few of the more conservative prefects by men of the centre. To rally support from both sides was its basic principle, as it had been Molé's; the difference lay in its stronger personal position in the Chamber of Deputies, and a more obvious centrist base. Thiers showed himself willing to practise Molé's "politics of the see-saw". He offered jobs to Dupont on the left and the conservative Martin, but both refused. He told the left that because Guizot was in London, a policy of liberalisation could be followed without his interference, and assured the conservatives that Guizot's willingness to represent his government proved how safe his foreign policy was. Two notable journalists, Granier de Cassagnac of the conservative *Presse* and Capo de Feuillide of the left, were sent on diplomatic missions which won their support. Thiers also managed to charm approval from Faucher of the *Courrier Français* and Chambolle of the *Siècle*. He thus reinforced a strong position in public opinion: he was, complained Lamartine, "a personification of the extra-parliamentary power of the press".[11] And he was the particular favourite of the National Guardsmen as well as popular in the world of high finance.

There were exceptions, however. The *Presse* waged an open war upon the ministry. Inside Parliament, Lamartine, Salvandy and Martin led a group of pro-Molé conservatives which was not reconciled to Thiers. The *Journal des Débats* objected to some of the concessions to the left and retreated into sulky disapproval. Guizot kept in close touch with those of his friends who feared and disliked Thiers: he regarded himself as directly responsible to the King in ensuring peace[12] and held himself ready to return to combat the ministry if necessary. He almost did this because of the apparent tolerance given to electoral reform. An independent deputy, a progressive conservative named

* *Ed. Note*. "A policy of transaction": one of ostensibly focusing upon measures most apt to reconcile the different factions within Parliament. In practice it amounted to a somewhat duplicitous attempt to build broad support by promising all things to all people. See J. P. T. Bury and R. P. Tombs, *Thiers 1797–1877, a Political Life* (London, 1986), pp. 63–4.

Rémilly, laid down a proposition which prohibited deputies from being promoted to paid public functions and being advanced in such during their period as deputy and for a year afterwards. Thiers spoke with embarrassment, not opposing the proposition, but asking for its adjournment. Refusal to countenance electoral or parliamentary reform had been part of the bargain with the doctrinaires, but he could not openly admit this to the left. Jaubert, very hostile to reform, wrote to all the doctrinaires asking them to help bury the proposition when the bureaux discussed it, and this occurred, but the Cabinet's weakness was manifest.

Thiers dominated his Cabinet in 1840 as he had in 1836. He spoke on every topic from sugar duties to the Eastern question, usually with brilliant success. He was presented with a gold medal by the Banque de France for protecting its privileges and helping win it the extension of its monopoly position. The session was fruitful in other economic measures. A concession was granted for steam navigation between France and America, railways were aided, the monopoly in salt manufacturing ended, and a large programme of public works implemented. The position of the Cabinet prevented measures more adventurous than this. Thiers was the prisoner of left and right. To retain the support of the *gauche dynastique*, he hinted that he might award Barrot with office. It is doubtful if King and conservative deputies would have tolerated this, but Thiers was saved from Molé's fate by the brevity of his ministry. As before, the King, who had given his minister loyal support, would remove him when he seemed a threat to peace.

It was Thiers's belief that Orleanist France needed a war: the throne to be made popular by an aura of military glory: the people themselves to be awakened from mediocrity and materialism by the excitement of combat.[13] Thiers himself enjoyed visiting battlefields and charting the campaigns of the Empire: to be Napoleon's biographer was insufficient. Thiers wished to emulate him, nor was he restrained by any of the humanitarianism or horror of war learnt from experience which so much affected Louis-Philippe. On the other hand, even Thiers could not but feel apprehension as to the possible course of war. So he was drawn two ways; enthusiastic enough to risk war, sufficiently timorous to fear it. An aggressive foreign policy seemed the solution: it would rally the left without upsetting the social order, and increase Thiers's own popularity. An encouragement to total conquest of Algeria, and the return of Napoleon's ashes from Saint Helena were useful achievements, but it was a more dramatic success which Thiers sought.

So in spite of warnings that Britain would act without France, Thiers refused a compromise of hereditary Egypt for Mehemet Ali, and Syria for his lifetime, and even an Austrian proposal that the southern half of Syria be given permanently to the Pasha, alienating the punctilious Metternich whom he had already offended by his disdain for diplomatic niceties. In the East, previous policy continued. Cochelet in Alexandria had the difficult task of restraining Mehemet Ali, whilst a friend of Thiers, the journalist Jacques Coste, editor of the *Temps*, had been corresponding with the brother-in-law of the Sultan, deviously pressing the latter to surrender Adana and Syria to different sons of Mehemet Ali, to win all back when they quarrelled, as they inevitably would. The French ambassador, like Coste, stressed British ambitions in the East, but Pontois was finding himself increasingly isolated.

The King and his minister thought that Guizot was too easily worried. Indeed, until July, Anglo-French relations remained superficially equable. When a British fleet blockaded Sicily in a quarrel over sulphur monopolies, Guizot persuaded his government to mediate, and after complicated negotiations Britain was extricated from an embarrassing affair. Palmerston's speedy, almost contemptuous, acquiescence to the restitution of the remains of the Emperor Napoleon when Thiers asked for them was a gesture in accord with an alliance which was becoming a façade concealing realities of power politics. Grievances simmered in the Foreign Secretary's mind: in Buenos Aires, in Spain, Portugal, Greece, Tunis and Persia as well as the Levant, France intrigued against Britain, he claimed, but dominating all was his prejudice against Louis-Philippe ("if he had been a very straightforward, scrupulous and highminded man, he would not now have been sitting on the French throne").[14]

Even Guizot, who exaggerates his own clear-sightedness in his memoirs, deluded himself in the strength of the *entente*. In London, the austere ambassador showed an excessive concern for precedence. The alacrity with which he would seize the arm of his hostess when going in to dinner was ascribed by English snobs to the social ignorance of a French bourgeois: perhaps it also symbolised a belief that he was not an ordinary ambassador, and determination that the alliance should be seen dominant in the salons of London. Certainly Guizot seemed to wish to show the *entente* in action. He retailed lists of all his guests and hosts to the Princesse de Lieven who would sometimes censor him for consorting with the unsuitable. He flung himself into the life of the English aristocracy to the extent of going to the races – a frivolity which astonished Paris: if the Duchesse de Dino is to be believed, his gambling was more successful than his diplomacy, since she reports his winning 200 guineas. But he was not a diplomat by nature, and failed to understand the English, in spite of all accusations by his compatriots that he was more English than French. He behaved in London like a Parisian politician, trying to split the Cabinet, to rouse the radicals against Palmerston, calculating support and forming alliances. He had no success: the French Cabinet system was different from the British, he did not understand Palmerston's character nor fully realise his paramountcy. Instead, his activities and those of the Princesse de Lieven, Guizot's Egeria, angered Palmerston. However, Thiers felt only relief in having a potential rival in voluntary exile. Guizot implemented the government's policy loyally: nevertheless, he was worried by concessions to the left within France, and continued to correspond with friends like Broglie and Léonce de Lavergne. He trusted Thiers so little that, fearing he might be blamed for any mistakes, he sent copies of his despatches to his political allies to be kept as a record.

At last it seemed as though the French policy "from Turk to Turk" was about to succeed: in June both Sultan and Pasha appeared to become more conciliatory. Eugène Périer, nephew of Casimir, was sent to push the Pasha into peace, to urge him to accept Egypt hereditarily and Syria for his lifetime, which Thiers had refused when proposed by others. He realised that the European situation was urgent, or at least pretended to do so, in order to extract concessions from Mehemet Ali. Périer spoke of a British blockade against Egypt, and the inability of France to protect her against this. Thiers, like Guizot, believed that the Prussian and Austrian envoys in London would force Palmerston to accept the negotiations, and therefore rejected an offer which was Palmerston's last, the pashalic of Acre, in south-west Syria.

While the French were active in the Near East, Guizot carefully avoiding the need to explain these activities to his diplomatic colleagues in London, the representatives of the Northern Courts were scurrying secretly to Palmerston's country home. Other European powers resented France's independent action. Irritation against the unmannerly Thiers and the unresponsive Guizot had pushed a somewhat unwilling Metternich, with Prussia in his train, into following the Anglo-Russian line. In late May, the fall of the Anglophile Grand Vizier seemed to give France in Constantinople a position similar to that which she possessed in Alexandria. Here was the motive which produced the four-power Convention against France and Egypt. Meanwhile events were occurring in the Levant which lessened Egyptian power. Fostered by British agents, a revolt broke out in Syria against Egyptian occupation. It was an embarrassment for France, for amongst the rebels were found Maronite Christians, traditional French protégés. The government showed its priorities by removing its consul from Beirut for having been unable to transfer his support from Maronites to Egyptians with sufficient celerity.

Guizot had warned Thiers and the King (by private correspondence through Général Baudrand) that Palmerston was preparing a four-power arrangement which would deprive Mehemet Ali of Syria, but he did not realise how imminent this was. Writing to Thiers on 14 July, the day before the signing of the Convention, Guizot noted the extreme reserve of his colleagues: however, he believed that when an arrangement came, it would be presented to the French for their approval. He was very mistaken. On 17 July, the French ambassador was summoned to the Foreign Office. Palmerston read Guizot a memorandum informing him of the Convention which he and the ambassadors of Russia, Prussia and Austria had signed on the 15th. Egypt was granted to Mehemet Ali and his descendants hereditarily, and, if the terms were accepted by Egypt within ten days, the Pasha should also possess Acre for his lifetime. If, within the following ten days, the proposals had not been accepted, the offer of hereditary Egypt would also be withdrawn. Separate acts provided for the surrender of the Ottoman fleet and for payment of tribute to the Sultan. The four allies promised to aid the Porte if Mehemet Ali should not surrender. Furthermore, it was agreed that the old rule forbidding entry of warships into the Dardanelles and Bosphorus would be returned to. Thus Unkiar-Skelessi, which France had relied upon to unite Britain to her, in opposition to Russia, had been voluntarily dismantled.

Palmerston stated his regret that France was not a party to the Convention.

He claimed that its terms were those once suggested by Sébastiani. Guizot could not deny this, but rightly stated that his predecessor had acted without the authorisation of his government. Guizot proceeded formally to protest against the conclusion of the convention to the exclusion of France. Beneath the diplomatic forms, the polite regrets and the cool protests, there was on one side malicious triumph, on the other shock and bitter resentment. Guizot and the Princesse de Lieven had "looked as cross as the devil for the last few days" remarked Palmerston gleefully to Bulwer a few days later: the ambassador, "when he dined here, . . . could scarcely keep up the outward appearances of civility".[15]

Thiers received the news of the Convention with astonished fury. When the King was informed in his study, he shouted so loudly, he could be heard some rooms away. At this moment, everyone was warlike; Marie-Amélie embarrassed her spouse by her bellicosity. The whole of the political world was shocked and surprised, and public opinion, in theatres and *cabarets*, reacted with spontaneous violence. The King seemed for once to be truly popular with all sections of society, and during the fête for the anniversary of *les trois glorieuses* cheers roared for him above the "Marseillaise". The press was more fervent still than the politicians. Thiers's *Constitutionnel* warned Palmerston that to thwart France meant European conflict. The *Siècle* and more moderate *Temps* spoke of a new revolutionary war against the aristocratic and absolutist Courts of Europe. The Bonapartist *Capitole* threatened to reduce Prussia to the boundaries of the old electorate. Even the *Journal des Débats* was angered by the "insolence" of the Convention. The left, however, found the government's response too moderate. The *National* spoke its scorn for a regime which did not fly into attack after such an insult: a worthy government would put 100,000 men on the Rhine, 50,000 would sit on the Alps, and another army would rouse Italy with revolution. Everywhere there was hatred for England, and rather unfairly as much for Austria and Prussia who had followed her into coalition. There were few exceptions to the general bellicosity: the legitimists could not approve a revolutionary war against Austria, however little they loved England, and the *Presse* was influenced by Molé who had never approved Mehemet Ali, in addition to disliking Thiers.

The Bourse panicked and fell at an unprecedented speed. However, it was rightly considered suspicious that Dosne, Thiers's father-in-law, and his ally, the banker Fould, had been able to speculate on the slump before it occurred. From London, the Comte de Flahaut had been able to warn his illegitimate son in time for Auguste de Morny to save a considerable sum. Palmerston noted this and the subsequent rumours that certain French politicians were buying English funds, speculating on peace, and it convinced him that France would never risk war: under the Empire, he remarked, war was the only way of making money; now, it was an infallible method of losing it.

The French government, in the absence of the Chambers, did all that was legally possible. Late in July, the classes of soldiers for the years 1836 to 1839 were called up, producing an army of 480,000 men in various states of preparation. An extraordinary credit of 8,120,000 francs was declared for the navy and plans for fortifying Paris were pressed forward. A problem which had confused Cabinets and commissions since 1833 was decided in a few days, to the delight of the King, and work began by ordinance. The War Minister, Général Cubières, and the rest of the Cabinet were pushed into the background. The Duc d'Orléans and Thiers, aided by Rémusat, took firm measures to repair the effects of inaction by previous war ministers and of budgetary controls. The army was organised for war in Algeria. Plans and materials alike were lacking for a European war. Supported by Rémusat, Orléans, who was acquainted with German military developments, forced innovations to produce greater speed and mobility upon Thiers, who believed that what sufficed for Napoleon was still valid.

Thiers, minister of 1 March, had become to the wits "Mars Ier". He pored over maps, his imagination sending Egyptians to Constantinople and Frenchmen to Berlin. With typically Orleanist contradiction, the *président* and his supporters spoke of revolutionary war against the Northern Courts, but the government was unwilling to trust to purely revolutionary means. Thus it was suggested to the reactionary King of Piedmont that an alliance with France could gain him Lombardy from Austria, and similar seductive attempts were made towards Naples.

Visiting Louis-Philippe and his president at the Château d'Eu in Normandy, Guizot found Thiers desiring peace but prepared for war: but he perceived that the King, however high his tone, was determined upon peace. He returned to London completely in accord with Thiers, and with two projects. One proposed a five-power guarantee of the status quo; the other project involved French mediation between the Pasha and the signatories of the London Convention. French terms were lower than before, but the essence of disagreement with Palmerston remained. Guizot and Thiers believed that if Egyptian troops defeated the Syrian revolt, the powers would not dare to attack. Their optimism rested upon an overestimate of Egyptian strength, encouraged by Cochelet,[16] divisions in the British Cabinet and amongst the four allies. Leopold, King of the Belgians, used his influence at the British Court to support the status quo proposal. There was some inclination to accept it, save from the vital quarter, Palmerston. He was convinced that France would not fight. He "likes to put his foot on their necks",[17] remarked Leopold to Queen Victoria, his niece.

Thiers tried to frighten the British chargé d'affaires, Bulwer. As they paced the gallery of his house at Auteil, he told the Englishman that the alliance of their two countries was at an end. France could withstand isolation; the whole population supported a government which would act with decision. Mehemet Ali was making concessions so France was bound to support him. "You understand, my dear friend, the gravity of what I have just said", he asked, his eyes fixed upon Bulwer. The other replied it would mean war. At the mention of the word, Thiers seemed to withdraw a little: the remarks were those of the private man, he could not speak for the Cabinet, but personally, he would not accept a passive role. When Bulwer showed that Britain believed that Louis-Philippe would prevent war occurring, Thiers asserted that, on the contrary, the King was more bellicose than he was.[18] Indeed, the latter raised his voice to embarrassed diplomats, complained bitterly of the ingratitude of European powers towards him, the only barrier to revolution, and threatened them with the dictatorship of Maréchal Clauzel as the outcome of conflict. If they gave him no choice between humiliation and war, he would unleash the tiger, he warned.[19]

Meanwhile, Pontois was trying to force the Porte to grant Mehemet Ali more generous terms than those of the London Convention, and attempting to prevent Turkish ratification of the treaty: he made menaces to achieve this, countenanced by the government, but later denied. The Porte refused, however, confident in British and Russian support. And Mehemet Ali, in spite of the urgings of Cochelet, was resisting abandoning hereditary possession of Syria. To reinforce him, Thiers sent to Alexandria Comte Walewski; it was a shrewd choice. To the Parisian world the young man was a bankrupt journalist, unsuccessful playwright, socialite and lover of Rachel, a gallant but dandified soldier in Algeria. But he was an illegitimate son of Napoleon and this, in Egypt where the Emperor's glory shone as brightly as in France and whose ruler addressed the King of the French as Emperor, gave him immense prestige, which, combined with his own tact and charm, enabled him to influence the Pasha. Walewski was told to moderate Mehemet Ali, to gain from him a *carte blanche* for French negotiations, and to maintain in him an alert defensiveness. France would not be militarily prepared until spring, nor could she fight in the East. She hoped that Egyptian force would deter the powers, and her own negotiations break triumphantly through the delay. In some respects French policy was too rational; it treated Turks, Austrians and Palmerston as opponents in a game, who would play by the same rules whilst condoning a little cheating. Yet while Walewski persuaded, Pontois threatened and Guizot remained ostentatiously and coldly confident, Palmerston prepared to call Louis-Philippe's bluff.

Thiers was deceiving Palmerston when he told him that Walewski had been despatched to persuade the Pasha to accede to the London Convention. The mission went beyond this. Walewski and Cochelet finally extracted a letter from Mehemet Ali, dated 7 November, to the "Very high, mighty and majestic seigneur, the august Emperor of the French nation",[20] in which the Egyptian ruler fulsomely put himself in French hands: he would even surrender Syria if France asked it, he declared, but in fact would hardly be satisfied with less than Syria for his lifetime. Walewski left to propose this to the Sultan's government, but the prevalence of British influence at the Sublime Porte doomed the second half of his mission to failure. By this time Palmerston was preparing methods of coercion. Thiers still hoped that resistance would break up the European coalition: his bluff was the more ill-founded, because he now knew from Walewski's despatches that Egyptian prepotence was largely illusory, yet still he encouraged the Pasha to hold firm.

In September an Anglo-Austrian force began assisting the Syrian rebellion. In Paris, the Bourse which had in August reached its lowest point since the revolutionary days of July 1831, sank still further. Crowds in theatres shouted the "Marseillaise" (although prudent managements tried to avoid this with mere orchestral versions) and anti-English slogans were chanted in the streets. Whatever the divisions in the political world, the people of Paris were crying with one voice, reinforcing the argument of those who believed only war could avoid revolution. The Duc d'Orléans was one such: "I prefer to fall on the banks of the Rhine or the Danube than in a gutter of the Rue Saint-Denis",[21] he cried. Many believed that the only alternative to Frenchmen killing Frenchmen was for them to kill Germans.

Such opinions did not pass unnoticed in Germany. At the beginning of the year, the Baron de Bourgoing had informed Soult from Bavaria, that German opinion was reacting against bellicose editorials in left-wing newspapers which spoke of reconquering the Rhine frontier. The semi-official approval given to expansionist sentiments, the concentration in October of French troops near the frontier at Thionville, turned these apprehensions into a conscious and sometimes furious patriotism. Small states, liberals, Catholics and nationalists who for various reasons had distrusted or detested Prussia now turned to her for protection. Very few Frenchmen understood this German nationalism, because so many of them saw their country as a revolutionary power and were unable to appreciate nationalism in others, save where, as in Italy or Poland, it was aimed against their enemies. German nationalism was a barrier to that aspiration, at once sacred and geographical, the Rhine frontier. "Sie sollen ihn nicht haben" had chanted Becker: his song which became respectable to sing and hugely popular, but was dedicated to Lamartine, who in articles in his *Journal de Saône-et-Loire* and in the *Presse* had criticised Thiers's bellicosity for placing France between humiliation and war. The poet, with *grand seigneurial* negligence, wrote (he claimed, in his bath) a high-minded mystical and pacific reply. Patriots were angered by its sentiments. Alfred de Musset responded with angry chauvinism: "We have had your German Rhine" he told Becker, conjuring up the victories of the Empire with braggadocio. Although Lamartine scoffed at it as a tavern song, it was vastly more popular than his. There was a rush to compose music for it, and one version was adopted by the army and sung in barracks. The Duc d'Orléans congratulated the poet warmly, whilst the effectiveness of his insolence was shown by a shower of challenges to duels from angry Prussian officers. Edgar Quinet also wrote a poem attacking Lamartine's new deity, human unity: France should not sacrifice her gods to this new Baal, he cried, in revealingly pagan terms. His pamphlet, *1815 et 1840*, was no less poetical. France remained the vanquished of 1815; she must rise from the tomb of Waterloo. Quinet's idea was that a free Germany would somehow surrender the left bank of the Rhine to France, but that if she did not, war would be necessary. A pacific monarchy denatured France: she would not be herself until she raised again the sword which repressive enemies had forced her to sheathe in 1815.

It was only Bonapartists and republicans who really desired war; the rest of the population were enjoying an outburst of noisy patriotism. Venting their Anglophobia in songs and slogans, few of them wished to extend it to the battlefield. As Léonce de Lavergne noted, the feeling was for war when it seemed distant, but veered away when war came closer.[22] The notables had recovered themselves and began to blame the ministry. The *Journal des Débats* divested itself of its former passion and began to praise the moderation of the King. Louis-Philippe had lent himself to the bluff, ignoring Rothschild and other financial proponents of peace, but he realised that it was not working, and he was not willing to slide into war. Long arguments took place in the Cabinet. Thiers wanted to adopt a more threatening stance, to increase the size of the army. Roussin, opponent of Mehemet Ali, now Minister of Marine, said the navy was not ready; it could not challenge Britain at sea. Général Cubières likewise declared the army unprepared for European war, and he asked to resign as did Pelet. When Thiers implied the possibility of war, the King grew emotional. "Nothing in the world will force me into it; I would abdicate a thousand times rather than consent to it."[23] He foresaw the destruction of French commerce and 100,000 Parisian workers dying of starvation. Unlike Thiers with his conception of Napoleonic glory, Louis-Philippe found war repugnant. "War, even successful, is fatal! It is a dunghill exhaling corruption!"[24]

The divided ministers, having exhausted the power of ordinances, agreed to convoke the Chambers for 28 October. Thiers still carried the majority of ministers, although where he was carrying them remained uncertain to them as to him, and when, after long arguments and much wavering, the King refused to agree to a manifesto to Europe (in which he feared a *casus belli*) the Cabinet resigned on 6 October. The ministers were not unhappy thus to lose responsibility. Louis-Philippe, however, was embarrassed: in circumstances which made Thiers appear a patriot to his detriment, a Cabinet crisis was added to diplomatic crisis. The strenuous persuasion of the Duc d'Orléans and the Duc de Broglie, who feared for the fate of the monarchy in the shock to public opinion, bore its results. The following day, the ministers returned. Thiers was perhaps still hoping for victory, or was fascinated by the prospect of war: whatever his motives for remaining *président*, he was determined to win popularity at the King's expense. Their former good relations were at an end. To his band of tame journalists, Thiers spoke maliciously of his sovereign: the newspapers were not slow to stress the divergences between the dishonourably pacific King and his patriotic minister.

However, the two did come to an agreement on the attitude to take towards Europe. Thiers drew up a note dated 8 October, for the French ambassadors to present to their courts. In measured tones, it declared that the deposition of Mehemet Ali (which the Sultan had decreed) would be taken as an alteration in the balance of power, and France would be forced to take action. Territorial terms were not touched upon explicitly, but the note showed France willing to allow Syria to be taken from the Pasha. If the later declarations Thiers made when out of office[25] were truthful, he would never have accepted the terms of 15 July: in this case, those who welcomed the moderation of his note were deceived. Probably he was not sincere and was playing for time, as he told Cochelet to encourage the Pasha who had fallen from boldness into fatalistic defeatism. The mildness of the note was primarily due to ministerial divisions and royal caution. Although the note at last put France on a defensible terrain, Guizot seems to have found it inconsistently mild, and placed it before Palmerston without defence or explanation. The latter could not but rejoice: he assured the French ambassador that Britain and the allies had no intention of deposing the Pasha, but military measures continued, and the surrender of Acre early in November marked the end of Egyptian power in Syria.

Meanwhile Thiers continued his confusing policy, speaking to Europe with the voice of Louis-Philippe, through the press with the voice of the anti-monarchical Thiers of the Coalition. He consulted Bugeaud and Clauzel on French chances of success in a European war. Measures were adopted to add 150,000 men of the 1841 class to the army, bringing it to almost 640,000 strong. Preparations were made to turn the National Guard into a military force, but the King refused to rouse Germany further by creating an armed camp at Metz. The withdrawal to Toulon of Amiral Hugon's fleet from the eastern Mediterranean seemed a pacific gesture; however, Granville heard from secret sources that an ambitious "Anconade" was proposed in the event of war – the seizure of the Balearic Islands. Credence was later given these rumours in a speech by Jaubert who had by then left office.[26] Warlike also were the negotiations with King Otto of Greece who was willing to invade Thessaly in the event of the Ottoman Empire becoming involved in war. Thus, whilst the note had lessened the chance of war, the ministry continued to prepare for it.

Meanwhile there was increasing apprehension over the internal situation. The *Journal des Débats* asked whether government and the rule of law still existed. "Or are we rather in a state of complete anarchy? The revolutionary party speaks as though it were the master. . . ."[27] There had been disorders in late August when republicans who had been banqueting, over 2,000 in number, at Chatillon, re-entered the capital. From late August there had been a rash of strikes in the workshops. Their origins lay in the hope of the republicans to gain from war or disorder, and from the economic slump which followed the diplomatic crisis. Many of the strikes were violent, some policemen were stabbed to death on 3 September in a munitions factory. Four days later, a protest march started by cabinet-makers of the Faubourg Saint-Antoine, joined by other workers, led to the building of barricades, but the speedy use of troops stifled insurrection at its birth. Shouting processions continued in the streets, and on 12 October a riotous crowd outside the War Ministry had to be dispersed by force. The left did not hesitate to fan the flames. The revolutionary *élan* of 1831 seemed to have been reborn; but this time a greater element of social division embittered it. The *National* and newspapers further to the left talked of the need to overthrow the existing order and to re-create society: pamphlets, the most notable being Louis Blanc's *Organisation du travail* and Lamennais's *Le Pays et le Gouvernement*, called upon the proletariat to organise itself for a struggle against the rich.

Then, on the evening of 15 October, as the King was driving along the

Quai des Tuileries, there was an explosion. Two footmen on the carriage were injured. The National Guard escort captured the would-be assassin, Darmès, who gave his profession as "conspirator": his aim was "to deliver France from the greatest tyrant of modern and ancient times".[28] He was a frequenter of republican wine-shops and communist clubs; the willing if unskilful tool of that permanent vague "conspiracy" decided the Court of Peers, which condemned him to death.

Louis-Philippe was deeply depressed by the event, a reminder of the hatreds felt towards him, a warning of the permanent insecurity of his position. But whereas the poor Queen suffered sleepless, tearful nights as a result, his political instincts quickly became dominant. He saw how the conservatives now felt the risks of Thiers remaining were greater than those of his being forced from office, how moderates became conservative in fearing anarchy, how Darmès had handed him a shield to protect him from the scorn of the patriots: he would have the approval of all who feared revolution more than they hated England.

All were now awaiting the speech from the throne. The King had told his *président* that he desired it to be vague: there must be no talk of war. "But Sire," protested Thiers, as reported by his mother-in-law, "you doubtless will not allow France to be humiliated. – Humiliate France! My dear minister, those are the words of the press."[29] When Thiers submitted a draft, the King refused to deliver it. It was too defiant in tone, equivalent to a declaration of war, he claimed. He read out his own proposals for a speech. There was a short, polite discussion; neither would give way. The *président du conseil* and his colleagues submitted their resignation, and with their accord, the King wrote to Soult, and, by telegraph, summoned Guizot to Paris.

Thiers left office with some relief. The *Constitutionnel* paved his way by praising his patriotism and deprecating the cowardly prudence of the King. Thiers's vacillation between the will to power and the wish to resign had reflected his inability to choose between the perils of war and the humiliation of peace. He had made mistakes more cleverly than Soult; none the less, they had been the same mistakes. Initial over-confidence in Mehemet Ali, delay intended to produce "between Turks" agreement turning into a bluff to frighten Europe and then into war preparations. Louis-Philippe was prepared to accept humiliation when he saw that the bluff had failed, and by appearing to force Thiers to resign had solved his problem for him and presented him with the role of the dismissed patriot. He convinced himself that he had been much more resolute than he had been. Yet it was his imagination which had wanted war: his desire, he later told Nassau Senior, had been a war by France and England against Austria and Russia, which would have liberated Italy from the former and established the independence of the Ottoman Empire. He blamed the King's "rage for peace"[30] for preventing this dream becoming reality. Out of power Thiers was more bellicose and expansionist than he had been as minister, and his demands for French influence in the Levant and description of the aim of his policy justified many of Palmerston's accusations of France's intentions.

Newspapers of the left and centre expressed horror at the King's action. Threatening manifestations continued; there was fear that the forces of insurrection would seize their opportunity. The politicians' minds were concentrated by this fear, as in May 1839. Guizot left London immediately, arriving in Paris on 26 October, and it took him only two days to form a Cabinet. Maréchal Soult was *président du conseil* and Minister of War in this ministry of doctrinaires and conservatives, but Guizot, Minister of Foreign Affairs, was its true head.

The advent of the ministry of 29 October (the date its nomination was published) did not remove all fear of war: many regarded it as doomed to a very brief and critical existence. The note of 8 October was a reality to Guizot, whereas to Thiers it was a ploy. Guizot gained the King's agreement to this, as to the seizure of Crete in the unlikely event of Russia taking Constantinople. He did not at once abandon the hope of some compromise from the allies. On leaving London he attempted to sway Palmerston with the habitual Orleanist argument: the French were dangerous revolutionaries, and their pacific government had the right to claim concessions to placate them. Through King Leopold, Louis-Philippe supported his minister's attempt to gain something in Syria for Mehemet Ali, to no avail, and Guizot instructed Cochelet to tell the Pasha that he would have to content himself with Egypt. Whilst using a calming influence in the East, France remained aloof from diplomacy in London. Guizot, whilst desiring that France should re-enter the European concert from which she had been so brutally ejected in July 1840, would do so only so long as no form of acceptance or condonation of the London Convention was involved. So Baron de Bourqueney, chargé d'affaires, was instructed to sign nothing until the powers had completely settled affairs between the Sultan and his vassal. Bourqueney was not altogether happy with this, fearing that exclusion might become permanent: but Guizot feared public opinion more. France would rejoin the other four powers over a convention which destroyed that of July 1840, once hereditary Egypt had been assured the Pasha.

Negotiations between Bourqueney and the four other representatives in London were rapidly successful on some points, due to the desire of the German powers for a speedy settlement. There would be no call for disarmament, the July Convention would be declared finished by its signatories, and the closure of the straits to warships would be restated. On other stipulations of lesser importance, France had less success, but once Bourqueney had convinced his chief that no more was possible, Guizot decided that further resistance would be harmful. Yet when he received in early March, the protocols by which the affair was to be terminated, he still had some objections. France could not admit that the London Convention had been "happily concluded": certain other adjectives which might displease national susceptibilities should be excised. This aroused some irritation, but eventually all the desired alterations were made. And when she signed the Straits Convention of 13 July 1841 with the other four powers, France re-entered the diplomatic world. Unkiar-Skelessi and the London Convention alike had been repudiated by Europe. Although Guizot asserted that Mehemet Ali owed the hereditary pashalic of Egypt to France, the truth in this claim could not conceal a humiliating defeat. Primarily this was due to faulty statescraft: for too long France had followed a dual policy, anti-Russian at Constantinople, anti-English at Alexandria. When Anglo-Russian *entente* emerged, France came to rely upon deviousness and delay. Desiring to maintain the Ottoman Empire in Turkey, whilst increasing her influence in Syria by means of Mehemet Ali, she prevented the latter from destroying the Empire after the disaster of Nezib: this was the Pasha's great opportunity, and France extinguished his chances, without gaining any credit from Britain. Palmerston had vowed to destroy French influence in the Levant, and showed himself unscrupulous and at times dishonest. But success cloaks dishonesty, and Palmerston's perception of his opponent's weak position, his decisive playing of his stronger hand, had made him victorious.

The King's refusal to be dragged into war was almost heroic, the prospect of war cleared his mind, but until then he had shared the illusions of his ministers. Desages, normally so astute, had fostered them, believing that Austrian desire for concession was stronger than British determination. He had helped compromise France with Egypt, and was then forced to admit late in 1840, that "the Pasha has played his hard miserably; we have played ours poorly; the game is lost".[31]

Rémusat described the crisis as "the critical moment of the Orleanist Monarchy".[32] Certainly its effects, direct and indirect, were enormous. Some blamed the King for the fright they had received and for their losses on the Bourse, others for the humiliation of retreat. Not only republicans felt this way; the Duc d'Orléans confessed himself ashamed to see his fellow soldiers when he knew the concessions made to keep the peace, and his brother Joinville, who believed that the French fleet could have defeated the British in the Mediterranean, felt similarly towards his sailors. Patriots believed that the regime had nothing to offer them: the King might consider some concessions, a small sacrifice of *amour propre*,[33] as of little import when peace was at risk, but there were many who found his "mania for peace" shameful. By the unpopularity of the foreign policy it encapsulated and reinforced, 1840 contributed to 1848. Louis-Philippe hoped to be able to say, when he died, that he left a realm "prosperous, free, rich, armed, redoubtable, without enemies and enjoying a strength that had cost humanity nothing",[34] but his ideal was not general. Many saw war as a good in itself: now they wanted revenge for 1840 as well as 1815. Yet Guizot was correct when he remarked that the forces of revolution retained their bitter hatreds but had lost their original *élan*. The republicans in their belief in easy victory at the end of a brief and glorious war, the nationalists with their ignorance of the nationalism of other nations being so intoxicated with their own, had illusions more powerful and more dangerous than those of the party of order. The majority were relieved, if shamefacedly: wrote Léon Faucher bitterly, "This country internally lacks resource and energy. It has charged opinion as quickly as the King, and, like him, it has been frightened."[35]

France learnt some lessons from the crisis. The army was maintained at a level of over 400,000, larger than before. French foreign policy changed in nature, and Guizot and Louis-Philippe did not attempt again to delay or bluff. Perhaps the most important and finally fatal result of the crisis, was that it placed Guizot in power and helped to maintain him there. For in 1840 France again seemed in a revolutionary situation: the financial effects of the crisis were worse than those of 1830, there were processions, revolutionary chants, conspiracies and the Darmés assassination attempt. The *parti de résistance* found again its *raison d'être*, and Guizot appeared as the man necessary to lead it.

REFERENCES

1. A. de Lamartine, *La Marseillaise de la Paix*, (*Recueillements Poétiques*, Editions Garnier Frères, 1960), 234.
2. H. L. Bulwer, *The Life of Viscount Palmerston* (London, 1870), II, 295.
3. Ibid.
4. Archives Parlementaires, 24 June 1840.
5. F. Guizot, *Lettres à la Princesse de Lieven* (1963), I, 248.
6. J. E. Driault, *L'Egypte et l'Europe* (1930), I, 305.
7. Comte C. de Rémusat, *Mémoires de ma vie* (1958), III, 297.
8. Ibid., 299.
9. Ibid.
10. Ibid.
11. A. de Lamartine, *Correspondence* (1882), II, 321.
12. Archives Nationales, 42.AP.4.
13. Duc E. de Noailles, *Le Comte Molé* (1925), VI, 183. Comte J. d'Eyragues, *Mémoires* (Falaise, 1875), 300. Affaires Étrangères, Correspondence politique Angleterre 655, 19, 20 April 1840.
14. Bulwer, op. cit., 310–12.
15. Ibid., 318.
16. Affaires Etrangères, Correspondance politique Angleterre 655, 19, 6 May 1840.
17. A. C. Benson and R. B. B. Esher (eds), *The Letters of Queen Victoria* (London, 1908), I, 294–6.
18. Bulwer, op. cit., 325.
19. Benson and Esher, *Queen Victoria*, I, 294–6.
20. Driault, op. cit., IV, 17.
21. Cited in P. Thureau-Dangin, *Histoire de la Monarchie de Juillet* (1897), IV, 277 and Rémusat, op. cit., III, 503.
22. E. Cartier, *Léonce de Lavergne* (1904), 43.
23. Comtesse S. A. Pelet de La Lozère, *Souvenirs* (1900), 302.
24. Ibid.
25. Archives Parlementaires, 28 November 1840.
26. Ibid., 3 December 1840.
27. *Journal des Débats*, 13 October 1840.
28. A. Trognon, *Vie de Marie–Amélie* (1872), 183.
29. Mme F. Dosne, *Mémoires* (1928), I, 215.

30. N. W. Senior, *Conversations with M. Thiers, M. Guizot and other Distinguished Persons during the Second Empire* (1878), 130–1.
31. F. Charles-Roux, *Thiers et Mehemet-Ali* (1951), 281.
32. Rémusat, op. cit., III, 448.
33. Ibid., 489.
34. Ibid.
35. L. Faucher, *Biographie et Correspondance* (1875), I, 101.

18

The Army: Bonapartism and Algerian Conquest

"On ne connait pas assez ces hommes de discipline dépourvus de pensée et prêts à tout faire pour le grade."

("Not enough is known of these men of discipline devoid of thought and ready to do anything for rank.")[1]

The army, more than any other institution except the peerage, represented France's changing regimes. Its commanders had often risen during the Revolution to serve the Empire, Restoration, and then to offer their services to Louis-Philippe. To some, this flexibility was a sign of unprincipled ambition; to others, proof of disinterested patriotism. The army presented itself as the servant of the nation rather than of a regime. So in Algeria, the Duc d'Orléans made a toast to the army, distant from the divisions of the fatherland, knowing of internal conflicts merely to curse them, and asking only to fight the enemy, be it Arab, climate or disease, in order to extend French civilisation.[2] Yet the army had been afflicted with purges quite as bitter as those which other institutions had undergone and, beneath a surface patriotism, lay political passions which existed with no less vehemence for being hidden. The legitimist Changarnier, republican Cavaignac, Orleanist La Moricière and Bonapartist Saint-Arnaud, could all fight bravely for France in Algeria, but of these generals, only the Orleanist could play a political role.

The government relied upon the army, but regarded it with some nervousness. Charles X had fallen partly because he could not utterly rely on his troops, and Louis-Philippe was forced to use the army more than the Restoration had done for internal purposes. In 1831 and 1834 in Paris and Lyons, it had protected his throne against insurrection. Louis Napoleon's attempted *putsch* failed, but it failed within the army itself, different sections of which had welcomed or crushed him. It was impossible to restrict the command simply to conservative Orleanists, and so the regime had to tolerate watchfully the presence of men whose loyalty was doubtful. Clauzel, for example, a general with prestige and popular with the left, was approached by republicans in 1831 to lead a coup. He refused, but, it would seem, after hesitation. Mangan, who appeared dangerously close to Lyons insurrectionists, was transferred and later promoted and, as general commanding in the north-west in 1840, played a very suspect role at the time of Louis Napoleon's Boulogne attempt. Algeria provided suitable territory for those whom the regime distrusted: thus Eugène Cavaignac, brother of the republican leader, made no secret of the fact that he would fight Carlist rebellion but not republican insurrection, pursued his career in North Africa, and progressed within the hierarchy, albeit more slowly than would a loyal Orleanist. To assist its influence over the army, the government sought as War Minister a prestigious soldier, in whom political or administrative competence was the least quality required. That is why Guizot felt that Général Bernard was too insignificant a minister (1836–39) and it was partially from fear that the military would learn from a bad example, that the King and Molé were so opposed to intervention in Spain after the radical *coup d'état* there in the summer of 1836.

It was the officers of lower grade that the government feared most. They felt the frustrations of the *petite bourgeoisie*; the failure to find a satisfactory niche in society whilst having left the settled ways of traditional order. In an army whose highest posts were occupied by men who had achieved their positions under the Empire, speedy promotion was rare. A war was attractive to many officers, not only for political or patriotic reasons, but because it promised advancement. Resentment was particularly felt against those superiors who had served the Restoration and much of the unrest in 1830 was due to indiscipline in the lower ranks who refused to accept orders from such men. The recruitment of many officers of the Empire who had opposed the Restoration strengthened the *parti du mouvement* in the army, and frequently made it a pressure group which acted against the prefect and gave support to radical elements. The poor behaviour of the army in Lyons in 1831 was largely due to the sympathy of some officers for opponents of the government and the General's disagreements with the prefects. Maréchal Soult as War Minister, using inspectors such as the martinet Général de Castellane, and the political action of Périer, strengthened discipline and removed many of the more untrustworthy elements from army command.

The army was still an obvious career for the children of good but impoverished families such as the Saint-Arnaud, but on the whole, the social rank of its officers was sinking, divorcing them from the ruling groups. The new officers entering the army frequently brought with them the republican or martially patriotic ideals common amongst much of the youth of the bourgeoisie. The École Polytechnique, which produced many artillery officers as well as civil engineers, was a seed-bed of Saint-Simonism and other radical causes. Disorders were endemic in it, on one occasion so serious that the government temporarily closed it down. Even at Saint-Cyr, where there was a strong aristocratic and landed-bourgeois element, there was an influx of *petit bourgeois*, frequently of republican conviction. There were serious disorders when the director refused to allow pupils to attend Général Lamarque's funeral. The July Monarchy, whose inception had caused the eradication of the predominance of traditional classes in the army leadership, was forced to educate a cadre which could well prove hostile to it.

Conservatives desired a small professional army whilst the left, true to the principles of 1792, desired a large force, informally organised and close to the population. The Soult army law of 1831 leant towards the former, although conscription provided the base of the 300,000 strong force. Conscripts could find suitable replacements to serve for them, and deliberate attempts were made to separate the army from the population. Parliament determined the number to be called up annually. Between 9 and 10 million francs annually were spent on defence, a quarter of total expenditure, but less in proportion to population than the other continental powers. The deputies were parsimonious on military matters, often causing ill feeling. "To be treated like this by an errand-boy after forty years of service"[3] raged Maréchal Soult after Dupin had led an almost successful attempt to reduce officers' pay. It led some soldiers to speak of the need for another 18 Brumaire.

Regiments were moved frequently, because to stay long in one place might lay the troops open to civilian influence. The government and military command looked disapprovingly at those cafés where the bourgeois bought the soldiers drinks; they could well be republican headquarters. There were also Bonapartist plots: Prince Louis Napoleon, in particular, corresponded with officers and met a few before attempting his *putsch* at Strasbourg in 1836. The Bonapartist pretender was right to take a particular initiative towards the artillery, because it was in their ranks that the largest proportion of young and impoverished officers was hostile to the regime, and at Strasbourg they formed a larger proportion of the army than elsewhere. Military unrest rarely had its origins in the ranks, where complaints were over pay, not politics. The political dangers, as manifest in Thomas's conspiracy at Lunéville in 1834 and the Vendôme mutiny two years later, were the work of the young low-ranking officers. Their belief that they could rouse the army to follow them, a similar illusion to that held by Louis Napoleon, was proved incorrect on the occasion of each attempt. Yet the case of the Bonapartist pretender showed that Louis-Philippe had no grounds for complacency.

On 30 October 1836, the Prince had ridden secretly into Strasbourg and met twenty officers assembled by the ringleader, Colonel Vaudrey, commander of an artillery regiment. The latter was easily roused and, having despatched various officers to seize the prefect and to print proclamations of victory, Louis Napoleon led the troops through the city. There were many signs of popular enthusiasm, for Strasbourg was a town of strong Bonapartist affections. The republicans applauded, ready to follow if the attempt proved successful. When the Prince attempted to win over an infantry regiment, some shouted "Long live the Emperor" or ran to kiss his hand, a few were completely hostile, but most wavered. It was a quick-thinking officer who shouted that the pretender was fooling them, and that in reality he was Colonel Vaudrey's nephew. Amidst the uproar, the barrack gates were closed, the Prince was separated from the mass of his followers and arrested. The ignominious failure should not conceal some real support for Louis Napoleon, shown again by the bourgeois jurists when they acquitted his fellow conspirators of charges of crimes against the state. The Prince was shipped to the United States, a political trial being considered too embarrassing.

Bonapartism owed much of its power to the position of the army in French society: the army represented unity in an age when division and conflict seemed rife. Under a regime based upon parliamentarianism, men who claimed to be loyal to the system propagated the myths of Bonapartism. Baron Bignon, cast from power with the *parti du mouvement*, wrote in his *Histoire de France depuis le 18 Brumaire* a chronicle of Napoleon's greatness, and Thiers, out of office in the 1840s, still less critically retailed the Napoleonic myths in his hagiographical volumes. The complaint Guizot made of Thiers's history of the Revolution, and which was even more true of his writing on Napoleon, was that it was superficially brilliant but in fact a spectacle of puppets, without choice, judgement or morality; this reflects a providential view of history, for which the Emperor was a hero and representative of his age.

Much of the willingness to worship in the cult of Napoleon was due to the fact that it no longer seemed a positive political creed. After the death of Napoleon's son in 1833, Prince Louis Napoleon Bonaparte, nephew of the Emperor, seemed to present no serious threat to the government. Louis-Philippe regarded the Duc de Reichstadt as presenting a real danger, but he did not believe Napoleon III a possibility, especially as he was convinced that Louis Napoleon was no Bonaparte, but that his father was the Comte de Flahaut. Even when the pretender became a sort of martyr, with the fortress of Ham as his Saint Helena, few could take him seriously. "To be a Bonaparte, prisoner of state, and expostulate on sugar-beet?"[4] sneered one former Bonapartist when the pretender published a pamphletary effusion on the merits of sugar beet. The July Monarchy has been blamed for lending itself to the Napoleonic cult by those who saw it as preparing the way for the Second Empire, but if there was danger, it was spiritual and not material. Thiers, discussing fears of a Bonapartist restoration, referred to the pretender as "a little fool who has no roots in this country",[5] and in political terms this was true.

So it appeared that the July Monarchy could be compared with the Empire to its disadvantage, to deliver a fundamental criticism of it, but without advocating its overthrow. Victor Hugo declaimed in the Chambers of Peers in 1847 against materialism and corruption, and, comparing the base present with the glorious past, he was tempted to tell them and all France "wait, let us talk a little of the Emperor, that would do us all some good".[6] And Duvergier de Hauranne, that fanatical parliamentarian, declared in his pamphlet *De la réprésentation Parlémentaire* (1847), "At the time of the Empire, it was the love of glory and national grandeur . . . today the thirst for riches."[7] As time passed, Waterloo was forgotten and Jena remembered, the tyranny neglected and only the glory remained.

Literature continued to reflect the strength of Bonapartism. The small dirty boulevard theatres constantly offered melodramas of which the Emperor was the hero. Dumas, by patching together a few dramatised scenes copied from the memoir writers, staged with expensive opulence and starring Lemaitre, had a huge success on his hands. The verses of Béranger and the lithographs of Charlet, both of them Emperor worshippers, were for most Frenchmen the only form of art they appreciated. The most famous invocation, however, was written by the royalist Balzac as a description of popular feeling. The old infantryman in the *Médecin de Campagne* tells the peasants gathered around him of the martial progress of the Emperor through Europe, awarding ranks, pensions and kingdoms. Napoleon was an enemy to the crooked lawyers, the voluble and futile politicians, but was eventually betrayed by the shopkeepers of Paris. This account, probably an accurate representation of Bonapartist anti-parliamentarianism, was turned into a pamphlet, without the author's permission, and sold 20,000 copies. Lamartine, Auguste Barbier (with a bitter attack on the liberticide "Corsican with straight hair"),[8] Chateaubriand and other legitimists, were a hostile minority. For most, the Emperor was the greatest Frenchman, and romantics adored in him the exaggeration of their own egos, and the tragic hero as man of action.

Bonapartism was thus a state of mind rather than a true party. A couple of short-lived newspapers with small sales, and a review, plus a Bonapartist tendency in certain republican newspapers, gave its viewpoint a small press representation. Some of the deputies of the left may be considered Bonapartist and it was Bonapartist sentiment rather than liberalism which dominated much of the *gauche dynastique*. Mauguin went to Russia in 1840 to try to interest the Tsar in a Napoleonic restoration, but no deputy sat frankly in the Bonapartist interest. Bonapartism had a text in *Les Idées Napoléoniennes*, written by Prince Louis Napoleon, published in Paris in 1839 and, sold cheaply at half a franc, achieving a large sale. It told the French that they felt a malaise because they were being prevented from fulfilling their destiny. Napoleon was "one of those extraordinary beings created by Providence to be the majestic instrument of her impenetrable designs".[9] The Empire was a synthesis of the principles of order and the principles of Revolution. Thus Louis Napoleon used the elements of Providence and compromise which were basic to Orleanist historicism, but added the essential ingredient of military glory. Bonapartism relied on no positive programme: it simply claimed to represent the essence of the nation. It fed upon Anglophobia. Napoleon's imprisonment on Saint Helena seemed a martyrdom, France humiliated in the person of her greatest ruler by the English.

> *"Sainte Hélène, leçon! chute! exemple! agonie!*
> *l'Angleterre, a la haine épuisant son génie,*
> *Se mit à devorer ce grand homme en plein jour."*[10]

> *("Saint Helena, lesson! fall! example! agony!*
> *England, exhausting her genius in hatred,*
> *Set about devouring this great man in broad daylight.")*

wrote Hugo, and there are many examples of still worse poetry and greater hatred.

Thiers sought the remedy for French sickness in an aggressive foreign policy. He believed that the return of Napoleon's remains to France would be a reconciliation with the past and inspiration for the future. Although the King feared encouraging Bonapartism he conceded, persuaded by his son and foreseeing adverse publicity that Thiers might give his refusal. Palmerston readily consented to the return of the remains from Saint Helena. To the surprised deputies on 12 May 1840, Rémusat, Thiers's Minister of the Interior, announced this. "He was Emperor and King," he declared, "he was the legitimate sovereign of our country" and could thus be buried at Saint-Denis, but the "usual resting place of kings" seemed unsuitable for such a man, and it was decided that the great soldier should lie in solitary grandeur at Les Invalides. Having proclaimed the legitimacy of the Emperor, Rémusat tried to present Orleanism as his heir, as it was of monarchy and liberal revolution. "Because there is something, the only thing, which can stand comparaison with glory: it is liberty!"[11]

When the Chamber debated the proposal, Lamartine delivered an eloquent attack upon it. He claimed that a cult of force was substituting itself for the religion of liberty, that the "men who parody Napoleon" were deifying warfare, and he mentioned the large sale of *Les Idées Napoléoniennes*.[12] The poet was to prove correct in his predictions, but he stood almost alone. Barrot replied that liberty was secure, that there was nothing to fear, yet the speeches proved in their emotion that military glory was more potent than constitutionalism. The left was especially fervent and reviled the sixty-five deputies who dared vote against any credits as traitors to the nation. There were criticisms that the governmental proposal was too meagre and the commission under Clauzel showed its liberality by doubling the proposed credit to 2 million. When the Chamber reduced this, a group presided over by Maréchal Gérard decided upon public subscription to supplement the deputies' parsimony. The King and Rémusat were becoming worried now that so many public figures and military men seemed to be attaching themselves to the excesses of the cult; Gérard was persuaded to resign and the plan came apart.

In the event, the return proved quite splendid enough. By the time it occurred, France had undergone the humiliation of the London treaty, Louis Napoleon's second attempt in October 1840 and the replacement of Thiers by Guizot. The pretender had decided that the defeat over the Eastern question provided him with an opportunity. Being in London, he decided to attack from Boulogne. He wrote to the general in command of the region, Général Magnan, who was not so firm in his refusal as the commander at Strasbourg had been; but in other respects circumstances were less favourable. Boulogne was not a Bonapartist town, and its inhabitants were unresponsive. As before, however, contact had been made with an officer who introduced the pretender to his troops, and the Prince made promotions and harangued the men. Once again, it was the decisive action of a loyal officer commanding his men to obedience which ended the attempt. Louis Napoleon and his band of followers fled to their boats, but National Guardsmen captured them with ease.

The government could not free him a second time and the Prince and his fellow conspirators were put on trial for treason in the Chamber of Peers. The accused made little impression: he was insignificant, he spoke sullenly and provocatively, almost inaudibly and with a German accent. His lawyer Berryer became the leading actor in the proceedings and made it a trial of Orleanism, using legitimist not Bonapartist arguments. The Orleanists had overthrown a centuries-old monarchy: by what right did they judge a Bonapartist pretender? Then Berryer, in common with all parties, contrasted the commonplace present with the glories of the past. How could this young man, seeing France humiliated whilst the government returned his uncle's ashes, do other than cry "That name held back, it is to me that it belongs"?[13] The emotional speech had reduced many of the more susceptible peers to tears. Berryer then commenced his final, devastating attack. "Who are you?" he asked the Chamber; and answered, counts, barons, ministers, generals and senators of the Empire who had taken an oath to Napoleon and his posterity. He challenged them "before those who know you",[14] which of them would not have rallied to the new Emperor had he been successful. (In 1851, still loyal to Henri V, Berryer amused himself by drawing up a list of peers who, voting the Prince guilty in 1840, had rallied to the new Emperor.) Embarrassed as they were, the peers found Louis Napoleon guilty (although it was noted that Flahaut and several others were absent). The pretender was sent to the fortress of Ham, whence he was able to escape after four years: he, but not the Empire, had been virtually forgotten.

Meanwhile the vast catafalque containing the remains of Napoleon I had been carried under the Arc de Triomphe, down the Champs-Élysées and across the Seine to Les Invalides. Here the preoccupation was to see who had taken precedence over whom (although Maréchal Soult was observed weeping), but outside there was a true spirit of devotion. In spite of the intense cold, thousands had filled the streets: there were cries of "Long live the Emperor" and scenes of emotion as the coffin moved past. The British embassy was protected by troops because an attack upon it was feared, due to the height of anti-English feeling in December 1840. In the event there was merely the shouting of slogans against the English and against Guizot. The only encouragement that Orleanists could derive from the occasion was that the Prince de Joinville, leading his sailors in procession, had been enthusiastically applauded. Ironically, the Orleanist princes were highly popular in the army, but this popularity could not be transferred into popularity for Orleanism in the country. The great emotional attractions of the Empire could not be rivalled by constitutional liberties, in spite of Rémusat and Barrot's confidence.

When the July Monarchy fell, the section of the French population which most wholeheartedly regretted it was found in Algeria. The acquisition of the North African colony was the longest-lasting achievement of Louis-Philippe's reign. This was ironical, for neither the King nor his leading ministers, with the exception of Thiers, were enthusiastic colonisers, and in 1830 the regime inherited a military presence in Algiers which it regarded as an embarrassment rather than a benefit. Indeed, Talleyrand, ambassador in London, had wished to abandon the occupation for the sake of the English alliance, but Molé, the Foreign Minister, had feared the effect on public opinion. And it was this and the pressure of interest groups, military and economic, which was to extend what Charles X had undertaken as a measure of national self-assertion against the insulting behaviour of the ruler of Algiers, into the colonisation of a vast area theoretically under Ottoman sovereignty.

The new regime sent to Algiers Général Clauzel, whose qualification was opposition to the Restoration. He took up command with no real instructions, but the chauvinistic and authoritarian General was not one to feel restrained by this. Although only two months had passed since Maréchal de Bourmont's brilliant entry into Algiers, he at once began a campaign in the surrounding areas. He removed an unfriendly bey and nominated a new one, which involved an expedition south to Médéa in the interior. Clauzel seemed to believe that he was in a war under the Empire where a victorious march into a capital subjugated a realm. He soon found that stray battalions were fallen upon, captured, killed or mutilated. The small garrison he left at Médéa suffered not only from attack but from the unfriendly climate, and it soon had to be reinforced. The next few years were to see the French army adjusting to this new style of campaign and each careless forward step led to defeat whose dishonour had to be wiped out by further advance.

The government, fearful of European war, found Clauzel's aggressive policy risky and recalled him. The military errors of a succession of incompetent commanders were exacerbated by indecision in Paris. It took the July Monarchy some time to decide what it desired: in 1832, as so often caught between the needs of a British alliance and fear of French opinion, it was still unprepared to declare whether occupation was permanent. Decisions tended to be taken by default. There was generally distrust between the commander at Algiers, whose powers, after Clauzel's initiatives, had been circumscribed, and the War Ministry, but the two were days' contact away. Under the military commander was a civilian intendant with slight powers who tried to organise an administration, although as yet there was little to administer. In 1833, a parliamentary commission under Duc Decazes voted by nineteen against two for the conservation of the northern coast of Algeria. It reserved French rights over the whole of the former Turkish possession, but found it convenient that only Oran, Algiers and two coastal towns further east should be occupied. It believed that a French army with native soldiers, 21,000 in all, would be sufficient. Although the government accepted the report, it took no initiative and the deputies reduced the credits demanded. Algeria seemed merely a drain of resources, and it was natural for Thiers and Guizot to use it in a political intrigue to rid themselves of Soult by contradicting his desire to retain it under military control and then to adopt this policy themselves.

The two dissenters on the Decazes commission, Passy and the Comte de

Sade, were representatives of a powerful group of deputies who opposed colonisation. The dominant factor in their hostility was expense, and liberal economists such as Passy and Duchâtel therefore frequently led opposition to North African involvement. And there was a school of thought which distrusted the military on principle. They were given many opportunities for attack. The information that Clauzel, whom Thiers replaced in Algerian command in 1836, had imposed a crippling tax upon the inhabitants of Tlemcen, using Turkish methods of punishment to collect it, caused an uproar in the Chamber of Deputies, which in 1837, voted reimbursement for the inhabitants. Algeria seemed to be a corrupting influence. Most of the generals, especially those with Napoleonic background, took bribes. When Général Brossard made a personal profit from the purchase of military equipment as well as taking bribes from Abd-el-Kader and was court-martialled and imprisoned, he was able to point out that other officers had profited from campaigns even if not in quite so heinous a fashion and that Bugeaud in particular had accepted large sums from the enemy and distributed it to his soldiers. Administration was chaotic, and frequently corrupt. (Thus Balzac's Hulot, in difficulties, sent an unfortunate relative to Algeria to make a quick fortune: it was only excessive speed which led to his downfall.)

If some commercial interests were against it, others were favourable. In Marseilles, all parties were united in enthusiasm for colonisation, and the wealthy merchant and deputy Reynaud and the chamber of commerce continually pressed the government to commit itself to complete occupation and the commercial exploitation of the territory which would increase the activity of its own port. More garrisons were moved to the Rhône valley and the Midi, increasing markets in those areas. Thiers was deputy for Aix and that Provence increasingly saw its prosperity linked with colonisation, doubtless encouraged his own enthusiasm, although his professed reasons were that this "training ground of warriors" provided the arena for "the sole instinct even slightly disinterested and heroic that remains in this country".[15] The most powerful pressure group, however, was the army. Deprived of European war, it found some compensation in North Africa. Général de Castellane was unusual, regarding it as "a school for disorganisation and indiscipline" where good soldiers were spoilt.[16] He could not, as did Aumale, delight in the "renowned chic" of Colonel de La Moricière's zouaves, an élite corps, long-bearded and turbaned, with a practical semi-arab uniform, still less could he approve the *légion étrangère*, both forces developed to match the tactics of the natives. Other enemies had to be contended with: extremes of climate, dysentry and cholera. It was an excellent field for displaying courage and flair, but the encouragement of verve at the expense of discipline may also have fitted the French army badly for future European battles.

As Léon Blondel, for a time director of finances in Algeria, wrote in a pamphlet favouring colonisation, it was "a distraction to keep our turbulent imaginations occupied": because it satisfied the national mind, it was an element of order.[17] The King came to accept this viewpoint. He, whose dominating characteristic was love of peace, realised it was a useful safety-valve. The left were quick to seize on anti-colonialism as yet another sacrifice to Britain. Louis-Philippe could not abandon Algeria and appear less patriotic than the Restoration, and battles in the desert prevented military impatience becoming a danger in France. The presence of his sons in the army in North Africa increased his enthusiasm by its effect on dynastic prestige. The Duc d'Orléans first campaigned in Algeria in 1835. He was horrified by the squalid living conditions of the soldiers. Although he shared the fighting with characteristic courage, he declared that he most prided himself on the improvements which were made in the following years.[18]

He was followed by his younger brother, Nemours, by which time the conquest of Algeria had entered a new phase. The politicians had desired limited coastal occupation of what were clumsily termed "French possessions in North Africa", but the hostile activities of native chieftains, especially Abd-el-Kader, rendered this impossible. After Clauzel had returned to command in 1835, he expanded the areas of occupation, undertaking conquests in land which he could not afterwards control. Thiers's imagination was caught by the very rashness of the scheme to replace the hostile Bey of Constantine, and permitted it. However, when Clauzel decided more troops were necessary, he had to apply to the Molé–Guizot ministry, which, depending upon many anti-colonialist doctrinaires, notably Duvergier and Jaubert, refused to send them, but was equally unwilling to incur the odium of countermanding the expedition. Thus in autumn 1836, the General set off for a distant town, of which he knew little, and which proved to be strongly fortified. His army suffered from the intense cold and could not undertake a long siege. "The Constantine expedition has not been a complete success" he telegraphed to Paris with impudent understatement.[19] The French army in Algeria often showed itself to its best advantage in retreat: Clauzel executed it better than he had the campaign; a young cavalry officer named Changarnier made his name in defending the retreat against ceaseless attacks of a larger enemy force, and the Duc de Nemours's sang-froid did much to maintain the morale of the vanquished army.

The public reaction was angry. The government published all relevant documents in an attempt to fix the blame on Clauzel who produced a brochure in his own defence which vehemently accused the ministry of wishing to abandon North Africa. Dupin attacked Clauzel's behaviour in Algeria so insultingly that the Marshal challenged the president of the Chamber to a duel, which was prevented only by the influence of Barrot. Although Clauzel retired angrily to the opposition benches, his policy had in reality conquered. A humiliation had to be avenged and public opinion satisfied. A better-prepared expedition was mounted under Général de Damrémont who in October 1837 led French troops to the capture of Constantine, although he himself perished in the final attack. The brave assault, in which Nemours distinguished himself, erased the shame of the preceding year.

Molé in Paris and Maréchal Valée, successor to Damrémont, accepted that the French presence in Algeria was definite, and, with the possession of Constantine, more than purely coastal. Garrisons linked by roads were established and a greater attempt made to win the loyalty of the natives: a protectorate was to replace the impossible client bey system. Valée successfully destroyed small-scale resistance, but in autumn 1839 when Abd-el-Kader began a new campaign, it became evident that coexistence with him was impossible, and against his tactics, Valée was to prove less successful. Although troops now numbered almost 60,000, he proved too slow-moving to protect the far-flung vulnerable garrisons he had established. His failure to put a speedy end to Abd-el-Kader for which he was unfairly blamed, led to a renewed debate in France. The opponents of colonisation argued that since *occupation restreinte* (limited occupation) had been shown to be impossible, withdrawal was better than total conquest. Others argued for this, and Bugeaud put himself forward, declaring in the Chamber the merits of his own system of conquest. Since Valée's political position was weak and Bugeaud had credit with Guizot, the former gave way to him in December 1840. Colonisation as such was slow to begin, in spite of Clauzel's criticism of governmental timidity in 1832 and his prophecy that cotton, sugar cane and cocoa could be cultivated. Yet even had Clauzel's absurd assessment of the climate not been untrue, it was scarcely possible to encourage cultivation when in 1838 the garrison cattle at the coastal town of Bougie had to be guarded while pasturing. Even in the vicinity of Algiers, where colonisation first began, the army had to protect the farms against raiders.

In spite of governmental instructions, Clauzel's first act in 1835 was to encourage colonisation. His proclamation declared, "By force of perseverance, we shall create a new people who will grow even more rapidly than those established on the other side of the Atlantic. . . ."[20] As the conquest extended, men began to leave Europe to seek a livelihood farming in North Africa, but were not officially encouraged. Instead, after the success at Constantine in 1837, when Molé declared that the era of provisional occupation had ended, most effort was spent on military improvements: barracks, military hospitals and forts were built, roads constructed, and a port begun north of Constantine, to be called Philippeville. The report of Blanqui, the economist, to the Académie des Sciences Morales et Politiques, was much less optimistic than the earlier predictions of Clauzel and other enthusiasts. He noted that those colonists, most of them Spanish and Italian, who had planted tobacco, cotton and other advanced crops, had ruined themselves, and he reassured the vine growers of Burgundy and Bordeaux that they had no competition to fear. Although he regretted the cupidity of many of the first immigrants, Blanqui could not doubt that the French colonists should take control in exploiting the territory: "We cannot give the slightest part of such a high and noble task back to the barbarians, except in the capacity of instruments."[21] In spite of his caution, many believed in an Eldorado. One colonisation society declared that Algeria would provide wealth equal to that of North America: "To become rich today, one need only become a colonist in Africa."[22] By 1840 there were 20,000 civilian Europeans in Algeria, half of them French, but there was so little produced that imports were worth seven times as much as exports. Within six years, however, the number of

Europeans had quadrupled and the colony was outgrowing its improvised military organisation.

Attitudes in France to the natives in Algeria and the methods applied in Africa itself, tended to differ. The initial impatience, as Clauzel put it, with "you natives . . . who so far have not sufficiently appreciated the advantage and honour of being considered equals by those who raised you up to their level",[23] often quickly turned to anger. Punishments and military measures could often be brutal, or certainly seem so, to those far from the environment wherein they were practised. The War Ministry disliked many of these measures and tried to impress upon the army that public opinion was a force to be reckoned with. Some saw Algeria primarily as a field for Christian endeavour. Catholics, and indeed some officers, argued that the Muhammadans would only respect men who were themselves faithful to a religion. Religion came to reinforce humanitarian prejudices, often to the annoyance of those who believed these principles could not be combined with military efficiency. In 1838, to the disgust of the anticlericals, the government asked the Pope to make Algiers a bishopric. The *Journal des Débats*, conservative but not religious, saw matters with unçonscious cynicism: "Tame them, if one can employ such a term, with the customs of Christian faith",[24] it wrote of the Muslim natives. The new bishop was more fervent and sincere; Dupuch, celebrated in France for his charitable works, set about converting the natives, and the scarcely more Christian French soldier, with only eleven priests and a small budget. He angered Général Bugeaud by speaking words of peace and charity and the two men were soon in conflict. The huge debts he ran up eventually necessitated a flight from his creditors. Catholicism in Algeria suffered from similar problems to those of civilian administration.

This administration was headed by a Cabinet, with civilian and military intendants, a director of finance and a *procureur général* heading a judicial system. Above it was the Governor-General who was also commander of the army, performing a dual role. He had enormous powers, especially if the Minister of War were a cipher. Clauzel blatantly disregarded Maison's orders to return troops to France as required by the military budget. Général Valée, who, under Molé, corresponded directly with the *président du conseil*, used to ignore or write insolently to Général Schneider, War Minister in the succeeding Cabinet. He also, according to Alphonse Karr, replied to the minister, when asked to suggest a choice of general to be sent to Algeria, "Send whoever you like into Africa, as long as it is not that —— de Cubières."[25] By the time the letter reached the War Ministry, the Cabinet had changed and Cubières was the new incumbent. Valée himself was undermined because Thiers, when president in 1840, corresponded with Colonel de La Moricière. With the ministry of 11 October, whose president, Maréchal Soult, was also War Minister, and a new governor in Bugeaud, minister and commander were both partisans of total conquest. The relationship of two such strong-minded men could not be easy, but in return for a degree of compromise, the old Marshal struggled against the politicians, overspending the military budget to provide troops with which the General gained glory.

Bugeaud commanded 60,000 French and indigenous troops (which itself was almost three times the number which it had been believed five years earlier could control and protect the coastal colony) and seven years later this had increased to over 100,000.

Général Bugeaud, although a military pillar of the monarchy, was unpopular with the King and many notable figures of the regime, as well as with its opponents. His blunt and authoritarian personality was uncongenial to Louis-Philippe and other politicians whose ways of compromise he despised. As gaoler to the Duchesse de Berry, he was "the man of Blaye" to legitimists and also to soldiers like Changarnier who found the role dishonourable to the army.[26] Unfairly, he had been blamed for the Rue Transnonain massacre by the republicans. Bugeaud was not one to ignore an insult, however, and when in the heated atmosphere of the 1834 session he had extolled obedience and received the reply "Is it necessary to obey so far as to become a gaoler? So far as ignominy?"[27] he challenged his interrupter to a duel. It was a young man named Dulong, the illegitimate son of Dupont (de l'Eure): he demanded pistols and received a bullet through the forehead. The General was thenceforth detested by the extremes and was not particularly popular in the centre. Nor was his conduct in Algeria without reproach. At the time of the trial of Général Brossard, it was shown that as part of a treaty with Abd-el-Kader, he had in a secret clause accepted a large sum of money, distributed some amongst his officers and used the rest for building roads in the department he represented as deputy. The opposition press had used the opportunity to attack the General who regarded journalists with apoplectic loathing. Bugeaud's undoubted loyalty to the regime and its conservative leaders made him a figure of importance, however. And as compensation for his unpopularity, he held the affection of his soldiers who liked his bluff familiarity.

Bugeaud evolved a strategy, the essence of which was mobility. La Moricière had shown how armies could live from the land if they were small, and had gained insight into tribal life. The French utilised this by replacing hostile chiefs, often with their relatives. Establishing garrisons, from which columns could comb the countryside, keeping communications open, they were able gradually to subjugate and pacify rebellious tribes. The razzia, the raid which burnt homes and crops and seized livestock, was a brutal but effective implementation of Arab methods of warfare. Bugeaud also established a directory of Arab affairs in which an élite corps of young officers who knew the country watched over the administration where it concerned the indigenous population. Care was taken to tax the natives less than Abd-el-Kader had done and to persuade them of the benefits of French protection. Whereas in 1841, Louis Veuillot had remarked ironically "Algiers is yours, and provided that evening is distant, you can even walk a couple of kilometres from it",[28] by 1845 Gustave de Beaumont was marvelling that it was safe to travel alone from Algiers to Médéa or Miliana in the interior. France began to become culturally aware of her colony; the Algerian paintings of Vernet, Delacroix and others appeared in salons; women wore imitations of Algerian costume; and the Duc d'Aumale gave his unappreciative father a dinner of couscous and honey cake.

Although the British came to accept the French presence in North Africa, the Turks would not resign themselves to the occupation of territory under theoretical Ottoman suzerainty. In 1836 and again in 1837, French fleets prevented their bringing aid to anti-French forces. Amidst farcical but bitter quarrels with the British consul, the French increased their influence in Tunis, symbolising it by building a memorial chapel where Saint-Louis had died. Visits by Montpensier and Joinville distributing largess with great effect, were repaid by the Bey of Tunis, whom the French treated as a friendly and independent ruler instead of the Turkish vassal which he supposedly was.

The ruler of Morocco was not so accommodating, and openly aided Abd-el-Kader. Eventually, fear of offending Britain having restrained the government for some time, Bugeaud forced it to act. The Sultan was presented with an ultimatum demanding that he cease assisting the rebels, and that the boundary be established as it had existed before 1830. Bugeaud was given reinforcements and the Prince de Joinville was sent with a fleet to Tangier. The greatest prudence was enjoined upon both, the government not wishing either to annoy Britain more than necessary or to involve itself in further military tasks. The General entered into some small battles with the Moroccans, and disobeying orders crossed the border slightly. Joinville behaved with greater circumspection: when the Sultan failed to make terms, he sent an ultimatum and embarked all French subjects from Tangier. Two weeks later, no satisfactory reply being received, he bombarded the fortress and then, in a well-mannered manœuvre, occupied the Island of Mogador, whence he could threaten the city. Meanwhile, on 14 August 1844, Bugeaud achieved what was the most striking, although not the most difficult, military victory of the July Monarchy. On the plains of the river Isly, his troops met a vastly greater body of Moroccans, and by superior discipline and strategy inflicted a crushing defeat upon them. The Sultan offered peace terms, upon which Joinville immediately suspended hostilities. To Bugeaud's anger, Mogador and his territorial gains were abandoned and he made insulting remarks about the Duc de Glücksberg and Joinville who had negotiated the treaty: "Bugeaud is only a vulgar corporal"[29] remarked Aumale. The moderation shown was profitable in the long run, for Morocco came increasingly within the French sphere of influence. Public opinion was delighted to have scored over Britain, and Joinville's popularity further increased. Bugeaud was made a duke, the only such honour granted by the regime, taking his title from his victory.

Military setbacks still occurred, however. The origin of most of the disorder, Abd-el-Kader, proved difficult to defeat. In 1843 he suffered a serious blow when the twenty-one-year-old Duc d'Aumale discovered his *smalah*, the vast mobile encampment of the rebel chief and his followers, and routed his forces in a brilliant cavalry charge. Thereafter, he was entirely nomadic, and when after September 1844, Morocco turned against him, he became a fugitive. He finally surrendered to the Duc d'Aumale in 1847. Two years previously another rebel chieftain, Bou-Maza, had for a time inspired tribes with religious fanaticism. As before, the French were caught off guard, Bugeaud's complacent belief that Algeria, except the far south, was secured, was shattered, and public opinion was horrified by the atrocities committed by the natives. Colonel de Saint-Arnaud prevented the rebellion gaining the town of Orléansville, and very gradually surrounded Bou-Maza, until in 1847, he too submitted. Another disaster occurred when at Biskra the Duc d'Aumale put too much trust in a native officer and a slaughter of French troops occurred. Aumale was much blamed in the opposition press for this, but his successful pacification of the province of Constantine won him a reputation largely unimpaired by this error of judgement. La Moricière, immensely popular with his troops, tried to restrict the savagery to which the irregular methods of warfare had accustomed them. Gradually French power pushed southwards into the mountainous regions and extension of influence made both disasters and the brutalities of the razzia rarer.

In April 1845, the government attempted to organise the territory, which was still under the theoretical control of the Minister of War and therefore ruled by ordinance. To satisfy the civilian susceptibilities of the deputies, Guizot and Soult wished to reduce the powers of the Governor-General and to create a civilian intendant. Maréchal Bugeaud threatened resignation and was only with great difficulty persuaded to remain, accepting certain changes such as European areas where military rule was limited, instituting an advisory council ("Chamber of second-rate deputies"[30] he grumbled) and regularising the bureaucracy. He refused to implement even this with good faith, however, and would not co-operate with the increased number of officials who admittedly were, for the most part, not of high quality. "Administrative anarchy"[31] continued in Algeria, until his successor, the Duc d'Aumale, instituted reforms.

Increasing security made possible colonisation, and military–civilian controversies again raged. Bugeaud published a brochure advocating that 100,000 married soldiers should be government aided: any limitation on occupation was dishonourable, but to hold the whole country, it was necessary for the colonisers to be disciplined and brave, qualities Bugeaud did not believe existed amongst civilians. They needed men who would farm six days a week and drill on Sundays. He put his plans into practice and went so far as to find wives for bachelor soldiers who wished to settle. The failure of these attempts merely proved to Bugeaud that his ideas should be applied more widely and with greater vigour. When in 1845 he publicly announced his intention to do this, there was uproar in Paris, accusations of rebellion by Bugeaud, whom Guizot eventually persuaded to retract his proposals.

The Marshal had in Général de La Moricière an able and vocal opponent with the ears of some influential members of the opposition, notably his relative, Gustave de Beaumont, and the latter's friend, Tocqueville. La Moricière believed in encouraging colonisation by civilians, granting concessions to anyone who seemed of good moral character and combining this with substantial self-government for the natives. There was something of a dream in the agrarian nostalgia of La Moricière's "Christian agricultural population"[32] which revealed the Vendean gentleman: Algeria was for many a *tabula rasa* on which to inscribe the civilisation in which they believed. Other soldiers became critical of Bugeaud's methods. Général Changarnier went into retirement after a quarrel with him. Canrobert wrote to Castellane about the barbarism of the razzias,[33] and the latter, a conservative peer, delivered a parliamentary attack upon Bugeaud, accusing him of using corrupting methods, of expending vast sums and using a large army to achieve harmful results. Dufaure and Tocqueville took up the theme, demanding a settled, disciplined administration. A public controversy began to rage. Bugeaud rushed into print to attack La Moricière with that readiness to enter a political affray which was characteristic of French generals. But it was he himself who forced the issue in 1847 by demanding extra credit for colonisation schemes. As with Clauzel and the Constantine expedition, the government feared to thwart a prestigious general, but feared also his unpopularity with its own supporters. They presented a demand for credit, but allowed their supporters full liberty in the vote. This freedom resulted in a commission hostile to Bugeaud, with Dufaure as its president and Tocqueville its rapporteur, which recommended that the proposal should be refused. As a result, the government withdrew the project. Bugeaud, furious at the Cabinet's unenthusiastic support, resigned. The ministry celebrated his achievements but was relieved by his departure. Without this autocratic figure, the July Monarchy in the last year of its life began to regularise the administration and to improve relations between Paris and Algiers.

The Duc d'Aumale's appointment as governor-general was of course attacked by the republican newspapers, but it was very popular in Algeria, where the Prince had won a considerable reputation. Aumale charmed the generals, even the republican Cavaignac and the recalcitrant Changarnier, whom he restored to command. As prince, he was not so completely a military man as his predecessor. He introduced a more liberal administration, gave greater powers to civilians and regularised the budget. He reversed Bugeaud's high-handed attitude to the natives and allowed colonisation only with strict regard to their rights. Bugeaud had scorned the liberal ideas echoed by humanitarians in North Africa, the journals, the sixty churches and ninety priests. Yet by 1848, Orleanist rule in Algeria was imparting to the conquest qualities above the merely military and commercial, and when revolution overthrew the regime, Aumale left Algiers with the regrets of its population.

Over slavery, still used in French West Indian colonies, the Orleanists were caught between the two modern forces of humanitarianism and commercial requirements. For once, the former proved the stronger, for there were many liberals who, bound by their hostility to radical social legislation within France as an example of unwarranted state interference, none the less were the more angry at the existence of an institution which infringed the laws of nature and liberty. Doctrinaires, such as the Duc de Broglie, and liberal economists, notably Passy, headed a powerful pressure group which included other such notable figures as Tocqueville and Beaumont, and Comte Agénor de

Gasparin, one of the many Protestants to concern themselves with emancipation. There was, however, a powerful collection of interest which were opposed, especially Bordelais, whether of the opposition or Orleanist, because of their town's West Indian links. The colonies also were highly hostile and had in Paris a council of delegates, presided by the influential Baron Dupin and employing as its spokesman in the Chamber of Deputies, the Bonapartist radical Mauguin.

Between these forces the question was debated, finally to be decided, as so often, by political expediency. In 1838 and 1839, commissions with Rémusat and Tocqueville as their rapporteurs submitted reports recommending emancipation, and Soult's ministry in 1839, which included Passy an ardent emancipator, accepted the proposals. However, ministerial changes and opposition prevented their fruition. Thiers cared little for such humanitarianism and Guizot was above all things a politician. The interest groups had to be placated, and so the government encouraged the Broglie commission which attempted to satisfy them. The compromise which was eventually adopted pleased few, but in 1845 it was finally decided that slavery would be abolished after a ten-year transitional period in all French colonies.

In its colonial policy in Algeria and the West Indies, Orleanist France was torn between its interest groups, military and commercial, and usually on the other side, religious, liberal and humanitarian. Of these the military was the most powerful, for it was seen by perhaps a majority as the guardian of French honour, as the only institution worthy of respect. Although the July Monarchy, so civilian in its mentality, restricted the huge latent power of the army, it suffered in popularity as a result. It had to accept the giant shadow of Napoleon, ever present; at once example and threat. "What the plunderer could not take by conquering, his fame usurps; alive he lost the world, dead he possesses it",[34] wrote Chateaubriand. Spiritually, France was predominantly Bonapartist, hence the July Monarchy's failure to root itself in national affection or respect.

REFERENCES

1. A. de Vigny, Cited in P. Flottes (ed.), *Pensée Politique d'Alfred de Vigny* (1927), 100–1.
2. Prince de Joinville, *Mémoires* (1894), Ch. IX.
3. Maréchal de Castellane, *Journal* (1895), II, 496.
4. A. Gayot, *Une ancienne Muscadine, Fortunée Hamelin* (1911), 153.
5. L. Viennet, *Journal*, (1955), 249.
6. Archives Parlementaires, Chambre des Pairs, 6 January 1847.
7. P. Duvergier de Hauranne, *De la représentation parlementaire et de la réforme électorale* (1847).
8. A. Barbier, "L'Idole", *Iambes* (1898), 34.
9. Prince Louis Napoleon Bonaparte, *Les idées Napoléoniennes* (1839), 146.
10. V. Hugo, *Hymne à la Colonne de Boulogne*.

11. Archives Parlementaires, 12 May 1840.
12. Ibid., 20 May 1840.
13. Ibid., 20 November 1840.
14. Ibid.
15. X. Doudan, *Mélanges et Lettres* (1876), I, 307.
16. Castellane, *Journal*, III 231.
17. Léon Blondel, *Nouvels Aperçus sur l'Algérie* (1838).
18. Duc d'Orléans, *Lettres* (1890), 186–7. Bibliothèque Nationale, nouvelles acquisitions françaises, 1369, F. 156.
19. C. Schefer, *La Politique coloniale de la Monarchie de Juillet* (1930), 257.
20. Maréchal Clauzel, *Correspondance* (1948), 29.
21. A. Blanqui, *Rapport sur la situation économique de nos possessions dans le nord d'Afrique* (1840), 31–3.
22. *Journal des Débats*, 6 October 1838.
23. Clauzel, op. cit., 29.
24. *Journal des Débats*, 5 September 1838.
25. A. Karr, *Les Guêpes* (1858), III, 172.
26. Maréchal E. V. E. de Castellane, *Lettres* (1898), 219.
27. Archives Parlementaires, 23 January 1834.
28. L. Veuillot, *Les Français en Algérie* (Tours, 1860).
29. A. Warnier in M. Emerit (ed.), *Le Conflit Franco-Marocain de 1844, d'après les notes de Warnier* (Algiers, 1950), 415.
30. Maréchal T.-R. Bugeaud, *Lettres inédits* (1923), 298.
31. Castellane, *Lettres*, 503, Maréchal T.-R. Bugeaud, *Des moyens de conserver la conquête de l'Algérie* (1844), 63–4, 110.
32. Castellane, *Lettres*, 462.
33. Ibid.
34. Vicomte F.-R. de Chateaubriand, *Mémoires d'Outre Tombe* (1948), IV, 89.

19

History and Philosophy

"Ce siècle de 1830, séparé par trois jours seulement de cet autre siècle 1829."

("This century of 1830, separated by three days only from that other century of 1829.")[1]

For men who had lived through events which overthrew traditions, history was of paramount importance. There was, as the Baron de Barante, himself a writer of history, said, a "fever for history",[2] a fever which infected art and philosophy. The dominance of political modes of thought made history of enormous significance: it could be used for and against kings and republics, to justify the rule of a class or predict the future, it was a pedestal for the idol of a great man or a vast altar for the religion of humanity. Less politically, it provided entertainment for a romantic generation, which enjoyed the picturesque, and which had been taught to regard itself as existing in transience. To write history could be an occupation of prestige or profit, and many of the leading figures of the July Monarchy had done so, notably Guizot, Thiers, Villemain, Barante, Sainte-Aulaire and Salvandy.

Guizot, regarding the July Monarchy as the inevitable and beneficent result of historical forces, wished to make the past understood and accepted. The 1830 system welded the monarchical and revolutionary pasts, and France had to come to terms with these traditions: "She will re-establish trouble and continuous abasement in her bosom if she remains hostile to her proper history."[3] He and other doctrinaires had a strong sense of the creative power of history and of the importance of institutions suiting tradition as well as conforming to philosophical principles.

This sympathy had its roots in an eclecticism of which the main exponent was the Baron de Barante. Although he had written his history of Burgundy during the Restoration, he remained the outstanding example of a school which put narrative first, not from laziness but from a scholarly equivalent of *laissez-faire*. He set out simply but fully to describe, believing that this would enable lessons to be drawn scientifically without the author's subjectivity obscuring the issue. The historian should not judge errors so much as ask what caused them, he argued, his premiss being that these would be apparent to all.[4] The narrative method, although colourful and dramatic in Barante's hands, thus was not history for art's sake, but didactic in aim if not in method. However, it understood that different ages have their individuality, and shared with romantic writers the belief that such individuality had charm and significance. Its popularity reflected an age of widened cultural sympathies.

For Augustin Thierry, the Baron's history was too aristocratic in its battles and ceremonies. He found a more democratic element in the struggle of races, in the conflict of unity with particularism. True to the broader historical sympathies of the time, he sought to rescue the humble, the vanquished, the forgotten. In his work on the Merovingians (1833–40), he used the original spelling of Gothic names and in other ways utilised local colour which gave his work popular success. He saw aristocrats in the conquering Franks, and the middle classes in the repressed Gallo-Romans, and in his *Considérations sur l'Histoire de France* traced the rise of the communal principle in the bourgeoisie, emerging from its Gallic obscurity. Augustin Thierry inspired others such as his brother Amédée to study the origins of the French nation, Granier de Cassagnac in his *Histoire des Classes Nobles* (1840) to see aristocratic origins in racial terms, and Henri Martin in his history of France which began to appear in 1833 to see race as a motivating historical force, in this case the leading role being given to the Celts. Thierry and his disciples believed that the story of contemporary France was a bourgeois epic in which old divisions were destroyed by progress: 1848 was to force them to revise these ideas.

The doctrinaire school was divided into several tendencies, therefore, but all stressed the primary of the text, faithful to their belief that the 1830 Charter embodied the constitutional monarchy. In 1833, Guizot, then Minister of Public Instruction, founded the Société de l'Histoire de France, an institution whose task was to select and publish important documents: Mignet, Cousin and Augustin Thierry were amongst the collaborators on this immense enterprise. For these men history was a directing force which they tried to combine with the particular fact. Their conservatism lay in seeing 1830 as some sort of completion, not a step or an inauguration. Thus for Thierry, it is the completion of the unfinished work of the Revolution of 1789 and the end of the conflict between Franks and Gauls. For him and Mignet, it is the final triumph of the bourgeoisie, of administrative centralisation and civil equality. This view finds an extreme in Cousin for whom progress was the inevitable result of crisis: since it triumphed, to pity the vanquished was to flout the forces of history. He differs from a superior historian like Thierry in this lack of sympathy, but both claimed the middle classes as the source of all real progress. The year 1830 put the men of this school, Guizot, Villemain and Cousin, in authority and further proved to them the truth of their theories. Their places as propagandising lecturers at the Collége de France were taken by radicals or democrats, Michelet, Quinet and Mickiewicz.

Whereas historians who were Orleanist tended to look at the particular, stressing the individuality of past ages with the hope that understanding would encourage compromise, there were others who sought the universal. Determinism was common to both, but was stronger in the latter. After 1789 humanity could not be the same: politics had become a mass experience, and whole societies and nations were seen in crisis, not individuals and classes. This tendency was found in conservative historians as well as progressives, but the latter more frequently presented humanity as a whole with universal values. Herder, whose work was translated and disseminated by Quinet, and Hegel were transformed into progressive and democratic influences. History was regarded as an epic of human progress, a view most clearly presented in poetical form by Quinet in *Ahasuerus* (1833) and by Lamartine in *Jocelyn* (1836).

For Michelet, the most important historian of this tendency, 1830 had been a seminal intellectual event. He ascribes to it a great light which made France visible to him: he undertook to write the history of that France whose national soul had not been described. The year 1830 had shown the people making history; there was no hero but the people itself, acting with a mass consciousness. When the new regime put him in charge of historical archives, he added a knowledge of sources to a historical philosophy which was nationalistic in inspiration. Whereas Thierry saw history as racial, others in terms of class or institutions, he saw it as national, with a superior harmony not a conglomeration of interests. "France has made France",[5] he declared: the idea came first. Thus Michelet worries little about the historical truth of the song of Roland, but takes it as true in its representation of heroic national spirit: similarly, Joan of Arc provides material for an emotional account of national virtues; she almost becomes the nation itself. "I saw her as a soul",[6] he said of the nation in the introduction to his *Histoire de France*. Mystical as he was, Michelet none the less was a passionate student of sources, and amongst the first to study the provinces. His democratic view that the popular, simple vision was true, occasionally led him into grave errors of partiality and omission. For him, as for Edgar Quinet, history was the struggle of mind against matter and liberty against fatality and obscurantism. Both were romantics in opposition to men like Thierry, believing that history, being a spiritual study, cannot be impartial. Quinet stressed more than Michelet the values of humanity and its constancy beneath the individuality of ages: all history was religious, and a deity provided the world unity through which the progressive force worked, but unlike Michelet he was primarily a philosopher.

With others of his time, Quinet believed in the great man as instrument of Providence. Even a conservative such as Comte Louis de Carné could speak of "men who embody principles, in whom the life of all is condensed" who not only made French history, but summarised their ages. Such were Suger and Richelieu, Louis IX, XI and XIV, who represented "the grand idea that has made France".[7] It was of course Napoleon, largely responsible for the prevalence of this idea, who was the great man most frequently described (notably by Baron Bignon and Thiers). The Revolution also provided its symbolic figures, Danton for Michelet, Robespierre for Buchez, Sieyès for Mignet, for in such men could be found what each historian regarded as its essential truth.

The particular subjects studied and written about reflect contemporary interests. Early France not only provided colour and excitement, it was examined in the hopes that it might provide answers and solutions for a nation confused as to its true identity. Not surprisingly, periods of civil war were much described; the wars of religion and the Fronde in France, and for Orleanist historians, the English seventeenth century. The latter seemed to resemble recent events in France, and encouraged the hope that 1830 would, like 1688, end an age of conflict. Guizot saw 1688 in England and 1789 in France not as isolated occurrences, but successful consummations of earlier attempts, whereas the less conservative Thiers and Mignet presented revolution as sudden, more foundation than culmination. The doctrinaires found examples in certain figures, notably Guizot's study of Washington, which presented him as a moderate conservative in an age of revolution. The Frenchman identified himself with the American president, and when accused in Parliament of corruption, compared his position with that of the other.[8] America was also the subject of a pioneering history by Comte Pelet de La Lozère who wrote a work which may be set beside those of Chevalier and Tocqueville.

It was, however, the revolutionary and Napoleonic eras which received most attention. This past was vital to the present, and whilst seeming distant, had many survivors. Thiers, when writing his *Histoire du consulat et de l'Empire*, consulted Gérard, Oudinot, Marmont, Cambacérès and others; Lamartine spoke to Danton's widow, a friend of Fouquier-Tinville, and used the memories of his own father and of other relatives. Thiers and his friend Mignet (whom the July Monarchy made director of archives at the Foreign Ministry) had written under the Restoration works presenting the French Revolution as a vital step in the story of the middle class, of which they were such successful and confident examples. They admired the liberal revolution, destructive of *ancient régime* caste restrictions, but disapproved its excesses. The year 1830 made historians of the French Revolution move leftwards, and as a liberal interpretation had been a form of opposition to the Restoration, so hostility to the July Monarchy was expressed by republicanism and a call to true revolutionary principles and scorn for mere constitutionalism. The cult of Robespierre and the publication of the works of Saint-Just in the 1830s, meant that for many republicans 1793 ceased to be an aberration and that the Jacobin regime became the Revolution's central event. Thus Buchez and Roux in their vast *Histoire parlementaire de la Révolution Française*, which began to be published in 1834, saw the Jacobins as the apostles of popular sovereignty. For Buchez, a Christian socialist, the Revolution was the consequence of Catholic principles of unity and fraternity, but he abhorred the Constituent Assembly as representing Protestant egoism and bourgeois individualism. Michelet's *Histoire de la Révolution Française*, the first two volumes of which were published in 1847 (in response to the fashion he had abandoned his history of France with Louis XI), was similarly democratic. Regarding the people as a force driven by philosophy, he sought the popular soul, a tendency to seek this in the amenable symbol rather than the idiosyncratic fact, presenting the fall of the Bastille as focal event and Danton as representative personality, although he regarded collective force as the true hero of the Revolution. The contemporary controversy over education also led him to present it as primarily anticlerical. Louis Blanc, like Michelet and Buchez, was prepared to condone the Terror in his hatred of the Girondins. The first two volumes of his work published in 1847 presented a specifically socialist interpretation. For him, the Revolution was itself a struggle between fraternity and individualism. The latter, the spirit of 1789, was represented by the Girondins, Voltaire their idol, whilst the socialist virtue of fraternity was found in Robespierre and Saint-Just whose mentor was Rousseau.

None of these, however, had the success of Lamartine's *Histoire des Girondins*, the eight volumes of which appeared between March and June 1847. Rarely can a work of history have been so popular or had such influence. It was bought by many who ordinarily would not have read history, as witness the vast sales and cheap popular editions. It was a frankly political work. "It is said 'Monsieur de Lamartine does not speak in the Chamber this year, but he has delivered a book in eight volumes'"[9] wrote its author pleasedly. He sought to rekindle the ideals of revolution and to educate people for another, a task Lamartine believed best served by concealing the horrors of the first. He had gilded the guillotine,[10] remarked Chateaubriand. In spite of its title, the Jacobin ethos is primarily reflected, and Robespierre, the dominant character, appears in a favourable light. Lamartine's desire to obtain leadership of dissatisfied and progressive forces in France, demanded no less. "My book needed a conclusion, and it is you who have given it!"[11] he told an audience at a radical banquet at Mâcon in July 1847. The *Girondins* not unnaturally suffered from the blatancy of this approach and from the haste with which its bankrupt and ambitious author wrote it, but even those who disapproved, often wallowed in its purple and gold verbosity.

Historians of the French Revolution could not avoid partisanship and other histories were written in a similar spirit to defend political heroes or attack philosophical enemies. So Nettement defended Louis XIV, and wrote a history of the Orléans family which could not have been other than unfavourable: other royalist historians attacked Jansenism, Crétineau-Joly wrote in praise of the Vendeans and the Jesuits, and Balzac, inaugurating a new tendency to royalist Machiavellism, admired Louis XI. The Comte de Montalembert's *Histoire de Sainte Elizabeth* is not only a hagiography but represents an aristocratic historian's dream of an age when hierarchy was charitable, and its unanimity withstood the forces of both anarchy and absolutism. The Catholic legitimist Comte de Falloux published in 1840 a biography of Louis XVI which paid more attention to the martyr than to the incompetent politician, although his willingness to blame the aristocracy for its part in the fall of the *ancien régime* was a more historical view than that of previous royalist Catholics who simply saw a Voltairean conspiracy.

Aurélien de Courson in his *Histoire des peuples Bretons* (1847) was less moderate than either of these: an admirer of feudalism, his was a work of particularism which ended in an attack on Thiers and on Bonapartist centralisation.

As politicians were frequently historians, so too were philosophers, notably Cousin, Michelet and Quinet. Thinkers as different as Comte and Tocqueville reflected the deterministic views current in political thought. There was a tendency to make history and philosophy positive sciences similar to sociology and the three subjects frequently became one. As Buchez wrote in his *Introduction à la science de l'histoire* (1833), doubt was fatal to societies, and scepticism encouraged egoism. It was necessary to find the principle which gave birth and life to societies. Buchez was not untypical in his belief that history was a science from which a philosophy that would organise society might be drawn.

During the July Monarchy, the change from the dominance of a liberal school of historians to a democratic school, from those who saw 1830 as a consummation of movement, to those who saw it as a small step, was paralleled by changes in philosophy. That which dominated in 1830, seeming to represent the regime and made almost official by the promotion its proponents received, was known as the "eclectic" school. Cousin, Jouffroy, Saint-Marc Girardin and Rémusat were the leading figures. Close to the doctrinaires and the latter a political member of the sect, their philosophical concepts could not be separated from contemporary events. Victor Cousin, son of an artisan, became the leading philosophical spokesman of the Orleanist bourgeoisie. Hegel and Royer-Collard dominated his intellectual development, and he added the constitutional liberalism of the latter to a modified historicism. His philosophy was largely a critical examination of all philosophies of the past: regarding error as partial truth, he believed the truth in all systems could be separated from the false and added together. As in philosophy, so in politics: one should take elements, stability, liberty, equality and aristocracy and combine them. This political eclecticism was well suited to the July Monarchy. In philosophy, it was not a dogma but rather a spirit of enquiry, deist but sceptical. His *régiment*, the men he trained to be teachers, were instructed to offer Christianity (in the person of its bishops) a bargain: philosophy would rule the lettered class, but religion was agreed to be necessary for the multitude. This hypocrisy was as unsatisfactory to aggressive Catholics as it was to agnostics, and as the 1830 Charter and political eclecticism lost intellectual prestige, so Cousin, while remaining an influential figure, began to cause a certain impatience in the young.

Theodore Jouffroy, having lost his faith, like his colleague Cousin sought a new religion in philosophy. Because he regretted the loss and was an unbeliever who disliked unbelief, eclecticism with its vagueness and religious tone suited his temperament. Epochs were founded on a creed, which was then increasingly seen as insufficient: an age of destruction followed, whilst a new creed emerged. They lived in a destructive age. "Today the destinies of man and humanity are the question; they are represented by the country that has always marched at the head of modern civilisation. . . ."[12] The world had a moral destiny and man was unhappy when he did not know it: philosophy should tell him what it was. But although he went further than Cousin who saw destinies accomplished in the Charter, he never really found any answers. Such was the problem of eclecticism. It led either to permanent scepticism, an inability to believe in anything for long, as with Charles de Rémusat who portrayed it in his work on the medieval philosopher Abelard, a human mind doubting, seeking but not finding: or else it became a sterile conservatism such as that of Saint-Marc Girardin, tied to the Charter, in art concerned less with aesthetics than with public ethics, trying to exist on a foundation of eighteenth-century liberalism without its politically dangerous irreligion.

Evidently the age was a poor one for philosophy. Metaphysics were unfashionable, and the dominance of politics destroyed liberty of thought. "Theories here are but verbal opinions, and not at all systems of well-pondered thought",[13] complained Emile de Girardin. And Lerminier, journalist, deputy and political commentator, noted the contrast at the root of this: "These days, vested interests are aggressive and intolerant, ideas are vague and indecisive."[14] Men knew what they wanted, but after a century of doubt, amidst proliferation of questions and answers, they no longer knew what they believed. Politics, the service of interest groups, and science, the exploitation of matter, predominated. As Jouffroy had seen, only religion was sufficiently strong to surmount these.

Edgar Quinet had originally been a disciple of Cousin, but had turned against him, largely for political reasons. Eclecticism he came to see as the child of the Restoration and he followed a development similar to Michelet's, putting democratic values above institutions and searching for a superhuman historical cause. Quinet was one of the breed of free-thinking mystics so prolific at this time, and also typical of the age was his search for unity. He adapted and developed Cousin's pantheistical deism, seeing a deity as motive force, and all history as the story of religions. In the *Génie des religions* he wrote that all creeds passed through a set of phases, from the simplicity of fear, through adoration to the complex diversities of explanation. A religion then became less cohesive and more individualistic and had to be replaced. Quinet argues in *Le Christianisme et la Révolution* that the French Revolution failed because it did not possess a new religion and was too rationalistic and too abstract. He himself, however, like so many others, had difficulties discovering this new religion, and after his period of vague deism he accepted a vague Protestantism which provided a suitable vehicle for his hatred of Roman Catholics.

The desire for synthesis and unity was taken to an extreme in Auguste Comte. Although termed a sociologist, he had little in common with the statisticians or investigators of particular ills, however radical some were in their solutions for the problems of industrialism. He believed that sociology was also history and philosophy and that on its scientific bases would be built a new religion. Comte's thought was rooted in Saint-Simonism, this son of a minor bureaucrat having been a brilliant pupil and then teacher at the

Polytechnique. He held the Saint-Simonist belief that scientists wielding spiritual power could solve society's problems; representing "a common social doctrine",[15] this priesthood would possess a political role between the governing capitalist "patriciate" and the producing proletariat. The *grand prêtre* had an order of knights at his disposal to discipline the latter, or alternatively to raise them in strike if the ruling class exceeded its role. Comte's massive *Cours de Philosophie Positive* (1830–42), in aiming at the removal of conflict, reaches the ultimate in denial, or rather, incomprehension of liberty. Because his sociology was a synthesis combining mystical elements with rational examination of society, Comte believed that it had all transcending rights. They were further justified by history, whose theological and fictitious, then metaphysical and abstract, phases had been succeeded by the last, in which "social science" attained the same positive quality as the physical sciences.

In common with Utopians, such as Fourier, he regulated all areas of existence. In positivist Europe, France would be divided into seventeen, although he was enough of a nationalist to claim that Paris was the natural headquarters for the *grand prêtre* of humanity. Nor did he scorn to organise the household, where woman, intellectually inferior but spiritually superior to the male, would play a dominant role. Comte's thought became less rational as time progressed, and when in 1846 passionate love came into his life, his work took a still more mystical turn.

At the time, Comte had little influence, but his attempt to produce a synthesis from conflicting forces and to create a new religion from a scientific examination of society is significant of a very strong tendency of thought during the period. Comte and Cousin were more alike than they would have admitted. Indeed, amongst conservatives and republicans, doctrinaires and democrats, Catholics and the prophets of new religions, there were many common factors. Eighteenth-century scepticism and revolutionary instability were seen as philosophically and politically impossible. In history there was an increased interest in the Middle Ages, in political philosophy a tendency to collectivism. There were many differing attempts to produce syntheses of romanticism and rationalism, science and mysticism, diversity and unity, all reflecting an age which hoped that, with the correct formula, from conflict could be brought harmony.

One man, however, and he was the greatest political thinker of this period, could not ally himself with the philosophers' theories nor accept the sociologists' equations. Comte Alexis de Tocqueville combined historical, political and sociological thinking but in a wholly individual manner. Whilst a determinist to the extent that he recognised the triumph of democracy as inevitable, he did not hold the common view that the inevitable was also the perfect. He foresaw no Utopia but rather the threats to liberty which the mass age might bring. His political philosophy was an attempt to ensure the survival of civilised values in this new world. Tocqueville was also a liberal compelled to rethink his creed. The liberalism of the Restoration as represented by the doctrinaires had become tarnished by power. Only Royer-Collard had retained the intellectual purity of the politically independent and impotent, and he was to recognise Tocqueville as his successor. Royer-Collard's ideas, however, were too much founded upon bases which had been overthrown in 1830. The exile of Charles X, which Tocqueville personally regretted, showed to him that the contemporary world was in a state of flux, and that the hopes of legitimists and those who believed that Orleanism ended the Revolution, were alike vain.

His clear-sightedness was to a great extent the result of his sense of being a member of a minority in the process of destruction. "You judge democracy as a conquered aristocrat convinced that the conqueror was right",[16] Guizot perspicaciously told him. Tocqueville, examining his fundamental instincts, found he had "a rational preference" for democratic institutions, "but I am by instinct an aristocrat, that is to say, I mistrust and fear the crowd".[17] He loved liberty and legality and believed only democracy could enable them to survive, but he believed democracy also brought its threats, and from this internal conflict came his great work of political philosophy. Scion of a royalist family, the Revolution of 1830 had sorrowed but not surprised him. After much conscience searching, he took the oath to Louis-Philippe, but found himself mistrusted by the more enthusiastic Orleanists and by radicals who disliked him as an aristocrat. He and his friend, Gustave de Beaumont, decided upon a temporary self-exile: in 1831 they obtained permission to visit the United States of America in order to study the penitentiary system. The results of their researches were published in 1833 and had some effect upon French prison reform.

More significant, however, was the work which stemmed from Tocqueville's main motive for the visit, the study of American democracy. *De la Démocratie en Amérique* was published in two parts: the first, in 1835, had an immediate success, went into several editions and won the Monthyon prize for its contribution to human well-being. The completion in 1840 was less popular: the early portions had satisfied the general curiosity about America, but this was more philosophical and more pessimistic. It warned the radicals that democracy was no automatic Utopia, whilst displeasing the conservatives by telling them that they could not resist its coming: indeed he stressed that to do so was dangerous. Some of the weaker aspects of Tocqueville's work result from his attempts to convince, as a politician, notably a tendency to evade necessary definition. He wished, by differentiating between fatalism and the realistic recognition of the inevitable, to create a programme for gradual democratisation, and addresses himself in particular to his fellow aristocrats and Catholics whose sense of personal honour and freedom, and whose anti-materialism he requires to counterbalance some of the worst effects of democracy. It presents a threat to the individual by its tendency to make a tyranny of public opinion. Tocqueville fears the crushing strength of a general mediocrity, of a despotism which comes not from one man but from the majority. He believed that decentralisation was a possible remedy for this and criticised the centralising tradition in France. Similarly he regretted that so many French liberals were hostile to religion, which he believed provided the morality, more necessary in a democratic society than in one founded upon hierarchical principles. His parliamentary career in the 1840s he found deeply frustrating in his inability to convert the *gauche dynastique*, with whom he sat, to his ideas of constructive liberal opposition.

Tocqueville believed, in spite of his prejudices, that the benefits of democracy outweighed the disadvantages. Egalitarianism gave all a stake in society and by making each man a property-owner, ensured thereby a respect for property and social responsibility.[18] The most important reason for accepting democracy, however, was the need to avoid conflict. It is here that Tocqueville's national background is clearly seen, and his aristocratic and royalist origins observed. Whereas Orleanist liberals saw compromise resulting from conflict, Tocqueville believed struggle to be potentially fatal to freedom. From class hatred, or the strife between revolutionary passion and conservatism, only dictatorship could emerge.

Democracy would bring increased regard for social justice: its laws would be made to help the greatest number. If it were somewhat vulgar and aesthetically unpleasing, there would be a more general compassion and a new humanitarianism. Yet he feared also personal vices encouraged by democracy, a selfish individualism, the narrow cosiness of the fireside, a mass vulgar materialism served by the growth of huge bureaucracy. Some signs of this he saw already in France, where the spread of wealth had created a bourgeoisie moderate in all things but its love of comfort. Yet this self-interest, "national self-interest", is the foundation of his democracy: it overcomes the anarchy he hates in contemporary France, and here he is revealed to be more concerned with his own country than with the Americans he is supposedly examining. However, if each man acts for the good of all by acting for his own good, and protects the rights of others in the belief that these rights may one day benefit him, morality becomes purely utilitarian, so Tocqueville wheels in religion to plaster over certain inconsistencies and gild the rather unpleasant doctrine of self-interest. This is somewhat hypocritical, for Tocqueville only returned to the Catholic faith later in life, and seems here to come dangerously close to the contemporary tendency to find religion useful as a bulwark to social order. In his case Christianity was fundamental to the historical movement which was leading to the triumph of democracy, and he hoped it would also prove a remedy to the excesses of egalitarian materialism. He resembles Royer-Collard in his belief in a transcendent religious idea of justice to which the individual may appeal, in his case, against the majority, in his predecessor's, against the state. For Tocqueville agreed moral views were necessary, but the problem which he, and other thinkers of his time, failed to solve, was that even as he wrote, such a body of ideas was breaking down.

For previous liberals, the limitation of the state's power had been a guarantee of the rights of the individual, but for Tocqueville, and herein lies one of the most important of his new ideas, this guarantee was to be found in the citizen's participation in political life. He fears the development of a bourgeois aristocracy within democracy, but hopes that general education will enable the worst effects of this to be overcome. To seek in liberty anything other than liberty itself, he warns, is to destroy it. Tocqueville seems to dare not truly express his pessimism lest he cause his fears to become reality. His failure as a politician was to a great extent due to his philosophical temperament and the faults in his philosophy are frequently the results of his desire to influence men's political action. With timid optimism he hoped that a gracefully dying nobility would bequeath a swan-song whose beauty might avert the vulgar mediocrity of the mass age he prophesied. The aristocrat watched democracy arrive with awe: "I sense my insight troubled and my reason staggering."[19] Gifted with the painful acuity of the man who observes and suffers from the sickness of the society in which he lives, he found in the advance of democracy a personal solution as much as a political good. The strength of the principle of equality will carry forward with it the disturbed and doubting individual: he can solve his difficulties by sharing its triumph. Like many of his contemporaries, Tocqueville looked to historical determinism to answer problems which seemed without solution.

REFERENCES

1. J. Janin, cited in J. Miège, *Jules Janin* (1933), 161.
2. Baron P. de Barante, *Mélanges* (1844), 44.
3. F. Guizot, *Mémoires pour servir à l'histoire de mon temps* (1858), I, 27–8.
4. Barante, op. cit., 45.
5. J. Michelet, *Histoire de France* (1833), I, introduction.
6. Ibid.
7. Comte L. de Carné, "Le Cardinal Richelieu", *Revue des Deux Mondes* (April 1843), 329–65, 729–53.
8. J. Naville (ed.), *Lettres de Francois Guizot et de la Princesse Lieven* (1963).
9. A. de Lamartine, *Correspondance* (1882), III, 85.
10. Vicomte F.-R. de Chateaubriand, cited in Marèchal E. D. E de Castellane, *Journal* (1895), III, 387.
11. Lamartine, *Discours politiques* (1878), 106.
12. T. Jouffroy, Archives Parlementaires, 22 December 1840.
13. E. de Girardin, *De l'instruction publique en France* (1842), 11.
14. J. L. E. Lerminier, "Du Gouvernement parlementaire", *Revue des Deux Mondes* (15 May 1837) 261–72.
15. A. Comte, *Cours de philosophie positive* (1845).
16. A. Redier, *Comme disait M. de Tocqueville* (1921), 15.
17. Comte A. de Tocqueville, *Œuvres*, ed. J. P. Mayer (1967), VIII, 84.
18. Idem, *Démocratie en Amerique* (*Œuvres*, ed. J. P. Mayer).
19. Ibid.

20

Art in Orleanist Society

"On ne lit guère en France, mais en révanche, tout le monde écrit."

("One reads but little in France, but on the other hand, everyone writes.")[1]

"Monsieur de Lamartine préside le conseil général de son département. Muses, pardonnez-lui!"

("Monsieur de Lamartine presides over the conseil général *of his department. Muses, pardon him!")*[2]

The crisis of religion and politics could not fail to affect art and literature. The men of nineteenth-century France believed they had undergone too many experiences. "Being civilised is very tedious"[3] wrote Madame de Girardin to Lamartine: the sense of ennui was as widely invoked as the vice of *égoisme*. Man was decadent, senile, asserted Charles Nodier: he had uselessly gorged himself upon the fruit of the tree of knowledge and would die of it.[4] He had sucked the sterile milk of impiety from the preceding century[5] lamented Alfred de Musset, but there seemed to be no palatable antidote. In a world of contradictions where each man was his own law, his own moral and aesthetic judge, a fact which caused, claimed Philarète Chasles, "a profound and universal weariness",[6] art was bound to reflect both the ardour of search and its despair. Whereas classicism had been the belief in a object of ideal beauty outside the creator, the romantic artist gave to his own subjective desires a value which rose above all other standards which he found academic or repressive. Yet the romantic also criticised the individualism of his age. Romanticism fully shared the contradictions of the period. It could be an expression of negativism – "Down with life!" cried one of Borel's heroes – or it might be optimistic, confident that from the death of old restrictions would emerge a new and unalloyed freedom. The same artist would in different moods celebrate decadent despair or joyful Utopianism.

The certainties of classicism had clashed with romanticism, values faced questions. Where classicism lingered on, it was frequently in debased form either as entertainment, in opera for example, utilitarian as in architecture, or for propaganda as in sculpture. Traces of classicism never disappeared, but with a few exceptions, failed to achieve original or important results. Opposed to conventions, romanticism was after 1830 happier on the left than allied to royalism as it had often been beneath the Restoration, but left and right agreed on hostility to the dull tyranny of a prosaic *juste milieu*, and almost all romantics were dissatisfied with society as organised and this dissatisfaction was a motive of their art. Extremism was natural to the romantic as a factor of his rebellion and an expression of his individuality.

Three months before the July Revolution, Hugo's *Hernani* had appeared, with its battle between the young *hugolâtres*, the fanatical supporters of romanticism, and the old classicists, horrified at their bold advocacy of artistic rebellion. Its preface declared romanticism to be liberalism in literature, and by liberalism Hugo meant not Orleanist constitutionalism, rather a freedom, undefined but permanently active. Literature was made the accompaniment of spiritual and political liberation. Sainte-Beuve's belief that "people and poets are going to march together . . ." as he expressed it in the Saint-Simonian *Globe* in October 1830,[7] held that art was revolutionary and democratic. The year 1830, wrote the critic Jules Janin, unleashed new forces in art as in politics: it broke rules and conventions, introduced new words as each author in his small domain made "his little July Revolution".[8] Some retained their belief in this as a potential source of inspiration, but for most the dreams of a popular art evaporated and left the artist feeling divorced from contemporary society and uprooted from the past. Many decided that since they could not believe anything, they wished to feel all. Experience for its own sake was an expression of an existence without philosophic certainty, but rarely did it resemble the hedonism of the eighteenth century. For romantics sexual pleasure was often associated with death. To avoid the boredom, that terrible *mal de siècle*, which was threatening to overwhelm him, the romantic, such as Alfred de Musset, would sacrifice much, but he realised, and perhaps rejoiced in it, that intense experience might lead even to the sacrifice of life itself.

When the nature of the new régime was revealed, some extreme romantics such as "Le Petit Cénacle", the young veterans of the battle of *Hernani*, commenced informal rebellion against society. They dressed with outlandish extravagance or cultivated a sinister conspiratorial aspect. The noise made by the *bouzingots* was not merely youthful exuberance but was a deliberate assault on bourgeois society. Such groups generally fell apart quickly, like the extreme romanticism of which they were an expression. Within a few years, Théophile Gautier, associated with the Petit Cénacle was, in such works as *Daniel Jouard ou la conversion d'un classique* (1833), mocking the war in which dull young men had deserted their bourgeois liberalism to become "Young France" republicans, to love the medieval, grow beards, use affected adjectives and write irregular verse under teutonic-sounding pseudonyms. The form of romanticism most directly associated with 1830 came to be disparaged, like the Revolution itself, but its sudden attack upon public sensibilities had changed the nature of art's relationship to society, making of it an assault rather than a solace.

There was, however, no such thing as "a Romanticism" but there were several traits and tendencies common to most romantics. Romanticism questioned the dogmas of society. The favourite romantic hero is in some way a rebel, and the author sympathises with his rebellion, even when it is unsuccessful. Dumas's *Antony*, as illegitimate, feels a grudge against society. It was, said its author, produced in a moment of "social licentiousness which follows revolutions".[9] To the literary critic and deputy Jay, this portrayal of rape, adultery and incest was worthy a *premier-Paris* in the *Constitutionnel*, attacking the play as "the most robustly obscene work that has appeared in these times of obscenity".[10] That the play had some popularity, and more notoriety, proved how society now expected to be shocked even whilst some of its members regarded their civilisation as being so fragile that a second-rate melodrama could overthrow it. Romanticism sought reality, outside the conventions, and tended to believe that by breaking the rules, a truth would emerge. It regarded this as applying to art as to morality, and so passion was exalted above worthless regulations and restrictions. Protesting against the materialism of the modern world, romantics attacked the bourgeois society which appeared to be its manifestation, but rarely felt much enthusiasm for the political rivals of Orleanism. A particular society, indeed several systems and concepts of society, had failed, and accordingly many artists undertook instead a search for the universal. The poetic epics of Lamartine are the expressions of the vague deism and humanitarianism in which many found answers to a mass of questions, and to make which more convincing, they covered with emotionalism.

Many authors chose to express in their art not one harmonious aspect of life, but the conflicts from which this desire for the universal had emerged. Hugo claimed in the prefaces to his plays that he was being true to nature when he passed from the tragic to the comic or from the sublime to the grotesque. Romanticism was an awareness of contrasts, the expression of a society which had lost cohesion. In a world where in each individual, doubt struggled with faith, and ambition was often irreconcilable with loyalty, it was natural that the artist should present his individual characters as reft by internal conflict. Rarely did romantic authors have the psychological knowledge which would have enabled them successfully to portray this, but they still delighted in presenting strongly contrasted qualities within one individual. Thus Hugo's Triboulet in *Le Roi s'amuse* is both malignant and a martyr to paternal affection; his Lucrèce Borgia combines the attributes of murderous monster with the sublime qualities of the perfect mother, and the pure-hearted prostitute recurs in the works of Hugo and other authors on innumerable occasions, symbol of the belief that virtue will be found in unconventional guise.

Romanticism was an aesthetic of conflict. The nature of the conflict varied according to fashion, 1830 especially giving it a political character. The struggle might be against a corrupt society or against nature or God. The rebel becomes a modern saint, and blasphemy and immorality are frequently treated as expressions of individuality, not, as in the past, as crimes which will receive human or divine punishment. Many believed it necessary to sink low in order to rise high. There was a search for rest through excess which harmonised with the belief in the decadence of civilisation. Whereas the classicist or conventional bourgeois regarded the romantic as a cause of this, he either enjoyed the decay or argued that society itself was guilty. He might use the contrasts he observed as a moral criticism. Thus Balzac will describe within one work both high and low society, the world of criminals and of *haute politique*. His view of life was that desire for power was a destructive struggle. As with so many romantics, his presentation of this in his heroes is not necessarily approval: indeed Balzac's own royalism was largely the intellectual adherence to an aristocratic society founded upon tradition and opposition to that, symbolised by Orleanist usurpation, in which individual wills competed without any personal loyalties.

The romantic hero varies between passivity and dynamism. He may be oppressed by society or rise above it to be anti- or super-social. This dissatisfaction is at the root of the idea of the *mal de siècle*. Most romantics lived in the shadow of Napoleon: they could not resign themselves to the petty promotions of the dull worlds of commerce or bureaucracy when the great examples of the Empire stood before them. A Byronic individualism was one response: another was to fight society with its own ruthless weapons and become a leader of it. A third response was to accuse society of persecution and seek to escape it. The latter accounts for the popularity amongst many young men of Alfred de Vigny's *Chatterton*. Eugène Labiche wanted to kiss the author, and declared mere words had never so moved him before: "My sleep will be a sublime nightmare."[11] Chatterton's suicide seemed to such enthusiasts to be the ultimate act of rebellion against a heartless society.

Romanticism exalted the creator, whose subjective desires and tastes became his leading standard. In overthrowing disciplines, the artist regarded himself as a liberator. Hugo welcomed the charge of being revolutionary in literature: he was proud to use new words, or to change semantic meanings – "He who unchains the word, unchains thought",[12] he pronounced. However, by 1840 many critics, not only the acerbic Chasles who disapproved of almost everything but also Sainte-Beuve, Nisard and Janin, were accusing the earlier generation of romantics, in particular Hugo and Lamartine, of having been destroyed by their own excessive liberalism: by freeing themselves of all disciplines, they claimed, these artists had become merely self-indulgent. Many of the effects of romanticism were thus criticised by men who had earlier identified themselves with it. What had been a school before 1830, had become a dominant but divided method of expression.

Romanticism demanded for the artist a special place in the world. Hugo claimed for him the role of leader, reformer and prophet. Lamartine regarded him as qualified to rule because understanding the forces of the world and having the duty to express them to a wide public. "She must popularise herself",[13] he cried of poetry. "I have wished to be read in the shops",[14] and, ever ready to believe his desires reality, he claimed from this the right to political leadership. Many other writers held similar political preoccupations. George Sand's idealising of the populace was based on the belief that fiction could predict and produce fact. Balzac on the contrary regarded it as his duty to present actuality, but neither he nor his age could yet comprehend the would-be scientific realism of a later period, and he regarded exaggeration of bad qualities to be a means of expressing the truth of society as he saw it. It was part of his role as "doctor of incurable diseases".[15] If the artist were priest he also was martyr, a comparison sometimes taken as far as an identification with Christ: "The misunderstood great artist who heroically fights his ungrateful public and bitter destiny"[16] wrote George Sand. Vigny constantly complained that society, with its measureless debt to the artist, not only starves him but persecutes him because of his divinity. Some believed that it was essential to be misunderstood, that public hostility was a proof of greatness, and that the greater the former, the more there was of the latter. Thus an extremist such as Pétrus Borel, the lycanthrope, deliberately insulted and attacked the public to make sure that there was no chance of his not being misunderstood and rejected by them. For him, art was a rebellion akin to that of a Fieschi.

Many of these artists could not decide whether they were democrats or members of an élite. It was typical of the period for them to try to be both. As Tocqueville hoped that fellow aristocrats would civilise the coming democracy, so George Sand romanticised love affairs between classes, Lamartine epitomised the *grand seigneur* convinced that he was egalitarian, and in music Berlioz sought a popular art in an uncompromisingly unpopular method. At a lower level, the artist who did not wish, or felt himself unable, to change society, was proud of his quality of apartness. *La Vie de Bohème*, celebrated by Henry Mürger in stories which began to appear from 1844 in the *Corsaire*, described a younger generation of artists without politics or salons open to them, not even able to afford the forays into bankruptcy of an Alfred de Musset, but inhabiting draughty garrets, hungry, neglected and unknown, lacking even the unpopular notoriety of older artists, but forming a distinctive and proud society. That the public read these tales showed how the myth of Bohemia had become more acceptable since the *bouzingots* had so shocked bourgeois susceptibilities in 1830.

The world seemed to become increasingly competitive, and official Orleanist philosophy welcomed this. Salvandy, at a prize-giving, told the pupils they were lucky to live in an age where society resembled a contest "where all life's rewards can be won".[17] The legitimist *Quotidienne* published this speech with regrets that nowhere had the speaker shown any understanding of the fact that society should be a moral organisation. There was, however, another reaction from those who were unable to stand with the Catholics nor wished to enter the competition. Art for art's sake was the product of a utilitarian and competitive system, a different form of rebellion, against other artists as well as against society. Utilitarians might ask where was the treatment of social problems, where were the arguments for progress:

Théophile Gautier would reply impertinently: "Several centuries ago, one had Raphael, one had Michelangelo, now one has M. Paul Delaroche; all of that because of progress."[18] He judged purely by aesthetic criteria, and democracy seemed only to mean an increase in bad taste.

A cynicism about politics after 1830 had led to studied indifference. Only the glass trade profited from revolution suggested Gautier; "a hero grows excellent green peas . . .".[19] This form of intellectual dandyism had the merit of shocking republicans and Orleanists alike. The younger writer Flaubert agreed, regretting that the artist had lost his freedom to a social mission when a sonnet had to explain a philosophy, a watercolour improve morals and a play dethrone a king, typical of a growing tendency in the 1840s to regard political involvement as an irrelevance or artistic danger.

Although later ages would regard with nostalgia an age when Stendhal, Mérimée and Gautier were flourishing, these men all claimed that their society was heavy and pedantic. They opposed many of the tendencies of romanticism but possessed others. Thus Stendhal's heroes, with their doubt and egoism, unleashing their wills against society, Gautier's determination to free his writing from moral convention or Mérimée's historical imagination and love of the grotesque, are representative of the age, but they and others began to mock the romantic poses, disapproved the murky obscurity cultivated by some artists, and attacked, overtly or by implication, the belief that writing was a political act.

The idea of art for art's sake was anathema to many, especially to republicans. A humanist such as David (d'Angers) believed the sculptor's duty was to portray the nobility of man, convinced, like George Sand, that this would make men noble. As a republican, he flattered his sitters, not from obsequiousness, but from political motives. For Lamennais, art existed to express the noblest tendencies of the epoch: the artist was the prophet of the religion of the future, his intent progress, his goal the perfection of the Being. Republican newspapers, notably the *National*, remained unsympathetic to the most progressive and original features in the art of the period because disapproving of the individualism or moral anarchy which was expressed there.

The novel was the form in which the age excelled, because it allowed freedom from formal constraints; it was a genre without convention which would prosper from the struggles of a hero in conflict with society or in portraying individualities and social dramas. The idea of history as a shifting of great forces inspired epic historical novels such as Balzac's *Chouans*, or Hugo's *Notre Dame de Paris*. The former's aspiration to narrate the hitherto untold epic of the middle class was a combination of this historical concept with the minutiae of contemporary realities. Others tried to put these ideas into poetry with much less success.

Lamartine suffered from his own affectations of negligence but also from the attempt to poeticise vague philosophical ideas. Never was nature more prodigal, and never were her gifts more abused, said Guizot.[20] In him the contradictions of the age jostled each other without merging: dandy and mystic, poet and politician, *grand seigneur* and democrat, Lamartine flitted from one rōle to another. One may ascribe to 1830 the personal disorder which affected his political career as well as his artistic, the latter becoming absorbed in the former. Thus in the *Chute d'un Ange* he set out to write a democratic and humanitarian epic, in which he, as Chasles said, "mistook size for grandeur",[21] an error of the age. The same critic complained that the poet would one moment evoke the wild bird winging its way to a sultry clime, the next he would be celebrating the steam engine. He, like so many of his contemporaries, had no personal private imagination but mingled themes and ideas pell-mell from Dante and Byron, the Bible and Pierre Leroux, Lamennais and Homer.

The theatre was where romantic writers were at their most extravagant and where, this being an age of virtuoso acting with such figures as Fréderic Lemaître and Rachel, ideas seemed to have the most immediate effect. It was this expression of the revolutionary or antisocial ideas which most disturbed conservatives. Frenchmen had once believed themselves elegant and refined, "One has to agree that for the last three years Providence has cruelly chastised that vanity", the Duc de Broglie told the deputies, to approving laughter. Nobody dared go to the theatre not knowing the play: it was a school of debauchery and crime whose disciples sooner or later appeared in the lawcourts.[22] Viennet declared that one could no longer take one's daughter to the Théâtre Français after the pro-romantic Baron Taylor had become its director. The deputies Fulchiron and Charlemagne delivered a parliamentary onslaught on Vigny for encouraging suicide in his *Chatterton*. When Dumas's *Antony* was produced at the state-subsidised Théâtre Français, the influence of the deputies Étienne and Jay (of the anti-romantic *Constitutionnel*) who threatened rebellion on the budget, led Thiers to forbid its performance. The government was sued by the author and lost. Seven years later, in 1840, with the September laws behind it, the government was on firmer ground in banning, after one performance at which an infuriated Duc d'Orléans was present, Balzac's *Vautrin* wherein Lemaitre as the robber chief imitated Louis-Philippe's appearance and mannerisms.

For Hugo, however, humanity was a religion and the theatre its church. Within it, the poet had charge of souls: the audience should take out with them "some austere and profound moral".[23] Yet Broglie, Viennet and other conservatives would have seen little sign of this in Hugo's own work. His attacks on Church and monarchy in such plays as *Le Roi s'amuse*, whilst condoning crime and depravity providing they were practised with passion, reflected a romantic ethos, where conventional virtues were shown as vices and social discipline was tyranny. However, the romantic theatre received a check with the failure of Hugo's *Les Burgraves*, and the enormous success Rachel achieved in reinterpreting the neglected classics revealed that many were beginning to tire of a romantic diet.

Public taste was poor. Nestor Roqueplan, as director of the Opéra-Comique, encouraged bad performances in an attempt to disgust the public with a genre he despised: he failed. Buloz, made *commissaire du roi* at the

Théâtre Français, dreamed of regenerating it, but the abject failure of George Sand's *Cosima* in 1840 enforced his surrender: henceforth he relied upon Scribe and Casimir Delavigne. The former was the most prolific and popular playwright of the period. The success of his plays, vaudevilles and opera libretti made him a rich man, with over 150 titles to his credit, including *La Xacarilla, Yelva* and *Zoë*, in order to cover the alphabet. Much of this success was due to an ability to avoid the excesses of warring literary schools, and to a fluent mediocrity. Scribe did however inject new life into the comedy of manners. The old conventions had broken down, and he led the way into new subjects such as the social effects of adultery or speculation, introducing new types such as the *puffeur*, the exploiter of commercial pretence. He also had the recommendation, rare in their epoch as Véron remarked,[24] of never having written a philosophical preface. The theatre reflected public taste, in a more direct way than any other art, and the popularity of Scribe's mildly amusing, unpretentious bourgeois dramas with their common-sense philosophy, was to be expected in an age when audiences were ceasing to be purely aristocratic or possessors of a traditional culture but demanded something more respectable than the vaudeville.

Many moderate romantics, a school well represented in the public or journals such as the *Revue des Deux Mondes*, believed that the struggle between romanticism and classicism was irrelevant to the service of art. "Any system is made very good by talent"; wrote Jules de Rességuier,

> *"For the worst to become the best,*
> *One thing suffices . . . it is a little genius."*[25]

The public was rarely classic or romantic. It wanted adventure, reading Scott and Cooper and their French imitators such as the legitimist Victomte d'Arlingcourt or Eugène Sue. A hardened classicist like Viennet was quite willing to turn out a historical novel in the style of Scott to satisfy public taste for his financial profit. The public loved Meyerbeer but never Berlioz. It rejoiced in Delaroche's glossy treatment of melodramatic and historical themes but never appreciated the new techniques of Delacroix. A certain conciliation towards romanticism was encouraged by the fact that time tamed and made respectable the former rebels. In the early 1830s, Hugo and his admirers had been regarded almost as outlaws, but in 1845 Vicomte Hugo was created a peer – "Le Roi s'amuse",* mocked one critic.[26] The entry of Hugo, Sainte-Beuve and Vigny to the Académie (although the latter's reception was stormy due to the fact that Comte Molé took exception to a condonation of Jacobinism), showed the rebellion in the process of becoming an orthodoxy.

In painting, the period is dominated, at least for posterity, by Delacroix and Ingres. The former, like Berlioz, whose music however he loathed, was a believer in colour and rhythm, whilst the older man put before all else the

* *Ed. Note.* Literally, "The King amuses himself", but more importantly, the title of one of Hugo's more notorious works.

beauty of form and line. To use labels in speaking of such figures is highly misleading, but to contemporaries they represented the romantic and classical poles, although it may be noted that there were many, such as the Duc d'Orléans, who admired both. Delacroix was romantic in his opposition to the conventional ideals. He sought a reality in the artist's subjective observation of nature, through which an emotional truth should be presented. He was no intellectual, however, and was embarrassed by his literary apologists, of whom the young Baudelaire is the most notable. Delacroix's *Liberty Guiding the People*, seemed for a moment to represent the pictorial celebrant of Orleanism. "She is a strong woman with a powerful bosom",[27] the poet Barbier had written of Liberty, and the artist was influenced by this conception. It represented the myths of the July Revolution, uniting on the barricades the top-hatted young bourgeois, a *polytechnicien*, an ardent worker and enthusiastic *gamin*, behind the figure of Liberty. The painting was a huge success in the 1831 salon and was bought by the King who soon chose to forget the revolutionary origin of his power and put it into storage until 1848 again brought it to light. In spite of this, Delacroix was a revolutionary only in painting. He disliked most new tendencies in literature and music. Fastidious and aristocratic by nature, he despised the vulgar commonplaces of the age and rarely portrayed contemporary subjects. Yet the reason why Baudelaire and others believed him "the true painter of the nineteenth century"[28] was for his contrasts in pigment, a rebellion against academic restraints. Delacroix also exhaled a sadness true to the *mal de siècle*.

Ingres, and his disciples such as Flandrin, regarded painting as a struggle between good and evil. Ingres revered Raphael and romanticised the classical past: he declared himself a dwarf in comparison with these, but aggressively considered himself a giant in comparison with his contemporaries. Such paintings as his *Stratonice* were declarations of an intention to reform art. None the less, in that most of his work was in portraiture, Ingres more frequently painted the contemporary world, or at least its wallpaper and mantelpiece ornaments. He brought the portrayal of elegance into great art, and gives to the fleeting and agitated moments of the July Monarchy a quality of permanence. Classicism had its followers, as did romanticism. There was the sensual school which celebrated the joys of the flesh. Thomas Couture's *Romains de la Décadence*, an orgy of classical bodies amidst a décor of grave antique dignity, was typical in at once feigning disapproval of the immorality it portrayed whilst doing so in a seductive way. Such paintings were very popular in large salons. On a higher level, Chassériau's nudes were yet more exotic and sensual than those of his master, Ingres. He attempted a *juste milieu* between opposing schools, seeking to combine Ingres's drawing with Delacroix's colouring, not always successfully. While some proceeded in this direction, there was also a reaction which sought greater purity, both of subject-matter and technique. A growth of taste for the Italian primitives was a rejection of romantic and voluptuary excesses and a reflection of the Catholic aesthetics of such men as the Comtes de Falloux and de Montalembert, who admired the simple faith which the nineteenth century envied but could not attain. Hippolyte Flandrin, admirer of Giotto, disciple of Ingres, to some extent began to regenerate religious painting in such works as his murals for Saint-Germain-des-Près.

One matter on which the admirers of Ingres and Delacroix were agreed was their disapproval of the middle way of painters such as Vernet, Delaroche and Scheffer. Because public taste appreciated the sentimentality of their subject-matter, these artists enjoyed a financial success, if not a critical vogue, which the greater painters did not achieve. "The troubadour style" of the historical artists was particularly viciously mocked by critics and connoisseurs. To admire Paul Delaroche's *La Mort de Jane Gray* [*sic*], which by its pathos and the meticulous reality of its every detail created a sensation at the 1834 salon, quickly branded the admirer with a *petit bourgeois* stigma. *The Princes in the Tower*, awaiting their murder with simpering apprehension, was a work of such popularity that it inspired Delavigne to write a play. A mass of other painters of lesser talent aped their styles, using themes of literature popular at the time (Hugo's *Le Roi s'amuse*, for example, was a favourite source) or those periods of civil and religious strife, rebellion and usurpation which interested historians and their readers.

Perhaps the greatest criticism which can be made of King Louis-Philippe was that Horace Vernet was his favourite artist. Although he showed better taste in assembling a superb collection of Spainish painting, the monarch shared with many of his subjects an enthusiasm for the panoramas of battle which Vernet produced by the score, every detail of each different uniform portrayed with accuracy, in vast unwieldy compositions. Baudelaire accused him of being "a soldier who poses as a painter", his art "improvised by the drum-roll, these canvases brushed over at a gallop, this painting manufactured by pistol-shots",[29] and indeed the vast sky of Vernet's panoramic *La Prise de la Smalah* was done in a day by eight pupils laying the blue paint on with sabres. Delacroix might find Vernet's decorations in the Palais Bourbon a horrific sign of "frightful decadence" of taste in the nineteenth century, Baudelaire in his *Salon de 1846* might load him with the most colourfully vituperative expressions at his disposal, but they had to admit that he was the most popular painter of the age: his work, original or in lithograph, hung in palace and brothel, student's attic and bourgeois salon. Baudelaire's comparison of Vernet's painting with the verse of Béranger was apt: both flattered the public love of glory and extolled the romance of battle. The contemporary admiration of virtuosity naturally adored the combination of detail and militarism. And public taste also appreciated the extraordinary craftsmanship of Meissonnier whose productions seemed more real than the daguerreotype itself. To combine this with period dress or sentimental subjects was a recipe for sure success.

Religious art often tended to be theatrical rather than religious. When the new church of Notre Dame de Lorette was completed in 1836, the art critic of the *Journal des Débats* wrote "I search for a portrait of a saint and I find . . . a woman of the world in monastic attire"[30] and this was a typical contemporary fault. When the Bible was used, it was as a literary, rather than a religious, source. One of the most successful religious painters was Ary Scheffer, who catered to public taste by giving a classical treatment to romantic themes. He was a true figure of the *juste milieu*, eclectic in painting and liberal in politics, playing minor roles in 1830 and 1848, drawing-master to the Comte de Paris and *chef de bataillon* in the National Guard. He specialised in pale sentimental Christs, lacrimose Virgins and luxuriously penitent Magdalenes (for in this age of prostitution and moralising, the repentant adulteress was a popular figure).

Neither religious painting nor what Baudelaire called "the heroism of modern life"[31] were successes of this age, which in other respects may be considered a high point in painting. A preference for the picturesque, for the historical, was shown in public taste and the eclectic artist turned to literature for inspiration. Because a dislike of their age was so strong in many romantics, they were rarely able to portray it with success. No romantic artist would wish to celebrate the poetry of cravat and patent leather, and the power of the machine, or Guizot withering his opponents with his scorn; themes which Baudelaire suggested. Those artists who approached Baudelaire's demands could hardly be considered of the romantic persuasion. Alfred de Dreux and Eugène Lami painted the grace of the Orleanist *haut monde*, portraying dandies and sleek horses, silk dresses and masked balls, *lions* and ballet dancers with an elegance to which Baudelaire applied that new word "chic". Gavarni and Devéria similarly made the fashion-plate a work of art. Ingres captured the sleek elegance of Comte Molé in his tight frock-coat, and Chassériau portrayed Lacordaire, newly become Franciscan, in a manner which its subject did not like, fearing perhaps that nervous intensity which the artist had so well understood and captured, ignoring that peace for which the Christian aspired. This age, more than any previous one, wished to escape its crises, and they were more often indirectly reflected than represented.

The July Monarchy was, unfortunately for the regime, the great age of caricature. Elements of romanticism encouraged it; exaggeration, contrast of light and dark, freedom of technique and disgust with the human form and mockery of it, by-product of current idealism and symbol of its breakdown, predisposed the artist towards caricature. The depth of political passions encouraged it. Although much caricature, such as that of Gavarni, is scarcely caricature at all but social comment, the works of others, notably Daumier, have never been surpassed in bitterness. His Robert Macaire, developed from a melodrama character created by Frédéric Lemaître, was a confidence trickster who becomes a banker using speech of smoothly hypocritical morality to conceal his unscrupulous trickery. Philipon, the brilliant organiser of the *Charivari*, had suggested the titles to Daumier, but after the September laws was forced to cease satirising Louis-Philippe and use Macaire as a vehicle for social satire. Less displeasing and more foolish, Henry Monnier's Monsieur Proudhomme presents the other face of contemporary mockery of the bourgeois: respectable, plump and owl-like, he cannot manipulate or ruthlessly speculate like Macaire. Anti-English and sentimentally Bonapartist, he feels foolish optimism about the future and naïve respect for the pillars of society. A spirit of introspection and criticism is shown by the popularity of physiologies such as *Les Français peints par eux-mêmes*, descriptions and prints by well-known artists and caricaturists. The most notable was Gavarni, who breathed life into the tiny hands and slim waists of fashion prints, and showed himself a master at portraying the elegant world of the dandy, of which he was an eminent example, and in drawing the other "types" who were impinging upon the French imagination, the student, the woman of fashion, and above all the *lorette*, the shop-girl who combined charm with relaxed morals.

The more abstract arts did not flower so well in a soil which was concerned with idea rather than with form. Music had its Berlioz, but architecture had no comparable genius. Eclecticism had full reign here. As in politics where the ideas of conservative and liberal constitutionalism had to compromise with the structure of the Napoleonic state, so in architecture the continuing dominance of a decayed classicism received additions of medieval or Renaissance styles. The regime completed various projects begun previously, Notre Dame de Lorette and the Madeleine also, with its vast painting in worship of Napoleon; Saint-Vincent de Paul rose to dominate its squalid area of Paris, its huge classical portico stuck incongruously on to the plain façade. There was utter failure to achieve an original Gothic style, in spite of the reaction against dry neo-classicism; Sainte-Clotilde, for example, owes its attractions to Cologne cathedral. Most common was a mongrel style with pointed arches applied to a classical body. However, there was growing an idea that architecture should submit to the nature of the material, a belief that from utilitarianism would derive a massive beauty which is best exemplified in Labrouste's Sainte-Geneviève library. Interior decoration represented an extension of architectural eclecticism. There were Renaissance and medieval vogues, but until the Revolution destroyed luxury and the Second Empire allowed the triumph of opulence to riot uncontained, the dominant style of the July Monarchy was based on the classical tradition of the Consulate. Armchairs, silks and velvets testified to the search for comfort, fringes and tassels to ostentation. The rich man aped Bohemian preciosity by displaying *objets de vertu* in glass cases. In lesser bourgeois families, industrial techniques allowed inexpensive copying and many homes pullulated with imitation antiquities.

A taste for the Middle Ages had been one of the hallmarks of early romanticism. The number of historians in positions of influence meant that this interest received official favour. In 1830 Guizot established the post of Inspector of Historical Monuments, given to Vitet and then in 1834 to Mérimée. In that year, again at Guizot's instigation, a further step to preserve the nation's cultural heritage was made with the foundation of a committee which in 1837 became the Comité Historique des Arts et des Monuments, of which Vatout was president and Vitet and Mérimée inspectors. Its task was the vast one of compiling a list of all the country's monuments and it had the right to veto demolitions voted by *conseils généraux* or *municipaux*. The work of this committee and of the Comte de Montalembert, a member (and author of such articles as *Le Vandalisme en France* in the *Revue des Deux Mondes*), changed the careless attitude towards the distant past. Victor Hugo, like Montalembert, admired medieval civilisation, defending Gothic architecture, not merely the arch for its own sake, but as a concept of society, contrasting the bell tower with the factory chimney, the graceful dignity of the abbey with the pompous solidity of a sub-prefecture. On the committee, some felt that the medieval was a superior culture and sought to recover its purity by removal of later additions and alterations if necessary; such were the architect Lassus who restored Chartres after the fire in 1836, Hugo, Montalembert and the fanatical collector Du Sommerard who, at the Hôtel de Cluny which he bequeathed as a museum to the state, gave dinners at which his guests ate with medieval implements. The others tended to represent the more prevalent eclecticism. As Musset claimed, "Our century has no rules"; it chose for convenience, antiquity, beauty, even ugliness.[32] Thus a drawing-room would mix Greek antiques, Renaissance paintings and Louis XIII furniture, men would wear hair-styles taken from Henri III or Jesus Christ, and architects erect classical structures with Gothic ornamentation. Political comparisons sprang to mind. In this century of disobedience, commented Baudelaire, whilst "everyone wants to rule, no one knows how to govern himself". The individuality so widely claimed destroyed the collective originality of the past, and but for a couple of geniuses, mediocrity was relieved only by eccentricity.[33]

Sculpture represented more than any other branch of art the dominance of classical styles, although there was a romantic sculpture which reached an extreme in the twisted, agonised figures of Préault, hated alike by public and academies. His opposite seemed to be personified in Pradier who continued a rigorous academic classicism, the dominant style. When the state made commissions, it automatically turned to this style, so Montalivet, as Minister of the Interior with responsibility for the Bureau des Beaux Arts, bought Etex's statue of Saint-Geneviève to present to Dupin's church at Clamecy. The same sculptor was commissioned by Thiers to create two panels for the Arc de Triomphe and he and Corot produced the undistinguished figures which accompany Rude's dramatic work. Like Etex, another republican, David (d'Angers) found Rude's *Marseillaise* too lacking in nobility,[34] and similarly objected to his powerful but unidealised tomb sculpture for Godefroy Cavaignac where the dead man's bearded head and shoulders thrust forward from under his shroud. David believed that art, especially sculpture whose material gave it permanence, existed to improve man and should illustrate only great examples. He refused to sculpt the traitor Murat or the corrupt Talleyrand but those whom he did portray he insisted on idealising. His small medallions have charm but his larger works are vapid because of this trait. In tune with his republican convictions he saw art as propaganda: he planned to democratise it, but in so doing made it empty and often crude. The seriousness with which republicans took the effect of art was shown when they forced Dantan, a brilliant caricaturist in sculpture, to break the bust he had made of Arago. The legitimists also had their sculptor in Mlle de Fauveau, a collaborator in the Vendean insurrection and whose *Judith holding Holofernes's Head* gave the heroine the features of the Duchesse de Berry and the head a striking resemblance to Louis-Philippe.

In its art commissions, the July Monarchy was fairly progressive, more so than the taste of many of its supporters would lead one to expect, such as the two great commissions from Berlioz, or Rude's sculpture on the Arc de Triomphe. In 1840, the Comte de Rémusat braved the classicism of the conservative peers and ordered Delacroix to decorate the cupola of the library of the Luxembourg. The salon which chose or rejected artists (in 1837 Delacroix and the sculptor Barye were banned from contributing) and had a system of prizes for young artists, notably the Prix de Rome, was directed for most of the period by anti-romantics, first Vernet then Ingres. This salon was a relic from more autocratic days, strongly resented by many artists, especially those excluded. Etex claimed that the jury should be selected by the submitting artists, but the forces of the artistic establishment with the state on their side as indirect supporter, were too strong. The King was slightly annoyed when his eldest son, an admirer of Delacroix, criticised the salon because it sounded almost like an attack on the government through the Bureau des Beaux Arts.

The role of the private patron was of far less importance than in the preceding century. The new rich tended to be more concerned with interior decoration and their buying of painting was a commercial speculation or result of an artist's success at a salon: they bought painting loose, and many criticised the fact that art was thereby becoming an industry, although this development was also a sign of the painter's independence. A few, however, commissioned important works. The Duc de Luynes, restoring the Château of Dampierre, commissioned architects, sculptors and painters to co-operate, but the difficulty of maintaining the tradition of the private patron and artist was shown when the touchy and very slow Ingres quarrelled with his employer and left his work unfinished.

French music presents two contemporary characteristics: the romantic desire for a message, expressed in theatricality or in literary programmes, and the pre-eminence of the virtuoso and the soloist in an age of public opinion which sought the spectacular and worshipped the fashionable. The French public was at once novelty-loving and conservative, demanding a supply of new works which adhered to old forms. In music as in painting, the artists split into two groups, one producing for a public and profiting from popularity, the other lacking mass approval but often supported vociferously by critics or *cognoscenti*. Musically, France was at her lowest ebb during this period, yet it was in the midst of the prevailing Italianate mediocrity and degenerate sub-romanticism that she produced her greatest composer, Hector Berlioz. He, and the still more individual albeit lesser figure Alkan, owe their originality to factors which depressed standards generally. The lack of a flourishing tradition, coexisting with strong academic conventions, the breakdown of traditional good taste giving way to sensationalism, produced even more than in painting a large amount of bad art which fell beneath the standards a surer, but less ambitious, age would have reached. Halévy, composer of *La Juive*, had a low view of his own capacity (shared by Berlioz and his admirers) and even less regard for French public taste which accounted for the small number of his compositions. The popularity of Bellini, Donizetti and lesser Italian composers, who at Le Théâtre Italien had a shrine consecrated solely to the performance of their works, was resented by some French composers and the fact that Auber, "the Scribe of Music",[35] was believed by many to be the greatest French composer of the age, shows that those who believed the nation's musical taste behind that of the Germans, may have been correct.

Music lacks the clearer divisions of politics, but the appearance of Rossini's last major work in 1829 and the performance of *Robert le Diable* in 1831, makes the July Monarchy contemporary with a new age in musical taste. Although the Italianate retained a strong hold in the affections of the conservative public, Meyerbeer's opera was for music similar to the battle of *Hernani* in literature. It was Berlioz who expressed in most literary form, notably in *Lélio*'s monologue, the new music's repudiation of the academic, and his contempt for those who believed it to be merely a sensual satisfaction, but Meyerbeer's sudden popularity broke traditions in a way more satisfactory to the majority. *Robert le Diable* presented a typically romantic subject in its fight of good and bad angels, its dancing nuns and officiating priests (for one of the minor results of the July Revolution was that it ended the prohibition of stage representation of religious ceremonies). If this opera meant the inauguration of a great age for stage settings, it also helped create as George Sand, an admirer, put it, "a music of true passion and realistic action", where heroes in their death-throes were not granted a final climactic aria.[36] Another admirer, Heine, said that Meyerbeer's operas were social rather than individual: *Les Huguenots* and *Le Prophète* present the people in a mass, as actors in the drama, as befitted a revolutionary age which found here the reflections of their own feuds, passions and enthusiasms.[37]

The French success of the German-born Meyerbeer breached Italian domination. Soon the French would be prepared to listen to Beethoven, at first with the "improvements" made by Castil-Blaze, or in the performances of Habeneck who would select movements and play lighter pieces between them. Gradually, however, concerts at the Conservatoire revealed Beethoven to audiences of enthusiasts for whom the discovery was similar to that of Shakespeare by an earlier generation. Another discovery, limited to an even smaller élite but similar to a widening of taste in the medieval cult in architecture and admiration for Italian primitive painters, was the enthusiasm, championed by the music critic d'Ortigues, for plainchant.

Nineteenth-century France had several important institutions where the state granted a man or group of men huge powers to make money or control thought or style by leasing to them a virtual monopoly: such were the Banque de France, the Université and the Opéra. The Opéra was more a social than a musical institution. Music took second place to the assignations made and seductions planned here. It was a habit to drift in during the first act, and it was said the music had to be especially loud at that time to be heard above the rustle of gowns. In the "devil's lodge" select members of the Jockey Club gathered to ogle the dancers and admire the bared shoulders and glitter of diamonds. Partly because of this particular audience, dancing was of immense importance, and with the Elssler sisters, Grisi and Taglioni, the ballet reached a peak of technical perfection. Display was of paramount importance and spectacular productions became the rule. Berlioz claimed that Duponchel, director of the Opéra for six years during this period, would only stage works with cardinals in them. The crowds came to *Robert le Diable* and its imitations such as Halévy's *La Juive* (1835), but *Don Giovanni* was poorly attended. For mediocrity of taste was encouraged by the fact that the Opéra, under the control of the state, was leased to entrepreneurs who undertook the risks. Véron, an immensely capable and jovially unscrupulous bon viveur who took charge in the difficult days of 1831, made it profitable in the way he was later to save the *Constitutionnel*. A brilliant act of publicity, a genius for advertisement made his expensive gamble in staging Meyerbeer's grand spectacle a profitable success which made the Opéra fashionable. He had received state aid as the government had seen it as a means of attracting the world to Paris and the public demonstration of a secure and elegant society: "The success and profit of the Opéra must give the lie to the riots", said Véron.[38] Thus the Opéra was bound to conservatism, in musical taste and politics, but Véron did something to make the institution more open. He diminished the number of large boxes, enlarging the number of seats which suited better the economical habits of the "new *grands seigneurs* of the third estate".[39]

The Opéra encouraged the star. It paid vast prices to its soloists (the Elssler sisters each received 20,000 francs a year) because this was what the public wanted. Malibran, Lablache, Rubini, Nourrit, were a few of the great names who won enormous popularity. Some, claimed Berlioz, would dictate to a composer or determine his success. The artists debased themselves for the gold of a tasteless materialistic society, he wrote bitterly. Technique freed from stylistic limitations appeared in the concert halls and thrived on the romantic belief in demoniac talent. Paganini on the violin and a throng of concert pianists, Chopin, Liszt and Thalberg the most famous, passed through Paris to waves of enthusiasm. An expansion of technique in playing was echoed by the composer. The romantic penalty of brilliance in language advancing beyond what the heart had to express, was not invariably avoided, even by such a great composer as Berlioz.

Berlioz represents the tendency in music, as there was in painting, to become literary. His admirer, Joseph d'Ortigues, said that he had made music a poetic art which was not content to entertain but spoke to souls using the ideas of the epoch. For the composer and his apologists, such as Gautier, Janin and d'Ortigues, the new liberty of rhythm and the stress upon orchestral colour was a bursting through convention, an assault upon academic standards. Berlioz was often highly programmatic, usually expressing typical romantic ideas such as the anguish of the artist facing an unappreciative society. But even those who probably did not appreciate Berlioz tended to treat music literarily. Berryer, for example, felt slightly guilty about his love of Chopin, "He digs up graves, and raises the dead!"; his music was "very unhealthy".[40]

Although the dreams of Nourrit who wanted a popular opera for the workers, remained in the realms of fantasy, and the concept of music as a universal language of the soul which united men and brought them nearer God, remained largely the idealism of men such as d'Ortigues and the *habitués* of the Comtesse d'Agoult's soirées, music, like so many other things, became democratised at this period. Primarily this was the effect of piano manufacturing by such as Erard and Pleyel where France led the world. Not all the instruments were of this quality – "What a scourge is the provincial piano! What an arena of false and squalling notes, of mediocre, bourgeois music!"[41] groaned Jules Janin, and much of the music performed was sentimental balladry which the new music-publishing industry began to produce in vast quantities.

Politics infected music as it did everything else. As Hippolyte Royer-Collard, nephew of the liberal conservative philosopher, was prevented from lecturing on surgery by republican medical students, so Louise Bertin's opera *Esmeralda* was never allowed a fair hearing because the composer was daughter of the proprietor of France's leading Orleanist newspaper. The shouts of "Down with the *Débats*" revealed the true source of hostility to the music. Berlioz, who had helped her in the orchestration of this work, also suffered from his journalistic connection with the *parti de résistance*. However, he also gained support from the Bertin's connections. The Ducs d'Orléans and de Montpensier were, as well as *hugolâtres*, admirers of Berlioz, and it was to the former that the performance of the massive requiem in the Invalides for Damrémont's funeral was owed. Indeed, although Berlioz disliked the bourgeois public of Paris and preferred the aristocrats of Saint Petersburg and Vienna, the government had treated him well. Not only did it grant him the immense forces for the Requiem, but it also commissioned the *Grand Symphonie Funèbre et Triomphale* for the tenth anniversary of the July Revolution and the inauguration of the July Monument, even though on the occasion of its first open-air performance the National Guard increased the composer's dislike of the *petite bourgeoisie* when, tired of standing still, it marched off to a loud tattoo.

Not only was it a great age of ballet, this was also an age of dance. A romantic generation wished to free the body from its fetters: a relaxed morality cast off restraint. The taste for the grotesque and the exaggerated invaded gesture, and a passion for frenzied enjoyment was shown in the Bals de l'Opéra where Musard, the Paganini of popular music, would conduct with drama a noisy band in such dances as the *valse éperdue* and the *galop infernale*. The dangerously intimate waltz, wild galop, the polka with its aura of pro-Polish emotion, expressed in a frivolous manner the liberation romanticism wished to achieve.

Another symbol of liberty was the enthusiasm for combat: literary men fought lawsuits, Hugo and Dumas against the Théâtre Français, Balzac against Buloz and Émile de Girardin over contracts, others fought duels, and there were also the purely literary quarrels of schools and parties. In France, commented Philarète Chasles, one fought to think, to love, to write poetry; "Even ink has to have the smell of gunpowder."[42] The need to win an audience or desire to gain support made writers aggressive. A larger public may have increased this tendency to literary as to political warfare. Parallel to the rise of cheaper journalism was the revolution in publishing where 18vo volumes in larger editions replaced the small editions of 8vo volumes and put books within the range of those of moderate means. Education encouraged both equality and individualism, making each man his own judge but also part of a literate public. Many complained at this expansion which they believed to have produced a lowering of standards. Custine remarked that only the bad critics whose careers depended upon them, read, or pretended to read, the excessive production of books.[43] Berlioz complained of the destructive power of the operatic tenor with an adoring public supporting his every whim, critics like Chasles believed that public approval had corrupted Lamartine, and Baudelaire inveighed against the Vernet-loving grocers. But public opinion created the critic as a journalistic power. The above examples wrote as critics, and so did Gautier, who lamented the fact that the critic separated the reader from the poet.

The machine literature, of which fastidious critics like Chasles and Custine complained, was shown in the serials which newspapers began to publish in quantity in the 1840s. In the *feuilleton*, the demands of a voracious and unselective public were catered for by a band of insouciant authors ready to churn out a diurnal instalment. The speed of their work might lend verve, but often led them to slipshod writing or careless errors. Within a week midwinter could blaze forth into summer: names might change – the author might choose, like many a bourgeois of the period, to add a particle to a surname, or the heroine might romantically grow younger or her hair change colour. More serious accusations were levelled at the serialised novel: it was a source of corruption, claimed its enemies, and brought depravity to the breakfast table. The belief that the novel, like the theatre, tended to corrupt, was widely held and sometimes appeared to be justified. For instance, Madame Lafarge, the murderess, claimed as an extenuating circumstance that reading novels had made her dissatisfied. Capo de Feuillide, a literary critic, told his readers that if they opened George Sand's *Lélia* they should do so only in the privacy of a locked study,[44] an accusation of immorality which brought him a duel with one of her more ardent defenders.

Under the Restoration, there had still existed an aristocratic public and a small artistic world. The expansion of journalism, economic growth with the increase of a middle class buying painting and attending the Opéra, changed the nature of the artistic world and created "public opinion". But no one could exactly define this new force. The journalist Méry declared it "a corporation full of mystery". The public was "a people apart in the middle of the people. The public watches the people pass by in its revolutions; it purchases engravings of the Bastille, but it does not take it." It could be right or wrong in its judgements (right or wrong according to "we") but nobody could tell why.[45] The public, like the bourgeois, the "egoist" or "individualist" was usually somebody else.

REFERENCES

1. A. Karr, *Les Guêpes* (1858), I, 27.
2. Mme D. de Girardin, *Lettres Parisiennes* (1857), IV, 73.
3. H. Malo, *La Gloire de Vicomte de Launay* (1925), 83.
4. C. Nodier, *Correspondance* (1876), 125.
5. A. de Musset, *La Confession d'un Enfant du siècle* (Larousse edition, 1870), 26.
6. P. Chasles, *Études sur les hommes* (1850), 212.
7. C. A. Sainte-Beuve, *Œuvres* (Pléïade edition, 1950), 337.
8. Cited in J. Miège, *Jules Janin* (1933), 184.
9. A. Dumas, *Mes Mémoires* (1962), II, 79.
10. *Le Constitutionnel*, 28 April 1834.
11. Bibliothèque Nationale, nouvelles acquisitions françaises, 20101, f. 6.
12. V. Hugo, "Réponse à un acte d'accusation", *Les Contemplations*. (Garnier edition, 1969), 23.
13. A. de Lamartine, *Premières Méditations poétiques* (*Œuvres*, 1903), 1xi.
14. L. Viennet, *Journal* (1955), 185.
15. H. de Balzac, *Cousine Bette* (Garnier edition, 1967), xxxi.
16. G. Sand, *Lettres d'un voyageur* (Pléïade edition, 1971), 935.
17. *La Quotidienne*, August 1837.
18. T. Gautier, *Mademoiselle de Maupin* (Charpentier edition, 1922), 28.
19. Idem, *Les Jeunes-France* (Pléïade edition, 1958), II, 25–6.
20. N. W. Senior, *Conversations with M. Thiers, M. Guizot and other Distinguished Persons during the Second Empire* (1878), 383.
21. X. Doudan, *Mélanges et Lettres* (1876), I, 180.
22. Archives Parlementaires, 24 August 1835.
23. E. Biré, *Victor Hugo après 1830* (1891), 98.
24. Dr L. Véron, *Mémoires d'un bourgeois de Paris* (1854), III, 61.
25. Cited in E. Asse (ed.), *Les Petits Romantiques* (1906), 167.
26. C. Maurice, *Le Courrier des Théâtres* (1845).
27. A. Barbier, *La Curée, Iambes et Poèmes* (1913), 11.
28. C. Baudelaire, *Le Salon de 1845, Curiosités aesthétiques* (1923), 7.
29. Ibid., 162.
30. *Le Journal des Débats*, 15 December 1836.
31. Baudelaire, op. cit., 7.
32. A. de Musset, op. cit., 26.
33. Baudelaire, *Le Salon de 1846*, op. cit., 194.
34. A. Etex, *Les Souvenirs d'un Artiste* (1877), 62.
35. "Fortunatus", *Le Rivarol de 1842* (1842), 16.
36. Sand, op. cit., 928.
37. H. Heine, "Musical feuilletons", *The Musical Quarterly*, New York, April 1922, 277.
38. Véron, op. cit., 172.

39. Ibid., 114.
40. Mme C. Jaubert, *Souvenirs* (1881), 41.
42. J. Janin, *Contes nouveaux* (1840), xxxvii.
42. Chasles, op. cit., 73.
43. Marquis A. L. de Custine, *Lettres du Marquis A. de Custine à Varnhagen d'Ense et Rahel Varnhagen d'Ense* (1870), 73.
44. M.-L. Pailleret, *François Buloz et ses amis* (1919), 386.
45. J. Méry, *Les Matinées du Louvre* (1856), 68.

21

The Supremacy of Guizot

"Comme un corbeau perché sur un maigre cyprès,
Il penche nuit et jour le nez dans sa poitrine
Sur un arbre sans fruit qu'il nomme sa doctrine."

("Like a crow perched on a meagre cypress tree
He leans night and day, nose on his chest,
On a fruitless tree he calls his doctrine.")[1]

During 1840, Louis-Philippe had grown increasingly conservative. The recrudescence of republican and Bonapartist activity, the labour unrest, demands for electoral reform and the diplomatic crisis had encouraged the opposition to speak in the revolutionary tones of the *parti du mouvement* in 1831. The King was less flexible than he had been then. Although initially he disliked Guizot for his part in the Coalition and believed Molé the natural leader of a pacific ministry because his friends had been foremost in the attack on Thiers, he turned to the former as the man best suited to pursue a policy of order at home and abroad. Guizot reunited the doctrinaires with the broad ranks of the conservative party, although not without difficulty, and by putting an end to the division which had agitated the political world since 1836, established a majority which was to prove fatally durable.*

With Montalivet as the King's representative and go-between, the Cabinet formed with remarkale speed and ease, the continuation of the European crisis persuading the politicians to lessen their pretensions and overcome their incompatibilities. Maréchal Soult became *président du conseil* and Minister of

* *Ed. Note.* David H. Pinkney, in his *Decisive Years in France 1840–47* (Princeton, New Jersey, 1986), has argued that historians generally have underestimated the importance of this period. Pinkney is on particularly strong ground regarding industrial take-off, diffusion of socialist thought, and the massive changes brought about by railway development. However, as the following chapters illustrate, from a political standpoint, the failure of the July Monarchy to adapt to change was perhaps the most significant element of the period.

War. Guizot regarded him as "a vulgar muddle-head"[2] but the prestige of the "illustrious sword" was needed to cover the unpopularity of the dominant figure who took the Ministry of Foreign Affairs. The price of Soult's co-operation was that his protégé, the clever but dishonest Teste, became responsible for Public Works. Comte Duchâtel was Minister of the Interior, Villemain Minister of Public Instruction and Amiral Duperré returned to the Navy Ministry. Humann, a difficult colleague but an effective administrator, took Finance, Cunin-Gridaine returned to Commerce and Martin was won over from the Molé group. The Cabinet was thus a talented and experienced one, not too biased towards the doctrinaires, but firmly conservative, consciously emulating Périer's imposition of authority after Laffitte's toleration of disorder. The ministry was announced on 29 October 1840 and the Bourse showed its approval by a rapid rise.

Guizot was an enigma to his compatriots. For the Parisian, he was doubly a foreigner, a mixture of meridional passion and of English "frigidity". Born of a bourgeois Protestant family at Nîmes, where the Revolution had manifested a violence from which his family suffered, he had spent a period at Geneva. In spite of his birth, he preferred septentrional populations, who had "more good sense, manliness, consistency and delicacy".[3] That he had been to Ghent to aid Louis XVIII against the falling Napoleon became a reiterated reproach of political opponents: his adherence to English ideas and membership of a religious minority alienated even some conservatives. Royer-Collard called him "an austere intriguer"[4] although he liked later to claim the qualification was unnecessary. Much of Guizot's unpopularity came from the combination of political skill and deviousness with an uncongenial stiffness and coldness. Beneath the exterior, he was in fact a man feeling strong jealousy and contempt and, more rarely, strong affection: but, albeit with passion, he believed in reason, logic and moderation. The intellectual approach, although frequently bent to personal advantage, dominated his political attitudes. "Guizot is capable of anything"[5] Thiers once remarked: his air of virtue made his political behaviour, no worse than his rival's, somehow more offensive. Because strongly convinced of the morality of his intentions, he was frequently unscrupulous in the means he used. Disinterested, except in the desire to wield power, leaving office poorer than he entered it and caring nothing for the honours or rewards of office, Guizot yet encouraged egoism and tolerated corruption: he allowed himself to be surrounded by men considerably less strict than himself, notably Génie, his secretary.

Guizot's passionate friendship with the Princesse de Lieven could not redeem him in the eyes of public opinion. This liaison, rooted in a shared grief at the death of children, loneliness and obsession with politics, seemed merely a ridiculous deviation on the part of the puritan he was believed to be. Louis-Philippe and the rest of Paris speculated on the degree of their intimacy, and laughed when they heard that the intellectual politician had persuaded the notoriously unbookish Princesse to read Dante. Guizot was determined to confront and conquer ridicule, and the Princesse added emotion to his struggle: "I love you; you love me," he wrote to her: "You are with me in everything I do, and, with you, everything is pleasing to me. Without you, my labours tire me, success quickly exhausts itself. . . . Thanks to you, there is not the least ennui, not the least lassitude."[6] The bourgeois also took pride in his intimacy with this *grande dame*, who provided him with a salon: she was pleased that her relationship with the French Foreign Minister brought the diplomats of Europe around her. Yet the fact that the Russian Princesse created an environment of cosmopolitan diplomatic high society, increased the patriots' suspicions, and her dislike for the commonplace and vulgar did much to remove Guizot from the realities of Parisian political life.

"I would much prefer to play tragedy with that man",[7] exclaimed Rachel observing Guizot at the tribune. Although not tall, he was able to dominate the Chamber, almost as Périer had done. Beneath a high brow of non-southern pallor, burned dark and piercing eyes: a sonorous voice was matched by an impression of scarcely restrained energy. There was none of Thiers's brilliance and flippancy, and Guizot at his worst would sermonise, but he could instil fear and respect, speak with a noble pride or make philosophy eloquent. He was equally capable of leaving his "presidential bench" for conspiratorial confabulations with back-bench supporters, but his true power over the governmental party rested in his oratory. And the success of this oratory depended upon a lack of qualifications and the transcendence of compromise by energy: Guizot's greatest speeches were prolonged and philosophical battle-cries. "I believe there is a sickness which besets our times . . . but I also believe in a remedy. . . . We are going to have to fight." Struggle was the condition of honour: "One must claim victory, not just peace".[8]

Guizot saw the July Monarchy as part of a historical movement, the progress of the middle classes. They were not merely a social phenomenon, but a beneficent and progressive force, a gregation of attributes, mostly virtuous; supporting both progress and stability, opposed alike to the disorders of socialism and the excesses of absolutism. "Enrich yourselves", Guizot's famous answer to demands for electoral reform, was not, therefore, a simple call to grab money. It was a Protestant's view that hard work and intelligence would be materially blessed, that civic virtue resided in a bourgeoisie whose earned rights could not be distributed to those of lesser ability. Now that legal equality and intellectual liberty were ensured, the old forces of nobility and Catholicism had ceased to be enemies, becoming necessary allies in the cause of order. He had not wished 1830 to take sovereignty from the Prince to give it to the people. Guizot's success lay in making negative sentiments inspiring. His personal courage concealed the timidity of his opinions, wrote Rémuset. "His speech is positive, even when his opinions are very little so."[9]

Guizot had learnt that no certainty could be based upon philosophies in an unsettled age, and that ideas were subservient to ambitions. Deviating from his doctrinaire past, he increasingly relied on interest groups, believing that the more powerful they were, the greater was their contribution to stability. Yet this reliance made immobility the basis of the ministerialist party. Whilst Guizot inspired it, Duchâtel, a more popular man, gave it organisation and persuaded where Guizot led. The Minister of the Interior had always considered "practical needs" more important than "abstraction and metaphysical fashionings".[10] The two men set about replacing themselves and their group at the head of the conservatives. However, they had lost to Thiers two of their leading followers, Rémusat and Duvergier, and some conservatives continued to regard the doctrinaires with dislike.

It was natural that the first attempt of Guizot to impose his domination should take an intellectual form. To create "a real and durable majority by knowledge of the harm its absence did us"[11], he attacked the forces of anarchy which Thiers had allowed to grow. He promised peace with honour abroad and strict action against strikes and riots at home. Thiers countered by attacking Guizot for humiliating France. Guizot was on weak ground, trying to separate himself from a policy he had served as ambassador, but Thiers, by the violence of his tone, seemed to prove the accusations against him, and he was further damaged by a hysterical speech from Jaubert, supporting him, in which the former minister attacked England in the most vitriolic terms. The *adresse* won a large majority, 247 to 161, an expression of the desire for peace. The Cabinet continued to fight a battle for the minds of the deputies, by encouraging Jouffroy, philosopher and deputy, to make his report on the *fonds secrets* in ideological terms. Political behaviour was pronounced inadequate to governmental institutions, an implication that no change would be made until the French became more conservative. There was no certain future for anyone in France, "the present always totters, the future remains an eternal enigma", the report stated, making pessimism part of a party programme.[12] The claim that the Cabinet would reconstruct the majority produced virulent debate in Chamber and press. Thiers claimed that governments should be formed in the centre, and advocated reforms in the September laws and electoral system which he had refused to consider when in power. Some moderate conservatives objected to the report as an attempt to make the governmental party doctrinaire. To the regret of the *Journal des Débats*, which had become almost hagiographic in its support of Guizot, the Cabinet retreated somewhat and made a less controversial call for unity, omitting the more debatable philosophical elements. Guizot was beginning to allow his ideas to be dominated by political tactics.

During 1841 the Foreign Minister was perpetually required to explain the difficult process of negotiating the Eastern question, but more embarrassing was the fact that Thiers had used the threat of war and absence of the Chambers, to publish an ordinance commencing the fortification of Paris. This, like the repeated parliamentary attempts to provide for Nemours, had become an obsession with the King who declared he thought to do more by it for French security than by changing frontiers. He also believed strongly in expenditure on projects using much labour. Napoleon made war to contain his army, Louis-Philippe told the Austrian ambassador: "Me, I must always provide a lot of work to restrain the heroes who are persuaded that I owe them my place."[13] But opponents claimed the *bastilles* were intended to repress insurrection, and the almost hysterical opposition led to the adoption of the plan for a continuous wall so positioned as to be of slight use against revolution. Indeed Guizot, Duchâtel and Montalivet lacked enthusiasm for the scheme, Humann feared its effect on the budget, and the *Débats* only supported it because Auguste Bertin de Vaux and Baron de Chabaud-Latour, shareholders of the newspaper, were aides-de-camp to the Duc d'Orléans.

The King persuaded the ministers to ask 140 million francs credit for the construction. When Soult spoke, he created renewed problems by advocating only his pet scheme of forts, which he believed superior to a wall. His retraction in face of royal annoyance gained the Marshal the nickname of "illustrious sword-sheath".[14] With Thiers's assistance, the measure was passed; he rallied the *gauche dynastique* to support the fortifications, which he proclaimed a patriotic duty, and he discussed with a strategic expertise which Guizot could not rival, the various plans, supporting that which had been accepted by the government and to which Soult was so unwillingly resigned. The measure passed with a large majority but for once the government had on its hands a struggle with the Upper House. Some peers had suburban properties whose charm would be spoilt by the fortifications, others objected to the expense, but most important was the opposition of Comte Molé and Chancelier Pasquier. This was largely the result of personal hostility to Guizot, but Molé justified it by presenting the fortifications as a challenge thrown at Europe and a threat to peace. His argument seemed proved by the speech which Bresson was persuaded to give, saying he knew by personal conversation with Prussian generals that they would fear such fortifications. This can hardly have improved the French European position and is one more sign of the inconvenience of parliamentary government in diplomacy. The King and the Duc d'Orléans (who wanted to speak in favour of the measure, but was prevented by the ministers) spared no efforts at persuasion. Molé and Pasquier responded by pressing legitimists who were usually absent, to come to express their hostility to the government. Although the issue could not really be in doubt, the vote of 148 to 91 none the less showed a remarkably large minority. The King was pleased with the result and grateful to Guizot for it, but it was one of those typically Orleanist victories where all parties emerged weakened. The King and Prince Royal were criticised by opponents of the measure for their interference, while the ministry had been shown divided and flexible before the royal will.

The government's promise of renewed dangerous opposition seemed to be proved by events of 1841. Although labour unrest had decreased and nothing paralleled the attempt of Prince Louis Napoleon, there was an attempt to kill one of the King's sons, there were severe disorders in southern France where troops had to be used, and the legimist and republican press increased their attacks on the regime and the King. The issue of electoral reform seemed to provide the opposition with a popular cause, and public opinion was making itself felt in protest and petition. Thiers had moved leftwards, effacing Barrot, many of whose followers were now looking to less moderate figures for leadership. Symptomatic was the election of the republican Ledru-Rollin as deputy for Le Mans after a campaign radically attacking the social order for which he was unsuccessfuly prosecuted. And in spite of the September laws, the regime remained vulnerable to journalistic attack. On 11 January 1841, the *Gazette de France* published three letters written in 1807 by the then Duc d'Orléans expressing hostility to Napoleon. This was embarrassing, because Louis-Philippe now liked to trade on the Empire, but a few days later, another legitimist paper published another three letters of greater import, but which were obvious forgeries. In one, Louis-Philippe promised to evacuate Algeria, in another congratulated himself for allowing the Poles to be crushed with such ease, and in a third stated that Paris was to be fortified so that the population could be crushed. The letters came at a time when the King's patriotism was daily impugned in the press as a result of the Eastern question collapse, and created a stir. Published in other legitimist and republican newspapers, they were the work of a woman who called herself Ida de Saint-Elme who, having lived a profitably immoral existence under the Empire, had since resorted to publishing fake memoirs and to blackmail. She had sold the letters which purported to have come from Talleyrand but were probably copied from a work of republican vituperation.

When the government decided to prosecute *La France* for its offence to the King, the editors could not produce the original letters. Berryer, defending the newspaper, made one of his best speeches in this poor cause. Because of the weakness of the libel laws, it was a political trial, and the jury acquitted. Since the prosecution had said that any king who had written such letters was a traitor, the opposition press was able to claim that the jury had found Louis-Philippe guilty of treachery. Although Guizot in the Chamber of Deputies pronounced the letters forgeries and formally protested against the lies therein, neither Berryer who had so successfully defended *La France*, nor Mauguin or Laffitte whose organs had retailed the libels as truth, dared rise to refute him. The opposition newspapers, however, acknowledged no defeat and it was the King's reputation which lost. The government continued its press trials, usually without much success. In September, a jury acquitted the *National* for a particularly vehement attack on the King. The appointment of the deputy Hébert, a strong doctrinaire and spiritual heir to Persil, as *procureur du roi* of Paris, was a sign of determination and it was Hébert who was charged with the prosecution of Dupoty, editor of the *Journal du Peuple*. This trial, for complicity in the Quénisset assassination attempt, was taken before the Chamber of Peers, as entitled by the September laws, rather than risk another acquittal.

In the summer of August 1841, the Duc d'Aumale was leading his troops which had served gloriously in Algeria, across France. At Marseilles and Lyons, cities not notable for their affection for the monarchy, he had been received with enthusiastic acclamation in working-class areas. In Paris, on 13 September, leading his regiment down one of the narrow streets of the Faubourg Saint-Antoine, a man shot at him from a few yards away; it missed, but killed the horse of the officer next to the Prince. "It appears that I begin to count for something"[15] remarked Aumale. The man who fired the pistol was an unintelligent fanatic named Quénisset, who frequented various secret societies, Les Travailleurs Égalitaires, Les Communistes, and Les Réformistes. Meeting at a wine merchant's, members of these groups read an inflammatory article by Dupoty in the communist *Journal du Peuple*, and Quénisset was pushed into his act of violence. Not only the failed assassin but two accomplices and Dupoty, charged with moral complicity, were taken before the Court of Peers. The journalist was jailed for five years: the others received the death sentence, which, as so often, was commuted by the King. Quénisset turned out to be the luckiest of the would-be assassins: having repented, he was deported to New Orleans where he married and named his son Gabriel, after Delessert, the prefect of police who had been kind to him.

Quénisset's act reminded men of the fragility of order. The provinces had recently been the scene of serious troubles. The "Humann census" had led, in the summer of 1841, to nation-wide disorders on a scale comparable to those of 1834. The Minister of Finance constantly complained of the budgetary deficit of 138 million francs, result of the war preparations of 1840, and of Thiers's extravagance. Humann, who had achieved a balance in the 1830s, was determined to do so again; he did not wish to have to impose a new tax, but to apply more strictly the existing taxes. His principal efforts were spent on the personal contribution and property taxes, which were based on an incompetently made registration dating from 1791. Humann's circular of February 1841 told the prefects to conduct a fresh registration of properties, their doors and windows, because many new buildings were not taxed. The minister found himself attacked for this by the opposition: "It is of a piece with the policy of contraband"[16] cried one deputy, in unsubtle reference to the rumoured origins of Humann's considerable fortune. The press wallowed in the emotional issue. The *Gazette de France* spoke of "the fiscal harpies about to pounce upon all house-tops, to enter every home": the proposals attacked small commerce by a reorganisation of the *patentes*, would lead to the demolition of buildings whose owners could not afford to pay tax on them, and would force the poor to brick up their windows.[17] Humann's bold and tactless speeches in Parliament, the government's foolishness in giving paid official financial posts to his nephew and to relatives of Guizot and Duperré, the decision to submit religious communities to taxation, led to a broad attack upon a justifiable reform.

At Toulouse in July, a secret society, Les Égalistes, pushed the population into rioting. The prefect made concessions to the unrest, and was immediately replaced. The municipal administration resigned in sympathy, and he was treated as a hero. The new prefect, Mahul, was greeted with a charivari of unusual violence, and the riots grew so threatening that he and other government representatives fled. This desertion was also punished by dismissal and order was restored by the army. Maurice Duval, *conseiller d'état* sent as government commissioner, dissolved the National Guard which had aided the protesters, and removed the municipal council which was dominated by legitimists and republicans. The legitimist domination of the local legal processes prevented any prosecution, but the census took place with cannon in evidence.

In other towns of the south-west there were similar but less violent disorders. At Albi and Montpellier there was stone-throwing and window-breaking. At Cahors crowds shouted "Long live Henri V! No census!" At Libourne, stones and seditious cries were hurled at tax collectors. All over France, in August and September, there were broken windows, and charivaris for prefects. Many owners closed workshops to allow their employees to protest. At Riom, the troops used the flats of their sabres to control stick-wielding crowds. At Clermont-Ferrand in September, there were grave disorders and rioters half-demolished the mayor's home and tried to burn the house of the chief of tax collection before troops fired at them. In the countryside around, elements of the *jacquerie* broke out where there was some communist influence amongst the peasantry. Elsewhere, as in 1830–31, a legitimist and Catholic peasantry attacked Orleanist and Protestant wealth. The *récensement* (census) was able to proceed once the army had mastered the serious protests: the results were a huge increase in receipts and proof that over half a million properties had previously escaped paying tax. The hatred he had aroused shortened the life of Humann, already unwell: in April 1842, he died at his desk, a martyr to the cause of a balanced budget.

The 1842 session opened in comparative calm, an opportunity for the deputies to enjoy political intrigue. Guizot's majority was not altogether firm. There were about 185 conservatives and 25 doctrinaires, about 20 each of republicans and legitimists and 100 each in the broad *gauche dynastique* and *centre gauche* groups. The government depended upon the support or at least the tolerance of various groups of the centre, for example the followers of Passy who numbered about thirty, and the smaller group around Dupin. Yet Dufaure and Passy were showing sympathy for electoral reform and early in 1841 voted against the government on this issue, nor could Guizot count on the loyalty of a group of about twenty conservatives who preferred Molé. Guizot attempted to ensure himself some of these by asking Passy to join the Cabinet as Minister of Finance. Passy refused, however, and it was Lacave-Laplagne, a previous occupant of the post, who took Humann's place.

A majority was least sure on the question of reciprocal "right of visit". France and Britain had agreed to allow each other's navies to detain ships sailing under their flags, suspected of participating in the slave trade. A new convention, altered to obtain European adhesion, had already been postponed by Guizot in personal revenge against Palmerston. The humanitarian measure would have probably passed easily enough had not Billault, deputy for Nantes, forced, in spite of his claim to liberalism, to represent the interests of its shipowners, made an eloquent speech against the proposal: the Chamber was easily roused by threats that England would be allowed to tyrannise the seas. Guizot doubtless remembered how Broglie in 1834 had been defeated by similar chauvinism over restitutions to the United States. When Jacques Lefebvre, rich banker and conservative deputy for Paris, doubtless thinking of his patriotic electors, proposed an amendment hostile to the measure, the Foreign Minister found it prudent to concede. He agreed to postpone French adhesion, and in spite of the annoyance of Europe, did not sign until 1845.

Elections were not only a means of trying to increase a majority, but also of strengthening loyalty by making its members dependent on the government. Those of July 1842 were held in a very calm atmosphere. The political crisis of 1839 and diplomatic crisis of 1840 were affairs of the past. Interests prevailed over issues: it was a fight over persons rather than over principles. However, because of the unpopularity of Guizot, many conservatives tended to separate themselves from the ministry, and many of them returned no more loyal than before. The resulting stalemate disappointed both government and opposition. Guizot blamed his party for the lack of success, accusing them of not fighting sufficiently boldly, but they realised that the electors did not want to be rallied to an uncompromising programme. The government majority remained theoretically sixty. The most threatening sign was the conservative collapse in Paris. Previously, five or six of the fourteen deputies of the Seine had been conservative: now there were only two, representing the wealthy Ier and IIe *arrondissements*. The dominance of the 200–300 franc taxpayers meant that Paris was *centre gauche*. There were also two republicans, Marie and Carnot, elected. This, announced the *National*, was a condemnation of the regime by the city which judged and executed governments.[18]

Scarcely were the elections over than the July Monarchy suffered a fatal blow. On 13 July 1840, the Duc d'Orléans decided to visit his parents at Neuilly: he drove himself from Paris in a low *calèche*. The horses were restive, and when they panicked at an obstacle, the frightened postilion ducked. The Duc, believing he had fallen off, leapt out: in doing so, he fell and hit his head on the cobbles, fracturing the skull. After a few hours he died, in the back room of the grocer's shop where he had been carried, his mother, father and other members of the family around him. The royal family was stricken by its grief. The Queen seemed to gain strength from the days and nights she spent beside the coffin, and tried to encourage her husband by reminding him of his duty to France. Louis-Philippe attempted to carry on administration, but would from time to time burst into uncontrollable sobbing: "Why is he dead, my poor son? I am the one who should have died!"[19] When the Prince, whom his brother Joinville called the "leader of tomorrow", had gone, the Orléans family lost much of its sense of purpose and malaise grew in the political world. The King's miraculous escapes from assassins had seemed to show the hand of God: now, Viennet asked, "Has God condemned us? Have we the right to overthrow one dynasty and replace it with a new one?"[20]

The tragedy occasioned a genuine display of public grief. An impressive requiem was chanted at Notre Dame which had been hung with black velvet: it was marred only by Laffitte who, as the oldest deputy, had to be granted the task of sprinkling the bier with holy water, and performed his duties in a perfunctory and undignified manner. The Duc d'Orléans was buried at Dreux, and at the spot where he had died, a funerary chapel was built. In it was erected an effigy of the Prince, watched over by an angel copied from a sculpture by his dead sister, Princesse Marie, and in the windows designed by Ingres, stood stained glass saints, whose faces were taken from members of the Orléans family, so that in Saint Philippe, the rather unsaintly features of the King gazed down on his son.

On 26 July 1842, Louis-Philippe gave a very emotional speech to the members of the two Chambers, telling them that it was necessary for France not to be exposed to an interruption in the exercise of royal authority. No regency had been provided for, and the government consulted various notabilities, Broglie, Thiers and even Barrot. The issue was hardly in doubt, for the wishes of the King and those of the deceased as expressed in his will were that the Duc de Nemours should become regent. Louis-Philippe imposed this choice on the Cabinet without discussion. The question was hardly academic, for the King was sixty-nine and his grandson, the Comte de Paris, heir to the throne, only four. Nemours had no ambition, which was in itself a recommendation. For the King and Guizot, he had the additional advantage of being a conservative who would do nothing to disturb the present government (indeed, Nemours shared his mother's regret at the occurrence of the July Revolution). The Duchesse d'Orléans was suspected of being too friendly with the opposition, and was credited with a feminine weakness more dangerous than Nemours's lack of popular appeal. Such factors influenced not only the government, but also Thiers. However, Lamartine took the opportunity of passing to the left and delivered a notable speech arguing that to grant the regency to Nemours was an abdication of national sovereignty. Barrot followed him and Tocqueville in asking that the Regent should be chosen by the Chamber: in presenting the choice "between the blind chance of birth and the judicious choice of the powers of the State"[21] he intended to attack merely the "quasi-legitimism" of conservative Orleanism, but inadvertently undermined the monarchical principle itself.

Guizot eloquently panegyrised the patriotism of the dead Prince and for once abandoned his party tactics to win support for Nemours by stressing that it was possible to be dynastic without being ministerial. Thiers brilliantly developed this theme, implicitly criticising the endemic French tendency to oppose not just a ministry but a constitution: the only way to improve a government was to show it that the advice given was that of a friend.[22] The speech was successful amongst the moderate opposition, and Thiers was warmly congratulated for it by Louis-Philippe. The majority for the Nemours regency was 310 to 94. A broad range of Orleanism had in these brief debates rallied to the bereaved King and what they believed the best interests of the regime. Dupin, Passy, Thiers and their followers had united with Guizot's ministerialists against the legitimists and republicans. The brief debate seemed to have strengthened the monarchy.

It also reinforced Guizot by dividing the opposition. Because Barrot had capitulated to the more radical elements in his party and spoken against Thiers, having promised he would be silent, relations between the two became very poor. Yet unexpectedly, this weakened opposition gained an important auxiliary. Concerning his poetry, Lamartine posed as a *grand seigneur*: he wrote quickly without deigning to revise. His politics were like this also, often poetic or romantic, with a certain lack of basic conviction, some good intention combined with much egoism, imagination predominating over realism. In the Chamber, his oratory was enjoyed, but he appeared too much the poet. Lamartine had tried to form a group which he called "the social party", which had some attraction for a few like himself who had formerly been legitimists and, whilst believing this a lost cause, found the bourgeois practicality of Orleanism distasteful. "The goal", declared Lamartine, for whom the goal was not only perfection but imminently attainable, "is the restoration of dignity and human morality to all the classes of which society is composed", by applying reason, justice and charity to political institutions.[23] He had hoped to do this through the conservative party and supported Molé in 1839 because he disliked both the doctrinaires and Thiers, and Molé seemed to offer the best chance for legitimists and Catholics to rally and bring their more spiritual conceptions to the regime, but became increasingly disillusioned with the conservatives. In 1842 Guizot tried to ensure his support by the offer of an embassy, but Lamartine wanted to become president of the Chamber and demanded ministerial aid. The Cabinet felt safer with Sauzet, however, who easily won, and Lamartine gained only the votes of the legitimists, a dozen Molé supporters and a few republicans.

Embittered by this humiliation, Lamartine moved to the opposition. Even whilst defending the King's government against the Coalition, he had warned that "France is bored" (a phrase which only attained its fame when repeated some years later) and stated the need for spiritual rebirth. Whereas Thiers found this in warfare, Lamartine believed in vague social and political changes, but found the ministers "implacable to all improvement".[24] By 1843, he had begun to attack "the reign in its entirety". To the bitterness of the former legitimist were added the resentments of thwarted ambition and the personal aspirations of the romantic. "I will turn boredom into insurrection, a revolution to drive away this nightmare",[25] he declared. This was *mal de siècle* made a political programme. His speech at the opening of the 1843 session announcing his conversion, created considerable effect. He put new life into the left, which, uninspired by the younger Garnier-Pagès's pallid leadership and rather worried by Ledru-Rollin's social radicalism, was inactive and depressed. The orator invoked the French Revolution, an event which had wracked every human soul, and created a torrent of ideas which could not be stemmed by a few interests grouped around a newly created monarchy.[26] Guizot powerfully defended his refusal to satisfy what he presented as demands for dangerous adventure. "Where do you come from then?" was his ironical question to Lamartine; one which however could be asked of many Orleanists, especially "the man of Ghent" himself.

More immediately dangerous was that Dufaure separated himself from the ministry, reducing its majority to thirty, worryingly vulnerable to the sudden squalls which could occur in the Chamber. Guizot and Duchâtel were pursuing the policy of buying off opposition which Thiers and Molé had previously used. Office was given to Molé supporters; first to Martin, then to Lacave-Laplagne, Amiral de Mackau became Minister of Marine in 1844, whilst Salvandy had been sent as ambassador to Madrid in 1841. Passy's acceptance of a peerage at the end of 1843 seriously weakened the new *tiers parti* which had formed around him and Dufaure. Also, the government made one appointment which would help to destroy the monarchy in the crisis of 1848. Until 1838 the National Guard had been well commanded by Général de Lobau, and from then until 1842 by Maréchal Gérard, who was at least prestigious and popular. Then a new commander had to be found, and Général Jacqueminot was chosen. Like his predecessors, he had served the Empire, but with little brilliance. He was chosen because of his wealth, the fact that he was typical of the Parisian bourgeois in his narrow but anti-aristocratic conservatism and had as a result become a spokesman for a large number of very average ministerial deputies: above all, he was the father-in-law of the Minister of the Interior.

In fact, Guizot, whilst giving the appearance of leadership, followed his majority, or at least, paid much respect to the opinions and prejudices of his most mediocre members. Such was the result of the silence of the Duc de Broglie, the loss of Rémusat and Duvergier, the alienation of Molé and other conservatives who differed from Guizot. The King complained that Guizot whilst not afraid of the parties of the opposition feared Jacques Lefebvre, and that this deputy feared the IIe *arrondissement*.[27] Thus the ministry of 29 October produced little of note in internal affairs, an economic improvement and the railway measures of 1842 being its only substantial achievements, but also made concessions to its friends on foreign affairs. It was to men like Lefebvre that Guizot sacrificed British goodwill over the right of visit, whilst Fulchiron and other protectionists forced him to abandon his, and the King's, desire for commercial agreement with Belgium.

Louis-Philippe had asked the Cabinet in 1842 to request again the grant for Nemours, and eventually in 1844 the ministers surrendered to the royal will. When the measure was considered by the bureaux, however, the ministerialists themselves caused the ministers to doubt their majority. The Cabinet behaved with embarrassed reticence, but the King forced the issue into the press, with damaging results. Guizot dared not proceed, and told the King that if he doubted his devotion, he would resign. Louis-Philippe grasped his minister's hands and told his "dear master" that he was more important to him than the Nemours's grant. On the occasion of the deputies' refusal to grant the King's request in 1840, Balzac had written in his *Revue Parisienne*, "everyone would firmly believe that the crown has the support of the bourgeois, that in all that which affects people there would exist a strong affection; this vote has been brought about by a cruel error".[28] This last attempt and its early withdrawal proved this still valid.

The ministry and the monarchy were morally, if not materially, weakened by another miscalculation, the "stigma". On coming of age, the Duc de Bordeaux, or Comte de Chambord as he was now known, had visited Rome in order, he said, to see the south of France. In November 1843, he installed himself in London in order to see the north. Over 800 legitimists travelled to the house in Belgrave Square to pay homage to Henri V. Although there were some workers and some women of Les Halles, intended to prove that legitimism was a national cause transcending the frontiers of class, over three-quarters of the visitors were aristocrats. There were many from families which also had Orleanist members – the Vicomte de Choiseul-Praslin, Comte Hippolyte de Tocqueville, a Broglie and a Montesquiou amongst others. There were two members of the Chamber of Peers, and Berryer, the Duc de Valmy, the Comte de La Rochejaquelein and two other deputies. As the speeches of Chateaubriand and others made obvious, this was an act of fealty to a king. Louis-Philippe was very angry. One deputy of the centre, a member of the commission on the 1844 *adresse*, had inserted the words "public conscience stigmatises culpable manifestations". The conservatives on the commission did not dare oppose this, nor did the King wish them to, and Jacqueminot threatened to introduce these words himself in an amendment if the Ministry did not officially endorse them. The use of the word "stigmatise" angered legitimists by insulting their aristocratic honour. None the less, Berryer was on weak ground when he tried to defend an act of allegiance to another monarch by men who had taken an oath to Louis-Philippe. The opposition of the left decided to support the legitimists in their defence, which became an attack on Guizot, although had the ministry opposed "stigma" they would doubtless have accused it of bowing to the legitimists.

The debate was extremely violent. Guizot was attacked for visiting Ghent in 1815 to carry the support of constitutional royalists to Louis XVIII, and was asked to explain the difference between his act and that of the legitimists. He rose amidst uproar. "I went to Ghent . . ." he began, provoking such cries of fury from the left that he could not make himself heard. The public galleries and legitimists joined to shout him down, and the ineffectual Sauzet, president of the Chamber, was unable to obtain order. Guizot remained calm and impassive, his head self-consciously high, defending his political integrity: "As for injuries, calumnies, words of wrath, you can multiply them, pile them up as much as you like; you will never raise them above the height of my disdain."[29]

The "stigmatisation" reopened the diminishing salon war. The debate between Orleanism and legitimism was resurrected with bitterness by such speeches as Dupin's attack on "an aristocracy too loyal to its antecedents".[30] Divisions within Orleanism were revealed: Guizot stood unhappily in the centre between those like Dupin and Jacqueminot who welcomed a chance to attack royalism, but others blamed his weakness in face of these bourgeois susceptibilities. The Comte de Carné, for example, refused to vote for the "stigmatisation", saying he did not wish to fight as many duels as he had cousins who had been to Belgrave Square; there were fourteen. Other conservative deputies, such as Janvier, who relied upon the votes of moderate legitimists, decided it was prudent to be absent during the vote. The most notable dissident, however, was Salvandy, who voted against the measure in spite of the fact that he had recently been nominated ambassador to Turin.

Louis-Philippe, who with old age was increasingly intolerant of opposition, drew his ambassador aside when he next visited the Tuileries, harangued him and seized his *grand cordon* of the Légion d'honneur saying "When I gave you this, Monsieur de Salvandy, I did not think that you would refuse to stigmatise men who violate their oath!"[31] The next day Salvandy resigned. As for "the stigmatised", as the five deputies were defiantly calling themselves, they stood for re-election after the vote and were triumphantly successful. The government made a serious tactical error in providing 3 millions for port improvements in Marseilles and Berryer was able to whip up his electorate against the attempt to bribe them. The left gave the legitimists their support, and in Brittany, La Rochejaquelein received the open assistance of the clergy, early signs of the problems which the government would shortly again face from the Church.

REFERENCES

1. A. de Vigny, *Journal* (1867), 90.
2. J. Naville (ed.), *Lettres de François Guizot et de la Princesse Lieven* (1963), III, 73.
3. Ibid., 84.
4. Baron P. de Barante, *Vie politique de M. Royer-Collard* (1861), 191.
5. Comte C. de Rémusat, *Mémoires de ma vie* (1958), IV, 60.
6. Naville, op. cit., III, 184.
7. A. de Faucigny-Lucinge, *Rachel et son temps* (1910), 94.
8. Archives Parlementaires, 3 January 1839, and Archives Nationales, 42.AP.35.
9. Rémusat, op. cit., III, 106.
10. L. Vitet, *Le Comte Duchâtel* (1895), 146.
11. Archives Nationales, 42.AP.35.
12. Archives Parlementaires, 23 December 1840.
13. Comte R. Apponyi, *Journal* (1913), III, 24.
14. L. Viennet, *Journal* (1955), 191.
15. G. Picot, *M. le duc d'Aumale* (1895), 146.
16. Archives Parlementaires, 21 July 1841.
17. *La Gazette de France*, 15 July 1841.
18. *Le National*, 29 July 1842.
19. Naville, op. cit., IV, 262.
20. Viennet, op. cit., 225..
21. Archives Parlementaires, 19 August 1842.
22. Ibid., 20 August 1842.
23. A. de Lamartine, *Discours politiques* (1878), 143.
24. Ibid., 145.
25. Lamartine, *Correspondance* (1882), III, 76.
26. Ibid., Archives Parlementaires, 4 January 1843.
27. Hugo, *Choses Vues* (1881), 83.
28. H. de Balzac, in *Revue Parisienne*, July 1840.
29. Archives Parlementaires, 8 January 1844.
30. Ibid., 7 January 1844.
31. Odilon Barrot, *Mémoires posthumes* (1875), II, 123.

22

Religion and Education

"Ni enfant, ni au collège, ni homme, je n'avais hanté les églises; ma réligion, si j'en avais une, n'avait ni rite ni symbole, et je ne croyais qu'à un Dieu sans forme, sans culte et sans révélation."

("Neither as a child, nor while at college, nor as a man, have I haunted churches; my religion, if I have one, has neither rites nor symbols, and I only believe in a God without form, without a cult, and without revelation.")[1]

After 1830, Pope Gregory XVI, desiring a quiet life for himself and his Church, had speedily recognised "carissimo in Christo Filio Nostro Ludovico-Philippo Francorum Regi Christianissimo". His nuncio attempted to reconcile royalists to the new regime and the radicalism of *L'Avenir* was repressed by Rome. The new Most Christian King, for whom the political role of religion was more important than its sacramental aspect, was sincere in wishing such Catholicism to flourish, but unfortunately for his regime, it was anathema both to those Catholics who refused a secondary role and to the anticlericalism not just of the *mouvement* but of many ministerialists. The need to humour the latter was responsible for petty persecutions which exacerbated mutual distrust. The destruction of Saint-Germain and the unfair blame attached to Archbishop de Quélen by the state which refused to repair the damage or even to allow the rebuilding of the Archbishop's palace, continued to rankle for some years. The laicisation of the Church of Sainte-Geneviève was another grievance: returned to the faith which built it by the Restoration but adopted by the crowd during *les glorieuses* as a resting place for their dead, the government surrendered and the church reverted to its revolutionary role as the Panthéon, secular shrine of the nation's heroes. In the 1832 budget, the payment to bishops was halved and in 1834, the opposition launched an attack on those bishoprics which had been added since Napoleon's Concordat. Broglie's government, embarrassed by the desertion of some of its supporters, tried, as Guizot would later over the attack on Jesuits, to persuade the Papacy to solve its problems for it: in this instance the Pope temporised, and the problem was submerged by other issues.

Such controversies made the episcopate a virtual enemy, moral and political. When, for example, Archbishop de Quélen fulminated against the secularisation of the Panthéon and the construction of a pediment which included anti-religious figures, "the crowned images of impious, licentious, corrupting writers",[2] the *Journal des Débats* replied with a vigorous defence of Voltaire and the secular state he stood for. Fieschi's assassination attempt brought the Archbishop to the Tuileries for the first time since 1830, but the King was enraged when in 1836, de Quélen announcing a Te Deum after the Alibaud attempt, did so without once referring to his royal rank. In 1837, the Garde des Sceaux, Persil, referred a statement made by de Quélen to the Conseil d'État which found it an abuse of the gallican laws. But after this, relations improved. The Molé government rebuilt Saint-Germain and created an archbishopric in Algeria. Archbishop de Quélen baptised the Comte de Paris in the royal chapel, although without making the event a demonstration of dynastic loyalty by the Church. His successor, Affre, had no loyalties to the *ancien régime*, but by this time educational controversies were causing a different mistrust between Church and state.

"Never has such an officially irreligious nation been seen",[3] Montalembert had written in 1830. This ceased to be true, but the July Monarchy never lost its secular prejudices. Some of its notabilities were genuine in their faith, but with varying degrees of sincerity or cynicism stressed the social utility of religion. The Protestant Guizot hoped that an alliance between Church and state, a system of education founded upon religious and moral principles would restrain the political disorders which derived from a search for earthly happiness. Tocqueville regarded religion as the answer to materialism: Cousin, speaking with less sincerity, saw it as a necessary consolation for the ignorant. Martin (du Nord), Minister of Justice and Religion, was a practising Catholic, but even he, wrote one satirist, appeared to consider "that priests can make excellent gendarmes".[4]

Gradually, the practice of Catholicism could emerge into a less obscure place in the nation's life, and adopt a positive posture. Laws of the Revolution had banned monastic orders from France without governmental authorisation, but the 1830 Charter appeared to remove this restriction. Dom Guéranger resuscitated the Benedictines at Solesmes in 1833, and Jesuits quietly returned without governmental obstacle. Lacordaire spoke from the pulpit of Notre Dame in the robes of the order of Saint Dominic which he had reintroduced into France: this would scarcely have been possible a few years earlier. In 1835, the Conférences de Notre Dame were inaugurated and crowds packed the cathedrals to hear sermons from Lacordaire and Ravignan, many of the younger generation amongst them; although the fact that there were twelve practising Catholics at the École Polytechnique in 1842 and that this was thought worthy of remark, testifies more perhaps to the previous irreligion than to the effect of the revival. Religion was no longer a subject for ridicule, the prerogative of women and peasants, but a force which appealed to many who felt that eighteenth-century scepticism had left emptiness behind it. The Garde des Sceaux's attendance at Lacordaire's sermons was a sign of governmental favour towards the Church: ironically it happened at a time when the demands of a section of Catholic opinion was increasingly embarrassing the government.

The regime was conscientious in its choice of bishops, and after two initial mistakes in its anxiety to promote men who were openly loyal to the new King, the majority of its appointees were worthy and apolitical, creating a younger, more intellectual and less aristocratic episcopate. To succeed de Quélen, in whom liberal Catholics found the Breton nobleman insufficiently absorbed in the priest,[5] Thiers, on the advice of Montalembert, chose Affre. There was hostility between the "Affreux" (Frightful), as their opponents termed those who appreciated the distance from the *ancien régime* which the new Archbishop represented, whilst high-society Catholics found unpleasing the manners, brusque to the point of coarseness, of this "upstart sacristan".[6] And Louis-Philippe, at first so delighted with "my archbishop" as he called him, would cry despairingly to the nuncio "Mio Dio! che sbaglio che abbiamo fatto! . . ." [My God! What a mistake we have made!][7] for Affre proved not to be a pliant tool to be charmed by royal disquisitions on the arcana of ecclesiastical ritual, but an obstinate defendant of Catholic demands. The Archbishop's position in fact resembled that of Louis-Philippe. Standing between the opposing forces of ultramontanism and gallicanism, amidst the conflict of political and Catholic demands in education, he trod a middle way with more honesty and less flexibility than the King. His career in the closing years of the July Monarchy was no more peaceful than de Quélen's had been, although very different, and his life ended violently during the 1848 Revolution.

Hostility between Church and state had been a crisis for those whose traditions had led them to believe in the alliance of throne and altar, but far greater problems faced Catholics in modern philosophy and industrial civilisation. Church recruitment was not keeping pace with the increase in population, still less with the growth of unbelief amongst the lower classes.* There were insufficient priests for existing churches, and many of the new towns were badly provided with churches, in spite of the government's building programme. Since the greater proportion of priests were of peasant origin, they preferred to minister in the countryside. The problems of class conflict and radical discontent had infiltrated the priesthood, notably the lower clergy, badly paid and often attracted by the ultramontanism preached earlier by *L'Avenir*.

The *Avenir* school had attacked the alliance of throne and altar, and they and their disciples continued to try to free Catholic action from all traces of

* *Ed. Note*. Edward Berenson, in *Populist Religion and Left-Wing Politics in France 1830–1852* (Princeton, New Jersey, 1984), recently has argued that "religiosity" was actually on the increase amongst members of the lower classes. However, this "religiosity" was not necessarily that of the orthodox Catholic Church. See Chapter 2 in particular.

royalism, often to the annoyance of legitimists. "These men cannot conceive that the good Lord can conduct his affairs in the absence of Henri V",[8] complained Lacordaire. However, many legitimists, such as Falloux, were willing to keep their politics out of their religion, and if the two creeds still often accompanied each other, they were no longer interdependent. At Madame de Swetchine's salon, irrespective of politics, gathered Montalembert, Lacordaire, the venerable Ballanche and young Vicomte de Falloux, Baron d'Eckstein, the grotesque Abbé de Genoude, and other representatives of progressive Catholic opinions.

Lacordaire was typical of a tendency in his century: he combined belief in progress with nostalgia for the distant past. Politically liberal and optimistic, he was spiritually anguished and practised methods of self-punishment more redolent of the Middle Ages which he romanticised than of the nineteenth century which he claimed to accept. His ideas of forming associations, creating a corporative society against egoism was a common reaction, but was more of the heart than the head. Yet it may well have been this contradiction and frequent vagueness which gave his oratory such power. The afternoon sermons which he delivered in Notre Dame became hugely popular events. Congregations of 10,000, which included political and artistic celebrities, crowded into the cathedral. It became as fashionable to go to hear him preach as it was to watch Rachel at the Théâtre Français. The latter reinterpreted classical drama for a romantic generation, the former revealed religion to it. Lacordaire made Catholicism a new crusade: he mixed ultramontanism with nationalism, giving France a role beside Rome in a fight for religion and democracy. He showed that he understood the pains of doubt and then overwhelmed with his emotional eloquence. Modern philosophy and psychology he injected into a theology whose dogmas he frequently made hazy. And in common with other romantics, his similes were daring, his metaphors frequently grotesque. Lacordiare was effective because he showed that he had understood the anguish of his age, and that he realised that France was in a state which was "irremedially new".[9] There were critics, however, the gallicans, the anti-romantics, many legitimists, and also Montalembert who, whilst electrified by the oratory, feared that a new idolatry of democracy would replace the old worship of monarchy.[10]

For the Comte de Montalembert, a liberal conservative with strong aristocratic reactions, did not share Lacordaire's optimistic assessment of the century. In 1835, he began to speak in the Chamber of Peers, using the language of *L'Avenir* to oppose the September laws, and demand full liberty in education and association for Catholics. Whilst sometimes shocked by his vehemence, many peers were pleased that heredity had delivered such an orator with its dying gasp. Montalembert believed that Catholics were in a position to make just demands of the state because they were no longer its enemy, but he quickly found that liberals distrusted him as a Catholic, whilst conservatives feared him as a revolutionary. He began to mobilise his support into a party.

Montalembert's preoccupations were political but *L'Avenir* had sown the seeds of "social Catholicism". Comte Charles de Coux continued to denounce the slavery and moral anarchy of industrialism in *L'Université Catholique* and *L'Univers*. He criticised the penal code which prevented workers' associations, which did not guarantee workers' rights, but which gave unlimited power to "captains of industry"[11] to buy labour as cheaply as they wished. Association and personal charity were the remedies, and it has to be admitted that his positive suggestions were more cautious than his criticisms. This was frequently to be the story of social Catholicism: its practitioners received from their religion a more penetrating insight into social ills, but the conservativism inherent in their upbringing and social station usually prevented the emergence of radical solutions. Many were aristocrats or legitimists, and whilst this made it easier for them to criticise industrial and bourgeois society, it meant that their proposals would tend to be paternalistic, with an agrarian bias. Even a political extremist such as the Vicomte de Cormenin could suggest no more than an increase in charity and, that typically Orleanist remedy for working-class problems, the *caisses d'épargnes*.

It was easier to attack a society whose pinnacle was not sacred, and the ending of Catholicism's political role opened the eyes of many believers to their social duties, in particular the young Fréderic Ozanam. Feeling himself and his friends to be in the situation of the early Christians in the decadent Roman Empire, he believed that social Catholicism would unite and strengthen them in zealous fervour. Thus he and his friends founded the Société de Saint-Vincent de Paul in 1833. The charitable organisation included all political beliefs, for Ozanam believed that France needed to lose her political spirit that religion might gain. He tried to model his association on the organisation of the early Christians, similar to the proselytising groups which republicans formed. Beginning in the slums of the Montagne de Sainte-Geneviève, he visited the poor at home, bringing them material assistance, helping with illness and bereavement whilst attempting to make conversions. By 1844 there were 32 centres in Paris, and another 109 in the provinces, the society as a whole having about 4,500 active members, and as many benefactors and honorary members. In 1847 it distributed nearly a million francs in charity. Working-class societies were formed in an attempt to have the poor help themselves, and successes were real even if only reaching a fragment of that indigent and irreligious mass which seemed to need moral and material assistance.

Vicomte Armand de Melun, believing that in Christian education lay the social regeneration of a diseased civilisation, created associations which provided formal teaching. L'Œuvre de Saint-Francis-Xavier organised courses of education which had a Christian bias, but gave also medical attention and material assistance, where workers such as Ledreuille and aristocrats like Falloux enrolled in a teaching body which instructed thousands. Melun, "on the same day haunting both garrets and salons",[12] was successful in bringing men of the world into charitable works and cognisance of proletarian problems. The society he created in 1846 assembled men of all parties such as Molé, Cormenin, Benoist d'Azy, Tocqueville and Montalembert with economists such as Blanqui, social Catholics such as Falloux, Coux and medical experts, notably Docteur Villermé. A pressure group was being formed which rivalled those which heretofore had thwarted isolated attempts at reform but 1848 destroyed its utility.

Much of the impulse came from upper-class guilt and fear. These charitable organisations worked with a new intensity and the contact they created between the privileged and the urban destitute was a striking innovation. These ministrations gave the poor more benevolence towards the rich, wrote Falloux; it familiarised the rich with the needs and the courageous qualities of the indigent; "in this reciprocal exchange, perhaps it is the rich who learn and gain the most".[13] These rich were, however, usually aristocrats or landowners; with the notable exception of the legitimist deputy Denis Benoist d'Azy, an industrialist and railway administrator, no important financiers or manufacturers were social Catholics. Although some notabilities such as Barante, Molé and Carné showed interest and gave patronage to some of their work, and Queen Marie-Amélie and the Prince de Joinville were generous contributors to Melun's Comité des Œuvres, a bureau which connected the charitable and the needy, Orleanist authorities were not often sympathetic, and looked with some suspicion at these associations. Social Catholicism began to influence opinion, but it achieved little in the way of legislation. The only notable product was the Child Labour Law of 1841, largely the work of Vicomte Alban de Villeneuve-Bargemont. Intended merely as a first step, the opposition it received prevented further progress, and his only other legislative achievement was the removal of official fees from the marriages of poor people.

Villeneuve-Bargemont and Melun realised that poverty in French society could not be solved by old methods, and social Catholicism was ahead of much other opinion in this. Many bishops were seriously concerned with charitable works, notably both the Paris archbishops of this period. Yet Affre's friendly review of Villeneuve-Bargemont's *Economie politique chrétienne* showed, by his stress on Christian virtues in the individual, that he had not understood the central point of the work; that the problems were so great that the state had to take action. The majority of leading churchmen restated the traditional attack upon usury, attacked materialism and egoism, which they associated with Protestantism and scepticism, and stressed the virtues of charity. Some of the bishops of the north where industrial problems were most evident, showed that they understood some of what was being argued. Cardinal de Croy, Archbishop of Rouen, took an initiative against the evils of child labour, and at Cambrai, Archbishop Giraud spoke forcibly of working-class problems, the insufficient pay and unemployment, and criticised the inhuman slavery into which employers forced so many of his flock. The police became worried by the activities of some priests. The most notable example was Abbé Ledreuille, himself of working-class origins, who warned the wealthy congregation of Saint-Roch that the gulf of hatred between rich and poor was widening, and that the poor, tired of waiting, would wreak vengeance if the rich failed to come to their aid. The government complained to Affre that this was an encouragement to social unrest, but the Archbishop excused it as a novel way of opening the purses of the wealthy. As working-class social and political agitation grew, the Church failed to play the sedative role which the government had expected of it.

The shadow of Napoleon fell over education as over so much else in France, in the form of the Université which had a monopoly position over education. This was attacked by Catholics for its secular influence and reviled or defended as symbolic of the modern state. Yet at the local level, education was often an arm of the Church. It seemed natural to the Restoration that the Minister of Public Instruction should also be responsible for religious affairs, and this was continued by the new regime until the Protestant Guizot decided it was unsuitable that he should hold this office and it became a fief of the Minister of Justice. For a while during the Restoration, the Catholics had succeeded in capturing the Université and it was then that three liberals who later became Ministers of Public Instruction under Louis-Philippe, Guizot, Cousin and Villemain, were dismissed. The year 1830 brought Cousin a hegemony in the world of education, but also strengthened the forces opposed to state interference in Catholic education. The new regime promised a reform of primary education, and this must count as one of its achievements, but it was the issue of religion and secondary education which really stirred passions.

In 1830, scarcely a quarter of the child population attended school, and the majority of adults were illiterate. The democratisation of society increased education for all age-groups. The Revolution inspired an interest in adult education, and the *Avenir* group had child instruction as one of its practical aims. The vast sales for Emile de Girardin's, and his emulators', self-education courses, revealed a public thirst for knowledge. Education seemed to more enlightened conservatives to be a necessary stabilising force in a society where disorder was endemic. "As soon as a people comes to know its rights, there is only one way to govern it, that is to instruct it",[14] proclaimed Girardin. Ignorance was destructive, literacy gave a man a share in civilisation. Guizot believed that only far in the future would education be politically relevant to the masses, but he believed that in the short term education, by being based on religion and morality, would teach the children of the poor to accept the foundations on which society was built. If they were taught to read when young, it was less likely that they would later take instruction from a republican like Martin Nadaud who used Lamennais's inflammatory *Paroles d'un croyant* as a textbook.

The succession of short-lived ministers meant that nothing was achieved until late in 1832 when Guizot obtained the post he was to occupy, with short interruptions, until 1836. The law of June 1833 for which he was responsible was intended to put primary education within the reach of all children. Each commune was obliged to possess a school or share it with neighbours, and provided lodging for a teacher to be paid at least 200 francs a year (not a very adequate sum). If the commune could not afford this, even with the imposition of a small extra tax authorised for the purpose, then the department or if necessary the state should meet the cost. Education was free for the poorest, and attendance was encouraged, although not compulsory. To supervise this, each commune should have a committee consisting of mayor, priest and three municipal councillors. The inclusion of the priest, which Guizot obtained from Parliament only with great difficulty, was intended to ensure that the education which the state was providing should be seen to be friendly to religion, but priest and mayor were often antipathetic, and the latter was given predominant power by the law, at the insistence of anticlerical deputies, creating here a microcosm of a national conflict. The establishment of a superior primary school in larger communes with a population of over 6,000, where more than the rudiments of reading and writing were taught, was intended to educate the children of the lower bourgeoisie, to prevent those parents who believed the average village school too rudimentary, from sending their children to the more prestigious colleges. These should be open to those whose parents could pay, wrote Cousin, whose observations on the Prussian system had some effect upon Guizot, "but it is necessary not to call them indiscreetly the inferior classes".[15] The law created a durable structure of primary education, which reflected the class basis of the July Monarchy.

It proved difficult to enforce even this very moderate reform. The mayors and local committees were often uneducated and parsimonious, and although it was a convention in rural areas that children attend only that half of the year they were unnecessary as labour, the population resisted attempts to educate the children. To overcome the resistance of the authorities, Guizot formed a body of inspectors who travelled the country, exhorting and reporting, but their effect was limited. And rarely were the teachers with their pittance, broad three-year course at the *école normale*, and certificate of morality from their home communes, figures of prestige. Guizot was frightened of educating them far above the low level at which they would have to teach. His circular describing the 1833 law to them, informed them that the government could not afford to pay them highly but that God would reward them if they performed their duties, which were to strengthen ideas of morality and order: "faith in Providence, the holiness of duty, submission to paternal authority, the respect due to the law, the prince, the rights of all, such are the sentiments that you will undertake to develop".[16]

The 1833 law made the foundation of Church independent schools easier, and the priest would naturally favour this rather than the communal school. Priest and teacher might be the only two literate men in the commune, and yet the difference between the philosophy of the seminary and of the *école normale* was considerable. None the less, with all these faults, Guizot's law did enable a considerable expansion in primary schooling. The number of primary schools increased by a third between 1833 and 1848, reaching about 40,000 in that year, but less than a fifth of these were for girls whose education continued to lag behind. Although about a quarter of boys, and more girls, still received no education, there were about 3.25 million children attending public and private schools by 1848, and literacy amongst conscripts had improved by over 10 per cent.

Secondary education was given to only about 69,000. Of these, 45 per cent were educated in private schools and the rest at the public colleges. The private institutions, however, existed by permission of the Université which imposed many restrictions upon them. It was able to control the route to higher education by obliging candidates for the *baccalauréat* to produce a certificate stating that they had prepared for the examination in a royal or communal college. Some of the private schools were *petits séminaires* where boys received instruction for the priesthood which many in fact did not enter, and which often gave an inadequate education. Thus both sides had complaints. Catholics claimed the 1830 Charter gave them liberty to teach, and to create their own schools without reference to the hostile Université: anticlericals argued that the existence of a separate education threatened national unity. Cousin asserted that the state was secular, so should be the Université which represented it, and its teaching.[17] He dominated the Université's *conseil royal*, a distinguished body (it included Villemain and Saint-Marc Girardin in literary departments and Thénard at the head of chemistry), which offended not only opponents but those within the Université who found their advancement closed by this oligarchy. A peer, Minister of Public Instruction in 1840, member of the Académie Française and Académie des Sciences Morales, president of various official bodies, Cousin had used his power, especially when director of the *écoles normales*, to propagate his eclectic system of philosophy which worshipped the Charter but was sceptical towards Christianity, and the teachers, "my regiment", were despatched to spread it in schools. There was increasing outcry at this. In 1837 Guizot attempted to end the Université monopoly, but this died with the Molé–Guizot Cabinet.

Three years later Cousin's proposals, less favourable to the Catholics, met a similar fate. He was succeeded by Villemain, a brilliant and popular lecturer in French literature, for whom the Chamber of Peers was merely a larger Academy and the Ministry of Public Instruction the highest academic accolade. Fully a product of the Université, Villemain believed in its monopoly and his project of 1841 retained independent schools under its irksome supervision in return for increasing their powers, and, moreover, brought the *petits séminaires* within its jurisdiction. The bishops, within whose charge these establishments lay, protested as one man. Brochures flooded the market, the *Univers* and *Ami de la Religion* vehemently attacked the proposals. Lacking the support of the other ministers, Villemain withdrew the bill, but a campaign had begun in the Catholic press and other newspapers, notably the *Presse*, which had some sympathy with the cause. In the Chamber of Deputies, the Comte de Carné, and in the Chamber of Peers, the Comte de Montalembert, continually harried the ministry, demanding the implementation of the promises of the Charter.

Montalembert became the Catholics' leading political figure and pamphleteer. His *Du Devoir des Catholiques dans la Question de la Liberté d'Enseignement* (1843) warned that the situation was urgent. France was becoming irreligious, the rule of scepticism was encouraged by the Université.

Catholics could not put their faith in King or Parliament, they must form their own party: "liberty is not received; it is conquered".[18] Montalembert had learnt from the failure of the *Avenir* that the co-operation of the hierarchy was important in forming a Catholic party. He was lucky that the threat to the *petits séminaires* had rallied the episcopate and that the new breed of bishops was willing to enter into the battle with the state whilst repudiating legitimism. Thus, Parisis, Bishop of Langres, in a brochure, *Du Silence et de la Publicité dans l'Eglise*, claimed that it was right that Catholics should use all means of publicity, and he admitted lay participation in Church matters and acknowledged in Montalembert the leader of a party. Learning from O'Connell and Cobden, the French peer showed himself their equal. He had a horror of timidity, a contempt for the bourgeois virtues of prudence and compromise. Vehement and provocative, he struggled remorselessly against the pusillanimity of his followers, and the compromises of the government. Many sympathisers found him too rash. Ozanam feared a Catholic party would prevent a Catholic nation. Montalembert himself later admitted the justice in some of the criticisms made of him, and regretted the extent of his opposition to the July Monarchy; for the Catholic party challenged the moral basis of the regime, although not in the interest of any other political opinion. Yet he was far from being the most violent. Respectable priests combed the Old Testament for insults, and claimed to find the works of Sade moral when compared with those of the anti-Jesuits Michelet and Libri.

Louis Veuillot took command of the *Univers* in 1842, and his caustic journalism imposed the heretofore obscure Catholic journal upon the attention of France, and envenomed the debate with his brutal attacks on the government and on Orleanist Voltaireanism. By 1844, the newspaper had a readership of 6,000: an extraordinary success for this, the first French religious daily paper. From a humble family which had suffered from the Revolution, Veuillot had pursued a career in Orleanist journalism, learning his trade as a polemicist, until a reconversion to Catholicism caused him to cease being the apologist of conservative politicians and to take a job on the *Univers*. becoming its principal editor after two years. It continued the work of *L'Avenir*: "The Gospel and the Charter, God and Liberty!"[19] was its battle cry. It was not merely concerned with liberty of education, although its most violent diatribes were inspired by this issue, but claimed complete liberty of the press and of association. In his radicalism, his loathing of Voltaireanism, there was a plebeian hatred of the bourgeoisie more extreme than Montalembert's aristocratic scorn. Opposition to certain aspects of the July Monarchy enabled him, like Genoude, to appear radical whilst being fundamentally reactionary. His journal appealed particularly to the lower clergy. He scorned the prudence of the ecclesiastical hierarchy, and disdained any qualified support.

It was not only such extreme Catholics who disliked the Université, but also opponents of the continuing Napoleonic state. The Catholics were not demanding the abolition of the Université, merely the ending of its monopoly position which extended over most education, primary and secondary. Thus

Tocqueville and his liberal supporters, Corcelles and Lasteyrie, lent support to the Catholic cause. Lamartine in his pamphlet, *L'État, l'Église, l'Enseignement*, argued like the *Avenir*: in return for surrendering power, the Church should be truly separate from the state and free from it. The left-wing *National*, disliking Cousin's Orleanist philosophy more than its Catholic opponents, agreed with the latter that the Université was a school of antisocial individualism. The moderates were increasingly isolated and the government with them, for the anticlericals, who had never completely ceased to warn of the terrifying spectacle of the "priest party", in their turn counter-attacked.

The Jesuits, the especial enemies of eighteenth-century sceptics and their spiritual heirs, provided an excellent target. Villemain treated the sober Académie to a polemic against them as opponents of liberty. Quinet and Michelet made many of their lectures anti-Jesuit diatribes and in their pamphlet, *Sur les Jésuites* (1843), presented the order as the permanent enemy of the French state, an organisation at the service of global reaction. Encouraged by the success of this and the enthusiasm of his "Marseillaise"-singing students, Michelet proceeded to publish *Du Prêtre, de la Femme, de la Famille*, which accused each priest of being a covert Jesuit, exerting power over France through women in the confessional. The government feared the jury too much to prosecute, but Salvandy, the new Minister of Public Instruction, dismissed Michelet and Quinet. In return, their admiring students howled abuse and anti-Jesuit slogans outside the minister's windows, and prevented a Catholic historian from lecturing at the Sorbonne. The most widely published and influential piece of propaganda opposed to the Jesuit order was, however, Eugène Sue's melodramatic serial *Le Juif Errant*, which portrayed members of the order stooping at nothing, as ready to indulge in a humble poisoning as to subvert the destiny of nations to achieve their hideous ends.

Thiers led the parliamentary attack against the Jesuits: for "the most beguiling of vulgar orators", as *L'Univers* called him, who knew how to be "Bonapartist, revolutionary, Voltairean, without ceasing in the least to be conservative",[20] this was an excellent issue which enabled him to represent the revolutionary tradition without threatening the social order. Dupin similarly, after his speeches of November 1843 and March 1844 demanding that the government be "implacable" towards the Jesuits (a word changed in the *Moniteur* to "inflexible"),[21] found himself more popular than at any time since his attacks on the Restoration. Since the Belgrave Square pilgrimage had put legitimism in the public mind again, Catholics were accused of attempting to subvert the regime, and a further wedge of division was introduced into the conflict.

Uneasily caught in this battle for the French soul, the government decided that only a measure closing or limiting the order would quieten the agitation, and after the bishops had refused, turned to the Papacy to save it. Comte Rossi, an academic of Italian origins and political friend of Guizot, was sent to Rome in March 1845 to try to persuade the Pope to close the Jesuit establishments in France. Eventually the persevering professor succeeded in wheedling from the Pope the agreement to tell the general of the order to ask the houses of Paris, Lyons and Avignon to disperse. Hearing rumours that Rossi's mission had failed, the *Constitutionnel* announced that the government would be interpellated and forced to a vote. The next day, however, the faces of the opposition fell; the *Moniteur* of 6 July 1845 announced that Rossi's negotiation "has achieved its goal. The Jesuit Congregation is going to cease existing in France and will disperse itself."[22] In fact, the *Moniteur* had exaggerated Rossi's despatch, itself an exaggeration of the Pope's concessions. The request to disperse meant that the Jesuits left their three largest centres, but not one of them had to leave France. It was a brilliant tactical success, but one of those victories which are signs of weakness. To win it, Rossi had warned the Pontiff of the fierceness of French anticlericalism, and Louis-Philippe threatened the nuncio with renewed uncontrollable violence such as that of February 1831. The Orleanist government also frightened the Pope by speaking of the schismatic and revolutionary threat of Mennaisianism, and the descendants of the *Avenir* were betrayed by the institution they exalted. Montalembert regretted the outcome, but had to admit the Jesuits were an embarrassment; he could now return to the fundamental issue, education, which in the meantime had reached a climax of bitterness.

Villemain, although less aggressive than Cousin, was no less a staunch upholder of the Université, and his second plan, produced early in 1844, preserved its predominance by making it the judge of all requests to open schools. The Catholic party agreed that this was unsatisfactory: almost all seventy-six bishops expressing the wish that teachers be examined by delegates of the state, but not of the hated Université, whilst anticlericals were furious that the *petits séminaires* had been left untouched.

When the peers debated the proposals, Montalembert showed that even with Broglie's alterations it was unacceptable to the Catholic party. Cousin, made eloquent with emotion over the attack on his revered institution, looking with horror at this glass of water, as if, scoffed Veuillot, he believed it poisoned by the Jesuits, begged Frenchmen to be united in education, in philosophy and in patriotism. Montalembert replied in his best vein with an attack on official eclecticism. Both men, opposing each other, reviled the government for its weakness, and the government, represented by Martin and Villemain, showed itself divided. Guizot's lofty generalities could not conceal the fact that his government dared take no firm decision. The proposal received a small majority, but only after an amendment which was almost a personal rebuff for Cousin by interfering with his philosophy teaching. Montalivet's support for this was seen as a reflection of the King's desire to placate the Catholics. The government, not having the courage to act for liberty, none the less found it politic to try to placate the Catholics by acting against the Université.

In the Lower Chamber, however, the commission, with the anticlerical Thiers as rapporteur and the *universitaires* in a majority, removed the amendments. The government foresaw the most embarrassing and violent clashes between Catholics and their opponents: it was rescued by an unfortunate event. Villemain was strained by the conflict and afflicted by family problems. The Jesuit menace which he had helped to raise had turned upon him. In his nervous delirium he would see the sinister black-cloaked forms advancing upon him, reproaching him for locking up his mad wife. With unseemly haste, Villemain was removed from the Cabinet (away from the battle, he soon recovered from his breakdown), his bill was withdrawn and the Comte de Salvandy, favourable to the Catholics, became Minister of Public Instruction. The government hoped a spell of inaction would end the confrontation, but neither side would allow this. And indeed, from fear of Dupin and its own anticlericals, by summoning Cardinal de Bonald of Lyons before the Conseil d'État for condemning a gallican manual, it did much to provoke Catholic opinion.

In 1846, Montalembert created a pressure group outside the party system, simply to achieve freedom of education. The Comité Electoral pour la Défense de la Liberté Religieuse sponsored candidates who declared themselves sympathetic to its aims. A central committee, which included Louis Veuillot and the legitimist journalist, Henri de Riancey, formed local branches. It aided journals and published pamphlets, of which Montalembert's *Du Devoir des Catholiques dans les Élections* was the most notable. In it, referring to his famous rallying call to the sons of the crusaders to battle against the sons of Voltaire, he attacked a third group, "the sons of Pontius Pilate".[23] The government which bought votes, which rested upon a sterile bureaucracy, which offered Catholics no more than the cheap bribery of bad sacred paintings for churches at election time, must be forced to grant their demands. "Go to the elections and, in exchange for your votes, demand that the deputies whom your votes will elect return the souls of your children to you."[24] Candidates who accepted the committee's line were returned in 146 *arrondissements*. A Protestant like Agénor de Gasparin who believed in liberty of education was preferred to an unenthusiastic Catholic, and party divisions were ignored in the spirit of the new religious politics.

It was difficult to transform this undoubted success into practical action, however, for the deputies favourable to the Catholic cause were divided between hostile parties. The initiative had to remain with the government, and eventually, in April 1847, Salvandy made new proposals. He attempted to satisfy everybody by orotund sentiments profusely thrown in all directions. The *petits séminaires* retained a privileged position: other independent schools would remain under surveillance from the state. Salvandy gave the Catholics a council as they had asked, but it was in fact strongly weighted in favour of the Université. Even moderate Catholics found the response to their campaign insulting, whilst the *universitaires* disliked the way in which their predominance was tortuously concealed. Not only the organs of the opposition attacked the proposals, but the *Journal des Débats* found it clumsy. Montalembert delivered a stinging attack upon it, and Affre had some sour interviews with the King: Church–state relations sank to a low point. Amidst general lack of enthusiasm, the proposals slumbered, to disappear in 1848: ironically the Revolution would provide the conservative majority which enabled Falloux to grant the Catholics their demands.

Shortly before the July Monarchy fell, Montalembert, in an oratorical duel with Guizot, had demanded liberty for the sake of the soul of a sick nation. The demand showed the distance which the Catholic Church had travelled since 1840. In spite of the failure to obtain liberty of education and defeat over the Jesuits, its position was vastly strengthened. If no mass conversion of the industrial lower classes had taken place, the former hatred had been diminished and Christianity been made intellectually respectable, positive and progressive. The July Monarchy failed to find a conservatism based upon tradition or upon morality. The bourgeoisie which was its mainstay was the product of revolution, and the monarchy fell because it failed to satisfy the lower echelons of this revolutionary bourgeoisie. Its attempts to do so had led to the sacrifice of the hereditary peerage, the lip-service to revolution, the various measures which offended the Church. It was over religion that its weakness was most clearly shown; from its hand-washing over the attack on Saint-Germain to its diplomatic transactions over the Jesuits. It hoped, mistakenly, by this to retain popular support, but it prevented itself from obtaining conservative or liberal credentials. A constitutional government which uses repressive measures is doubly weakened: it deserts its principles, and its petty repressions are usually doomed to be ineffectual.

REFERENCES

1. A. de Musset, *La Confession d'un enfant du siècle* (Larousse edition, 1870), 17.
2. *Journal des Débats*, 9 December 1837.
3. Comte C. de Montalembert, *Journal* (1911), 28.
4. "Fortunatus", *Le Rivarol de 1842* (1842), 8.
5. Count A. von Nesselrode, *Lettres et papiers du chancelier comte de Nesselrode, 1760–1850* (1908), VII, 281–2.
6. "Fortunatus", op. cit., 8.
7. R. P. Droulers, "La nonciature de Paris et les troubles sociaux-politiques sous la Monarchie de Juillet", *Saggi storico intorno di Papato* (Rome, 1959), 124.
8. H. D. Noble, *Lacordaire* (1935), 67.
9. Cited in P. Thureau-Dangin, *Histoire de la Monarchie de Juillet* (1897), V, 31.
10. Montalembert, *Correspondance* (1905), 463.
11. *L'Avenir*, 21 April 1831.
12. Vicomte A. de Melun, *Mémoires* (1891), II, 152.
13. Comte A. de Falloux, *Mémoires d'un royaliste* (1888), I, 160.
14. Emile de Girardin, *De l'Instruction publique en France* (1842), 7.
15. Victor Cousin, *De l'Instruction publique dans quelques pays de l'Allemagne* (*Œuvres*, 5e Série, 1855), I, 172.
16. J. Naville (ed.), *Lettres de François Guizot et de la Princesse Lieven* (1963), III, 348.
17. Cousin, op. cit., II, 134.

18. Montalembert, *Du Devoir des Catholiques dans les élections* (1842), 76.
19. *L'Univers*, 21 January 1845; *Journal des Débats*, 4 January 1839.
20. Ibid., 30 January 1846.
21. Archives Parlementaires, 16 March 1844.
22. *Le Moniteur*, 6 July 1845.
23. Montalembert, *Du devoir des catholiques dans les élections*, 37.
24. Ibid., 58.

23

Foreign Policy, 1841–1848

"La famille des Bourbons est un poignard que l'étranger en 1814 a laissé dans le coeur de la France: changez le manche comme il vous plaira, dorez la lame si vous voulez, le poignard reste poignard."

("The Bourbon family is a dagger which the foreigner left in the heart of France in 1814: change the haft if you please, gild the blade if you will, the dagger remains a dagger.")[1]

Threats of war receded after the crisis of 1840 had passed, and with internal disorder seemingly repressed and prosperity increasing, attention turned to Europe. It became habitual to lament the decline in French valour and prestige, and a nationalistic republicanism prevailed amongst the intelligentsia. In his opening lecture at the Collège de France in 1842, Quinet asked the French people if they were finished, answering for them with a resounding negative, to the applause of his students. Thiers's claim that his dream of a war, with British co-operation, to free Italy and Poland, was constantly thwarted by Louis-Philippe's "rage for peace",[2] was merely a milder version. It rested upon the same illusion, that Europe looked to France for leadership, and that Germans would surrender land to retain French friendship.[3] Victor Hugo, for example, believed that France could gain the Rhine frontier if she allowed the Germans to expand eastwards. This would usher in an age of eternal peace, "the Ocean under your eyes, England at your feet".[4]

The poem in which Hugo wrote these lines, commissioned for the inauguration of a statue to Napoleon but never publicly performed because of their Anglophobia, was an example of the way most Frenchmen looked at the world. For Michelet, Britain was "l'anti-France", the national spirits of the two countries were antithetical; the one, mercantile and egoistic, the other fraternal and libertarian. Even such a rational liberal as Tocqueville in a report to the *conseil général* of his department argued for a railway from the interior to the Channel, linked to steamships, so that a French army could be quickly landed on the English coast. The Eastern crisis turned dislike into loathing, later directed at the French government. In 1840 Faucher promised an English friend that there were many like himself who preferred greatness to liberty, and that France would soon revenge herself on her enemies.[5] Yet within a few months he was bitterly admitting that the English need not fear this "as long as the king lives and Monsieur Guizot remains his very humble instrument".[6] Even ministerialists made ritual anti-English statements in their electoral programmes, but commercial and financial interests held war in horror, and conservatives were divided between those who believed it would strengthen Orleanism and those who believed it would destroy all social order. Louis-Philippe declared that war would unleash anarchy: "the present state of all human minds would settle for nothing and would overthrow everything. The world shall be unkinged."[7] The relationship between Guizot and the King was one of confidence because they were in agreement; he interfered less and co-operated more, knowing that he could trust his Foreign Minister.

Guizot told Sainte-Aulaire that France had made too much noise in Europe, preferring the appearance to the reality, proposing to discard the old war cries and pursue partnership with the other powers.[8] The result was to make diplomacy more dependent upon personalities. Guizot strongly believed that "it is individuals who determine things"[9] and acted accordingly. His personal friendship with Lord Aberdeen, the British Tory Foreign Secretary, is the prime example: the cultivation of the Greek Prime Minister, Colettis, was another. The French ambassador to Greece was Piscatory, a political friend of Guizot's and the use of Rossi in Rome and Broglie in London were other instances where close political colleagues were used abroad and ties were strongest where ties of common political principle existed. "The success of the moderate party is everywhere our success",[10] Guizot told Broglie. France thus opposed Palmerston's encouragement of Italian nationalists and radicals in Switzerland and Spain. Such a policy was very vulnerable to political change, however. In Prussia, for example, Bresson's dominance in the late 1830s came to an end when a new king ascended the throne.

With Russia, relations remained as bad as ever. In 1841, the Russian ambassador was withdrawn from Paris because he had become doyen of the diplomatic corps, and the Tsar did not wish him to present the compliments of the New Year to Louis-Philippe as was the custom. France replied similarly, and a "cold war" resulted. Relations worsened further in 1843 when the Marquis de Custine published his book, *La Russie en 1839*, criticising from a conservative and Christian viewpoint the absolutism which reigned over a corrupt aristocracy and barbarous peasantry. Russian opinion was very angry and the French government somewhat embarrassed by the popularity of the work within France, and the approval given it by the *Journal des Débats*. If France was to have an alliance with a great power other than Britain, it had therefore to be with Austria, as in times of previous difficulties in 1835 and 1837. Guizot told Metternich that France was a conservative power: "We are placed upon very different points of the horizon, but we share the same horizon."[11]

Guizot opened the 1842 session declaring that although France was grateful to Britain for the *entente* in 1830, the alliance was no longer intimate. He sought good relations with all but no exclusive ties. In fact, the first actions taken by the man whom the opposition would later claim to be the servant of the British were hostile towards Britain. Bearing a grudge against Palmerston, Guizot obstructed the right of visit, which France had in principle accepted in 1833. He hastened to accept it when the Tories came to power, only to find that many deputies were uninterested in distinguishing between Palmerston and Aberdeen. Naval and mercantile pressure and simple chauvinism postponed agreement until 1845, when Broglie went to London and a new convention was signed substituting concerted naval action against the slave trade for the right of visit, a considerable success for the government.

It had been assisted by the fact that Lord Aberdeen shared with Guizot a contempt for chauvinism, and an academic frame of mind, and through meeting and correspondence created an amity extended to diplomacy. In the speech from the throne in December 1843, Louis-Philippe used the phrase which Aberdeen had applied to the friendly Anglo-French relationship, "the *entente cordiale*".[12] Cementing the *entente*, the visit of Queen Victoria and Prince Albert to France was a huge personal success. Legitimists were annoyed that a fellow sovereign had at last granted this recognition: diplomatists felt that France had attained a European respectability. Guizot compared himself with Joan of Arc having seen her king consecrated at Rheims, but predicted, "I will be burned some day, as she was. Not by the English however, I think."[13] Louis-Philippe showed he understood the inconveniences of the *entente* when he told Victor Hugo with his usual melancholy irony, that in returning the visit, he feared both a bad reception and too good a one. One would please the legitimists, the other would displease patriots: it was not easy to move when one was Louis-Philippe, he said.[14]

Constant friction threatened the *entente*, in Athens, Constantinople, Lisbon and Madrid, which the two foreign ministers overcame. But the greatest source of rivalry was colonial and led to a crisis whose effects in France resembled those of the Egyptian crisis. Guizot himself was no enthusiastic coloniser, but there were powerful pressure groups which demanded a world-wide presence for France: mercantile interests (especially in Bordeaux), Catholic missionaries, and above all the navy. Amiral Lalande used to communicate directly with journalists, often critically of the government, and he and other such strong-minded commanders as Dupetit-Thouars and de Hell would follow their own policies far away from the eyes of the government. Thiers had encouraged expansionism and ordered Amiral de Hell, governor of the Ile Bourbon, to extend French influence on Madagascar. To retain British friendship, Guizot retreated from the engagements made, after two ministers of marine had been forced to resign over the matter. Their replacement, Amiral de Mackau, himself developed expansionist ideas and had to be controlled through a limited budget. Guizot attempted to satisfy the pressure groups with a policy of maritime strongholds and trading posts, treaties being signed with chieftains on the Guinea and Gabon coasts. So much was colonisation subjugated to European affairs that France, for fear of alienating Spain, speedily renounced the intent to occupy an archipelago near the Philippines. As public opinion was uninterested in distant islands and the navy had not the power of the army, Guizot's conservative colonial policy created little outcry.

The great exception to this indifference was the Pritchard affair, because it involved national pride. Failing to gain a foothold in New Zealand, Admiral Dupetit-Thouars had been allowed to occupy the Marchesas Islands; thence he proceeded, without authorisation, to extend French protection over the Society Islands, then used the excuse of protecting French missionaries to annex Tahiti in November 1843. In the process, Dupetit-Thouars had ill-treated an unpleasant missionary, George Pritchard, fanatical Protestant and British consul. Expelled from Tahiti for rousing hostility to the French, Pritchard appeared in English eyes as a martyr. Aberdeen was forced to demand reparation, and Guizot, ever ready to sacrifice the appearance to the reality and who realised that Pritchard, who had been imprisoned for six days, should have been treated "more gentlemanlikely",[15] was prepared to make them. In the *Moniteur* on 26 February 1844, the French government disavowed Dupetit-Thouars's action and returned Tahiti to its previous state of protectorate. The opposition represented this as a gross humiliation. Carné, spokesman for dissident conservatives, questioned the Cabinet on its surrender, and Billault and Dufaure, leaders of the moderate opposition, attacked Guizot for betraying national interests to English arrogance. Thiers marked his return to politics after a long silence by a virulent attack and an unfavourable comparison of Guizot's ministry with the Restoration. Although the government defeated an attempt to censure it by 233 votes to 187, many of its own supporters were unhappy. Public opinion was roused to fury. In the theatres of Paris the audiences sang a chorus from Halévy's *Charles VI*, "Never in France, never will the English reign." The Prince de Joinville published his pamphlet, *L'État des forces navales de la France*, complaining that the French navy was incapable of fighting Britain: the *Journal des Débats* published a ministerial reproof to the Prince's criticism of his father's government. The *National* opened a subscription to offer a sword of honour to Dupetit-Thouars and students of the Ecole Polytechnique went publicly to the offices of the republican newspaper to add their names to the list.

Guizot, as with the right of visit, waited for passions to cool somewhat. Then, to maintain the *entente*, he agreed to award Pritchard an indemnity, which was never paid. The King and Guizot had been worried that this affair and rivalry for influence in Morocco, would end the *entente*, but it survived, and in October, the two paid a successful visit to England. The King was able to announce, in his speech in December 1844, the continued health of the *entente*, but the Chamber hardly rejoiced. Billault, who made a speciality of attacks on the government's submission to Britain, blamed the so-called ally for providing the arms with which the Moroccans had killed French soldiers. He was supported by other leaders of the moderate opposition who attacked with quite as much violence as the far left. The ministry received a very small majority of eight votes. Those who voted for the ministry became known as "pritchardistes", their names published in the opposition press and subject to obloquy.

The Pritchard affair dominated the last years of the reign. It became the leading item in the opposition's programme. A moral coalition formed between republicans and legitimists, members of the *centre gauche, gauche dynastique* and dissident conservatives. "Oh yes!" cried Lamartine, "peace! but one wants it to be dignified and solid; one prepares it; one does not ask for it!"[16] Molé attacked Guizot's "extreme policy, extreme even in its weaknesses".[17] The election addresses of 1846 were frequently anti-English, and the further left the more violent. Thus the republican Arago limited his manifesto to an attack on the British and Guizot, their servant. They had shot at the tricolour in Syria in 1840, humiliated his country in the Pritchard affair, and in Morocco were responsible for shedding French blood: "They have dared to tell France, the France of Marengo, of Austerlitz, of 1830: 'You will not go further!'"[18]

However, the hated alliance, for which Guizot and Louis-Philippe had sacrificed so much popularity, was falling apart, and as in 1836, Spain was the cause. The government was determined to follow what Louis-Philippe called "a policy of abstaining",[19] by which was meant the desire to influence events without being compromised by them. France continued to support the moderates against the radicals. The Comte de Salvandy, sent as ambassador to Madrid in 1841, refused to hand his letters of credence to the radical soldier who had grasped the regency: unable to hand them to the Queen herself, he returned to Paris. The problem was no longer the Carlists, but the conflict between radicals and moderates, and the marriage of Queen Isabella, who, now aged eleven, was thought to be marriageable within a year. The girl's mother wished for the Duc d'Aumale, but Louis-Philippe knew such a marriage would ruin the *entente*, and, worse, commit France to support for Spain: a revolution in Madrid which forced Aumale and his wife to flee across the border would play into the hands of Thiers and Barrot. However, the King was determined to avoid the British and Spanish radical choice, Leopold of Saxe-Coburg, and insisted that a husband should be drawn from the ranks of the Spanish and Neapolitan Bourbons. The French fostered a proposal that the son of Don Carlos should marry Isabella, and to please Metternich even tolerated the Austrian suggestion that the two should hold equal rights. Britain, however, rejected this, but in 1843 agreed with France to promote the candidature of the Duke of Cadiz, the Queen's cousin, a demonstration of the *entente cordiale*. The Tories were willing to see the French-supported *moderados* attain power, Sainte-Aulaire was on good terms with Aberdeen, and in all areas where there had been differences, an attempt was being made to heal them. Aberdeen allowed Guizot to understand that he favoured a Bourbon marriage but would not commit himself on paper, both sides fearing a conflict of interests if they were too concrete: thus, out of a wish to placate, grew the origins of the fatal misunderstanding.

The French now began to favour a Neapolitan candidate. In 1843 Aumale undertook a socially successful visit through Italy. France, skilfully and opulently represented at Naples by the Duc de Montebello, was gaining influence and such a marriage would prove the close links between the three Bourbon courts. Bresson, who had been successful in negotiating the marriage of the Duc d'Orléans, was sent to Madrid as ambassador in order to promote the desired alliance. Negotiations continued in London, Paris and Naples; Bresson and Bulwer, his English counterpart, intrigued against each other in Madrid whilst the *entente* underwent the Pritchard crisis. Guizot had seen the marriage of his sovereign's youngest son, the Duc de Montpensier, to Isabella's younger sister as a trump to be used against a Saxe-Coburg. Bresson, his position somewhat weakened by attacks on him in the French press and by the *Débats* criticising the Spanish government (not the first time the conservative newspaper had thus embarrassed the ministry it supported), used this card in his individual brand of negotiation. The neurotic diplomatist, struggling for influence against Bulwer, saw the very existence of the Orléans dynasty at stake. He encouraged the Queen Mother to request the Duc for her younger daughter. The French government welcomed this but, worried by British reactions, wanted to postpone it until Isabella had produced a child. When Guizot saw Aberdeen at Eu in September 1845, he assured him that the Montpensier marriage was out of the question for three or four years, whilst Aberdeen promised that Britain would not encourage the Coburg candidature. This visit marked the illusory high point of the *entente*: "It is even more than an *entente*; it is concord",[20] wrote Guizot. Nevertheless when Spain turned against a Neapolitan prince, with Bulwer continuing his intrigues, Sainte-Aulaire in February 1846 gave Aberdeen a memorandum stating that if Isabella seemed about to marry a prince not blessed with Bourbon blood, France considered herself free to offer Montpensier either to the Queen or her sister.

The crisis broke in June when the Queen Mother decided to espouse the Saxe-Coburg cause, finding her daughter's cousin neither prestigious nor attractive. Worse, the Tories fell and Palmerston reoccupied the Foreign Office. "He is the enemy of my house"[21] Louis-Philippe said of him, with justification. He and Guizot were quick to believe the worst of Palmerston, and given his previous behaviour, there was no reason for them to have done otherwise.[22] Only Bresson rejoiced, for he saw that at last his opportunity had come: "You are a thousand times disengaged and freed by the conduct of the English agents",[23] he told Guizot.

Guizot would not immediately break the Eu agreement, considerably modified though it had been, but he allowed Bresson enough latitude for the ambassador to assure the Spanish that Montpensier could marry the younger daughter at the same time as the Queen's marriage. Louis-Philippe was shocked when he heard of this engagement, and it needed proof that Palmerston was supporting the radicals in Madrid and proposing the Saxe-Coburg Prince for Isabella's sister, to make him alter his determination to disavow Bresson. "I have never betrayed anyone, and I will not today begin to allow anyone to be betrayed under my name",[24] he had written angrily to Guizot: now the Foreign Minister convinced the King that it was he who was being deceived. "It is necessary to trade blow for blow with him"[25] he decided, but word still went to try to restrain Bresson on simultaneity of the marriages. Palmerston had blundered: thinking to frighten France, he had in fact given Guizot a reason to break a verbal agreement, welcomed joyfully by Bresson, but accepted only with great reluctance by Louis-Philippe. Palmerston had also frightened the Spanish Queen Mother: she put herself in Bresson's hands, and accepted the Duke of Cadiz for Isabella on condition that her younger daughter was allowed to marry the Duc de Montpensier at the same time.

"Let us dare to merit victory. The throne of Spain is worth this gamble"[26] Bresson encouraged Guizot. The urging of his Foreign Minister and a letter from Queen Cristina, finally overcame the King's scruples. On 15 August he made a family decision consulting his wife, sister and eldest son. He had little choice: a refusal would have led to Palmerston's triumph. On the 17th, Guizot was able to tell Bresson that the Montpensier marriage might be associated with the Isabella–Cadiz contract, but that this should be signed and celebrated first. The decision once made, the formalities were quickly completed, and on 10 October, in spite of Palmerston's threats, the youngest son of Louis-Philippe married the Infanta of Spain. Guizot's hope that only Palmerston would be seriously annoyed was proved false. Palmerston was furious, but so was Queen Victoria; so were the Tories, and even Aberdeen wrote a wounded letter to Guizot. Yet the British accusations of French bad faith had no justification. Guizot had repeated that a Saxe-Coburg marriage released the French from their agreement to postpone Montpensier's marriage, and to know that Palmerston was trying to have his candidate marry the younger daughter to prevent this altogether, may be considered excellent grounds for breaking a gentleman's agreement when one of the gentlemen was no longer in office. Palmerston did not easily accept defeat. He tried to have Isabella's marriage annulled on the grounds of the poor quality of the Duke of Cadiz (had the choice been left to the unfortunate young Queen, she would undoubtedly have taken Montpensier): the French ambassador at Rome, Comte Rossi, made sure that the Papacy would resist any such intrigue. Bresson, compromised by his ascendancy at Madrid, had to be moved, but could only be transferred to a capital where relations with Britain were not of great importance, and was therefore sent to Naples. The unfortunate man felt this to be demotion and, shortly after arriving at his new embassy, cut his throat.

Guizot's triumph was almost as embarrassing as his retreat over Pritchard. Public opinion did not thank him for obtaining a good marriage for Montpensier although it would undoubtedly have raged over any humiliation. Those ministers who believed most strongly in the value of the British alliance, notably Duchâtel, criticised the sacrifice made for a small piece of dynastic prestige. Thiers and other members of the opposition now made themselves the champions of the alliance, and Molé cultivated the acquaintance of the British ambassador. The latter, Lord Normanby, behaved in a fashion which heretofore Louis-Philippe had to suffer only from the Russians: he refused to be presented to the Duc and Duchesse de Montpensier and delivered a calculated insult to Guizot by withdrawing an invitation to an embassy reception. Ministerialists therefore boycotted that event and went instead to the Foreign Ministry. After Guizot's speech on the matter, Palmerston demanded an apology threatening to withdraw ambassadors, but was overruled by his colleagues, and Apponyi, Austrian ambassador to France, obtained from Guizot and Normanby expressions of regret which passed as apologies. Palmerston attempted a diplomatic attack on France, but it failed because the conservative powers by this time had come to prefer Guizot. The sending of the Duc de Broglie to London as ambassador in July 1847 helped to normalise relations somewhat, but even Broglie, who earlier had been apostle and ideologue of the English alliance, now understood the difficulties of any satisfactory alliance with a country represented by Palmerston.

As before, when relations with England were poor, Austria was regarded more favourably. Guizot wrote to his ambassador in Vienna, the Comte de Flahaut, hoping that Metternich would observe the contrast between himself and Palmerston, and distinguish "the conservative minister from the muddle-headed minister".[27] France and Austria co-operated against what Guizot called Swiss "provocative radicalism".[28] In the war of the Sonderbund, the French government was opposed to the radical cantons, and its attempts at mediation tended to favour the pro-clerical cantons. Guizot was attacked by all sides: the left believed in aid to the radicals, and the Catholic party, Montalembert eloquently at their head, demanded assistance for the dissidents. But he could not allow Austria to act for fear of alienating French liberal opinion, whilst Palmerston opposed constructive action because he wanted the radicals to win the conflict. In the war, France gave secret aid to conservative and Catholic cantons, but with no success. Fundamentally she was impotent as on other occasions where Britain would not support her and public opinion opposed Austria. She had, for example been powerless when Cracow, the last tiny relic of Polish independence, had been swallowed up by Austria. With Britain refusing to co-operate, Guizot made a restrained protest. The Paris press, however, displayed its usual pro-Polish fervour, with the *Débats* rivalling the newspapers of the left in angry emotionalism. In Italy also, the conservatism in Orleanist foreign policy had come to predominate over the early encouragements to constitutionalism. Louis-Philippe regretted the death of the moderate but conservative Pope Gregory XVI, and hoped for a similar replacement. "What I want is a peaceful Pope; there is enough trouble in the world",[29] he told Prince Albert de Broglie, leaving for Rome to take up a diplomatic appointment. France was surprised by Pius IX and up to a point encouraged him, whilst finding certain of his actions excessively radical. By late 1847, the French government was worried by signs of revolutionary activity, and Rossi was instructed to try to dampen these developments. France's position in Italy remained as weak as it had been since 1830, too cautious for the nationalists, too liberal for the conservatives.

That she did not desire a change in the boundaries established by the Congress of Vienna meant that France inevitably was more a conservative than a liberal power. Guizot did not share the illusions of the left that German nationalism was compatible with French expansion. Instead, France sought to maintain the independence of the smaller states of Italy and Germany. This realism was combined with a strong pacific principle and belief in a European legality. Regretting a rivalry between British and French agents in Syria which exacerbated conflict between sects, Guizot asked himself wearily whether he and Aberdeen could ever suppress "that which gains nothing for our two countries and causes much harm to thousands of men who pay with their lives for the egoism" of their agents.[30] French gunboat diplomacy had always been moderate and justified, taken after grievous ill treatment of French subjects: thus Louis-Philippe refused to claim war costs from Morocco in 1844. "That would be repugnant to my feelings as a man and as the leader of a state such as France",[31] because poor Moroccans would be forced to pay for the crimes of their sovereign. Unfortunately, the King's humanitarianism and his moderation, both of which he imprinted upon the foreign policy of the period, were unfashionable qualities. Haussonville's claim that by 1848 France was the arbiter of Europe because Palmerston had isolated Britain,[32] was perhaps an exaggeration: none the less France was almost wholly accepted as a partner in the European consort. Now Britain attracted the odium of the conservative powers but, possessing greater material strength and internal unity than Orleanist France, she was better equipped to stand alone. Yet at the moment when it seemed that Europe had finally accepted the July Monarchy, it collapsed from within.

REFERENCES

1. E. Quinet, *Œuvres*, (1877–1879) III, 267.
2. Ibid., 290. N. W. Senior, *Conversations with M. Thiers, M. Guizot and other Distinguished Persons during the Second Empire* (1878), I, 130–1.
3. Gérard de Nerval, *L'Allemagne* (*Œuvres*, 1960), 731.
4. V. Hugo, *Poésies complètes* (1890), 210.
5. L. Faucher, *Biographie et correspondance* (1875), 262.
6. Ibid., 258.
7. *Revue Rétrospective* (1848), 364 and 380.
8. Cited by Comte de Saint-Aulaire in *La Revue de Paris*, 15 March 1925, 259–60.
9. Baron P. de Barante, *Souvenirs* (1890), VI, 586.
10. Archives Nationales, 42.AP.214, Guizot to Broglie, 30 July 1847.
11. Prince C. W. von Metternich-Winneburg, *Mémoires* (1883), VII, 400–1.
12. Archives Parlementaires, 27 December 1843.
13. J. Naville (ed.), *Lettres de François Guizot et de la Princesse de Lieven* (1963), III, 96.
14. Hugo, *Choses Vues* (1887), 83.
15. Naville, op. cit., III, 98.

16. Archives Parlementaires, 3 January 1845.
17. Ibid., Chambre des Pairs, 2 January 1845.
18. Archives Nationales, 220.AP.18.
19. *Revue Rétrospective*, 151.
20. Affaires étrangères, Angleterre, 665 no. 66, 13 September 1845.
21. C. F. Greville, *Memoirs* (1874), iii, 345.
22. Naville, op. cit., iii, 246.
23. *Revue Rétrospective*, 181.
24. Ibid., 182.
25. Ibid., 185.
26. Ibid., 320.
27. Archives Nationales, 42.AP.9, Guizot to Flahaut, 14 November 1846.
28. Comte J. O. d'Haussonville, *Histoire de la politique extérieure du gouvernement François* (1850), ii, 325.
29. Prince A. de Broglie, "Souvenirs", *Revue des Deux Mondes* (April 1895), 345.
30. Naville, op. cit., iii, 171–2.
31. *Revue Rétrospective*, 249.
32. D'Haussonville, op. cit., ii, 380.

24

The Structure of Society

"Il n'y a plus de bourgeois depuis que le bourgeois se sert lui-même de cette injure."
"There are no more bourgeois ever since the bourgeois gave himself that insult."[1]

"Il est, il est sur terre une infernale cuve:
On la nomme Paris; c'est une large étuve,
Une fosse de pierre aux immenses contours
Qu'une eau jaune et terreuse enferme à triples tours;
C'est un volcan fumeux et toujours en haleine
Qui remue à longs flots de la matière humaine. . . ."

"There is, there is on earth an infernal cistern:
It is named Paris; it is a large sweating-room,
A pit of stone with immense circumference
Which a dirty yellow water encloses in three turns;
It is a fuming volcano always active
Which spews long waves of human material. . . ."[3]

The population of France was 35,402,000 in 1846, representing an increase of almost 30 per cent since 1801. This growth was felt most in the countryside where rural over-population became a problem of which the authorities were increasingly aware. Some, like the prefect Dunoyer, advocated birth-control and late marriage: simple starvation was the real check on population, however. The mortality figures per 1,000 were 34 in the cholera years, falling to 27.4 in the prosperous years of the 1840s, rising to 31.1 in 1846–48. Rural families emigrated to towns in search of work or charity, and in a dozen overwhelmingly agricultural departments the population diminished or was stationary. Thus the July Monarchy was a period of considerable urban expansion. Between 1831, with one commercial crisis, and 1846, when another began, the population of larger towns, the 363 prefectures and sub-prefectures, increased by about 22 per cent, considerably more than the proportional increase in French population during this period, or than the increase in the previous thirty years.[3]

In spite of the cholera in 1832 and other, smaller, more localised outbreaks, the population was becoming less unhealthy. Horrific as industrial conditions often were, purpose-built factories were more hygienic and safer than attics crammed with machines. Although an ignorant population was opposed to it, the campaign for vaccination was having some effect, as were more doctors, hospitals and a greater use of soap. The breakdown of morality as traditional rural society began in some places to dissolve, may have increased the birth-rate. Infant mortality was still high, 23 per 1,000 and about 28 per 1,000 in industrial towns, but this was an improvement on previous proportions. France was a country of emigration, from country to town, from town abroad. The numbers congregating at Le Havre waiting for the boat to New York, were a reflection of the economic condition of France. The United States, the destination of most French *émigrés*, took between 3,000 and 4,000 Frenchmen a year, but more in the bad years 1832–33, 1839–41 and the number shot up to 20,000 in 1847.[4] Algeria began to provide another destination when, in the 1840s, colonisation at last became possible there. But most of those who left the countryside flocked to overcrowded Paris or Lyons.

In spite of this movement, France remained predominantly an agricultural nation. Of the 25 per cent who may be termed town-dwellers, over half lived in towns with less than 10,000 inhabitants, and there were 15 departments which had no towns this size. Over 60 per cent of Frenchmen were directly involved in farming and many more worked in trades reliant upon it. Agriculture and its industries were highly vulnerable to climate, and especially so the owners of small plots which, although they occupied one-fifth of French agricultural land, were four-fifths of the landowners. In the 1830s, almost half was cultivated by share-cropping, although simple tenancy was tending to replace this everywhere. This inefficient division of land was attacked by most commentators from the reactionary Rubichon to the rationalist *Journal des Débats*, but, sanctified by custom and recent political change, could not easily be reversed. Improved farming methods and efforts by wealthier landowners began to compensate for it. The "internal emigration" of legitimist aristocrats led to much land improvement and greater interest in farming. Many improved the roads to estates which previously they had visited only in summer and which winter weather rendered impassable mud tracks: they attempted to link scattered possessions and introduced new crops and machinery.

There were also attempts to begin cultivation of common land, but the government hesitated to undertake reform itself for fear of popular resistance, being told by the *conseils généraux* that the poorest peasants relied upon it. However, it supported this and other methods of land reclamation and rationalisation. There was a general tendency to replace the triennial fallow with a rotation system involving potatoes. Although in north and central France, wheat was replacing rye, rye bread remained most peasants' staple food. Increasingly, potatoes were a vital part of the diet, especially in the north, yet agricultural improvements could scarcely keep pace with the growth in population, and bore fruit only later in the century. Famine remained a real threat, and a bad harvest brought thousands to the edge of starvation, most notably in 1846 and 1847.

The routines, rituals and risks of rural life still impinged on industry, in workers' traditions, reliance upon raw materials or climatic energy sources. As in agriculture itself the old seasonal habits continued, so in some small towns industrial production virtually ceased at harvest time. Yet mechanisation of methods and the demands of the industrial system were changing farming substantially. Especially in the north, the metal plough began to replace wooden instruments. Improved techniques made gleaning, one of the traditional privileges of the worker, an increasingly jejune endeavour. And industry affected the crops grown: sugar beet production rose almost ninefold during the July Monarchy to supply the northern factories which were turning sugar from a luxury into a common article. Silk production in the Rhône valley increased to feed the workshops of Nimes and Lyons. Around the new industrial towns intensive vegetable growing provided the populations with potatoes, and cows were brought nearer the towns to enable the wealthier inhabitants to drink fresh milk.

The government established a Conseil Général de l'Agriculture, beside those of commerce and manufacture, over half of whose members were deputies or peers, including the president Duc Decazes, an influential landowner and industrialist, and Général Bugeaud. Mathieu de Dombasle, the leading agronomist, was a member and lent his support to the proponents of reform. In the 1840s it was reft by a division between the protectionist majority, of which Decazes as cattle-raiser and metallurgist was doubly a strong supporter, and a free-trade minority, notably of viticulturists. Beneath this body, the *conseils généraux* were much concerned with farming, and there were local agricultural societies which encouraged research and publication, disseminated propaganda for innovations and awarded prizes: they might provide the legitimist with his only public role.

Orleanists with agricultural interests usually showed themselves progressive, such as Decazes with his model farm, or Comte Adrien de Gasparin in the Vaucluse, but in a conservative area like the latter, as with Bugeaud's primitive Dordogne, they were often isolated by their political or religious ideas. To change agricultural systems where they were at their most backward, on the tiny peasant plots, or where production was at its lowest as was the case where *métayage* prevailed, needed a measure of radical state action which no limited government could have undertaken, and it made little attempt to do more than educate. Many of the ministers of commerce and agriculture, notably the textile manufacturer Cunin-Gridaine, knew more about industry than about farming. As was shown in 1846, the government's information on agriculture, mostly obtained from the prefects, men often of legal training with no knowledge of farming, could be dangerously inadequate. Nor could they understand this world where aristocrat and peasant alike reverenced the soil and past ways, in many places dining together at harvest time, the former leading the assembly in prayer. It was a world where, as Stendhal said, the doctor had not replaced the priest as a confessor,[5] especially in the south and west. Often the authorities found the priesthood the only available force for order, as the prefect reported in the Dordogne in 1838 when serious disturbances were provoked by rumours that the rich would make the poor eat straw.[6] However, where a rural middle class had established itself on land taken from monasteries or from *émigrés*, aristocracy and clergy alike had lost their prepotence.

The railway was beginning to create a cultural unity which was leading to the disappearance of patois and other regional distinctions, although there was a growth in academic appreciation of these. George Sand used patois in some of her novels in peasant life, and Jasmin's Provençal poetry had a Parisian vogue. When, in 1846, the first Breton dictionary was published, it was significantly in the capital. Parisian standards dominated increasingly. When, at Vézelay, Merimée finds an inn without ink and serving black bread, it provokes him to express the wish that Napoleonic dictatorship had been prolonged until his compatriots had been thoroughly civilised.[7] Stendhal stressed the terrible monotony of provincial life. In a small town, the sub-prefecture provides the meeting place for the Orleanist bourgeois, the legitimist gentry congregate in another salon and around their sterile conflict exist the masses of peasantry, little higher than the animal world. At Lyons there were salons which could draw on men like Sauzet and Fulchiron to provide a pale imitation of Parisian society; Bordeaux possessed a successful opera house, but was very conventional in its repertoire. The cultural and political dominance of Paris had never been more obvious. The murderer Lacenaire exemplified this anti-provincial snobbery when he expressed relief when told he was to be executed, not at Beaune where he had been captured, but at Paris: it would have been most disagreeable to suffer a provincial executioner.

In some ways, the capital retained the aspect of a country town, ringed by royal palaces and country residences. On Montmartre, vineyards provided the cheap rough wine for Parisian *cabarets*, rabbits were shot on the Plaine Saint-Denis, milk came fresh from cows pastured within the walls of 1840 and the Champs-Elyseés remained wooded and somewhat dangerous, the haunt of vagabonds and prostitutes. And within there lay the self-contained villages of the Faubourgs Saint-Germain and Saint-Honoré, the former legitimist, the latter essentially Orleanist. To its north had developed the world of the boulevardier with the fashionable Cafés Anglais and de Paris, the tobacconists and dandies' tailors. Across the river lay the Latin quarter, increasingly the bastion of the scholar and the artist. The residential quarters were becoming stratified; many blocks were still bourgeois on the ground floor and inhabited by paupers in their attics, with various gradations of class and wealth between, but the middle classes were moving from the poorer areas. New *beaux quartiers* were created to house them, such as Maisons, now adorned by the addition of the name Laffitte, who developed the area and christened its streets after his friends. Expansion often meant specialisation and districts became associated with classes or types. The shopgirls whom Gavarni immortalised became known as *Lorettes* from the church which overshadowed their small world, whilst the new rich gathered close to the Bourse.

But contemporaries did not notice the traditional aspects of the city as much as its seemingly uncontrollable growth (from around 785,000 in 1831 to slightly beyond a million on the eve of the 1848 Revolution). Working men crowded into cheap and sordid furnished rooms, and suburbs of shanties such as the inaptly named Belleville were thrown up to house the influx. None the less, accommodation was insufficient. Gabriel Delessert, prefect of police, appealed vainly to pedestrians and carriages to travel on the right, to minimise congestion. More serious were moral and hygienic problems which the rapid population increase brought with it.

Traditional morality and religious belief had broken down. One-third of all births were illegitimate, and child murder or abandonment were the frequent recourse. Dr Parent-Duchâtelet's immensely thorough study, *De la Prostitution dans la ville de Paris* (1836), describes the phenomenon as a vast reflection of social problems, linked with pauperism and expanding in times of unemployment. One contemporary claimed that a third of those dying in Paris left no money for their burial, for which the government paid, and considered one in thirteen destitute and many others living scarcely above the subsistence level. A commission appointed to examine the 1832 cholera epidemic discovered that one-fifth of the total area of Paris had half the population, that in many places sixty people lived in five-storey houses without courtyards, that in the Rue des Arcis, every inhabitant had only 7 square metres living-space. Such streets had 45 deaths for every 1,000 people, which was twice the average. Even without the cholera, Paris in the 1830s was more unhealthy than it had been in 1820, and had a death-rate which compared very unfavourably with that of France as a whole. The commission, which included Docteurs Villermé and Parent-Duchâtelet, published a report, inspired by the cholera, forming the first scientific total statistic of the Paris population, although its claims that Sunday's excesses caused a greater rate of decease early in the week and that political passions weakened the body, perhaps owed more to bourgeois prejudice than to objective observation. The findings caused the implementation of what was, for the age, a massive programme of public hygiene, the creation of a Conseil de Salubrité, the undertaking of a vast new sewerage system, and the building of many new fountains, increasing tenfold the length of existing waterpipe.

Reform was held back because the government of Paris reflected the constitutional monarchy. The prefect, the Comte de Rambuteau, ruled the Hôtel de Ville in considerable splendour, but his powers were restricted by an unimaginative city council whose thirty-six members tended to be small tradesmen representing the views of *petit bourgeois* electors. The expense of compensation prevented many improvements, such as the authorities' plans to improve the unhygienic Halles. The Rue de Rambuteau, of which the prefect was so proud, was a long, straight, but still narrow street plunging through the east Parisian slums, and which took several years to negotiate and then to build. The government could only complete, not emulate, the ambitions of Napoleon. The Place de la Concorde (previously Louis XV and scene of the guillotine) was turned from a shapeless patch of mud into a square with statues of towns and rivers, and the central obelisk, testimony to Mehemet Ali's Francophilia, sign of the government's wish to obliterate political memories. With the exception of the July monument, its other constructions lacked an overt political message: the churches of Saint-Vincent de Paul and Notre Dame de Lorette were completed, and Sainte-Clothilde begun, whilst the first great station, the Gare Saint-Lazare, was opened in 1843. And gradually, the city was becoming gaslit.

However, Paris was often seen as a city of dark forces, for poets a "hell' or "cesspool" to be likened to Sodom or Babylon. Insurrection and conspiracy, notably the massacre effected by Fieschi's machine, suggested that this was a volcano whose civilised crust barely contained crime and anarchy; Gisquet's "fifth class" or the "dangerous classes" described by the Parisian bureaucrat Frégier, immoral and revolutionary. They seemed to have no answer, but that of Rubichon was at least bold. Like many legitimists he bore a grudge against the revolutionary city and argued that Bourges be made capital of France. He admitted it was dreary and boring, but this was a positive recommendation because it enabled the government to concentrate on the huge task of regenerating France, whilst Paris fulfilled its cosmopolitan role.[8] De Vigny's line, "Towards the unknown end she ceaselessly advances",[9] suggests he would have agreed that Paris was a mindless machine driving France towards destruction, but it is of course Balzac who made himself the chronicler of "sea-like agitation"[10] which so quickly covered the constant suicides, bankruptcies and other catastrophes. "Paris then is a slough"[11] is the lesson his heroes have to learn when into their provincial minds sinks the realisation that the city of their ambitions is a jungle.

Contemporaries felt that in their time, more than previously, money was the key to all doors. But unfortunately for the régime, it could not depend upon money as a political cement: Orleanism lacked the tradition and religious or aesthetic foundation to override differences of class and wealth. More than any other previous society, France in this period possesses both horizontal and vertical divisions. It had no true ruling class. Tudesq's *grand notable* is essentially a historian's term to define the addition of new wealth and power to that of a traditional group, but its limitations are themselves a point of importance to the historian. Some *grands notables* welcomed the Revolution of 1848, but many, perhaps the majority, were horrified by it. And within the great bourgeoisie of the July Monarchy the variations in style and idea are enormous. Between the Delessert or the de Laborde families, wealthy under the *ancien regime* and with aristocratic connections, and the self-made Gisquet or Laffitte, there were deep differences. Charles X had threatened the political interests of all and temporarily united them, but besides the interests common to all bankers, they had little in common. Such old bourgeois families as the Delessert had often become cultured and philanthropic: their newly arrived rivals were usually less conservative and more attached to capitalist values. Yet in spite of the obvious differences and deep enmity often felt between such groups, the July Monarchy is frequently defined as being bourgeois.

When, in 1835, the republican Garnier-Pagès asserted in the Chamber of Deputies that the bourgeoisie was withdrawing its approval from the regime, it was not his contention but his terminology which provoked a small uproar. "What is the bourgeoisie?" demanded the banker Fulchiron: "There is no bourgeoisie in France"[12] stated another deputy. Yet others who were similarly both bourgeois and Orleanist, Gisquet or Barrot or Guizot, blithely used the word as if self-explanatory. "Everyone knows what the bourgeoisie is; it represents the vast majority of the population",[13] declared Gisquet, but he confuses numerical majority with a body he chooses to find representative. Similarly, Baudelaire addressed them, "You are the majority – in number and intelligence."[14] Presumably Fulchiron meant there was no caste beneath the aristocracy, that the middle classes were too complex a grouping simply to be labelled bourgeoisie: whilst the others were using the word to express a very real phenomenon, but one hard to define, that of a literate, politically conscious public possessing a certain prosperity and not manually employed. Louis Blanc defined the bourgeois as a man who works for himself, possessing capital and implements: the people are dependent upon others. Such a definition would include many artisans who could not properly be considered in this category but Blanc adds to his objective, if inaccurate, description various characteristics. The bourgeois, he claims, puts himself before society, prefers wealth to glory: he betrayed Napoleon, but he also hates the monarchy because jealous of aristocrats. If they differed on its merits, such dissimilar men as Louis Blanc and Louis-Philippe, Guizot and Garnier-Pagès, all agreed that the bourgeoisie was the dominant class.

This could not have been stated with such certainty under the Restoration. The bourgeoisie in 1830 had captured political power, it was asserted, even by those who regretted it. Some members of the middle class, for instance Bugeaud the soldier and landowner, or Royer-Collard, liberal philosopher and scion of an established professional family, disliked the dominance of the middle class. However well the bourgeoisie governed its own affairs, asserted Royer-Collard, it lacked the ability to govern France.[15] The journalist Désiré Nisard criticises the King for an excessive regard for the bourgeoisie and adds, "Personally, the excellent king Louis-Philippe does not give me the satisfaction to believe that he does not take me for an ironmaster."[16] There was a strong division between commercial and professional, and the former, with the exception of a Périer or Laffitte, tended to be under-represented at the highest levels.

Whilst for the republicans or legitimists, as the latter's *Gazette* wrote, the bourgeois worshipped money, and this idolatry was "the disease of the epoch",[17] others saw wealth as sign of virtue. For Guizot this class, whilst successful, had not attempted to become a caste: desiring liberty for itself, it desired it for all. And Saint-Marc Girardin saw wealth as almost democratic in its sign of capacity. The public went to the best lawyer or doctor, by its confidence and its payment making him an elector.[18] So the right to vote accompanied wealth and economic liberalism, testimony to a society of freedom and just rewards.

Of course, some were rewarded more than others. As Barrot remarked, the bourgeoisie "rises very high and falls very low"[19] and increasingly the poorer grew resentful of the political and financial power of the wealthier. But as well as the horizontal strata of wealth, there were the vertical barriers of profession and tradition. In the old market towns and legal centres of France existed a class, frequently Catholic or legitimist, which new political and economic currents were slow to affect. Sometimes they showed hostility to capitalist forces, as when, during the 1845 Toulon shipyard strikes, many bourgeois were sympathetic to the workers' case and the clergy's attempts at mediation. And, in reverse, business often opposed a government which it considered tolerant of royalism and clericalism. At Rouen, for example, a city dominated by capitalist industry whose newspaper the *Mémorial* believed the *Journal des Débats* excessively indulgent towards working-class disorder, all four deputies were in commerce but only one was ministerial and one was the republican Laffitte. In an area of prosperous small landowners such as the Aisne, the voters chose as their deputies men of the opposition like the *centre gauche* Vivien, Odilon Barrot or the extreme anticlerical Lherbette. In Lille, similarly, the middle bourgeoisie had exiled the *grand bourgeois* from parliamentary representation, although at Sedan where a few rich industrialists, for example Gendarme the great iron manufacturer, dominated a small electorate, Cunin-Gridaine was the deputy. For the most part, unless the *notable* were a member of the opposition, he did not represent an *arrondissement* where the smaller commercial bourgeoisie were powerful.

The King reassured Salvandy who feared socialist revolution: "The middle classes are not all of society, but they are the force within it."[20] When the majority possessed property, a Jacobin revolution was impossible. He was partly correct: the Second Republic would show that most republicans were not socialists. But the King was misled in seeing no further than the *haute bourgeoisie*: because he disliked or despised Général Jacqueminot or Jacques Lefebvre, he considered his tolerance of them a virtue and he took them as representative of a class he misunderstood the more dangerously because he half understood it. He became convinced by the complacent expressions of the rich that the lesser members of the middle class were also satisfied. Like many others, he failed to understand the hatred of a section of the middle class for the bourgeois concept, and the dissatisfaction amongst others with their place in society, and that this could take them to the lengths of countenancing revolution. A class which hated to be pushed lower but which had difficulty in moving into the more prestigious positions, tended to produce large numbers of displaced young men, dissatisfied with the structure of a society where connection seemed the best qualification for promotion. As for their fathers, often without a vote, yet, as National Guardsmen, performing the night duty from which the more prosperous cavalry were spared, at the mercy of economic crises which could deplete their savings or remove them from the franchise or the jury, they too had dissatisfactions. The inaction of the *petit bourgeois* National Guardsmen in 1848 was more fatal to the July Monarchy than the activity of the republicans. Having enlarged the political world, the Orleanists divided between those like Guizot to whom the *petite bourgeoisie* threatened the conservative bases of society, and those such as Barrot for whom they were the heirs of the Revolution. The monarchy, he later claimed, fell because the mass of the middle class was excluded from political participation.[21]

The Duchesse de Dino, albeit niece of Talleyrand, whom 1830 had restored to influence, felt that the Revolution had already gone too far: tasteful Restoration society had disappeared and they had to suffer deputies "of a complacency, of a self-assurance, of an unparalleled pedantry, with the fashion of speaking incomprehensibly".[22] These hostilities, and the differences of speech and manner, may have declined before 1848 but had not disappeared.

The new monied classes no longer aped the aristocracy or felt their manifest inferiority to the previous extent. Thus the old nobility felt a real decline in their position. "There is the aristocracy of the epoch",[23] exclaimed Général de Castellane, having seen the incredible gilded luxury of the hotel of the banker Benoît Fould. And although he no doubt enjoyed receiving noblemen and would marry his daughter to one, the millionaire deputy felt inferior to nobody. In the Moselle area, the de Wendel family, prospering from their forges, was pushing the fortune of the Comte d'Hunolstein, great landowner and previously by far the richest man, into second position. And although most wealth was still in aristocratic hands, of the fifteen men paying over 15,000 francs tax, five, including the two richest, Joseph Périer and Gendarme, were bourgeois. The other ten were members of the ancient nobility, and included three peers, the Duc de Choiseul-Praslin (the murderer), Talleyrand's heir, the Duc de Valençay, and the Marquis de Boissy. Similar proportions, Tudesq has shown, are found in the group of about 550 paying over 5,000 francs. Here is a greater proportion of nobles of the Empire, but almost three-quarters were property-owners. The wealth of bankers was striking and seemed novel and was therefore much commented upon, but it remained secondary to landownership. This great wealth was predominately Orleanist, and was concentrated in certain areas, primarily Paris and the Seine, followed by other departments of the north–centre. Lesser landed wealth was predominately legitimist.

Within smaller geographical areas, the proportions of different social groups vary greatly, and differ also according to the historian's definitions. Ibarrola gives Grenoble a miniscule working class of 7 per cent, a similar proportion of servants, and the rest of the population various forms of middle class; the small shopkeepers and artisans (many of whom Louis Blanc would have termed working class) with about 30 per cent, larger commerce and industry at about 5 per cent, liberal professions the same, state employment and the army a little more, and proprietors and *rentiers* the fairly high proportion of 21 per cent. Such figures reflect a town of traditional crafts (in this case hat and glove making) and a society where money once earned was put into land, property or state bonds.

Paris presents a more complex structure, but still one economically dominated by the workshop, not the factory. Daumard calculates that 17.5 per cent of the Parisian population was bourgeois.[24] Of the group paying over 1,000 francs *cens*, half were *propriétaires* (but of this large proportion, many were retired or had inherited) and the economic professions came next with 30 per cent, the remainder being the liberal professions (12 per cent) and public services (8 per cent). Professional groups were still high in proportion to economic professions; the more so, the less industrialised the town. Clermont-Ferrand, for example, at this early stage in its expansion, had about 500 electors, with *propriétaires* and economic professions equal – about 35 per cent of the population each. Although liberal professions came behind official functions, they still made a remarkably high proportion in most towns and were dominant in some. In almost every urban *arrondissement*, voters in commerce were outnumbered by the professional classes, official or independent, although it would appear that they were advancing at their expense. And the restrictions in the capitalist nature of the wealth of the Orleanist wealthy, is shown by the estimation that about 43 per cent of their wealth was in land or property, 18 per cent in state bonds, slightly over 4 per cent in the Banque de France, 14 per cent lent to individuals and only 3.7 per cent in company shares. Yet whatever the exact nature of this wealth, there remained a large gap between its possessors and the envious *petite bourgeoisie*.

The aristocracy was scarcely more a united class, divided as bitterly on politics, it was also extended by the imperial nobility, scarcely absorbed into the traditional groups of the *ancien régime*. The huge creation of titles granted to parvenu families – "One does not dare to be merely a baron, at least to truly be one"[25] wrote Karr acidly – had obscured the nature of aristocracy. The loss of political power, even though 1830 was no complete deprivation, especially of pre-eminence in the provinces, had removed from the aristocracy its last means of controlling society. Middle-class snobbery still gave it a social role outside its own ranks, and an impoverished aristocrat might be considered by the wealthy bourgeois parent a suitable spouse for his offspring, thus Fould's daughter married a Breteuil, and Madame Clicquot, the Champagne widow, gave her daughter to the Comte de Chévigné. Yet this was growing rarer, and it is significant that the Clicquots were legitimist, for as the *haute bourgeoisie* grew more powerful, noble marriages became unnecessary as a means to social position.

In a world where their values were disappearing, their wealth rivalled or overtaken, their social position challenged, the July Revolution had removed the political power of a class, even if individual members retained importance. The principle of heredity was attacked in the monarchy of Charles X, to be followed by the ending of hereditary peerage, whilst many suffered in purely material terms from the loss of jobs or pensions. Even the aristocracy who rallied to Orleanism, found themselves on the defensive, and the increase in voting, tiny though it was, in some areas delivered power into the hands of the bourgeoisie. The plebeian proprietors near Paris told Comte Molé when they voted against him in the *conseil général* elections, that they preferred one of themselves.[26] Further from Paris, however, in areas where landed wealth had only rarely been shared with the bourgeoisie, aristocratic dominance remained intact. Thus the young and extravagant Comte Henri de Castellane could still array forty servants in his livery with candelabra in their hands to light the way to his château for the nocturnal arrival of an Orleanist prince. In the Cantal he presided feudally, giving huge hospitality to all around, and the population found it quite natural that he should be elected twice, and overwhelmingly, for Murat, before he was even of age to take his seat. The La Fayette family, if less flamboyant, retained huge local preponderance because great landed wealth added to progressive politics was such a powerful combination. Yet it was obvious that such wealth was becoming rarer. The Dupin family rivalled the Comte de Chastellux in their area, although the former's power was urban and the latter's rural. In the Eure department, the Passy brothers, Antoine as prefect, Hippolyte as deputy, had built up such influence by a client system, that in 1839 not even the Duc de Choiseul-Praslin could obtain election against their candidate, even though a vastly wealthy landowner with governmental support.

For the Orleanist aristocracy, although it tended to be more open to the imperial nobility, to marry wealth or accept talent as a form of social equality, these developments were almost as displeasing as for legitimists. The Baron de Barante complained of the masses "our gracious sovereign, who has neither taste for, nor confidence in, the aristocrats of birth or spirit".[27] For 1830 represented a divorce between culture and the ruling class. A figure like Molé was isolated because, despite having served the Empire, he was hostile to patriotic and revolutionary prejudice: "in him we have had the aristocracy that loves ideas and letters".[28] The last short flowering of the salon under the July Monarchy occurred partly because 1830 had freed the aristocracy from political orthodoxy, and because in a world of public opinion with a bourgeois Chamber of Deputies, they had lost much of their power over opinion.

It was rare for the old aristocracy to marry completely new wealth, but alliance between the latter and the imperial nobility was common; the Prince de La Moskowa, for example, eldest son of Maréchal Ney, married Laffitte's daughter. For the highest families, however, both impeccable ancestry and wealth were required. In theory, the Duchesse de Dino gave her daughter complete freedom concerning suitors, but the exclusivity of her salon was such that the choice was bound to be restricted and the successful candidate, Henri de Castellane, was superficially in every way a highly desirable choice. Amongst the less wealthy provincial nobility, the nature of marital alliance had changed little. For a Breton like Carné, to marry the descendant of one who went on a crusade with his own ancestor seemed entirely natural. Yet in every piece of journalism emanating from the perspicuous Comte de Carné comes the message that the bourgeoisie, with their own financial aristocracy, were the new rulers. The nobility was beginning to feel itself anomalous, even while often upholding its old traditions and prejudices. The Duc de Luxembourg-Montmorency congratulated himself on being the last of his line, and rejoiced whenever he saw an ancient family extinguished, as there was no longer a place for them, and continuation only besmirched the glory of their ancestors.[29]

The July Revolution had its effect on fashion as well as on politics. The year 1830 freed the beard: no longer was it the outrageous appurtenance of the lazy Bohemian, but carefully cultivated, it became an adornment to the man of fashion. A few aged and fanatical legitimists wore wigs, Bonapartists liked the military effect of a moustache, and a profusion of side-whiskers spoke a willingness to resemble the citizen King. Dandyism was a manifestation of rebellion, a protest against the dull clothes and conventional pleasures of the mediocre bourgeoisie. The dandy, an urban aristocrat, would make an idyll of the townscape: he had to extract every ounce of pleasure from the life of the city, he had to cultivate grace and impertinence, to mock society whilst showing it to be vulgar. The rules were elegantly but dogmatically laid down by Barbey d'Aurevilly in his treatise *Du Dandysme et de Georges Brummell*. Product of a bored society, the dandy had to be slightly cruel. It was vital to cultivate every detail of dress in a society which seemed to think money more important than pleasure: so Lautour-Mézeray, in the happy days before his tailor's bills forced him to become a prefect, would fully change his costume thrice a day. Nestor Roqueplan claimed that he could never sleep the day before an appointment with his tailor, such was the importance of the occasion, and wore jackboots at home because slippers were bourgeois. The dandy's whole way of life was a protest against commercial professionalism: he would arise at midday, pay some calls or stroll in the boulevards, change his dress, dine and attend the opera. To disarrange the bourgeois world, the dandy would sometimes be obstructive: for example the Marquis de Saint-Cricq delighted in bringing the traffic to a standstill by hiring strings of empty cabs.

A certain amount of money was necessary for these pursuits, although it was virtually obligatory to owe considerable sums to tradespeople. The Duc d'Abrantès, son of Maréchal Junot, having squandered his fortune, lived three days a month as a dandy, dining at the Café de Paris and ogling the dancers at the Opéra, and would then return to spend the remainder in the poverty of the Latin Quarter. The life of *un lion* or *un fashionable*, for it was chic to be English in one's dress and deportment if not in political opinions, involved being also *un sportsman*, or at least feigning an interest in sport. Membership of the Jockey Club was an important qualification for the dandy: theoreticaly founded to encourage the breeding of pedigree horses, the club received the patronage of the Ducs d' Orléans and d'Aumale who encouraged the fashion for elegant society to attend horseracing at Chantilly.

This was the most rural that the world of the dandy became. If forced from Paris, he had to do his best to behave as if he were still in the city. So in Algeria Comte Napoléon Bertrand put on a pair of new white gloves at the moment the assault on Constantine commenced. This loyalty to the capital and the essential *épater le bourgeois* (flabbergast the bourgeois) were the only political requirements. It was possible to be legitimist, republican or even Orleanist in politics, as long as these opinions were held with some iconoclasm. The dandy's world extended from the great hotels of the Faubourg Saint-Germain into the Bohemian dens of the Latin Quarter. It was possible to think only of dancers at the Opéra or cards at the Jockey Club, or alternatively to be a poet like Alfred de Musset, author like Eugéne Sue or journalist like Roqueplan or Villemessant. Perhaps it was preferable to combine as many factors as possible, for the dandy was heir to the eighteenth century, but rendered aggressive by the new age's disapproval of amateurism. So the Prince de La Moskowa, and composer, patron of a society for the encouragement of church music and president of the Jockey Club, anti-governmental in the Chamber of Peers and personal friend of the Orléans princes, was exemplary. Also like d'Abrantès he was a son of a great man of the Empire. They were particularly prone to dandyism as an expression of *mal de siècle*, feeling most directly the impossibility of emulating their fathers.

Yet the world of the dandy was disappearing before the forces against which he elegantly protested. The small world of Paris was being distended: the railways brought in hordes of provincials, and, worse, Americans. Under the Second Empire, the banks and great stores began to dominate the boulevards where formerly had stood the cafés, the glove shops, tobacconists and *bains chinois* (Chinese baths). The dandy with his grey trousers, lemon yellow gloves and waistcoat, blue coat and elegant cane was protesting against the uniform of the black frock-coat. "That black attire worn by the men of our times is a terrible symbol; . . . It is the human reason that has trampled all our illusions"[30] lamented Alfred de Musset.

But because woman was without professional function, to her was allowed the display of which the male was deprived. Indeed fashion became more than ever important because in a society where the earning of money was a more obvious function of existence, the female became a spending organism as the male's counterpart: fashion was a subject to which whole journals were devoted. Carefully arranged curls beneath the beribboned bonnet, the corset into which the recalcitrant female form had to be squeezed, spoke of leisure and a servant. Whilst the details signified wealth, a certain carelessness was carefully cultivated, sign of a conscious moral relaxation. Abbé de Ravignan inveighed against low-cut dresses from the pulpit. Woman, however, was beginning to resent what came to be seen as a secondary place in society, to which the growth of a male professional existence was relegating her. Divorce, which an attempt to make which easier by Barrot and Schonen in 1831 had been defeated by the Chamber of Peers, remained the foremost demand of the more emancipated women such as George Sand, Flora Tristan and the Comtesse d'Agoult. Not all women approved the aggresiveness of these female liberators. "It is Omphala fuming at the feet of Hercules"[31] remarked Louise Bertin of George Sand: she herself believed that the traditional role of women in society, forming opinion in the salon, acting as a civilising influence on the male world, was more honourable than equality. Yet for women there were increased possibilities of self-expression even if marital equality were denied them, and the *lionnes* seized with an enthusiasm most thought excessive the right to behave publicly with an abandon similar to that of their menfolk.

The *bals masqués* for students and *grisettes*, the *bals musards* for a wider range of society, where licentious behaviour in dances such as the galop and polka was encouraged, seemed to symbolise the new social freedoms. "There," wrote Gavarni who frequented them, "to be of the people, one plays the commoner",[32] sign of an upper class tired of restrictions. Society was becoming self-conscious, examining its customs and often accusing itself of hypocrisy. The popularity of law cases testified to a fascination with its seamier side: the *Gazette des Tribunaux*, much used by authors such as Stendhal and Balzac, was more widely read than many newspapers. Two of the greatest cases of the period closely concerned the question of female place in society. Lieutenant de la Roncière was found guilty of rape, largely because the jury would not believe the evidence of four handwriting experts who suggested that the letters convicting the accused were in fact written by the young woman concerned, and they preferred to believe that she, as her parents claimed, was so pure as never to have read a novel. La Roncière went to prison because delicacy towards the female sex prevented all facts being fully known, but Madame Lafarge, who poisoned her husband, claimed that a male jury could not try her, because of their sexual prejudice. In fact, they were highly indulgent in finding extenuating circumstances which did not prevent the murderess from writing self-justificatory memoirs which became a gospel of feminine liberation. Elsewhere on the sexual compass, greater interest, if rarely tolerance, was shown in homosexuality. If Custine's perversion was too notorious and unconcealed for him to be admitted to most houses to which his rank and literary distinction would otherwise have gained him automatic admittance, sexual deviations began to be increasingly treated in literature, by Dumas, Balzac and Gautier for example, and more scientifically by such physiologists of society as Parent-Duchâtelet.

If the unmentionable began to be mentioned, it is also true that society became embarrassed by certain things. The growing fears of criminality, depravity or sickness of mind or body led to their sequestration. Executions were transferred from the highly public showplace of the Place de Grève to a suburb where they were held in the very early morning. Abolitionists such as Hugo argued that this removed all the deterrent effect claimed for capital punishment. Increased humanitarianism and also fastidiousness led to laws which obliged the departments to make arrangements for housing lunatics, and provided for governmental inspection of establishments. Growing more conscious of crime and madness, men ascribed it to a society out of joint. Suicide in particular become increasingly popular, especially in times of economic depression; there were 918 in Paris in 1847, almost twice as many as in years before 1830, and in France as a whole a similar progression took place. Tocqueville ascribed it to the melancholy due to material greed and loss of faith. One deputy blamed it upon romantic literature, in particular

Alfred de Vigny's *Chatterton*: Vigny inevitably replied that if the artist were prone to self-destruction, this was the fault of society.

Romantic man believed that society oppressed the individual. "Does society today no longer have a place for those from whom it does not profit? I believe it",[38] asked and answered Balzac, and his central thesis was that society was immoral. Vautrin, his great criminal, can be used for law and order because in contemporary society there is frequently no difference between good and evil, and in a world of revolutions, today's lawbreaker may be tomorrow's lawmaker. Ambition and greed war on family loyalty and individual integrity throughout the *Comédie Humaine*: old standards have been destroyed to leave only money. Delacroix agreed, comparing modern society with a horde of bandits, equal amongst themselves in sharing their rapine, but failing, more than any previous society, to observe the Christian laws of charity because "material welfare is the sole concern of modern men".[34] Others of all parties, even Orleanists not seduced by the charms of capitalism, agreed, but all tended to place the blame in a different place.

There were two complaints seemingly contradictory. On the one hand, men complained at increased levelling, the growth of the average and the mediocre. The triumph of the bourgeoisie, pronounced the Marquis de Custine, was a conquest by ants. "Profitable work" would soon banish the liberal professions in the name of liberalism.[35] Fears that rulers and ruled were both sacrificing to the tyranny of the mediocre were repeatedly expressed by Tocqueville, and as usual Mme de Girardin produced a maxim: "The great abase themselves in order again to count for something; the small raise themselves only because they are small."[36] On the other hand there were no less common laments that the individual had become selfish and undisciplined, concerned only with his own interests. Corporate feelings, it was claimed, were the only remedy to this destructive spirit, and so "association" was frequently invoked as the answer to "individualism". Both complaints, which contemporaries perhaps exaggerated, stem from the novelty of a society which frankly had no religious or spiritual foundation but which attempted, perhaps unconsciously, to maintain itself by the increase of prosperity and education. It became a presupposition that wealth was a standard. In 1839, the Garde des Sceaux, defending low pay for magistrates, argued that the poor were not expected to enter this career: "Justice is encharged with the protection of property; it participates in the interests of property and order by the composition of its personnel."[37] In a fragmented society, belief in the protection of property was the only factor which united all property-owners. The spirit of aristocratic France, lamented Barante, had been extinguished in the struggle of "merchants against *bousingots* [rebels]",[38] whereby the need of order had compelled men of taste and intelligence to accept the materialistic thesis which reduced everything to the satisfaction of interests. But this did not suffice. If it is an exaggeration to describe the bourgeoisie as possessed by a demon of destruction, as did Heine, he was surely correct in seeing many Orleanists as being conservative by material necessity rather than true conviction: thus the popularity of Lamartine who appealed to revolutionary emotion without threatening the social order.

Perhaps one is in danger of overstating the crisis of this society. Men would look back on it from the Second Empire as an age when vulgarity had not completely triumphed, when there was still a real identity between the peak of society and the aristocracy of artistic and intellectual talent. The period of the July Monarchy was not more corrupt or degenerate than other periods, in many ways it was more innocent and vital, but it firmly believed that it was in decay. Men had not become resigned to living in a fragmented society, they were afflicted by the loss of all certainties which later ages have come to accept, and they continually wondered how society could survive without the disciplines of religion, hierarchy and generally accepted principles.

REFERENCES

1. C. Baudelaire, *Le Salon de 1845, Curiosités aesthétiques* (1923), 4.
2. A. Barbier, *Iambes* (1898), 60.
3. C. Pouthas, *La Population française* (1956).
4. R. Rémond; *Les États-Unis devant l'Opinion Française* (1962), I, 65.
5. Stendhal, *Lucien Leuwen* (Martineau edition), 330.
6. Archives Nationales, BB^{18} 1254 A^{8} 6636.
7. P. Mérimée, *Correspondance générale* (1941), I, 308.
8. M. Rubichon, *Du mécanisme de la société en France et en Angleterre* (1833), 420.
9. A. de Vigny, *Poésies Complètes*, (1903), 199.
10. H. de Balzac, *Père Goriot* (Pléïade edition), II, 886.
11. Ibid.
12. Archives Parlementaires, 17 August 1835.
13. H. J. Gisquet, *Mémoires* (1840) I, 247.
14. Baudelaire, *Le Salon de 1846*, (1846) 81.
15. Baron P. de Barante, *Souvenirs* (1890), III, 145.
16. D. Nisard, *Souvenirs* (1888), I, 36.
17. *La Gazette de France*, 22 August 1837.
18. *Journal des Débats*, 8 December 1831, 3 January 1833.
19. Odilon Barrot, *Mémoires posthumes* (1875), I, 209.
20. Comte C. de Rémusat, *Mémoires de ma vie* (1958), Rémusat, III, 226.
21. Barrot, op. cit., 226.
22. Duchesse D. de Dino, *Chroniques* (1909).
23. Maréchal de Castellane, *Journal* (1895), III, 382. Vicomte de Beaumont-Vassy, *Les Salons de Paris* (1879), 27.
24. A. Daumard, *La Bourgeoise parisienne* (1963).
25. A. Karr; *Les Guêpes* (1858), III, 99.
26. Barante, op. cit., III, 89.
27. Ibid., V, 35.
28. Comte A. de Tocqueville, *Correspondance* (*Œuvres*, ed. J. P. Mayer, 1954), XI, 304–5.

29. Dr F. L. Poumiès de la Siboutie, *Souvenirs d'un Médecin de Paris* (1910), 248–9.
30. A. de Musset, *La Confession d'un enfant du siècle* (Garnier edition, 1968), 11.
31. Marquis A. L. de Custine, *Lettres du Marquis A. de Custine à Varnhagen d'Ense et Rahel Varnhagen d'Ense* (Brussels, 1870), 443.
32. P. A. Lemoisne, *Gavarni* (1924), I, 108.
33. Balzac, *Le Lys dans la vallée* (Garnier edition), 174.
34. E. Delacroix, *Journal* (1832), 227–8.
35. Custine, *Souvenirs et Portraits* (1956), 242.
36. Mme D. de Girardin, *École des Journalistes* (Brussels, 1840), 2.
37. Archives Parlementaires, 4 April 1839.
38. Barante, op. cit., IV, 28.

25

Industrialisation and the Economy

"On s'obstine à nourrir de gélatine les malades des hôpitaux qui s'obstine à en mourrir de faim.
On découvre un nouveau cerfeuil vénéneux.
On attaque la pyrale, insecte qui nuit à la vigne, au moyen d'une composition qui détruit les ceps – et brûle les mains qui l'emploient.
La gaz éclate.
Les chemins de fer causent d'horribles catastrophes.
On propose d'employer la vapeur et les rails à marcher plus lentement qu'un fiacre sur le pavé.
Dieu protège la France."

("One persists in nourishing with gelatine hospital patients who persist in dying of hunger because of it.
One discovers a new poisonous chervil.
One attacks the meal-moth, an insect which blackens the vine, by means of a composition which destroys the vine-stock – and burns the hands that apply it.
Gas explodes.
Railways cause horrible catastrophes.
One proposes to use steam and rails to progress more slowly than a hackney-carriage on the pavement.
God save France.")[1]

Optimists believed that the principles of science might be applied to society where its laws alone would initiate progress and unite conflicting creeds. Yet during the July Monarchy, science, as virtually every other facet of human existence, was invaded by politics. It was to be expected that men's views on Geoffroy Sainte-Hilaire's ideas on evolution as a constant upward movement and Cuvier's which posited a fixity in the animal world, depended upon their religious and philosophical beliefs, but even where theories were more easily proved, men often preferred beliefs which supported political prejudices. Raspail used parasitology in socialist attack; his belief in camphor as a remedy for all infectious diseases was the wishful thinking of a democrat in opposition to the orthodox establishment. Because Orfila, dean of the Paris medical faculty and a vocal Orleanist, spoke for the prosecution in the Lafarge poisoning case, Raspail aided the defence by claiming that arsenic could be absorbed from the ground by a corpse. The Université and its monopoly were placed at the service of a Napoleonic scientific establishment: Orfila in medicine, the peers Poisson in mathematics and Baron Thénard in chemistry, caused a conflict in the scientific world, similar to that over freedom of education.

The cholera epidemic provided a blow to the self-confidence of science. Medicine was helpless and divided, and it was not known whether or not the disease was contagious. Chlorine was the official preservative, but many doctors poured scorn on it: some swore by leeches, others by alcohol: some forbade vegetables, others believed that a voracious vegetable intake would repel the disease. Some cruel spirit was deriding "the insolent bravado of science . . ."[2] suggested Nodier. He himself proliferated remedies, mint cordial with pepper, heady doses of opium, ether and brandy: more pleasant, if not more efficacious, he insisted on a regimen of absinthe, and rare steak washed down with plenty of wine. But although cholera had exposed science, it gave an impetus to scientific developments. The state encouraged medical improvements and began to pay more attention to urban problems. Cholera caused scientists such as d'Arcet to apply themselves to practical problems of hygiene and to develop the collection of statistics, that religion of exactitude of which Parent-Duchâtelet had such expectations.[3] The government fostered scientific education, but its attitudes remained distinctly conservative and uncommercial. Only in photography, with Daguerre and Bayard, was France a rival to England. This may have been due to the academic dominance of men whose view of science was philosophical rather than practical. The upper classes, unlike their eighteenth-century forebears, were rarely interested in a subject allied to a rationalism and capitalism of which most of them now disapproved. (One of Dumas's characters realises that the Comte de Monte-Cristo is not a nobleman only because he knows too much about science.) In spite of efforts by such men as Girardin or the astronomer Arago, French education remained firmly rooted in the classics, and turned its back on technology. Whilst Saint-Simonians and Fourierists believed that science and industry were beneficent forces in a well-organised society, Orleanists tended to see them as natural forces to be accepted, whose morality or effect was scarcely relevant. There were some like Chevalier or Girardin who fervently believed that industrial development improved human welfare, and that the struggle to perfect the machine and increase production could end social conflicts. Others looked more intently at the immediate effects: "We purchase at frightful cost the progress reserved for the future to enjoy",[4] wrote Eugène Buret.

Industry in France was primarily based upon the workshop. Large factories employed only about 1,300,000 of the 5 million Frenchmen who were supported by industry, found mostly in the north and north-east, in towns which had grown up around new industries, primarily textile manufacture. Industry was usually little mechanised or was highly specialised. Niort, for example, depended on chamois gloves and when the sale of these declined, the whole town suffered. Lyons was the most striking example of specialisation, entirely dominated as it was by the silk industry; in spite of mechanisation, it remained traditional in its commercial structure. The majority of industrial concerns in Lyons and Paris employed between two and ten workers, although for the north-east the average unit was thirty-five. In Lille, in the technically advanced spinning industry, the average factory employed 150 men but most of the town's workers were employed in smaller, more primitive concerns. Even in so-called great industry, the top 125,000 employers in France employed only an average of 10 men each.

The period is one of irregular progress, fast in some areas, slow in others, towards a fully capitalist system. From factories dependent on the weather, stopping production when demand slackened, there increasingly emerged industries not content to remain static, but with expansion as a rule of existence, less dependent on local or natural factors, seeking to capture a national or international market. New sources of energy, primarily coal, and the machines which replaced practised expertise and human skills, enabled unvarying production. Because the north had the labour supply, water, iron and coal, it was best suited to industrialisation, and factories spread from Alsace towards more backward Normandy. Textile industries, especially cotton, led the way: others lagged behind. In 1848, most pig-iron was still made by charcoal, although France, producing 5 million tons of coal a year herself, had to import 2 million tons to fuel expansion. Even in the progressive metallurgical industry, the majority of engines were hydraulic, whereas in England, steam was in command. Railways gradually geographically expanded the use of coal but it remained an expensive commodity, profitable only where mass production and new engines demanded it.

French industry thus retained ancient restrictions, adding to them the uncertainties of early capitalism. Industries vulnerable to local specialisation now suffered more from national factors. In 1832 and 1833, recovering from the slump, towns such as Tourcoing and Roubaix passed from huge unemployment to a severe labour shortage, only to find themselves in 1834 suffering a small slump resulting from overproduction. A similar phenomenon occurred after 1842, with technical innovation and expansion succeeded by falling demand and retraction. In the crises of 1837–39 and 1846–48, mechanised industries suffered more from international market forces whilst competition by them in times of prosperity, harmed those who relied upon more primitive methods.

Yet although a later generation will note the dominance of economic traditionalism, contemporaries were struck by changes such as the huge increase in iron production and coal-mining, the mushroom growth of new towns, the steam engine, iron ship and mechanised loom. That Cunin-Gridaine had over 500 workers in his sheet factories, responsible for an annual production worth over 5 million francs, or that Nicolas Schlumberger, who paid over 4,000 francs in *patente*, employed almost 700 workers in his metallurgical factory, and half as many in two other linen and cotton mills, were facts which impressed contemporaries by their immensity. That the majority of manufacturers remained workshop owners was a less dramatic fact. Roubaix's growth seemed prodigious but was exceptional. The number of looms multiplied more than sixfold during the July Monarchy, but it was the progressive cotton industry which was most affected and the wool industry changed little. Great industry might remain a minority but in many places its effects were startling. Not least, its competition damaged the small industry of agricultural areas, increased rural poverty and rendered irrelevant the traditional skills of the French worker. Whilst it improved the quality of clothing for all members of the community and brought fashion to a wider public (the first department stores selling ready-made clothes were founded in Paris in the 1840s), much of the old workmanship was no longer economical. Finer and slower hand-spinning had virtually disappeared by 1848 and a similar loss of quality was experienced elsewhere, in paper-making, for example, which became almost entirely mechanised. Often, as in the Lyons silk industry, masters and men alike opposed mechanised production and, although the Jacquard looms were in increasing use during the period, it was not until shortly before 1848 that mechanical power was applied to them in a few of the larger workshops.

For the worker, hours were long and pay usually inadequate, the need to withstand British competition being at least as important a factor as entrepreneurial greed. Hours of work in a cotton factory at Lille, probably the scene of the worst conditions, were generally fourteen or fifteen hours a day of which two were free for meals: but a seventeen-hour day was not unknown. Artisans' hours were not quite as appalling although still long, and many of the strikes in Paris in 1840 had a ten-hour day as their primary demand.

The skilled worker earned 3 or 4 francs a day: printers, carpenters or masons might aspire to an annual income of 1,000 francs. Where great physical strength was necessary, in mining or metallurgy, the worker could earn more. The growth of machinism involved increasing use of female and child labour, especially in the cotton industry, where weak limbs could work a machine as well as the strong. This lowered wages: at Lille in 1847, the man was usually paid a little over 2 francs a day, the woman half as much and as child scarcely half as much as this, a sum which was not enough to feed it. The wool industry paid rather better, and linen, because in decline whilst affected by mechanisation, rather worse. Wages varied from area to area: for example pay at Saint-Quentin was a quarter lower than at Lille, but the cost of living was also lower, and conditions better. Villeneuve-Bargemont noted that 22,000 of the 70,000 inhabitants of Lille were paupers and that a sixth of the population of the Nord department were receiving public assistance. Rouen and Mulhouse were almost as bad with three-fifths of the work-force earning insufficient to support themselves. A family was lucky to have meat and wine twice a month, potatoes and bread were their basic diet, although at Sedan a higher-paid work-force ate meat almost daily. Conditions varied, therefore, but even the authorities admitted that in the towns, one man in twenty-nine was "indigent" and that many of those who received public assistance were in employment. The effects of industrialisation were to lower wages, often paying less than the 12 francs a week necessary to maintain a family at subsistence level. On the other hand, it did provide better clothing and put household goods such as glass, soap and utensils within the reach of many of the poor. What it seemed to do was to make life more precarious for many of those industrial workers who, living on the edge of penury, were thrown into it when an economic slump lowered their wages or made them unemployed, and, in this period, economic slump on a national level became more frequent than before.

It has been estimated on a very broad definition, that in large manufacturing industry on average there were only four or five strikes a year. There were twice as many artisans as industrial workers, and Stearns and Aguet have estimated that they accounted for over three times the number of strikes. The worker in industry was in an environment where his low level of education and economic conditions made strike action difficult. As Villermé remarked of one weaving area where the workers were very low paid, their discontent was "never much to fear"[5] because they lacked the energy to protest. However, amongst the literate, there was an increased awareness of their powers. For instance, the Anzin miners in 1837 struck because they believed they should profit from the higher prices coal was fetching. Strikes in factories, where they did occur, showed primitive motivation and method. They appealed either to the good nature of the employer or to the fairness of a governmental representative: or they could be violent, with an attack on the employer or his property; new machinery, frequently the cause of complaint, was often smashed. There was no real proletarian consciousness or industrial understanding, but a dull despair which would very occasionally break into violent and short-lived action. This was very different from the disciplined strikes of the Anzin and Saint-Étienne miners. Where new industry showed such understanding, it was due to the presence of workers with a background of organisation. When Lyonnais went to Elbeuf to work the new machines, they took with them their "mutualist" tradition, and the large-scale strike of October 1847 showed its effect, although even this owed much of its impressiveness to Parisian leadership. The true weakness of strikes arose from the economic situation which produced them. In a period which, despite temporary and local labour shortages, was one of unemployment, the power of the worker was limited. Moreover, he was rarely able to have saved sufficient to enable him to cease work for any prolonged period and he received little support from workers outside his industry or town. The industrial worker could only accept harsh economic realities. This is shown in the difference between 1839 in Lille when cotton workers struck because the bread price was high but there was little unemployment, and 1847 when, although the high price of bread led to a small riot, there was no serious strike because of the high unemployment.

One of the first to describe the social effects of industrialisation was Vicomte Alban de Villeneuve-Bargemont, who as prefect of the Nord before his resignation in 1830, was already horrified by the living conditions of the poor in Lille. After involvement in the Vendean insurrection, he published in 1834 his influential *Economie politique chrétienne*, in which he popularised the English term, pauperism. He distinguished it from poverty: the new indigence was an absolute, irremediable state, "the general, permanent and growing distress of worker populations".[6] He was amongst the first to predict the danger of class warfare. He attacked Say's law which asserted that supply and demand created an equilibrium. Overproduction, rather than lower prices and increasing prosperity, actually caused stagnation, and decreased wages. He claimed the need for a minimum wage which would enable a family to live without struggle and to save enough for an economic or personal crisis. He believed that taxes should be removed on working-class necessities. Like other aristocrats, he proposed farm colonies as a remedy, but made other, more modern, suggestions such as health departments, working-class associations to organise mutual aid and education. He wished the state to take more positive action in providing relief, inspecting working conditions and prohibiting child labour.

There were other legitimist critics of industrialism. The Protestant La Farelle noted working-class vices of alcoholism and immorality but claimed they were the result of bad laws and a corrupt society. The legitimist press paid more attention to such problems than the Orleanist press, or indeed many republican organs, because it harmonised with their political hatred of bankers and merchants. Gougenet des Mousseaux asked ironically why liberals worried so much about slavery when the working classes of France lived in a worse state. Admirer of O'Connell, as were other Catholics in the 1840s, he argued in his *Des Prolétaires, nécessité et moyens d'améliorer leur sort* (1846) that not only was working-class immorality the result of poverty, but that the working-class élite was worth more than businessmen and should be brought into the political system. Cardinal de Bonald, Archbishop of Lyons, son of the legitimist theorist, not only attacked manufacturers' cupidity but made fewer exhortations to resignation, formerly the Church's answer to the problems of the poor, one of many social Catholics who believed that remedies had to be more than purely religious. Social Christianity began to influence many of the *grands notables* and even some of the Orleanist upper classes.

Doctor Villermé is of significance as an observer because he was an Orleanist: whilst influenced by Villeneuve-Bargemont, he remained an economic liberal. A respected figure, member of the Académie de Médecine and the Académie des Sciences Morales et Politiques, the body which had ordered his inquiry into causes of working-class discontent, his report was one of the most influential descriptions of working-class conditions of the period. Entitled *Tableau de l'État morale et physique des ouvriers employés dans les manufactures de laine, de coton et de soie* (1840), it was the first work to apply statistics concerning hygiene and living standards on a large scale. Villermé went beyond statistics, to enter homes, to examine conditions there, not only physical but spiritual. He tried to argue that the state of the working classes was not as abject as some claimed, but the facts he retailed, or descriptions such as that of pale, thin, barefooted women and children traipsing to work in the factories of Mulhouse, clothed in rags oily with grease that dropped from the machines, grasping the piece of bread which was to sustain them during the day,[7] often disproved this optimism. His claim that the lot of the worker had improved ignored the devastating effects of industrial crises, crises which, as Buret said, were "the normal state of our industry".[8] Eugène Buret, who at the age of thirty published his *De la misère des classes laborieuses en Angleterre et en France* and died two years later, went further than Villermé, who was the rapporteur when Buret's work was awarded a gold medal by the Académie des Sciences Morales et Politiques (which had in fact not read it all, and considered many of its proposals impractical). Buret in his turn criticised the body, dominated by liberal ideas, for limiting the question to one of savings, in which they liked to see the answer to industrial problems, which he believed had advanced far beyond the stage of simple equilibrium. The proponents of *laissez-faire* had drawn laws which they claimed to be eternal from the youth of the industrial age, and they were now in its maturity.

Although owing much to social Catholics, believing with them that work could not be treated as a simple commodity, Buret was neither Christian nor revolutionary. He blamed society, not one particular class, and his work is coloured by a striking note of urgency; "It is up to us to sow the seeds of calm or tempest for future generations."[9] His recommendations are more radical than those of any other non-communist. He believed Fourierism to be impossibly Utopian, but wished to see some *phalanstères* tried (which reveals how Fourier's ideas might be taken seriously by practical men). He advocated co-operative societies selling cheap food, and state aid to assist working-class industry. Buret is unusual in that he was committed neither to large- or small-scale industry, but believed in their coexistence. He advocated increased taxation for the rich, beyond the proportion of their wealth, and more state intervention to prevent unemployment. Buret was the first to believe that the ill effects of mechanisation could be remedied within industrialisation itself.

This was to demand too much of a regime whose inception destroyed the moral principles of legitimism, and was equally opposed to visionary Utopias. As Orleanism was politically necessary, so *laissez-faire* was economically necessary. Rules of supply and demand regulated industry and finance, and government intervention would falsify a system, largely satisfactory and wholly inevitable. When in 1837 a crisis loomed, the *Journal des Débats* hoped that the government would not make large-scale grants as in 1830. This mass charity did not befit "a century which prides itself upon having perfected the science of government" and would suggest that Spanish Carlists fighting to maintain convents were leading civilisation.[10] Because it could not be admitted that royalist paternalist and Christian ideals had any merit, governmental welfare action was suspect. Jean-Baptiste Say was almost a patron saint, invoked not only by Orleanist economists, but often by moderate republicans as well.

There was an equilibrium in economics, argued such thinkers: the population would grow with wealth and decrease in response to reductions in salary. As prefect, Charles Dunoyer practised this theory, discouraging charity which he thought encouraged over-population, and further disgusted the clergy by advocating coitus interruptus. Lestiboudois, a *centre gauche* deputy, opposed the reduction of livestock tariffs, arguing that if prices decreased the number of workers would multiply dangerously. Such illogical use of laissez-faire arguments to defend tariffs is perhaps more typical of the thought of the average man of commerce than are the more intellectual concepts of the economists. Men like Dunoyer and Bastiat found to their own satisfaction a happy identification of private and public interests. Bastiat's anti-protectionist *Les Harmonies économiques* proclaims that progress and order are permitted only by the unregulated economy: the consumer's good must also be the general good. Since this was a new science, the economist's job was to observe and explain its laws. Thus Baron Charles Dupin, "Dupin-the-calculator" a peer and brother of the president of the Chamber of Deputies, claimed statistics would become the infallible determinant of all governmental action. As paid spokesman for colonial interests, his *laissez-faire* was combined with protectionism, and in his economic liberalism there was manifest greater disapproval of workers' coalitions than of common action by commercial concerns. Also influential was Adolphe Blanqui (brother of the revolutionary conspirator). He led the liberal majority in the political economy section of the Académie des Sciences Morales (it included Dupin, Hippolyte Passy, Rossi and Villermé) and tried to exclude Villeneuve-Bargemont and others hostile to his doctrines.

In spite of that, these were increasingly influential. Sismondi had attacked Say's optimism, using as evidence slumps and pauperism, and claimed that greater industrial power led to monopolies, not to freedom. Villeneuve-Bargemont developed these ideas further, showing that increased production did not mean increased prosperity if wages were decreased, and answered the liberals' rule of equilibrium with a new law: "The more rich entrepreneurs a country possesses, the more poor workers it confines."[11] Another legitimist, Rubichon, showed how Malthusian prophecies were being realised in France, with industrial overproduction combined with pauperism, against Horace Say who, guarding the liberal dogmas of his older brother, argued that a growth in population would lead to industrial expansion. Rubichon's *Du Mécanisme de la Société en France et en Angleterre* (1833), in spite of its royalist and religious remedies for a landowning hierarchy and Christian corporation, was an influential work, on Louis Blanc amongst others. Similar in its analysis, less reactionary in its recommendations, was the work of the agronomist Baron Bigot de Morogues, typical of his class in regretting that France was turning from its agricultural mission to an industrial state, who suggested state-aided agricultural colonies reclaim land, with high wages to force manufacturers to follow suit.

Because of these attacks and the socialist challenge, the liberal school transferred its ground somewhat: if all was not perfect, this was because equilibrium was prevented from establishing itself: if the lot of the poor appeared to worsen, this was due to the remaining restrictions which the government tolerated. Remove these last barriers and the Utopia of the liberal economists would establish itself. Following the English example, an offensive against protectionism was launched. Springing from a society of Bordeaux viticulturists, l'Association Centrale pour la Liberté d'Échanges became a national organ for free trade. Presided over by the *gauche dynastique* peer, the Duc d'Harcourt (a landowner with metallurgical interests who attacked his fellow owners for self-interest in keeping tariffs high), it had the support of d'Eichtal and a bevy of distinguished economists, Blanqui, Chevalier, Horace Say, Faucher and Bastiat. Rather like Catholicism in the struggle for freedom of education, *laissez-faire*, a force inherently conservative, often sounded radical when attacking a government. Thus Adolphe Blanqui, who became a deputy for Bordeaux, attacked "an aristocracy of tariff supporters",[12] a group of selfish rich men who put up the price of working-class food. Bastiat, although he like Blanqui would have opposed any direct government aid to the poor, similarly posed as their defender. Free trade was a humanitarian question, "the most humanitarian of all the questions posed in our century".[13] It embraced the causes of justice, peace, human unity and fraternity. This apostle of the consumer society argued that protectionists were the enemies of abundance.[14] Free trade was not simply an economic theory: as freedom of education for Montalembert's Catholics, or the community for Utopians, it was a moral necessity. In spite of the English influence which lay behind his ideas and action, Bastiat typified a complex society which chose to believe that one solution would solve all ills, and that there were natural, scientific laws which produced this solution.

Orleanist governments believed in reducing tariffs where possible. Duchâtel, as Minister of Commerce in 1834 and 1835, was able to achieve some results, but throughout the period customs proposals were blocked in the bureaux by deputies whose regional or personal interests were opposed to reforms. Chambers of commerce of many towns provided powerful pressure against allowing increased imports. Sugar-beet growers formed a committee to protect their interests against those of the Bordeaux importers of Caribbean sugar, both trying to win the government to penalise the trade of the other by higher tariffs. Most powerful was the Comité des Intérêts Métallurgiques, a body including forgemasters, timber and coal owners; on its board a Schneider and a de Wendel, deputies and peers, such as the Duc de Mortemart. They were able to help prevent the Belgian customs union, desired for political reasons by Louis-Philippe and Guizot in 1843: the government was not the willing servant of the bourgeoisie, but when such a strong group existed with the support of the Banque and of important deputies such as Jaubert and peers like Decazes, it could only give way to them. Protection was the more powerful because it could feed on Anglophobia, represented genuine fears of foreign competition, and by forming in 1847 a Société pour la Défense du Travail National proved that it too understood the importance of public opinion.

Legitimist, Catholic or aristocratic economic thinkers opposed industrial capitalists as the emanation of a world they disliked, which followed amoral, scientific rules. There was a growth of those who saw neither public or private charity as effective and who demanded radical state action to remedy a growing evil. They came from right and left, but rarely from within the ranks of Orleanism. Being the men in power, Orleanists were obviously less likely to be radical or dissatisfied, but their liberal ideas also predisposed them to avoid much state intervention. That which they did believe in was expansionist rather than reforming in intention. A substantial body of Orleanist opinion, notably the King, Thiers and Molé, and in journalism the *Presse* and *Journal des Débats*, believed in the efficacy of public works programmes. Others such as Bastiat opposed them and all state interference and increased taxation, and many deputies, not necessarily the most conservative, agreed and were sometimes able to limit costly government schemes. In verse as pleasing as the remedy it advocated, Delphine de Girardin in the *Presse* informed her readers that "luxury is charity". Spending money produced employment, she told the economists,

> *"The paradox is great, and I beg pardon for it,*
> *But the poor man is happy when the rich man amuses himself."*[15]

They should theorise less and change their silk cravats more frequently. No doubt this was an economic doctrine most of the middle classes found themselves able to accept.

The problems of industrialisation were so vast that it seemed difficult to reform without destruction. The machine, working, it seemed, in accordance with its own rules, following its own laws not men's, could not be limited in its action without destroying the system which gave it birth. Solutions thus tended to be either Utopian, reactionary as in the case of Rubichon, or communist in Cabet, or mere modifications of existing behaviour which could have had little effect. In between lie various attempts, by Buret, Buchez or Villeneuve-Bargemont, to combine radical state action with a degree of economic freedom, but all were more potent in criticism than suggestion. "We assist in the birth of a new world",[16] declared Buret, and they needed to organise it. Many others would have agreed, in opposition to the liberal economists, that this new world would be hideous if left to itself. Reformers were searching for the idea of a moral community. Buret was apolitical, but most other radical commentators were anti-Orleanist. France could not easily reconcile herself to becoming an industrial civilisation, and within those who accepted it, there were political and cultural divisions on the form industry should take.

The ardent statistician and hygiene expert, Parent-Duchâtelet, a Catholic but an Orleanist, claimed that not all reformers were purely disinterested. Amongst them were many opponents of the regime, those jealous of any authority which did not follow their direction, the Utopians, who dreamed of an impossible future; these, he argued, damaged the cause of the poor by their attacks on the government – "they become philanthropists only to embarrass and obstruct it in its march".[17] In fact, the central government and its agents sometimes emerge better than bourgeois republicans in reforming zeal, and urban and industrial representatives who were politically on the left refused to co-operate with attempts by the prefects just as much as did their Orleanist counterparts.

The bill on child labour, introduced by Cunin-Gridaine in January 1840, was a strictly limited measure, not only in its terms but in its application solely to large-scale industry. The family unit rested upon child labour, and no government would dare to challenge the principle at the base of most of industry. The law affected only a minority, and not necessarily that with the worst conditions. The paternalistic manufacturers of Mulhouse had attempted a voluntary limitation of child labour but it had failed, and they favoured a law. Cunin-Gridaine, himself a great employer, was not only the proponent of the bill, but a believer in inspection. On the other hand, humane men such as Docteur Villermé pointed out that many parents relied upon the income the child might earn. A law, to be acceptable to great industry and to be realistic within the circumstances of the period, could scarcely be radical. Even so, those, often in the opposition, such as Taillandier and Lestiboudois, who believed the state should not interfere in industry and who opposed the bill, achieved by their opposition the wholly inadequate provision of inspectors, not to be appointed by the state but unpaid, chosen by the industrialists. Gay-Lussac, the famous scientist and peer, argued that industry was a sacred untouchable thing, whilst another peer, the doctrinaire liberal Rossi, asserted that children had the right to work. The bill received, however, the support of Montalembert and of Villeneuve-Bargemont, deputy for the Nord, whose writings had done much to prepare opinion for such a measure, although he found it inadequate. It passed because so many ministerialists represented country towns, where machines had scarcely penetrated and child labour on a large scale was unknown, and could therefore follow the dictates of humanitarianism or at least see the illogicality of manufacturers who demanded protection, refusing to countenance state intervention.

The bill which became law in March 1841 concerned factories which employed over twenty workers. There was to be no labour for children under eight years old, a maximum of eight hours for those under twelve, and twelve hours for those under sixteen. Under twelve, they had to go to school, and there were further limitations on night-time working, but because the onus was put on the parents and not on the manufacturer, these restrictions were not always applied. In some departments, the law was poorly observed, for example in the Eure where the former prefect Antoine Passy, *sous-secrétaire d'état* at the Ministry of the Interior, was a person of influence and aided the industrialists in their protests. On the other hand, the Société Industrielle de Mulhouse, a manufacturers' association, protested that the law was insufficiently enforced and asked for independent state-paid inspectors. Due to growing pressure, in 1847 the government decided on a new bill making the minimum age ten, and creating an independent inspectorate, but the regime fell before this became law.

The great Orleanist palliative was the *caisse d'épargne*. That the working classes should save and help themselves was the general answer to those who advocated public assistance. In vain did Villeneuve-Bargemont and Buret stress how difficult it was for workers to save on wages which scarcely paid for their food. Cunin-Gridaine, a conscientious employer, said his employees were unwilling for him to put a proportion of their wages straight into the savings banks because they feared he would then argue that they were earning too much: Buret commented how the need to respond to the tenets of economic liberalism had sunk to the workers. Although limited, the *caisses d'épargne* did expand hugely in number during the July Monarchy, having about 200,000 depositors, with an average of almost 600 francs each by 1848. It was only the childless working-class couple or the better paid, such as the domestic servant, who could thus afford to save. Only 90,000 of the 320,000 Parisian workers made deposits. The fact of expansion was seized upon, however, by such as Charles Dupin who in his pamphlet *Bien-être et concorde des classes du peuple français* (1840), intended for a plebeian readership, argued that antisocial agitators were at the root of all social problems. The workers should not listen to them, nor be coddled with charity, but submit to economic laws and save when they could.

When Buret wrote that "industry has become a war and commerce a game",[18] the commerce he wrote of existed in a financial world whose foundations arose in the previous century. Indeed it was the existence of institutionalised finance governed by men with the Protestant morality of the Delessert family (and almost half the regents of the Banque were Protestant), which led to the two forms of finance, one highly conservative, the other divorced from state control. Banking under the July Monarchy was divided into two forms. One tried to satisfy the demands of expanding industry; the other was one of the great institutions of state, a financial force created by Napoleon. The Banque de France, structure and personnel untouched by the 1830 Revolution, represented the world of government. The notabilities of high finance were on its ruling body, fifteen regents elected by the 200 greatest *actionnaires*. In the 1840s, five were deputies, including Jacques Lefebvre, Joseph Périer and Benjamin Delessert. Four peers, including the Comte d'Argout, the governor, were also regents. Thiers was the son-in-law of another, Dosne, and it was his ministry that renewed the Banque's monopoly to issue nationally valid bills of exchange. It represented inherited fortune and traditional finance rather than new industrial enterprise: in origin, Adolphe d'Eichtal was no exception, but having been influenced by Saint-Simonism, he was usually alone in adherence to more progressive ideas. Although industrial expansion made it necessary for the Banque to create branches, it was not very helpful to industrial enterprise. In the 1846 slump, for example, d'Eichtal wished to reduce interest rates to encourage trade, but the more conservative, led by Odier, feared this would increase speculation and financial disorder. The fact that *rentes*, the state bonds, were 5 per cent and remained so in spite of repeated attempts to lower the interest, shows the power of conservative finance and those such as the King who had political motivations. That interest rates should be high was to the advantage of the *petit bourgeois rentier* as it was for those bankers for whom it was an orthodoxy that low interest rates were financially dangerous. The demands of industrialists and economical progressives could not prevail against this political force.

Banking remained at its head a traditional organisation. Banks were very much family concerns. When Casimir Périer was a regent of the Banque, two of his brothers also sat on the board. They and the Delessert family looked askance at newcomers, of whom the most striking was Jacques Laffitte. His career was astounding and its frequent proximity to disaster and the severe retrenchment forced upon the ostentatious parvenu towards the end of his career, doubtless proved to his more conservative counterparts that they were right not to follow his example. Having become director of the bank he had joined in a very humble capacity, Laffitte considerably expanded and diversified its activity. The year 1830 caused its collapse, but when he had rearranged his affairs he, in 1837, founded his Caisse Général du Commerce et de l'Industrie, built on the belief that credit, at a price, was everybody's right. He tried to attract all capital, even from the small investor, by his terms, which meant that interest rates were high, but he lent with less guarantee from the borrower. Hippolyte Ganneron's Caisse Central du Commerce et des Chemins de Fer followed in 1842, one of many more credit suppliers. The Banque was unfriendly to these, refused them permission to call themselves banks and limited their powers. They did, by their competition, force the banks to lower their interest rates somewhat, but French finance remained very much a closed world and investment banking only became respectable after 1850. Although there were other sources of credit, a growing number of provincial banks and specifically industrial credit societies, it remained an expensive commodity. Bankers preferred speculation in government bonds and railway shares to the risky business of helping industry.

The importance of family assistance or connections is shown by that great success of the period, untypical only in its magnitude, the Schneider brothers' company. Adolphe Schneider, of a banking and mercantile family, began his career in the Seillière bank, and in 1836 he acquired the Le Creusot iron foundry. The money came from Seillière, from another financier known to the family, and from Adolphe Schneider's father-in-law, whilst his brother Eugène had married the grand-daughter of a great iron manufacturer, and thereby gained experience and a dowry. Adolphe directed the commercial side whilst Eugène was responsible for the technical innovations such as the huge presses forging vast pieces of steel. This use of traditional methods of finance for technically progressive manufacturing for locomotives and iron ships was symptomatic of early-nineteenth-century France. It is worth noting that although Adolphe Schneider became a deputy in 1842, the brothers had received no assistance from their cousin, the peer and, for a brief period, minister, Général Schneider. The worlds of industry and politics were still separate.

Indeed some suspicion of capitalism was shown by company legislation.

In this intermediary period between the simple family firm or partnership and the concern which encouraged or relied upon public financial involvement, it was not easy to become legally a company. A *société anonyme* had to gain a government permit for the limited liability of its directors: if refused, the projectors could form a *société en commandite*, where the active partner assumed unlimited liability and other subscribers stood only to lose their capital. Between 1830 and 1840, only 150 companies were allowed into the first category, almost ten times as many into the latter. The Conseil d'État, charged with the task of examining submissions, was strict: primarily a body of conservative lawyers, often landowners, they were unsympathetic towards capitalist enterprises. At one point, even the Chamber of Deputies, disturbed by speculation, considered abolishing *sociétés en commandite*. The companies of this period, although allowing increased public involvement, still put enormous responsibilities upon the manager. Great concerns of mixed interests tended to be formed by the family alliances and close personal links of finance and industry. There was a frequent tendency to extend horizontally: thus the Compagnie des Mines de La Loire had gained control of two-thirds of the mines of the area, a canal and the railway from Saint-Étienne to Lyons. It brought together ironmasters, financiers and railway managers. Accusations of a new feudalism often seem partially justified. The Anzin mines company, connected with the Périer family, virtually controlled Valenciennes, owning its railway, its newspaper and, one might say, its deputy.

The means by which the French industrial revolution most impinged upon the life of the majority, the most striking industrial changes of the period, lie in transport. The reign of Louis-Philippe is notable for railways, but improvements effected in other fields of transport, if less sensational, perhaps had more effect. Canal tariffs were made uniform and moderate; 2,000 kilometres of waterway were built; in particular the river Aisne was linked to the Marne and the Marne to the Rhine. The government paid great attention to roads which the Restoration had rather neglected. During these eighteen years, the distance covered by the *routes royales* almost doubled to reach 35,000 kilometres. The law on *chemins vicinaux* of May 1836 improved local roads enormously by making it statutory for the local authority to maintain them: labour or a tax contribution proportionate to wealth was required from every male in order to perform this. The attention to repair, combined with improvement in carriage building, halved travelling time. The postal service doubled its traffic and the telegraph system, although remaining in government hands, made France a country of improved communication and greater uniformity.

Cuvillier-Fleury, having travelled from Paris to Rouen, marvelled at the courage of himself and his fellow passengers. They had hurtled through dark tunnels for five minutes at a time, suffocating with the smoke, journeying onwards with "an unrelenting rapidity".[19] It was this which made the railway such a symbol of the age, representative of the wonders and horrors of progress, seemingly unstoppable. There had been those, notably Thiers, who dismissed railways as a useless toy, but by 1848 they were an important part of French commercial and social life. The director of Ponts et Chaussées, Legrand, was a strong enthusiast for them: interested in the writings of Michel Chevalier and impressed by the financier Péreire's achievements in constructing a line from Paris to Versailles, he and the Molé government attempted a state-planned railway network. The government's proposal for six lines reaching in all directions from the capital, fell apart because the deputies felt that such a great plan should be undertaken by the state and not by private companies profiting from government aid. New proposals in 1838 which suggested that the state perform the major part, were defeated because now the majority decided it preferred private companies. Political opinions were to the fore: neither Thiers, the president of the commission chosen to examine the measure, nor Arago, its rapporteur, were friendly either to the Molé Ministry or to railways. Indeed the republican astronomer believed that railways were uneconomical because they could not run during the night. Many deputies feared that rival towns to those they represented, would profit, and so the government plan was defeated by sectional interest, the *lutte de clochers*[20] as Viennet called it, small-minded caution and political hostilities.

However, the greater stability of the Soult–Guizot ministry enabled a plan to be drawn up which provided for lines to the Channel, to Belgium, to the Rhine via Strasbourg and Nancy, to Bordeaux and to the Mediterranean via Lyons. Most of this was built by 1848. In the boom which followed the 1842 law in which companies were given large powers in return for certain guarantees, many monopolies formed: the Rothschild–Hottinguer company controlled the Paris–Valenciennes–Lille line which extended to Belgium and then expanded to Dunkirk and Boulogne. The fact that many other concessions of branch lines were granted to smaller companies did not enable them to rival the dominance of this great concern with such powerful interests behind it, which became the Société des Chemins de Fer du Nord, controlling the main lines. The deputies were torn between fear of the great financiers and their dislike of government expenditure.

Those hostile to railways felt justified when in 1838 the first serious accident occurred, on the Saint-Germain line. The next, in 1842, on the route to Versailles was even worse, killing forty people, amongst them men of note, for railway travel was still the prerogative of the wealthy. Contemporaries were unprepared for the carnage of mangled bodies and mechanical wreckage. Guizot forbade the Princesse de Lieven to travel by train after this. However, public interest in the new technology could not long be stifled and the railway boom continued and contemporary willingness to idealise the machine removed political obstacles. The railways profited from ex-Saint-Simonist interest. Arlès Dufour and Enfantin were guiding forces of the great company which in 1844 united important financiers (Charles Laffitte, Péreire, James de Rothschild and others, under the presidency of Gouin) to build a railway from Paris to Lyons. With the respectability of a progressive public enterprise, small investors hurried to place their funds and rich men to sit on the boards of railway companies. The railway boom began to arouse hostility in those who feared an alliance of politics and finance. In 1844, a deputy of the left, Crémieux, attacked those parliamentarians who had joined railway companies. From the Chamber of Peers, Comte Molé responded with an attack upon the spirit of levelling and the destructive jealousies for which Crémieux had become spokesman. He argued that he and Maréchal Gérard, in placing themselves at the head of a national enterprise, were ensuring the honesty of the concern and encouraging the confidence of the public. Molé believed that "powerful industrial associations are the elements of order, stability and conservation",[21] and men of the left were not far from agreeing, thence their hostility. In spite of his lofty defence, Molé resigned his railway directorship, proof primarily of his personal susceptibility but also a sign that involvement in industry was still unusual for a politician. By this time railways were popular however, and every small town wanted one. Proposals for new lines passed easily before the 1846 elections because all feared the unpopularity which might be incurred by resistance to them. It was only the recession beginning that year which slowed the frenetic pace of track building. Industrialists often disliked railways, accusing them of absorbing capital, and they were frequently blamed for causing the slump.

Severe crises were almost a rule of economic life in this period. In 1830, the shock of revolution was added to a recession produced by poor harvests, and created unemployment which was blamed by the workers primarily on the machine, and made 1831 a year of machine-breaking. A period of recovery then ensued, interrupted by a slump which, beginning in 1837, reached its peak early in 1839. This was blamed by the press on speculation, and investment fever, and it is probably true that over-extension of borrowing made the economy vulnerable to a recession which emanated from America. Further years of prosperity followed and then the final crisis of the July Monarchy where economic slump coincided with growing political discontent. Again there was general belief that *agiotage*, speculation and invesment were at fault, although a few, as in 1838, blamed the Banque de France for its failure to provide credit when most needed to save firms from bankruptcy and prevent unemployment. A sign of growing industrial dominance of the economy was that it was increasingly agreed that poor harvests were an aggravating, but not initiating, factor. These crises show the vulnerability of early capitalist society to sudden recession. The closeness of industrial economy to agriculture, the specialisation in which many towns indulged and the weakness in facilities for preventing bankruptcy, meant that a national crisis could emerge from a localised problem.

In autumn 1846, fears of a food shortage began to affect trade. Although bankers ascribed the decline to the Spanish diplomatic crisis, far more important was the slump in England. Because of the bad harvests of 1845 and 1846 and the great floods of the Loire which had caused considerable losses in property and production, there were bankruptcies and borrowing leading to restrictions in credit and a cessation of building programmes which increased unemployment. Bertrand Gille has suggested that there is more than coincidence in the fact that the poorest harvests of the period came in

1839 and 1846 after investment booms, and that proprietors were neglecting fertilisers for speculation. This should show more failures on great properties if it were so, and the drought of 1846 was a more important factor. Although the government made considerable attempts to prevent starvation, it could do little to improve the industrial situation. Governmental action was criticised for its insufficiency, but with such an industrial structure as France possessed, the public works which were intended as remedy could be no more than a palliative. The financial foundations were insufficient to support healthy industrial growth.

Bread prices had in fact decreased during the July Monarchy. In the bad years 1830–32 and 1839–40, it passed 75 centimes for 4 livres, between 1833 and 1837 it was less than 58 centimes, in the prosperous years from 1841 to 1845, it sank to under 34 centimes and then rose to 49 centimes in 1847. It is probable that the poor were better off on the morrow of revolution than they had been seven years before, but the fact of these fluctuations caused extreme suffering. The disaster of 1846–47 was that bad harvests of 1845–47 coincided with potato disease. The latter brought poverty and hunger to areas like Flanders where the peasantry had usually been fairly prosperous. In some areas peasants were forced to eat their rotten potatoes, sometimes dying as a result. Central France, furthest from the ports and grain depots, suffered the most. The department of the Indre saw the worst scenes of violence; there were riots, pillaging and occasionally murders as agricultural unemployment led to a rise in vagabondage. In many areas merchants were afraid to move sacks of cereals. Not only in the country but also in Paris, bakeries were plundered, as often happened in times of famine. In June 1847 in Mulhouse, the "fête of the bakers" saw a workers' strike turn into serious riots: to prevent looting, troops were used and five rioters were shot when they refused to retreat. The government sent rainforcements by rail to Strasbourg: troubles spread to the neighbouring towns but soon died out. None the less, this had been the first sign of radical class-consciousness amongst the hitherto apathetic spinners of that area.

By spring 1847, massive imports had relieved the shortage and the 1847 harvest brought prices down but the financial crisis took longer to disappear. A depletion of state reserves and loss of confidence had caused the Banque to raise its interest rate, improving its reserves but harming enterprise. The budget went into heavy deficit due to the government's enormous borrowing and grain buying. The railways were most vulnerable because they had hugely borrowed at high rates. The government came to the rescue of some companies threatened with collapse but could not prevent several dramatic bankruptcies. The consequence for the rich and middle classes was not as painful as for the poor, but many families met disaster. A rise in bankruptcies, 462 in 1845 when the first credit stringency was felt, 531 in 1847, was accompanied by an increase in bourgeois suicides. The *petit bourgeoisie* blamed the rich or the government for unemployment or reduction in living standards, and became more radical in its political beliefs. The electoral victory late in 1847 of the *gauche dynastique* Berger, replacing a rich conservative in a previously governmental Paris *arrondissement*, was a warning to the government of disaffection amongst the bourgeoisie, to be shown fatally by the National Guard in February 1848.

The July Monarchy has been seen as the apotheosis of *laissez-faire* but was not in fact so. The government interfered considerably in most aspects of the nation's economic life. The child labour law of 1841 and the proposed extensions of 1847 may seem a very inadequate response to the horrors of industrialism, although the French record compares favourably with the British. Many small reforms were performed by ordinance, such as rigid measures on colouring of food and matters of hygiene. The 1838 law which regulated the exploitation of mines, subjecting the holders of concessions to many rules to ensure safety and co-ordination of exploitation, and the law on local roads of 1836, were substantial pieces of governmental interference in local prerogatives and personal economic liberties. State intervention in railways, the sewerage programme, construction of fortifications and other public works show a positive attitude towards the governmental economic role. This is not surprising, given the tradition of the Napoleonic state and the fact that although some, like Guizot, mistrusted it, others, notably Thiers, positively intended that the constitutional regime should emulate the achievements of this forerunner. A lack of uniformity, a certain incoherence limited possibilities of action, as the growing complexities of the capitalist system under a constitutional regime created a proliferation of conflicting economic interests. Writing to his son, the Baron de Barante agreed, without enthusiasm, that "politics becomes almost exclusively a matter of commerce" and admitted to him that "the authority of the government is not strong enough to fight against the clamour of private interests",[22] thinking primarily of the government's failure to withstand the protectionists.

The tax structure represented the dominance of the wealthy, and was sanctified by liberal ideas. When a deputy of the left in April 1832 demanded suppression of taxes on salt and wine and, in return, a tax on revenue from property, Thiers replied that direct taxation was as blind as the war of which it was the expression and the result – "that tax of passion, it is the spirit of '93 in administration!"[23] Indirect taxation, on the other hand, was the child of liberty because it taxed appetites which could be restricted. And on workers' attempts to coalesce against their employers, bourgeois interests similarly converged with liberal ideology. On the morrow of 1830, Odilon Barrot was surprised that workers who had fought for liberty on the barricades should so forget its principles as to associate to demand higher wages. Only very slowly throughout the regime did Orleanists come to revise the dogmatic liberalism with which they came to power in 1830. Amongst prefects, the Vicomte de Saint-Aignan, in the department of the Nord, was unusual in seeing the causes of working-class discontent elsewhere than in the evil nature of the workers, and in understanding that wealth went to the wealthy and believing that it was the government's duty to try to improve relations between employer and worker. The articles by Granier de Cassagnac in the *Presse*, the Duc de Montpensier's awareness of proletarian problems, the growth of a pressure group around the Comte de Melun are signs of changing attitudes, but the July Monarchy was given no opportunity for them to fructify.

Commerce became increasingly democratised. If the Banque retained its immense powers, the credit institutions and railways put speculation within the reach of many a bourgeois who previously would have remained cautiously within the bounds of his profession. Bonds were no longer 1,000 francs or more, but 100 or less, sometimes as low as 20 francs, to attract the increasing number of small investors. Every pressure group had behind it a number of lesser fry whose electoral importance was huge. "Gold is the only idol to which one burns incense" wrote Scribe in one of his plays. The July Monarchy had already gained that characteristic factor of modern societies, a democratic cupidity and widespread expectation of wealth, combined with the belief that greed was the besetting fault of others. Each group saw egoism rampant in another. The disciple of Buchez, Auguste Ott, in *Des conséquences de l'égoisme en politique et en industrie* (1840), and the legitimist Rubichon in his works against mechanisation, agreed in criticising a society in which only the strong man prospered, whilst Orleanists blamed the individualism of anarchists who sowed dissension, and the *petit bourgeois* accused the *haute bourgeoisie* of rapacity. Tocqueville, like other opponents of *laissez-faire*, asked what happened to the spirit of a man who spent his life making pin-heads. And from this malign industrialism emerged a new aristocracy, "one of the harshest to appear on the face of the Earth",[24] which brutalised its work-force and in times of crisis threw them on to public charity. For most outside their number, the upper-middle classes became the prime culprits of civilisation's ills, and this class was primarily associated with Orleanism. The economic crisis made the *petits bourgeois* feel like revolutionaries, adding social grievances to their political dissatisfaction with the regime. In spite of the horrors of industrialism, it was not the suffering proletariat of Lille or Roubaix which rose in February 1848, but that traditional revolutionary class, the artisans of Paris.

REFERENCES

1. A. Karr, *Les Guêpes* (1858), IV, 22.
2. C. Nodier, *Correspondance* (1876), 252.
3. A. J. B. Parent-Duchâtelet, *De la Prostitution dans la Ville de Paris* (1836), I, 16.
4. E. Buret, *De la Misère des classes laborieuses en Angleterre et en France* (1840), III, 162–3.
5. L. Villermé, *Tableau de l'état physique et moral des ouvriers* (1840), I, 96.
6. Comte A. de Villeneuve-Bargemont, *Economie Politique Chrétienne* (1834), 12.
7. Villermé, op. cit., 72.
8. Buret, op. cit., I, 186.
9. Ibid., 58.
10. *Journal des Débats*, 24 March 1837.

11. Villeneuve-Bargemont, op. cit., 379.
12. A. Blanqui, *Histoire de l'économie politique en Europe* (1845), II, 320.
13. F. Bastiat, *Œuvres complètes* (1881), I, 109.
14. Ibid., IV, 5.
15. *La Presse*, 29 March 1837.
16. Buret, op. cit., I, 62.
17. Parent-Duchâtelet, op. cit., I, 11.
18. Buret, op. cit., I, 62.
19. F. H. G. Limbourg (ed.), *Correspondance du duc d'Aumale et de Cuvillier-Fleury* (1910–14), I, 154.
20. L. Viennet, *Journal* (1955), 277–8.
21. *Journal des Débats*, 27 May 1838.
22. Baron P. de Barante, *Souvenirs* (1890), VII, 84.
23. Archives Parlementaires, 15 Avril 1832.
24. A. de Tocqueville, *Démocratie en Amerique* (1835), 298.

26

Republics and Utopias

"Venez, peuples, venez au banquet social!
Venez, sceller la loi nouvelle."

("Come, people, come to the social banquet!
Come, to seal the new law.")[1]

"Ah! philosophe, tu veux nous séduire; nous vivrons cent quarante-quatre ans, dis-tu, si nous réalisons ton système."

("Ah! philosopher, you wish to seduce us; we will live one hundred and forty-four years, you say, if we carry out your system.")[2]

Republicanism was a divided creed. In the 1840s, the new issues of socialism and communism added themselves to the previous divisions between the patient and the activists. There were many republicans like Béranger (who had helped bring the July Monarchy into existence) who attacked the government, yet felt the French were not ready for a republic: a weak constitutional regime, he believed, would disgust them, enabling a republic to arrive by peaceful, not revolutionary, means.[3] Or Victor Hugo, in the early years of the regime only half an Orleanist regretted the fear of the Republic for which he blamed the violence of its devotees, whilst looking forward to its eventual appearance. Thus a romantic genaration scanned the horizon and found there a glimmering chimera, but often recoiled from those who rushed into action. Even the less moderate had difficulty deciding when action was justified. The republicans would mock the *juste milieu* for worshipping its own revolution and disapproving of others, but fundamentally their own view was similar: revolution was justified by success. When the *Tribune* believed successful insurrection possible, it would support it, as in 1834, but at other times, it used only vague revolutionary rhetoric – an encouragement from which it could dissociate itself, politically if not morally.

Liberal republicans such as Carrel, felt increasing disgust or fear with their party. Francois de Corcelles left the Association de la Presse in 1833, saying he could not accept the dictatorship and suspension of individual rights which the majority of the committee deemed necessary. In so far as there was a republican orthodoxy, it had become a vague Jacobinism, but in reality there were as many republican theories as there were republican leaders. The *Revue Républicaine* in 1834 anounced that equality was the aim of society, and significantly viewed this equality in economic as much as in political terms. But its practical suggestions for reforms were moderate: a maximum twelve-hour working day and minimum wage which would cover the cost of living for a man and his family and allow a small surplus for savings. In spite of talk of equality, Jacobin social and economic reform was still in the age of Robespierre. None the less, the necessity of replying to the social formulae of Saint-Simonism and Fourierism encouraged the diluted influence of Buonarroti to spread throughout the republican movement: equality became more important than liberty, whilst fraternity was advocated against Orleanist individualism and bourgeois egoism. The ground lost in 1830 could only be recaptured by becoming "popular" and so, inspired by Argenson and others, the republicans began to pay more attention to purely working-class movements. The republican press began to convert bourgeois republicans from liberalism to a combination of socialism and Jacobinism. So Thomas, prefect of the Bouches-du-Rhône, complained that there was no village in his department but had its advocate of the merits of the sharing of goods, and of the guillotine.[4]

The débâcle of 1834 left the party without leadership, and until 1839 the conspiratorial tradition was maintained and dominated by one man, Auguste Blanqui. Opposed to Utopias, unconcerned with future constitutions or economic principles, his obsession was to destroy what existed. Not only the monarchy but religion also had to be uprooted, and then a dictatorship brought into being by creating equality and educating the people in republican virtue. Blanqui worried little about the details. He conspired to produce the destruction from which he believed the perfect Republic would emerge, and in 1834 he began to try to implement his vocation. The Société des Familles was a more disciplined body than the Droits de l'Homme, and purely Parisian. At the peak was Blanqui who appointed the "families", sections of six who were separate and ignorant of each other. The leadership was in the hands of intellectuals and propertied men, the members usually young shopkeepers or artisans. Blanqui's lieutenant was Armand Barbès, a young southerner of independent means, enthusiastic but undisciplined, with an extrovert warmth completely lacking in the cold fanatical Blanqui, with whom he was later to come into bitter conflict. The Familles recruited members, tried to infiltrate the National Guard, and collected ammunition, until Pépin, the accomplice of Fieschi, betrayed the existence of their arsenal to the police. The leaders of the conspiracy received only short sentences, and in 1837 Blanqui began creating a new but similar organisation, the Société des Saisons. A "week" had seven members, four week leaders made a month, three of these formed a season, four of these a year, and, at the top, each representing a year, were Blanqui, Barbès and Bernard. The society probably never reached the 1,000 members which this structure was designed to hold. Because of its secrecy, there was little activity it could undertake save the practising of certain rituals, repetition of bloodthirsty slogans and the amassing of weapons. It had to remain disciplined, waiting for the opportunity to initiate the revolution.

Blanqui tried to prevent useless individual assassination attempts, but Champion, arrested with plans to kill Louis-Philippe, was a member of the Saisons, and the Grouvelle powder factory which intended to blow up the King was closely connected with it. Members of the Saisons were probably also connected with the very violent, secretly and irregularly published, *Moniteur républicain* and *L'Homme libre*. This underground activity had few external effects, however. The years 1836 to 1839 form a period of superficial quiescence in France. The Champion and Grouvelle plots, like that of Aloysius Hüber who had invented an improved *machine infernale* with which to dispose of the monarch, were discovered by the police before they could reach fruition.

The difficulty confronting republican leaders was that in order to rouse enthusiasm they spoke violently, to encourage confidence they spoke of triumph as inevitable and to maintain readiness they had to present the final struggle as imminent, all of which made it difficult to discipline their troops. There was growing impatience late in 1838 amongst the members of the Saisons and a group demanding action emerged. Blanqui had to admit the time was ripe: in 1839, an economic slump was accompanied by a political crisis initiated by the downfall of the Molé ministry. As the ministerial crisis dragged on throughout the spring with unemployment in Paris increasing, Blanqui decided to accede to his followers' impatience, overruling Barbès who believed victory impossible. He prepared a battle plan for 12 May which directed even where the barricades, normally the improvised strategy of urban warfare, should be constructed: "We are going to fight"[5] Blanqui announced to his surprised staff on the Sunday morning. So little were the authorities expecting any manifestation, that Gabriel Delessert, the prefect of police, like most of fashionable Paris, was at the races at Chantilly.

Scarcely 500 were present of the presumed 1,000 members, and very few joined them from the streets. It was the first time that most of them had seen their leaders, and the unimpressive sight may have disillusioned some and lessened their fighting spirit. After the necessary pillaging of an arms shop, Barbès led one section to the Palais de Justice where the outnumbered guard were disarmed: in the mêlée an officer was shot, an unprovoked crime of which Barbès, possibly wrongly, was later accused. The next strategic point, the Prefecture of Police, defended itself, and Barbès, deciding not to risk his small force in battle, proceeded to the Hôtel de Ville. Here, while the insurgents forced the guard to yield their weapons, he was able to read, from the balcony where La Fayette had embraced the Duc d'Orléans, a proclamation signed by himself, Blanqui, Bernard and, without their knowledge, by d'Argenson, La Mennais and Laponneraye. "The cowardly tyrant of the

Tuileries mocks the hunger that tears the bowels of the people, but the measure of his crimes has reached its peak. They are finally going to receive their chastisement."[6] He called upon the people to rise in revolt. But none showed a sign of so doing, and the *garde municipale* and troops were able to surround the insurgents and capture most of them, including Barbès, fighting to the last. On 13 May, all final scattered resistance collapsed: the last hope of the insurrection, the students, failed to join the dead cause. The effort cost the lives of thirty soldiers and twice as many insurgents. The role of Blanqui was inglorious: the men supposedly under his command had built a few barricades before being arrested, but Blanqui seems to have been too frightened to show himself and temporarily escaped.

This pathetic attempt to return to the days of 1834 received strong disapproval in the depleted republican press. Both Blanc's *Revue du Progrès* and the *National* found it foolhardy and blameworthy. At the trial, Barbès refused to defend himself, appointing himself judge of the peers who faced him, denying responsibility for the death of the shot lieutenant and, with an egoistic chivalry which displeased Blanqui, claiming entire responsibility for the insurrection. He received the death sentence, the others lesser penalties. Barbès's penalty raised considerable emotion in the Latin Quarter. More than 2,000 students protested to the Ministry of Justice, and Victor Hugo produced an emotional poem asking the King to spare Barbès's life. But before he presented it, Louis-Philipps had persuaded the Cabinet to commute the sentence, although the ministry had acted on the peers to obtain a severe sentence and it put up determined resistance to the King's desire for clemency. Barbès was sent to Mont-Saint-Michel, where he would later be joined by Blanqui. The prison was cellular; no more were the jovial evenings of Sainte-Pélagie, until in 1844 public opinion forced the government to relent, allowing the prisoners to mingle. The Second Republic was to see the two conspirators return to public life, although their mutual recriminations for the failure had made them bitter enemies.

Some who had escaped capture in May 1839 reassembled in a new organisation called the Nouvelles Saisons. It had less than 600 members and was poorly led, the appearance of its members linking arms at Garnier-Pagès's funeral being its only public manifestation. Under the leadership of Flocon, then Caussidière, then the worker Martin (who as Albert was a minister in 1848), attempts were made to inject some spirit into the republican underworld. But it was not only small but divided; a Société Dissidente emerged – the old division between the violent and the more violent. However, these societies were predominantly working class, a change from 1831. In 1847, a rival group engaged in manufacturing bombs was caught. These movements presented no great threat as long as police agents discovered such conspiracies before fruition. In the eyes of many, they discredited republicanism by their violence and made it ridiculous by their ineffectiveness. Even the spirit seemed to go out of assassination attempts, for the two remaining attempts to kill the King were the work of unbalanced individuals rather than political manifestations.

In 1840, the more moderate republicans made an effort to re-create the movement as a national force after the conspiratorial years. There was an attempt to create in Paris a party organisation with local committees: although it failed, about 100 candidates fought the 1842 elections in the republican interest. Meanwhile, they presented their ideology in a *Dictionnaire politique*. This work, which went into several editions, was introduced by Étienne Garnier-Pagès, who died before it was published, and contained, amongst others, contributions from its publisher Pagnerre, Marrast, Blanc and Thoré. Its basic creed was universal suffrage, and its historical views were Jacobin. Garnier-Pagès justified revolt against despotism, but did not recommend it. Socially, it was vague, reflecting tendencies of the time in diluted forms. The usual attacks on bourgeois egoism, criticisms of the Utopias of Fourier and Saint-Simonism, and of communism were included. It recommended tax reforms, ending tax on non-luxury consumption, and a progressive income tax, but no real socialism appeared in these pages, whilst the inclusion of an article by Lamennais testified to a decrease in hostility to religion amongst republicans.

This restatement of moderate republicanism was paralleled by an improvement in the fortunes of the *National*. Whereas the secret societies were dominated by the *déclassé* bourgeois, the young men on the *National* lived an existence which was typical of the middle-class dandy. These journalists paid themselves such large salaries that they almost bankrupted the paper for which they wrote. After the death of Carrel, replaced very briefly by Sainte-Beuve, Armand Marrast became its editor. Writing as elegantly as he dressed, he forgot his demands for revolutionary action made when an editor of the *Tribune*. Although the *National* violently scorned the government, it was moderate in its economic and social policies, which were rooted in liberalism, giving the state only a role of arbitration. Most of its readers were middle class, and many of them were not truly republican. Ironically, it was the most purely free-trade newspaper, following Jean-Baptiste Say in his attack on financial oligarchies, but remaining unsympathetic to state intervention. Such policies were shared by many followers of Barrot who feared a Jacobin republic but delighted in vivacious attacks on Guizot and Louis-Philippe.

Étienne Garnier-Pagès had led the small parliamentary republican contingent with tactical skill: his wry humour and moderation in debate had made his death regretted outside his own party. The successor who inherited his seat symbolised some of the changes taking place in republicanism in the 1840s. The lawyer, Ledru-Rollin, was a scion of a prosperous Parisian medical family, of typically Orleanist background, but he spoke with radical accents. Le Mans, for which he became deputy, was a town of strong republican activity: the *Courrier de la Sarthe* was a successful republican daily and the mayor, Trouvé-Chauvel, and his deputy were republicans. His electoral speech was a demand for radical reform, in economic as well as political terms. Universal suffrage was the means to a social end. In the Chamber of Deputies, François Arago had already spoken of the need to "organise work"[7] but in spite of the fact that both he and Ledru-Rollin thus adopted the phrase of the socialist Louis Blanc, neither meant much more than a vague recommendation to state intervention. Ledru-Rollin was always more violent in style than in substance, but he was prosecuted for his electoral speech, which naturally increased its effect. The jury found him guilty on a minor charge, but after an appeal acquitted him on a technicality. He was never much respected by his party or by fellow deputies. The campaign for electoral reform, however, gave the republicans a national platform, and his tendency to rant proved an advantage.

Through his private wealth and as parliamentary representative of the more radical republicans, Ledru-Rollin was able to gain control of a newspaper. The *Réforme*, which, with 2,000 subscribers, obtained only half the circulation of the *National*, spoke for his group, including Cavaignac (until his early death), Beaune, Flocon and Caussidière. Although more radical than the *National*, neither it nor the *Journal du Peuple* espoused violence, and the danger to their existence was less governmental action than unprofitability. At Châlons, this group gained control of the reformist banquet: Lamartine, Antoine Garnier-Pagès and other moderates stayed away. Ledru-Rollin fervently praised Robespierre, and Flocon announced "We are the reds."[8] The cheers they received, like the readers of their newspaper, were mostly lower middle class. As Orleanist conservatism became increasingly associated with the *haute bourgeoisie*, the dissatisfied increasingly found the radical accents of Jacobinical republicanism acceptable. Although he claimed to be a socialist, in fact Ledru-Rollin believed that small property was sacrosanct, and that only great wealth was politically undesirable.

As a new term, "socialism" was being used to describe a broad variety of suggestions for reforming society: the significance lies not in any meaning of the word but in that so many chose to pin this label on themselves. It had been introduced into the French vocabulary by Pierre Leroux who presented it as a moral communion for society, a transcendent common cause. It thus tended to become very vague. "Charity is socialism",[9] announced Lamartine in 1834. Thus for many, socialism was simply the contrary to bourgeois individualism, and no further definition was found necessary.

Its foremost proponent in France was Louis Blanc. The diminutive theoretician, a former teacher from a middle-class official family, became famous when he published his *Histoire des Dix Ans*, an eloquent, if unreliable, account of the first half of the July Monarchy. For a time he was editor of a republican newspaper, the *Bon Sens*, until, too radical for its owners, he was dismissed. In 1839 he published his *L'Organisation du Travail* (which sold 6,000 copies within a few weeks and had gone into five editions by 1848). It was responsible for spreading socialist ideas amongst the Parisian artisans, whilst Chevalier's criticism and Blanc's response in the *Journal des Débats* in February 1845, brought them before an educated bourgeois readership. The views Blanc propounded combined social radicalism with a hostility to the violent revolution desired by most extreme republicans. He aimed to avert it by the state extending credit to groups to purchase the materials of their labour. In this way, capitalism would gradually disappear. Blanc tried to persuade the bourgeoisie that private enterprise and unfettered competition would, by bankruptcy, impoverish them. The people, however, were the force behind change, and by the "people" he meant not the broad peasant mass which constituted the majority of the French population, nor women who would not be allowed to vote because of their superstitious proclivities, but a revolutionary crowd of artisans, small farmers and *petite bourgeoisie*. In the associations and workshops they created, co-operation, not competition, would be the basis of behaviour and profit would serve the common good, not private pleasures. Whereas Buchez and *L'Atelier* desired a mixed economy, Blanc's mixture was purely transitional. The new society would provide an education for citizenship: Blanc, like other republicans, believed in the necessity to root out old ideas, spiritual as well as political. Also, with other republicans (a notable exception being Raspail), he demanded an aggressive foreign and colonial policy. Frenchmen, he believed, were superior to other peoples: France, progressive and unselfish, should lead all nations. It was his complaint that bourgeois civilisation, self-centred and unpatriotic, sacrificed too much to peace. Blanc, however, was not as rigidly centralist as many Jacobins. His workshops were to have substantial powers of self-government; an *atelier*-based society being an especially French, or Parisian, form of socialism.

Raspail might be unusual in his pacifism, but his eccentric and quarrelsome character isolated him from his fellow republicans, although not from the poor whom, as a doctor, he devotedly served. With 500 subscribers or less, his *Réformateur* depended upon private assistance, and its readership was scarcely more than the loyalty of friends and disciples. Followers such as Marc Dufraisse and Jean-Jacques Vignerte had, under the auspices of the Société des Droits de l'Homme, published pamphlets suggesting state finance for workers' associations, attacking the conception of property as a natural right, but none of these publications had much effect outside a narrow circle.

In Pierre Leroux, former polytechnician and Saint-Simonian, socialism was more a religious than a political programme. He believed that man was perfectible and that humanity, dead and living together, was God: individualism and egoism destroyed the essential unity of mankind and prevented its progress. This romanticised version of deism, combined with nineteenth-century historicism, predicted a future of complete concord. Leroux preferred the word "communionism", the ultimate in fraternity, to "communism" with its drier political sound. Since all shared in the state, the community would reflect the perfection of everyman which the destruction of a corrupt society had released. The exact arrangement of this state was vague, but Leroux would presumably have argued that politics would disappear with the conflicts they represented. He had a passionate admirer and apologist in George Sand. His ideas harmonised with her belief in the sacerdotal role of the artist. In *Consuelo*, Leroux's philosophy receives exposition in the forms of the sentimental romantic novel: the doom of the House of Rudolstadt is symbolic of an aristocracy which has to expiate past crimes against the workers and good triumphs in the fictional happiness of socialist heroes. The philosopher and the novelist published the *Revue Indépendante* and then the *Revue Sociale*, and a local newspaper in Sand's province, *L'Éclaireur de l'Indre*, which had readers in the small manufacturing towns of the area. Leroux's belief that society could not live without religion was an obsession of the age, and his mystical conception of humanity was popular with many. Those students who found Cousin's historicism too bourgeois, found attractions in Leroux's eloquent predictions of a perfect proletarian future. Others, disgusted by the ugliness of a world in which, as George Sand put it, "wealth has suffocated beauty",[10] accepted Leroux's assurances that perfect art would emanate from a perfectly organised society.

Frenchmen first noticed communism in 1840. In July, in Belleville, as a counterpart to the reformist banquet from which they had been excluded as too extreme, those who put social revolution, violent of necessity, before political change, held their own gathering. Not all the 1,200 present were necessarily communist, but they heard from the platform several speeches expressing extreme ideas. Dezamy attacked those like Ledru-Rollin who believed that universal suffrage was a panacea: inequality, he asserted, could only be destroyed if social and political revolution went hand in hand. Pillot reviled the bourgeoisie and spoke of the workers' rights. Various other speeches, ranging from sloganising to sophisticated social analysis, present the same views.

In May and June 1840 had appeared the only two copies of *L'Égalitaire*; its editor was Théodore Dezamy, later the author of the *Code de la Communauté* (1843). In these publications, he tried to prove that inequality is the source of evil, whilst "Community! Community! All possible good is summarised in that single word."[11] Communes of about 10,000 would be created, whose inhabitants would live in one huge habitation and take meals in common in groups of 1,000. Dezamy, like Cabet, was convinced that the organisation of his communist Utopia would enable men to work less and consume more, but his was a puritan regime where luxury and smoking were banned, marriage prohibited and sexual intercourse made purely functional. Although Latin was proposed as the language of communist society whose sweet habits would enable beasts like the zebra to be tamed, Dezamy dared criticise Fourier for irrationality. His communism was scientific he claimed, being based upon material things, and it was inexcusable to disagree with the obvious. Jean-Jacques Pillot would have agreed, and in his pamphlet, *Ni Châteaux, ni chaumières* (1840), advocated violent revolution but showed less concern with the exact details of the result. Implicated in the Saisons plot, Pillot also served six months in prison, found guilty of having encouraged Quénisset to shoot Aumale.

Other communists were not so materialist. For Alphonse Esquiros, writer and journalist, communism had a religious basis. God's own unity commanded human unity, nationally and socially. Jesus Christ was the first *sans-culotte*, and he developed this idea in his *L'Évangile du Peuple*, one of those mixtures of biblical style and political content which show the influence of Lamennais. For calling the poor to revolt in violent terms, Esquiros was imprisoned for six months. Similarly punished, and even more extreme, was the unbalanced priest Abbé Constant who, in *La Bible de la Liberté* (1841), counselled would-be suicides to murder a rich man before their self-inflicted demise.

Communist ideas were also found in certain clubs. The Saisons survived as the Nouvelles Saisons or Travailleurs Égalitaires, more explicitly communist than before, with *métiers* (trades), *ateliers* (workshops) and *fabriques* (factories) replacing the former divisions. As in other republican organisations, however extreme, some groups would find their fellows excessively moderate, and so a section of activists split off to call itself the Société Communiste Révolutionnaire. Members tried to start an insurrection by shooting at police at the Garnier-Pagès funeral in 1841. Darmès, who tried to assassinate the King in the autumn of 1840, had been a member of a communist club, but had acted alone. The *procureur général* prosecuted two members of the Travailleurs Égalitaires but the peers refused to accept their complicity, although in 1841 they sentenced the journalist Dupoty and other communists for encouraging Quénisset. The rash of writings and outbreak of communist activity in 1840 was probably the result of Blanqui's political failure and of the labour unrest of that year. It certainly frightened the government which took measures to try to stamp it down. Sometimes as a result of prosecutions for illegal association, the clubs became mere drinking parties. The Club de la Chopinette, meeting at a suburban wine merchant's shop, sang bloodthirsty songs and put their principles into practice by sharing their womenfolk. The Société Matérialiste preached an extreme of violence, amorality and atheism.

> *"With the guts of the last of the priests,*
> *Let us strangle the last of the kings"*[12]

a couplet from one of their songs, is a summary of their creed. Accepting Proudhon's maxim that property is theft, they stole. These and other groups, straddling the worlds of politics and crime, talked long of bloody plans to overthrow order.

Although Marx was active in Paris between 1843 and 1845 (when Guizot expelled him in response to Prussian demands), his writings had no effect either on French intellectuals or on the insular French communists. They had a very vague conception of class. Their recruitment was artisanal and *petite bourgeois* rather than truly proletarian. "Orleanist communism" participated in the common obsessions of this period in France: rather than a class struggle, it saw a conflict of interest groups, a mass of individuals who needed to have a common will imposed upon them. They reflected anticlerical, nationalist and terrorist traditions of the French Revolution taken to an extreme. These traditions, which had earlier informed the republican societies, now became more purely communist and terrorist. By 1848 the state had won the battle against the secret societies. The 500 men of the disorganised Société Dissidente or the Société Communiste were too much a minority: although gradually increasing their influence, they seemed in no way comparable to the mammoth conspiracy of the Société des Droits de l'Homme. But in a revolutionary situation, 500 determined men, or indeed, one gunshot, may prove decisive.

For the broad masses of the industrial working classes the arid violence of such communists held as little attraction as did the cerebral politicising of the *National*. Perhaps it was the hopelessness of their condition which made perfection seem scarcely more unlikely than amelioration, perhaps the need for vision of a people enslaved to machines, or the desire for religion of a displaced class recently torn from its traditional beliefs, attracted the workers to Utopianism. The majority of visionaries foresaw an idealised agrarian society, and in this the prophets of the proletariat resembled more the social Catholics than the technocratic young bourgeois of Saint-Simonism. Yet with the latter, they shared a limitless belief in the perfectibility of man placed in a beneficent environment. A recent tradition of revolutions had engendered a belief in the ability to change society radically; a faith in historical forces made these changes appear irresistible. Utopianism was the inheritance of eighteenth-century optimism combined with hostility to its individualism; for whatever separated the various proponents of perfection, all were agreed that a communal and socialist existence would uproot egoism from the human soul.

Étienne Cabet was of working-class origin, unlike most other republican or socialist leaders. The gifted child of prosperous artisans, he had entered the law and joined the Charbonnerie under the Restoration. One of those promoted by Dupont and removed by Périer, he became a deputy for Dijon, qualifying by means of a friend's transferring property to his name. He joined the extreme section of the *mouvement*, became secretary-general of the Association Libre which instituted educational courses for workers and editor of *Le Populaire*, a newspaper with a wide sale, aimed particularly at the working man. During the spell in exile to avoid prosecution over the violent attacks his newspaper had delivered on Louis-Philippe, Cabet moved from advocacy of working-class self-help towards socialism. In his *Histoire Populaire de la Révolution Française* (1839–40), he justified Robespierre and presented him as a man of communist vision. In 1840 he published the work which made him famous, the *Voyage en Icarie*, a lengthy account of a Utopian state founded by Icar, a benevolent Napoleon or super-Robespierre, who, brought to power by popular revolution, embarks on a programme of radical reform. Within fifty years, without violence but through propaganda, Icar has transformed the state and human nature by establishing equality. The people wish to worship Icar as a second Christ, but he had not wished this (Cabet, who obviously saw himself in this role, felt he might not aspire to deity) so instead the people named the country after its reformer. In this land of joyful labour and noble ceremony, egoism, avarice and immorality would disappear. A moral education having reformed human nature, newspapers might give only facts, not opinions, the theatre would show the crimes of the past and joys of the present, and all art must be approved by the elected authorities. In the *Voyage* and *Le Vrai Christianisme* (1846) Cabet, although anticlerical, presented Icaria as the development of the teaching of Christ, "the bravest revolutionary to have appeared on the face of the Earth".[13] To the title *Père*, sign of working-class affectionate respect, he, like Enfantin before him, gave a mystical significance.

Cabet's *Voyage* was a considerable success and in March 1841 he published the first issue of his monthly *Le Populaire*, the organ of pacific communism. It avoided the governmental prosecution which had destroyed the violent and anarchistical *L'Humanitaire* after only two issues. Parisian workers co-operated in its financing, but the enterprise was firmly conducted by Cabet who used its offices as a party headquarters. *Le Populaire* was the most successful journal for the working class, reaching a printing of 4,500 in 1847, many of which would have been shared copies or read in *cabarets*: its rivals, *La Fraternité, La Ruche Populaire* and *L'Atelier*, sold less than 1,000 copies each. Cabet's paper was more entertaining and less theoretical than these, but it did have a subdivision headed "social disorder" where it described working conditions, proletarian hardships, capitalist crimes, upper-class debauchery and other manifestations of inegalitarian society. Correspondents and travelling propagandists, led by the indefatigable Cabet, spread the gospel and formed cells in the provinces. Lyons and Paris were the foremost centres, then after 1843 his influence grew in Toulouse, Vienne and in the declining port of Nantes. The skilled, and often literate, artisan was the usual follower. Icarianism was successful, probably having about 100,000 followers at its peak, because it catered for the family: children were welcomed, games were played and songs sung at meetings.

However, like other movements, it began to split. Cabet had promised Utopia within fifty years, but even this seemed too long for some. There were many who felt that Icaria would have to be created by violent means, and advocated immediately doing so. By 1848 many of the sections were no longer under Cabet's control. The largest communist association, it seriously worried the government, and in 1847, Duchâtel, Minister of the Interior, decided that its dangerous principles had to be eradicated by preventing the publication of the *Populaire*. A period of persecution began, and Cabet decided to found his Icaria in liberty. A few days before the February Revolution, a band of hopeful Icarians embarked for New Orleans.

Cabet's main rival in Utopia was Charles Fourier, who as unsuccessful business man was personally acquainted with the woes of capitalist existence. Although his theories were formulated well before 1830, they only became celebrated after the July Revolution when ambitious and fantastic remedies for society's problems were voraciously sought, and profited by the collapse of Saint-Simonism because he appealed to the same combination of scientism, mysticism and sensualism, but taking them still further. Fourier, typical of the age, combined a craving for harmony with unwillingness to restrict the passions; what the community was for Dezamy and Cabet, the *phalange* was for Fourier. Man individually is imperfect but, he claims, an organisation created on rational and scientific lines makes him a perfect organism, like the bee in the hive. The *phalange*, an area of 500 acres, a large edifice of varied rooms for 2,000 people, is the universal remedy. Within it, inequality of wealth would be permitted, but a minimum standard of living was guaranteed. He planned to end the drudgery of work, with more powerful machines, and an organised system which would allow an endless variety of pleasurable tasks. Because children love filth, small boys would joyfully accept the tasks of cleaning the slaughterhouses or purifying the sewers. Similarly all tastes would be catered for in a society properly organised for consumption. Fourier produces complicated plans for ensuring that those who like tough chickens or mealy pears (a taste which would create discord in the households of unsatisfactory bourgeois civilisation) could easily be satisfied in a planned community. Sexual liberation was to be institutionalised: a "court of love" would arrange a partner or partners, and all proclivities could be gratified by open arrangement. Those who failed the community by refusing to conform to its orders would be used in a service not wholly congenial; for example, young girls would be given temporarily to elderly phalanx members. All perversions could be catered for, although the most unusual might require global organisation. Fourier, if in a more fantastic way, agreed with other sociologists in seeing human relations as formulae which could be logically decided, and his determination to produce freedom leads to the most extraordinary and complicated regimentation.

Much of this may be considered the ridiculous dreaming of an eccentric bachelor, but the forms of Fourier's dreams reflect his age. That he was taken seriously by so many stems partly from the acuity with which he saw the mean horrors of *petite bourgeois* life and the ugly consequences of industrial capitalism. Fourier's search for mathematical formulae satisfied the current faith in scientific solutions. Every part of his work is governed by a law of proportion (and it is proportion, not equality, which is the rule of reward in the *phalange* as it was to be in the Saint-Simonist state). The whole of his writing contains graphs, proofs, tables and calculations; extraordinary neologisms are invented to prove its scientific nature. The mathematical proportions show the best way of doing everything and make liberty an irrelevance. Man as a being had thirty-six stages to complete, and he was in the fifth, that of "repugnant, fragmented industry": society was becoming hideously corrupt because staying too long in this stage. It needed to move into *garantisme*, where "guarantees" were given against the unpleasant consequences of industrialisation, and when, in three stages, complete association would be introduced and the *phalanges* become the basis of civilisation. Fourier was not strictly a revolutionary: the communists believed in a violent seizure of power, Cabet in years of propaganda, but Fourier, the unsuccessful capitalist, hoped for a rich man to inaugurate his system. He wrote to King Louis-Philippe, asking him to commence its application, and spent many of his days waiting for the chance arrival of a benefactor. His followers were less patient. Some disciples tried in 1832 to create a *phalange*: they included Alexandre Baudet-Dulary, a doctor, and for a while deputy for Étampes, who provided land and money for the experiment which could not emulate Fourier's grandiose vision, and failed ignominiously.

The most important disciple was Victor Considérant, who became unchallenged leader after the master's death. Whilst removing some of Fourier's most lunatic ideas such as the proposal to harness ships to giant whales in order to save energy or for a chemical to turn the sea into a potable substance tasting of lemonade, he retained the essential quality, the mysticising of science. All philosophies of the past were untrue, he declared, because they contradicted each other: nothing from the past could save their rotten civilisation. The "Science of Humanity" would found a new system, and it led to the *phalange* as method of reformation. Considérant produced descriptions, plans and drawings of vast buildings, the *phalanstères*, which would house these large communities. The family was obsolete because it was not an economic unit: "the function, or the wordly destiny of man is the administration of his planet"[14] he declared in Saint-Simonist terms, and the community being the most effective economic organisation was also a moral imperative. Considérant was the editor of the Fourierist journals, *La Phalange* (1836–43), and *Démocratie Pacifique* (1843–51), which had a circulation of about 2,000 copies, and these together with the works of Fourier and Considérant reached a small public. Since Fourierism, unlike Cabetism, was largely restricted to intellectuals or dissatisfied members of the professional classes, it did not disturb the authorities.

These Utopians all believed in the abolition of politics. Fourier allowed the political instincts to have an outlet in group negotiations in the *bourse* of the *phalange* in order to obtain goods they themselves had not produced, and regional conferences and a world congress would organise vast public works. But since the communists and Utopians were reacting so strongly against the division of French society, in their determination to create an authority to override the anarchy of individual wills, they had no intention of regularising these by allowing their expression. Harmony abolished political disagreement, and government became purely concerned with economic planning. Utopians shared the socialist hostility to the "financial barons",[15] the belief that industrial competition was not only unjust but inefficient, the preoccupation with work and machinism differentiating them from earlier visionaries. The Utopians had unlimited faith in the ability of science and mechanics to solve all the problems of society, whilst many socialists were hostile to the machine which damaged the position of the traditional craftsman. One school had visions of vast factories of mechanical mass production, the other was firmly rooted in the *atelier* and the small-scale industry of the individual workers. For men such as Blanc and Proudhon, the *atelier* was to be the foundation of the new socialist state as it was of French industry. Most workers would probably have agreed, but economic facts were against them. Reformers set out to change men's nature and give him a more satisfying emotional life. Not all followed Fourier and the communists in their attack on marriage (bourgeois paternalism being associated with monarchism), Cabetism in particular basing itself on the family unit. United on what they would destroy, they were often angrily divided on what should replace it. Socialism, said Louis Reybaud, in his hostile *Études sur les*

Réformateurs Contemporains (1842), was "the art of improvising faultless societies"[16] numerous sects attacked society, covering chimeras with statistics.

As he wrote, a completely different form of socialism was being advocated. Pierre-Joseph Proudhon (1809–65) was very much an individualist, and like many such, he was little heeded. A typographer, like Cabet born into an artisan family, a prize awarded for an early literary effort was withdrawn on the publication of his *Qu'est-ce que la Propriété?*, to which question he gave the famous answer, "It is theft."[17] His *Avertissement aux Propriétaires* attacked the capitalist who did not reward the collective achievement of his workers, but paid them only as individuals. Capitalist division of labour is degrading machinism which alienates man from his work: the aim of the social revolution is to return him to it. The anti-religious Proudhon opposed the mysticism of Utopians but unlike the communist materialists he hated centralisation. Like Blanc he believed in the workshop, but not merely as an economic entity: for him the *atelier* is the universal unit, the state an enemy, in whosoever hands it rests. Workers' associations would be the directing force, and work being god, the organisation of industry replaces government and the identity of interest guarantees good behaviour. So Proudhon is Utopian in his own way, and, in spite of his contempt for Fourier, even he feels the need for a scientific justification for his ideas, in his case a geometrical "series" deciding functions in society by calculation.

By 1848, left-wing anticlericalism had been considerably modified: the dissociation of throne and altar, the increased awareness by many Catholics of the depths of social problems and the influence of men such as Lamennais and Buchez, had effected this change. Lamennais believed that "the people" was a sacred concept. Virtue in a materialistic society existed only in the poor. Although he was willing to allow the government to be overthrown by force, the violence and amorality of the communists were alien to him. He believed in small proprietors, and his socialism lay in criticism of existing society rather than in his proposals. Buchez, a former Saint-Simonist, had found the movement too élitist and pantheist. He believed that only Christianity could resolve the conflict between the individual and society: the Gospels contained those moral truths which would establish collectivism. Catholic in that he saw in Protestantism the forces of individualistic selfishness (represented by England), and although not strictly orthodox, his Christianity was more than the vague deism professed by many republicans. Buchez thus stands between the social Catholics and republican socialists, and was of course disliked by both. None the less he had followers amongst those who wished to reconcile religion and science, revolution and society. Buchez influenced the first successful truly working-class journal, *L'Atelier*, founded in 1840. (The Saint-Simonian *Ruche Populaire* could claim priority but had lived a precarious existence amidst the divisions which rent the school.) It claimed to be written by workers for workers and liked to insult the theorists of opposing socialist schools for being bourgeois. Its offices formed a discussion centre where the craftsmen to whom Buchez's ideas appealed (jewellers, mechanics, carpenters and especially typographers – accounting for the high quality of production) met to debate and plan the paper. True to its name, it regarded the workshop as the economic unit and like other socialists was politically radical whilst conservative in its proposals for industrial organisation.

Strikes tended to show these traditional economic attitudes, whilst only very slowly obtaining a political note. There was a Luddite tendency in many of them, especially during the first years of the July Monarchy. In the summer of 1830, weavers around Rouen who were badly hit by mechanisation in the city, broke up many of the machines which threatened their livelihood. In Paris, the troubles amongst printing workers seemed more advanced in that the demands were made within a capitalised industry, and extended to shorter hours and higher salaries, but hostility to new machines was the predominant feature. The following year, as a climax of machine-breaking throughout France, 1,500 women protested against mechanisation in shawl-making in Montmartre and the disorder was so great that troops were used. Although Rheims, suffering from mechanisation in clothes-making, or Niort, too closely dependent on the susceptible glove-making industry, had significant Cabetist groups, the agitations of socialists often seem to have penetrated little beneath the surface. At Toulon, for example, an old established working class, frequently legitimist, with its own traditions and mutual societies, had received an influx of peasants to fill the labour needs of the expanding port and arsenal. The associations split, but even in those which accepted the new lower-paid workers, the will to undertake a political struggle was lacking. The prefect blamed Flora Tristan, the upper-class agitator, for the large-scale strike at the arsenal in 1845, and its leaders were members of her Union Ouvrière. Nevertheless, the strikers preferred to put their trust in the traditional leadership: a priest was given full powers to mediate by the workers and they accepted the concessions made by the Admiral in charge of the arsenal, although most of his promises were overruled by the government, as had been those of the prefect of Lyons in 1831.

Most working-class associations were friendly societies, providing mutual aid, helping when unemployment or illness struck or paying for funerals, in return for regular contributions. Most of these mutual societies were restricted to towns and to traditional crafts, and outside Paris and Lyons they were weak. The Parisian typographers took an initiative in inviting representatives of other typographical associations to their meetings to try to create a national organisation, but this unusual sign of political sophistication had no results. The problem of communication allied to the limited localised nature of men's thinking doomed such attempts for the moment.

The action of the authorities varied according to circumstances. In theory all coalitions in economic interest were banned by a law of 1791, reinforced in the *Code Civil*. Sometimes, if as in the case of the six-week strike of the porcelain makers of Limoges the activity was peaceful, the legal officials prevented the prefect intervening, and in this case the manifestation was often successful. Occasionally prefects tried to mediate and occasionally blamed the employers for their greed or harshness, but on the whole the authorities allowed strikes, which were still unusual occurrences, to continue until an agreement was reached. Most strikes were peaceable but unsuccessful. The authorities would act against violent strikes or working-class associations where these seemed to be politically active.

Saint-Simonism began to express itself in terms such as *prolétaire* and *socialisme*, but outside Paris and Lyons they were scarcely understood. The Société des Droits de l'Homme propaganda commission (Berryer-Fontaine, Lebon and Vignerte) tried to place members in working-class associations and produced pamphlets which claimed to be written by working men but were the product of republican intellectuals. The lawyer Marc Dufraisse, for example, posing as a "shoemaker's apprentice", told the workers that their local associations should merge in order to obtain national power of negotiation, significant of a growing realisation that the working classes needed to be organised by themselves. Republican activity was rife amongst the journeymen tailors: their leader was Grignon whose association had links with provincial bodies and for a while had about 6,000 members, according to Gisquet. This posed a threat which the government could not ignore: it made a large number of arrests and harsher penalties than usual were applied, Grignon receiving three years in prison. Similar organisation occurred amongst typographers and shoemakers, and, in these trades at least, trade unions advanced from mutual self-help organisations to politically minded associations.

Outside Paris, the new industries were generally quiescent, but the workers of the Anzin and Rive-de-Gier coal-mines had organisations which led to strikes for higher pay, which were often extremely violent and where the workers' discipline made them difficult to break. The 1840s witnessed a considerable expansion in activity. In 1844 a huge, if temporary, organisation was created in the Rive-de-Gier basin, near Lyons. Secret societies and the republican leader, Kersausie, helped to mould the various associations into one strike which lasted three months before it collapsed. Even where a well-disciplined and determined force of workers existed, it was difficult for them to overcome employers who generally had governmental support. The improvement in organisation and greater sophistication of demands, testified to the effect which socialism was beginning to produce amongst the working classes in a few areas. In Metz in 1834 a republican factory owner and former mayor, prosecuted for defamation by the prefect and acquitted, was borne through the streets by his workers to cries of "Long live the Republic". But in the 1840s, his popularity had completely disappeared: to be a republican was no longer enough and he merely appeared as another employer and not an unduly generous one.

Various crafts, carpentry and construction especially, had associations which resembled freemasonry more than trade-unionism, with colourful ceremonies and social gatherings. *Compagnonnage* gave the travelling craftsmen centres where they could find both immediate warm hospitality and enemies from traditional rival sects, whom it was their duty to insult and fight, customs rooted in the past, which proved to some that it was irrelevant in an age of capitalism. Agricol Perdiguier, a joiner, had made that *tour de France* which was the duty of every *compagnon* and, having participated in the traditional activities, described his tour, suggesting that the craft rivalries which *compagnonnage* fostered were foolish relics, and that all workers should unite and turn their bellicosity against their employers. George Sand's novel, *Le Compagnon du Tour de France*, drew much on this work. Sand's hero refuses to marry a young noblewoman because her father has insulted him and it takes her voluntary impoverishment to make him overlook this attack upon his class. Although the message of Perdiguier was thus sentimentalised, it was also popularised and it began to become fashionable for the prosperous to admire the lower orders. Sand, in her *Revues*, published the work of working-class poets, the stonemason Louis-Charles Poncy for example. A similar service was performed by the former Saint-Simonian, Olinde Rodrigues, who published a volume entitled *Poésies Sociales des Ouvriers* (1841). It would seem, however, that these poets would often have preferred to be treated as social equals by the bourgeois who so praised their work, rather than as representative of a working class they were frequently pleased to be able to escape from.

A figure in many ways similar to George Sand was Flora Tristan. Also from a background of aristocratic pretensions, her attitude strongly influenced by her feminism, she conducted as woman and revolutionary, aristocrat and romantic, a war against society which had ill-treated her, hoping to find allies in the poor. Tristan was influenced by the statisticians and investigators, notably Buret whom she recommended her working-class audiences to read, but she was an activist more than a social critic. Although she spoke of working-class palaces, resembling *phalanstères*, where work would be varied and enjoyable and advocated sexual equality as a means to human unity, Utopianism took second place. "To organise the working class"[18] was her overriding aim. To this end she published *L'Union Ouvrière*, and travelled indefatigably preaching the merits of national organisation for working men. Her achievements, restricted though they were, are the greater in that she was often disgusted by those she tried to help. Disillusioned with the bourgeois democrats who would sacrifice no more than the time they spent in cafés, saddened to find at Agen that the working-class Gascon poet Jasmin had become *embourgeoisé* and hostile to her ideas, depressed by the frequent conservatism or indifference of the working man, her exertions contributed to an early death in 1844. Flora Tristan's was the difficulty of the intellectual involved in the cause of a lower social rank and, in her case, was increased by her femininity.

The republicans were becoming aware of the reproaches of socialists such as Buchez and Tristan. "What do we do for the people, whilst talking incessantly of the people?"[19] the Vicomte de Cormenin asked his fellow republicans. As a party, they did little, nor suggested doing much, because positive proposals created disunity, and parties were maintained by negative factors. In November 1844, *La Réforme*, copied by sympathetic journals, published Ledru-Rollin's appeal for a *pétition de travailleurs* to ask the deputies to inquire into the situation of the working classes, to observe their sufferings and take requisite action, including radical social reform and universal suffrage. The petition received 130,000 signatures, many fewer than its proponents had expected, and when he presented it to the Chamber he found no one to second the petition, not even from amongst the men of the left. An echoing voice in the Chamber of Peers, although Vicomte Dubouchage was no republican, was of little assistance. Dubouchage led a number of peers, and in the Lower Chamber Garnier-Pagès and the moderate republicans undertook a successful delaying campaign to prevent the government proceeding with its attempt to make the *livret*, the worker's identity card, obligatory. The moderate republicans found it easier to stand up for liberty against the Orleanist government than to make positive proposals for governmental action.

The 1848 Revolution surprised the republicans. Their newspapers had been growing somewhat indifferent to the electoral reform campaign of banquets. Flocon and Ledru-Rollin were disturbed by the nameless extremists, heirs to the Société Dissidente of 1834, who they believed would, by creating a futile insurrection, put them in an impossible or dangerous position. "Men of the people," announced Flocon on 21 February, "take guard tomorrow against all rash undertakings; do not furnish the powers with a sought-after pretext for a bloody success."[20] Louis Blanc told a republican meeting that riots would simply open themselves to the shots of the army and National Guard.[21] The majority of leading republicans agreed but when insurrection was put into their hands, they grasped it, rather as their enemies had done in 1830.

The republicans were victorious by default in 1848. If the Orleanists captured the 1830 Revolution, no less did a section of the republican party capture the Revolution in 1848. The self-appointed provisional government did not represent the working classes, but the lawyers and journalists, the politicians of Paris. The republicans were a minority of the French population. De la Hodde's estimate of 4,000 republicans in Paris is a figure which refers only to the active: presumably there were many more; d'Alton-Shée suggests 10,000 but even this was a tiny minority. Besides Paris, only Lyons had a substantial party. The secret societies were enervated and torn by dissension in 1848. The relics of the Société des Saisons had about 600 men, the Société Dissidente, more violent and more dogmatically communist, about another 400. The banquet campaign and increase in labour unrest due to the economic crisis, caused governmental apprehensions. The authorities began to speak of communism as a threat. They blamed some grain riots on the influence of *les Cabet* amongst the peasantry. In January 1848 Cabet himself was arrested, although soon freed, and a Cabetist journal was forced to close.

The *gauche dynastique* Faucher testified to the fears of the bourgeoisie: "Communism grows and extends itself in the inferior ranks as do weakness and political immorality in the superior ranks." Good citizens were caught between desire for order and scorn for the government.[22] Yet most republicans were men like the prosperous lawyer and deputy Adolphe Crémieux who dismissed all talk of better treatment for workers as erroneous; was not he who started work at five in the morning, a worker as much as any peasant? As long as there were no legal barriers, differences in wealth were inherently necessary in society. Many bourgeois felt this way but agreed with Crémieux that the July Monarchy had moved too far from its revolutionary origins and should be reminded of them.

Although socialists used figures from Leroux's *De La Plutocratie* (1843), claiming that fewer than a million Frenchmen dominated 34 million others, they had little appeal for many of these millions. The peasantry had only begun to be infected by socialism in a few areas where the countryside met a radical town. The proletariat of the northern manufacturing towns remained sunk in indifferent despair, whilst in towns like Toulon, Marseilles and Nimes, many workers retained their royalist predilections. On his second *tour*, in 1847, not this time as a worker but as a propagandist financed by George Sand with the mission to reform the *compagnonnage* and to moralise the working classes, Perdiguier found agitation amongst "our bourgeois democrats" and working-class dissatisfaction: "But the standards of so many saviours offer themselves to his eye that he does not know under which to range himself"; lacking faith in their leaders, the workers could not successfully revolt, he feared, but he was encouraged that they were beginning to think as a class.[23] By this time socialism, from having been a conspiracy by a set of eccentrics, had become a real, if highly divided, force with working-class and *petit bourgeois* support.

For men who so constantly attacked egoism and individualism, republicans and socialists manifested both these qualities to an extreme extent. Those who preached the beauties of unity, such as Cabet or Buchez, were notoriously intolerant of any rivals to their influence or dissentients from their ideas. A creed extolling the virtues of equality was frequently preached by men who claimed to be heeded as prophets and obeyed as Messiahs: George Sand worshipped Michel (de Bourges) and Leroux as demigods, and other leaders, such as Cabet and Blanqui, demanded and often received the most complete obedience from their followers. Romanticism had infected republicanism with its belief in the hero, to obey whose will was freedom. Much in republicanism, or at least in its more eccentric varieties, was simply romanticism divorced from any possible reality. Intellectuals felt dissatisfied, members of the upper classes sometimes had guilt feelings. The "so-called enlightened classes", wrote George Sand, had always oppressed the masses: now it was for "holy common people"[24] to lead the nations and to reform civilisation. Whilst advocating the rule of the people, intellectuals still imposed their own values upon them, most especially when they reproached the workers for not living up to their own ideals of them. Yet if by 1848, socialism had gained the adherence of a small minority only, it had at least forced republicans to treat it with respect, and conservatives to regard it with fear.

REFERENCES

1. Mathieu d'Épinal, *Mes Nuits au Mont Saint-Michel* (1844).
2. Mme de Girardin, *Lettres parisiennes* (1857), III, 68.

3. P. J. David d'Angers, *Souvenirs de David d'Angers sur ses contemporaines* (1929), 147.
4. J. Vidalenc, (ed.), *Lettres de J. A. M. Thomas* (1953), 65.
5. L. de la Hodde, *Histoire des sociétés secrètes* (1850), 239.
6. Ibid., 245.
7. Archives Parlementaires, 17 May 1840.
8. H. de Lacretelle, *Lamartine et ses amis* (1878), 111.
9. A. de Lamartine, *Voyage en Orient* (Hachette edition), II, 477–8.
10. George Sand, in the preface to P. Leroux's translation of J. W. von Goethe, *Werther* (1845), XII.
11. T. Dézamy, *Code de la Communauté* (1846), 13, 27.
12. G. Sencier, *Le Babouvisme* (1912), 305.
13. E. Cabet, *Voyage en Icarie* (1842), 215.
14. V. Considérant, *Destinée Sociale* (1848), 113.
15. Ibid.
16. L. Reybaud, *Études sur les réformateurs contemporains* (1842), II, 49.
17. P. J. Proudhon, *Qu'est-ce que la propriété?* (1840), 131.
18. F. Tristan, *L'Union Ouvrière* (1843), 108.
19. "Timon" (Vicomte L. M. Cormenin), *Livre des orateurs* (1847), 23.
20. *La Réforme*, 21 February 1848.
21. De la Hodde, op. cit.
22. L. Faucher, *Biographie et Correspondance* (1875), II, 38.
23. A. Perdiguier, *Correspondance inédite avec George Sand et ses amis* (1966), 89.
24. Ibid., 51.

27

Banquets, Scandals and Revolution

"Les grands citoyens, les amis du peuple, les forts, les sérieux, les habiles, les grands politiques, se sont alors dit: 'Le peuple a peur de la famine, le pain est cher; c'est le moment de demander pour lui . . . des droits politiques.'"

"The great citizens, the friends of the people, the strong, the serious, the able, the great politicians then said to themselves: 'The people fear famine, bread is dear; it is the moment to demand for them . . . political rights.'"[1]

"Déjà près d'eux l'Ocean sur ses grèves
Mugit, se gonfle; il vient, maitres, voyez!
Voyez, leur dis-je. Ils répondent: tu rêves.
Ces pauvres rois, ils seront tous noyés."

"Already close to them the Ocean on its shores
Bellows, swells itself; it comes, masters, see!
See, I tell them. They respond: you dream.
These poor kings, they will all be drowned."[2]

By 1845 there was widespread dissatisfaction, both amongst the conservatives and their opponents. The unprecedented length of survival of the ministry of 29 October 1840, the continued dominance of Guizot and Duchâtel, lend to the last years of the July Monarchy an air of misleading stability. Although the ministerial majority was usually around thirty, small rebellions persistently threatened it. Duchâtel, Minister of the Interior, told Vitet, a fellow doctrinaire, that the ministerialists grew lax, forgetting "those salutory fears, those memoires of 1840 which rendered them vigilant and docile. Without a little fear, no sagacity at all."[3] This had always been the strategic dogma of the doctrinaires. Duchâtel considered resignation in order to reform the conservatives by a spell of opposition. The risks, however, seemed too great, because the opposition "is dragged along, unconsciously, into serving as the avant-garde of the revolution".[4] Although Duchâtel realised that the July Monarchy could only live by basing itself on the two centres, the conservative centre had come to regard the left centre as too dangerous to be allowed not only political power, but even an administrative role. The *centre gauche*, amalgam of the former *tiers parti* and of conservatives allied to Thiers, was driven, like the *gauche dynastique*, into political exile.

Comte Beugnot, an associate of Montalembert, wrote in the Catholic *Le Correspondant* in 1845 a reasoned criticism of Guizot which also applies to the regime. As a result of constant efforts against unworthy opponents, the minister had contracted "not the taste for, but the habit of expedients which form the basis of parliamentary tactics".[5] Broglie spoke similarly, recommending that Guizot demand loyalty and discipline, and failing to gain them, should resign,[6] a "doctrinaire" criticism that governmental authority was decaying in the hands of pragmatists. Yet the spirit was going from the doctrinaires who, when Dumon replaced Teste as Garde des Sceaux in December 1844, dominated the Cabinet. Rémusat noted their decline: no measure had been passed that the most limited provincial bourgeois could not have conceived. His accusation that Guizot had reduced government to maintaining a majority is slightly unfair, for the violent debates caused by the various controversies in foreign affairs, education, as well as the routine passions of Orleanist politics, created plenty of parliamentary excitement. Even such a limited affair as the children's labour law had proved difficult, because it, and the attempts to further free trade, had confronted certain interest groups. Because of its intention to be a coalition of conciliated interests, Orleanism had never possessed a reforming impulse. Thiers had attempted to create excitement, not by reforms but by foreign policy adventures. Guizot had dispensed even with this. Thiers complained that this did not suit the French temperament. "It is not a government; it is an administration." By its concentration on routine economic matters, the government alienated support. "The government is far too bourgeois. . . . It is poetry that it lacks. It is only cane, beetroot and budget."[7] Even the apologia of Barante, writing to his dissatisfied son, reads like criticism, contemptuous of the political world and bourgeoisie, "But what would you have? After fifty-five years of revolution, opinions are worn and collapsing." Private interests ruled: the opposition wanted ministries; ministerialists demanded rewarding functions; electors chose deputies who most suited their interests. This might be degrading but "the dynasty takes root", and the only alternatives were reaction or republican anarchy.[8]

The desire for peace and continuation reflected itself in the debates on the *adresse* early in 1845. If some conservatives were dissatisfied, the majority, owing their places to Guizot or fearful of the electoral reform or aggressive foreign policy promised by the opposition, could only hope for the maintenance of his government. Thus when Molé, in an effective speech to the peers, launched an attack upon Guizot for betraying the conservative party by imposing upon it his uncompromising negativism, and was supported in the Lower Chamber by a few dissidents such as Carné and Saint-Marc Girardin, the majority only drew itself more tightly together. A *réunion* at the home of Hartmann gathered 190 ministerial deputies to protest against the coalition which seemed to be forming, and created a permanent committee to watch over the interests of their party and maintain the ministry firmly. Reinforced by this manifestation and with the King's support, Guizot resisted the advice of those who advocated a temporary retreat from power. Instead he disciplined the dissentients in his majority. The deputy Drouyn de Lhuys, director of commercial affairs at the Foreign Ministry who had voted against the Cabinet on the Pritchard paragraph where the ministerial majority had been only eight, and Comte Alexis de Saint-Priest, minister at Copenhagen, who had shown opposition in the Chamber of Peers, were dismissed from their posts. He also weakened the dissentient conservatives by recruiting Salvandy as Minister of Public Instruction. And the government's survival was aided by the decision taken by a slight majority, representing all parties, to make public voting the rule which, salutary in itself, gave the government greater control over the "civil service deputies". Ministerial control was further enhanced in the 1846 session when the governmental intention to hold elections became known, for no deputy wished to risk losing the assistance which might assure him his seat. There were no obvious issues in the two sessions, once the potentialities of the Pritchard affair had been exploited: the question of religious education was raging and occupied the attention of many. Thiers, who in 1846 had almost replaced Barrot as leader of the *gauche dynastique* as well as of his own centre, made corruption an issue, although his own hands were not spotless. France was not ready to be roused, however, 1846 was quiet, and few yet realised that the prosperous years were ending. The monotony was only briefly broken by two assassination attempts on the King, both of them the work of unbalanced individuals.

The elections of July 1846 therefore took place in an atmosphere which could only profit the ministry. Thiers and Barrot had drawn up a common programme, involving an extension of the franchise and the incompatibility of being a deputy and holding a paid official post. Outside Paris and one or two other political centres, however, few were interested in such technicalities. It was personal matters and commercial interests which dominated: the *gauche dynastique* had exploited the dissatisfaction of northern sugar-beet growers and the government profited from the programme of railway building. The novel factor of a specifically Catholic vote also had considerable impact; 275 candidates bound themselves to support freedom of education, and 146 of them were elected. Chaix d'Est-Ange at Rheims had previously won because of his promise; but he had broken it, so Catholic and legitimist votes went to his *gauche dynastique* opponent, Faucher, who won. The republican Vicomte de Cormenin, on the contrary, lost because his commitment to the Catholic cause alienated many radicals who had previously voted for him. The issue tended to separate republicans and legitimists, and both lost seats because they co-operated less than in 1842.

The government was highly content. The King congratulated Duchâtel whose organisational ability had contributed to the result. "These are the first truly governmental elections that have been seen since 1814"[9] announced Guizot. The opposition lost twenty-five or thirty seats, which, won by the ministerialists and conservatives, increased them to the seemingly invulnerable number of 290. It was estimated that they obtained about 104,000 votes to the opposition's 94,000. However, in Paris the opposition had 9,000 of the total 14,000 votes, and eleven of the twelve *arrondissements*. The *gauche dynastique* dominated not only the capital but other areas of the north and centre, the Aisne, Oise and Somme departments. The ministerialists were increasingly found in the smaller towns, especially of the south. As Gustave de Beaumont told the deputies, soon all electoral colleges of under 200 voters would be governmental preserves – "it is only a question of time and knowing how to go about it, of good or bad prefects".[10] The number of "civil service deputies" had increased because of the larger governmental majority from 142 to 188, almost all of them ministerial. The elections thus fuelled demands for electoral reform, for if the governmental hold on patronage were not removed, it seemed unlikely that the opposition could win a majority.

The year 1846 also brought many figures of note into the Chamber. The Abbé de Genoude and Comte de Falloux added talent to the legitimists whose numbers had sunk below twenty. The republicans had done poorly, but the *gauche dynastique* had a welcome recruit in Général de La Moricière who provided them with a rival to Bugeaud in military prestige. The opposition gained influential free-traders in the persons of Léon Faucher, Adolphe Blanqui and Louis Reybaud. A new generation appeared, children of the founding fathers of the July Monarchy, Oscar de La Fayette for example, or of the notables of the Empire, such as Charles Lebrun, Paul Daru, the Duc d'Elchingen and Comte de Morny. And there were also many additions to the ranks of the dissident conservatives, for example Montalembert's brother-in-law, Charles de Mérode.

In 1830 even the most radical found the lowering of the voting qualification to 200 francs satisfied their demands. Universal suffrage was opposed by all but the most extreme. The fact that the legitimist Genoude demanded it, seemed to prove fears of the landlords' dominance in rural France to be correct. Electoral reform was more attractive to those in opposition than for those enjoying office: Thiers and Rémusat, when ministers, refused reforms which they later demanded. The narrower the basis of power became, the more politicians demanded change. During the 1839 attack on Molé, Faucher criticised the "civil service deputies" as representatives of royal power. And the emergence of the *gauche dynastique Siècle* as the most widely read newspaper made the *petite bourgeoisie*, especially National Guardsmen who congratulated themselves on serving the state, question their exclusion from the *pays légal*. Petitions were submitted to the Chamber demanding that all National Guardsmen be enfranchised. Parliament, however, in 1839 was more interested in destroying ministries, and Thiers's Cabinet was too dependent on conservative support to consider reform, whilst the *gauche dynastique* for its own tactical reasons had no wish to embarrass Thiers by demanding it.

After 1840, however, Thiers was in opposition with his two lieutenants, Rémusat and Duvergier, who, if they were inclined to adopt double standards as to the expedient moments for reform, were none the less genuinely concerned with efficient parliamentary government. The combined inactivity and stability of Guizot's rule seemed to suggest that reform was necessary, not, early in the 1840s, in response to an irresistible demand, but simply to improve the workings of Parliament. Until 1842 the annual propositions of Gauguier, trying to suppress pay to "civil service deputies" during the session, and Rémilly's which extended the period of prohibition, had been primarily concerned with this. In February 1842, the deputies debated a proposition by Ducos to enfranchise those inscribed on the second part of the jury list. A week later, a proposal by Ganneron was debated which resembled that of Rémilly. The debates made electoral and parliamentary reform an urgent issue, and part of the programme of the opposition. It is noteworthy that Gauguier, Rémilly, Ducos and Ganneron were all representatives of the centre, and that in 1842 the proposals were supported by Dufaure who was then a part of Guizot's majority. Guizot, however, firmly laid down the principles on which he would oppose all attempts to change the system for the following years. The July Monarchy was too young, he claimed, for it to be able to risk the dislocations of reform. In an age of growing prosperity more would climb, by their merits, into the *pays légal*; and so there was no need to alter a system working well, merely to satisfy the ambitions of the opposition. However, governmental majorities were small, only eight against Ganneron's proposal.

The far left found these propositions inadequate. In May 1840, Arago supported by Garnier-Pagès, demanded universal suffrage, whilst Barrot and the *gauche dynastique* sat in embarrassed silence. A few days later, a procession of workers walked to the Observatoire to thank the republican astronomer for his speech which had also demanded work for the unemployed. Arago promised to defend their interests, but his advocacy of moderation suggests apprehensions at this proletarian manifestation. That electoral reform was becoming a popular cause is reflected also in various banquets held during 1840. That on the Plaine de Chatillon in August, after the government had prevented its being held in the VIIIe *arrondissement* on Bastille day, was attended by about 3,000, many of them National Guardsmen. Rich bankers, Laffitte and Goudchaux, and moderate republicans such as Arago, began to use socialistic expressions. At the National Guard review of 1840, there had been cries of "Up with reform" and shouts of groups demanding electoral change were heard even through Berlioz's funeral march when the Bastille column was inaugurated in July. Trouvé-Chauvel, radical mayor of Le Mans, took the opportunity of a visit by the Duc de Nemours to criticise governmental immobility and demand reform, Nemours replying with cold politeness that the position of mayor was not intended to be political. The government clumsily over-reacted, dismissing mayor and municipal council. In the Saône-et-Loire department, Lamartine told the *conseil général* that the age of the masses approached[11] and persuaded them to demand an extension of electoral rights. On the whole, however, between 1841 and 1846, the issue of electoral reform slumbered and Guizot could claim that only a minority of trouble-makers demanded it.

When Rémusat reopened the question of parliamentary reform early in 1846, it was with a proposition even less radical than that of the dissident conservative, Rémilly, six years earlier. Those with legal and administrative positions of political importance were to be ineligible for election, nor could a deputy accept such a paid post. Limited though it was, Guizot, Duchâtel and Hébert (*procureur général* and reporter of the commission examining the proposition), attacked it vigorously. Regarding the Chamber as representative of a certain set of interests and not as the organ of national sovereignty, it seemed entirely logical to them to argue that it was unjust to deprive of their rights an important section of the community. One conservative, however, warned the government that the functionaries would come to form the majority of the majority: the prediction was already fact. Other conservatives were agreed in their regrets, but in a pre-electoral period were unwilling to thwart the government. And because Thiers's eloquent speech attacked the monarch, he helped the ministry to a large majority. The proposition had been part of the electoral programme of Barrot and Thiers which also advocated enfranchising the voters for the *conseils généraux*, and certain other *capacités*, and a minimum of 300 voters for each *arrondissement*, mild suggestions in comparison with Thiers's verbal violence.

Thiers was a poor party leader: he distrusted any rival, and relied upon outbursts of oratory and violent attempts to charm, to re-create periodically a party always threatening to fall apart. For much of the 1840s he was discourged and inactive, putting his energy into writing his history of Napoleon and visiting the battlefields of the Empire. He and Barrot, tired of sterile opposition, entered into distrustful alliance, both also expecting that the demise of Louis-Philippe would, in spite of the conservatism of Nemours, the Regent, bring their ambitions to fruition, and sometimes attended the soirées of the Duchesse d'Orléans to cultivate their future prospects. Barrot too had difficulty uniting his party. With good nature and integrity, he was a man differentiated from the ordinary only in his oratorical gifts, and led the disparate groups of the moderate left because there was no obvious rival. He was more conservative and pessimistic than he sounded, confiding to Tocqueville his fears that they too greatly honoured humanity "and place too much confidence in moral forces, and that in doing battle with the bad inclinations that all governments for so long have developed and survived by in our country, she has run aground".[12]

Tocqueville deeply disliked the alliance of Barrot with Thiers for which his friend Beaumont and Duvergier worked so hard. Partly this was a personal dislike of Napoleon's biographer, but it was also a hostility to the amoral attitudes and centralising tendencies which Thiers represented. Tocqueville also objected to the way Faucher's *Courrier* and Chambolle's *Siècle* gave radical accents to *petit bourgeois* prejudice by chauvinism and attacks on the monarch. He gathered around him a small group who desired liberalism without revolutionary language, progressive in social and economic questions. They tended to sympathise with Catholic dislike of the Université monopoly, and attacked the *Siècle* for its anticlericalism. Chambolle riposted with the old accusations of crypto-legitimism, a charge to which Tocqueville, Francisque de Corcelles and other aristocratic sympathisers remained vulnerable, even if it was unjustified.

It was a miserable epoch, lamented Tocqueville, "when no one knows where he is going or with whom. There is the disease, the incurable disease that eats away at us."[13] The isolated group could not have much influence on a party which all too often seemed a reflection of the conventionality, the prevalence of negative ideas over creative reform, to be found in ministerial ranks. The "new left" of Tocqueville did, however, form links with those liberals who found in Dufaure and Billault leaders who, whilst criticising the immobility of the ministry, found Thiers and the left uncongenial. Certain dissident conservatives looked with some favour on these groups in the centre, and Molé lost credit with the more uncompromising conservatives by forming an alliance with Billault shortly before the 1846 elections. Thus in the 1840s, when two massive blocs opposed each other with increasing hostility, the Orleanist party system, as before, fostered the growth of "third parties".

Guizot's majority was huge, but at its heart was weak. The 1846 elections had returned a large number of conservatives, fully aware of Guizot's unpopularity, free of the discipline of fear which Périer and Broglie had wielded. Comte Henri de Castellane had formally introduced the group during the *adresse* debates which began the 1847 session. Because of the patronage of Comte Molé, his mother's lover, he was the informal leader during his brief parliamentary career. The group tended to consist of young aristocrats such as Castellane, the dandified Comte de Morny, or rich men, notably Sallandrouze, the carpet manufacturer, who had no need to defer to the ministry in order to gain official positions. They chafed at the domination of the doctrinaire establishment. When Hébert became a minister, they showed their potential destructive power by producing their own candidate for the vice-presidency of the Chamber: the split in the conservative vote allowed the opposition candidate, Léon de Malleville, to triumph. Adding insult to this, one of the dissident conservatives, Desmousseaux de Givré, launched an attack upon the ministry for splitting the party by its uncompromising opposition to all reform. What positive actions had Guizot's government to its credit, he asked, and resoundingly answered to left, centre and right of the Chamber, "Nothing! Nothing! Nothing!"[14] The phrase was adopted by the opposition and used by the *Presse* as a watchword. Guizot told these critics either to become loyally ministerial or to join the opposition. He was misled by his almost invulnerable majority. The government was increasingly isolated in the country, especially in Paris. The defection of the *Presse* meant that newspapers supporting the ministry, notably the *Journal des Débats*, had a tiny minority of the total readership.

Guizot's power inside the Cabinet seemed greater than ever, and he retained the unalloyed support of the King. Maréchal Soult, although he still had the power to make himself a nuisance, had become increasingly feeble, even as a figure-head, and late in 1845 was forced to realise that he could no longer conduct the administrative business of the War Department, which was transferred to Général Moline de Saint-Yon. Then in September 1847, Guizot expelled him from the presidency, compensating him with the decorative title of "Maréchal général", taking for himself officially the position he had for long occupied in fact.

The Baron de Barante wrote from the Auvergne in the summer of 1847 telling Guizot that although the *conseil général* session had been calm, he noticed amongst the electorate a reaction against the dominance of private interests and the distribution of jobs, and he asked the minister to take greater care over promotion and dismissals.[15] The severe electoral defeat of an aide-de-camp of the King who received a promotion, thereby having to submit himself to a by-election, was a rebuff for the Court and the government which seemed to substantiate this. Even the *Journal des Débats* which had criticised Desmousseaux repeated his accusation in polite language, suggesting the government was insufficiently positive. In the *Revue des Deux Mondes*, d'Haussonville noted further weaknesses, especially the difficulties in finding new ministers.

Guizot's answer to criticism had been to reshuffle his Cabinet, a manœuvre as obvious in parliamentary regimes as it is usually ineffectual. The weak Moline de Saint-Yon, much of whose administration had been controlled by the Duc de Nemours, and Mackau were persuaded to resign but Lacave-Laplagne obliged Guizot to dismiss him. This sacrifice was an attempt to placate Duchâtel, who, resentful of Guizot's primacy, had retreated into a sulky indolence. He bore a grudge against Lacave-Laplagne who had refused to promote his client to the directorship of the postal services. After some problems, three peers (none of them experienced parliamentarians) were brought into the Cabinet. Dumon left Public Works for Finances, and Jayr, former prefect for Lyons, took his portfolio. Général Trézel and the Duc de Montebello went to the War and Marine Ministries. The earlier appointment of Hébert and the introduction of Jayr strengthened the doctrinaire element in the Cabinet and resistance to reform, but its parliamentary position was not improved.

The July Monarchy was not an abnormally corrupt regime, but suffered from many weaknesses which made it appear so. Lacking automatic loyalty, it had to do much persuading, make many compromises and buying support followed naturally. It also had a number of oppositions which had the freedom to seize upon, and to exaggerate, every fault committed. Regimes in which the state held vast sums for which it did not have to account, where criticism dared not raise its voice, whilst essentially more corrupt in themselves, could conceal their use of reward for political service. The art of political survival had demanded a certain flexibility of conscience, whilst the absence of party discipline made interest a predominant factor. Rémusat confessed that abuses, whilst those of Louis-Philippe's government were peccadilloes compared with those of governments before and since, seemed a less acceptable accompaniment to constitutionalism, to politicians in opposition.[16] Even the conservative Carné agreed with Tocqueville and his associates, Lanjuinais and Corcelles, in their preoccupation with this problem, and the conservative deputy, Comte

Agénor de Gasparin, son of the former minister, turned against Guizot who, by opposition to parliamentary reform, was maintaining a system which compromised all within it. "Never has one corrupted so shamelessly"[17] wrote Général de Castellane, particularly shocked that Guizot's secretary, the "lowly esteemed" Génie, was made a commander of the Légion d'honneur, and that this honour, military in origin, should be distributed to ministerial journalists.

Scandals in 1847 touched the highest levels of government. Émile de Girardin, compelled by the deep impulses of his illegitimacy, coveted a peerage for his father, but, resentful of Guizot's demand that his *Presse* surrender all indepedence, turned against the Premier and described how the government had financed *L'Époque* two years earlier. The ministers, he claimed, had allowed it to traffic a theatre concession for a large sum paid to the paper, and a peerage was sold for 80,000 francs. The latter accusation caused the peers to command Girardin to answer a charge of insulting their dignity. Although unable to prove his more dramatic charges save on the theatre concession, the peers accepted that he had not intended to impugn their honour and their refusal to prosecute, against ministerial wishes, was a sign of disapproval of Guizot's government. During angry debates Guizot was able to show that Girardin had lent himself to transactions, but the fact that the government had not fulfilled its bargain was no justification. Moreover, Guizot temporarily lost his characteristic calm, made insulting reference to Girardin's ancestry and had to be hustled from a back entrance when the furious deputy came to challenge him. Eventually, after Duchâtel had tried to blame the irregularity of minor officials, a majority of deputies declared themselves, in the word supplied with the contemptuous assistance of Morny, "satisfied" with the explanation.

The government emerged enfeebled from this to face the Teste–Cubières scandal. A lawsuit initiated by the director of a salt-mining company revealed letters written to him by a shareholder, former War Minister, Général Cubières, referring to large bribes to a minister in 1842 for a mining concession. This could only be Teste who, at Public Works, had responsibility for these. Yet before the peers, to which both he and Cubières belonged, he strongly denied these imputations. The General was little more than a glamorous, but rather stupid and greedy, cavalry officer whose typicality of the military establishment had inevitably led him to the brief honour of the War Ministry under Thiers, whose friend he had remained. Teste was a more considerable figure: an opponent of the Bourbons, a successful lawyer and *tiers parti* deputy who had made himself the fluent mouthpiece of the clumsy Soult. It was the latter who introduced him into the Cabinet of 12 May, and forced Guizot to keep him as Minister of Public Works, in spite of his colleagues' mistrust, until December 1843 when he was removed and compensated by a peerage and the presidency of a Chamber of the Cour de Cassation.

Chancelier Pasquier had instituted a long and searching inquiry. There was no doubt that the director and the General had agreed to bribe a minister, but there were doubts as to whether the money had reached him. None the less it was decided that Teste would stand trial in July beside his fellow peer and two lesser figures, unscrupulous capitalists, the director and a shareholder, a former *receveur-général*. The reading of papers left the question of Teste's participation in doubt until the deputy Malleville presented Pasquier with letters from Cubières after they had been used by Marrast in the *National* to whom they had been given by Cubières himself, anxious that he should not appear a thief rather than merely a corruptor. It was increasingly obvious that the former minister had received 100,000 francs from the director of the salt-mine by means of the other two accused. Cubières was a pitiful figure, but even as his guilt became plain, Teste, the lawyer, defended himself with aplomb. But on the fourth day direct proof of his receipt of the money was found. That evening in prison Teste tried to kill himself with a pistol brought him by his son: he only succeeded in wounding himself. For once Dumas's *Comte de Monte-Cristo*, a work with which Teste would later while away some of the hours of imprisonment, had been almost prophetic, rather than a reflection of the melodrama of the July Monarchy. The four received civil degradation and fines, Teste's being severest, although more than he could afford, for it was his indebtedness which led to his crime, and he also went to prison for three years. The trial conducted openly and fairly, honoured the regime, but could not compensate for the fact that two of its most notable servants had trafficked their influence. Men blamed the corruption on Guizot's system. "What horrors! What misery!" exclaimed Thiers. "The blood spilled at Eylau was a misfortune less great than the grave consequences of peace at any price."[18]

The crime of the Duc de Choiseul-Praslin had greater popular impact. His branch of the family had lost its royalist purity by serving Napoleon, and the Duc had mingled with those liberal aristocrats who became Orleanists. He had married the only daughter of Maréchal Sébastiani (obtaining a large dowry, necessary to the depleted Praslin finances). Although unpopular, such a great name could not be ignored, and he became *chevalier d'honneur* to the Queen and a peer at the request of his father-in-law. Beneath his cold exterior, the Duc became consumed with hatred for his emotional wife. On 18 August 1847 he murdered her in the most horrifying manner: failing to slit her throat, he clubbed her to death with a candelabra. The exact motives remain unclear, but the murder was at once discovered and his guilt was evident.

As a peer, Praslin could not be arrested without the agreement of his colleagues who were in recess. The King at Eu hurriedly convoked the Chamber. Praslin was transferred to the Luxembourg, but the delicacy of his guards had enabled him whilst in the latrine at his home, to swallow arsenic. Desperate and horrifying attempts were made by bleeding and pumping the stomach to save the murderer's life. They were in vain: Praslin bore his suffering in silence and died, to the fury of public opinion. Class hatred was roused and paid no attention to the sufferings of the Sébastiani family who were booed. Republican newspapers encouraged the belief that the King and

Sébastiani had saved the life of the murderer who was living in comfort in England. The *Constitutionnel* claimed to see in this domestic murder the result of Guizot's politics. In an attempt to quiet public dissatisfaction, peers took the unusual step of publishing an account of the crime and of their proceedings.

Other horrors and scandals followed, as if omens presaging the fall of the monarchy itself. The Prince d'Eckmühl was incarcerated in a lunatic asylum for stabbing his mistress. A peer, and former ambassador, Mortier, in a fit of insanity, threatened to kill his children: Pasquier, using the authority of the president of the Chamber of Peers, persuaded him to unlock the door, upon which the police were able to seize the razor-wielding madman. Another ambassador, Bresson, his ambitions thwarted and his mind disturbed, committed suicide by cutting his throat. The deputy, Henri de Castellane, dying prematurely, left an excessively affectionate correspondence with footmen which was discovered by his wife. Rumours flew about the more conventional immoralities of the dead Minister of Justice, the seemingly irreproachable Martin (du Nord). At a card game at which one of the royal princes was present, a royal aide-de-camp was discovered cheating; he fled the country.

Les Mystères de Paris which had recently been published in the *Journal des Débats* seemed in its portrayal of the dark corners of a glittering but corrupt society to be no more than realistic. "There are moments when everything serves those who wish to draw the worst conclusions, when everything can envenom", wrote Pasquier, who was so closely involved in the Praslin and Mortier affairs.[19] "Our civilisation is very sick", wrote Molé to Barante on hearing of the Praslin murder, "and nothing would astonish me less than a good cataclysm which would put an end to all of that."[20] Some, more scientific than the emotional pessimistic Molé, Tocqueville for example, felt they were in a situation which could lead to a revolt. Others dismissed these fears. Xavier Doudan, late in 1847, whilst noting the succession of calamities which would in more superstitious days have been taken as omens of great public catastrophe, believed that the world would continue as before, "the number of passengers who fall into the sea presages nothing about the sailing of the ship".[21]

Thus the feeling of malaise increased amongst the governing classes. Chancelier Pasquier, who bore a gurdge against the King and Cabinet for making his Chamber of Peers "a great coach-house for all the incapable", believed there was no more direction or will in the government, and that after all his years on the throne Louise-Philippe was in a weaker position than in 1830.[22] Or there was the Duc de Mortemart who complained of the "shameful spectacle" of their Parliament which wasted its energies in intrigues and spared no time for necessary reforms: he told Général de Castellane that he believed the first bold man with "a strong hand" could sweep it away.[23] In these criticisms, of course, there was much aristocratic disapproval of bourgeois behaviour. Pasquier and Mortemart, like Molé, a more purely political critic is government, were men who regretted the change of regime in 1830, and now felt justified in their predictions that no regime born of revolution could obtain stability.

The corruption wearied Guizot, emotionally and physically. Then the Petit affair invaded his own office. He may have disliked Teste, Cubières was Thiers's minister and not his, but their corruption had besmirched the regime of which Guizot now seemed the embodiment, nor was his impeccable personal behaviour able to save his reputation. His secretary, Génie, had been approached by Auguste Bertin de Vaux, fils, former deputy, a peer and the most important shareholder of the *Journal des Débats*, lover of a certain Madame Petit, who wished to obtain a better position for her husband, a *receveur des finances*. Petit was told that if he wanted a position on the Cour des Comptes, he would have to buy the resignation of a member, but the resistance of the then Minister of Finances, Lacave-Laplagne, prevented a satisfactory outcome. The ambitious cuckold reverted to the role of jealous husband, and began a case against his wife, employing a left-wing deputy as his lawyer. The affair became public, and on 21 January 1848, Barrot interpellated the ministers on it. The previous day the ministry had banned payment for resignations. Guizot's line was to condemn such actions, to admit they had taken place under Louis-Philippe and the previous regime, but he was very silent on all that concerned Génie and Bertin. He promised a law to forbid the sale of places. The Chamber was little satisfied, but Guizot demanded a vote of confidence and received a large majority, but only after independent conservatives had declared themselves "distressed and malcontent". By this time, however, the question of the Parisian reform banquet had become the dominant political issue.

The evidence of corruption, coinciding with an economic depression, produced outbreaks of class hatred. Whilst the Teste–Cubières trial was taking place, on 5 July 1847, the Duc de Montpensier gave a large fête at Vincennes. Elegantly dressed Parisian society drove in its magnificent carriages through Paris and instead of curiosity, were greeted in the Faubourg Saint-Antoine by loudly expressed hostility, "Down with thieves!" Nor was this limited to the town. In some departments late in 1847, there were peasant riots and manifestations against "the monopolists". In 1847, politics moved outside the Chambers. The effect of Lamartine ("I speak through the window"[24]), the example of the English Anti-Corn Law League reinforced by a visit to Paris in 1846 of Cobden, much courted by the opposition (although Montalembert had been the first to copy the movement), made French politicians more aware of the public. To whip up demand for reform, leaders of the Orleanist opposition, Barrot, Beaumont, Duvergier and Malleville, met with two republicans, Carnot and Garnier-Pagès, and agreed that the Comité Central Électoral de Paris, a group of extreme left and republican figures, should be given support by the parliamentary opposition. Duvergier, most extreme of the spokesmen of the 1839 coalition, most ardent of the centre for change, had in his brochure *De la réforme électorale* (1847) advocated alliance of *centre gauche* with republicans to achieve this and to restrict the royal prerogative, attempting to pull the unenthusiastic Thiers into the campaign, by an arrangement with Marrast that the *National* should cease its attacks on him. The petition drawn up by Pagnerre to represent this alliance was violent in denunciation of abuses and vague in proposals for reform. They agreed to hold banquets to publicise their demands, but the first which resulted was a very cautious exercise. The price of admission was high, only electors might attend, and it was held in a private place to evade the law on public meetings. The government, whilst believing it had the legal right to prohibit it, felt it inopportune to do so.

At the large Parisian banquet held on 9 July 1847, a republican colour dominated, and no toast was made to the King, although republicans moderated their language in consideration for the dynastic deputies present. Barrot spoke of the destruction of the spirit of 1830 by corruption and egoism. Duvergier followed him, referring to the falsification of the Constitution, the buying of consciences, and attacked his *bête noire*, the personal power of the King. The campaign continued after this, albeit with no great verve. The Comité Central sent out many letters urging their provincial friends to emulate Paris. A few banquets were held that summer, many more in autumn, and sixteen *conseils généraux* expressed the criticism of corruption and desire for reform as its remedy for the administrative problems on which they were called to deliberate. The campaign was localised. The departments of the Aisne, Côte-d'Or, Moselle, Haut-Rhin, Saône-et-Loire, Vosges, Seine and Nord were to the fore, but the south and west showed little interest.

Odilon Barrot was present at many, haranguing the assembled provincials, bringing them a night of Parisian oratory, claiming that the uncompromising ministers, not the banquets, were weakening the monarchy.[25] Although the most radical reform which his *gauche dynastique* had demanded, the halving of the *cens* to 100 francs and the addition of *capacitées*, would have enfranchised only 200,000, Thiers had not supported it and even Barrot himself seems to have considered it excessive. Yet many, notably Guizot and the King, saw the heirs of Robespierre standing behind the gentle Odilon Barrot, as they had in 1831. And indeed, in his battle for moderation, he lacked the support of the leading opposition moderates, Thiers, Billault and Dufaure, who abstained from the campaign. When the organising committee at Lille invited radicals to participate, Barrot made his presence conditional upon a toast to the 1830 settlement, which was refused. As a result, the *gauche dynastique* was absent and the radicals were left in command.

Republican elements began to establish a preponderance in the campaign which, as a result, lost some favour amongst moderates. Often Barrot, Malleville or Duvergier would find themselves present or even presiding at banquets where no toast was made to the King nor even to the July settlement and where mention was made of the organisation of labour and revolutionary duties of the people. Some radicals attacked not only "the man of Ghent" but also "the royal volunteer of 1815", Odilon Barrot himself. At Autun, at Chalon-sur-Saône, at Dijon in November and December, the republicans held their own banquets, where moderates were openly mocked. Ledru-Rollin demanded universal suffrage and promised revolution: "When the fruit is rotten, it only takes the touch of the wind to detach it from the tree."[26] The republicans invoked 1793, using Jacobin phrases: those demands enunciated in secret councils in the 1830s were now shouted from dining tables in public halls across the country. From confidence in this growth of republican manifestation and a fear of losing his more extreme followers, the moderate republican Garnier-Pagès refused to attend banquets where a toast was made to the King or the July settlement. The coalition of the summer had fallen apart as previous coalitions had done.

It was Lamartine who lent the campaign its most revolutionary tone. At Mâcon on 18 July, he spoke to an audience of over 3,000, gathered to celebrate the author of the *Girondins*. After a toast from the mayor, Lamartine held an audience of hero-worshippers captive with his eloquence whilst a storm stripped the canvas shelter from around them. He attacked "the spirit of materialism and trafficking" which infected this "Regency of the bourgeoisie".[27] He had said "France grows weary", now he declared "France is distressed! . . .", distressed by corruption. "After having had the revolutions of liberty and the counter-revolutions of glory, you will have the revolution of public conscience, and the revolution of contempt!" This was greeted with huge applause. The whole speech was an invocation of the revolutionary spirit: "My book had need of a conclusion; it is you who give it."[28] Performances at a theatre in the popular quarter of Paris of a drama, *Le Chevalier du Maison rouge*, inspired by Lamartine's history, presented scenes of the Revolution whose violence was well received by the audience. It probably had a greater effect than all the banquets, about 180, which took place in 1847.

The session opened on 28 December with the majority in disarray. From within it had come expressions of dissatisfaction, the effect of the scandals of the previous session and the fears engendered by the reformist banquets. Barante referred to the "troubled lifelessness"[29] with which conservatives would follow Guizot from fear of the opposition, although not only a few "progressive conservatives" but many other ministerial followers now believed a measure of change to be necessary. Increasingly they felt that Guizot should resign if he would continue to refuse reform, whilst Duchâtel, often critical and jealous of Guizot but too lazy to be actively disloyal, also believed that the Cabinet should resign for different reasons. Those who desired a change of ministry faced the inflexible will of the King who, fixed in his belief that politicians were cowards, that the opposition would dissolve if resisted, not only insisted that Guizot remain, but refused to tolerate any thought of concessions which his minister tentatively suggested might be necessary. Nor would he listen to those who advocated change even when they were such considerable conservatives as Pasquier, Sébastiani, Rambuteau or even Montalivet, his former confidant and still intendant of the civil list. In the King's mind, he was an ally of Molé, whom the King feared would lead to Thiers, and Thiers to war or the entry of Barrot. Even when Montalivet, a colonel in the National Guard, spoke to him of disaffection in that body, the King was not worried for long. A meeting with Général Jacqueminot told him what he wished to believe. Besides, Louis-Philippe had developed a mystical belief in the powers of the Charter: as long as he was true to it, he was invulnerable, he believed. The ministry had a majority and it was constitutionally unnecessary and undesirable to change it.

The King would not even listen to his family. Through her mother, Queen Louise of the Belgians had tried to give warnings as early as 1839; "The excellent Father takes a little too much account of the opinion of Europe, and thinks too little of conforming to that of the country."[30] The Duchesse d'Orleans believed that the identification of the monarchy with the unpopular Guizot would endanger her son's throne. In her salon in the Tuileries gathered an artistic, political and social rival to the increasingly dull and conservative Court, where notabilities of the opposition, Victor Hugo, Billault, Alfred de Musset, Thiers and Barrot congregated, and which Montpensier and Joinville also frequented. Indeed, the most urgent criticism came from the younger princes. Largely because of their opposition to the course of government, both were sent into an honourable exile: Joinville was given a Mediterranean command and Aumale made governor of Algeria. Meeting the former in Italy in 1847, the Marquis de Boissy discussed with the Prince the decadence of the political class, corruption and governmental insufficiency – "two malcontents chatting together".[31] The Prince de Joinville's letter to his younger brother blamed their father for the course of events. "There no longer are ministers; they have no responsibilities; all goes up to the King. The King has reached an age where one no longer accepts observations; he is accustomed to governing. . . . This immense experience, his courage and his great qualities lead him to confront danger boldly, but danger exists none the less. . . .": he regarded the future with foreboding.[32] The death of Madame Adélaïde on 31 December 1847 severely grieved Louis-Philippe: it also removed the only member of his family whose advice to rid himself of Guizot, he might have taken.

As for Guizot, in spite of advice from some of his friends to retire, he was convinced of his indispensability. In a European situation where revolution threatened, Guizot feared to leave France at the mercy of Thiers and Palmerston. The domination of foreign affairs in his mind and the King's, led them to misunderstand the internal situation. With his belief in life and politics as a battle, proud to bear the burden, he determined not to waver. "We will have, inside and outside, a recrudescence of 1831",[33] he told a friend. He saw himself as another Périer, leading the resistance to revolution. He would do nothing to disorganise the conservative army of which he considered himself the general. And the speech from the throne, 29 December 1847, in referring to the agitation fomented by "enemy or blind passions"[34] deliberately challenged even the moderates. All nuances of opposition agreed to be very angry about what they chose to see as a royal insult. Some suggested a mass resignation in order to force the country to choose between the accusation and the opposition, but the majority believed that the government would triumph as in 1846. However, they failed to attend the Tuileries to present their condolences to the King on the death of Madame Adélaïde.

The first debates on the *adresse* took place in the Chamber of Peers. It was a far more agitated event than usual. Montalembert and Pelet de La Lozère criticised Guizot's illiberalism and pro-Austrian policy in Italy. The Marquis de Boissy attacked corruption and those he called "self-styled conservatives". "Conservative, it seems to me, signifies, must signify, he who wishes to conserve, not just portfolios in certain hands, but all that which it is useful to conserve." And he warned the government that if nothing was done they would all face a revolutionary situation. "I am an aristocrat, and therefore truly liberal", he declared, supporting Vicomte Dubouchage in the fight for improving the conditions of the working classes: "Let us agree upon something: if you accord us nothing, we will take all; we will treat you as conquered. . . ."[35] Pasquier warned him against using threatening language. The Comte d'Alton-Shée spoke with even greater violence and was forced to stand down when his praise for the 1793 Convention produced an uproar unusual for the Chamber. More moderate critics were the Duc d'Harcourt, Prince de La Moskowa, Comtes de La Redorte and Molé, whose chances of replacing Guizot seemed good. Through them all came a demand for reform, and the belief that if there were no change a more than purely political crisis would result.

When the Chamber of Deputies came to discuss its *adresse*, the first attack was on finances, which seemed for once a profitable ground for criticism, due to the deficit into which two poor harvests had forced the government. Thiers who led the attack here even managed to blame this on humiliating foreign policy. He exaggerated a problem, due partly to the railway budget and largely temporary, but which combined with other factors to present a society in decadence. Billault's amendment enabled him to detail the corruptions for which the opposition blamed the ministry. The Petit affair had given fresh ammunition and Guizot perceptibly withered under the vituperation of Malleville and Girardin. Yet he would allow no compromise. The attempts by Morny and others to remove the provocative phrase on "blind passions" had no results. The King who saw the debates merely as "storm in a teacup"[36] refused to be concerned with an opposition he despised. Nor had he any sympathy for the dissident conservatives. When Sallandrouze told him of fears in the business world and need for reform, the King asked ironically, "Do your carpets sell well, Monsieur Sallandrouze?"[37]

Many conservatives were asking that the Cabinet undertake some measure of parliamentary reform; Morny and members of the progressive conservative group were joined by traditionally ministerialist deputies such as Liadières. Two representatives asked Guizot to replace the provocative and uncompromising Garde des Sceaux Hébert, to remove the besmirched Génie and to introduce a measure of parliamentary reform to deal with incompatibilities. Guizot seemed to consider sacrificing Génie, and even suggested that reform was a possibility but that it should not be seen to be at the behest of the opposition. The demands of combat and Cabinet unity decided his attitude, and he resisted the mild Sallandrouze amendment which attempted to bind the Cabinet to "the initiative of sage and moderate reforms demanded by public opinion",[38] approved not only by the Duchesse d'Orleans but even by the Duc de Nemours. Guizot did not move from his refusal to grant immediate reform, but even his implicit suggestion that if the unity of the conservative party demanded it, he would consider introducing a measure, annoyed the King who expected firmer resistance. The Sallandrouze amendment was defeated by a majority of thirty-three, a sign that the ministry was safe but that forty conservatives had abstained or voted against the Cabinet.

The debate on the Sallandrouze amendment revealed the problem of Orleanist conservatism. Guizot's determination to assure "the maintenance of the unity of the conservative party"[39] was to make an idol of something which scarcely existed. His rigidity was a natural result of a conservatism which had no traditions: trying to establish them, he had adopted the dangerous policy of resistance in a mobile society. To promise reform, to make an engagement, Guizot said was doubly destructive, weakening what existed without replacing it. A prudent government might make reforms but awaited the right moment to do so. He promised that the Cabinet would take account of the country's feelings: it was for the party to come to an agreement, for the natural protectors of Orleanism. In other words, an embarrassed Guizot gave an oratorical gloss to his imprisonment by the King and divisions within his own party. Guizot justified himself to Louis-Philippe by telling him that without his hints of reform, the Cabinet would probably have been defeated. Without gaining support from reformists, he had incurred the disapproval of the unyielding, especially the King who stated that if reforms were implemented and not defeated by the Chamber of Peers, he would use his veto for the first time. A belief that reform was an attack upon his prerogative was his primary motive. As in 1838 he had refused to allow Molé to make ministerial concessions and forced him into a battle against the Coalition in order to defend the Crown's prerogatives, so ten years later he refused to allow Guizot to countenance reform, forcing him likewise into battle, and one which this time would prove fatal. Obviously Guizot realised that he either had to produce reform or his resignation would become necessary, but he failed, as did many others of all opinions, to regard the situation as urgent. The *Débats* expressed his attitude when it declared that Guizot's words meant reform of Parliament in this legislature.[40] He was decided on extensions of incompatibilities, and electoral reform, the addition of the second jury list, but whether he would have resigned rather than bow to the King's certain refusal cannot be known.

Amongst all speeches on the *adresse*, two had been outstanding: one received with rapturous applause in the Chamber of Peers and gaining huge publicity, the other, delivered in the Chamber of Deputies, with less verve, more rational and intellectual; both were cries of alarm. Montalembert portrayed might defeating right in the Swiss Sonderbund. And in France he spoke of the revolutionary spirit in men's minds, that revolution which threatened true freedom. He asked that "honest men open their eyes"[41] to fight it with courage and conviction, and attacked the government's encouragement of material interests, its failure to support morality and religion. Tocqueville also spoke of his fears for the future. He noted in the country "the instinct of instability': there was surface calm, but disorder had entered men's spirits. Working-class passions were no longer political so much as social, indeed there was a growth of ideas which were antisocial: property divisions were seen as unjust, and when such ideas came to be generally held as now they were, there were dangers of revolution. "We sleep now that we are on top of a volcano."[42] Like Montalembert, Tocqueville felt the soil of Europe trembling. His remedy was less spiritual; electoral reform and the resignation of Guizot, and so as a party politician he was less respected. Both men observed the weakness of bourgeois civilisation as represented by the July Monarchy: whilst disliking its corruption and materialism, both feared in its destruction the growth of a creed which would destroy freedom and wage war on individuality.

Tocqueville told the Orleanists that they were sleeping on a volcano, as Salvandy had remarked shortly before the 1830 Revolution that the royalists were dancing on one. Contemporaries were worried by a growth in revolutionary feelings, but many remembered how often before they had been worried and how the regime had survived. Duchâtel visited one of the plays about the French Revolution, and found it deplorable but still slept through most of it. Conservatives could console themselves that the left was increasingly disunited. Their customary divisions seemed to have been deepened by the open involvement of the republicans in the banquet campaign. The *Réforme* was losing money and subscribers. Republicans were openly contemptuous of the *gauche dynastique*, but were themselves divided. Those like Caussidière who desired insurrection were fiercely opposed by Ledru-Rollin and others who believed it would prove fatal to their party. On the morrow of the Republic most republicans believed the monarchy was firmly established.

The swing towards the opposition amongst the middle classes of Paris was shown when the IIe *arrondissement*, an area of lesser tradesmen and business men which had provided an anti-revolutionary National Guard in 1830–31, had to choose a mayor. All the names on the list were of the opposition and the government had to appoint one, Berger, whom it strongly disliked and who had defeated the ministerialist Lefebvre in the parliamentary elections. The 1848 Revolution triumphed not because of the republicans but through the sort of men who elected the *gauche dynastique* Berger. As Lucien Delahodde said, conspiracies had been crushed in 1832 and 1839. For revolution to succeed, "the bourgeois must in anger, as in 1830, unwittingly, as in 1848, bring insurrection into play."[43] The selection of Berger caused the Bourse to sink by 40 centimes, a measure of panic by the financial class. The lack of confidence caused the suffering of small commerce, which voted revenge upon the government, and the tendency to move towards the left thus fed upon itself. The *petite bourgeoisie* who formed the ranks of the National Guard blamed the King for the time he spent in his residence at Eu, where he continued to conduct affairs with his customary conscientiousness, but which profited in trade at the expense of the capital. Court mourning for Madame Adélaïde further decreased expenditure by Orleanist society and it was the shopkeepers who suffered. They felt little gratitude to a regime which refused them a vote, but it did not cause them to become actively republican. There were, however, active republicans in the ranks of the National Guard which they were determinedly infiltrating. The fact that since 1840 the King had not passed the National Guard in review for fear of hearing cries for reform, meant that a gap had grown between the monarch and his civilian militia.

A group of left-wing Parisians decided to hold a banquet. National Guard officers of the XIIe *arrondissement* (the Observatoire–Panthéon area) were the organisers, and on the refusal of Arago to preside, their deputy Boissel, a chemist, agreed to do so, on the condition that it was reformist and not revolutionary; but with Marie, Garnier-Pagès and Pagnerre on the committee, it was evidently republican, although Ledru-Rollin, too radical, had been excluded. The government was wondering whether its tolerance of the banquets had not been misplaced. Weakened during the *adresse* debates, it needed to prove its strength, and on 14 January therefore, Duchâtel prohibited it, using a law of 1790 which gave the government power to forbid such meetings if they threatened order. Rémusat had acted similarly in 1840 without massive uproar: on this occasion the opposition chose to see it as a sign of arbitrary government. As a result, Barrot's party revoked their previous refusal and agreed to attend the banquet. Duvergier, moving spirit of the alliance of convenience between dynastic opposition and republicans, on 7 February challenged the ministry on the right to ban the banquet. He called Duchâtel's prohibition "a ministerial fiat"[44] and in a pre-arranged drama, with the opposition shouting their solidarity around him, declared he would attend the banquet. The debate resembled those of the Coalition in its deliberate evocation of a revolutionary atmosphere, although Guizot was more unpopular than Molé had ever been. Louis-Philippe was compared with Charles X, and Guizot with Polignac, his blind servant in the implementation of absolutism. The replies of Hébert helped to increase the bitterness of the argument, claiming as he did that all *réunions* were illegal. Duchâtel was dismayed by the effect of Hébert's doctrinaire absolutism: he himself had preferred to establish the government's right to ban *réunions* which seemed dangerous, and to point out that the ministry of the Interior in 1840 under Messieurs dé Remusat and de Malleville, had given him a precedent. He assured the deputies that the government had no intention of banning all such reform banquets.

Although many members of the opposition felt uneasy, and some were partially satisfied by the ministry's vague assurances, it was difficult, having made such vehement threats and promises, to withdraw. On 13 February, Barrot presided over an unruly discussion. A few still demanded a mass resignation to force elections: notably Marrast and Marie who expressed the fear of many republicans that a mere riot would be crushed by the authorities, who would thereby strengthen themselves. The vote was 70 to 18 for proceeding with the banquet.

Thiers agreed with Marie, but he felt unwilling to damage his authority by restraining his more enthusiastic associates. Besides, he hoped that riots might weaken the government and lead to the abdication of "the old man". "The National Guard is going to give Guizot a good lesson; the King has good ears, he will hear reason and give way in time."[45] As he was to assure Falloux on 19 February, with his customary obliviousness to the possibility of bloodshed, the government had forces ten times superior to those of any possible riot: "With several thousand men under the guiding hand of Maréchal Bugeaud, I would answer for all. . . .[46] He hoped for the regency of the Duchesse d'Orléans and it was wrongly believed in some areas that the Princesse had lent herself to this.

The *gauche dynastique* having made the banquet a political manœuvre, now did their best to stifle its excessively radical nature. They doubled the subscription to 6 francs (some had wanted it still higher), transferred the date to a weekday, 22 February, hoping thereby to lessen the numbers of working men. But the republicans demanded as compensation a procession, in which Blanc and Guinard claimed a part for a workers' contingent of up to 300. The leaders of the banquet accepted, realising that the procession they intended could still be largely a National Guard manifestation. As the date grew nearer, however, and the politicians observed the agitation in student quarters and in some *ateliers*, pressure for retreat made itself felt. On 19 February, almost 200 members of the opposition met at Durand's restaurant near the Madeleine. Chambolle and Barrot expressed their doubts and fears, and Berryer's legitimists found at the last moment that they feared the destruction of the social order more than they desired to destroy the government. Berryer's speech had considerable effect, until Lamartine managed to make himself heard and in an effective harangue inflamed passions and inculcated, at least temporarily, feelings of bravado which caused a large majority of those present to decide to proceed with the banquet, against their true convictions.

Most were confident in the power of the government to put down any riots. Gabriel Delessert, prefect of police, receiving reports of surface tranquillity albeit with underlying inquietude, felt that his preparations would suffice. The army in and around Paris had 31,000 men who, unlike those in 1830, were well armed and provisioned. They were, however, commanded by the ineffectual Général Tiburce Sébastiani, brother of the Marshal, who was scarcely on speaking terms with Général Jacqueminot, commander of the National Guard (similar in owing his position to a relative rather than to talent). Jacqueminot, completely out of touch with the men he led, was foolishly confident. Even the King realised his inefficiency but could not dismiss him for fear of upsetting his son-in-law, the Minister of the Interior, and listened to him because he heard what he wished to hear.

Amidst the increasing apprehensions, a movement for compromise emerged. Delegates of the opposition proposed a transaction to two influential conservatives, Vitet and Morny. Their informal treaty of 19 February provided for a highly ritualised confrontation whereby opposition deputies would attend the banquet, but leave when requested by the police, Barrot having made a restrained protest: then the Cour de Cassation would judge the issue. The King was unenthusiastic, but agreed, facing increasingly urgent requests by the Queen and Duc de Montpensier to replace Guizot with a more conciliatory figure. Whilst the more extreme ministerialists and members of the opposition objected to what they considered a surrender, others were still worried. Molé tried to persuade the opposition leaders to cancel the banquet or hold it outside Paris. Rambuteau and Delessert spoke of their fears in the salon of Mme de Lieven, who, convinced by them of the threat of riots, annoyed Guizot by summoning him from conversation with the British ambassador. "And it is for this, princess, that you have interrupted my conversation with Lord Normanby? Let these messieurs calm themselves and, just like you, they will rest very tranquilly."[47]

On 20 February, the prefect of police received the order from the Cabinet to forbid the banquet, Duchâtel being confident that matters would work out according to the agreement. On the 21st, Delessert thus had posted throughout Paris a declaration that the banquet was illegal. Republican journalists, annoyed by the caution of Ledru-Rollin and other deputies, published events planned for the 22nd, enhancing the role of the procession. Marrast, after a pretence at consulting the *gauche dynastique*, placated extremists in the *National* on 21 February, by asking the people and uniformed guard to march behind the deputies to the place of the banquet. In doing this, he destroyed the agreement and set in train events which led to revolution. The assumption of such authority by a republican journalist infuriated conservatives. At the government's request, Vitet and Morny drew up a new proclamation explaining that the government had desired a judicial issue, but that after the opposition manifesto convoking the national guard and threatening order, tolerance was no longer possible. Barrot begged them to have the government reconsider, agreeing that the protest was highly unwelcome but pointing out that there would be dangerous protests in the streets on the morrow. But the Cabinet would not alter its resolution. Guizot realised that concession could destroy the ministry and overrode the weak protests of Delessert. In the Chamber, his majority supported firmness, and Barrot's inability to divorce himself from the republicans enabled Duchâtel to score a debating point in claiming that no government could allow itself to be dictated to by a group of opposition journalists.

In the late afternoon of 21 February, as the governmental prohibition of the banquet was being posted on street walls, about 100 deputies and members of the banquet committee gathered at Barrot's home. Most wished to withdraw and were angry with the republican journalists who had made them choose between possibly dangerous riots and retreat. There were a group of "irreconcilables", notably Lherbette, d'Alton-Shée and Lamartine who dramatically declared his willingness to go to the banquet attended only by his shadow if necessary, but a majority of 80 to 17 decided that the deputies of the opposition should not attend, deciding instead upon a vote of censure against the government. The banquet committee itself, partially swayed by an emotional plea from the inconsistent Marrast not to lay the population open to the fury of the government, seconded the decision. However, radical National Guardsmen assembled at the *Siècle* office were angry when Chambolle informed them of this, and students and other inflammable republicans were furious that their leaders would not act without the *gauche dynastique*. Republican divisions were manifested at a rowdy meeting at the *Réforme* offices. D'Alton-Shée, who had left Barrot in disgust, argued forcibly that their honour compelled them to proceed with the banquet, and was supported by Caussidière and Étienne Arago. Louis Blanc and Ledru-Rollin replied that any riot would be defeated. The prudent dominated and the *Réforme* on 22 February appeared with an article by Flocon attacking *gauche dynastique* pusillanimity, but also with strong advice to the people to behave with moderation, not to provide the government with the occasion for "a bloody success": "when it pleases the democratic party to take a similar initiative, one will see whether it will fall back when it has advanced!"[48] So the republican leaders followed the *gauche dynastique* in their flight, covering the fleeing pack with insults as it joined their retreat.

The King exulted at the decision: he felt justified in his prediction that the opposition would not have the courage to carry out their threats. Duchâtel, equally pleased, on his own authority countermanded earlier orders which he believed might appear provocative. He instructed Jacqueminot and Sébastiani to withdraw all troops to their barracks and cancelled orders for the arrests of Caussidière and twenty other republicans it was believed might try to lead a riot. Delessert, in possession of reports from his agent Delahodde, fully encouraged these dispositions, and the King approved, but no other member of the *conseil*, even the *président*, was informed. All troops were in their barracks by morning, when crowds began to gather. There was an air of expectation rather than determination amongst those who came into central Paris from the suburbs and the slums. Some activists there were, and others unaware of the cancellation when they set out were angry when they heard of it, but the huge crowds in the Place de la Concorde seemed peaceful enough. The deputies in the Chamber opposite were not unduly worried and began the day's business with a discussion on the affairs of the Banque de Bordeaux. The King was still complacent and when Horace Vernet expressed apprehensions to him, the favourite royal painter was impatiently silenced: His Majesty's greater concern appeared to be the portrait of Abd-el-Kader he was commissioning. Nor could Jayr, worried by the growing number of working-class smocks apparent in the streets, frighten the King; Louis-Philippe, like so many, felt that nothing could occur without leadership of the deputies, and since the opposition had retreated, he did not fear the Paris mob.

A crowd in the Boulevard des Capucines attacked the Ministry of Foreign Affairs with stones but was forced to withdraw by the troops. However, the municipal guard could not clear the Place de la Concorde. The government was convinced that the crowds, lacking leadership, would disperse and therefore took great care not to provoke them. The opposition, for the most part, concurred: they were concerned to salvage what they could with the project of accusation, attacking the government for betraying French honour, disobeying the Constitution and practising systematic corruption. Thiers mocked Duvergier and Barrot for this, which he said should be an extreme measure, but they claimed it was necessary to calm emotions. Inside the Chamber only fifty-three signed the "impeachment" which was handed to the president and its discussion was fixed for the following day. After the desultory debates on finance, the deputies left the Palais Bourbon to discover that during the afternoon the situation had worsened slightly. Children had begun building small barricades from the portable chairs of the Champs-Elyseés. In the Rue de Rivoli and Rue Royale groups of workers were shouting against the government. Some bands had seized rifles from arms shops – although the government had been sufficiently far-sighted to remove gunpowder. The republican leaders were sceptical spectators, not believing in the possibility of a serious riot. The authorities seemed to agree, for they still avoided strong military measures.

However, at 5 p.m. it was decided that circumstances necessitated a stronger attitude: the army was put into positions laid down by Maréchal Gérard's plan for repressing a Parisian uprising. But the call to arms of the National Guard was a disaster: many guardsmen did not appear for duty and those who came were often disgruntled. Some leaders of the National Guard met members of the opposition at the offices of the *Siècle*, and it was decided that the National Guard would oppose rioters but also show that it desired a change of ministry. At the offices of the *Réforme* and *National*, the republican leaders and journalists were rather depressed. The government seemed to be in full control as the intending rioters retreated before the army. The King remained confident and the ministers shared his feeling that the next day would see all traces of disorder vanish.

The morning of the 23rd, however, disappointed the government's hopes. Some barricades had been erected in the west-central districts although troops dismantled them without too much difficulty. A few clashes occurred but the rioters were as yet small leaderless bands. But during the night, clubbists had told followers to go on to the streets, and many appeared with weapons. The government felt the need also to call the National Guard, and it was this search for extra strength, in fact indicative of weakness, which was perhaps its greatest error. When the call to arms was beaten through Paris, most guards decided not to answer. Delessert remarked sourly that if he let fifty shops be pillaged, the sullen *petite bourgeoisie* would soon answer the call.[49] Much of their inaction was indeed laziness and complacency rather than radical protest. They felt little disposition to risk injury protecting a ministry they disliked. However, those republicans who were in the National Guard took care to appear to rouse hostility towards the government, and others who were not, like Flocon, dressed in the uniform so as better to embarrass the army and discourage the population. When the National Guards met, there were demands for political change: many appeared to have come to discuss the situation rather than take orders. The general political will was to arbitrate between the ministry and the rioters, who in the early morning did not seem a great danger. Jacqueminot was prostrate at his home and the militia leaderless. The Second and Third Legions drawn from the Faubourgs Montmartre and Poissonière showed more interest in shouting "Down with Guizot!" and "Up with reform" than in protecting the strategic positions to which they had been sent. Other legions signed political manifestations to the King and the Chambers. None save the loyal First (drawn from a prosperous area of the right bank) and half of the Tenth (of the Faubourg Saint-Germain) obeyed orders: the others served as a force aiding disorder by preventing the troops from repressing the rioters by standing between them. This naturally spread discouragement in the badly led army.

As the news of the trouble arrived at the Tuileries, those around the King, his son Montpensier and Marie-Amélie, supported by Dupin and Montalivet, called for a change of ministry. The King was by this time no longer sublimely confident but had sunk into a kind of paralysis. He had been so certain, that the shock of being proved wrong seemed to remove all motive force. Moreover, he would not be responsible for bloodshed. "I have seen enough blood" was his constant refrain. He told Duchâtel that the army must not fire, declaring that he could not use it when the National Guard had turned against him.[50] A combination of humanitarianism and shock at the realisation that the base of his regime "the National Guard, that force upon which I have been pleased to support myself . . . which . . . said to me in 1830: Take the Crown and save us from the Republic!"[51] had turned against him. Eventually ceding, Louis-Philippe sent for Guizot and told him that with bitter regret he was sending for Molé: "to you the honour, to me the shame."[52] Guizot, not unhappy to be removed from office whilst undefeated, returned to a Chamber which had again been vainly trying to discuss the Banque de Bordeaux. He mounted the tribune and announced "the King has just had Monsieur le Comte Molé called to exchange him . . .",[53] to be interrupted by tumultuous applause from the left. The conservatives were mostly angry, an anger which turned against the King when they learnt that it was he who had abandoned the ministry. Some even wanted to go to the Tuileries to protest but Guizot persuaded them otherwise. Men of the moderate opposition such as Rémusat and Dufaure were very worried that the insurrection should have triumphed in this way. Certainly Guizot's resignation occurred at the worst time for the monarchy – to resign before the insurrection or to stay on with a firm military policy, would both have been better.

The July Monarchy now repeated in quick motion its last ministerial crisis. Molé was found at the Chamber of Peers and brought to the Tuileries: it was by now 4 p.m. He rightly told the King that it would be safer to summon Thiers and Barrot. Louis-Philippe was aghast at the effect this would have in Europe, but Molé told him it was a question of saving the monarchy. However, when pressed, perhaps fearful of seeming to shirk a duty, he gave in to the King's demands. It was a mistake: he had difficulty even in making the King accept Bugeaud in charge of the troops in Paris. Molé, having spoken to Dufaure, Passy and Billault, received their support and, having received no response to a hasty letter, went to see Thiers in person. Thiers, who at this moment felt in command of the situation, demanded electoral and parliamentary reform which Molé agreed to, but humiliatingly demanded also a dissolution which would hand power to him. At Barrot's home, an agitated meeting was beginning to find Molé insufficient, as were many of the Parisian crowds to whom the news had been brought by loyal National Guards sent out by Montalivet.

The mood of Paris was strange, a combination of simple joy, of hesitation and of revolutionary fervour. In some places there was public dancing to celebrate the fall of Guizot. Elsewhere crowds sang the "Marseillaise" and marched through the dark streets with flares. At the offices of the *National* and of the *Réforme*, republicans were haranguing the crowds. Ledru-Rollin told his audience they must not disarm until they received universal suffrage. Mobs arriving at the Boulevard des Capucines to boo Guizot, the aim of unsuccessful hostilities earlier, found themselves against a solid wall of soldiers, and were pushed against them from behind. In the chaos amidst the slogan-shouting and missile-throwing, the commander trying at once to retain discipline amongst his troops and to send back the crowds, a shot rang out. Who fired it will never be known: it may have been a nervous soldier, but it was possibly Lagrange, later to become a republican deputy – at least he would claim the honour.[54] Panicking, the soldiers, not waiting for an order, immediately replied with gunfire. Several dead lay on the pavement. Both soldiers and crowd then panicked and ran in different directions into the surrounding streets.

The republicans quickly profited from the error. The sixteen bodies were put on to a cart which was pulled through the streets of Saint-Denis and Montmartre. At the offices of the *Réforme*, Flocon promised vengeance. There were cries of "To arms! To the barricades!" During its procession the cortège of corpses imparted that necessary extra force of hatred. Throughout the night barricades were built and ammunition prepared. When Molé, returning from his fruitless mission to Thiers, heard of the killings outside the Foreign Ministry, he decided that the situation destroyed his effectiveness, and Montalivet carried his renunciation to the King. The futile attempt had cost valuable hours. Meanwhile the King had accepted the pressing advice of Guizot and Duchâtel, to put Maréchal Bugeaud in charge of the army and National Guard, and prepared to accept Thiers.

Bugeaud arrived at the military headquarters before 2 a.m. on 24 February. His first task was to instill spirit into the staff which he was able to do. Ignoring the National Guard, for which he had always the greatest contempt, he planned a strategy whose main focus was sending two strong columns through the insurrectionary districts, one to the Hôtel de Ville by way of the Rues Montmartre, Saint-Denis and Saint-Martin, the other to the Bastille by way of the boulevards. Whilst Bugeaud was planning this strategy, Thiers was having a stormy interview with the King. Louis-Philippe alternately resisted Thiers's proposals and exaggerated the humiliation of having to submit to them. He resisted Thiers's determination to recruit Barrot, expressed disgust at the addition of Duvergier whom he heartily disliked, and angrily refused dissolution. None the less the two agreed to publish in the *Moniteur* that Thiers had been charged with forming a Cabinet and had received the King's approval for the addition of Barrot.

Thiers, on leaving the King, visited Bugeaud with whom he had an unsatisfactory interview. The Marshal was enthusiastic to get on with the job of destroying rioters but Thiers gave him to understand that his own ministry and, by implication, Bugeaud's command was provisional. Rémusat expressed to Thiers the conviction that Bugeaud's appointment was a provocation and the two men went to the King and argued the matter with him for two hours. Duvergier and Barrot were persuaded to enter the Cabinet but both objected strongly to Bugeaud, believing that the conservative general's unpopularity with republicans would prevent the success of their concessions. Finally Général de La Moricière was recruited. It was by now 7 a.m. The provisional Cabinet assembled at the Tuileries; Thiers, Barrot, Duvergier, Malleville, Beaumont, Rémusat and Abbatucci, the last a figure of very doubtful loyalty.

Bugeaud's troops had a certain success, but at about 8 a.m. he ordered them not to fire. Général Bedeau's column, at the entrance to the Rue Saint-Denis, had come to a very solid barricade. He had been persuaded not to worsen the conflict by an attack, when, if the defenders were convinced that Thiers and Barrot were ministers, bloodshed might not be necessary. Bugeaud seems to have felt that, given Barrot's presence in the Cabinet, to stamp out insurrection by force as he had formerly proposed would split the Cabinet, lose him his post and probably destroy his career. Although it is possible that like Marmont before him, Bugeaud would have failed (and indeed the first signs were appearing that temporarily repelling the forces of insurrection would not prevent their immediately re-forming), it was at this point that insurrection gained control of the capital. The retreat of Bedeau's column was disastrous for its morale: soldiers mingled with the crowds and often gave them their weapons and ammunition. Somewhat depleted, the exhausted and demoralised troops arrived at the Place de la Concorde in mid-morning. Bugeaud, to avoid responsibility, for the success of the Revolution, later claimed that he had received the order from above. Louis-Philippe later admitted, such was his horror of bloodshed and civil war, that he approved the cease-fire, but denied giving such an order. Bugeaud's exact motives, like the exact time of his confused directions to Bedeau, must remain enclosed in the chaos of that wet and dark February morning.

The new ministers found the exhausted and aged King more conciliatory than previously. He readily accepted that La Moricière should take charge of the National Guard under Bugeaud, a measure which Thiers hoped would mitigate the effect of the Marshal's unpopularity, and that the troops should be brought back to surround the Tuileries. Barrot, Beaumont and La Moricière rode out into the streets to try to rally support. The further east towards Porte Saint-Denis Barrot and Beaumont travelled, the more hostility they met, and red flags were observed hanging from windows. Previously they had persuaded some barricades to be demolished: now Barrot met cries not only of "Down with Bugeaud!" but against Thiers also, and the mocking contempt of men who accused him of allowing himself to be deceived. Nevertheless there were few signs of republicanism or of revolutionary leadership. Returning exhausted he met La Moricière whose mission had been similarly fruitless. "M. Thiers is no longer possible, and I will not be much longer",[55] Barrot declared.

At the Tuileries, Thiers, Rémusat and Duvergier continued to act like politicians: they obtained the King's permission and made a proclamation to the "Citizens of Paris" announcing armistice, reform and dissolution, but were unable to print it as the presses were now behind enemy lines.

News came that the palace was in danger of being cut off. Duvergier declared that it had become a matter of saving the throne of the Comte de Paris: "You wish to say that I must abdicate",[56] replied the King. Duvergier protested that this was not his intention, but the idea had come into the King's mind and was expressed by him first. At about 11 a.m., to improve the courage of the defenders of the palace, Louis-Philippe rode into the Place du Carrousel, accompanied by Bugeaud and La Moricière, Thiers and Rémusat. The troops welcomed the King, but from the National Guard the cries were mixed: from the First and and Tenth Legions came cries of "Long live the King! Up with reform!" but from the Fourth Legion the cries were hostile. At this moment, the King lost hope, swung his horse round and returned to the palace. Here he slumped into a chair in despair whilst courtiers, soldiers and politicians milled around, some in useless activity and consultation, others like their sovereign sunk in inactive hopelessness. The left-wing deputy Crémieux entered, claiming that disorder would end if Thiers were replaced by Barrot and Bugeaud by Gérard. Both men showed themselves only too happy to relinquish their commands, more theoretical than actual. Thiers, who in 1830 had taken an initiative that created the July Monarchy, now led the flight from responsibility. "I see that the tide rises and we all could be engulfed."[57] The King accepted with ironical fatalism. "Well then, my dear minister," he said to Thiers, "there you are in your turn of unpopularity, what would you counsel me to do?"[58] Barrot, *président* by default, was unaware of his appointment: he was at the Ministry of the Interior attempting to harangue crowds crying for the death of Guizot.

Whilst the sound of nearby gunfire proved that violent insurrectionaries were penetrating ever nearer, Girardin burst in to declare the necessity of immediate abdication and the regency of the Duchesse d'Orleáns. The Duc de Montpensier and several others present supported this vigorously, but the Duchesse implored the King not to abdicate and the Queen commanded him to stay and fight. "Better to die here than to leave by that door!"[59] Piscatory and Montalivet were the only politicians present to support her: abdication meant the Republic, they said. With renewed gunfire, the urging of Montpensier, the assurance that defence was becoming impossible, Louis-Philippe declared that rather than shed blood he would abdicate. Slowly he wrote, "I abdicate this Crown that the national will called upon me to wear, in favour of my grandson, the comte de Paris. Let him be able to succeed in the great task that falls to him today!"[60] The paper was hurriedly borne to Maréchal Gérard who had gone out to inform the crowd, but it never reached him. Nor did the news calm the riot but merely encouraged it. Those inside the beleaguered palace heard that a mob had murdered members of the *garde municipale* whilst National Guards stood by inactive, that Général Bedeau was making no attempt to control the crowds in the Place de la Concorde, and that Général de La Moriciére, trying to stop an attack on the Tuileries had been wounded and captured by the insurgents. Retreat became flight. At 1.30 a.m. the King, Queen, their family and some friends left the palace and entered three inconspicuous carriages which Nemours had positioned outside. With an escort of National Guards on horseback commanded by Montalivet, they left along the quais towards Saint-Cloud, scarcely noticed amidst the chaos of the excited crowds.

Nemours, who remained, had retained his habitual calm gravity. The politicians were disappearing; Bugeaud and Gérard had likewise left. The Prince arranged a brief defence to protect the royal retreat. He found to his surprise that the Duchesse d'Orléans and her two sons had not left: they were in the pavilion de Marsan, where the Princesse was praying beneath a portrait of her husband, preparing to die there, or hoping that the crowd would somehow recognise her child as their king. It was here that Dupin and Grammont found her. The two deputies, the Duchesse, her children and some close friends, including Ary Scheffer, then left the palace escorted by officers, for the Chamber of Deputies. Dupin convinced the Princesse that the declaration of her regency by the deputies might yet save the throne of the Comte de Paris. But at the Palais Bourbon, affairs were in chaos: Orleanism was disintegrating. Leaderless, the conservatives were willing to accept the regency of the Duchesse, but the defeats of the last two days had sapped their wills: they had no ideology to sustain them in defeat. The fleeting presence of Thiers, almost hysterical, had merely increased despair. In this situation, the republicans' and legitimists' powers of destruction at last became effective.

The republicans had been taken by surprise. At about midday, the leadership finally decided that the Republic was possible. So lacking in confidence had they previously been that Garnier-Pagès had agreed to accompany Beaumont and Malleville to the Hôtel de Ville to work for the regency and prepare for the Duchesse's arrival there, which Barrot had desired in the naive hope that 1830 could be repeated from its balcony. But earlier in the afternoon republicans unprepared for compromise penetrated the Chamber, determined to end the monarchy. Lamartine was taken aside and converted to the idea of a republic: he was promised the first place in it. Thus when Dupin mounted the tribune to announce the abdication of the King and the regency of the Duchesse, and Président Sauzet ordered to be entered in the records the acclamations which this had received, the republicans and legitimists determined that no speedy decision should be made which might re-establish the monarchy. Lamartine asked the president to suspend the sitting until the Princesse had left. Sauzet, believing him favourable, initially agreed and called for all those not deputies to leave, but had not the strength to enforce this. The Duchesse d'Orléans rose to appeal to the deputies, but from her balcony could not make herself heard. Sauzet, having failed to obtain silence for her, allowed the republican Marie to speak, who sophistically argued the illegality of the proposed regency which by law should be in the hands of Nemours. He demanded a provisional government, and was supported by Crémieux, who, realising the probability of a republican issue to events, had changed sides since the morning. The legitimist Genoude demanded that the people should be consulted. Barrot had now arrived breathlessly: refusing republican offers of a place in a provisional government, he made an appeal for the regency and the majority of deputies applauded. The Duchesse again rose and tried to speak, but again uproar prevented her from making herself heard. Barrot continued, but was unable to conclude: he had most deputies behind him, but he could not sway the crowd which had been allowed to flow into the Chamber whilst he spoke. "You are nothing here; you are no longer anything . . .", La Rochejacquelein shouted at the Orleanists. A new flood of republicans entered, led by Emmanuel Arago. Ledru-Rollin addressed them, denying the Chamber the right to create a regency, and announcing that the armed people were "master of Paris, whatever happens".[61] From the ministerial benches, Berryer supported him, demanding a provisional government. Lamartine now mounted the tribune. In fact, Sauzet had declared the *séance* closed, but the deputies applauded Lamartine, believing that his oratorical talent might yet save the monarchy. Lamartine made a brief poetical reference to the sufferings of the Princesse and her innocent son, but when he invoked respect for "the glorious people who have fought for three days to redress a perfidious government",[62] the Orleanists knew their cause was lost. Amidst the applause from his supporters, a new invasion of the Chamber took place. The arrivals were not republican students and journalists as before, but a mob brandishing weapons, many of them drunk on wine from the Tuileries which was being sacked. They were screaming "No deputies! Long live the Republic!" Sauzet and the deputies escaped by the nearest doors, and Nemours escorted the Duchesse through a corridor into the courtyard.

Whilst from the Chamber, Lamartine led the names acclaimed by the crowd to the Hôtel de Ville where they were to be sanctified by further acclamations, Barrot made a last hopeless attempt from the Ministry of the Interior before Marie and Carnot entered to take possession of it for the republican provisional government. The Duchesse d'Orléans and her children were helped by the Comte de Mornay to reach the German frontier on 26 February. That night, Nemours secretly embarked for England but the rest of the royal family had greater difficulty. King Louis-Philippe had thought it best to establish himself far from the capital at Eu, but the news that the

Republic had swept away the regency forced him into exile. Through the agency of the British consul, the King and Queen left Trouville for England on 2 March.

In spite of Nemours's reiterated orders, Général Ruhlières in the Place de la Concorde had failed to protect the Palais Bourbon. The 4,000 troops there were never used. Bedeau believed that the order to avoid conflict was still in force. Thus the mob had been able to sack the Tuileries and then run through the gardens and Place de la Concorde to enter the Palais Bourbon. Both generals had proved capable on the battlefield, but both feared civilian responsibility, and Sauzet, with a restricted view of his duties, failed to instruct them to protect the Chamber. Nemours had tried to act as commander but had no official position, and his priority, a task he fulfilled with cool courage, was the protection of his sister-in-law and nephews. In Algeria, the Duc d'Aumale heard on 1 March that the Republic had been proclaimed: he considered transporting the army to France to recover the throne but was dissuaded by Joinville. On 3 March, the princes left Algeria, to the grief of the army and population of Algiers. Orleanism thus collapsed, not because it was defeated by superior force, but because the population of Paris would not protect it against its enemies. Even then all was not necessarily lost, but the division of authority and responsibility, typical of all constitutional regimes, but particularly developed in the July Monarchy, prevented determined and coherent action. At the end, Orleanism wished to be civilian in a military situation, and fell because it had not been able to decide in time whether to use force or concession. "Napoleon fell for waging too much war, Charles X for having violated the law. But at least the causes of the fall of Louis-Philippe have been outside of him, and do not at all accuse his memory",[63] wrote Pelet de La Lòzère. It is, however, difficult not to blame the King for his obstinacy in the last years of his reign, and for the fatalism with which he then allowed his monarchy to collapse. He, like Charles X, had shared his authority with an unpopular man and fell because he failed to sacrifice him with sufficient speed.

For years Louis-Philippe had manœuvred and struggled. He had sacrificed popularity for peace, had braved bullets and endured ministerial crises. It is not surprising that the ageing monarch had tired of crises and in his fatigue become immobile and obstinate. He himself blamed the legitimists who prevented his being a successful conservative monarch struggling against the forces of revolution. In his exile, he had few reproaches to offer himself. He believed he had always been a constitutional king who kept his oaths, that he had maintained the peace of Europe, and finally he congratulated himself on not saving his throne at the price of bloodshed. There have always been some who accepted this verdict. "And when one thinks that his reward for eighteen years of peace and prosperity is a little burial vault in an obscure English village, that gives good pause for some sad reflections",[64] wrote King Leopold when, in 1850, Louis-Philippe died after two years' exile.

Very few republicans had expected, or plotted, a revolution and many republican leaders believed in their regime only as a distant dream. "No conspiracy",[65] stated Marie: there had been no preparation. Marrast had feared a collision and done his best to avoid it, and this was true not only of moderates but of socialists like Louis Blanc. The republicans were so unready and so little confident of their ability that they sent word to England to ask Prince Louis Napoléon Bonaparte to hold himself in readiness.[66] In republican discussions, there was a mood almost of passivity: like the Orleanists, they believed in the forces of history and waited upon them. It was only when they heard that the King had abdicated that the republican leaders, Blanc, Arago, Marrast, Bastide, Thomas and others, meeting at the offices of the *National*, believed that their dream could become reality. They decided to oppose the regency and demand a provisional government. Marrast then led some of them to the Chamber of Deputies where they conferred with Ledru-Rollin, Garnier-Pagès and the man who, more than any other, was responsible for the Republic, Lamartine. The latter's motives will always remain obscure. It was perhaps ironical justice which made arbiter of the monarchy's fate a man who began and ended his life as a legitimist, and in between times vaguely covered most colours of the political spectrum. As many dissatisfied men who later became Orleanists for want of any other conviction had undermined the Restoration, so the July Monarchy had its strength sapped by the mobile opinions and sullen disloyalties of those it failed to satisfy.

Orleanism believed in its necessity, but necessity does not mean invulnerability. Most Orleanists believed that compromise was a strength, but failed to understand that it is not easy for a compromise to stand still. Compromise eventually obscured any point of resistance, or vital principle. Orleanist parliamentary policy had always been to pull rivals or opponents towards itself, infiltration rather than conflict: thus Thiers approached Molé in 1838, and the *gauche dynastique* drew close to Thiers in 1840. In 1848, within two days the July Monarchy ran desperately through its parties and their leaders, trying to discover one which would guarantee its existence. From Guizot to Barrot, none could find that strategic point on which to plant the flag and fight. A vital moment came when men like Crémieux who had used the policy of infiltration to propel Barrot to power, decided that they would be safest in supporting the Republic.

As Guizot said, they had "collected a very tangled heritage from our stormy times".[67] The July Monarchy had failed to establish itself in the shifting and unstable society which had emerged from revolution and war, but nor did the Second Republic or Second Empire succeed. Only when passions were exhausting themselves, when conservativism and republicanism came together in the face of communism and military defeat, could a regime of compromise establish itself. Whilst passions were still strong and each alternative believed itself possible, the establishment of a constitutional regime was unlikely to prove successful. As Rémusat said, the liberties provided by the July Monarchy helped to undermine it: "The greatest merit of the establishment of 1830 has perceptibly contributed to its ruin."[68]

REFERENCES

1. A. Karr *Les Guêpes* (1858).
2. Béranger, cited in E. Hamel, *Histoire du Règne de Louis–Philippe* (1890), II, 680.
3. L. Viter, *Le Comte Duchâtel* (1895), 179.
4. Ibid.
5. Comte J. C. Beugnot, *Le Correspondant* (1845), 345.
6. *Revue Rétrospective* (1848) III.
7. Papiers Thiers, nouvelles acquisitions françaises, 20602, no. 146. f. 244.
8. Baron P. de Barante, *Souvenirs* (1890) VII, 123.
9. J. Naville (ed.), *Lettres de François Guizot et de la Princesse Lieven* (1963), II, 243.
10. Archives Parlementaires, 25 August 1846.
11. A. de Lamartine, *Discours politiques* (1888), II, 92.
12. Comte A. de Tocqueville, *Correspondance* (*Œuvres*, ed. J. P. Mayer, 1967), VIII, 485.
13. Ibid., 370–1.
14. Archives Parlementaires, 27 April 1847.
15. Barante, op. cit., VII, 229.
16. Comte C. de Rémusat, *Mémoires de ma vie* (1958), III, 262.
17. Castellane, *Journal* (1895), III 273.
18. L. Thiers, *Correspondances. M. Thiers à Mme Thiers et à Mme Dosne* (1904), 158.
19. Duc E. A. G. de Pasquier, *La Révolution de 1848* (1944), 131–2.
20. Barante, op. cit., VII, 84.
21. X. Doudan, *Mélanges et lettres* (1876), II, 137.
22. Comtesse C. de Boigne, *Récits d'une tante* (1921), V, 91.
23. Castellane, op. cit., III, 281.
24. C. A. Sainte-Beuve, *Causeries du Lundi*, (1868), XI, 458.
25. C. Almeras, *Odilon Barrot* (1951), 158, 161, 164.
26. Comte E. d'Alton-Shée, *Souvenirs de 1847* (1879), 70.
27. Lamartine, op. cit., 265.
28. Ibid.
29. Barante, op. cit., VI, 220. Comte A. de Morny, "Quelques réflexions sur la politique actuelle", *Revue des Deux Mondes* (January 1848), 151–63.
30. Louis-Marie d'Orléans, *La Cour de Belgique et la Cour de France* (1933), 67.
31. Marquis M. E. O. de Boissy, *Mémoires* (1870), II, 32.
32. *Revue Réstrospective*, (1848) 481–2.
33. Archives Nationales, 42.AP.35.
34. Archives Parlementaires, 28 December 1847.
35. Ibid., Chambre des Pairs, 3 January 1848.
36. Odilon Barrot, *Mémoires posthumes* (1875), 500.
37. Ibid., 504.
38. Archives Parlementaires, 12 January 1848.
39. Ibid.
40. *Journal des Débats*, 14 January 1848.
41. Archives Parlementaires, Chambre des Pairs, 15 January 1848.
42. Archives Parlementaires, Chambre des Députés, 15 January 1848.
43. L. de la Hodde, *Histoire des sociétés secrètes* (1850), 193.
44. Archives Parlementaires, 7 February 1848.
45. Comte A. de Falloux, *Mémoires d'un royaliste* (1888), I, 264.
46. Ibid.

47. Boigne, op. cit., v, 101.
48. De la Hodde, op. cit., 196.
49. Dr F. L. Poumiès de la Siboutie, *Souvenirs d'un médecin de Paris* (1910), 293.
50. Pasquier, op. cit., 212.
51. E. Lemoine, *L'Abdication du Roi Louis–Philippe* (1851).
52. Pasquier, op. cit., 213, and Guizot *Mémoires pour servir à l'histoire de mon temps* (1858), VIII, 583–5.
53. Archives Parlementaires, 23 February 1848.
54. Dr L. Véron, *Mémoires d'un bourgeois de Paris* (1854), v, 273.
55. Rémusat, op. cit., IV, 220.
56. N. W. Senior, *Conversations with M. Thiers, M. Guizot and other Distinguished Persons during the Second Empire* (1880), 74–5.
57. Pasquier, op. cit., 239.
58. Rémusat, op. cit., IV, 224.
59. Bibliothèque Nationale, nouvelles acquisitions françaises, 726, f. 1.
60. Archives Parlementaires, 24 February 1848.
61. Ibid.
62. Ibid.
63. Comte J. Pelet de La Lozère, *Pensées morales et politiques* (1873), 74.
64. J. J. Dupin, Archives Nationales, Fichier des Ventes, 7 September 1850.
65. A. A. Cherest, *La Vie et les œuvres de A.–T. Marie* (1873), 94.
66. B. Sarrans, *Histoire de la Révolution de Février 1848* (1850), I, 291–3.
67. Archives Parlementaires, 21 January 1847.
68. Rémusat, op. cit., IV, 247.

Further Reading

Although what follows is by no means a complete bibliography of the July Monarchy, a serious attempt has been made to be thorough. It has proven necessary, therefore, to cite many works written in French; nevertheless, whenever possible, works in English have been brought to the fore.

For the sake of convenience, this essay has been arranged to correspond with the chapters in the text. This has necessitated a certain amount of repetition, but the reader should note that the further readings of certain chapters should be read in combination with those of others. For instance, the reader interested in religious history should combine the sources cited for Chaptor 4 (on the *Avenir*) with those cited for Chapter 22 (Religion and Education). The reader should also take note of the primary sources, particularly the memoirs, cited in the notes to Collingham's text.

There is no recent, standard bibliography of the July Monarchy. The reader can, however, turn to the relevant sections of the *Bibliographie annuelle de l'histoire de France* and should note that the journal *French Historical Studies* publishes a list of recent works in French history in each edition.

The following abbreviations for journals have been used in this essay.

AHR	*American Historical Review*
AHRF	*Annales Historiques de la Révolution Française*
AM	*Annales du Midi*
EHR	*English Historical Review*
ESR	*European Studies Review*
FHS	*French Historical Studies*
HJ	*Historical Journal*
JEEH	*Journal of European Economic History*
JEH	*Journal of Economic History*
JIH	*Journal of Interdisciplinary History*
JMH	*Journal of Modern History*
JPE	*Journal of Political Economy*
JSH	*Journal of Social History*
MS	*Mouvement Social*

RE	*Revue Économique*
RH	*Revue Historique*
RHES	*Revue d'Histoire Économique et Sociale*
RHM	*Revue d'Histoire Moderne*
RHMC	*Revue d'Histoire Moderne et Contemporaine*
SH	*Social History*

GENERAL WORKS

In general, the July Monarchy has not been given the attention that it deserves. Nevertheless, the reader can place it within its general historical context by turning to broad surveys which cover modern French history. Amongst these, G. Wright, *France in Modern Times* (London, 1960), A. Cobban, *A History of Modern France* (London, 1962–65), II, and J. P. T. Bury, *France 1814–1940* (5th edn, London, 1985), all provide useful, standard narratives. R. Rémond, in *La Vie Politique en France* (Paris, 1965), takes a more overtly analytical approach. R. Magraw's *France 1814–1815: the bourgeois century* (Oxford, 1983) is essentially a social history. From its opening sentence it is a provocative and stimulating work, and when read in conjuction with the work of Cobban previously cited, will give the reader a good idea of the Marxist–Liberal revisionist debate that has dominated French history for the last couple of decades.

Many historians have focused upon both the Bourbon Restoration and July Monarchy in order to discuss the French experiment in constitutional monarchy. J. Lucas-Dubreton' s *The Restoration and the July Monarchy* (London, 1929) is an amusing read due to its many anecdotes, but it has not weathered the test of time well and is occasionally wrong. I. Collins's *Government and Society in France 1814–1848* (London, 1970) is a more reliable, standard account. The book to read, however, is A. Jardin and A.-J. Tudesq's *Restoration and Reaction, 1815–1848* (Cambridge, 1983); it combines a relatively up-to-date narrative with an excellent account of the diversity of the different French regions.

There are two fairly recent texts which focus upon the July Monarchy. Neither P. Vigier in *La Monarchie de Juillet* (Paris, 1962), nor P. H. Beik in *Louis-Philippe and the July Monarchy* (New York and London, 1965) go into much detail, but both works do provide a simple, fluid narrative. Beik's work contains some very valuable translations of important documents of the period. P. Thureau-Dangin's *Histoire de la monarchie de Juillet* (Paris, 1884–92) contains a wealth of detail in its seven volumes, as attested by the number of times that later historians refer to it.

INTRODUCTION

To set the scene for the July Monarchy, one can turn to studies of the Bourbon Restoration. G. de Bertier de Sauvigny's *The Bourbon Restoration* (Philadelphia, 1966) remains the standard account. Bertier is exceedingly sympathetic to the Bourbon Monarchy and his interpretation should be balanced by reading F. B. Artz, *France under the Bourbon Restoration* (Cambridge, Massachusetts, 1930), which is very strong on constitutional history and contains an excellent examination of the Charter. J. Hall Stewart's *The Restoration Era in France (1814–1830)* (Princeton, New Jersey and London, 1968) contains valuable translations of important documents. One can also approach the period by combining P. Mansel's *Louis XVIII* (London, 1981) with V. W. Beach's *Charles X of France, his Life and Times* (Boulder, Colorado, 1971).

To get some notion of how French royalists viewed the world, one can read N. Hudson's *Ultra-Royalism and the French Revolution* (Cambridge, 1936) or J.-J. Oechslin's, *Le mouvement ultra-royaliste sous la restauration: son idéologie et son action politique, 1814–1830* (Paris, 1960). D. Higgs, in *Ultraroyalism in Toulouse: from its origins to the Revolution of 1830* (Baltimore, 1973) gives an excellent local study. For the reverse side of the coin, one can read P. Pilbeam's "The growth of liberalism and the crisis of the Bourbon Restoration, 1827–1830", *HJ* 25(2) (1982), 351–66 and E. Newman's "The blouse and the frock coat: the alliance of the common people of Paris with the liberal leadership and the middle class during the last years of the Bourbon Restoration", *JMH*, 46(1) (1974), 26–59. Newman has also described the waning fortunes of republicans during the early years of the Bourbon Restoration in "Lost illusions: the regicides in France during the Bourbon Restoration", *Nineteenth-Century French Studies*, 10(1) (1981) 45–74. To view republicans, Bonapartists and liberals working in common opposition, one can turn to A. Spitzer, *Old Hatreds and Young Hopes* (Cambridge, Massachusetts, 1971) and R. S. Alexander, "The *fédérés* of Dijon in 1815", *HJ* 30(2) (1987) 367–90. For opposition within the military, one can read E. Guillon, *Les Complots militaires sous la restauration* (Paris, 1895), 2 vols, and J. Vidalenc, *Les Demi-Soldes* (Paris, 1955). R. Holroyd describes relations between the monarchy and the army in "The Bourbon Army, 1815–1830", *HJ*, 14(3) (1971), 529–52.

CHAPTER 1: THE REVOLUTION OF JULY 1830

The book to read for this and the following chapter is D. H. Pinkney's *The French Revolution of 1830* (Princeton, New Jersey, 1972) and one should combine this with the same author's "Pacification of Paris: the military lessons of 1830" in J. M. Merriman (ed.), *1830 in France* (London and New York, 1975), pp. 191–202. J.-L. Bory, *La Révolution de Juillet* (Paris, 1972) presents an action-packed narrative of the three glorious days and M. Aguhlon, "La révolution de 1830 dans l'histoire du XIXe siècle français", *AHRF*, année 52 (1980), no. 242, 483–98, gives a broad interpretation of the meaning of the event.

E. L. Newman describes those who did the actual fighting in "What the crowd wanted in the French Revolution of 1830" in J. M. Merriman (ed.), *1830 in France*, pp. 17–40, and "L'image de foule dans la révolution de 1830", *AHRF*, année 52 (1980), no. 242, 499–509. The important role of journalists prior to and during the Revolution is analysed by D. L. Rader, *The Journalists and the July Revolution in France* (The Hague, 1973), and R. D. Price discusses the reaction of the army in "The French army and the Revolution of 1830", *ESR*, 3(3) (1973), 243–67. For the arch-kingmaker and his apprentice, one can turn to P. Mantoux, "Talleyrand en 1830", *RH*, 78 (Jan.–April 1902), 266–87, and M. L. Lifka, "Thiers' role in the July Revolution", *Second Annual Meeting of the Western Society for French History* (1974–75), pp. 245–51.

The *RHM* published a series of articles on the Revolution in various provincial cities in vols XXXII–XXXIV (1934), but for a more recent, analytical account, the reader should turn to P. Pilbeam, "The 'three glorious days': the Revolution of 1830 in provincial France", *HJ*, 26(4) (1983), pp. 831–44. J. M. Merriman has described the events of the Revolution in a small departmental capital in "Restoration town, bourgeois city: changing urban politics in industrialising Limoges", in J. Merriman (ed.), *French Cities in the Nineteenth Century* (London, 1982), pp. 42–72, and in *The Red City: Limoges and the French nineteenth century* (New York and Oxford, 1985).

CHAPTER 2: THE FOUNDATION OF A REGIME

One should commence by reading the relevant documents translated by J. H. Stewart, *The Restoration Era in France (1814–1830)* (Princeton, New Jersey and London, 1968) and P. H. Beik, *Louis-Philippe and the July Monarchy* (New York and London, 1965). V. E. Starzinger discusses the nature of the regime in *Middlingness: juste-milieu political theory in France and England, 1815–1848* (Charlottesville, Virginia, 1965), and D. H. Pinkney describes the first tentative steps of the government in "*Laissez-faire* or intervention? Labor policy in the first months of the July Monarchy", *FHS*, 3(1) (Spring 1963), 123–28. Lafayette's ineffectual attempts to influence the regime are described by L. S. Kramer, "La Fayette in 1830: a center that could not hold", *Canadian Historical Journal* 17(3) (1982), 469–92.

On the massive administrative changes brought by the Revolution, one can read J. Tulard, "Les épurations administratives en France de 1800 à 1830", in P. Gerbod *et al.*, *Les Épurations Administratives XIXe et XXe Siècles* (Geneva, 1977), pp. 49–62, and C. H. Pouthas, "La réorganisation du ministère de l'intérieur et la réconstitution de l'administration préfectorale par Guizot en

1830", *RHMC*, 9(1962), 241–63. P.-B. Higonnet, "La composition de la Chambre des Députés de 1827 à 1831", *RH*, 239(1968), 351–78, and L. Girard, "La réélection des députés promus à des fonctions publiques (1828–1831)", in *Mélanges offerts à Charles H. Pouthas* (Paris, 1973), pp. 227–44, describe changes in Parliament.

CHAPTER 3: POST-REVOLUTIONARY DISORDERS, 1830–1831

On relations between Louis-Philippe and the supposed bulwark of order, see L. Girard, *La Garde Nationale 1814–1871* (Paris, 1964). The National Guard was not always reliable during this period, however; see P. Pilbeam, "Popular violence in provincial France after the 1830 revolution", *EHR*, 91 (1976), 278–97, R. D. Price, "Popular disturbances in the French provinces after the July Revolution of 1830", *ESR*, 1(4) (1971), 323–50, and Price's "Techniques of repression: the control of popular protest in mid-nineteenth-century France", *HJ*, 25(4) (1982), 859–87.

In the introduction to J. M. Merriman (ed.), *1830 in France* (London and New York, 1975) Merriman persuasively puts forward the argument that the Revolution of 1830 was not simply a matter of three glorious days in Paris. The argument is furthered in the same book by J. Rule and C. Tilley, "Political process in revolutionary France, 1830–1832", pp. 41–85, and Merriman, "The demoiselles of the Ariège, 1829–1831", pp. 87–118.

On the role of students and young men as an opposition group, see A. Esler, "Youth in revolt: the French generation of the 1830's", in R. J. Bezucha (ed.), *Modern European Social History* (London, 1972), pp. 301–34. M. Brown describes the widespread sympathy for Polish nationalists in "The comité franco-polonais and the French reaction to the Polish rising of November 1830", *EHR*, 93(369) (1978), pp. 774–93. The trial of the ministers of Charles X tested the regime of Louis-Philippe severely; see P. Bastide, "Le procès des ministres de Charles X", *RHMC* (July–September 1957), 171–211.

CHAPTER 4: THE ATTACK ON LIBERALISM: SAINT-SIMONISM AND THE *AVENIR*

The best approach to Saint-Simon is to read what he actually wrote. K. Taylor's *Henri de Saint-Simon (1760–1825). Selected writings on science, industry, and social organisation* (New York, 1975) is a useful starting-point. F. E. Manuel, *The Prophets of Paris* (Cambridge, Massachusetts, 1962) describes the writings and actions of Saint-Simon and his followers. On the influence of Saint-Simonist thought, see B. M. Ratcliffe, "Saint-Simonism and messianism: the case of Gustave d'Eichthal", *FHS* 9(3) (1976), 484–502, S. A. Hanna, "The Saint-Simonians and their application of state socialism in Egypt", in S. A. Hanna (ed.), *Medieval and Middle Eastern Studies in Honor of Aziz Suryal Atiya* (Leiden, 1972), pp. 199–210, and C. G. Moses, "Saint-Simonian men – Saint-Simonian women: the transformation of feminist thought in 1830's France", *JMH*, 54(2) (1982), 240–67.

The religious aspects of socialist thought are analysed in E. Berenson, *Populist Religion and Left-Wing Politics in France, 1830–1852* (Princeton, New Jersey, 1984), and J. Droz discusses the impact of religious thought upon certain revolutionaries in "Religious aspects of the revolutions of 1848 in Europe", in E. M. Acomb and M. L. Brown (eds), *French Society and Culture since the Old Regime* (New York, 1966), pp. 134–49. One can place the *Avenir* in its historical context by reading B. Reardon, *Liberalism and Tradition: aspects of Catholic thought in nineteenth-century France* (Cambridge, 1975). One should also read P. N. Stearns, "The nature of the *Avenir* movement (1830–31)", *AHR*, LXV (July 1960), 837–47, and *Priest and Revolutionary: Lammenais* (New York, 1967), by the same author.

CHAPTER 5: *MOUVEMENT* AND *RÉSISTANCE*: THE TRIUMPH OF PÉRIER

For discussion of works concerning legitimist opposition, please turn to Chapter 10. On the *mouvement* party, see J. Nantet, "Royer-Collard, Guizot, Tocqueville et le parti du mouvement", *La Nouvelle Revue des Deux Mondes*, no. 3 (1972), pp. 570–81. T. D. Beck gives a thorough statistical analysis of the deputies elected in 1831 in *French Legislators, 1800–1834* (Los Angeles and London, 1974). The iron grip of Périer may be seen in C. Breunig, "Casimir Périer and the troubles of Grenoble, March 11–13, 1832", *FHS*, 2(4) (1962), 469–89. The triumph of Périer was not without its costs however; see P. Pilbeam, "The emergence of opposition to the Orleanist monarchy, August 1830–April 1831", *EHR*, LXXXV, no. 334 (January 1970), 12–28.

For the background to the violent upheavals of this period, see C. H. Johnson, "The Revolution of 1830 in French economic history", in J. M. Merriman (ed.), *1830 in France* (London and New York, 1975), pp. 139–89, P. Gonnet, "Esquisse de la crise économique en France de 1827–32", *RHES*, XXXIII (1955), 249–92, J. Lucas-Dubreton, *La grande peur de 1832 (la choléra et l'émeute)* (Paris, 1932), and F. Delaporte, *Disease and Civilisation: the cholera in Paris, 1832* (Cambridge, Massachusetts, 1986). For the result in Paris, see A. Faure, "Mouvements populaires et mouvement ouvrier à Paris (1830–34)", *MS*, no. 88 (July–September 1974), pp. 51–92; for Lyons, see R. J. Bezucha, "The Revolution of 1830 and the city of Lyons", in J. M. Merriman (ed.), *1830 in France*, pp. 119–38.

CHAPTER 6: THE ORLEANIST CONSTITUTION

The focus here is upon government personnel and administration, but the reader is advised to combine the works cited in this chapter with those of the following. The place to start is P. Bastide's *Les Institutions politiques de la Monarchie Parlementaire française* (Paris, 1954). To learn about the upper echelons of government, one should read the relevant chapters of *Le Conseil d'État: son histoire à travers les documents d'époque* (Paris, 1974), published as part of the Histoire de l'Administration Française series by Éditions du Centre National de la Recherche Scientifique. Moving down a level in the administration, one can read A.-J. Tudesq, "Les chefs de cabinet sous la monarchie de juillet: l'exemple d'Alphonse Génie", in M. Antoine *et al.*, *Origines et Histoire des Cabinets des Ministres en France* (Geneva, 1975), pp. 39–53. J. Baillou discusses the men who executed foreign policy in *Histoire de l'administration française. Les affaires etrangères et le corps diplomatique français* (Paris, 1984), I. The judiciary is discussed in J. P. Royer and R. Martinage (eds), *Juges et notables au XIXe siècle* (Paris, 1982). C. H. Church discusses the men who made the government run in *Revolution and Red Tape: the French ministerial bureaucracy 1770–1850* (Oxford, 1981). Tax officials are the subject of J. Clinquart in *L'Administration des douanes en France sous la Restauration et la Monarchie de Juillet (1815–48)* (Neuilly, 1981).

B. Chapman's *The Prefects and Provincial France* (London, 1955), helps to explain the difficult task of these men who served as bridges between local and central government. B. Bergerot discusses recruitment in "De la création des préfets", *Revue administrative*, année 36, special no. (1983), 21–115. The problems of bringing about change and centralisation are discussed in P. A. Gourevitch, *Paris and the Provinces: the politics of local government reform in France* (Los Angeles, 1980). A.-J. Tudesq discusses local authorities in *Les Conseillers Généraux en France au temps de Guizot, 1840–1848* (Paris, 1967), and "De la monarchie à la République: le maire, petit ou grand notable", *Pouvoirs*, no. 24 (1983), 5–17.

CHAPTER 7: PARLIAMENT: DEPUTIES AND PEERS

P. Campbell, in *French Electoral Systems and Elections since 1789* (London, 1958), outlines the rules of the game and gives a broad account of the results; S. Kent in *Electoral Procedure under Louis-Philippe* (New Haven and London, 1937) explains how the system worked during the July Monarchy. S. Kent, "Electoral lists of France's July Monarchy, 1830–1848", *FHS*, 17(1) (1971), 117–27, discusses who participated in the voting, and A.-J. Tudesq, "Parlement et administration sous la monarchie de juillet", in M. Brugière *et al.*, *Administration et Parlement depuis 1815* (Paris, 1982), describes the role of deputies.

For a thorough examination of the background of the deputies, one can turn to L. Girard *et al.*, *La Chambre des Députés en 1837–1839* (Paris, 1976), for the peers, A.-J. Tudesq, "Les Pairs de France au temps de Guizot", *RHMC*, 3 (1956), 262–83. The latter two works should be read in conjunction with A.-J. Tudesq's classic social study *Les Grands Notables en France* (Paris, 1964), 2 vols. On the difficult judicial role of the peers, see L. Devance, "Chambre haute et pouvior judiciare en France: la cour des pairs pendant la Monarchie constitutionnelle", *Parliaments, Estates and Representation*, 4(2) (1984), 147–56.

On elections and political life in general at the local level, see P. M. Jones, "An improbable democracy: 19th century elections in the Massif Central", *EHR*, 97(384) (1982), 530–57, P. McPhee, "On rural politics in 19th century France: the example of Rodès, 1789–1815", *Comparative Studies in Society and History*, 23(2) (1981), 248–77, and P. McPhee, "Social change and political conflict in Mediterrean France: Canet in the XIXth century", *FHS*, 12(1) (1981), 68–97.

CHAPTER 8: LOUIS-PHILIPPE AND HIS COURT

Despite the fact that Louis-Philippe was a very complex character who lived a fascinating life, there has not been a great deal of substance written about him. Of two English biographies, T. E. B. Howarth, *Citizen-King* (London, 1961) and Agnès de Stoeckl, *King of France. A portrait of Louis-Philippe, 1773–1850* (London, 1957), the former is the better work, but we still await the definitive biography. For those able to read French, Duc de Castries, *Louis-Philippe* (Paris, 1972) is recommended. For details of king and court life, one can turn to D. Cochin, *Louis-Philippe* (Paris, 1918), or J. Bertaut, *Le Roi bourgeois (Louis-Philippe Intime)* (Paris, 1936). For the early years, there is J. Lucas-Dubreton, "La jeunesse de Louis-Philippe", *La Revue des Deux Mondes*, no. 11 (1963), 336–48 and R. Recouly, *Louis-Philippe, roi des francais. Le chemin vers le trône* (Paris, 1936). Several articles have been written on personal relations; see J.-P. Garnier, "Louis-Philippe et le duc de Bordeaux", *La Revue des Deux Mondes*, no. 1 (1968), 38–52, J. Duhamel, "Louis-Philippe et Victoria", *La Revue des Deux Mondes*, no. 1 (1969), 38–44, J. Tonnelé, "Le mariage de Louis-Philippe", *Aux carrefours de l'histoire*, no. 25 (1959), 1139–44, and R. Burnand, "Marie-Amélie, reine des Français", *Historia*, no. 77 (1958), 608–18. J. J. Baughman takes a very sympathetic view of a king beset by a miserly Chamber of Deputies in "Financial resources of Louis-Philippe", *FHS*, 4(1) (Spring 1965), 63–83. On a similar theme is A. Colling, "La liste civile de Louis-Philippe", *La Revue des Deux Mondes*, no. 4 (1966), 571–82.

CHAPTER 9: THE DOCTRINES OF ORLEANISM

There has been much discussion about the nature of the regime. For the traditional interpretation, see J. L'homme, "Bourgeois supremacy during the July Monarchy", in J. Friguglietti and E. Kennedy (eds), *The Shaping of Modern France* (London, 1969), pp. 228–35, C. Morazé, *The Triumph of the Middle Classes* (London, 1966), and the same author's *La France Bourgeoise XVIIIe–XXe Siècles* (Paris, 1952). L. O'Boyle put forward a similar interpretation in "The middle class in Western Europe, 1815–1848", *AHR*, LXXI(3) (April 1966), 827–45, but came under attack from the arch-revisionist A. Cobban, "The 'middle class' in France, 1815–48" and O'Boyle gave her rejoinder in "The middle class reconsidered: a reply to Professor Cobban"; both of the latter articles can be found in *FHS*, 5(1) (Spring 1967), pp. 41–56. S. Grunor entered the fray with "The Revolution of July 1830 and the expression 'bourgeoisie'", *HJ*, 11(3) (1968), 462–71, and R. Magraw has restated the Marxist position in *France 1814–1915: the bourgeois century* (Oxford, 1983). Perhaps the simplest way for the reader to make sense of all of this is to read the relevant chapters of R. Rémond, *The Right Wing in France from 1815 to De Gaulle* (Philadelphia, 1969).

In further regard to doctrine, one can turn to A. Jardin, *Histoire du Libéralisme Politique* (Paris, 1985), and L. Girard, *Les libéraux français, 1814–1875* (Paris, 1985). Girard's "Political liberalism in France, 1840–1875", in E. M. Acomb and M. L. Brown (eds), *French Society and Culture since the Old Regime* (New York, 1966), pp. 120–32, is brief but useful.

CHAPTER 10: LEGITIMISM AND THE VENDÉE, 1832

R. Price, in "Legitimist opposition to the Revolution of 1830 in the French provinces", *HJ*, 17(4) (1974), pp. 755–78, has discussed the conflicting interests that reduced the likelihood of serious legitimist revolt, and this is a point ably demonstrated in B. Fitzpatrick, *Catholic Royalism in the Department of the Gard, 1814–1852* (Cambridge, 1983). Legitimist ideology is discussed in R. Rémond, *The Right Wing in France from 1815 to De Gaulle* (Philadelphia, 1969) and S. Rials, "Contribution à l'étude de la naissance des partis politiques en France: le parti légitimiste de 1830 à 1883", *Revue de la Recherche juridique. Droit prospectif (Aix-en-Provence)*, v. 8 (1983), pp. 383–408.

On the attempt to organise revolt, see E. Gabory, *Les Bourbons et la Vendée* (Paris, 1923), G. de Bertier de Sauvigny, *Le Comte Ferdinand de Bertier (1782–1864)* (Paris, 1948), and the collection of documents in Bertier's *La Conspiration des légitimistes et de la duchesse de Berry contre Louis-Philippe, 1830–1832* (Paris, 1950). The book to read on the attempted insurrection is H. de Changy, *La Soulèvement de la duchesse de Berry: 1830–1832; les royalistes dans la tourmente (Paris, 1986)*, and to this one can add J. Lucas-Dubreton, *La Princesse Captive: La Duchesse de Berry, 1832–1833* (Paris, 1925).

CHAPTER 11: THE REPUBLICANS 1831–1834

G. Weill, *Histoire du parti républicain en France 1814–1870* (Paris, 1928), gives the broad background, and G. Perreux, *Au temps des sociétés secrètes. La propagande républicaine au début de la monarchie de juillet* (Paris, 1931), provides the more immediate context. Much interesting and picturesque detail can be gleaned from J. Lucas-Dubreton, *Louis–Philippe et la machine infernale* (Paris, 1951). B. H. Moss, "Parisian workers and the origins of republican socialism, 1830–1833" in J. M. Merriman (ed.), *1830 in France* (London and New York, 1975), pp. 203–17, and A. Faure, "Mouvements populaires et mouvement ouvrier à Paris (1830–34)", *MS*, no. 88 (July–September 1974), 51–92, describe the growth of republicanism in the capital and D. B. Weiner, "Francois-Vincent Raspail: doctor and champion of the poor", *FHS*, 1(2) (1959), 149–71, describes one cause for this. For republicanism outside of Paris, one can turn to M. Agulhon's brilliant *The Republic in the Village: the people of the Var from the French Revolution to the Second Republic* (Cambridge, 1982), and the same author's *Une Ville ouvrière au temps du socialisme utopique: Toulon de 1815 à 1851* (Paris, 1970). W. H. Sewell, "Social change and the rise of working-class politics in nineteenth-century Marseille", *Past and Present*, no. 65 (November 1974), 75–109, analyses the changes in the artisan community that would pave the way for republican recruitment. D. Porch describes republican recruitment and secret societies in *Army and Revolution, France 1815–1848* (London, 1974), and M. Agulhon describes republican symbolism in *Marianne into Battle* (Cambridge, 1981).

CHAPTER 12: THE MINISTRY OF 11 OCTOBER 1832 AND MINISTERIAL INSTABILITY, 1834–1835

On the subject of ministerial changes, for this and subsequent chapters, see C. Pouthas, "Les ministères de Louis-Philippe", *RHMC*, 1(1954), 102–30. For the role of Guizot, see E. Brush, *Guizot in the Early Years of the Orleanist monarchy* (New York, 1974). For Thiers, see J. P. T. Bury and R. P. Tombs, *Thiers 1797–1877, a Political Life* (London, 1986). P. O'Brien gives an account of the often embittered debate over fortifying Paris in "L'embastillement de Paris: the fortification of Paris during the July Monarchy", *FHS*, 9(1) (1975), 63–82. Tariff reform was also the subject of much discussion; see B. M. Ratcliffe, "The tariff reform campaign in France, 1831–1836", *JEEH*, 7 (1978), 61–138.

CHAPTER 13: APRIL INSURRECTION AND SEPTEMBER LAWS

The sources cited for this chapter should be read in conjunction with those for Chapter 11, and, once again, G. Weill, *Histoire du parti républicain en France 1814–1870* should be used for general background. The revolt in

Lyons has been studied in detail by R. J. Bezucha in *The Lyon Uprising of 1834* (Cambridge, 1974) and F. Rude, *Les révoltes des canuts, novembre 1831–avril 1834* (Paris, 1982). The resultant trial is described in P. Bastide, "Les accusés d'avril 1834 devant la cour des pairs", *Politique*, no. 3 (1958), 260–70. The attack upon the King is narrated in J. Lucas-Dubreton, *Louis-Philippe et la machine infernale* (Paris, 1951), and discussed by D. Monney, "L'attentat de Fieschi", *Liaisons*, no. 249 (1980), 16–22.

CHAPTER 14: THE PRESS

The great influence of the press is a subject upon which all historians concur. I. Collins, *The Government and the Newspaper Press in France, 1814–1881* (Oxford, 1959), shows that the government of Louis-Philippe was almost as censorious with the fractious press as that of Charles X, but possibly less effective. For a shorter version of the same material, see I. Collins, "The government and the press in France during the reign of Louis-Philippe", *EHR*, 49(1954), 262–82. The government attempt to exert control is discussed in J.-P. Aguet, "Remarques sur les procès intentés à la presse périodique française sous la Monarchie de Juillet (1831–1847)", *Cahiers Vilfredo Paredo*, nos. 22–23 (1970), 63–75.

The changes brought by technological advance are described by A. J. George, "The romantic revolution and the industrial revolution in France", in J. Friguglietti and E. Kennedy (eds), *The Shaping of Modern France* (London, 1969), pp. 242–8, and J. Smith Allen discusses the attitudes of those who may or may not have benefited from such progress in "The moral universe of 19th-century Parisian readers", *Proceedings of the 10th Metting of the Western Society for French History* (1982, 1984), pp. 362–72. The impact of the serialised novel is the subject of E. R. Tannenbaum, "The beginnings of bleeding-heart liberalism: Eugène Sue's *Les Mystères de Paris* (1842–1843)", *Isis*, 23(3) (1981), 491–507.

Studies of individual journalists include M. L. Brown, *Louis Veuillot, French Ultramontane Catholic Journalist and Layman, 1813–1883* (Durham, North Carolina, 1977), J. Richardson, "Émile de Girardin 1806–1881", *History Today*, XXVI (1976), 811–17, and J. J. Hémardinquer, "Henri Fonfrède ou l'homme du Midi révolté", *AM*, 88(129) (1976), 451–64.

CHAPTER 15: FOREIGN POLICY, 1830–1835

R. Bullen's "France and Europe, 1815–48: the problems of defeat and recovery", in A. Sked (ed.), *Europe's Balance of Power* (London, 1979), pp. 122–44 helps to explain why it was virtually impossible for Louis-

Philippe to conduct a successful and popular foreign policy. On the politics of *entente*, the book to read is R. Bullen, *Palmerston, Guizot and the Collapse of the Entente Cordiale* (London, 1974), and to this can be added J. Duhamel, *Louis-Philippe et la première entente cordiale* (Paris, 1951), and S. Mellon, "Entente, diplomacy and fantasy", *Reviews in European History*, II (September 1976), 373–80. For the role of Talleyrand in this regard, see M. Schumann, *Talleyrand, Prophet of the Entente Cordiale* (Oxford, 1977); on the career of this extraordinary man, see L. Madelin, *Talleyrand* (Paris, 1979).

R. Bullen has analysed one of the more complicated issues of the period in "France and the problem of intervention in Spain, 1834–1836", *HJ*, 20(2) (1977), 363–93. On the separate questions of Poland and tariff reform, the following sources should be read in combination with those cited for Chapter 12: M. L. Brown, "The Polish question and public opinion in France, 1830–1846", *Antemurale*, 14 (1980), 77–299, L. S. Kramer, "The rights of man: Lafayette and the Polish national revolution, 1830–1834", *FHS*, 14(4) (Fall 1986), pp. 521–46, and B. M. Ratcliffe, "The politics of tariff reform in the 1830's", *Proceedings of the 6th Meeting of the Western Society for French History* (1978–1979), pp. 318–26. On Franco-Belgian relations, see H. Deschamps, *La Belgique devant la France de Juillet* (Paris, 1956).

CHAPTER 16: THE BRIEF SUPREMACY OF THIERS AND PARLIAMENTARY DISORDER, 1836–1839

For a more sympathetic view of Thiers, see J. P. T Bury and R. P. Tombs, *Thiers 1797–1877, a Political Life* (London, 1986). R. Albrecht-Carrié, *Adolphe Thiers or the Triumph of the Bourgeoisie* (Boston, 1977) gives a fairly standard interpretation of the minister and the times. On the Finance Minister Humann, see F. Ponteil, *Un type de grand bourgeois sous la Monarchie de Juillet, Georges Humann, 1780–1842* (Paris, 1977).

The question of intervention in Spain is discussed in R. Bullen, "The Great Powers and the Iberian peninsula, 1815–48", in A. Sked (ed.), *Europe's Balance of Power* (London, 1979), pp. 54–78, and J.-C. Jauffert, "M. Thiers, l'Espagne et la légion étrangère, 1835–1837", *Revue historique des Armées*, no. 3 (1979), 145–72. The use of force in settling disputes is discussed by N. N. Barker, "France and the 'pastry war' of 1838–39: the futility of gunboat diplomacy", *Proceedings of the 4th Meeting of the French Colonial History Society* (1978–1979), pp. 99–108. Relations between France and South America and Mexico have come under a good deal of recent discussion. See I. Morgan, "French ideas of a civilising mission in South America, 1830–1848", *Canadian Journal of History*, 16(3) (1981), 379–403, I. Morgan, "French policy in Spanish America, 1830–1848", *Journal of Latin American Studies*, 10(2) (1978), 309–28, N. N. Barker, "The factor of 'race' in the French experience in Mexico, 1821–1861", *The Hispanic American*

Historical Review, 59(1) (1979), 64–80, and *The French Experience in Mexico, 1821–1861: a history of constant misunderstanding* (Chapel Hill, 1979), by the same author.

On the troubled domestic front, see R. Girard *et al.*, *La Chambre des Députés en 1837–1839* (Paris, 1976), and J. Lucas-Dubreton, *L'Affaire Alibaud ou Louis-Philippe Traqué (1836)* (Paris, 1927). On two of the more inveterate revolutionaries, see A. B. Spitzer, *The Revolutionary Theories of Auguste Blanqui* (New York and Oxford, 1957), S. Bernstein, *Auguste Blanqui and the Art of Insurrection* (London, 1971), and R. Merle, *Armand Barbès, un révolutionnaire romantique* (Toulouse, 1977).

CHAPTER 17: DIPLOMATIC DISASTER, 1840

The general context for the 'disaster' can be found in C. Drault, *L'Egypte et l'Europe* (Paris, 1930), I, and R. Owen, "Egypt and Europe from French expedition to British occupation", *Studies in the Theory of Imperialism* (1972), pp. 195–209. Particular studies of the misguided role of Thiers include F. Charles-Roux, *Thiers et Mehemet-Ali* (Paris, 1951), C. Pouthas, "La politique de Thiers pendant la crise de 1840", *RH*, 182 (1938), 72–96, and L. Nettier, "Heine, Thiers et la presse parisienne en 1840", *Revue d'Allemagne*, 4(1) (1972), 113–53. Guizot does not emerge from this episode entirely untarnished either. See the relevant chapters of D. Johnson, *Guizot* (London and Toronto, 1963), and P. Rosenvallon, *Le moment Guizot* (Paris, 1985).

Relations with Germany declined precipitously. See R. Poidevin and J. Bariéty, *Les relations franco-allemandes, 1815–1975* (Paris, 1977), R. Poidevin and K. G. Faber, *Les relations franco-allemandes, 1830–1848* (Metz, 1977), and A. Owsinska, *La Politique de la France envers l'Allemagne, 1830–1848* (Warsaw, 1974).

CHAPTER 18: THE ARMY: BONAPARTISM AND ALGERIAN CONQUEST

One can start by reading the relevant chapters of P.-M. De La Gorce, *The French Army* (London, 1963), but the best sources to consult are D. Porch, *Army and Revolution, France 1815–1848* (London, 1974), and Porch's "The French army law of 1832", *HJ*, 14(4) (1971), 751–69. C. Schefer, *La Politique coloniale de la Monarchie de Juillet: l'Algérie et l'évolution de la colonisation française* (Paris, 1928), remains a valuable study, but to it should be added two recent works: P. Montagnon, *La Conquête de l'Algérie: 1830–1871* (Paris, 1986) and A. T. Sullivan, *Thomas-Robert Bugeaud: France and Algeria, 1784–1849: politics, power and the good society* (Hamden, Connecticut, 1983).

Not a great deal has been written in English on Bonapartism recently. Although H. A. L. Fisher, *Bonapartism* (Oxford, 1908) remains valuable and can be combined with A.-J. Tudesq, "The Napoleonic legend in France in 1848", in J. Friguglietti and E. Kennedy (eds), *The Shaping of Modern France* (London, 1969), pp. 255–61, the best studies are J. Lucas-Dubreton, *Le Culte de Napoleon, 1815–48* (Paris, 1960) and, especially, F. Bluche, *Le Bonapartisme* (Paris, 1980). On the return of the Emperor's ashes, one can read J. Boisson, *La retour des Cendres* (Paris, 1973), and J. Vidalenc, "L'opinion publique en Normandie et le retour des restes de Napoléon en décembre 1840", in *La France au XIXe Siècle: Mélanges offerts à Charles-Hippolyte Pouthas* (Paris, 1973). For the initial failures of the man who ultimately would profit by all of this, see A. Cobban, "Louis Napoleon Bonaparte in 1838", *EHR*, 83(328) (1968), 537–41, and A. Dansette, "Les premières conspirations de Napoléon III, 1830–1833", *La Revue de Paris*, année 66, no. 11 (1959), 57–70.

CHAPTER 19: HISTORY AND PHILOSOPHY

The three following studies can be used as an introduction to the subjects discussed in this chapter: E. Coornaert, *Destins de Clio en France depuis 1800* (Paris, 1977), F. Engel-Jánosi, *Four Studies in French Romantic Historical Writing* (Baltimore, 1955), and C. Rearick, *Beyond the Enlightenment: historians and folklore in nineteenth-century France* (Bloomington and London, 1974). K. Offen, "The beginnings of 'scientific' women's history in France, 1830–48", *Proceedings of the XIth Meeting of the Western Society for French History* (1983, 1984), pp. 255–64, and D. R. Kelley, *Historians and the Law in Postrevolutionary France* (Princeton, New Jersey, 1984), can also be consulted for more particular considerations.

The writings of Guizot and Thiers are analysed by their respective biographers in D. Johnson, *Guizot* (London and Toronto, 1963), and J. P. T. Bury and R. P. Tombs, *Thiers 1797–1877, a Political Life* (London, 1986). Michelet has always evoked a strong response from his readers. Two recent works are fairly sympathetic; see L. Orr, *Jules Michelet: nature, history and language* (Ithaca, New York, and London, 1976), and E. K. Kaplan, *Michelet's Poetic Vision. A romantic philosophy of nature, man and woman* (Amherst, 1985), but note also the authors' bibliographies. Quinet has attracted much less attention, but see R. H. Powers, *Edgar Quinet: a study in French patriotism* (Dallas, 1957). Tocqueville was the great French thinker of the age. J. P. Mayer, *Prophet of the Mass Age: a study of Alexis de Tocqueville* (London, 1939), is the standard account, but one should also read D. S. Goldstein, *Trial of Faith: religion and politics in Tocqueville's thought* (New York, 1975). The biography to read is A. Jardin, *Alexis De Tocqueville 1805–1859* (Paris, 1984).

CHAPTER 20: ART IN ORLEANIST SOCIETY

To gain an impression of what a remarkable period this was, one need only glance at (but one should read!) D. G. Charleton (ed.), *The French Romantics*, I and II (Cambridge, 1985), and one can combine this with P. E. Chauvet, *A Literary History of France* (London, 1967), IV, by way of introduction. F. W. Jennings, *Culture and Society in France 1789–1848* (Leicester, 1987), gives the broad context. D. Owen Evans, *Social Romanticism in France 1830–48* (Oxford, 1951) remains thought-provoking, as does A. J. George, *The Development of French Romanticism* (Syracuse, New York, 1955). J. Smith Allen's discussion of the changes brought by technological advance in *Popular French Romanticism: authors, readers and books in the 19th century* (Syracuse, New York, 1981) is basic for the cultural historian; for a shorter version, one can turn to the same author's "Towards a social history of French romanticism, authors, readers and book trade in Paris, 1820–1840", *Journal of Social History*, 13(2) (1979), 253–76. E. N. Schamber, *The Relation between the Art and the Politics of the French Romantics* (Washington, 1984) helps to explain why artists played such a dramatic role during this period.

There is a vast array of studies of individual artists; one can only hope to point to a limited number of works which will serve to get the reader started. M. Crouzet, *Nature et société chez Stendhal: La Révolte romantique* (Lille, 1985) is the most recent study of a brilliant and ascerbic social critic. Three recent articles focus upon individual artists and their politics: K. G. McWatters, "Stendhal, the novelist and politics", *Essays in French Literature*, no. 6 (1969), 57–73, H. Redman, "Chateaubriand and French politics of the 1830's and 1840's", *Chateaubriand Congrès* (Wisconsin, 1968, 1970), pp. 193–200, and S. Raphael, "Balzac and social history", *ESR*, 1(1) (1971), 23–33. In the field of music, the work to turn to remains J. Barzun's comprehensive *Berlioz and the Romantic Century* (New York and London, 1969), 2 vols, and, for a more specific study, one can read R. P. Locke, *Music, Musicians and the Saint-Simonians* (Chicago, 1985). R. Middleton (ed.), *The Beaux Arts and Nineteenth-Century French Architecture* (Cambridge, Massachusetts, 1982), offers an introduction to that field of study. Both Ingres and Delacroix are discussed in N. Bryson, *Tradition and Desire; from David to Delacroix* (Cambridge, 1984). On the master of the cruel art of caricature see R. Passeron, *Daumier* (Oxford 1981).

CHAPTER 21: THE SUPREMACY OF GUIZOT

D. H. Pinkney, in *Decisive Years in France 1840–47* (Princeton, New Jersey, 1986), has depicted the immense economic, technological, social and demographic changes that France was undergoing during this period. But from the political standpoint, these were also years of stultification and lost opportunities. R. L. Koepke discusses the failure of the government to bring about reform in "The failure of parliamentary government in France, 1840–1848", *ESR*, 9 (1979), 433–55. The government did not fare much better on the diplomatic front, and this seriously undermined the Crown; see R. Bullen, *Palmerston, Guizot and the Collapse of the Entente Cordiale* (London, 1974).

On the man who would be Prime Minister, see D. Johnson, *Guizot* (London and Toronto, 1963), P. Rosenvallon, *Le moment Guizot* (Paris, 1985), and the series of articles in *Actes Colloques François Guizot* (Paris, 1974) published by the *Bulletin de la Société de l'histoire du Protestantisme français*. For an analysis that throws a fairly favourable light upon Guizot, see A. Roubaud, "Les élections de 1842 et 1846 sous le ministère Guizot", *RHM*, XIV (1939), 261–87. On the acrimonious debate over fortification, see P. O'Brien, "L'embastillement de Paris: the fortification of Paris during the July Monarchy", *FHS*, 9(1) (1975), 63–82.

CHAPTER 22: RELIGION AND EDUCATION

There are numerous works to which one can turn for the general background. Two standard account are C. S. Phillips, *The Church in France, 1789–1848: a study in revival* (Oxford, 1929) and A. Dansette, *Religious History of Modern France* (London, 1961), I, and to these should be added B. M. G. Reardon, *Religion in the Age of Romanticism: studies in early nineteenth-century thought* (Cambridge, 1985). Two studies by P. Droulers, "La nonciature de Paris et les troubles sociaux-politiques sous la Monarchie de Juillet", in *Saggi storico intorno di Papato* (Rome, 1959), pp. 401–63, and *Action pastorale et problèmes sociaux sous la Monarchie de Juillet chez Mgr. d'Astros, Archévêque de Toulouse, censeur de Lammenais* (Paris, 1954), are also useful. J. N. Moody's "French liberal Catholics, 1840–1875", in E. Acomb and M. L. Brown (eds), *French Society and Culture since the Old Regime* (New York, 1966), is brief but helpful, and his "French anticlericalism: image and reality", *The Catholic Historical Review*, 56(4) (1971), 630–48, is a valuable discussion of a difficult subject. E. Berenson's *Populist Religion and Left-Wing Politics in France, 1830–1852* (Princeton, New Jersey, 1984), shows how the Church was coming under competition from republicans, socialists and democrats. Charity was a vital concern for both the Church and the state; see D. Higgs, "Politics and charity in Toulouse, 1750–1850", in J. F. Bosher (ed.), *French Government and Society 1500–1850* (London, 1973), pp. 191–207, and R. Price, "Poor relief and social crisis in mid-nineteenth-century France", *ESR*, 13(4) (1983), 423–54. For studies of leading individuals, see H. D. Noble, *Lacordaire* (Paris, 1935), W. Gurian, "Montalembert, leader du 'parti catholique'", *Politique*, nos 49–52 (1970), pp. 117–46, and M. L. Brown, *Louis Veuillot, French Ultramontane Catholic Journalist and Layman, 1813–1883* (Durham, North Carolina, 1977).

The subject of education is undergoing much discussion at present; see the collection of articles in D. N. Baker and P. Harrigan (eds), *The Making of*

Frenchmen: current directions in higher education in France, 1679–1979 (Waterloo, Ontario, 1980), and R. Gildea, *Education in provincial France, 1800–1914: a study of three departments* (Oxford, 1983). Schools, teachers and students are the subjects of R. Grew, P. Harrigan and J. Whitney, "The availability of schooling in nineteenth-century France", *JIH*, xiv(1) (Summer 1983), 25–63 and P. V. Meyers, "Professionalisation and social change: rural teachers in nineteenth-century France", *JSH*, 9(1976), 542–8. C. R. Day tackles the question of social mobility in "The making of mechanical engineers in France: the *ecoles d'arts et métiers*", *FHS*, 10 (1978), 439–60.

CHAPTER 23: FOREIGN POLICY, 1841–1848

For a general analysis, see D. Johnson, "The foreign policy of Guizot, 1840–1848", *University of Birmingham Historical Journal*, 6(1) (1958), 62–87. On the decline of *entente*, see D. McLean, "The Greek Revolution and the Anglo-France entente, 1843–4", *EHR*, 96(378) (1981), 117–29, and two articles by R. Bullen: "Guizot and the 'Sonderbund' crisis, 1846–48", *EHR*, 86(346) (1971), 497–526, and "Anglo-French rivalry and Spanish politics, 1846–1848", *EHR*, 89(350) (1974), 25–47. On an ultimately pyrrhic victory, see E. J. Parry, *The Spanish Marriages, 1841–1846* (London, 1936). The slave trade was also an important issue during this period; see two articles by L. C. Jennings, "French views on slavery and abolitionism in the U.S., 1830–48", *Slavery and Abolition*, 4(1) (1983), 19–40, and "France, Great Britain and the repression of the slave trade, 1841–1845," *FHS*, 10(1) (1977), 101–25.

CHAPTER 24: THE STRUCTURE OF SOCIETY

The standard general survey is F. Braudel and E. Labrousse (eds), *Histoire économique et sociale de la France* (Paris, 1976), III, and this can be combined with C. Pouthas, *La Population française pendant la première moitié du XIXe siècle* (Paris, 1956). Three recent local studies can be recommended: W. H. Sewell, *Structure and Mobility: The men and women of Marseille, 1820–1870* (Cambridge, 1984), P. M. Jones, *Politics and Rural Society: the southern Massif Central c. 1750–1880* (Cambridge, 1985) and G. L. Gullickson, *Spinners and Weavers of Auffray* (Cambridge, 1986).

For an introduction to the study of rural life, one can turn to M. Agulhon, G. Desert and R. Specklin, *Histoire de la France rurale* (Paris, 1976), III. R. Price discusses the massive effects of the development of communications networks on rural life in *The Modernization of Rural France* (London, 1983). There are numerous works on agricultural development; one can start with H. D. Clout, *Agriculture in France on the Eve of the Railway Age* (London,

1980). Similar ground is covered by W. H. Newell in "The agricultural revolution in nineteenth-century France", *JEH*, XXXIII (December 1973), 697–732, and *Population Change and Agricultural Development in XIXth Century France* (New York, 1977). Changes in the peasant community are outlined by E. Labrousse in "The evolution of peasant society in France from the eighteenth-century to the present", in E. M. Acomb and M. L. Brown (eds), *French Society and Culture since the Old Regime* (New York, 1966), pp. 44–64. G. W. Grantham discusses farm economics in "Scale and organisation in French farming, 1840–1880", in W. N. Parker and E. L. Jones (eds), *European Peasants and their Markets* (Princeton, New Jersey, 1975).

Works on the various social classes are legion; it is hoped that the following will at least point the reader in the right direction. D. Higgs, *Nobles in Nineteenth-Century France* (Baltimore, 1987), discusses the long-term recovery of the nobility from the ravages of the Revolution. For a specific discussion of this class under the July Monarchy, see T. D. Beck, "Occupation, taxes and a distinct nobility under Louis-Philippe", *ESR*, 13(4) (1983), pp. 403–22. The nobility was also a part of a broad élite known as the *notables*; the book to read is A.-J. Tudesq, *Les Grands Notables en France* (Paris, 1964), 2 vols. B. Singer, *Village Notable in Nineteenth-Century France: priests, mayors, schoolmasters* (Albany, New York, 1983), discusses a much less elevated but important group. On the topics of wealth and the bourgeoisie, one can read A. Daumard, "Wealth and affluence in France since the beginning of the 19th century", in W. D. Rubinstein (ed.), *Wealth and the Wealthy in the Modern World* (London, 1980), and the same author's *La Bourgeoisie parisienne de 1815 à 1848* (Paris, 1963). P. N. Stearns, *Paths to Authority: the middle class and the industrial labor force in France, 1820–48* (Urbana, Illinois, 1978) is laudable for its objectivity. On bourgeois society, one should also read M. Agulhon, *Le cercle dans la France bourgeoise 1810–1848* (Paris 1977).

L. Chevalier's *Labouring Classes and Dangerous Classes in Paris during the First Half of the 19th Century* (New York, 1973), remains perhaps the most influential work on its topic, but it should be read in combination with G. Rudé, "The growth of cities and popular revolt, 1750–1850, with particular reference to Paris", in J. F. Bosher (ed.), *French Government and Society 1500–1850* (London, 1973), pp. 166–90. On the subject of crime, one can also read J. M. Donovan, "The uprooting theory of crime and the Corsicans of Marseille, 1825–1880", *FHS*, 13(4) (1984), 500–28, and L. Berlanstein, "Vagrants, beggars and thieves: delinquent boys in mid-nineteenth-century Paris", *JSH*, 12(4) (1979), 531–52. On the response to crime, see G. Wright, *Between the Guillotine and Liberty: two centuries of the crime problem in France* (New York and Oxford, 1983), J. M. Donovan, "Justice unblind: the juries and the criminal classes in France, 1825–1914", *JSH*, 15(1) (1981), pp. 89–107, and T. J. Duesterberg, "The politics of criminal justice reform: 19th century France", in J. A. Inciardi and C. E. Faupel (eds), *History and Crime: implications for criminal justice policy* (Beverly Hills and London, 1980), pp. 135–52.

On the professions and social mobility, see G. Weisz, "The politics of medical professionalisation in France 1845–1848", *JSH*, 12 (1978), 3–30, and G. L. Geison (ed.), *Professions and the French State, 1700–1900* (Philadelphia, 1984). The role of women has attracted the attention of several authors: see H. D. Lewis, "The legal status of women in nineteenth-century France", *Journal of European Studies*, 10(39) (1980), 178–88, C. G. Moses, *French Feminism in the XIXth Century* (New York, 1984), and D. Zimmerman, "George Sand and the feminists of the 1830's and 1840's in France", *Friends of George Sand*, 4(2) (1981), pp. 20–4. The subject of cultural revolt is discussed in C. Grana, *Bohemian versus Bourgeois* (New York and London, 1964).

CHAPTER 25: INDUSTRIALISATION AND THE ECONOMY

The basic text is F. Braudel and E. Labrousse (eds), *Histoire économique et sociale de la France* (Paris, 1976). A. L. Dunham, *The Industrial Revolution in France* (New York, 1955), remains a valuable book, but it has in certain regards been superseded by R. Price, *An Economic History of Modern France 1730–1914* (London, 1981).

Economic historians have made an industry out of comparing French economic growth with that of other countries. Whilst such comparisons can be very valuable, they also can be confusing and misleading. One is advised, therefore, to begin by considering the words of warning in F. Crouzet, "French economic growth in the 19th century reconsidered", *History*, 59 (1974), 167–79. One can then proceed to work one's way through the following: R. Cameron, *France and the Economic Development of Europe, 1800–1914* (Princeton, New Jersey, 1961), J. Marczewski, "The take-off hypothesis and the French experience", in W. W. Rostow (ed.), *The Economics of Take-Off into Sustained Growth* (London, 1964), pp. 119–33, M. Lévy-Leboyer, "Le processus d'industrialisation: le cas d'Angleterre et de la France", *RH*, 239 (1968), 281–98, R. Roehl, "French industrialisation: a reconsideration", *Explorations in Economic History*, 13 (1976), 233–81, and P. O'Brien and C. Keyder, *Economic Growth in Britian and France 1780–1914* (London, 1978).

Although certain details on banking in France can be gleaned from B. Gille, *Banking and Industrialisation in Europe, 1730–1914* (London, 1970), the book to read on this subject is the same author's *La Banque en France au XIXe Siècle* (Geneva, 1970). On those with the money to invest, see E. C. Carter *et al.*, *Enterprise and Entrepreneurs in Nineteenth- and Twentieth-Century France* (Baltimore, 1976), L. Bergeron, *Les Capitalistes en France, 1780–1914* (Paris, 1978), and A. Muhlstein, *Baron James: the rise of the French Rothschilds* (London, 1983).

Dramatic changes in textile production affected all of France; see W. M. Reddy, *The Rise of Market Culture: the textile trade and French culture,*

1750–1900 (New York, 1984). The conditions of labour and the effects of rapid change upon the working classes are discussed in J. Wallach Scott, "Men and women in the Parisian garment trades: discussions of family and work in the 1830's and 1840's", in P. Thane, G. Crossick and R. Floud (eds), *The Power of the Past: essays for Eric Hobsbawm* (Cambridge, 1984), pp. 67–94, C. H. Johnson, "Economic change and artisan discontent: the tailor's history, 1800–1848", in R. Price (ed.), *Revolution and Reaction* (London and New York, 1975), pp. 87–115, and F. Furet and J. Ozouf, "Literacy and industrialisation: the case of the department du Nord in France", *JEEH*, 5(1) (1976), 5–44. One of the most distressing aspects of the industrial revolution is discussed in the following: "The problem of child labor reform and the working-class family in France during the July Monarchy", *Proceedings of the 5th Meeting of the Western Society for French History* (1977, 1978), pp. 228–36, and C. Heywood, "The market for child labour in 19th-century France", *History*, 66(216) (1981), 34–49.

Strikes were one of the results of increased worker organisation; see E. L. Shorter and C. Tilly, *Strikes in France, 1830–1968* (Cambridge, 1974), P. N. Stearns, "Patterns of industrial strike activity in France during the July Monarchy", *AHR*, LXX (October 1964), 371–94, and J.-P. Aguet, *Les Grèves sous la Monarchie de Juillet (1830–1847)* (Geneva, 1954). Strikes were part of the modernisation of forms of protest; see C. Tilly, "Charivaris, repertoires and urban politics", in J. M. Merriman (ed.), *French Cities in the Nineteenth Century* (London, 1982), pp. 73–91.

CHAPTER 26: REPUBLICS AND UTOPIAS

Historians interested in the subjects of the origins of the labour movement and working-class organisation have found their investigations complicated by the fact that artisans almost inevitably were at the forefront of political agitation and industrial action; thus, it is more appropriate to speak of political consciousness than class-consciousness in this period. The end result has been some very sophisticated analyses which are well worth considering.

M. D. Sibalis, "The evolution of the Parisian labor movement, 1789–1834", *Proceedings of the 10th Meeting of the Western Society for French History* (1982, 1984), pp. 345–54, can be used by way of introduction to the period of the July Monarchy, but the standard reference is E. Dolléans, *Histoire du mouvement ouvrier* (Paris, 1947), I. J.-P. Bayard, *Le compagnonnage en France* (Paris, 1977), discusses a highly traditional form of artisanal organisation. W. H. Sewell, *Work and Revolution in France: the language of labor from the Old Regime to 1848* (Cambridge, 1980), discusses the long-term effects of the institution of *compagnonnage* and suggests that it seriously hindered the development of class-consciousness. B. H. Moss, in "The Parisian producers associations (1830–1851)", in R. Price (ed.), *Revolution and Reaction* (London and New York, 1975), pp. 73–83, and *The Origins of the French Labor Movement 1830–1914* (Berkeley, California, 1976) discusses some of the characteristics of the French experience which help to explain why worker organisations in France never quite fit into the Marxist model. E. Berenson's *Populist Religion and Left-Wing Politics in France, 1830–1852* (Princeton, New Jersey, 1984) also illustrates the highly individual nature of the French experience. Two articles by E. L. Newman, "The new world of the French socialist worker poets", *Stanford French Review*, 3(3) (1979), 357–68, and "Sounds in the desert: the socialist worker-poets of the bourgeois monarchy, 1836–1848", *Proceedings of the 3rd Meeting of the Western Society for French History* (1976), pp. 269–99, can usefully be read in conjunction with Berenson's monograph. On the working-class community, one should also read M. Agulhon, "Working-class and sociability in France before 1848", in P. Thane, G. Crossick and R. Floud (eds), *The Power of the Past: essays in honour of Eric Hobsbawm* (Cambridge, 1984), pp. 37–66.

Lyons, because of the precocity of the *canuts* in organising to fight for their own interests, has been the focus of many studies. See the following three articles by M. L. McDougall, "Consciousness and community: the workers of Lyon, 1830–1850, *JSH*, 12(1) (1978), 129–46, "Experiments in organisation, workers society in Lyon 1835–1848", *Proceedings of the 8th Meeting of the Western Society for French History* (1981), pp. 346–55, and "Popular culture, political culture: the case of Lyon, 1830–1850", *Historical Reflections*, 8(2) (1981), 27–41. Women often played a vital part; see L. S. Strumhingher, *Women and the Making of the Working Class: Lyon, 1830–1870* (St Alans, 1979).

There is a plethora of works on individual Utopian socialists, radicals and republicans, The strange mixture of insight and eccentricity that was Fourier can be followed in J. Beecher and R. Bienvenu (eds), *The Utopian Vision of Charles Fourier: selected texts in work, love and passionate attraction* (Columbia, Missouri, 1983), N. V. Riasanovsky, *The Teaching of Charles Fourier* (Los Angeles, 1969), and M. C. Spencer, *Charles Fourier* (Boston, 1981). Cabet was probably the best organiser of the lot, but he was also authoritarian and given to flights of fantasy; see C. H. Johnson, *Utopian Communism in France: Cabet and the Icarians, 1839–1851* (Ithaca, New York, 1974). Raspail dedicated his life to helping the poor and furthering the cause of republicanism; see D. B. Weiner, *Raspail: scientist and reformer* (New York, 1968), and L. Veluz, *Raspail: un contestaire au XIXe siècle* (Périgueux, 1974). Buchez and Leroux both played important roles in broadening the appeal of socialism and republicanism. On Buchez see M. Reardon, "The reconciliation of christianity with progress: Philippe Buchez", *The Review of Politics*, 33(4) (1971), 512–37, and B. A. Cook, "The Christian socialism of Philippe Buchez", *1st Meeting of the Western Society for French History* (1974), pp. 214–24. On Leroux see J. Bakunin, *Pierre Leroux and the Birth of Democratic Socialism, 1797–1848* (New York, 1976), and the same author's "Pierre Leroux on democracy, socialism and the Enlightenment", *Journal of the History of Ideas*, 37(3) (1976), 455–74, and "Pierre Leroux, a democratic religion for a new world", *Church History*,

44(1) (1975), 57–72. P.-J. Proudhon's writing was to have significant subsequent effect upon syndicalism, see R. L. Hoffman, *Revolutionary Justice: the social and political theory of P. J. Proudhon* (Urbana, Illinois, 1972); Louis Blanc had more immediate impact, see L. A. Loubère, *Louis Blanc* (Evanston, Illinois, 1961). The troubled life and writing of Flora Tristan are discussed by S. Joan Moon, "Feminism and socialism: the utopian synthesis of Flora Tristan", in M. Boxer and J. Quataert (eds), *Socialist Women* (New York, 1978), pp. 19–50.

CHAPTER 27: BANQUETS, SCANDALS AND REVOLUTION

With the notable exception of D. H. Pinkney, *Decisive Years in France 1840–47* (Princeton, New Jersey, 1986), historians have tended to focus upon the causes of subsequent revolution when analysing this period. Such analyses generally have not shown the leading politicians in a favourable light; see three articles by R. L. Koepke: "The failure of parliamentary government in France, 1840–1848", *ESR*, 9 (1979), 433–55, "The short, unhappy history of progressive conservativism in France, 1846–1848", *Canadian Journal of History*, 18(2) (1983), 187–216, and "Charles Tanneguy Duchâtel and the Revolution of 1848", *FHS*, 7(2) (Fall 1973), 236–54. Nevertheless, the government made itself unpopular at least as much by what it failed to do as what it did; see A. Roubaud, "Les élections de 1842 et 1846 sous le ministère Guizot", *RHM*, XIV (1939), 261–87, and P. Higgonnet and T. Higgonnet, "Class, corruption and politics in the French Chamber of Deputies, 1846–1848", *FHS*, 5(2) (Fall 1967), 204–24. Despite the grim economic background discussed in E. Labrousse (ed.), *Aspects de la crise et de la dépression de l'économie française au milieu du 19ᵉ siècle* (Paris, 1956), the revolution was brought about by a relatively minor matter; see J. L. Baughman, "The French banquet campaign of 1847–48", *JMH*, 31 (March 1959), 1–15. On the actions of Louis-Philippe during the crisis, see J.-F. Lemaire, "Le roi dans les trois journées de février 1848", *La Revue des Deux Mondes*, no. 3 (1969), 551–68. On the role of one of the main actors, see W. Fortescue, *Alphonse de Lamartine: a political biography* (New York, 1983).

The broad context of the Revolution can be gleaned from L. C. Jennings, *France and Europe in 1848* (Oxford, 1973), M. Traugott, "The mid-19th-century crisis in France and England", *Theory and Society*, 12(4) (1983), 455–68, and W. L. Langer, "The pattern of urban revolution in 1848", in E. M. Acomb and M. L. Brown (eds), *French Society and Culture since the Old Regime* (New York, 1966), pp. 90–118. P. Amann's "The changing outlines of 1848", in J. Friguglietti and E. Kennedy (eds), *The Making of Modern France* (London, 1969), pp. 248–55, offers a useful introduction to the subject of writing on the Revolution. One can then proceed to G. Duveau, *The Making of a Revolution* (New York, 1967) and R. Price (ed.), *Revolution and Reaction* (London and New York, 1975). R. Price has translated many important documents in *1848 in France* (London, 1975). For two more particular studies, see J. G. Gallaher, *The Students of Paris and the Revolution of 1848* (Carbondale, Illinois, 1980) and D. Fiesta-McCormick, "Literary impact upon a revolution: Paris 1848", *The American Society Legion of Honor Magazine*, 49(3) (1978), 167–76.

A Short Cast of the Principal Characters

Due to the broad nature of his work, the author has discussed a large number of individuals and the reader previously unfamiliar with the July Monarchy may at times find himself somewhat bewildered. It is hoped that the following brief descriptions of leading political personages and commentators will prove of assistance should the reader become confused about the role of any one individual. For descriptions of the members of the royal family, the reader should turn to Chapter 8.

Affre, Denis-Auguste, Archbishop of Paris (1793–1848)
Made archbishop in 1840, Affre's initial friendly relations with Louis-Philippe soon deteriorated as he repeatedly criticised the government over a series of issues, particularly in the areas of education and the role of the universities. He saw the July Monarchy fall without regret, but was killed whilst on a mission of peace during the June Days of 1848.

Arago, Dominique-François (1786–1853)
An eminent scientist, he was elected to the Chamber of Deputies in 1830 and thereafter sat on the far left. President of a republican teaching society, he also involved himself in economic matters, especially transport. He favoured electoral reform and consistently opposed government measures, but did not support violent revolution.

Balzac, Honoré de (1799–1850)
Journalist, trenchant social critic and a great novelist, Balzac was Catholic and legitimist in political orientation.

Barante, Amable-Prosper-Guillaume, Baron de (1782–1866)
Historian and biographer, Barante was a leading liberal peer during the Restoration and, although he played no part in the Revolution of 1830, went on to become French ambassador in Turin (1830–35) and St Petersburg (1835–1842) under Louis-Philippe and supported constitutional monarchy.

Barbès, Armand (1809–1870)
Republican and revolutionary, Barbès played an active role in the Société des Droits de l'Homme. Friend of Auguste Blanqui, he also helped organise the Société des Familles and was subsequently imprisoned for his part in the insurrection of May 1839. He was not released until after the Revolution of 1848, and then returned to his old ways.

Barrot, Camille-Hyacinthe-Odilon (1791–1873)
Lawyer, prefect of the Seine (1830–31) until the sacking of Saint-Germain-l'Auxerrois and deputy in the Chamber, Barrot was leader of the *gauche dynastique*. He generally sided with the opposition, except during the Thiers ministries, became a determined opponent of Guizot and played a leading role in the banquet campaign that triggered the Revolution of 1848.

Berryer, Pierre-Antoine (1790–1868)
Author, lawyer and member of the Chamber of Deputies, he was an eloquent spokesman for the legitimists. In 1832 he counselled against the attempt to raise royalist revolt in the Vendée, but subsequently defended legitimists and the Catholic Church in numerous court cases.

Bertin, Louis-François (1766–1841)
Journalist, under whose direction the *Journal des débats* grew rapidly. He was tried for offences against the King in 1829, but was acquitted.

Blanc, Jean-Joseph-Louis (1811–1882)
Socialist, author and journalist, Blanc opposed the Orleanist Monarchy, supported the banquet compaign of 1847–48 and emerged as a major actor in the Second Republic.

Blanqui, Adolphe (1798–1854)
Economist and professor, he was a member of the Académie des Sciences Morales et Politiques. In 1840 he carried out an inquiry into the condition of the working classes which subsequently became the basis of his *Des classes ouvrières en France*. He became a deputy in 1846 and, unlike his brother Auguste, supported the government of Louis-Philippe.

Blanqui, Louis-Auguste (1805–1881)
Arch-conspirator and determined republican, he perhaps was the most famous of contemporary professional revolutionaries. Active within a series of republican secret societies, he took part in the insurrection of 1839, for which he was imprisoned. His publications and his trials made him the focus of much attention and gained him a certain devoted following.

Broglie, Achille-Léon-Victor, Duc de (1785–1870)
A leading doctrinaire and liberal, Broglie constantly opposed the ministries of Charles X as a peer and member of the Aide-toi, le Ciel t'aidera society.

He entered the first July Monarchy Cabinet as Minister of Public Instruction and thereafter was a leading political figure with conservative tendencies. He became president of the Conseil d'État in March 1835. The September laws were passed under his presidency, but his government fell over the question of a conversion of *rentes*. Thereafter he remained outside of the various Orleanist Cabinets, although he did carry out several government commissions.

Buchez, Philippe-Joseph-Benjamin (1796–1865)
Historian, journalist and democrat, during the Second Restoration he was involved with both the *carbonari* and the Saint-Simonians. Buchez helped to found the Amis du Peuple society, but after it suppression, focused his attention upon developing a doctrine which reconciled democracy with Catholicism and his writings proved highly influential.

Bugeaud, Thomas-Robert, Marshal of France (1784–1849)
Known as a strict disciplinarian within the army, his part in the imprisonment of the Duchesse de Berry at Blaye (1832) and suppression of revolt in Paris (1834) made him extremely unpopular with both legitimists and radicals. He played an important part in the French colonisation of Algeria. Bugeaud was placed in command of the troops in Paris in 1848, but was prevented from acting decisively by Louis-Philippe.

Cabet, Étienne (1788–1857)
Journalist, historian and Utopian socialist, Cabet was a member of the *carbonari* and liberal opposition during the Restoration and became a republican shortly after the Revolution of 1830. Actively engaged in educating the masses, he was an excellent organiser and, although authoritarian, enjoyed a good deal more support amongst the lower classes than most socialist writers. In 1847 he began the first of several attempts to found an ideal community, based on his *Voyage en Icarie*, in North America.

Carnot, Lazare-Hippolyte (1801–1888)
Republican journalist and deputy in the Chamber (1839–48), he sat on the extreme left and constantly opposed government policies. Carnot played an active part in the banquet campaign and published several pamphlets supporting *rapprochement* between republicans and the constitutional left.

Carrel, Armand (1800–1836)
Journalist, historian and co-founder of the *National*, Carrel contributed to the Revolution of 1830, but rapidly grew disenchanted with the government of Louis-Philippe and passed over to the republicans. Repeatedly brought to trial by the government for his writings, Carrel's tempestuous career came to an untimely end due to a duel with Émile de Girardin.

Cavaignac, Godefroy-Élénore-Louis (1801–1843)
Dissatisfied by the results of the Revolution of 1830, he emerged as one of

the leading republicans under the July Monarchy. Frequently brought to trial for his organising activities in such societies as the Amis du Peuple, he usually was acquitted. Cavaignac became a contributor to *La Réforme* and was elected president of the Société des Droits de l'Homme. He was extremely popular with the left at the time of his death and his funeral became the scene of a large political manifestation.

Chateaubriand, François-René, Vicomte de (1768–1848)
One of the great writers of the era and a peer, Chateaubriand was a devout Catholic and royalist; nevertheless, he clashed repeatedly with the *ultra* ministries of Charles X, particularly over the issue of press censorship. After the Revolution of 1830 he remained legitimist and was arrested at the time of the attempted revolt in the Vendée. He was acquitted, but he ceased to be a leading political figure.

Clauzel, Bertrand, Marshal of France (1772–1842)
Forced into exile in 1815 because he had supported Napoleon during the Hundred Days, an amnesty allowed his return in 1820; he became a member of the liberal opposition in the Chamber of Deputies in 1829. Clauzel commanded the army of Africa (1830–31) and served as Governor-General of Algeria (1835–36), but returned after waging a disastrous campaign which brought him much criticism. He served in the Chamber of Deputies until 1842, consistently voting with the liberals.

Considérant, Prosper-Victor (1808–1893)
Utopian socialist author and journalist, he became the leading follower of Fourier and upon several occasions unsuccessfully attempted to form his own version of the *phalanges*. Suspicious of industrial centralisation, Considérant criticised government railway ventures, but remained sympathetic to the monarchy until February 1848.

Cousin, Victor (1792–1867)
Philosopher, academic and member of the Académie Française, he made popular the philosophy of eclecticism. Throughout the July Monarchy he was influential in the administration of the Université and he served briefly as Minister of Public Instruction in the second Thiers ministry (1840).

Duchâtel, Charles-Marie-Tanneguy (1803–1867)
A liberal under the Bourbon Monarchy, he entered the Conseil d'État in November 1831 and subsequently held several ministries, most notably Finance under Molé and the Interior under Guizot. Renowned for his ability to organise government electoral victories, he had to take flight after the Revolution of 1848.

Dupin, André-Marie-Jean-Jacques (1783–1865)
A lawyer, he entered Parliament in 1828 and became a member of the liberal

opposition. He helped convince Louis-Philippe to become king and remained an Orleanist until 1848, pleading the case of the Comte de Paris after the King's abdication. Dupin was president of the Chamber of Deputies (1832–40), but refused repeated invitations to join government Cabinets.

Dupin, François-Pierre-Charles (1784–1873)
Liberal, author and parliamentarian, he vigorously opposed the government of Polignac during the Restoration and became a member of the Conseil d'État under Louis-Philippe. Particularly active in government commissions regarding finance and the marine, he became a peer in 1837, slowly becoming more conservative as time passed.

Duvergier de Hauranne, Prosper-Léon (1798–1881)
Journalist, author and deputy in the Chamber, he firmly supported Périer against republican insurrection. After the death of Périer (1832) however, he steadily drifted leftwards, occasionally siding with Thiers and often opposing Guizot. Though not a republican, Duvergier helped organise the banquet campaign that led to the fall of the July Monarchy.

Falloux de Coudray, Alfred-Frédéric-Pierre, Comte de (1811–1886)
Historian and author, he was a legitimist and Catholic apologist. Under the influence of Lacordaire and Montalembert, Falloux became a liberal Catholic and championed freedom of education. He entered Parliament in 1846 and sat with the legitimists; in 1848 he welcomed revolution, hoping that a broadened franchise would lead to a return of the Bourbon Monarchy.

Fourier, François-Marie-Charles (1772–1837)
Utopian socialist, journalist and author, his idea of the *phalange* brought him a following of disciples, but failed to attract the necessary patron who might have funded the agricultural colonies. Fourier's imagination was exceedingly wide-ranging and some of his ideas were bizarre, but they did have influence upon other social critics and theorists.

Garnier-Pagès, Étienne (1801–1841)
A leading republican, Garnier-Pagès fought in the streets of Paris during the Revolution of 1830. Quickly disenchanted by the government of Louis-Philippe, he reorganised the Aide-toi, le Ciel t'aidera society along anti-dynastic lines and became a member of the Amis du Peuple society. He entered the Chamber in 1831 and became a leading spokesman of the radical left. He demanded electoral reform and consistently opposed the government until his untimely death deprived the republicans of an important leader.

Garnier-Pagès, Louis-Antoine (1803–1878)
Republican and democrat like his brother Étienne, he also fought in the Revolution of 1830. Shortly after the death of his brother, he entered the Chamber of Deputies as a member of the opposition and worked to bring

about accord between republicans and the *gauche dynastique*. He spoke at several reform banquets, but distanced himself from the extreme positions of radicals such as Ledru-Rollin and Louis Blanc.

Girardin, Émile de (1806–1881)
Writer, journalist and founder of *La Presse*, Girardin entered Parliament in 1837. He and his influential newspaper supported the Molé ministry, but bitterly opposed Guizot. Perhaps his greatest influence was as an innovator in the newspaper trade.

Guizot, François-Pierre-Guillaume (1787–1874)
Professor, historian, journalist, government *fonctionnaire* and deputy in the Chamber at different points of the Restoration, Guizot played a vital role in organising opposition to Charles X as a doctrinaire and member of the Aide-toi, le Ciel t'aidera society. Despite his part in bringing about the fall of the Bourbons, Guizot deeply feared violent revolution and saw the July Monarchy as the culminating achievement of the Revolution. He served in various capacities in the ministries of the first decade of the July Monarchy; perhaps his greatest contribution was the education law of 1833. Despite his part in engineering the fall of the Molé ministry, Guizot gradually gained the favour of Louis-Philippe and dominated French government from 1840 to 1848. Although his success in maintaining parliamentary majorities gave France the appearance of stability, his opposition to electoral reform and unpopularity contributed significantly to the Revolution of 1848.

Hugo, Victor (1802–1885)
Novelist, poet, playwright and leader of the "romantic revolt", Hugo in his early years was a supporter of Bourbon government, but his political position moved steadily leftwards. Although he rallied to the government of Louis-Philippe shortly after the Revolution of 1830 and became a peer in 1845, Hugo's writing did much to encourage the spread of Bonapartism.

Humann, Jean-Georges (1780–1842)
A wealthy merchant, reputed to have made his fortune from smuggling, he was a liberal in the Restoration Chamber of Deputies and acquired a reputation for knowledge in financial matters. He supported the Revolution of 1830, was part of the commission that revised the Charter and emerged as a loyal Orleanist. He served as Finance Minister in three ministries and was associated with the doctrinaires.

Lacordaire, Jean-Auguste-Philibert-Alexandre, Abbé de (1789–1860)
A gifted orator and redoubtable polemicist, Père Lacordaire was repeatedly at the centre of religious controversies. His writings for the *Avenir* and a Catholic school organised in conjunction with Montalembert brought him to trial before the Chamber of Peers and enhanced his reputation. However,

unlike Lammenais, he submitted to the Pope's encyclical letter of 1832 which rejected many of the *Avenir's* more radical views. Lacordaire subsequently made a great name for himself by his sermons at Notre Dame, simultaneously giving conservative Catholics cause for concern.

La Fayette, Marie-Joseph, Marquis de (1757–1834)
Veteran of the Revolution and liberal deputy under the Restoration, La Fayette played a crucial role as commander of the Parisian National Guard in bringing about the July Monarchy. He did so in spite of his republican principles, however, and soon became alienated from the government. He was re-elected as a deputy in 1831 and became part of the *gauche dynastique* opposition to Périer.

Laffitte, Jacques (1767–1844)
Banker and opposition deputy under the Restoration, Laffitte made his *hôtel* a centre for the Revolution of 1830 and pressed Louis-Philippe to accept the title of lieutenant-general and then king. As a member of the *mouvement*, Laffitte was made president of the Conseil d'État in November 1830 when Louis-Philippe wished to conciliate left-wing opinion. But Laffitte soon found himself compromised by his conservative fellow ministers and resigned in April 1831. He returned to his seat on the left of the Chamber and consistently opposed subsequent ministries.

Lamartine, Marie-Louis-Alphonse de (1790–1869)
Poet and historian, Lamartine gave up his support of the Bourbons shortly after the Revolution of 1830 and, after several unsuccessful attempts, was elected to Parliament in 1833. Known essentially for his eloquence, Lamartine focused his attention upon the "social question". In the 1840s he grew increasingly disgusted with Guizot's government and joined the banquet campaign of 1847–48, declaring himself republican once the Revolution of 1848 had succeeded.

Lammenais, Jean-Marie-Félicité, Robert de (1782–1854)
Liberal Catholic, author and polemicist, Lammenais was one of the founders of the *Avenir*. He wished to see the Catholic Church free of the state and argued on behalf of extension of the franchise, liberty of the press, and freedom of association and education. His views were too radical for conservative Catholics and were several times rejected by the Papacy. This did not stop Lammenais from increasing his attacks upon King and Court, as he made himself a champion of the "people".

Ledru-Rollin, Alexandre-Auguste (1807–1874)
Lawyer and democrat, Ledru-Rollin made his name in the 1830s by defending individuals and newspapers brought to trial by the state. Elected into the Chamber in 1841, he rapidly became known for his attacks upon the govern-

ment and continued to defend opponents of the regime. He was a major actor in the banquet campaign, his demands for electoral reform making him one of the more radical participants.

Leroux, Pierre-Henri (1797–1871)
Journalist, author and democrat, Leroux sought to develop a philosophy which combined Christianity with socialism and egalitarianism. His doctrine was popularised by George Sand in several novels.

Michelet, Jules (1798–1874)
Historian and professor, Michelet gained reknown for the emphasis that he placed on the "people". Despite enjoying much favour during the early years of the regime, Michelet's radicalism, extreme nationalism and anticlericalism eventually led the government to suspend his lectures in January 1848. A favourite of the students, this increased general discontent with the government.

Molé, Louis-Mathieu, Comte de (1781–1855)
Minister of the Marine in the Richelieu Cabinet (1817–18), Molé subsequently became a moderate but telling critic of the Villèle and Polignac ministries. As Minister of Foreign Affairs in the first July Monarchy government, he pursued the policy of non-intervention preferred by Louis-Philippe. A conservative, he became president of the Conseil d'État (1836–39) but his government fell due to a remarkable coalition led by Guizot, Thiers and Barrot. Molé thereafter remained out of office, but continued to be a bitter opponent of Guizot in Parliament.

Montalembert, Charles Forbes de Tryon, Comte de (1810–1870)
Another co-founder of the *Avenir*, Montalembert, as well as pursuing the fusion of Catholicism and liberalism, was an ardent defender of repressed nationalities. He and Lacordaire opened a school without authorisation and were tried and fined for it. He took his place in Parliament as a peer in 1835 and rapidly established himself as an orator, especially in defence of liberty of education and freedom for Poland.

Montalivet, Marthe-Camille Bacheson, Comte de (1801–1880)
Politician and author, Montalivet was a constitutional monarchist under the Restoration and rallied to the government of Louis-Philippe shortly after the Revolution of 1830. He held several portfolios during the July Monarchy, including the Interior and Public Instruction. After the fall of the Molé ministry, Montalivet's liberal principles distanced him from the doctrinaires and he refused to serve in the Guizot government despite appeals from the King.

Périer, Casimir (1777–1832)
A wealthy banker and liberal under the Restoration, Périer emerged as a

champion of order and *résistance* after the Revolution of 1830. His ministry (1831–32) saw the suppression of the Association Nationale, repression of legitimists plots and repression of popular uprisings in Lyons and Grenoble. In foreign affairs he pursued a policy of non-intervention until he determined to aid the Belgians free themselves from the Dutch. When Périer died of cholera, Orleanist conservatives lost their strongest spokesman.

Persil, Jean-Charles (1785–1870)
Lawyer and leading opponent of the Polignac ministry, Persil was one of the deputies who offered Louis-Philippe the *lieutenance-générale* of the realm in 1830. He twice served as Minister of Justice (1834 and 1836) and was made a peer in 1839. Throughout the July Monarchy Persil was known as an opponent of government reform.

Proudhon, Pierre-Joseph (1809–1865)
Revolutionary, author and journalist, Proudhon became famous for his assertion that property was theft. His writings ranged from political economy to social analysis and he was a harsh critic of the Utopian socialists and liberal economists of the times.

Quélan, Hyacinthe-Louis, Comte de (1778–1839)
Archbishop of Paris, his relations with the July Monarchy were unfriendly. He was threatened by the populace when the archbishopric was sacked after a commemoration of the death of the Duc de Berry. During the cholera epidemic of 1832 he did much work for the victims and established an orphanage.

Quinet, Edgar (1803–1875)
Historian and philosopher, the extreme anticlericalism of his *Les Jésuites* lost him a chair at the Collège de France in 1846. In the following year he was elected a deputy and sat in the Chamber with the opposition.

Raspail, François-Vincent (1794–1874)
Doctor, scientist and republican, Raspail was president of the Amis du Peuple and editor of the *Réformateur*. As a result, most of his scientific publications were written whilst in prison. He was particularly concerned with treating the poor and championed the use of camphor as an antiseptic.

Rémusat, Charles-François-Marie, Comte de (1797–1875)
Author and journalist, Rémusat was one of the most distinguished contributors to the *Globe* and his liberalism led him to sign the journalists' protest against Charles X's *ordonnances* of July 1830. After the Revolution, Rémusat entered the Chamber and supported the party of order, becoming associated with the doctrinaires. However, his closest tie was with Thiers and from 1840 to 1848 he was part of the opposition.

Rigny, Henri Gauthier, Comte de (1783–1835)
Admiral with a distinguished record under the Restoration, he refused to enter the Polignac ministry. Under the July Monarchy he became Minister of the Marine (1831–34), then Minister of Foreign Affairs and ambassador at Naples in his final year.

Salvandy, Narcisse-Achille de (1795–1856)
Military officer, author and consitutional monarchist, Salvandy was Minister of Public Instruction (1837–39) and ambassador to Madrid (1841–42) and Turin (1843); he resigned the latter post after a dispute with Louis-Philippe over his refusal to support an address in the Chamber against legitimists. Nevertheless, he returned to the Ministry of Public Instruction in 1845 and remained there until February 1848.

Sand, Armandine-Lucille-Aurore (George) (1804–1876)
Celebrated novelist, democrat and bluestocking, Sand was an influential social critic who, for a time, showed the influence of Lammenais and Pierre Leroux.

Soult, Nicolas-Jean-De-Dieu, Marshal of France (1769–1852)
Having fought in the wars of the Revolution and First Empire, Soult supported Napoleon during the Hundred Days and consequently was exiled from France until 1819. Under the July Monarchy, he served as War Minister (1832–34, 1839, 1840–47) and president of the Conseil d'État (same dates). Numerous important army reforms were passed under his ministry and he was directly involved in the construction of fortifications around Paris.

Talleyrand-Périgord, Charles-Maurice de, Prince de Bénévent (1754–1838)
A principal actor in the Revolution, First Empire and Restoration, Talleyrand was the leading French diplomat during the early years of the July Monarchy. As ambassador to Great Britain, he sought to gain acceptance of the July Revolution by the European powers and his efforts brought about the Quadruple Alliance of 1834.

Thiers, Marie-Joseph-Louis-Adolphe (1797–1877)
Historian, journalist, parliamentary deputy and minister at different points, Thiers was a central figure of the July Monarchy. He was the chief proponent of Louis-Philippe during the Revolution of 1830. He played a major part in the capture and subsequent exposure of the Duchesse de Berry in 1832, showed himself to be a man of order during the uprisings of 1834 and supported the resultant September laws. Thiers led two ministries (February–August 1836 and March–October 1840), but his bellicose foreign policy made amicable relations with the King impossible. He passed the following years in opposition to the ministry of Guizot and was unable to rescue the monarchy when called upon at the last moment in 1848.

Tocqueville, Alexis-Charles-Henri, Clérel de (1805–1859)
One of the great writers of the age, Tocqueville was a constitutional monarchist who recognised that the advance of democracy was inevitable. As a judge, he received a government commission in 1830 to study the penal system in the United States. He became a deputy in the Chamber in 1839 and remained there until 1848.

Tristan, Flora (1803–1844)
Socialist and feminist author, Tristan sought to bring about a union of workers of all trades and all nations. Although her l'Union Ouvrière enjoyed a certain success, her efforts gained few adherents amongst workers.

Veuillot, Louis (1813–1883)
Writer and journalist, the conservative Veuillot supported the *résistance* in Guizot's journal the *Charte de 1830*. When the journal changed political orientation, Veuillot left to travel in Italy and returned a fervent Catholic. He then took over the *Univers* and made it popular with his polemics.

Villemain, Abel-François (1790–1870)
Professor at the Sorbonne and member of the Académie Française, Villemain opposed censorship under Charles X. He became a deputy in the Chamber in 1830 and a peer in 1832. He was Minister of Public Instruction during the Soult ministry of 1839, was replaced in the following Thiers ministry and returned to the post under Guizot until ill health forced him to retire in 1843.

Voyer de Paulmy d'Argenson, Marc-René-Marie, Comte (1771–1842)
One of the leading liberals of the Restoration, he was disappointed by the outcome of the Revolution of 1830 and sat with the opposition in the Chamber of Deputies. In 1832 he signed the *Compte rendu* of the opposition and in 1833 he signed a manifesto of the Société des Droits de l'Homme.

Maps

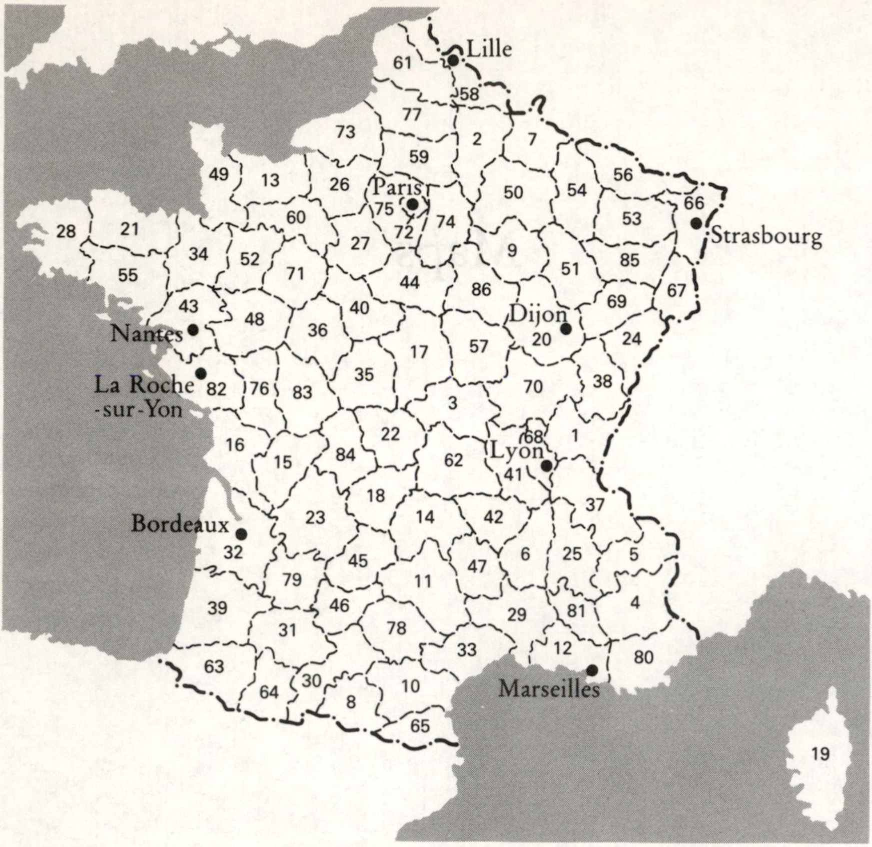

1 Ain
2 Aisne
3 Allier
4 Basses-Alpes
5 Hautes-Alpes
6 Ardèche
7 Ardennes
8 Ariège
9 Aube
10 Aude
11 Aveyron
12 Bouches-du-Rhône
13 Calvados
14 Cantal
15 Charante
16 Charante-Inférieure
17 Cher
18 Corrèze
19 Corsica
20 Côte-d'Or
21 Côtes-du-Nord
22 Creuse
23 Dordogne
24 Doubs
25 Drôme
26 Eure
27 Eure-et-Loire
28 Finistère
29 Gard
30 Haute-Garonne
31 Gers
32 Gironde
33 Hérault
34 Ille-et-Vilaine
35 Indre
36 Indre-et-Loire
37 Isère
38 Jura
39 Landes
40 Loir-et-Cher
41 Loire
42 Haute-Loire
43 Loire-Inférieure
44 Loiret
45 Lot
46 Tarn-et-Garonne
47 Lozère
48 Maine-et-Loire
49 Manche
50 Marne
51 Haute-Marne
52 Mayenne
53 Meurthe
54 Meuse
55 Morbihan
56 Moselle
57 Nièvre
58 Nord
59 Oise
60 Orne
61 Pas-de-Calais
62 Puy-de-Dome
63 Basses-Pyrénées
64 Hautes-Pyrénées
65 Pyrénées-Orientales
66 Bas-Rhin
67 Haut-Rhin
68 Rhône
69 Haute-Saône
70 Saône-et-Loire
71 Sarthe
72 Paris
73 Seine-Inférieure
74 Seine-et-Marne
75 Seine-et-Oise
76 Deux-Sevres
77 Somme
78 Tarn
79 Lot-et-Garonne
80 Var
81 Vaucluse
82 Vendée
83 Vienne
84 Haute-Vienne
85 Vosges
86 Yonne

Map 1 The departments of France in 1833 (after V. Manin, *Petit Atlas National des Départements de la France* (1833)).

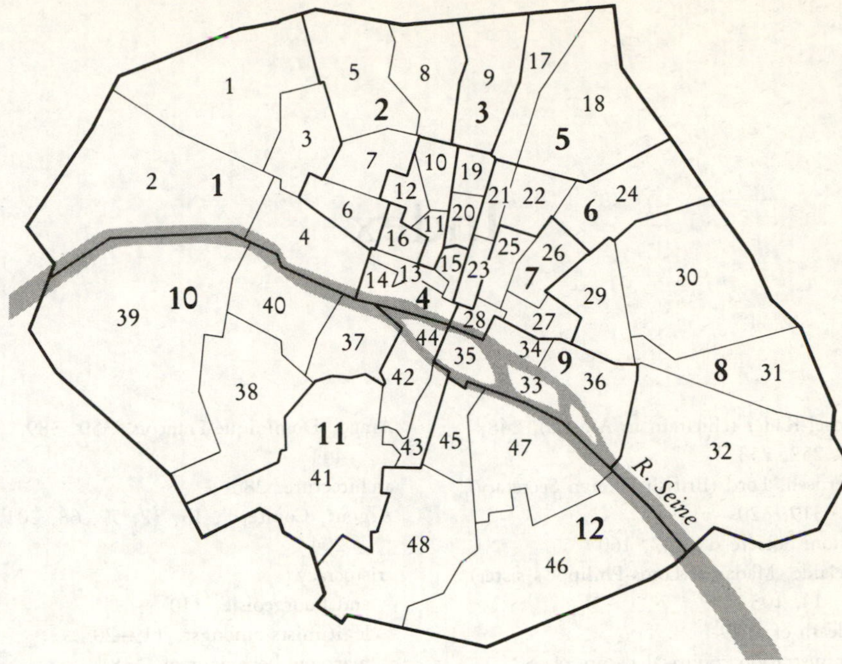

arrondissement
quartier

Ier
1 Roule
2 Champs-Elysées
3 Place Vendôme
4 Tuileries

IIe
5 Chaussée d'Antin
6 Palais-Royal
7 Feydeau
8 Faubourg Montmartre

IIIe
9 Faubourg Poissonnière
10 Montmartre
11 Saint-Eustache
12 Mail

IVe
13 Saint-Honoré
14 Louvre
15 Marchés
16 Banque de France

V^e^
17 Faubourg Saint-Denis
18 Porte Saint-Martin
19 Bonne-Nouvelle
20 Montorgueil

VIe
21 Port Saint Denis
22 Saint-Martin-des-Champs
23 Lombards
24 Temple

VIIe
25 Sainte-Avoye
26 Mont-de-Piéte
27 Marche Saint-Jean
28 Les Arcis

VIIIe
29 Marais
30 Popincourt
31 Faubourg Saint-Antoine
32 Quinze-Vingts

IXe
33 Ile Saint-Louis
34 Hôtel de Ville
35 Cité
36 Arsenal

X^e^
37 La Monnaie
38 Saint-Thomas
39 Invalides
40 Faubourg Saint-Germain

XIe
41 Luxembourg
42 Ecole de médecine
43 Sorbonne
44 Palais de justice

XIIe
45 Saint-Jacques
46 Saint-Marcel
47 Jardin du Roi
48 Observatoire

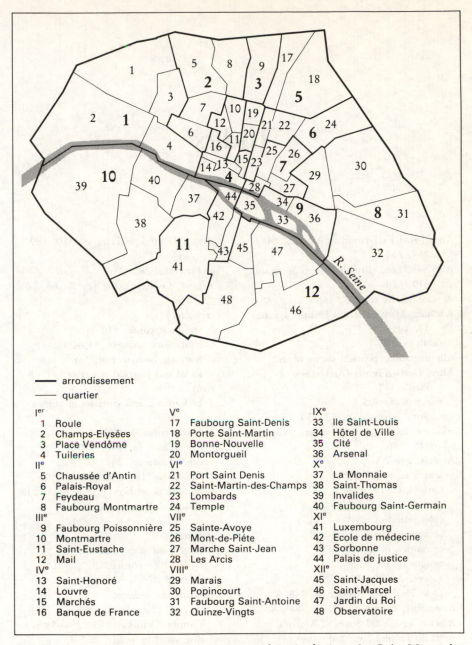

Map 2 The *arrondissements* and *quartiers* of Paris during the July Monarchy (after A. de Bertier de Sauvigny, "La Restauration" in *Nouvelle*

Index